Psychological Consultation and Collaboration in School and Community Settings

SIXTH EDITION

A. MICHAEL DOUGHERTY
Western Carolina University

BROOKS/COLE
CENGAGE Learning·

Australia • Brazil • Japan • Korea • Mexico • Singapore • Spain • United Kingdom • United States

BROOKS/COLE
CENGAGE Learning

Psychological Consultation and Collaboration in School and Community Settings, **Sixth Edition**
A. Michael Dougherty

Publisher: Jon-David Hague

Assistant Editor: Naomi Dreyer

Editorial Assistant: Amelia Blevins

Managing Media Editor: Elizabeth Momb

Senior Director, Brand Management:
Kim Russell

Senior Brand Manager: Elisabeth Rhoden

Senior Market Development Manager:
Kara Kindstrom

Senior MarComm Manager: Linda Yip

Manufacturing Planner: Judy Inouye

Rights Acquisitions Specialist:
Thomas McDonough

Design, Production Services, and Composition:
PreMediaGlobal

Cover Image: © Marilyn Volan

For product information and technology assistance, contact us at
Cengage Learning Customer & Sales Support, 1-800-354-9706.

For permission to use material from this text or product,
submit all requests online at **www.cengage.com/permissions**.
Further permissions questions can be e-mailed to
permissionrequest@cengage.com.

Library of Congress Control Number: 2012955416

Student Edition:

ISBN-13: 978-1-285-09856-2

ISBN-10: 1-285-09856-0

Brooks/Cole
20 Davis Drive
Belmont, CA 94002-3098
USA

Cengage Learning is a leading provider of customized learning solutions with office locations around the globe, including Singapore, the United Kingdom, Australia, Mexico, Brazil, and Japan. Locate your local office at **www.cengage.com/global**.

Cengage Learning products are represented in Canada by
Nelson Education, Ltd.

To learn more about Brooks/Cole, visit **www.cengage.com/brookscole**

Purchase any of our products at your local college store or at our preferred online store **www.cengagebrain.com**.

Printed in the United States of America
1 2 3 4 5 6 7 22 21 20 19 18

＊

Dedicated with love to my parents, Arthur and Cecilia;
and to my family, Leslie, Matt, and Ashley

Contents

PART IV   Professional Issues and Epilogue   340

14 Ethical and Legal Issues   341

Preface

*P*sychological Consultation and Collaboration in School and Community Settings* is written for graduate and undergraduate students in the helping professions. Students in counseling, psychology, social work, human resource development, and other helping-profession training programs will find this book helpful as they seek to acquire the knowledge and skill bases that lead to the effective practice of consultation and collaboration. This book can be used either as the primary text in consultation and collaboration courses or as a supplemental text in courses in the helping professions. In addition to the book's use in consultation and collaboration courses, many instructors have found the text useful in introductory and "roles and settings" courses in counseling psychology, school counseling, school psychology, student development, mental health and community counseling, social work, and human resource development. Moreover, practicing consultants and collaborators can find in this book a wealth of practical and theoretical information to help guide their practice.

In addition, this text can be used in conjunction with *Casebook of Psychological Consultation and Collaboration in School and Community Settings*, Sixth Edition, also published by Cengage Learning. The casebook contains several cases that describe real-life examples of consultation and collaboration and illustrate various approaches.

I spend a good deal of time having students work in small groups analyzing the case studies presented at the end of each chapter and in the casebook (Cengage-Brooks/Cole, 2014). Frequently, a great number of excellent discussions are held based on the students' insights and questions concerning these case studies. Below is a table that aligns the chapters of *Psychological Consultation and Collaboration in School and Community Settings* (referred to as "Core Text") with those in the *Casebook of Psychological Consultation and Collaboration* (referred to as "Casebook"). This table assists the instructor in effectively using the two texts together.

CORE TEXT CHAPTER	CASEBOOK CHAPTER
Chapter 1: The Foundations of Consultation and Collaboration	Chapter 1: Foundations of Consultation and Collaboration
Chapter 2: Consultants, Consultees, and Collaborators	Chapter 1: Foundations of Consultation and Collaboration (cont'd)
Chapter 3: The Generic Model of Consultation and Collaboration	Chapter 9: Implications for Effective Practice
Chapter 4: Entry Stage	Chapter 9: Implications for Effective Practice (cont'd)
Chapter 5: Diagnosis Stage	Chapter 9: Implications for Effective Practice (cont'd)
Chapter 6: Implementation Stage	Chapter 9: Implications for Effective Practice (cont'd)
Chapter 7: Disengagement Stage	Chapter 9: Implications for Effective Practice (cont'd)
Chapter 8: Pragmatic Issues	Chapter 6: Systems Consultation: Working with a Metropolitan Police Department
Chapter 9: Mental Health Consultation and Collaboration	Chapter 3: Mental Health Case Consultation
Chapter 10: Behavioral Consultation and Collaboration	Chapter 2: Problem-Solving (Behavioral) Consultation: School-Based Applications
Chapter 11: Organizational Consultation and Collaboration	Chapter 5: Education/Training Consultation with School Personnel Chapter 7: Process Consultation in a Workplace Setting
Chapter 12: School-Based Consultation and Collaboration	Chapter 2: Problem-Solving (Behavioral) Consultation: School-Based Applications (cont'd) Chapter 4: Adlerian Case Consultation with a Teacher Chapter 8: Schoolwide Collaboration to Implement a PBIS Program
Chapter 13: Case Study Illustrations of Consultation and Collaboration	Chapter 10: Cases for Further Practice
Chapter 14: Ethical and Legal Issues	NA

An instructor's manual and PowerPoint slides are also available at this text's website; instructors can create a free login at login.cengage.com. The website will be a valuable resource for your instruction and contains a variety of materials, including test question banks, suggested class activities, and recommendations for teaching/learning. I believe this instructor's manual and the related slides will be very helpful to you in teaching the concepts and skills of consultation and collaboration.

In this text, I use *human service professional* and *mental health professional* as general terms that encompass counselors, psychologists, social workers, human resource development specialists, and members of other helping professions.

At the same time, I have tried to respect the terminology used by the professions covered in this text.

PURPOSE

This book provides a thorough overview of what students and practicing mental health/human service professionals need to know and be able to do to effectively practice consultation and collaboration in a culturally competent manner. It provides a balance of theory and practice and illustrates their interrelationship. The book presents a generic model for application, surveys the various models to consultation and collaboration, discusses their organizational context, and reviews the many ethical and professional issues faced in delivering these services.

I have found that students learning about consultation and collaboration appreciate a practical, general model for delivering these services before they study specific approaches. As a result, I have provided a culturally sensitive generic model of consultation and collaboration at the beginning of the text before discussing specific models. Students will also find a large number of case studies that illustrate how to deliver consultation and collaboration services in real life. Furthermore, many professors note that the greatest challenge in teaching consultation and collaboration is to make them practical; therefore, I have included the numerous case studies to bring their concepts to life.

Finally, students say they benefit more from learning about consultation and collaboration when they are involved personally. As a result, I have structured the book so students can develop a personal model of consultation and collaboration. Each chapter begins and ends with questions that stimulate and encourage the reader to reflect on the material in that chapter. In the case studies, students are asked to make decisions about a particular consultant's or collaborator's behavior. Each chapter ends with some recommendations for effective practice. I have attempted to write a text that is interesting, current, informative, multiculturally sensitive, and oriented toward practice with a solid grounding in theory and research.

ABOUT THE SIXTH EDITION

The attention paid to consultation and collaboration by members of the helping professions and their organizations since the first edition of this text in 1990 has been nothing short of amazing. I am very excited about the sixth edition. I have kept the topics and format that professors have found most helpful in their instruction and students in their learning, while adding new topics (e.g., social justice) and formats (e.g., even more case studies and constructivist viewpoints).

In my opinion, it is critical that any text in the helping professions be aligned with the standards of organizations to which those members may belong. Consequently, in this edition, I have made revisions with several documents in mind that will continue to affect the practice of consultation and collaboration. I have closely reviewed the *Council for Accreditation of Counseling and Related Educational Programs 2009 Standards* (CACREP, 2009) to ensure that the specific competencies related to consultation and collaboration and related material are effectively covered. This text covers, in varying degrees, demonstrated knowledge in some of the CACREP core curricular areas including:

1. Professional Orientation and Ethical Practice (i) advocacy processes needed to address institutional and social barriers that impede access, equity, and success for clients; and (j) ethical standards of professional organizations and credentialing bodies, and applications of ethical and legal considerations in professional counseling.

2. Cultural and Social Diversity: (b) attitudes, beliefs, understandings, and acculturative experiences, including specific experiential learning activities designed to foster students' understanding of self and culturally diverse clients; (c) theories of multicultural counseling, identity development, and social justice; (e) counselors' roles in developing cultural self-awareness, promoting cultural social justice, advocacy and conflict resolution, and other culturally supported behaviors that promote optimal wellness and growth of the human spirit, mind, or body.

5. Helping Relationships: (a) an orientation to wellness and prevention as desired counseling goals; (b) counselor characteristics and behaviors that influence helping processes; (f) a general framework for understanding and practicing consultation.

8. Research and Program Evaluation: (b) research methods such as qualitative, quantitative, single-case designs, action research, and outcome-based research; (d) principles, models, and applications of needs assessment, program evaluation, and the use of findings to effect program modifications.

Due to the increasing popularity of school-based consultation and collaboration, along with master's degree programs in counseling adding coursework in consultation and collaboration due to professional organization competencies, I have carefully considered material such as the CACREP Standards for School Counselors, the *National Model: A Framework for Comprehensive School Counseling Programs* (ASCA, 2005), the *Standards for Graduate Preparation of School Psychologists* (NASP, 2010b), the *Model for Comprehensive and Integrated School Psychological Services* (NASP, 2010c), and *School Psychology: A Blueprint for Training and Practice III* (Ysseldyke et al. 2006) to assist in the revision. In one example, consultation can be viewed as part of the responsive service and systems support elements of the *National Model: A Framework for Comprehensive School Counseling Programs* (ASCA, 2005). In another example, this text provides detailed coverage in addition to the aforementioned CACREP common core curricular experiences, the following elements of the CACREP (2009) Standard for School Counselors under the heading COLLABORATION AND CONSULTATION:

M. Knowledge

1. Understands the ways in which student development, well-being, and learning are enhanced by family–school–community collaboration.

2. Knows strategies to promote, develop, and enhance effective teamwork within the school and the larger community.

3. Knows how to build effective working teams of school staff, parents, and community members to promote the academic, career, and personal/social development of students.

4. Understands systems theories, models, and processes of consultation in school system settings.

5. Knows strategies and methods for working with parents, guardians, families, and communities to empower them to act on behalf of their children.

6. Understands the various peer programming interventions (e.g., peer mediation, peer mentoring, peer tutoring) and how to coordinate them.

7. Knows school and community collaboration models for crisis/disaster preparedness and response.

N. Skills and Practices

1. Works with parents, guardians, and families to act on behalf of their children to address problems that affect student success in school.

2. Locates resources in the community that can be used in the school to improve student achievement and success.

3. Consults with teachers, staff, and community-based organizations to promote student academic, career, and personal/social development.

4. Uses peer-helping strategies in the school counseling program.

5. Uses referral procedures with helping agents in the community (e.g., mental health centers, businesses, service groups) to secure assistance for students and their families.

In another example this text covers, in varying degrees, information related to the following elements of the *Standards for Graduate Preparation of School Psychologists* (NASP, 2010b): 2.2 Consultation and Collaboration; 2.4 Interventions and Mental Health Services to Develop Social and Life Skills; 2.5 School-Wide Practices to Promote Learning; 2.6 Preventive and Responsive Services; 2.7 Family–School Collaboration Services; 2.8 Diversity in Development and Learning; and 2.10 Legal, Ethical, and Professional Practice.

In addition, I have studied material from the taskforce from Division 13 of the American Psychological Association (APA), which developed *Guidelines for Education and Training at the Doctoral and Postdoctoral Levels in Consulting Psychology/Organizational Consulting Psychology* that recommend consultation proficiencies for psychologists.

In this edition, I have updated the material and refined the discussion of the topics. Each page of the text has been thoroughly reviewed to ensure clarity and currency. I have also included many new topics and more extensive coverage than in the fifth edition. At the same time I have avoided trendy topics that do not have a strong evidence-based relationship between theory and practice. On the other hand, critically important topics related to multicultural competence (e.g., advocacy consultation and social justice) have received the attention they clearly deserve. The introduction to each of the four parts of the text has been thoroughly revised to make even clearer the purpose of each chapter in that part of the text. The chapters of text now include a great number of examples that illustrate how internal and external consultants would approach a consultation situation. Throughout the text, I have again provided significant additional coverage of cultural diversity, advocacy, social justice, systems theory, and ecological variables as they affect consultation and collaboration in both counseling and psychology. Collaboration has asserted itself as a major force in the consultation/collaboration arena. As a result, this edition provides more extensive coverage and examples related to collaboration. More examples and coverage of systems-level intervention are included to reflect the increasing view that ecological factors may impact the individual and, as a result, more systems-level interventions are needed. In many chapters I have provided an example on individual consultation followed immediately with an example or organizational consultation. This allows the reader to not only better understand the nature of how these processes are different, but also provides better coverage of organizational consultation, which is on the increase in the helping professions. I have included a significant amount of additional material throughout the text on prevention as there is a trend to increasingly view consultation and collaboration in this way. I have provided more information and guidance on how professionals internal or external to an organization function when providing consultation and collaboration. Expanded coverage has been added on response to intervention (RTI), multicultural consultation/collaboration, and treatment integrity of interventions. The most broad-based change is an increased focus on school-based consultation. I have again revised Chapter 12, which focuses on school-based consultation and collaboration with administrators, teachers, and parents. Chapters 4–10 each contain a detailed case study on school consultation and community consultation.

Each chapter has been carefully examined and reviewed. I have updated the introductory chapter and have added coverage of promoting consultation and collaboration in the work setting, the multicultural limitations of consultation and collaboration, and the levels of prevention. Some major specific changes for each chapter include:

Chapter 1: The Foundations of Consultation and Collaboration

- A new section on the promise of consultation and collaboration
- Revision of some of the case studies to better illustrate consultation, collaboration, and their differences
- Expanded coverage of the concept of prevention
- New material to guide choosing between consultation and collaboration

Chapter 2: Consultants, Consultees, and Collaborators

- Significant updating of the section on research
- New material on culturally sensitive empathy
- Expanded coverage of skills related to cultural diversity
- Addition of new material on the advocate role as it relates to social justice initiatives

- A new section which provides an orientation to the models of consultation
- A new section on the consultee as a variable in the consultation process

Chapter 3: An Overview of the Generic Model of Consultation and Collaboration

- This is an all-new chapter that introduces the generic model of consultation and covers, in addition, multicultural competence, consultee readiness for change, resistance, and how to personalize the generic model.

Chapter 4: Entry Stage

- New material on entry for internal and external consultants
- New material on formal versus informal entry
- Additional case studies reflecting each phase of entry for both organizational and individual consultation
- Additional discussions of the implications of cultural diversity on the entry stage
- New information about the social influence process
- Additional case studies

Chapter 5: Diagnosis Stage

- New material on diagnosis for internal and external consultants
- Additional case studies reflecting each phase of diagnosis for both organizational and individual consultation
- Additional detailed description of data-gathering methods using multiple methods/sources
- Additional discussion of the implications of cultural diversity on the diagnosis stage
- Additional coverage of functional behavioral analysis (FBA)
- New material on qualitative data gathering
- Additional case studies

Chapter 6: Implementation Stage

- New material on implementation for internal and external consultants
- Additional case studies reflecting each phase of implementation for both organizational and individual consultation
- Additional discussion of the implications of cultural diversity on the implementation stage
- New material on monitoring and assessing treatment integrity

- Expanded coverage of evidence-based interventions
- Expanded coverage of adapting interventions to its multicultural context
- Additional case studies

Chapter 7: Disengagement Stage

- New material on disengagement for internal and external consultants
- Additional case studies reflecting each phase of disengagement for both organizational and individual consultation
- Additional discussion of the implications of cultural diversity on the disengagement stage
- New conceptualization of the use of qualitative methods
- Additional information on maintenance planning

Chapter 8: Pragmatic Issues of Working Within an Organization

- Addition of a new case study
- A new section with material on social justice
- New material added regarding changes in the nature of organizations
- New material regarding systems theory and implications for consultants
- New material added on the ecological perspective on consultation
- New material added on the culturally competent organization

Chapter 9: Mental Health Consultation and Collaboration

- Increased coverage of innovations in consultee-centered consultation that move beyond Caplan's contributions to an eclectic approach
- Increased coverage of modifications to Caplan's model
- Inclusion of material on advocacy in mental health consultation

Chapter 10: Behavioral Consultation and Collaboration

- New material on behavioral technology training as it relates to preparing consultees
- Expanded coverage of conjoint behavioral consultation
- Inclusion of material reflecting the increasing eclectic nature of problem-solving consultation

Chapter 11: Organizational Consultation and Collaboration

- New information on the organization as the client system
- New material on process consultation

- New material on performance consultation
- New material on multicultural organizational consultation

Chapter 12: School-Based Consultation and Collaboration

- New material on response to intervention and consultation
- Expanded coverage of school collaboration
- New material on interagency collaboration
- New material on cross-cultural collaboration with parents
- New material on multicultural school consultation and collaboration
- New material on consultation/collaboration and special education
- New material on systems-level change
- New material on prevention in school consultation

Chapter 13: Case Study Illustrations of Consultation and Collaboration

- Moved ecological example to a generic category

Chapter 14: Ethical and Legal Issues

- New case on ethical decision making
- Incorporated material from organizational consultation ethics and school-based ethics into the chapter
- Additional coverage on aspirational (virtue) ethics
- Additional coverage of organizational consultation ethics
- New material on ethics and collaboration

In addition, I have retained the glossary at the end of the text. I hope that these additions will help the text become even more valuable and practical for the reader.

OVERVIEW

What will you discover as you read this book? *Psychological Consultation and Collaboration in School and Community Settings* is divided into four parts. All four parts thoroughly emphasize cultural competence. Part I sets the stage for understanding consultation and collaboration as services and how they are practiced with competence, including multicultural competence. Chapter 1 is an orientation to the practice of consultation and collaboration: It contains an introduction, a definition of consultation and collaboration, a brief historical overview, and information on how you can promote consultation and collaboration within your work setting. Chapter 2 includes a discussion of the characteristics of effective consultants and collaborators and of the roles in which they engage; it also reviews the current status of research in consultation and collaboration.

Part II describes in detail the ins and outs of the consultation and collaboration processes using a model that involves four stages: entry, diagnosis, implementation, and disengagement.

Chapter 3 provides an orientation to the generic model of consultation and collaboration; Chapter 4 is about the entry stage—that is, how the consultation or collaboration process starts.

Chapter 5 discusses diagnosis—how the consultant or collaborator can help determine the problem to be solved. Chapter 6 describes the implementation stage—how the parties involved attempt to solve the problem. Chapter 7 examines the ending of the consultation or collaboration process, including the difficulty consultants and collaborators face in conducting evaluation, assessing success and how they can say goodbye in a personal yet professional manner. Chapter 8 deals with the pragmatic issues of working within an organization. This chapter emphasizes that all consultation or collaboration takes place within some type of organization and that the forces in that organization impact, for better or worse, your efforts.

Part III surveys mental health, behavioral, organizational, school-based consultation and collaboration, and provides a chapter on case study illustrations. Chapter 9 reviews mental health consultation; because of the traditional popularity of Caplan's model, I have made it the central focus of the chapter, while recognizing the increasing eclecticism in this model. Chapter 10 explores behavioral consultation, which uses behavioral technology, including cognitive behavioral approaches, both to benefit clients and organizations and also as an aid in training human service professionals and others such as teachers and parents. Chapter 11 discusses organizational consultation, including four specialized applications: education/training, program, doctor-patient, and process. Chapter 12 covers school-based consultation and collaboration, including how these services can be provided to administrators, teachers, and parents. Chapter 13 presents case study applications to give a better sense of the nuts and bolts of consultation and collaboration.

Part IV of this text is designed to familiarize you with professional issues. Chapter 14 focuses on the ethical, legal, and professional issues consultants and collaborators encounter in their practices, such as those related to confidentiality, diversity, and crisis situations.

HOW TO USE THIS TEXT

This text can be used in several ways. Some instructors might want students who are preparing for work in schools to read Chapter 12 first and students who are training for work in community settings to read Chapter 13 first. This would give each student a sense of how consultation and collaboration are practiced in his or her field. Other instructors might want to begin with Chapter 14 to instill an understanding of the complexity and seriousness of the ethical and professional issues faced in the process of providing consultation or collaboration. Still others might want to start with the generic model and cover the specific approaches later, or vice versa. I have designed this book so that the material can be covered in the most logical order regardless of how a particular course is taught.

ACKNOWLEDGMENTS

I would like to thank the many graduate students in counseling and psychology—as well as college student personnel and human resources at Western Carolina University who contributed indirectly yet significantly to the development of this text. Their feedback on the consultation and collaboration course I teach was an invaluable asset in determining the final form this text would take. I also wish to thank Mary Rompf, a graduate student at Western Carolina University, who provided invaluable assistance throughout the revision process. I extend many thanks to Meagan Karvonen, Western Carolina University, for reviewing the evaluation sections of Chapters 6 and 7. I continue to thank Gerald Corey, professor emeritus of California State University at Fullerton, and Mary Deck, professor emeritus of Western Carolina University, for their suggestions over the years concerning the organization of the text and the instructor's manual. In addition, I thank the large number of professors and students who provided their opinions about the text over the years.

I would also like to acknowledge my reviewers, among them Nicholas Benson, University of South Dakota; Kimberly Booker, Texas Woman's University; Sherrie Foster, Tennessee Tech University; Elaine Kies, National Louis University; and Stacy Van Horn, University of Central Florida. These individuals furnished me with a wealth of helpful ideas and many valuable comments.

To my wife and life partner, Leslie, my deepest appreciation for her love, support, and understanding during the preparation of this text and for helping me remember that work is always there and love is not always as accessible. To our children, Ashley and Matt, thanks for helping me remember how to play.

Finally, to the talented people at Cengage–Brooks/Cole, I extend my gratitude for being able to work with a first-class group of professionals. It was a true pleasure to work with them and others who helped make this book a reality.

✳

To the Student

Consultation and collaboration are "head, heart, and hands" processes. You come to understand them, then you become a strong advocate for them, then you do them with a passion.

The often-used metaphor of the bicycle rider sheds light on what it takes to be an effective consultant and collaborator. The front wheel provides direction, the back wheel provides the force, and the rider guides the bike to its destination. The rear wheel represents your technical skills (what you do when you consult or collaborate), the front wheel represents your skill with people (how you consult or collaborate), and the rider represents your personhood (who you are). When all three elements are in sync, it becomes more probable that you will succeed in your consulting and collaborating endeavors. This book will help you become an even better "bicycle rider." You might want to take special note of the questions at the beginning of each chapter. They are designed to stimulate thought about each chapter's main points as you read. In addition, the questions at the end of each chapter will assist you in applying what you have learned through your reading. I hope you will take the time to reflect on these questions after you have completed each chapter. Each chapter concludes with a few suggestions for effective practice, which will help you determine how to use the chapter's material in your practice of consultation and collaboration.

In addition, supplementary readings are suggested at the end of each chapter. I have chosen these readings carefully and encourage you to read those that interest you. You will note that there are a variety of case studies throughout the text. The focus of some cases will not be in your professional training area. Nonetheless, the analysis of these cases can be quite beneficial to you, because it is the process of the analysis and not the cases themselves that is critical.

I also suggest that you look over Chapters 8, 13, and 14 after you read Chapters 1 and 2.

Even a cursory glance at these chapters will show you the many important issues you will face in your practice of consultation and collaboration.

Chapter 8 covers a variety of issues related to working in an organizational context. By skimming through this chapter, you can appreciate the complexity of organizations and, consequently, of consultation and collaboration within them. Chapter 13 presents the case of Acme Human Services Center and illustrates how various consultation approaches can be applied to that case. This chapter also includes a case study transcript of both a consultation session and a collaboration session. By looking through this chapter, you can get a feel for the nuts and bolts of real-life consultation and collaboration. Chapter 14 discusses ethical, professional, and legal issues.

Once you have obtained a perspective on how consultants actually consult and how collaborators actually collaborate, you can more readily see the critical importance of such procedures as creating relationships with the people with whom you are going to work and determining the interventions that emerge for use with the client system.

This is a book about consultation and collaboration: what these services are, how they are effectively practiced, and the forms they can take. I sincerely hope that after reading this book you will be motivated and empowered to perform consultation and collaboration confidently and effectively.

✳

Consultation and Consultants, Collaboration, and Collaborators

Consultation and collaboration are forms of service delivery that are expected from members of the helping professions in a variety of settings. These services are continually developing as their research base develops. What kinds of things might you do as a consultant or collaborator? The purpose of Part I of this text is to offer you an answer to this question by providing a snapshot of consultation and collaboration and what the people who effectively engage in these services actually do. This section is designed to assist you to develop a basic sense for these services both conceptually and practically while preparing you for the chapters that follow.

In Chapter 1, consultation and collaboration are defined, contrasted with other helping relationships, and examined in several contexts, including their multicultural limitations, historical development, and social influences such as systems theory. Chapter 2 provides a frame of reference for the effective practice of consultation and collaboration by focusing on the knowledge, skills, attitudes, roles, and research base necessary to provide these services effectively and in a culturally competent manner.

1

＊

The Foundations of Consultation and Collaboration

The goal of this chapter is to introduce the concepts of consultation and collaboration, define them, and show how they differ from one other and from other services performed by mental health and human service professionals. Here are five questions to consider as you read this chapter:

- How would you define *consultation* and *collaboration* so that a layperson could easily define them?
- What are the key differences between consultation and collaboration?
- What do consultants and collaborators actually do when they provide services?
- What are the implications of the multicultural limitations of consultation and collaboration for effective practice?
- How can consultation and collaboration be both remedial and preventive?

What is consultation? What is collaboration? What do psychologists, counselors, social workers, college student personnel, human resource specialists, and other members of the helping professions do when they consult and collaborate? What special knowledge and skills do consultants and collaborators need to practice effectively? What roles do consultants and collaborators take on in their work? How do issues related to diversity, social justice, multiculturalism, and prevention figure into their effective practice? Students can begin to develop a personal style of providing consultation and collaboration by developing answers to the aforementioned questions.

When professionals in the helping relationships engage in *consultation*, they assist individuals and groups for the purpose of helping them to be more effective in their jobs, whether on the individual, group, organizational, or community level. Consultation is a helping relationship in which those in the helping professions provide the conditions so that individuals and/or groups in a variety of settings (e.g., agencies, schools, and businesses) improve their effectiveness. Simply put, consultation is an interpersonal helping relationship that uses problem solving to achieve its ends.

This apparently simple process is actually quite complex. You'll learn that consultants provide assistance to the people with whom they are working (called *consultees*) with their immediate problems with the parties the consultees are charged with helping (called the *client system*). Said another way, in these relationships, the consultee is the individual seeking assistance with an immediate problem in their work with another individual or group, which is referred to as the client system. Consultants also try to improve their consultees' professional functioning with current and future client systems with similar problems, thus having a preventive effect. You'll discover that the client system can consist of an individual, a group, a system, an entire organization, or the community at large. As we will see, this is an important fact to remember when dealing with multicultural, diversity, and social justice issues.

Part of this assistance is in helping consultees become more aware of additional choices or alternatives for working with their client systems. Consultants engage consultees in joint problem solving, typically of a collaborative nature, and consultees are free to accept or reject any consultant recommendations. The consultant typically tries to be a facilitator in the process whenever possible as opposed to taking on the expert role.

Consultation is practiced by counselors, psychologists, and social workers in a variety of settings for a variety of reasons. Consider the following examples:

- A psychologist helps a therapist deal with problems she is having with one or more clients in her caseload.
- A school counselor works with a school teacher to improve classroom management techniques.
- A school psychologist facilitates team efforts to implement a response to intervention (RTI) program.

- A counseling psychologist consults with a nursing home director about recreation programs for patients suffering from Alzheimer's disease.
- A family therapist trains school counselors in family systems theory for use in their work.
- A professor of human services assists a job corps center staff in developing culturally competent practice.
- A team of school-based consultants assists teachers in finding ways to help students cope with school violence.
- A psychologist diagnoses the reasons for high turnover in a social services agency.
- A counselor assists the staff of a counseling center in identifying its major work concerns and in making plans to solve them.
- A mental health worker assists a Head Start program in developing evaluation strategies for its parent training program.
- A social worker assists a group of rural human service agencies to build a network for responding to common issues.
- A community mental health worker facilitates a group of other mental health professionals in developing an ecological approach and practice that emphasizes outreach and client advocacy strategies for assisting ethnic minorities.
- A group of mental health consultants assists a university in examining and revising the mental health aspects of its crisis communication plan.

As you will note as you read this text, *collaboration* is quite similar to consultation. Those parties with whom the member of the helping professions collaborates are termed *fellow collaborators*. The majority of what holds for consultation in terms of underlying assumptions and characteristics also holds for collaboration. For example, both are problem-solving activities. However, as we will learn in detail, there is one distinctive area in which consultation and collaboration differ. This major differentiating point is that, in collaboration, it is assumed that *direct service* from the member of the helping professions (as well as fellow collaborators) to the client system is integral to successful outcomes. That is, in collaboration, all of the collaborators provide *direct service* to the client system. In consultation, on the other hand, the consultant acts as a facilitator who guides and serves as a resource to the consultee in the consultee's *direct service* to the client system. In its most generic form, collaboration involves a process in which two or more parties work together to assist a client system toward some desired outcome. These parties can be of different disciplines (Finello, 2011); for example, a school counselor, a school psychologist, and a teacher mutually provide distinct, yet coordinated, service to a student.

Consider these examples that illustrate how members of the helping professions can provide assistance to others (as well as receive assistance) through collaboration:

- A community counselor serves on an inter-agency team to design an ecological approach to developing social supports within a human services agency.

- A school psychologist serves as part of a site-based management team in an urban school.

- A human resource management specialist serves as a member of a self-directed work team that is a permanent structure in a health care setting.

- A psychologist works with a group of managers to examine the turnover of women in leadership positions.

- A school counselor and teacher collaborate to assist a student, with the counselor providing counseling services to the student and the teacher changing the way she instructs the student in the classroom.

- Two mental health professionals in the same agency team up to help a client suffering from AIDS, each working with a different (yet coordinated) aspect of the case.

- A school psychologist facilitates a schoolwide team in implementing a RTI program at an elementary school.

- A community psychologist advocates with a community group to ensure that group's access to services.

Now consider these real-life examples of consultation and collaboration, which are similar to those that you will encounter in your professional practice.

The Case of Billie: Consultation

Billie is a therapist working with a client who reveals during a session that he has AIDS. As therapy continues, Billie is increasingly aware that there are several AIDS-related issues, including one of cultural competence, which may need to be dealt with in subsequent therapy sessions. Billie notes her anxiety about working with a client who has AIDS and her lack of knowledge about AIDS-related issues. By taking advantage of the consultation opportunities that her employer provides, Billie meets for three consultation sessions with a psychologist, who helps her examine her knowledge, skills, and attitudes concerning people who have AIDS and related multicultural competence issues. The psychologist then recommends a variety of resources that provide pertinent assistance. In addition, the psychologist helps Billie develop both short- and long-term plans to become more effective in dealing with clients with AIDS.

The Case of Chris: Collaboration

Chris Gonzalez is the head counselor at a large urban secondary school that has a severe substance-abuse problem among its student body. The counseling department of the school has a well-defined procedure for referring substance-abuse cases to community resources. At the request of the school administration, Chris has been studying several drug-prevention programs but is uncertain about which one would be best for the school. Chris contacts Leslie, who is a substance-abuse counselor at the community mental health center, and invites her to collaborate with him.

Leslie is quite familiar with a number of substance-abuse programs for schools. Chris and

Leslie agree to team up and meet for three two-hour sessions over a three-week period. During the first meeting, they explore the school's substance-abuse problem in detail, and Leslie observes the overall operation of the school. In the second meeting, Leslie provides Chris information on possible substance-abuse programs with which Chris was not familiar. Chris helps Leslie understand the unique characteristics of the school and how they would affect any program. In the final meeting, Leslie and Chris problem solve and decide which programs might be good fits for the school. They then develop a plan together for engaging all stakeholders to examine their recommendations.

In conclusion, consultation has become an increasingly powerful force in the helping professions (Gutkin & Curtis, 2009), and collaboration has significantly grown in its importance as a stand-alone service. A tremendous social demand for these services has developed, in part due to the effects of the realignment of the world's economy, the increasing demographic changes in our society, the importance of multicultural and social justice issues, increases in mental health issues across our society along with a shortened supply of mental health professionals to address those issues, and federal legislation such as *No Child Left Behind* as well as that related to special education. Whereas some decades ago consultation was considered an "emerging role" (Kurpius, 1978, p. 335), today it is an accepted, routinely practiced, and valued service provided by psychologists, counselors, social workers, and other professionals. However, as I will discuss throughout this text, the effective practice of consultation and collaboration can be limited by multicultural issues and variables. The ever-changing makeup of American and other societies dictates the necessity of ensuring cultural competence in the work of consultants and collaborators. This creates opportunities for initiatives related to advocacy, social justice initiatives, prevention, empowerment, systems-level interventions, and an ecological perspective on consultation and collaboration.

THE PROMISE OF CONSULTATION AND COLLABORATION

Although the promise of consultation and collaboration has yet to be fulfilled, substantial progress has been made in integrating these services into the roles of members of the helping professions. In essence, consultation has emerged as a primary service provided by helping professionals to assist a variety of other professionals (such as teachers) and caregivers (such as parents). Just as in counseling and psychotherapy, consultation and collaboration have their roots in a Eurocentric framework. However, there is a significant literature emerging (e.g., advocacy consultation and social justice consultation) that promotes cultural competence in consultation and collaboration. Collaboration has emerged as an alternative to consultation, particularly in settings where both the would-be consultant and consultee are employed in the same work setting. This situation results in the notion that the prospective internal consultant might well be required to take some aspect of the responsibility for the direct service to the client system and, as a result, become a fellow collaborator (Pryzwansky, 2011). Collaboration has also been considered to be a more proactive than reactive service. For example, collaboration may be the service of choice in developing and implementing prevention programs that deal with ecological variables, as the various collaborators will have expertise in at least one environment that may be impacting the client system's behavior (Ysseldyke, Lekwa, Klingbeil, & Cormier, 2012). Collaboration continues to grow in its literature base and in its use by members of the helping professions. There has been an increase over the past decade in the number of research studies conducted on consultation and collaboration validating their practice (see, e.g., Erchul & Sheridan, 2008).

Consultation continues to be a cornerstone activity for members of the helping professions. Consider, for example, school consultation. School consultation can focus on a child, classroom, or the system (in this case, the school itself and its ecology). The school psychology profession has had consultation in its role for over 50 years, including dealing with issues related to special education in the schools (Reschly & Bergstrom, 2009). School psychologists, by consulting with the significant adults in the lives of children, can thereby effectively serve those children (Gutkin & Curtis, 2009); thus, consultation is a central role in their practice (Ball, Pierson, & McIntosh, 2011; Truscott et al., 2012). For example, the *School Psychology: A Blueprint for Training and Practice III* (Ysseldyke, et al., 2006) suggests that school psychologists add even more consultation activities to their roles (Newell, 2012). In recent years, a unique role in consultation and collaboration for pediatric school psychologists has emerged (Sheridan, Swanger-Gagne, Welch, Kwon, & Garbacz, 2009). School psychologists, though consulting more than ever before, indicate a desire to do even more (Anton-LaHart & Rosenfield, 2004; Stoiber & Vanderwood, 2008) and most likely will in the future (Cummings, Harrison, Dawson, Short, Gorin, & Palomares, 2004a; Finello, 2011; Merrell, Ervin, & Gimpel, 2006; Sheridan et al., 2009). School psychologists are increasingly being called upon to provide consultation on a variety of issues related to school, home, and community (Finello, 2011; Newell, 2012; Tomes, 2011; Truscott et al., 2012). Gravois (2012), however, makes one note of caution: Consultation is often seen as an "add-on," not a mainstream function of school-based professionals.

Still considering school consultation, school counselors spend a significant proportion of their time performing consultation (Dahir & Stone, 2012; Neukrug, 2012; Perera-Diltz, Moe, & Mason, 2011). School counselors tend to desire to engage in more consultation than they are actually able to do (Nelson, Robles-Pina, & Nichter, 2008; Scarborough & Culbreth, 2008). The *American School Counselor Association National Model: A Framework for School Counselor Programs* (ASCA, 2005) promotes consultation as an essential school counselor competency. The current emphasis on RTI and prevention in schools results in a likely greater emphasis on consultation by school-based professionals, including school counselors (Racine Gilles, Kratochwill, Felt, Schienbeck, & Vaccarello, 2011; Stoiber & Vanderwood, 2008; Truscott, 2008). It is this author's opinion that counselors in general, including school counselors, will increasingly provide more and more consultation services in this and the following decades.

Mental health professionals frequently seek consultation primarily for the purpose of assisting their clients in an ethical manner, with a secondary goal of avoiding possible lawsuits based on malpractice. The onset of managed care and limited counseling sessions has led to the increased need for consultation among clinical mental health counselors, psychologists, and social workers (Sperry, 2005). For example, clinical mental health consultants may assist with organizational downsizing, creating multiculturally competent organizations, mental health policy, violence prevention, social justice initiatives, and conflict resolution. Community consultants from the helping professions are called upon to assist in a variety of programs (Phelps, 2011; Staton et al., 2007), such as those designed to prevent elder abuse (Wolf & Pillemer, 1994).

A special workgroup on consultation and interprofessional collaboration across the specialty areas of psychology [see Arredondo, Shealy, Neale, & Winfrey (2004)] validated consultation and interprofessional collaboration as important activities for psychologists. Serious social issues like the AIDS epidemic have led many psychologists to take on community involvement through education/training consultation (Douce, 1993; House & Walker, 1993) as well as by providing mental health consultation services to primary care physicians (Gongora, 2004) and in pediatric care (Truscott, 2008). Community psychologists and clinical mental health counselors have been expanding their application of consultation (Mellin et al., 2010; Neukrug, 2012) by engaging in areas such as trial consultation (Myers & Arena, 2001), systems consultation and prevention programs (Lewis, Lewis, Daniels, & D'Andrea, 2011), mental health consultation with juvenile correction facilities (Cowles &

Washburn, 2005), collaborating with community fire service personnel (Henderson, MacKay, & Peterson-Badali, 2010), and acting as cultural mediators to close the gap between mainstream schools and nonmainstream families (Nastasi, 2005).

Whereas social workers used to be only the recipients of consultation, they now have provided consultation services to a variety of constituencies for over three decades. The 1980s saw a significant rise in the number of counselors providing services to organizations and their personnel (Maher, 1993). Human resource development specialists, as well as members of other helping professions, are frequently being called on to consult with organizational programs such as those related to employee assistance. Student affairs specialists are increasingly being asked to provide consultation in postsecondary educational settings (Knotek, 2006). Music therapists spend a significant amount of their time consulting and collaborating (Register, 2002). Consultation is increasingly used in early childhood classrooms and family childcare homes (Wesley et al., 2010).

Collaboration is increasingly being seen as an important service provided by members of the helping professions. Collaboration is used as a service to assist youth, families, schools, health agencies, and other community agencies and communities at large (Henderson et al., 2010; Shaw & Brown, 2011). Collaboration by school counselors with other community providers has been promoted (ASCA, 2005) and has taken on increased importance in practice (Epstein & Van Voorhis, 2010; Mellin, Hunt, & Nichols, 2011; Steen & Noguera, 2010). Recent reviews of the role of school psychologists indicate increased attention to collaboration as a service (Pryzwansky, 2011; Ysseldyke, Burns, & Rosenfield, 2009; Zins & Erchul, 2002), including collaboration with community agencies (Finello, 2011). Collaboration is increasingly viewed as a significant role in the work of counselors in promoting social justice (Lopez-Baez & Paylo, 2009). Interdisciplinary collaboration between community mental health providers has experienced significant emphasis in the literature (Mellin, Anderson-Butcher, & Bronstein, 2011).

Managed care has also given impetus to interagency collaboration.

As the discussion above illustrates, consultation and collaboration have become important roles for many professionals; practicing these roles has become increasingly scientifically based with the increasing emphasis on evidenced-based interventions (Cowan, 2007; Erchul & Sheridan, 2008; Truscott, 2008). Members of the helping professions provide consultation to, or collaborate with, individuals, groups, and organizations, usually in one of three organizational settings. In one setting, professionals work "in-house" and consult and collaborate within the organization that employs them—for example, a school psychologist or school counselor consulting with a teacher about a student's behavior. A second setting for practice is within some type of human service agency, whose mission in part is to provide consultation/collaboration services to the community, such as a community mental health center. A private firm or independent practitioner offering consultation/collaboration services to the community—for instance, a psychologist in private practice offering stress management training to the employees of a job corps center—constitutes a third setting.

CONSULTATION DEFINED

What is consultation? This simple question has a complex answer. For example, later in this book, you will be exposed to definitions of mental health, behavioral, and organizational consultation. Defining the term *consultation* is as difficult as defining such terms as *counseling, psychotherapy*, and *collaboration*. There is no widespread agreement on the definition of *consultation* (Gutkin & Curtis, 2009; Snyder, Quirk, & Dematteo, 2011; Truscott & Albritton, 2011). In fact, the continued ambiguous use of this term makes quality research on the subject difficult (Erchul & Sheridan, 2008; Zins, 2002).

Generally speaking, "Consultation is a complex and sophisticated set of service delivery methodologies" (Gutkin & Curtis, 2009, p. 595). Consultation is a helping relationship that is interpersonal and has a problem-solving focus in which the consultant and consultee meet to assist a third party called the client system. When members of the helping professions consult, their primary purpose is to help others work more effectively to fulfill their professional or caregiving responsibilities to an individual, group, organization, or community. The typical focus in consultation is changing behavior in some way, whether it is the behavior of a client or the behavior of program participants. The consultant's role varies with the needs of the consultee (Williams, 2000). Whereas the consultee maintains responsibility for managing the problem and carrying out any intervention procedures, the consultant maintains the ethical responsibility of making appropriate recommendations and overseeing the professional well-being of the consultee and client system.

Consultation tends to be defined in terms of the role and function of the consultant. However, this method de-emphasizes the *process* of consultation. A variety of generic definitions of consultation have been suggested over the years (e.g., see Parsons, 1996). These definitions generally agree about the role of consultation, but they differ on such issues as whether the consultee must be a human service professional or whether the consultant must be from outside the system in which consultation occurs.

A general and widely accepted definition of consultation is: *Consultation is an indirect process in which a human service professional assists a consultee with a work-related (or caretaking-related) problem with a client system, with the goal of helping both the consultee and the client system in some specified way.* The *content* of consultation deals with what is discussed, and the *process* refers to the problem-solving process and the nature of the interaction between consultant and consultee (Kurpius & Fuqua, 1993a). The consultant and consultee pool their expertise to assist the client system. Consultation is achieved via "… structured interviews and the implementation of interventions with progress monitoring" (Reschly & Bergstrom, 2009, p. 440). The aforementioned interviewing strategies engage the consultee in collaborative decision making/problem solving. The consultant's job in a nutshell is to "…elicit a

description of the problem, assist in analyzing the problem, co-construct a plan for intervention, and establish a monitoring system once the program is implemented" (Kratochwill, 2008, p. 1674). It is important to remember that successful consultation implies that there will be some sort of change in the consultee, such as new skills or a reconceptualization of the problem and its context, as a result of consultation (Neukrug, 2012).

COMMON CHARACTERISTICS OF CONSULTATION

Can consultation be identified by certain common characteristics? A survey of the literature on the nature of consultation (e.g., Gutkin & Curtis, 2009; Kratochwill, 2008) suggests it can. Some general agreement exists on the following characteristics of consultation.

First, most authors consider consultation to be a problem-solving activity. What constitutes a problem can, of course, vary significantly. An organization could seek a consultant to assist in such problems as alleviating poor staff morale or determining how best to evaluate the effects of a substance-abuse program. The term *problem* does not necessarily imply that something is *wrong*. It may simply refer to a situation that needs attention or enhancement. That is, consultants not only assist consultees in developing solutions to defined problems (such as assisting an administrator in working out the glitches in a program), but also empower consultees by assisting them in recognizing their needs and tapping the unused potential and resources necessary to meet those needs (such as through strategic planning) (Egan, 2010; Knoff, 2008). The positive psychology framework (Gerstein, 2006; Meyers, Roach, & Meyers, 2009) has influenced consultation with an increased focus on strengths and optimal human functioning. From this perspective, consultants approach their work with an emphasis on wellness, social competence, life skills, and prevention (Meyers et al., 2009).

The consultee's problem with the client system can be dealt with in either a remedial or a developmental manner, depending on what the situation dictates. An example of a remedial case is a consultant working with a teacher in order to assist a student in reducing bullying behaviors. In an example of a developmental approach, a consultant assists a teacher in tweaking a classroom-based antibullying program.

Consultants facilitate consultees' views of the problem to include a part of a larger system, in order to understand how the problem has developed, is maintained, and may be solved (Kurpius & Fuqua, 1993b). On the other hand, consultants will want to pay close attention to what the consultee's story is (Pryzwansky, 2011). Hence, consultation can occur in a very broad range of problem-solving situations. In this sense, consultation is a unique activity (Auster, Feeney-Kettler, & Kratochwill, 2006; Kratochwill, 2008).

A second commonly accepted characteristic of consultation is that the client system receives indirect service from the consultant through an intermediary (the consultee). Thus, the consultant provides assistance to the consultee that can positively affect the consultee's work with the client system. Figure 1.1 shows the relationships among the parties involved in consultation. The solid lines represent direct service; the broken line represents indirect service. The reader should not assume from Figure 1.1 that the relationship among the consultant, consultee, and client system is a linear one. There are times when the consultant may want access to the client system (e.g., for assessment, testing, or observation). Further, the consultant has an ethical and moral obligation to ensure that interventions designed to assist the client system are appropriately carried out (Kurpius & Fuqua, 1993b).

A third characteristic is its tripartite nature (Kratochwill, 2008); that is, it involves three parties: a *consultant*, a *consultee*, and a *client system*. The consultant delivers direct service to a consultee, who delivers direct service to a client system. Both the consultant and the consultee are presumed to have competencies to use in the consultation situation (Rimehaug & Helmersberg, 2010). Consultees, for example, may have unique knowledge about the client system. As a result, consultation typically is characterized by shared expertise and joint involvement on the part of the consultant and consultee (Wesley & Buysse, 2006), with the consultee being responsible for carrying out the intervention.

A fourth characteristic of consultation on which there is substantial agreement is its goal of improving both the client system and the consultee (Zins & Erchul, 2002). The term *improve* can, of course, mean many things, and hence a large number of approaches to consultation and a great many interventions become available to consultants. For example, a consultant might help a consultee, not only to work more effectively with a given moderately depressed client, but also to empower the consultee to effectively assist similar clients in the future. This characteristic of consultation puts the preventive effect of consultation into focus.

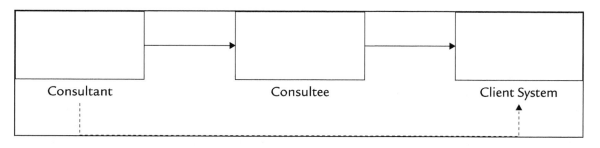

F I G U R E 1.1 Relationships of the parties involved in consultation

In addition to these characteristics, there are several more on which there is common agreement:

- Either the consultee or the client system may be given priority over the other at a given time, depending on the nature of consultation and the approach that is taken.

- The consultant provides indirect service to the client system by providing direct service to the consultee.

- Consultation can be remedial or preventive. In remedial consultation, the consultant helps the consultee develop an effective intervention. In preventive consultation, a main focus is to assist consultees to increase knowledge and skills for future use.

- Consultants can be either separate from or part of the system in which consultation is to occur; that is, external consultants or internal consultants.

- Participation in consultation is voluntary for all parties involved.

- Consultees are free to do whatever they wish with the consultant's suggestions and recommendations. They are under no obligation to follow the consultant's recommendations. The need for monitoring or being on call when the consultee implements the consultant's recommendations is necessary to ensure treatment integrity, which is the appropriate implementation of the recommendation by the consultee.

- The relationship between the consultee and consultant is one of peers, of two equals.

Although the consultation relationship is equal in terms of the power and decision making, it is unequal in terms of need and often expertise; that is, the consultee needs help with a problem and the consultant does not (at least as far as the consultation relationship is concerned). However, the consultee typically possesses the ability to accurately assess input from the consultant (Rimehaug & Helmersberg, 2010). Consultant–consultee relationships, as noted by Gutkin and Curtis (2009, p. 600) note: "... should be collegial and collaborative rather than hierarchical and coercive." Kratochwill (2008) adds that the focus of consultation should be on building consultee strengths rather than focusing on their professional weaknesses. The primary reason for consultation occurring is that the consultee expects the expertise of the consultant to be of some value with the situation at hand. Hence, a consultant can be both directive and collaborative (Gutkin & Curtis, 2009; Hylander, 2012; Kratochwill & Pittman, 2002).

- The consultation relationship is temporary. Depending on the type, consultation may range from a single session to weekly sessions for more than a year. Whatever its length, however, the relationship is always temporary (the consultant does not replace the consultee).

- Consultation deals exclusively with the consultee's work-related or caretaking-related problems. By definition, it does not deal with the personal concerns of the consultee.

- The consultant can take on a variety of roles in consultation, depending on the nature of the problem, the skills of the consultee, the purpose and desired outcomes of consultation, and the skills of the consultant.

- Consultation tends to be collaborative in nature; that is, consultants and consultees work together to complement each other in solving the problems defined in consultation and the consultant takes on the collaborator role whenever possible. The consultant brings expertise and social influence to bear on the problem and engages the expertise of the consultee to solve the problem (Gutkin & Curtis, 2009). Wesley and Buysse (2006, p. 132) note that consultants "... must manage the sequence of consultation tasks while concentrating on maintaining the interpersonal aspects of a trusting relationship with the consultee." One cardinal exception is in carrying out the agreed-upon consultation plan. The consultee carries out the plan with the consultant remaining on call for further assistance. Another exception is when consultees have the skills but not the time to do a given task. For example, a consultee might ask a consultant to lead a workshop on substance-abuse counseling for the consultee's organization, even though the consultee is skilled in that task.

■ Consultation usually occurs in an organizational context. Three key variables within an organization can influence the success of consultation: the people involved in consultation, how the process of consultation unfolds, and how change procedures are implemented. It is quite important that consultants understand the dynamics of the consultee's workplace.

These characteristics are not without controversy and need to be reviewed periodically in light of research findings and new models (Gutkin & Curtis, 2009).

In summary, the basic rationale for consultation is that the vast increase in mental health and educational needs in our society has not been met with an adequate increase in the numbers of professionals to assist in handling these needs. As a result of consultation, consultants are able to effectively assist, through indirect means, a larger number of clients, programs, and organizations than with a more direct approach such as one-on-one counseling. In addition, you will discover that consultants and collaborators are required to be experts on the issues that are brought forth and also experts on the ecological subsystems that are related to the client system. Further, conducting effective consultation can be a challenge because there are a large number of variables involved in the process over which the consultants have no control (Vanderheyden & Witt, 2008).

COLLABORATION DEFINED

As noted above, collaboration is increasingly viewed as a necessary competency of members of the helping professions, including school-based professionals (Cook & Friend, 2010; Ysseldyke

et al., 2009). Collaboration as an option for service delivery has been around since the early 1970s and has been steadily growing in popularity ever since (see ASCA, 2005; Cook & Friend, 2010; Pryzwansky, 2011). It emerged as a way to help the parties involved to take on a greater sense of ownership in the problem-solving process, most particularly, the carrying out of interventions (Finello, 2011).

Collaboration can occur in a variety of settings (Conoley & Conoley, 2010). For example, in schools, collaboration can occur during screening for special education services, development of individualized education plans (IEP), RTI, periodic review of students, and also with problem-solving intervention teams and site-based management teams (Mellin et al., 2011). In another example, mental health professionals collaborate with members of community systems to provide more integrated services. The increased focus on collaboration suggests that mental health professionals see the importance of an interdependent approach for tackling social issues and client needs (Mellin et al., 2011; Sink, 2011b).

Collaboration is increasingly being used as a service that is designed to be an alternative to consultation—school-based collaboration, for example, was first viewed as an alternative to school-based consultation (Pryzwansky, 2011). At the same time, collaboration has emerged as an effective service among community-based mental health professionals. In many ways, collaboration emerged as an alternative to consultation as a result of criticism of the older literature written about consultation. This early literature was written from the perspective that the consultant was external to the organization, while the number of internal consultants was growing significantly (e.g., increase in school counselors and school psychologists). Further, there was criticism that organization-based consultants did not provide direct service to the client system—that was the responsibility of the consultee. The emphasis on the use of teams who had responsibility for problem solving led to a focus on the mutual responsibility of team members for the outcomes of problem solving, including any interventions. Finally, the structures and processes of some organizations, such as schools, dictated the need for both indirect and direct services from organization-based mental health professionals (Racine Gilles et al., 2011). Criticisms like these fostered the emergence of collaboration as a service distinct from consultation.

Collaboration is very similar to consultation in that, as a stand-alone service, it follows the same problem-solving process. Collaboration permits people with diverse expertise to combine efforts to accomplish the shared goal of helping a client, program, or organization. Collaboration improves upon the solutions the parties may have come up with independently (Petri, 2010).

Like consultation, collaboration has many definitional issues surrounding it (Cook & Friend, 2010; Mellin, 2009; Petri, 2010). A commonly accepted general definition of collaboration is "two or more people working together, using systematic planning and problem-solving procedures, to achieve desired outcomes" (Curtis, Castillo, & Cohen, 2008, p. 890). It has also been defined as where professionals "…engage in a nonhierarchical relationship to develop interventions" (Burns, Wiley, & Viglietta, 2008, p. 1636). A defining benchmark of collaboration is that the parties involved not only provide expertise but also solicit input from fellow collaborators (Ysseldyke et al., 2009). In collaboration, each participant "alternately plays the consultant/expert and the consultee/recipient role in a forum where solution finding is jointly and equally shared among people with different knowledge and experience" (Thousand, Villa, Paolucci-Whitcomb, & Nevin, 1996). Collaboration involves shared ownership of problem definition and solutions, a shared knowledge and expertise, and the increased willingness to work together.

Thus, collaboration is a service in which the collaborator from the helping professions accepts responsibility for the mental health aspects of a case, including carrying out some of the planned interventions and assuming joint responsibility for the case (Schulte & Osborne, 2003). For example, a school counselor might work with a student on decreasing verbal aggression while consulting with the teacher about decreasing the student's verbal aggression in the teacher's classroom. The teacher, in turn, provides consultation to the counselor about the behavior of the student and works with the student in the classroom. Figure 1.2 illustrates the relationships of the parties involved in collaboration.

Similar to consultation, support for collaboration by organizational leadership is essential to its successful use (Petri, 2010). Typically, collaboration involves the interactive exchange of resources, interdependence between collaborators, and a focus on decision making (Rubin, 2002; Welch, 2000). Collaboration requires the development of shared goals, bidirectional communication, and joint problem solving (Minke, 2006). There is an inherent respect of the views and skills of fellow collaborators (Arredondo et al., 2004; Pryzwansky, 2011). As a result, the parties involved in collaboration build up each other's capacity for achieving the goals of collaboration (Conoley & Conley, 2010). A key element in collaboration is focus on the end result and the connection between the purpose of collaboration and its goals (Gibbons & Silberglitt, 2008).

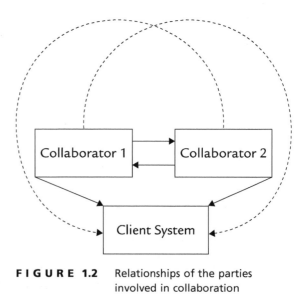

FIGURE 1.2 Relationships of the parties involved in collaboration

In collaboration, the parties involved share the power in the decision-making process (Macmann et al., 1996; Pryzwansky, 2011). In a school setting, a teacher's perspective is involved as well as that of the school counselor and school psychologist. Further, the teacher influences their behavior through his or her input. All collaborators are considered to have unique expertise, expected to apply that expertise in helping the client system, and be held accountable (Welch, 2000). Again, in collaboration, both parties reciprocally influence one another in all aspects of the case, engage in joint problem solving, and have responsibility for some aspects of the case related to its outcome.

Collaboration sometimes remains a one-on-one experience, but most frequently is a small group process that emphasizes teams (Mellin et al., 2011; Paisley & Milsom, 2007). For example, many schools have an Instructional Consultation Team (IC-Team) (Gravois, Groff, & Rosenfield, 2009; Rosenfield & Gravois, 1999), prereferral intervention teams (PIT) (Young & Gaughan, 2010), or multidisciplinary problem-solving teams (PST) (Burns et al., 2008). In some work settings, collaboration teams are established whenever there is a collective effort to accomplish a goal such as helping the client system (Kirst-Ashman & Hull, 2012; McNamara, Rasheed, & Delamatre, 2008). In school-based collaboration, teams can promote student assistance, teacher support, and school-wide support (Adelman & Taylor, 2008; Gravois et al., 2009). Some federal legislation focused on schools [e.g., Individuals with Disabilities Education Improvement Act (IDEIA, 2004)] require the use of multidisciplinary teams for some student-related decisions (McNamara et al., 2008; Yetter, 2010). In nonschool settings, teams in which collaboration is the primary activity include task forces, work groups, and multidisciplinary teams. Teams are an increasing popular outcome of school reform, including reform aimed at cultural competency (Simcox, Nuijens, & Lee, 2006) or in improving morale in an agency.

Successful teams have certain characteristics (Gravois et al., 2009). To be effective, teams have to manage their business activities (e.g., problem solving and evaluation) and maintenance (giving and receiving feedback) activities well (Barnett, Hawkins, & Lentz, 2011; Rosenfield & Gravois, 1999). Teams engaging in collaboration will need a mechanism for dealing with issues such as conflict among members (Finello, 2011) and have strong leadership qualities, commitment, and focus among members (Gravois et al., 2009; Yetter, 2010). Further, teams will want to ensure that participant input is valued, interventions are well defined, and the team has some accountability for outcomes (Kirst-Ashman & Hull, 2012; Slonski-Fowler & Truscott, 2003).

Why does collaboration work? Conoley and Conoley (2010) provide an interesting perspective on this question that employs the principles of positive psychology. The basic point is that effective collaboration can provide social support to the parties involved. This support is twofold. First, fellow collaborators feel more productive when they are in trusting relationships such as those provided by positive support. Second, collaborations avail to the parties involved access to more tools to deal with the tasks involved in collaboration. The result of social support, then, is to increase the collaborators' "personal resources and skills" (Conoley & Conoley, 2010, p. 77). These authors conclude that "… a positive collaborative relationship expands the competence of all involved and predicts enhanced functioning for all involved" (p. 77). Collaboration also works if there is an established conceptual framework for its implementation that is followed appropriately (Mellin et al., 2011). There are four elements to one popular conceptual framework: role interdependence, professional flexibility, reflection on process, and newly created professional opportunities (Mellin et al., 2010). Role interdependence refers to the degree that fellow collaborators rely upon one another to meet the goal of collaboration. Professional flexibility deals with how fellow collaborators adapt and adjust their roles based on the collaboration process. Reflection on the process involves evaluation of the collaborative process with an intent to improve each collaborator's practice in future collaborations. Newly created professional opportunities pertain to collectively determined intervention that may be more helpful to the client system than those derived by the fellow collaborators individually and in isolation from one another. There is, however, limited empirical research to support the importance of these elements in effective collaboration efforts.

Like consultation, the context or setting of collaboration can shape its nature. There are typically two contexts in which collaboration can occur: intraagency and interagency. For example, in intraagency collaboration, people from the same school setting work together to help some children and their families in increasing the children's academic achievement.

In interagency collaboration, a group from two or more agencies attempts to help a child make a successful transition from a juvenile evaluation center to a public school setting.

Interagency collaboration is particularly common in early childhood settings (Harris & Klein, 2004) and in public education (Mellin, 2009), and has received significant attention among professionals (Tseng, Liu, & Wang, 2011). Collaboration in both these contexts presents its own unique challenges. In interagency collaboration, the term *interdisciplinary collaboration* is receiving increased attention in the literature (D'Amour, Ferrada-Videla, Rodriguez, & Beaulieu, 2005). Interdisciplinary collaboration involves two or more professionals pooling their expertise to reach a defined goal in an intervention in which decision making and intervention are shared (Mellin, 2009). In interdisciplinary collaboration, high levels of communication, cooperation, coordination, and accountability are essential (Mellin, 2009). Due to its complexity, interdisciplinary collaboration can be a challenge to implement. In intraagency collaboration, the major challenge is for the parties-at-interest to find the time to actually meet and implement the nuts and bolts of the collaborative process. In interagency collaboration, the major challenge is one of coordination of the efforts of two or more organizations to a common end (Dedrick & Greenbaum, 2011; Mellin et al., 2011).

As we have seen, defining the parameters of collaboration can sometimes be difficult. When the would-be consultant and prospective consultees are employed in the same setting, it is difficult to meet some of the fundamental assumptions underlying consultation, resulting in collaboration most likely being the method of choice. For example, maintaining confidentiality at necessary levels in consultation can be challenging, the voluntary nature of consultation becomes questionable, and it is often difficult to relieve the consultant of *any* responsibility for the outcome of consultation (Zins & Erchul, 2002). Again, considering some of the challenges a school counselor or school psychologist might face in attempting to provide consultation services in a school, some authors (e.g., Caplan & Caplan, 1993) have suggested that collaboration is the intervention of choice over consultation when the mental health professional is internal to the organization.

One trend in collaboration is an increased emphasis on community collaboration in which stakeholders from various community entities such as schools and mental health services engage in community collaboration to assist client systems (James & Crews, 2014; Mellin, 2009; Mellin et al., 2011). Another trend is for collaboration to be a useful service in achieving social justice initiatives (Lopez-Baez & Paylo, 2009). Further, collaboration may be useful in situations where a consultee does not have the skill or time to effectively take total responsibility for implementation of the intervention (Kratochwill & Pittman, 2002; Pryzwansky, 2011). Some research on collaboration as a service has socially validated collaboration as a valued service by practitioners (Welch & Tulbert, 2000) but additional and higher quality research is needed (Mellin, 2009; Petri, 2010). In conclusion, it is important to remember that a distinguishing difference between consultation and collaboration is that, in *consultation*, the consultee retains responsibility for the outcome, is considered to be the determiner of the suitability of possible interventions, and is responsible for adequate implementation of the intervention (i.e., ensuring treatment integrity) (Zins & Erchul, 2002).

The following three brief and general examples illustrate the scope of consultation and collaboration:

Case Example 1: Consulting with Another Human Service Professional

George is a clinical mental health professional providing therapy to a family who has a dying child, a new situation for him. George asks you, a mental health consultant with expertise in this area, for some recommendations for helping the family deal directly with the impending death of the child since this is causing severe problems within the family. You interview the family for the purposes of data collection without performing any therapy. You then provide George with specific written recommendations for him to assist the family in dealing with this issue. George agrees with your recommendations and implements them, although he is free to reject them if he chooses. You then follow up and help George assess the progress he has made with the family relative to the recommendations. [*Note that in this example of consultation, the consultant takes on an expert role of assessing and diagnosing the client system to assist with the clinician's methods of working with the client system (family).*]

Case Example 2: Consulting with a Juvenile Court Counselor

A probation counselor approaches you, a mental health professional assigned to her workplace, for consultation regarding challenges the counselor is having in providing counseling to a parolee. Through your discussions of the nature of her problems with this case, you sense that the behaviors of the consultee significantly impact the difficulty experienced in working with the client system. You are first empathic with consultee regarding his conceptualization of the case. You then ask some judicious, neutral questions about the client system and then make some observations about other ways to conceptualize the issues of the client system. In this case, you help the consultee to see that the parolee's failure in finding a job is not so much due to lack of

effort as the need for improved job interviewing skills. You support the resulting consultee reconceptualization of the case, which has resulted in a broadened perspective on the treatment options available to assist the parolee. Your consultation then turns to having the consultee select, implement, and evaluate the intervention that she thinks has the best chance of helping the youth. (*Note that in this example of consultation, the consultant acts in a facilitator role with the result that the consultee having a broadened perspective on the treatment options while retaining the responsibility for implementing the intervention.*)

Case Example 3: Collaborating with a Teacher

Mary Smith, a teacher, and you, a school counselor, agree on trying to assist a student who Mary says is "incorrigible" and whom you view as lacking proper social skills with adults. You and Mary meet and establish a relationship. Mary describes what the student does that makes her label him as "incorrigible" and how often these negative behaviors occur. You give your opinions about the student's behavior. You make classroom observations and Mary gathers additional classroom data regarding her instructional techniques with the student. With that data in hand, you and Mary critically analyze the data and determine the acceptable level of the negative behaviors to be sought as well as the level of new desirable behaviors. You and the teacher also determine that a change in instructional procedures may be in order to assist the student. For example, together you determine that the student would benefit from being a team leader for his group's team project. You discuss the strengths of the student and how those might be used in meeting the goals of collaboration. Together, you then select a behavior change program with empirical validation from the research literature that has Mary implementing some positive reinforcement procedures with the student in the classroom while you provide related counseling services to the student. You help her with the development of the positive reinforcement procedures and she assists you by providing information that is helpful to you in counseling the student. You monitor the progress of the student on a weekly basis for two weeks and adjust the intervention accordingly. At a later date, you both evaluate the effectiveness of the collaborative experience. You have been responsible for implementing the mental health aspect of the case, while the teacher has been in charge of assisting the student in developing appropriate social skills in the classroom. *(Note that in this example of collaboration, both collaborators have some specific responsibility for implementing the interventions.)*

MULTICULTURAL LIMITATIONS OF CONSULTATION AND COLLABORATION

It is very likely that you will practice consultation and collaboration in multicultural and cross-cultural settings (Sue, 2008). For example, the 2000 U.S. Census showed that the society in the United States is already very diverse. By 2050, the majority of the population in the United States will be people of color (Romney, 2008). This diversity is, and will be, further reflected in all of the institutions in U.S. society and thus requires culturally competent practice on the part of consultants and collaborators. The same can be said for many societies throughout the world.

In and of themselves, cultural differences are complex and subjective (Hall, 2005; LaRoche & Maxie, 2003). Further, there is a complex connection between culture and consultation. Culture is viewed as a context that permeates all aspects of consultation rather than simply a related variable (Hoffman et al., 2006; Ingraham, 2000, 2008; Tarver Behring & Ingraham, 1998). In other words, the culture of the consultant, the consultee, and the client system are all aspects of the ecology dealt with in consultation (Cooper & Leong, 2008; Ortiz, 2006; Ramirez & Smith, 2007). Most models of consultation are ethnocentric and therefore are limited (Nastasi, 2006). As a result, consultants and collaborators will want to not only be culturally sensitive in their practice but also have the skills

and knowledge to respond to diversity (Meyers et al., 2009; Romney, 2008). Knotek (2012) cites an example that illustrates that not all cultural groups, in this case Native Americans, necessarily adhere to the common assumptions regarding consultation such as interpersonal relations and problem-solving styles.

Ingraham (2000, 2004, 2008) has built a framework that conceptualizes consultation from multicultural and cross-cultural perspectives, thus promoting cultural competence. Ingraham's model brings multicultural competence to the forefront and traditional consultation models are adapted accordingly (Ingraham, 2004, 2007). This framework, which can be applied to all models of consultation, considers the influence of culture on the consultation process and the individuals involved in it. In *multicultural consultation*, the consultant, in a culturally sensitive manner, adjusts services to accommodate and value cultural differences (Ingraham, 2003, 2008). *Cross-cultural consultation* is consultation that occurs across cultures. Ingraham's comprehensive framework focuses on structures and processes of consultation, thus allowing consultants to identify and reflect upon multicultural issues and increase the chances of a successful consultation experience. This framework has five components:

a) consultant knowledge, skills, and dispositions related to cultural competence in consultation;

b) understanding consultee needs for development in knowledge, skill, confidence, and objectivity;

c) cultural variations in the parties involved in consultation (e.g., consultant–consultee similarity);

d) contextual influence (e.g., organizational culture) and power influences (difference in power among parties in the consultation relationship); and

e) methods for supporting consultee success in multicultural situations.

Nastasi (2006) points out the necessity of cultural specificity in delivering services such as consultation and collaboration. Cultural specificity refers to the idea that all aspects of services such as consultation and collaboration are relevant to the targeted culture (Nastasi, 2006).

Hoffman et al. (2006), although not developing a framework for consultation as such, have presented major ideas that could lead to the development of a feminist and multicultural framework. The major themes include (p. 127):

a) a nonhierarchical approach that provides greater benefits than a hierarchical one;

b) a hierarchy in the consultation relationship is not inevitable;

c) an open triad structure examines the complex interplay of interpersonal and extrapersonal forces within the context of the system;

d) the consultation experience is used as an opportunity to transform the system;

e) patriarchal structures in organizations are based on greater privilege for some rather than all;

f) the consultant's expertise and skills should be used to empower;

g) the role of the consultant is that of an active agent for change;

h) the consultation process can prevent similar systemic problems in the future; and

i) informed advocacy on the part of the consultant for the consultee and client system is appropriate.

Through employing the framework and/or concepts like those described above, consultants are in a better position to provide services with multicultural competence. Without such a framework, the chances for successful consultation and collaboration are diminished (Ramirez & Smith, 2007). As Salzman (2005) notes: "… no symptom or observation can be accurately interpreted without due consideration to social, historical, political and cultural considerations" (p. 235). Consultants will want to ensure that they are culturally sensitive and competent at each phase of the consultation process. As an example, the concept of "happiness" for the client system may vary by culture (Gerstein, 2007).

In addition to striving to be multiculturally competent, consultants will want to bear in mind that the traditional models of consultation, which are typically derived from models of counseling and psychotherapy, may be based on worldviews that are irrelevant to some cultural groups (Corey, 2009; Hoffman et al., 2006). As Corey (2009) notes: "With respect to many of the traditional theories, assumptions made about mental health, optimum human development, the nature of psychopathology, and the nature of effective treatment may have little relevance for some clients" (p. 42). For example, many cultural groups do not embrace the emphasis on individualism that many counseling theories value. As a result, consultants need to take a "person-in-the-environment perspective" (Corey, 2009; Lum, 2011). By focusing on both individual and environmental factors, consultants can modify and adjust the model they are using (Diller, 2007; Ramirez & Smith, 2007) to accommodate consultees and their client systems. For example, a consultant might adjust working with a consultee of a culturally different group by reconceptualizing treatment goals by taking the consultee's cultural beliefs into consideration (Diller, 2007). In other examples, a consultant may suggest that a consultee spend more time in relationship building with the client system or making recommendations regarding how to approach a culturally different client from a cultural style perspective (Ramirez & Smith, 2007). According to Diller (2007), another possibility is adding to existing models, as appropriate, culture-specific helping strategies. By behaving in this manner, consultants ensure that they take into account the subtle variables influencing the consultation process. The use of a multicultural framework will help consultees with a variety of issues that block consultee objectivity such as intervention paralysis in which consultees are multiculturally aware, yet afraid of acting due to concern over making a multicultural blunder or making a cultural blunder in which a consultee acts in such a way as to be culturally insensitive (Ingraham, 2004). This can result from the common predicament of a consultee knowing that each case is individual and also that common cultural variables may be at play (Ramirez & Smith, 2007). A bottom-line approach to multicultural consultation and collaboration is that all local cultural situations need to be examined in terms of how they interact with the members of the system being addressed (Meyers et al., 2009; Sue, 2008). In other multicultural frameworks, cultural competence is the effective practice of consultation and collaboration in different cultural contexts.

CONSULTATION, COLLABORATION, AND LEVELS OF PREVENTION

U.S. society faces more incidences of mental health and behavioral disorders than it can handle in part because existing resources are typically targeted at treating existing maladies rather than preventing them (Gutkin, 2009). Simply put, more behavioral and psychological problems emerge due to the fact that the resources available cannot eradicate problems faster than they are created. Consultation and collaboration are services that deal simultaneously with both remediation of current problems and prevention of incidences of future problems (Baker & Shaw, 1987). The idea behind prevention is that consultation enhances consultee's abilities to successfully deal with or prevent similar issues in the future and serves as a method of delivering prevention services through the intermediary of the consultee (Zins, 1995). Therefore, the consultee becomes an agent of prevention from having gone through consultation.

The remedial perspective is reactive, while the preventative perspective is proactive and typically considers environmental events as they impact individuals (Blom-Hoffman & Rose, 2007). As you know, a remedial approach fixes a problem after it occurs with the idea of preventing occurrences in the future. For example, a consultant assists a consultee to select and implement an intervention for a client system with an existing problem. Preventive approaches attempt to stop problems from

occurring in the first place and hopefully result in a decrease in the need for services and resources (Love, 2007). For example, a school-based consultant facilitates a group of stakeholders implementing a school-wide antibullying program. There is increasing empirical support that consultation can have a preventive effect (Gutkin & Curtis, 2009; Gutkin, 2012).

Prevention in consultation is based on human ecology (Gutkin, 2009). In essence, the ecological perspective states that human behavior has to be examined in some context in order to be adequately understood. For consultation and collaboration, this suggests that defining the client system accurately involves not only looking at an individual's behavior but also the environments in which that behavior occurs. Examples of variables include school climate and increasing the capacity of human service organizations. The preventive approach to consultation has been underdeveloped (Hughes, Lloyd, & Buss, 2008; Meyers, Proctor, Graybill, & Meyers, 2009), most likely due to the continued focus on remediation as well as difficulties in implementation (Gutkin, 2012; Erchul & Sheridan, 2008). Throughout this text, you will read examples that illustrate consultation and collaboration as either remedial or preventative.

One of the founders of consultation, Gerald Caplan, stressed prevention utilizing the public health model. The practice of consultation and collaboration feels the impact of his findings even today. The public health model includes three levels of prevention: primary, secondary, and tertiary (remedial). As Lewis, Lewis, Daniels, and D'Andrea (2003) note: "Primary prevention focuses lowering the incidence of emotional problems and on promoting positive mental health among people not identified as having any special difficulty. It can be distinguished from secondary prevention, which aims at early identification and treatment of problems, and from tertiary prevention, which attempts to decrease the long-term effects of disabilities" (p. 25). Primary prevention tries to prevent problems from occurring in the first place, secondary prevention tries to prevent problems from occurring in at-risk populations, and tertiary prevention (remedial) tries to prevent problems from reoccurring once they have been effectively resolved with a given client system. For example, a school-based consultant might engage in primary prevention by working to effect a system-level change in a school that creates a safe and caring school climate conducive to all students learning at optimal levels; secondary prevention by working with an administrator to develop a special program for students at risk for dropping out of school; and tertiary prevention by working with a teacher to assist a student with a history of acting out in the classroom. In another example, a community-based consultant might engage in primary prevention by consulting with neighborhood organizations to promote human development and self-advocacy; secondary prevention by working with a community-based alternative mental health program to prevent teenage pregnancies; and tertiary prevention by consulting with the counselors of pregnant teens and their partners. As you might guess, preventive consultation can have the broadest effect when an entire system such as a school or a community agency is the target for change.

While Caplan's classification scheme for prevention remains popular, the nomenclature in prevention is undergoing change and a newer set of prevention categories has emerged. Though understandable, this change has led to some confusion regarding levels of prevention in the prevention literature. Strein and Koehler (2008) note that in the mid-1990s the Institute of Medicine (IOM) endorsed prevention terminology based upon which portion of the population the prevention intervention is focused on. The categories are *universal*, *selective,* and *indicated*. Universal interventions, like those of primary prevention, are designed for a population as a whole. One example would be a substance abuse prevention program for all students. Selective interventions target subpopulations that may be at risk. An example is a substance abuse prevention program for children of alcoholics. Indicated intervention strategies involve special strategies for segments of the population who are exhibiting early signs of a problem. Following our other example, a group of students exhibiting the early signs of

substance abuse are provided with a substance abuse prevention program tailored to their needs. The school-based consultation and collaboration literature has increasingly categorized interventions within this three-tiered model that matches resource intensity with problem intensity (Strein & Koehler, 2008). This categorization scheme has implications in that consultants and collaborators will need to ensure that the stakeholders, both internal and external to the organization, understand the terminology being used in the prevention effort.

There is increasing consensus among mental health specialists in our society that we need to focus more on the psychological health and well-being of our society during the 21st century (Gutkin, 2009; Meyers et al., 2009). As a result, prevention focuses not only on eliminating the incidences of problems (e.g., bullying) but also the enhancement competencies in a population (e.g., social skills) (Durlak, 2009).

In conclusion, consultation and collaboration, because they can focus on both remediation and prevention, are ideal services for mental health providers as they attempt to better meet the needs of people in a rapidly changing, culturally diverse, and technological society. For example, as we will see later in the text, these myriad societal changes have also given rise to an increased body of literature that focuses on the ecological perspective in consultation and its related emphasis on prevention (Gutkin, 2012). All models of consultation and collaboration have both remedial and preventative aspects, but they do vary in the degree to which one or the other is emphasized (Zins, 1995). There is a wealth of prevention programs that consultants and collaborators can impact in a variety of roles and ways, ranging from assisting stakeholders in interpreting program data to facilitating efforts for advocating for a program within an organization.

HISTORICAL OVERVIEW

Now that we have defined and described consultation and collaboration, let's examine their historical context. Like any other human service function, the roots of consultation and collaboration go back to ancient times.

Decades ago, Gallessich (1982) pointed out two prototypical roles of consultation that emerged: the healer and the technological advisor. The healer had the power to improve well-being, and the technological advisor could tell someone how to fix something or how to proceed to the next step in solving a problem. As human knowledge expanded, so too did the need for people who could help solve problems and provide technical expertise. A third role gaining increasing prominence is that of social change agent in which consultants actively advocate for systems-level change to accomplish, for example, social justice (Moe, Perera-Diltz, & Sepulveda, 2010).

As consultation developed into a tool of mental health professionals, the familiar medical consultation provided a model. If a physician noticed something about a patient that might require the attention of a specialist, he or she consulted with the specialist. Frequently, the results of that consultation meant turning the patient over to the specialist (in other words, the consultant). The physician who originally handled the case frequently did not treat the patient again. Hence, in the original form of consultation, the consultant saw and treated the patient.

Such was the state of consultation around the turn of the 20th century. Then it became increasingly apparent to medical professionals that the referring personnel could benefit from participating in treating the patient further. This change in perspective fostered the emergence in the human service professions of consultation as we now know it. It has been around since the 1950s (Meyers, Truscott, Meyers, Varjas, & Collins, 2008). Additional forces that contributed to the emergence of human service consultation were the growth of the organization development movement and the community mental health movement (Brown, Kurpius, & Morris, 1988).These forces viewed the consultee as an active participant in the consultation process and viewed consultation as a developmental, preventative force that would continue to balance direct and indirect service activities. This shift led

to the idea of consultant as trainer, that is, a professional party who would give away the skills of helping. The basic essence of consultation, as it emerged as a service delivery, was to enhance the methodological repertoires of consultees (Johnson & Pugach, 1996). The consultant was the expert who accomplished this task in a series of transactions with the consultee. Gerald Caplan's 1970 landmark book *The Theory and Practice of Mental Health Consultation* promoted mental health consultation as a primary prevention service to mental health providers. This book was, in part, based on Caplan's professional experiences in the late 1940s and early 1950s. Consultation became a primary activity for workers in the schools such as counselors and psychologists. The community counselor's role as a consultant has been less well-established (Keys, Bemak, Carpenter, & King-Sear, 1998). Along with these developments, there has been a great expansion of the empirical literature on consultation (Sheridan & Erchul, 2008).

Consultation today, common in such human service professions as psychology, counseling, social work, and human resource development, has developed into three broad types: organizational, mental health, and behavioral. I will cover the historical development of each of these types in later chapters.

More recently, the changing nature of organizations such as schools has changed the amount of emphasis placed on the expert role (e.g., a counselor helping a teacher improve classroom management skills) to a more collaborative approach (e.g., a counselor and teacher working simultaneously on goals related to improved classroom behavior) (Bradley, 1994).

Collaboration as a distinct service emerged in education as a response to legislation involving the education of students identified as eligible for special education services. It was viewed as being distinct from consultation and involved stakeholders in a partnership to assist students, primarily those with disabilities (Cook & Friend, 2010).

There has been a parallel increase in interest in collaboration as a mode of service delivery in profit and nonprofit organizations. In other organizations, collaboration emerged as the idea of teams and joint responsibility for implementing mental health programs emerged. For example, in the mental health arena, collaboration emerged as an alternative to traditional consultation, primarily for internal consultants. In fact, the increase in having providers and recipients of consultation employed in the same organization made it increasingly difficult for some of the assumptions of consultation to be met and thereby gave impetus to the popularity of collaboration.

Finally, the complexity of organizations, a renewed focus on prevention and ecological constructs, the increased recognition of multicultural issues in our society, and the emergence of social justice all have demanded a more system-level approach to problem solving. The literature concerning consultation and collaboration has reflected increased interest in providing these services at the systems level. It is now common for consultants and collaborators to work on organization-wide issues and deal with problems that affect the entire organization (Merrell et al., 2006). For example, counselors and psychologists are involved as consultants and collaborators in dealing with system-level issues such as those related to school reform or organizational cultural competence.

CONSULTATION AND COLLABORATION COMPARED WITH OTHER HUMAN SERVICE ACTIVITIES

As noted above, consultation and collaboration each have a set of central elements and characteristics. Comparing consultation and collaboration with the four other common human service functions—counseling and psychotherapy, supervision, teaching, and mediation—is beneficial as a way of making the concepts underlying consultation and collaboration more clear. Caplan, in the 1970s, popularized such comparisons (see, e.g., Caplan, 1970).

Consultation and collaboration are different from *counseling and psychotherapy* in two fairly obvious ways. First, counseling and psychotherapy are dyadic in nature (they involve two parties: the therapist and the client), whereas consultation and collaboration are triadic (Neukrug, 2012). Second, counseling and psychotherapy deal with the personal problems of the client, whereas consultation/collaboration deal with work-related or caretaking-related concerns only. This is not to say that the effects of resolving a work-related problem cannot be therapeutic to the consultee or fellow collaborators or that consultants/collaboration do not acknowledge consultee affect. Still, consultants and collaborators, even if they are trained therapists, do not provide counseling or psychotherapy to consultees or fellow collaborators as part of consultation or collaboration services, even if the work- or caretaking-related problem being solved is determined to be due to a personal problem of the other professional or caregiver. In such cases, the human service professional brings up his or her concerns and then refers the other party for assistance or, as we will see later in the text, if necessary, engages in an ethical dual relationship with the consultee. A final point to remember is that when the consultant or collaborator is trained in counseling and psychotherapy, it is quite easy to inadvertently turn the consultation or collaboration session into a therapy session.

Another function that is different from consultation and collaboration is *supervision*. Supervision can be either clinical or administrative. Clinical supervision involves "consistent observation and evaluation of the counseling process ... provided by a trained and experienced professional" (Haynes, Corey & Moulton, 2003, p. 3). Administrative supervision focuses "on the issues surrounding the supervisee's role and the responsibilities in the organization as an employee" (Haynes et al., 2003, p. 3). Supervision tends to be performed in dyads and implies an ongoing relationship, whereas consultation and collaboration are usually temporary, tripartite relationships (Kirst-Ashman & Hull, 2012). More significantly, supervision implies the power of one person over another and the legal and clinical accountability for the behavior of the supervisee (Thomas, 2010). If I am your supervisor, I have the power to perform ongoing evaluations of your effectiveness on the job. These evaluations will be used in personnel decisions that affect you in many ways at work and thus create inequity in the relationship. Therefore, consultants or collaborators do not become supervisors of the people to whom they provide these services.

Teaching is also different from consultation and collaboration. Traditional teaching involves a predetermined, detailed lesson plan, whereas events in consultation and collaboration often dictate more spontaneous behavior by the parties involved. Further, teaching is an unequal relationship in which teachers have power over students and evaluate them, traditionally by some grading process. Human service professionals may assess consultee or fellow collaborator learning, but in a manner different from that used by teachers. A consultant or collaborator may, however, take on a teaching role on occasion. For example, a mental health collaborator might teach a fellow collaborator how to perform a behavioral counseling technique with a client, or an organizational consultant might teach a consultee the basics of survey design. Later in this text, you will read about education/training consultation; it is one of the most commonly requested approaches to consultation.

Mediation is different from consultation and collaboration, although many consultants and collaborators use mediation techniques in group or organizational work. Mediation is a form of conflict resolution (Fisher, Ury, & Patton, 1991) in which the mediator takes on the role of a third-party, neutral observer. Mediation is similar to consultation and collaboration in that it has a problem-solving orientation, is tripartite in nature, uses collaboration extensively, and involves a peer relationship among the parties. Mediation is different from consultation and collaboration in that it necessarily deals with conflict, never uses a teaching role, and does not allow room for suggestions or recommendations by the third-party neutral.

WHETHER TO CHOOSE CONSULTATION OR COLLABORATION

A discussion of how to choose between consultation and collaboration is important as they are closely related services. You will frequently be faced with the decision to choose between consultation and collaboration as the service of choice in particular situations. Below I describe some guidelines to assist you in this choice process.

First, ask and answer the question, "How does the organizational culture view each of these services in terms of preference?" In some instances, it might well be that collaboration is regarded as the "new kid on the block" and therefore is not perceived to be as legitimate as consultation. On the other hand, for professionals who are internal to the organization in which services are to be provided, collaboration may be preferred because it presents many stakeholders with a piece of the action of implementation.

Second, ask yourself, "How do I really feel about consultation and collaboration? Do I think consultation puts me too much in the expert role? Do I think collaboration forces me to give up too much power in the case?" It is important for you to know where you stand on issues like these as they will affect your choice of services. Before you proceed with consultation, you need to determine if the assumptions underlying consultation (e.g., confidentiality, the voluntary nature of the relationship, nonhierarchical status within the relationship) are met. If they are not met, collaboration may well be the method of choice.

Your own skill level will also influence your decision to use consultation or collaboration. On the one hand, consultation demands the ability to guide and control the problem-solving process while empowering the consultee. On the other hand, collaboration demands the ability to balance the reciprocal influence that the parties exert on each other in collaboration. As you gain experience in both consultation and collaboration, you will become equally comfortable with both processes.

The level of skill of the prospective consultee or collaborator will influence your choice of services.

If the other party is not skilled in what is most likely to be implemented and time for training is not feasible, then collaboration is in order. If time is not a factor or the other party is relatively highly skilled in terms of possible interventions, then consultation may well be in order.

The bottom line is that the choice between using consultation or collaboration is frequently a judgment call with either choice being an adequate one. As in determining whether to provide any other service, the nature of the problem, the cultural and organizational contexts in which it occurs, and the skills of the parties involved interact together to influence your choice. The circumstances surrounding the problem at hand will most likely determine the choice between consultation and collaboration.

BASIC ASSUMPTIONS
OF THIS TEXT

To set the stage for the remainder of the text, I now share five basic assumptions about consultation and collaboration. First, I assume that consultation and collaboration are very similar in terms of the skills needed and the processes engaged in. Throughout this text, what I write about consultation basically holds for collaboration. The main point to remember is that in collaboration, as opposed to consultation, the mental health professional assists in the intervention and also receives and gives consultation to other collaborators. In order to enhance the readability of the text, I will frequently use the term *consultation* instead of phrases like *consultation and collaboration*. When it is necessary to differentiate consultation from collaboration, I do this explicitly in the text.

The second assumption is that *how* a consultant or collaborator performs is as important as *what* he or she does. This is very important because the perceptions of these processes by the parties involved are critical in determining their success. For example, as a consultant, I might know what I need to do to help a particular consultee, but if I don't know how to do it in a way that he or she sees as helpful, then the consultation is less likely to be successful. Of importance is how the working relationship is established (Gutkin & Curtis, 2009). By consulting and collaborating under the supervision of well-trained professionals, you will understand *how* you consult and collaborate and the impact your behavior has on the effectiveness of these processes.

The third assumption is that consultation and collaboration are human, helping relationships. Consultants and collaborators work *with* people. The personal sides of these services become as important as their professional sides. Human service professionals need to identify and clarify their values about both life and the professional services they offer so that they do not fall into the trap of inadvertently imposing those values when providing these services. Such an imposition, in addition to being unethical, can restrict the professional growth of the persons with whom they are working. In addition, a lack of self-knowledge about values can place blinders on a professional and lead to mistakes during the course of consultation and collaboration. However, when consultation and collaboration are viewed as human, helping relationships, the respect, dignity, and welfare of the parties involved become paramount. Effective professionals excel by behaving in ways that demonstrate respect for their consultees and fellow collaborators and protect their welfare.

The fourth assumption is that human services professionals need training in these services. In the past, many people consulted and collaborated without ever having any proper training; they learned to provide these services through a series of consulting and collaborating experiences alone. Only by chance do they develop a frame of reference for approaching consultation and collaboration opportunities. Flying by the seat of one's pants is dangerous in the delivery of any professional service; the professional (and sometimes the personal) aspects of other people's lives are involved. Consultants should not view their counseling/psychotherapy skills as sufficient to get them by when consulting (Welfel, 2002) as that is a very slippery slope. Consequently, human service professionals need to be well-grounded in models and interventions related to consultation and collaboration (Alpert & Taufique, 2002a; NASP, 2010c; ASCA, 2005). This knowledge creates an objective frame of reference for delivering professional services. Further, only such knowledgeable and skillful professionals lend credibility to consultation and collaboration as legitimate services for human service professionals to provide.

The fifth assumption is that how one goes about effectively practicing consultation and collaboration depends on a large number of factors. To consult and collaborate effectively, you need to develop an understanding of how these services are practiced. A general framework for understanding and practicing consultation and collaboration will help you develop a cognitive map and a sense of direction for performing these services. A familiarity with the types of consultation and collaboration—usually categorized as mental health, behavioral, and organizational—will provide you with models that have some applicability in particular situations. Acquiring a broad repertoire of skills and a strong knowledge base from which to provide service permits consultants and collaborators to employ the most current, pertinent knowledge, and appropriate skills available. I encourage a systems view of events. Maintaining a systems view of events allows you to not only see the big picture but also to see the interconnectedness of events, their multicausal nature and the great realm of possible ways of intervening. By focusing on systems, consultants and collaborators can often determine the conditions inherent within the organization that contribute to the development and maintenance of problems within individuals (Lopez-Baez & Paylo, 2009; Zins & Erchul, 2002). Developing cultural competence is a must for practicing consultants and collaborators as practice needs to be adapted to the cultural context of the consultee and client system. You will consult and collaborate most effectively when you have integrated your knowledge and skills with your unique personality.

SUGGESTIONS FOR EFFECTIVE PRACTICE

- Know the focus points in your work environment that can be improved through your services.

- Develop a working definition of *consultation* and *collaboration* with which you feel comfortable.

- Become very familiar with the characteristics of both consultation and collaboration so that you can do both well and differentiate between the two when necessary.

- Give the highest priority to culturally competent practice.

- Make a point to differentiate consultation and collaboration from the other professional services you will be providing.

- Strive to take into account the social and cultural factors affecting your consultees and their client systems.

QUESTIONS FOR REFLECTION

1. How do the roles of consultant, consultee, and client differ from one another?

2. What is the basic difference between indirect and direct service that consultants and collaborators provide?

3. In what ways can consultation and collaboration be called problem-solving processes?

4. Why is it important for consultants and collaborators to have a personal theory of these two services?

5. In what ways are consultation and collaboration similar? Different?

6. How can you promote consultation and collaboration services in your work setting and also emphasize both the preventative and remedial aspects of these services?

7. How can consultation and collaboration have the goal of improving the consultee or fellow collaborator and the client system at the same time?

8. Because consultants, by definition, work with consultees who have work-related problems, how can the consultation relationship be that of equals?

9. How would you as a collaborator determine which roles to take on during collaboration?

10. How can you practice consultation and collaboration in a culturally competent manner?

SUGGESTED SUPPLEMENTARY READINGS

Started in 1990, the *Journal of Educational and Psychological Consultation* is sponsored by the Association for Educational and Psychological Consultants and published quarterly by Lawrence Erlbaum Associates. This journal serves as a forum for the exchange of ideas, theories, and research among professionals in the human services and education.

Consulting Psychology Journal: Practice and Research. This quarterly is the official journal of Division 13, Consulting Psychology, of the American Psychological Association (APA). It presents various ideas related to the practice of consultation. In recent years, the journal has tended to emphasize organizational consultation.

Dougherty, A. M. (2014). *Casebook of psychological consultation and collaboration* (6th ed.). Belmont, CA: Brooks/Cole, Cengage. Following an introductory chapter on the foundations of consultation and collaboration, this text provides seven detailed case studies illustrating consultation and collaboration in action. Each case study includes selected learning exercises to enhance the reader's reflection on the case and to facilitate pertinent group discussion. After the case study chapters, Chapter 9 draws implications for effective practice based upon material drawn from the cases. The final chapter provides several practice cases. Designed in workbook format with a large number of interactive learning exercises, this case studies text is designed to accompany the present text. Its focus is to provide, in an interactive format, a nuts-and-bolts approach to understanding how members of the helping professions provide service consultation and collaboration services.

SUGGESTED WEBSITE

http://www.nasponline.org   This is the website of the National Association of School Psychologists. It contains a wealth of invaluable information, including information on consultation and collaboration.

2

✳

Consultants, Consultees, and Collaborators

I f you were looking for a consultant or collaborator to work with people in your human service organization, what type of person would you hire? If you were going to permanently hire a mental health professional in your organization and part of his or her job was to consult and collaborate, what would you be looking for in candidates? What kinds of professional knowledge and skills would be needed in such a person, and how would you be able to tell if the consultant/collaborator truly possessed them? What roles would you want this person to take during his or her activities? What would be the most critical factor for you in determining whether or not to hire this prospective helper?

This chapter provides some answers to these questions—it discusses the characteristics that effective consultants and collaborators possess, the skills critical to successful consultation and collaboration, the various roles that professionals take on when providing these services, and get a brief understanding of the models they use. In addition, I will examine two other important areas: the position (internal or external) of the consultant/collaborator to the organization in which service is to occur and the current status of research on consultation and collaboration. I will look briefly at consultees and their role in the consultation process. However, to provide a more authentic perspective on the nature of the consultee in the consultation process, I have incorporated the consultee's experience in consultation into each chapter of this text.

As you read this chapter, consider the following questions:

■ How are the personal characteristics of consultants and collaborators likely to influence the delivery of their services?

- What skills seem necessary for consultants and collaborators, regardless of the role they assume in delivering their services?

- Do any of the roles of consultants and collaborators tend to conflict with one another (e.g., expert and collaborator)?

- In what ways should consultants and collaborators be multiculturally skilled?

- To what degree can the research related to these services guide your practice?

As I have noted in Chapter 1, you can assume in this and the following chapters that the discussion of a given topic applies equally to consultation and collaboration unless I make a distinction. I avoid using the terms *consultation* and *collaboration* together in order to enhance the readability of this text.

Consider the following two cases:

Case Example 1:
An Ineffective Consultant

Dale Jones, a counselor, and Jackie Cheng, a social worker, work together in a community mental health center. Jackie approaches Dale for consultation regarding a migrant family that is part of Jackie's caseload. It seems that the family has had difficulty adjusting to the community, which consists primarily of retirees who have their summer homes there. When Jackie asks Dale for help in facilitating the family's adjustment, Dale makes light of the request by noting that by late fall, both the retirees and the migrant family will be long gone.

Case Example 2:
An Effective Consultant

Terri Brodski, a psychologist, and Jamie Stewart, a social worker, work together in a community mental health center. Jamie approaches Terri for consultation regarding a migrant family that is part of Jamie's caseload. It seems that the family has had difficulty adjusting to the community, which consists primarily of retirees who have their summer homes there. When Jamie approaches Terri about the family's problems, Terri asks her to present her concerns about the family in detail, and she listens to and clarifies Jamie's concerns. When Jamie shares discouragement about the possibilities of helping the family, Terri offers encouragement and support, and asks how Jamie's work with the family ties into their agency's role and mission. Finally, they establish a verbal contract between them and agree to meet twice more about how Jamie can work more effectively with the family.

First, Terri observes Jamie working with the family. During the next consultation session, they exchange their impressions about the family; divide the family's adjustment problem into three smaller, more specific problems; and set goals to solve them. Terri then leads Jamie through a brainstorming session during which possible interventions are generated. Once they agree on an intervention for each problem, Terri assists Jamie in formulating their ideas into a feasible plan, which Jamie agrees to carry out.

During their final consultation session one month later, Terri and Jamie formally evaluate the degree to which each problem was solved and the effectiveness of the consultation process itself (i.e., how well they worked together).

They plan additional follow-up strategies for Jamie to use in later contacts with the family and agree that, within 30 days, Terri will make a follow-up call to Jamie concerning the family's progress. Then they say their goodbyes.

Terri clearly spent much more time and used more skills with Jamie than Dale did with Jackie. Terri displayed many of the characteristics of effective consultants. She used interpersonal skills when offering support and encouragement to Jamie. When Terri listened to and clarified Jamie's concerns, she used effective communication skills. She used several problem-solving skills with Jamie to identify ways to help the migrant family. Terri showed the skills of a multiculturally competent consultant when she asked Jamie to share in detail her views of the family's problems. Terri also showed skill in working with organizations when she asked how Jamie's work with the family tied into the agency's role and mission, and she displayed ethical and professional behavior skills by spending the time and effort needed to help Jamie. As you can see from these two cases, there are characteristics and skills that differentiate effective consultants from ineffective ones. Let's examine these characteristics next.

CHARACTERISTICS OF EFFECTIVE CONSULTANTS AND COLLABORATORS

Because consultation and collaboration are demanding, the requirements to perform them successfully are a challenge. Some research suggests that the best consultants seem to be guided by the need to make a difference in the lives of others (Bianco-Mathis & Veazey, 1996).

But, beyond an internal motivation, effective consultants must possess the following:

- a personal and professional growth orientation
- knowledge of the content and process of consultation and collaboration as well as human behavior
- consultation and collaboration skills

What Arredondo, Shealy, Neale, and Winfrey (2004) pointed out for psychologists applies to all consultants and collaborators in that they "… need to acquire and demonstrate the knowledge, skills, attitudes and values necessary to work in a collegial, integrative, and informed manner across specialty and practice areas" (p. 791).

A *personal growth orientation* involves the willingness of a consultant to grow and change as a person. This includes understanding oneself as a racial and cultural being (Sue, 2008). Because consultation involves problem solving, which requires change on the part of the consultee, consultants need to be willing to model that change. A personal growth orientation does not necessarily mean that consultants must experience personal growth counseling or therapy, although such experiences can be quite

beneficial. Rather, the concept of personal growth orientation entails any aspect of a consultant's life in which he or she endeavors to "stretch" in attempting to realize their potential. For example, one consultant might decide to accomplish the feat of hiking to every waterfall in a national park within a certain time frame; another consultant might volunteer 10 hours a week of free consultation services to a church group; whereas another consultant might participate in a personal growth group to improve his or her interpersonal effectiveness. In short, personal growth orientation is an attitude toward life that helps consultants become more effective human beings by periodically "stretching" themselves in some way.

A *professional growth orientation* refers to consultants' participation in activities that enhance the effectiveness of their consultation practices (Cooper, Monarch, Serviss, Gordick, & Leonard, 2007). Consultants often participate in workshops, training programs, academic courses, and supervised practice so as to remain current in their fields. In addition, many consultants seek additional training and knowledge to expand the parameters of their consultation practices. For example, one consultant, a university professor by training, might take a series of management and organizational behavior courses and so expand her consultation services to include human service agencies. Thus, a personal and professional growth orientation helps consultants to "practice what they preach" more effectively. By experiencing growth in their own lives, consultants are better able to empathize with consultees about the barriers to growth that consultees normally experience, and to be more authentic role models for those with whom they work.

Effective consultants, of course, also possess *knowledge of consultation* and a basic *knowledge of human behavior* (Arredondo et al., 2004). Effective consultants know the ins and outs of consultation; that is, they possess a general model of consultation and are knowledgeable about the various types of consultation and related multicultural and ethical issues. Such knowledge provides them with a sense of meaningfulness and adds direction to their practice.

Effective consultants must also possess knowledge about human behavior—including both individual and group behavior—for consultation involves, first and foremost, a human, helping relationship. Because consultants spend much of their time working with individual consultees, they need to know the basics of personality theory, normal and abnormal behavior, interpersonal relationships, and human communication. Knowledge of these topics is essential for maximizing the effectiveness with which each stage of consultation is accomplished. A basic knowledge of group dynamics, organizational theory, and ecological perspectives is a necessity for almost all consultants because most consultation occurs in and is affected by an organizational setting.

Even when consultants have a growth orientation and are knowledgeable, if they are to be effective, they need to possess *skills in consulting*. Consultants must be able to *do* as well as *know*. Effective consultants have a broad repertoire of consultation skills that range from basic communication skills to sophisticated problem-solving intervention skills. There is a research base developing to support these notions (McGivern, Ray-Subramanian, & Auster, 2008).

SKILLS NECESSARY FOR CONSULTATION AND COLLABORATION

Many skills are required of effective consultants and collaborators. Factors such as the readiness for change on the part of the consultee and the degree to which the consultant manifests attributes such as empathy impact the consultation relationship (McGivern et al., 2008). Consultants and collaborators will want to ensure that all of the process elements of their respective services are met (Gutkin & Curtis, 2009), such as interpersonal and collaborative skills (McGivern et al., 2008). You will want to remember that the skills described below are not the consultation process itself. Rather they are the tools with which you

will implement the process. Many authors point out the importance of competent interpersonal and communication skills (see, e.g., Dougherty, Henderson, & Lindsey, 1997; Egan, 2010; Kratochwill, 2008). Skills in working with culturally diverse populations are important (Ingraham, 2004, 2008; Lum, 2011; Miranda, 2008). Competence in problem-solving skills is also essential (Welch, 2000). Skills in working with organizations are increasingly needed (Knoff, 2008). Because consultants, and even more so collaborators, are increasingly being called on to work with groups of consultees, skills in group work are a must (Paisley & Milsom, 2007). Finally, well-developed ethical and professional behavior skills are essential to competency (Corey, Corey, & Callanan, 2011). The limited empirical research on the importance of the skill areas also supports the hypothesis that they are related to consultation success (see Knoff, McKenna, & Riser, 1991; Knoff, Sullivan, & Liu, 1995; Randolph & D'Ilio, 1990). For example, Knoff and coauthors (1995) found that there were two primary skill areas when prospective consultees were queried regarding consultant effectiveness: consultant knowledge, process, and application skills; and, consultant interpersonal and problem-solving skills. It is very likely that the same holds for collaboration as its skill sets represent the same competencies (Arredondo et al., 2004).

Interpersonal and Communication Attitudes

Consultation is a human, helping relationship that involves extensive communication. Interpersonal and communication skills, which are related to creating and maintaining effective human relationships, are essential for a consultant (Snyder, Quirk, & Dematteo, 2011). Furthermore, the attitudes from which these skills flow are as essential as the skills themselves (Dixon & Tucker, 2008; Kurpius & Rozecki, 1993; Martens & DiGennaro, 2008).

In the early 1960s, Carl Rogers (1961) demonstrated that the desirable underpinnings for these skills are unconditional regard, empathy, and genuineness. These attitudes form the core conditions on which an effective consultation relationship can be built. Without these attitudes in the consultant, the development of rapport with the consultee may take longer to achieve or may not occur at all. These attitudes exist on a continuum; their presence in a person is not an all-or-nothing proposition (Egan, 2010). However, to the degree that consultants possess these attitudes, the conditions for successful consultation will be established (Kurpius & Rozecki, 1993).

Unconditional regard (often referred to as *acceptance*, *positive regard*, or *respect*) refers to the ongoing appraisal that a person deserves our respect (Raines & Dibble, 2011). Unconditional regard reflects the willingness of the consultant to respect and accept the consultee as a human being who is worthwhile, has dignity, and can be liked or cared for by the consultant, in spite of the consultee's imperfections. The consultant often manifests regard as nonjudgmental and nonpossessive behavior toward the consultee (e.g., assuming the consultee's and client system's goodwill). Positive regard is related to positive helping relationships (McGivern et al., 2008).

Empathy refers to the consultant's ability to understand—to tune in to and accurately perceive the consultee's experience without losing his or her objectivity. It is a posture of putting oneself in another person's shoes. Empathy helps in establishing rapport, trust, open communication, and a common ground from which a relationship like consultation can proceed (Raines & Dibble, 2011). Empathy is significantly related to positively influencing a helping relationship (McGivern et al., 2008). Empathy is both a value and a communication skill. Recent conceptualizations of empathy have included the concept of what is called *inclusive cultural empathy* (Egan, 2010) and *objective empathy*, which allows the consultant to use a multicultural frame-of-reference in being empathic (Clark, 2010). These perspectives on empathy are diversity-oriented and involve an understanding of not only the person but also the cultural context of the person. The consultant's empathic experience is positively impacted by the consultee (Comstock et al., 2008).

Genuineness is demonstrated when consultants feel free to be themselves in the consultation relationship—when they need not hide behind roles, become defensive, or lose spontaneity with the consultee (Egan, 2010). Perhaps one of the greatest contributions of genuineness to successful consultation is the modeling effect it can have for the consultee (Bellman, 1990). When consultees view consultants as genuine, they too can become more genuine (Block, 2000).

In summary, although your skills are critical to your success as a consultant, your perspective may be just as important (Bellman, 1990). For decades, these attitudes and the behavioral characteristics that reflect them are linked to professional skills and knowledge in such a way that they affect how a consultee perceives a consultant's helpfulness (e.g., see Bardon, 1986).

Interpersonal Skills

The interpersonal skills of creating, maintaining, and terminating relationships refer to our ability to get along with other human beings. Because consultation is a helping relationship, consultants need relatively high levels of these skills (Arredondo et al., 2004; Dixon & Tucker, 2008; Getty & Erchul, 2009; Meyers, Proctor, Graybill, & Meyers 2009).

The creation and maintenance of consultation relationships require the following major interpersonal skills:

- putting the consultee at ease (e.g., making small talk)
- setting expectations about the relationship (e.g., contracting behaviors)
- creating an environment conducive to mutual collaboration (e.g., determining early on what the consultee can and cannot do)
- creating an environment conducive to change (e.g., talking implicitly and explicitly about how consultation is related to change)
- creating an appropriate image of the consultant in the eyes of the consultee (e.g., explaining

early on who the consultant is and what he or she can do for the consultee)

- developing a social influence base built on prestige, trustworthiness, and similarity (e.g., making explicit use of expertise, benign intent, and similarities to the consultee)

- being comfortable with oneself as consultant (e.g., exuding confidence)

- noting and responding not only to consultee verbalizations, but also to emotions and non-verbal behaviors (e.g., reflecting a therapist's anxiety about working with a client who has AIDS)

- using appropriate humor (e.g., being willing to laugh at oneself)

Interpersonal skills assist consultants in developing and sustaining strong relationships with their consultees. The strength and outcome of the consultation relationship are often directly related to consultee motivation, a commitment to change, and a positive attitude toward consultation (see Curtis, Castillo, & Cohen, 2008; Newell, 2012). Gibbs (1980) was one of the first authors to note that consultant interpersonal skills are integral to working effectively in cross-cultural consultation. Kurpius and Rozecki (1992) note that "if the consultant does not have a mastery of the art of communication and an understanding of the intricacies of interpersonal interaction, the consultation process will most often appear lifeless and unlikely to be of long-lasting help" (p. 143).

Communication Skills

The communication process between consultant and consultee can be considered central to the process of successful consultation (Benn, Jones, & Rosenfield, 2008; Newell, 2012; Rosenfield, 2002, 2008). Communication skills, then, act as tools that help the consultant to guide and manage the consultation process because the patterns of communication can impact what happens in the consultation process and how the consultee perceives things (Benn et al., 2008; Sheridan & Kratochwill, 2008). Everything

consultants do when they consult involves a system of language constructs (Daniels & DeWine, 1990); that is, a system of symbols used to make sense of life events and experiences. Communication skills refer to people's ability to send and receive meaningful messages. Such skills tend to be more specific than relationship skills. As you know from your experiences with others, communicating is sometimes quite difficult.

Consultants need to use a broad repertoire of communication skills to increase the probability of a successful outcome to consultation. There is some research that highlights the importance of communication in consultation (Dougherty et al., 1997; Rosenfield, 2008).

There are many "basic" communication skills (Ivey, Ivey, & Zalaquett, 2012). Among the more important ones for consultants are:

- nonverbal attending (e.g., keeping an open body posture)

- listening (e.g., actively discerning a consultee's intended meaning)

- expressing empathy (e.g., understanding the consultee's experience as well as his or her cultural context and accurately communicating that understanding back to the consultee)

- questioning (e.g., asking consultees to expand on a subject or be more specific)

- clarifying or paraphrasing (e.g., putting consultees' expressions into the consultant's own words to demonstrate understanding or to help consultees understand themselves better)

- summarizing (e.g., putting together the main points of discussion in order to determine the next step in the consultation process)

- providing feedback (e.g., providing consultees with information about themselves for the purposes of examination and change)

- giving information (e.g., informing the consultee of the possible ways a given client might be effectively helped)

- "speaking the same language" (e.g., choosing plain language that avoids jargon)

Communication skills such as these are related to a successful consultation outcome in that they allow the consultant and consultee to exchange meaningful and accurate information, which facilitates more effective problem solving and aids relationship maintenance throughout the consultation process. Jargon should be used with caution (Knotek, 2003). Through the use of effective communication skills, the consultant is able to view the situation and the consultee from a variety of perspectives and enhance the possibilities of a successful outcome to consultation (Kurpius & Rozecki, 1992). In fact, communication and interpersonal skills build the foundation for the success of all of the stages of consultation.

Skills Related to Cultural Diversity

Cultural considerations can affect consultation practice (Arra, 2010; Lopez & Truesdell, 2007; Nastasi, 2006; Newell, 2012). Several organizations such as the American Psychological Association, the American Counseling Association, the Council on Social Work Education, and the National Organization of Human Service Education have developed materials on multicultural preparation and practice. The helping professions have experienced a significant impact from multicultural movements both from within and without those professions (Arredondo, Tovar-Blank, & Parham, 2008; D'Andrea & Heckman, 2008). The increasing diversity within American society as well as other societies demands values and related skills on the part of consultants in dealing with that diversity: "Consultants almost inevitably provide services to individuals who are different from themselves in their culture of origin" (Ramirez, Lepage, Kratochwill, & Duffy, 1998, p. 479). The term *multicultural* pertains to "… individuals who possess elements of racial and/or cultural diversity that are not fully reflected in mainstream American culture" (Li & Vazquez-Nuttall, 2009, p. 27). One of the major challenges human service professionals encounter is discerning the complex role cultural diversity takes on in their work (APA, 1993, 2003; Egan, 2010; Hays, 2001; Tomes, 2011). As

early as 1970, Caplan pointed out how cultural variables could adversely affect communication in consultation.

Indeed, the culture of the parties involved in consultation may well affect the efficacy of the mode of consultation being used (see Brown, 1997; Knotek, 2012). There is no doubt that consultants need to be culturally competent and take cultural differences into account and prize them (Clare, 2009; Cooper, Wilson-Stark, Peterson, O'Roark, & Pennington, 2008; Meyers et al., 2009; Ortiz, 2006; Sherblom & Bahr, 2008). For example, by the year 2025, the Hispanic and Asian combined population will approximate one-quarter of the population in the United States. Consultants will increasingly be asked to consult with and about culturally diverse people and with organizations owned, managed, or populated by culturally diverse people (Jackson & Hayes, 1993). Competencies in becoming multiculturally skilled as a consultant include those related to beliefs, attitudes, knowledge, and skills (Arredondo et al., 2004; Holcomb-McCoy, 2009; Lewis, Lewis, Daniels, & D'Andrea, 2011; Nastasi, 2005; Newell, 2012), as well as assessment and intervention (Quintana, Castillo, & Zamarripa, 2000; Rogers, 2000).

Multicultural competence is basic to effective consultation (Cooper & Leong, 2008; Holcomb-McCoy & Bryan, 2010; Romney, 2008; Tomes, 2011). Corey et al. (2011) note that one of the major issues facing human service professionals is understanding the complex role that cultural diversity plays in their work. Sue (1998) suggests that cultural competency involves making hypotheses rather than premature judgments about culturally different people, knowing when to generalize and when to individualize regarding culturally different people, and having culture-specific expertise. When consultants work from a multicultural perspective, they attempt to understand and deal with the sociocultural forces affecting the helping relationship (Gibbs, 1980; Newell, 2010b; Sue, 2008). There are a significant number of multicultural competencies that have been established for human service professionals by Arredondo and her colleagues (1996, 2004). Ingraham (2000) has developed eight domains for consultant competency in multicultural consultation. Consultants should bear in mind that all consultation is multicultural if the concept of culture is broadened to include diversity indicators such as gender and age (Das, 1995).

Understanding your own cultural framework provides a context for understanding different cultural contexts (ACA, 2005; APA, 2002, 2003; Ivey et al., 2012). Being multiculturally skilled is essential for consultants and involves interpersonal, communication, problem-solving, ethical, and professional behavior skills such as the following (Ramirez et al., 1998):

- understanding the impact of one's own culture, including values, attitudes, and beliefs on practice
- valuing, respecting, and understanding the impact of other cultures
- adapting a culturally responsive consultation style
- integrating a knowledge of cultural diversity into effective practice
- not making value judgments about consultees (or client systems) who are culturally different
- challenging any stereotypic beliefs about culturally diverse groups
- viewing cultural differences as issues to meet, not as impediments
- using methods consistent with the life experiences and values of different minority groups
- possessing specific knowledge about the particular minority group served in consultation
- ensuring that definition of problems and development of goals take place within a cultural context

Although consultation models tend to be deficient in the areas related to cultural diversity (Ingraham, 2000, 2003, 2004, 2008), including gender issues (Henning-Stout, 1994), the literature related to multicultural issues in consultation has expanded greatly since the turn of the millennium (Cooper & Leong, 2008; Lopez & Truesdell, 2007).

By increasing the level of your skills in working with those from different cultures, and addressing the complexities of culture and gender as they relate to consultation, you can move toward effective consultation practice. For excellent resources for working with people from different cultures, see Atkinson (2004), Diller (2007), Hall (2005), Lum (2011), Romney (2008), and Salzman (2002).

The bottom-line in dealing with diversity is pointed out by Ortiz (2006, p. 159): "… the development and application of interventions in a diverse setting or with a multiethnic population does not automatically make it an example of multicultural practice."

Problem-Solving Skills

Because consultation is by nature a problem-solving activity, consultants need to be highly skilled in problem solving (Arredondo et al., 2004; Meyers, 2002; Meyers, Truscott, Meyers, Varjas, & Collins, 2008). There is some empirical evidence that problem-solving skills are essential even in the presence of effective interpersonal and communication skills (Curtis et al., 2008). Some of the many problem-solving skills available to consultants are:

- setting the stage for problem solving (e.g., defining consultation as a problem-solving activity)
- defining the problem (i.e., isolating "what is to be fixed" during consultation)
- examining the conditions surrounding the problem (e.g., noting antecedents and consequences)
- gathering, analyzing, and interpreting data pertinent to the problem (e.g., surveying organizational personnel and providing feedback on the results)
- identifying any facilitating and restraining forces (i.e., determining which forces are working for and against a given plan)
- designing interventions for a particular situation (e.g., identifying consultee strengths that increase the likelihood of successful plan implementation)

- evaluating problem-solving attempts (i.e., determining the degree to which a selected intervention worked)

- determining who will do what, how, and when during the problem-solving process (i.e., arranging the responsibilities involved in carrying out the plan)

- predicting the ramifications and implications of solving the problem (i.e., examining how change can affect other parts of the system)

Consultants use problem-solving skills such as these to assist their consultees in solving work-related problems. Many consultants attempt to facilitate the development of more sophisticated problem-solving skills in their consultees. The critical implications of these skills for successful consultation will become apparent in later chapters (Chapters 4 and 5) that discuss specific problem-solving skills.

Skills in Working with Organizations

As the cases presented at the beginning of this chapter indicate, almost all consultation occurs within some organizational context. Because of this, consultants need to have some basic skills—specific behaviors— in working with an organization as a whole including contextualizing the problem relative to its environment (Arredondo et al., 2004; Vanderheyden & Witt, 2008). When successfully demonstrated, these skills increase the likelihood of a successful outcome of consultation. Further, the increased emphasis on systems-level change in organizations (Ysseldyke, Burns, & Rosenfield, 2009) dictate that consultants and collaborators have expertise in organizational constructs such as systems theory and ecology (Gutkin, 2012). Ecology, for example, can assist the consultant in determining whether the client system is the individual student with a problem or the organization (e.g., the school) which is not meeting the individual student's needs and is thus precipitating the problem.

Without these skills, consultants and the consultation process itself can become victims of those organizational forces that have negative effects. Some of the more important skills consultants need when they work with organizations are:

- becoming accepted by the members of the organization in which consultation is to occur (e.g., creating working relationships with prospective consultees)

- understanding ecological variables as they affect the context of consultation

- using organizational analysis (e.g., determining who talks to whom under what conditions)

- providing feedback (e.g., giving the consultee objective information about some aspect of the organization's functioning)

- using systems theory (e.g., dealing with complex organizational issues)

- gathering information (e.g., using surveys to determine the attitudes of the organization's members)

- using a repertoire of organization-wide interventions for capacity building (e.g., providing a stress management program)

- determining the cultural competence of an organization (i.e., its working atmosphere related to cultural differences)

- determining the culture of the organization (i.e., its norms, standards, and values)

- using program planning (e.g., assisting consultees in executing effective programs)

- determining how to utilize human resources within the organization (e.g., assisting consultees in improving managerial styles)

As the list suggests, consultants need not have all the skills required to give the organization with which they consult everything it needs. However, such consultants do need selected skills that allow them to operate at an optimal level within the organization and assist with selected organization-wide changes.

Group Skills

Because they are increasingly being called on to work with groups of consultees and on teams, effective consultants need to be skilled in working with a variety of groups (Conyne & Mazza, 2007;

Webster, Knotek, Babinski, Rogers, & Barnett, 2003; Yetter, 2010). In spite of this trend, little attention has been paid to training in consulting with groups (Pryzwansky, 2011; Thomas, 2010). Several of the types of consultation you will be reading about later—such as education/training consultation, program consultation, process consultation, and behavioral system consultation—frequently demand the use of group work on the part of consultants.

Furthermore, group skills are particularly critical for collaborators because most collaboration occurs in teams (Meyers, Meyers, & Grogg, 2004; Paisley & Milsom, 2007). Some of the many group skills needed include:

- focusing and maintaining attention on task and work issues (e.g., gently reminding the group when it gets off task)

- managing conflict within a group of consultees (e.g., using mediation skills in assisting two conflicting group members)

- managing agendas of meetings (e.g., helping group members determine what items should be on an agenda and how those items are to be dealt with)

- providing feedback to group members (e.g., confronting members, avoidance of important issues)

- facilitating concrete and specific communication among group members (e.g., reflecting the true meaning of vague generalities)

- linking the comments of one group member to pertinent comments from others (e.g., tying in a consultee's statement about one of her clients to another consultee's remark about one of his clients)

- facilitating the development of the group process (e.g., knowing when to move from the getting acquainted stage to the working stage)

- using group management skills (e.g., knowing how to terminate a group session)

- sensing and using group dynamics to help consultee groups meet their goals (e.g., calling attention to the emotional current running through the group)

Increasingly consultants and collaborators are interacting in group modalities, such as teams, thus amplifying the importance of group-related skills.

Ethical and Professional Behavior Skills

To be successful, consultants need to behave ethically and professionally. The necessary skills are often associated with internal feelings or beliefs that are explicitly demonstrated in consultants' behavior. Throughout their careers, all consultants encounter professional situations that require a set of skills based on sound ethical judgment (Corey et al., 2011). For example, what would you do if, as a consultant, you were "over your head" in trying to help a consultee work with a difficult client?

Some of the myriad important skills that can help consultants act in an ethical and professional manner are:

- acting with integrity (e.g., maintaining confidentiality)

- adhering to an ethical code (i.e., adhering to accepted guidelines for professional behavior)

- engaging in consultation only within one's professional limits (i.e., declining consultations for which one is not qualified)

- maintaining personal and professional growth (e.g., engaging in professional development activities)

- having the intent to help (e.g., being as thorough as possible)

- effectively coping with the stress of consulting (e.g., using stress management skills)

- ensuring cultural competence (e.g., adapting procedures to cultural context)

- using effective writing skills (e.g., writing high-quality reports)

- using power for legitimate purposes only (i.e., using one's skills to influence others appropriately)

Acting in an ethical, professional manner creates positive perceptions among the consultant's coworkers and contacts. Such perceptions contribute to the successful outcome of consultation because consultees are able to attribute to the consultant the social influence necessary for maximum effectiveness during consultation. I will deal extensively with the ethical and professional behavior of consultants later in this text.

Possessing all of the skills mentioned above seems a tall order. The extent of a consultant's skills is best understood if they are seen as part of a continuum; no consultant either lacks or completely possesses each skill. And although it is important to note that effective consultants are not expert in all of these skills, they possess most of these skills to a moderate or high degree. Developing the skills to be even more effective is a process that continues for the entire career of every consultant. With this in mind, it is reasonable to note that, for consultants to be effective, they need to be "… able to define problems, introduce strategies, facilitate correct implementation, and attain desired outcomes … someone who can deliver results" (Vanderheyden & Witt, 2008, p. 120).

ROLES CONSULTANTS AND COLLABORATORS ASSUME

The Nature of Consultant Roles

Consultants can wear many hats. They use the skills described in the preceding sections in a variety of consultation roles or functions performed at any given time during the consultation relationship. Just as consultation is not easily defined, neither are the roles in which consultants function.

Consultants can take on any number of roles during a particular consultation relationship.

The nature of the roles is usually defined in the consultation contract but there needs to be flexibility in role selection as events in the consultation may dictate such. Effective consultants are able to determine which roles are necessary, define them to the satisfaction of all parties involved, and then perform those roles. At the same time, consultant roles

can change as part of adapting to what is going on in a given consultation session.

The primary role a consultant takes on depends on several factors, including his or her abilities and frame of reference, the model used; the consultee's characteristics related to the expectations, coping style, commitment to change, skill levels; the nature of the problem that consultation is attempting to solve; and the ecological context in which consultation occurs (McGivern et al., 2008). Based on this assessment, the consultant will be directive or nondirective as appropriate (Kratochwill, 2008; Rimehaug & Helmersberg, 2010).

The Categorization of Roles

Most categorization schemes put consultation roles on some sort of continuum. The most popular categorization approach still used today was developed in the 1980s by Lippitt and Lippitt (1986), in which consultants' roles lie on a continuum ranging from directive to nondirective. In directive roles the consultant is something of a technical expert, whereas in nondirective roles consultants tend to facilitate the consultee's expertise. Another popular approach to consultants' roles, developed by Margulies and Raia (1972) in the 1970s, includes task roles (those related to expertise) at one end of a continuum and process roles (those related to facilitation) at the other. Regardless of how consulting roles are categorized, the bottom line is that categorization schemes tend to reflect the consultant's degree of involvement in the consultation process relative to that of the consultee. They guide the consultant in determining who is responsible for what tasks and how the consultant should proceed in consultation. For most human service professionals, the directive–nondirective categorization scheme of Lippitt and Lippitt (1986) seems most appropriate; the terms are familiar to most human service professionals, and they provide a very helpful rule of thumb because they imply the amount of control the consultant should have over the consultation process. The following discussion of common consultation roles is grounded in the categorization scheme of Lippitt and Lippitt (1986).

Common Consultation Roles

Consultants can engage in the consultation process in a broad range of roles that vary in terms of how much the consultant directs the activity occurring in consultation (Lippitt & Lippitt, 1986); that is, some roles are more directive than others. Next we'll consider six consultation roles: advocate, expert, trainer/educator, collaborator, fact finder, and process specialist.

Advocate.   The most directive consulting role is that of advocate. It has received a great deal of attention in the consultation literature in the past decade. At first glance you would think that advocacy would not be a typical role the consultant takes on. From one perspective, as an advocate, the consultant attempts to persuade the consultee to do something the consultant deems highly desirable. Persuasion is a primary activity in this role (Kirst-Ashman & Hull, 2012).

For example, a consultant relying on her superior knowledge about data collection in organizations might advocate the use of several methods in addition to what the consultee thinks is necessary. In another example, a consultant may advocate by identifying organizational stakeholders and recommending systems level interventions to managers.

Recently, the advocacy role has been defined more in terms of advocating for the rights of those who are unable to help themselves (see, e.g., Clare, 2009; Hoffman et al., 2006; Lewis et al., 2011; Lopez-Baez & Paylo, 2009; Sherblom & Bahr, 2008; Smith, Reynolds, & Rovnak, 2009). In this sense, advocacy is often combined with outreach: the promotion of available services to selected populations (Buerkle, Whitehouse, & Christenson, 2009; Dixon, Tucker, & Clark, 2010; Holcomb-McCoy & Bryan, 2010; Toporek, Lewis, & Crethar, 2009). For example, a mental health professional may advocate at a variety of levels to get barriers related to client access or growth examined (ACA, 2005). In another example, a consultant advocates for community change by dealing with the media to create a sense of urgency for change and creating new alliances with existing and new stakeholders in the community (Lee & Rodgers, 2009). In yet another example, school-based professionals, through consultation and collaboration, advocate for positive school environments that promote student academic success, psychological well-being, and physical health (Williams & Greenleaf, 2012).

Consultants can act as advocates in a variety of ways (Dahir & Stone, 2012; Dixon & Tucker, 2008; Kurpius & Lewis, 1988; Lewis et al., 2011; Li & Vazquez-Nuttall, 2009): as process consultants assisting groups in working effectively or becoming self-advocates; as identifiers of target groups needing advocacy, as locators of necessary resources, and as facilitators of advocacy attempts; and as agents who attempt to prevent target groups from needing advocacy at a later time. Lopez-Baez and Paylo (2009) add that advocacy can be used in community collaboration when, for example, a counselor who is knowledgeable about issues within an organization or group that create barriers for clients works with others to facilitate change. Further, when school-based professionals engage in a leadership role in systems change initiatives while engaging in community collaboration, they are thereby participating in systems advocacy (Lopez-Baez & Paylo, 2009). Finally, advocacy can be looked at as the facilitation by consultants of the empowerment on individuals to advocate for themselves (Speight & Vera, 2009).

On the one hand, consultants have a professional obligation not to engage in inappropriate advocacy roles (Remley, 1988). Yet they should not avoid situations that dictate that they become advocates, for example, in a social justice situation.

There are times, situations, and issues for which advocacy is the most appropriate role for a consultant. One common example of an appropriate advocacy role is when the consultant detects within an organization a discrepancy between the way an organization is supposed to treat its clients and the way it actually treats them (Lott & Rogers, 2005). As noted above, engaging in social justice issues is another example (Sander, Sharkey, Olivarri, Tanigawa, & Mauseth, 2010). Consultants can avoid misusing the advocacy role by maintaining a high level of self-awareness and skills about such matters as poverty, racism, and value-related issues and by maintaining a collaborative relationship with the consultee and community organizations. In a final note, it is important to remember that advocacy has emerged as a competency set approved by the American Counseling Association that far transcends the use of advocacy in consultation and collaboration. See, for example, Toporek, Lewis, and Crethar (2009).

Expert. A common role that consultants take on is that of expert or technical advisor. The expert role on occasion receives criticism because it does not necessarily empower consultees. However, there are occasions, like in crises or knowledge/skill deficits, when the expertise of the consultant is a necessary part of consultation.

In this circumstance, the consultee needs some knowledge, advice, or service that the consultant can provide on request (Stroh & Johnson, 2006). A bottom-line way to look at this is to simultaneously keep these two maxims in mind: (1) "Never tie a helping hand behind your back"; (2) "Do not do for consultees what they can do for themselves." This can be particularly true when dealing in multicultural situations in which it is incumbent upon the consultant to recognize the vastness of knowledge that potential consultees can bring to the process (Holcomb-McCoy, 2009). That said, when in the expert role, consultants often provide content expertise that is specialized and that is often a need for which consultees solicit consultation (Anderson-Butcher et al., 2010; Vanderheyden & Witt, 2008). As Vanderheyden and Witt (2008, p. 122) note: "Whether consultation is effective may depend on actions of the consultant that include (a) identifying an appropriate intervention target, (b) selecting an effective intervention, (c) ensuring correct implementation of the intervention, and (d) correctly monitoring the effectiveness of the intervention and responding formatively to facilitate effectiveness." When consultants are retained as experts over a long period of time, it seems apparent that the consultees (or organizations) retaining the consultants know what they

need from the consultants. However, this is often not the case (Schein, 1988).

In comparison to the collaborative role in consultation (see below), the expert role has the consultant showing greater control during the consultation process in terms of directing the process, selecting topics and data collection strategies, and determining the most appropriate intervention (Tysinger, Tysinger, & Diamanduros, 2009). In other words, the consultant is basically in charge of the decision making in consultation while the consultee provides his or her views and related information. There is limited empirical evidence that supports the expert approach to consultation as legitimate and beneficial (Tysinger et al., 2009).

Consultants who consult with agencies about their programs—perhaps they are asked to make a diagnosis of what is wrong with an agency's client system—typically act in the role of expert. Consultants also function as experts when they are asked to recommend solutions to previously defined problems. For example, a consultant might recommend a training program in stress management for the members of the counseling department at a large secondary school. As in any other consulting role, the consultant does not treat the client system directly.

Consultants who engage in the role of expert need to be aware of the possibility that they can create dependence on the part of their consultees (Lippitt & Lippitt, 1986). The consultee can get used to having the consultant do the work and can effectively give the problem away to the consultant. As a result, consultants will want to maintain behavior that does not appear to suggest that the consultant is superior to and/or has power over the consultee (Rimehaug & Helmersberg, 2010). To accomplish this, these authors suggest presenting several viable alternatives when engaging the consultee in decision making.

In addition, consultants engaging in the expert role will want to realize that under such circumstances their consultees may not improve their own problem-solving abilities, especially if the consultant does not take the time and effort to help them to do so. Indeed, perhaps the most common mistake consultants make when using the expert role is to underestimate their consultees' abilities and consult in such a way that consultees' knowledge and skills are not adequately utilized.

However, there is a body of literature that suggests that, at least in school consultation, consultees prefer greater consultant directiveness and control during the consultation process (Erchul & Chewning, 1990; Gutkin, 1996). In addition, consultants often take on the expert role when engaging in systems-level consultation due to their ability to make recommendations based upon local context for removing barriers to proposed change (Anderson-Butcher et al., 2010).

Here is an example using the expert role: Mary's parents ask you for assistance with their daughter, who is nine years old and has only one friend. The friend frequently has Mary give up her toys and part of her lunch at school. You observe Mary at school four times in differing contexts and watch her interact with many of her peers. You then write a brief report with specific suggestions for the parents to follow.

Trainer/Educator. Very closely related to the role of expert is that of trainer/educator. Whereas the role of "technological advisor" does not imply change in the professional functioning of consultees, the role of a trainer/educator does. Consultants can engage in both formal and informal training and/or educating. Some authors (e.g., Conoley & Conoley, 1992) contend that formal education/training activities such as workshops are not truly consultation because of the amount of preplanning involved. Others (e.g., Lippitt & Lippitt, 1986) see the trainer/educator role as a legitimate and distinct approach to consultation itself. Perhaps these differences in viewpoint result because education is compared with consultation as if it were a different human service. One way to reconcile these different perspectives is to take the view that whereas consultants frequently train and educate, both formally and informally, this role is only one of several in which they engage.

Consultants are often asked to act in the capacity of trainer/educator. The role of trainer implies

that the consultant has both the expertise in certain skills and the ability to create the conditions under which consultees can acquire those skills. The role of educator implies that the consultant possesses a body of knowledge that consultees desire and has the ability to teach them that knowledge. Formal training and education sessions usually take the form of workshops and seminars. For example, a consultant might train a group of program leaders in a human service agency in methods of motivating subordinates. Informal training/educating usually occurs between the consultant and the consultee during some other aspect of the consultation relationship. Thus, a consultant might teach a consultee how to gather baseline data on certain client behaviors.

One advantage of the trainer/educator role is that the consultee receives skills and/or knowledge that can perhaps be used repeatedly in the future, and thus the consultee's professional development is enhanced in some specific way. However, it is possible to erroneously assume that the consultee will actually use the newly acquired skills and knowledge in some way. Unless the consultant incorporates into the training the context in which the skills and knowledge are most useful, there is a strong likelihood that they will not be adequately put into practice in the future.

Consider this example, which uses the trainer/educator role: You are a practicing school consultant in a middle school. Your principal asks you to conduct some in-service training for the school staff on "Motivating the Underachieving Middle School Child." You agree to conduct the workshop and follow through.

Collaborator. Nowhere in the consultation literature is there more confusion than that over the term of *collaborator* (Schulte & Osborne, 2003). However, consultants generally take a collaborative role in consultation in that the consultant and consultee pool their resources and work together on the task of creating a successful consultation experience. Whereas the expert role in consultation acknowledges the consultee's need for assistance and direction, the collaborator role acknowledges the consultant's need for the consultee's assistance during the consultation process (Snyder et al., 2011). It is important to note that the collaborator role is not the opposite of the expert role (Gutkin, 1999b; Tysinger et al., 2009). When a consultant engages in the collaborative role, the consultee is encouraged to express his or her own ideas and modify the consultant's contributions (Meyers et al., 2009). This role has been related to a positive working relationship between the consultant and the consultee (McGivern et al., 2008). The collaborator role taken on the consultant engages the consultee more deeply in the consultation process, thereby increasing the consultee's investment in consultation and the likelihood that consultation will have preventive effect on the consultee that will transfer to similar situations in the future.

The collaborative role can take on two dimensions: directive and nondirective (Gutkin, 1999a, 1999b). It has been argued that when consultation is successful, consultants take on a collaborative role that varies along a dimension from directive to nondirective (Tysinger et al., 2009). In the collaborative directive role, the consultant could be viewed "… as (a) being prescriptive when appropriate, (b) settling disputes through shared decision making, (c) using interpersonal influence techniques as necessary, and (d) being respectful of consultees' right to reject ideas" (Tysinger et al., 2009, p. 322). The collaborative nondirective role, on the other hand, has the consultant "… (a) assisting consultees in developing their own solutions to presenting problems, (b) attempting to minimize their own directiveness and control over consultation sessions, and (c) accepting consultee leads throughout the process" (Tysinger et al., 2009, p. 322). There is limited research which suggests that consultees prefer a collaborative directive to collaborative nondirective role from consultants, suggesting that consultees prefer more consultant input in the consultation process (Tysinger et al., 2009).

When used to describe consultation, the *collaborator* role describes consultant behavior that engages the consultee in a joint endeavor to accomplish a particular task at a particular time.

The concept of complementarity is important in the collaborator role. The consultee has a large say in determining what is discussed in consultation and how the consultation process transpires (Tysinger et al., 2009). Consultants do not perform for consultees tasks that the consultees could perform for themselves; they contribute expertise that consultees need to accomplish those tasks. Collaboration is frequently needed in identifying alternative solutions to a problem, in determining the positive and negative forces operating on various alternatives, and in making decisions about how to approach a given problem. There is significant research that suggests that consultees should be active participants in the consultation process, and for a variety of reasons ranging from collecting richer and deeper data on the client system to enhancing the consultee's investment in the consultation process (Gutkin & Curtis, 2009).

You should note that the *role* of collaborator for a consultant is distinct from the *service* of collaboration. As I have noted earlier, in the service of collaboration, each collaborator takes responsibility for some aspect of direct service to the client system. In any role that a consultant takes on, including that of collaborator, the consultee retains sole responsibility for direct service to the client system.

In one example of a collaborative role, a consultant and a consultee might compare their observations of a client and come to a mutually agreed-upon identification of the client's problem. In another case, they might mutually agree on how much and what kinds of data need to be gathered about the consultee's organization.

Among the relatively few risks involved in engaging in the collaborator role is that consultants may not realize that they are affected by consultees' behavior. Perhaps the most common mistake consultants make when using the collaborator role is to overestimate their consultees' abilities and consult in such a way that consultees' knowledge and skill inputs hinder effective consultation. To avoid this pitfall, consultants need some assessment of consultees' problem-solving abilities before assuming the collaborator role.

Conditions to enhance consultees' professional development are built into the role of collaborator. When the consultant takes on a collaborative role, consultees' problem-solving skills are enriched for the future. In addition, their confidence is likely to increase because they feel a sense of contribution to the consultation process. Some limited empirical evidence suggests that consultees prefer a collaborative approach by consultants (Gutkin, 1999a). At the same time, there is an ongoing debate about whether collaboration is an integral element in consultation (Erchul, 1999; Gutkin, 1999a, 1999b). Further, there is little agreement in the field as to the definitions of the terms *collaborator* and *collaborative* (see Schulte & Osborne, 2003). This lack of agreement has stifled research on the collaborator role and its effective implementation.

The following example uses the collaborator role: You are a consultant working in a community mental health center with a colleague who has difficulty with a client. Together, you and the colleague pool your resources and contribute your respective strengths and abilities to resolve the difficulty.

Fact Finder.   The role of fact finder is one every consultant takes on frequently. In its simplest form, it merely involves obtaining information. In the typical fact-finding role, the consultant gathers information, analyzes it, and feeds it back to the consultee (Lippitt & Lippitt, 1986).

The consultant often takes on the fact-finding role to collect information necessary in clarifying or diagnosing a problem. Methods for gathering information include reading records, interviewing, observing, and surveying. (I will discuss several ways to gather information in Chapter 4.) Consultants can gather information on a consultee's client or on an entire organization.

Fact finding can range from a simple, quickly accomplished task to a very complex, time-consuming one. A school psychologist (consultant) might administer an individual intelligence test to a student (client system) who is being seen by a school counselor (consultee) and report the findings back to the counselor. In another example, a consultant might design and send out a survey to an organization's members to determine the level of morale within the organization.

One question the consultant should ask before beginning fact-finding activities is, "Why am I (and not the consultee) gathering this information?" If the answers relate to lack of consultee expertise, political sensitivities, time constraints, or the consultant's need to learn more about the environment in which the problem is occurring, then the role of fact finder is a legitimate one. If the answer is because it's the consultant's job—not that of the consultee—to gather the facts, then the consultant should reexamine whether or not that role is appropriate.

Consider this example of a fact-finding role: You are consulting to determine why the personnel at a human service agency are exhibiting poor morale. You spend a great deal of time in the agency observing and interviewing personnel concerning the quality of work life. You put the data together and interpret it for the head of the agency.

Process Specialist.   The least directive role of the consultant is that of process specialist. When consultants take on the role of process expert, they focus more on the *how* than the *what*.

Instead of asking, "What's going on?," the process specialist asks, "How are things going?" When a problem is being solved, the consultant as process specialist does not examine the content but rather the problem-solving process itself (Rimehaug & Helmersberg, 2010). The focus is not so much on the nature of the problem-solving steps but on how those steps are accomplished. One approach to consultation with organizations, called process consultation, was developed in the 1980s by Edgar Schein (1987, 1988). Process consultation has as its major goal the enhancement of the consultee's understanding of the process events that affect everyday behavior. Two process roles seem to be emerging: the *process observer* role and the *process facilitator* role (Kormanski & Eschbach, 1997).

In the process observer role, the consultant provides periodic feedback concerning the group's process, models problem-solving processes, assists the group in dealing with communication issues, and facilitates the group process. There has been some discussion that process consultation, although primarily a group consultation model, can be used with individual consultees and focus on the consultant–consultee interaction as a source of data. The point is, the process specialist works in such a manner that the consultee becomes a better and more independent problem solver in the future. I will discuss process consultation again in Chapter 11.

In one example of a process specialist role, a consultant might sit in on a school's faculty meeting and, at the end, ask the faculty questions to assist them in analyzing their interpersonal behavior relative to what was accomplished in the meeting. In this example, the consultant merely puts in exploratory questions what he or she observed. In another case, a consultant might help an administrator learn how to have more effective meetings by using agendas. In this instance, the consultant assists the consultee in making an intervention designed to give people more time to participate in meetings.

Because consultants typically focus on structure and content, they are often uncomfortable in the process specialist role. And because the role of process specialist frequently requires the consultant to work with more than one consultee, group process skills are essential.

One common mistake consultants make in the process specialist role is to assume they have permission to bring up interpersonal issues (Schein, 1988). Consultees should first ask if feedback is wanted or raise questions concerning interpersonal issues.

The following example illustrates the process specialist role: You are a consultant called on to help a team of middle-school teachers work "more effectively." You sit in on the group's meetings several times, get a sense for the group's "process," that is, how they do what they do, and then invite the group to examine their own functioning in a nondefensive manner.

In school-based consultation, an emerging role not in the Lippitt and Lippitt (1986) list is that of *change facilitator* (Roach, Kratochwill, & Frank, 2009). The change facilitator role has developed in the context of consultants facilitating the acceptance of research-based practices (including interventions and programs) by teachers and administrators. Among other things, this role involves "… communicating

with potential adopters, developing rapport and empathy with consultees, and carefully matching research-based practices to consultee and student needs" (Roach et al., 2009, pp. 301–302).

Clearly, consultants need to be able to move easily among the various roles described in this section, or at least know their limitations to the degree that they can make referrals when appropriate (Schein, 1990c).

INTERNAL AND EXTERNAL CONSULTANTS

Consultants may or may not belong to the system in which consultation is to occur. An *internal consultant* is part of the organization in which consultation occurs. An *external consultant* consults within an organization to which she or he is not permanently employed on a temporary basis. The entire consultation process remains the same regardless of the locus of the consultant. Whether the consultant is internal or external is determined to some degree by the perceptions of the members of the organization served by the consultation. For example, an itinerant elementary school counselor may serve three different schools. Depending on one's viewpoint, the consultant can be seen as internal or external. A staff member at the school system's central office may note that, because the school counselor is employed by the system that runs the three schools and because everyone involved in the consultation also belongs to the school system, the counselor functions as an internal consultant.

But consider another point of view: Because the counselor is at a given school only infrequently, he or she is not really a part of that school. Thus, to most of the school's staff—those at the school every workday—the counselor is seen as an outsider, an external consultant.

One could argue that the internal–external distinction receives too much attention; a consultant is always external to the problem to be resolved whether or not he or she is external or internal to the organization itself. Also, having expertise in a problem area may be more important than whether a consultant is internal or external (Meyers et al., 2009).

It seems reasonable to suggest that effective consultants are effective whether or not they are permanently attached to the system receiving consultation (Stroh & Johnson, 2006). This contention is further supported by the fact that internal consultants are taking on many of the functions historically reserved for external consultants (Caplan, Caplan, & Erchul, 1994; Meyers et al., 2009). There are, however, advantages and related disadvantages to being either an internal or an external consultant (Harris, 2007; McLean, 2006). External consultants seem to be characterized by marginality; that is, they are only marginally admitted into the organization. They are likely to be objective, neutral, and comfortable with conflict, ambiguity, and stress (Stroh & Johnson, 2006; Tobias, 1990). On the other hand, internal consultants are affected by the hierarchy (Caplan & Caplan-Moskovich, 2004) and the politics of the organization; that is, they "operate more by mandate than by choice" (Block, 2000, p. 131). As a result, internal consultants may be better suited for program consultation (e.g., consulting about an antibullying program) than broader organizational issues such as leadership (Meyers et al., 2009).

Many organizations with internal consultants hire external consultants with the expectation that the two work as a team (Kelley, 1981). Such a team approach can blend the objectivity, expertise, and "newness" of the external consultant with the knowledge of the organization, expertise, and continuity provided by the internal consultant.

There has been an interesting twist in the literature on internal consultants. Since the mid-1990s, there has been a movement to suggest that collaboration is preferred to consultation when delivered by professionals who are internal to the system. Because mental health or human resource specialists are considered experts in their area, they can provide and receive assistance from their fellow collaborators while also directly serving the client system. A driving force for this shift in thinking is that in organizations such as schools there is a very limited amount of time to assist clients and multiple

treatment options can help compensate for this potential barrier to success.

AN ORIENTATION TO THE MODELS OF CONSULTATION AND COLLABORATION

Although Part III of this text provides extensive coverage of models of consultation and collaboration, I introduce them here to provide you with a snapshot of how the knowledge, skills, attitudes, and roles discussed earlier in this chapter can be viewed from different perspectives.

A model of consultation provides a conceptual definition for practice. The models of consultation I will cover have the common characteristics and assumptions of all consultation (Gutkin & Curtis, 2009; Kennedy, Frederickson, & Monsen, 2008) as well as the common trait of informing consultation research. All models of consultation can help consultees deal with a work-related concern through a problem-solving process and stress the problem-solving skills of the consultant (Kratochwill, 2008; Racine Gilles, Kratochwill, Felt, Schienebeck, & Vaccarello, 2011). The ways problem solving is accomplished varies according to the model under consideration. In addition, these models can have a preventive effect and help consultees become more effective with similar or related problems in the future. For example, these models are being challenged to adequately deal with ecological variables as they are strongly connected to prevention concepts.

Some models of consultation are more structured than others, and the consultant may act in the role of technical expert, expert diagnostician, or expert facilitator. Models of consultation can also vary in terms of the conceptualization of the problem and the goals of consultation. Although all models have a well-defined approach to solving problems, no model has developed an adequate theoretical basis from research to prescribe how the consultant and consultee should interact with each other. Unfortunately, there is one other similarity among the models—a lack of an adequate body of literature on how they apply multicultural consultation situations (Ingraham, 2008; Ingraham & Meyers, 2000b).

Part III of this text discusses three popular models of consultation—mental health, behavioral, and organizational. Mental health consultation (see Chapter 9) conceptualizes a problem in terms of mental health constructs. The goal of alleviating the mental health problem is accomplished by helping consultees work with their clients or with the mental health implications of their programs. The consultant acts either as facilitator or technical advisor in advocating the value of enhancing the mental health functioning of all involved in consultation. Mental health consultation focuses both on helping consultees help their clients and on helping consultees become more effective professionals. In the past, mental health consultation was strongly influenced by psychodynamic theory, but today is practiced from a variety of theoretical points of view.

Behavioral consultation (see Chapter 10) conceptualizes the problem in terms of reducing the difference between the current frequency of some problem behavior and the desired frequency of that behavior. This behavioral goal is accomplished through the use of interventions based on the principles of learning. The consultant acts as both expert and guide and advocates that behavior be changed in a precise, scientific manner. Behavioral consultation is based on social learning theory. The range of behavior change can be from the individual level to that of an entire organization.

Organizational consultation (see Chapter 11) conceptualizes the problem in terms of an organization's structure and processes, and has the goal of modifying those structures and processes to ameliorate some problem through carefully designed interventions that affect the organization's system. The consultant takes on one or more roles to assist consultees. Values are advocated that enhance the organization's overall effectiveness by helping its members become more satisfied and productive. An increasing number of human service and educational organizations use organizational consultation to enhance their effectiveness.

Although models can help consultants guide their practice, models can also overly focus their attention on aspects of the model instead of the features of the consultation setting. Further, practicing consultants, irrespective of what model they employ, will want to be aware that "consultation represents an ongoing process that is often mediated by factors such as interpersonal skills, relationship dynamics, problem severity, willingness of participants, competencies of consultees and clients, and many other issues" (Sheridan, Kratochwill, & Bergan, 1996, p. viii).

THE CONSULTEE AS A VARIABLE IN THE CONSULTATION PROCESS

In consultation, the consultee is a major variable that affects the process for better or worse. To address this issue, I have incorporated the consultee's experience in consultation into each chapter of this text. In this section, I briefly overview the issues that consultants will want to consider as the consult with their consultees. First and foremost, consultants will want to promote the use of effective knowledge, skills, and attitudes of the part of the consultee. To that end, consultants will want to assess their consultee's expertise in these areas relative to the problem at hand at the outset of the consultation process. To what degree is the consultee familiar with the consultation process, assessment, and possible interventions? To what degree does the consultee have the desired skill sets to assess the client system and implement a plan with adequate treatment integrity? To what degree and how are the values and attitudes of the consultee a factor in influencing the consultation process? More specifically, consultants will want to consider the degree to which multicultural, system-level, and ecological factors are likely to impact the consultee's performance in the consultation situation. Throughout the remainder of this text, I consider the consultee's experience in consultation as a variable that impacts the consultation process. In particular, Chapter 3 covers two important concepts related to consultees—consultee readiness for change and resistance to consultation.

RESEARCH IN CONSULTATION AND COLLABORATION

As a practicing consultant, you will want to verify that your practice is legitimate. With the increasing attention being paid to consultation and collaboration, it is important to scrutinize the research base for these services. One way to verify this is through examining the empirical foundations of consultation (Erchul & Sheridan, 2008). Research in consultation is less than six decades old, and is therefore not yet very sophisticated. But there is a growing body of research supporting the efficacy of consultation. School consultation is far and away the area in which the majority of consultation and collaboration research has been conducted. That said, it is reasonable to extrapolate from that literature to at least examine consultation and collaboration in other settings. Armenakis and Burdg (1988) note four types of consultation research, numbered in terms of increasing sophistication. First, there are experience-based writings (e.g., case studies), typically written by the consultant, that describe a given consultation experience. Second, there is quasi-scientific research in which there is not adequate control over the variable being assessed, as distinguished from the third type, scientific research, which requires adequate control over the experimental conditions. The fourth type of research is meta-analysis, which attempts to tie together the results of several studies (Kratochwill & Stoiber, 2000a).

Research on consultation usually involves one or more of the following areas: what consultants do (i.e., consultant practice), the interaction between consultant and consultee (i.e., consultation process), and the effectiveness of interventions (Froehle & Rominger, 1993). Meyers et al. (2008) add the areas of ecological and sociopolitical context and prevention.

What do the results of the various types of research suggest about consultation? Meade, Hamilton, and Yuen (1982) pointed out long ago the difficulties surrounding research in consultation. In summarizing the research to date, these authors suggested that outcome studies found consultation to be effective (although they questioned the methodological soundness of most studies), that process studies were so limited that very few conclusions could be made, and that research on consultant characteristics was methodologically so poor that the whole area of research should be reconceptualized. They recommended that future research use time-series designs in outcome studies, that consultation process studies utilize the case study method, and that multiple measures be used.

In reviewing the research on school consultation, which appears to be more or less representative of research in other areas of human service consultation, Gresham and Kendall (1987) noted some of the more important things learned about consultation from research include the following:

- Most outcome research is conducted on behavioral consultation.

- The empirical research support base is strongest for behavioral consultation.

- Dependent variables tend to include the frequency of consultation use by consultees and changes in clients, consultees, or both as a result of consultation.

- Long-term follow-up is typically a part of outcomes research.

- In process research, problem identification is the best predictor of problem solutions.

- Consultee perceptions of the effectiveness of consultants' communication skills are related to consultee perceptions of overall consultant effectiveness.

- Consultees dislike jargon.

In a later review, Gibson and Chard (1994) evaluated 1,643 consultation outcomes using meta-analysis. These authors concluded that consultation is at least moderately effective.

Sheridan, Welch, and Orme (1996) reviewed consultation outcome research in educational settings from 1985 to 1995. They found that three-fourths of studies reported positive outcomes and that behavioral consultation research studies were most prevalent. The authors point out advances in methodological aspects of research such as design and multiple measures. Sheridan, Kratochwill, and Bergan (1996) found empirical support for change in both client system and consultee behaviors. These same authors investigated the research on consultation processes and determined that successful behavioral consultation was characterized by variables that included a cooperative attitude, clearly defined roles, and active involvement by all parties.

How can research in consultation continue to evolve? First cited by Froehle and Rominger (1993), five topics still need attention in consultation research: (1) agreeing on a definition of consultation, (2) encouraging methodological diversity in consultation research, (3) addressing multi- and cross-cultural issues in consultation research, (4) enhancing the connection between research and practice, and (5) training consultants in research (pp. 694–695). Others (see, e.g., Alpert & Taufique, 2002a; Gutkin & Curtis, 2009; Love, 2007; Meyers, 2002; Zins, 1995) point out the need for research in the areas such as consultant training, consulting with groups and in teams, consultation's effectiveness in providing preventative-oriented services, and consultee resistance.

Dixon and Dixon (1993) add that consultation research can be improved through expanding the measures used to evaluate it and by defining its "boundary" conditions. They suggest that consultation outcome research should measure changes in the consultant and the consultee; in the interactions between the consultant, consultee, and client system; and in the system in which consultation occurs. Gutkin (1993) notes that consultation research needs to move from defining the broad boundaries of consultation services to "qualitatively more refined and sophisticated levels of research … that will move us closer to answering questions such as what forms of consultation are most effective with which types of consultees having what kind of clients with which sort of problems under what sets of circumstances" (p. 241).

Kratochwill, Elliot, and Busse (1995), Kratochwill (2008), and Truscott (2008) have suggested that future research in consultation needs to ensure stricter data presentation, collection procedures, and more sophisticated designs. These authors have also recommended that future research expand the use of effect sizes to allow for single-case and within-study meta-analyses, thus allowing for an examination of connections between training and treatment outcomes.

There is limited research related to multicultural consultation due to the fact that it is a relatively new area of investigation in consultation (Holcomb-McCoy & Coker, 2009; Ingraham, 2000, 2003, 2008; Newell, 2010b). However, research using quantitative, and especially, qualitative and mixed methods, is on the increase (Ingraham, 2008). Empirical research addressing cultural factors, however difficult it is to conduct, must be performed (Ramirez et al., 1998). There is very little research in this area, especially that related to Hispanics (Ramirez & Smith, 2007). To date, most of the research in this area is analogue research and qualitative case studies. Results suggest that the sensitivity of the consultant to racial issues is more important than the race of the consultant, and that consultants may want to specifically address racial issues in the consultation session. More sophisticated research that identifies consultation methods that are effective in multicultural contexts is sorely needed (Ingraham, 2000; Ingraham & Meyers, 2000b). As Ingraham (2000) notes: "Empirical research with real consultation sessions is needed to investigate fully the influence of race, consultant style, and consultee perceptions of consultant effectiveness" (p. 322). This need holds for cultural variables in addition to race. Researchers should also consider investigating traditional consultation approaches and modifications with culturally diverse consultees and client systems (Tarver Behring, Cabello, Kushida, & Murguia, 2000) such as parents (Cox, 2005; Guli, 2005; Hoard & Shepard, 2005). For example, does it take more time for the consultant to build rapport with consultees from certain cultural groups? In another example noted by Ingraham (2008), research is needed in exploring how the cultural context of consultation impacts its processes? Ingraham and Meyers (2000b) add that research is needed in the area of culturally different communication styles in the consultation relationship. Meyers (2002), Ingraham (2003, 2008), and Ingraham and Meyers (2000b) have suggested that qualitative research methodology may be particularly appropriate for research on multicultural consultation in terms of clarifying relationships among variables. The limited qualitative research to date is promising (see, e.g., Goldstein & Harris, 2000; Ingraham, 2003), but more is needed (Ingraham, 2008; Tysinger et al., 2009).

Several authors, including Newell (2010a) and Conoley, Conoley, & Reese (2009), have pointed out the necessity for consultation research to have practical applicability. There needs to be a stronger link between academic research and professional practice as the use of increasingly sophisticated research methodologies does not necessarily imply enhanced practice (Conoley et al., 2009). For example, Henning-Stout (1994) and Sandoval (2004) suggested research on the communication of expert consultants as they relate to their impact on consultees. In another example, there has been a call for improved research on how well interventions are delivered by consultees (i.e., treatment integrity) (Hagermoser Sanetti & Kratochwill, 2009; McLeod, Southam-Gerow, & Weisz, 2009) by, for example, developing psychometric properties for treatment integrity measures (Sheridan et al., 2009). Kratochwill and Stoiber (2000b) recommend that consultation research examine which interventions provide evidence-based outcomes and encourage the use of multiple measures. Truscott (2008) points out that there has been an increase in interdisciplinary research regarding consultation. Qualitative research in consultation also has been on the rise (Benn et al., 2008). However, Gutkin and Curtis (2009) point out the need for more and better research on the preventive aspects of consultation. Erchul and Sheridan (2008) note that process variables, such as relationship building, have been increasingly examined.

There has been very limited research on collaboration as a service. One study (Welch & Tulbert, 2000) socially validates some of the aspects of collaboration that have been espoused by practitioners. Other research (see Meyers, Meyers, &

Gelzheiser, 2001) stresses the importance of clarity of the roles of team members, shared decision making, and the necessity of a school vision for collaboration to be optimally effective. But there are major definitional issues surrounding terms like *collaborative*, *collaboration*, and *collaborator*, all of which create major difficulties in conducting pertinent research. Schulte and Osborne (2003) raise issues that need to be addressed in research on collaboration such as: (a) how should collaboration be defined; (b) which definitions of collaboration are linked to specific outcomes in consultation; and (c) how does, if at all, direct service tie into definitions of consultation. Cox (2005) points out that the research on parent collaboration is promising but that additional research needs to be conducted. Conoley and Conoley (2010) recommend that research on collaboration consider the findings from positive psychology. There is a movement in interagency collaboration to develop an overarching framework for use in evaluating interagency collaboration (Tseng, Liu, & Wang, 2011). Related to this initiative is the need for research on interdisciplinary collaboration (Mellin, 2009; Mellin, Hunt, & Nichols, 2011). Results of research on interagency collaboration suggest that it provides increased interagency linkages, increased information sharing, and more diverse interagency activities (Tseng et al., 2011) and research on developing scales to assess its effectiveness (Dedrick & Greenbaum, 2011).

A summative view of the research, however limited, suggests that consultation has efficacy even if consultation practice has far outpaced the body of research on consultation (Dunson, Hughes, & Jackson, 1994; Erchul & Martens, 2002; Gravois, 2012) and the amount of research in this area has actually declined since the mid-2000s (Pryzwansky, 2011). However, qualitative research efforts in consultation are increasing (Berrios & Lucca, 2006; Newell, 2010a), and they may be particularly useful when combined with quantitative approaches into a hybrid model (Kratochwill & Stoiber, 2000b). A final conclusion on the state of research in school consultation is that it is "... promising but undeveloped" (Erchul & Sheridan, 2008, p. 3). These authors suggest that consultation research be forward-looking and include evidence-based inter-ventions, advanced statistical processes, and special computer programs.

SUMMARY

The characteristics of effective consultants and collaborators result from their desire to grow personally and professionally, to acquire knowledge in consultation and human behavior, and to enhance their consulting skills. When they consult and collaborate, members of the helping professions need interpersonal and communication skills that flow from a genuine attitude based on respect, as well as problem-solving skills, skills in working with groups and organizations, skills in dealing with cultural diversity, and skills in maintaining ethical and professional behavior.

Consultants and consultees can take on a variety of roles, ranging from nondirective ones, such as process specialist, to directive ones, such as advocate. The role taken is a result of his or her abilities, the needs of stakeholders, and the nature of the problem.

The research on consultation and collaboration is limited. Although there is general support for the fact that consultation and collaboration are effective services, there is relatively little specific guidance for practitioners.

SUGGESTIONS FOR EFFECTIVE PRACTICE

- Make a commitment to try to consistently grow personally and professionally, increasingly learn about the knowledge of human behavior and consultation, and develop the skills of consultation.

- Practice the various roles that consultants and collaborators take on so that you can become comfortable with them.

- Develop each of the skills areas identified for effective consultants and collaborators.

- Become familiar with the empirical and qualitative research on consultation and collaboration as means to guide your practice.

- Remember the maxim: "The magic is that there is no magic." In other words, effective consultation or collaboration is the result of hard work, effort, and technical application.

- Remember a second maxim: "Do not tie a helping hand behind your back; but do not do for consultees or fellow collaborators what they can do for themselves." In other words, take on the expert role when you need to, but take on a collaborator whenever possible; use what you know and can do when necessary, but empower others whenever possible.

QUESTIONS FOR REFLECTION

1. Which criteria indicate that you have an adequate personal and professional growth orientation as a consultant?

2. The basic attitudes from which a consultant's interpersonal and communication skills flow are critical to effective consulting practice. Why?

3. Why are interpersonal skills as important for the consultant as communication skills?

4. What are the most essential problem-solving skills for a consultant to possess? Why?

5. With which of the consultant roles discussed in this chapter do you feel most comfortable? Why?

6. Why are the skills in working with cultural diversity so critical?

7. What are the basic differences in consultant and consultee behavior when a consultant changes from a directive to a nondirective role?

8. What are the factors that determine the role a consultant will take on?

9. If you were a consultant starting a relationship with a consultee, what consultee characteristics would you consider especially crucial for successful consultation?

10. If the research results on consultation are limited, how can consultants use them to enhance their effectiveness?

SUGGESTED SUPPLEMENTARY READINGS

Dougherty, A. M. (2014). Foundations of consultation and collaboration. In A. M. Dougherty (Ed.), *Casebook of psychological consultation and collaboration* (6th ed.). Belmont, CA: Brooks/Cole Cengage. This introductory chapter to a case studies text with an interactive format concisely examines the "nuts and bolts" of consultation and collaboration.

Erchul, W. P., & Sheridan, S. M. (2008). *Handbook of research in school consultation: Empirical foundations from the field*. New York: Lawrence Erlbaum Associates. The book provides an analysis of the state of research in school consultation. The book discusses related research perspectives and methodologies, findings, and future research directions. This is an excellent resource if you are interested in research in consultation.

Ingraham, C. L., & Meyers, J. (2000). Annotated bibliography for the miniseries on multicultural and cross-cultural consultation in schools. *School Psychology Review, 29,* 426–428. This bibliography continues to be a source for citing some of the cutting-edge thinking in multicultural consultation.

It puts in one place a list of important articles that will help you better understand the nature of multicultural consultation.

Lippitt, G., & Lippitt, R. (1986). *The consulting process in action* (2nd ed.). La Jolla, CA: University Associates. Although focused on organizational consultation, this book remains a classic in the consultation literature. Chapter 3, "Multiple Roles of the Consultant," presents a comprehensive approach to categorizing the many roles that consultants can take on. This article is a classic about consultation roles. The authors discuss each role and then speculate on the factors that influence when a given role will be taken on. Chapter 7, "The Consultant's Skills, Competencies, and Development," reflects a survey performed by the authors concerning the necessary components of an effective consultant. These two chapters present a concise overview of the roles consultants can take on and the skills and attitudes necessary to fulfill them effectively. They are as informative today as they were when first published.

PART II

✳

The Stages of Consultation and Collaboration

N ow that you have an idea of what consultation and collaboration are, and what skills and roles professionals use when they provide these services, let's examine a generic model of consultation/collaboration. The purpose of Part II of this text is to explain in detail a generic model of consultation and collaboration that you can use to guide your practice. Both theoretical and practical perspectives are brought together in the ensuing chapters. This section is designed to acquaint you with methods of providing the indirect services of consultation and collaboration using a problem-solving format. The main goal in this part of the book is to provide you with an understanding of how to effectively go about the practice of consultation and collaboration. A second goal is to discuss some pragmatic issues such as resistance to consultation and the influence of cultural, ecological, and organizational variables on the consultation process.

In Chapter 3, the generic model is explained in terms of four stages—entry, diagnosis, implementation, and disengagement—and the four phases within each of those stages. The chapter also examines resistance to consultation and collaboration, a common phenomenon. Chapter 4 highlights the entry stage with special attention being paid to interpersonal influence on the part of the helping professional. Chapter 5 focuses on diagnosis stage and contains essential information on data gathering. In Chapter 6, you will learn about the implementation stage with consideration being given to the increasingly important concept of treatment integrity. Chapter 7 explores the disengagement stage with an emphasis on evaluation. In Chapter 8, coverage is provided of the pragmatic issues of working within an organization such as cultural, organizational, and ecological influences.

As you read these chapters, I ask that you pay particular attention to the multicultural issues that can arise. Also of importance is remembering that the generic model needs to implemented in a personal and meaningful way with a genuine intention of helping others. Further, recall that the model describes a process for use by both external and internal consultants. When functioning as an internal consultant, most of the organizational aspects related to the model, for example, those related to physical entry, have been dealt with. Put briefly, the external consultant deals with the model in its organizational and individual consultee aspects, while the internal consultant most frequently deals exclusively with the individual consultee aspects. Finally, let me remind you that I will not use the phrase *consultation and collaboration* continuously throughout the remainder of this text; if there are differences between the two services at any of the stages, I will use the individual terms to differentiate.

3

＊

An Overview of the Generic Model of Consultation and Collaboration

The purpose of this chapter is to provide an overview of the generic model. The model consists of four stages—entry, diagnosis, implementation, and disengagement. Each of these four stages, in turn, consists of four unique phases. The chapter also covers the importance of having a multicultural framework for implementing this model as well as discussing issues related to resistance to consultation and collaboration.

You may find it beneficial to consider these five questions when reading this chapter:

- In what ways is the generic model easily explained to consultees and fellow collaborators?

- For each stage, what cautions should be taken to ensure multicultural competence in its application?

- What is your position on the following statement? "Resistance to consultation is normal."

- What strengths do you have as an individual that will enable you to personalize the generic model when you are implementing it?

- Why do you think it is normal during the course of consultation for the participants to move back and forth among the stages?

This straightforward generic model provides a framework for performing consultation and collaboration and allows for the inclusion of their intricacies and the complexities. This model puts a research-based, general structure around the consultation and collaboration processes. It represents what counselors,

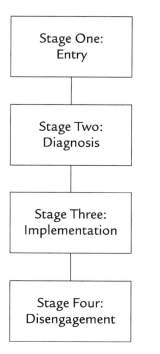

FIGURE 3.1 The stages of consultation and collaboration

psychologists, college student personnel professionals, social workers, human resource specialists, and other members of the helping professions need to know to effectively consult and collaborate. As you can see in Figure 3.1, consultation and collaboration follow a problem-solving format consisting of four stages: a relationship-building or entry process, the definition of the problem or diagnosis stage, an implementation stage, and a termination stage called *disengagement*. This model parallels for the most part the stages of other problem-solving models such as that of Bergan & Kratochwill (1990) and Kratochwill (2008).

Although there are an increasing number of research studies performed on the processes of consultation and collaboration, there are still very few evidence-based guidelines for effective practice. However, there is a substantial amount of evidence in the literature that indicates that a formal problem-solving approach to consultation can be effective (Erchul & Sheridan, 2008; Meyers, 2002;

Sheridan & Kratochwill, 2008). The generic model provides a literature-informed direction and focus while allowing for the flexibility necessary for effective consultation.

In a nutshell, in a problem-solving approach to consultation, different aspects of the problem brought to consultation or collaboration are examined and a plan for remediating the problem is developed, implemented, and evaluated. The expectation is that there will be a preventive effect in that consultees, by going through the consultation process, will not only deal effectively with the problem at hand, but also be better able to deal with similar problems on their own currently and in the future (Young & Gaughan, 2010). Furthermore, you will note that, in every aspect of the problem-solving endeavor, the way consultees and fellow collaborators perceive your communication is every bit as important as what you actually say. You will note that a stage model of consultation by itself does not deal with the important dynamics between the consultant and consultee that impact the consultation process (Hylander, 2012). Consequently, I describe such dynamics throughout the chapters that cover the generic model. Finally, there is a phenomenon called *resistance* in which the consultee or fellow collaborators do not engage in the problem-solving process constructively. Maintaining effective communication is one method of minimizing resistance.

Stage One of the generic model represents the starting up of the consultation process. It is called *entry* because the consultant enters the organization and/or enters into relationships with individual consultees. In this stage, relationships are built, the parameters of the problem are examined, and a contract is agreed upon and made with consultees within the organization or individual consultees. This stage lays the foundation on which the remainder of the consultation rests. The stage can range from very formal for external consultants to informal for internal consultants.

Stage Two of this model is concerned with shedding light on the problem that was broadly examined during entry. In this stage, the problem is understood more clearly and deeply. The consultant and consultee set goals based on this understanding and begin to think of ways to meet those goals. The term *diagnosis* is used (as opposed to *problem definition*) because it implies an ongoing process.

Stage Three involves taking action to solve the problem: A plan is formulated, implemented, and evaluated. This stage is called *implementation* to reflect its primary focus on action and its secondary emphasis on planning.

Stage Four winds down the process; it is the period of disengagement. Consultation is evaluated and consultant involvement is reduced. Goodbyes are said and leave is taken. The term *disengagement* implies that the process of consultation goes through a gradual reduction in activity and is used instead of *termination*, which implies a more abrupt ending to the process.

Each of the four stages in the consultation process consists of four phases. I have chosen the term *phase* because it implies process, whereas terms like *step* imply more static events and fail to acknowledge that consultation is a very dynamic endeavor that goes through its own life cycle.

There is nothing magical in having four phases for each stage; they merely result from the way I choose to view both consultation and collaboration after an extensive review of the literature. The important thing to remember at this point is that consultation can be divided into certain stages and phases. The model can be applied in a reiterative manner. That is, the stages (and the phases within them) frequently can overlap and interact with one another, depending on what happens during consultation. Consultation is a flexible and dynamic process; it rarely proceeds in textbook fashion. You should note that it is normal, in real-life consultation and collaboration, for there to be movement back and forth between the various phases and stages (Allen & Graden, 2002; Egan, 2010). Consultation is typically a *recursive process*. That is, new information or additional data obtained in the consultation process may lead to a change in problem definition or a switching to a new goal or intervention (Meyers, Proctor,

Graybill, & Meyers, 2009). For example, while a consultant and consultee are in the process of implementing a plan, a different aspect of the problem might emerge that would require returning to the diagnosis stage. Furthermore, some experts consider the implementation stage to occur continuously; that is, each of the consultant's actions during the entire consultation process is viewed as an implementation.

THE PHASES OF THE ENTRY STAGE

Stage One, entry, consists of the following phases:

- exploring organizational needs
- contracting
- physically entering the system
- psychologically entering the system

Exploring organizational needs refers to the process in which the consultant, consultee, and perhaps other parties-at-interest discuss the concerns that brought them together and then determine whether consultation should proceed.

Contracting refers to the process of formalizing the agreement that consultation should take place. Expectations for all parties involved are stated in the contract, as are fees for services to be rendered and deadlines to be met. You will want to remember that consultants who are internal to the organization often engage in informal contracting. When a consultant *physically enters the system*, relationships are built, a work site is obtained, the organization is studied, and contact with the consultee begins. *Psychologically entering the system* entails the ongoing process in which an external consultant gains acceptance as a temporary member of the organization and the internal consultant builds strong rapport with a given consultee. This phase actually lasts the duration of the consultation process, and it is a task that requires continual attention if consultation is to be fully successful.

THE PHASES OF THE DIAGNOSIS STAGE

Once the entry stage is accomplished, the consultation process proceeds to the diagnosis stage, which consists of the following phases:

- gathering information
- defining the problem
- setting goals
- generating possible interventions

When *gathering information*, the consultant and consultee also attempt to increase the chances of understanding the problem by isolating factors that precipitate it. Data can be gathered through a variety of means, including surveys, interviews, observations, and examination of records. When *defining the problem*, the consultant and consultee analyze and interpret the data that have been gathered. It is especially important for the consultant and consultee to remain objective during this phase. A biased interpretation of the data can lead to an erroneous definition of the problem. Once the problem has been defined to the satisfaction of the parties involved, *setting goals* to overcome the problem occurs. The consultant has the responsibility to make sure that any goal that is set meets the criteria of being an effective goal. Once goals have been set, the consultant and consultee move on to *generating possible interventions* that could resolve the problem.

THE PHASES OF THE IMPLEMENTATION STAGE

Once a list of possible strategies has been generated, the consultation process moves to Stage Three, implementation, which includes:

- choosing an intervention
- formulating a plan
- implementing the plan
- evaluating the plan

This stage begins with *choosing an intervention* or group of interventions—activities the consultant and consultee think have the best chance of effectively solving the problem. Using these interventions, the consultant and consultee embark on *formulating a plan* that incorporates these interventions.

The pros and cons of a variety of possible plans are carefully scrutinized until a plan that is likely to succeed is chosen and tailored to the unique requirements, including those of culture, of the consultee, client system, and/or the organization. In collaboration, each party involved is assigned to and responsible for carrying out a part of the plan. The third phase is *implementing the plan*, and the consultant usually monitors the plan's progress once it has been implemented. In collaboration, unlike consultation, the human service/mental health professional takes responsibility for the mental health aspects of the case and hence participates directly in the implementation process. In collaboration, the parties involved carry out their pieces of the plan implementation and provide ongoing assistance to one another as necessary. The final phase is *evaluating the plan* once implementation has been completed. Based on the results of the evaluation, the consultation process moves either back to a previous phase of some stage (e.g., defining the problem) or on to the stage of disengagement.

THE PHASES OF THE DISENGAGEMENT STAGE

Stage Four, disengagement, consists of the following phases:

- evaluating the consultation process
- planning postconsultation matters
- reducing involvement and following up
- terminating

Evaluating the consultation process can range from assessing consultee satisfaction with consultation to measuring the impact of a system-wide intervention on the behavior of the members of an organization. Evaluation must be a planned event so that consultant and consultee alike will know what will be evaluated, by whom, how, and when. There is a trend toward the increased use of qualitative measures of consultation effectiveness. *Planning postconsultation matters* involves deciding how the effects of consultation are going to be maintained by the consultee and/or the organization. This phase is essential in increasing the probability that follow-through occurs after the consultant's involvement ends. *Reducing involvement* is the phase in which the consultant creates conditions of decreasing contact with the consultee. This is also the time when more and more responsibility for the results of consultation is taken on by the consultee. *Follow-up* is the process in which the consultant monitors this transfer of responsibility so as to iron out any unforeseen problems.

Terminating is the formal ending of the consultation process. It has professional aspects (e.g., collecting final fees) and a personal side (e.g., saying goodbye). Effective consultants successfully accomplish both the professional and personal sides of termination (Dougherty, Tack, Fullam, & Hammer, 1996).

PUTTING THE GENERIC MODEL INTO PRACTICE

There are three important points to make about putting the generic model of consultation into practice. First, consultation is a dynamic, interactive process that uses the various stages as needed (Meyers & Yelich, 1989). Things rarely, if ever, go in a textbook fashion. Equal attention should be paid both to *what* you are doing and to *how* you are doing those things. Different consultees and different fellow collaborators engage in the use of the generic model differently. Some try to tell you everything they can at the outset of consultation, while others share information about the problem at different intervals. You will want to pace yourself by taking the people you assist where they are and then sensitively guide them through the generic model.

Second, it is very important to get supervised practice in consultation. By "trying on" the model and putting it into practice, you can get a sense of yourself as a consultant. The more experience you get, the higher the probability that you will increase your effectiveness as a consultant.

Third, there is limited empirical support for the notion that the generic model be implemented in a collaborative manner whenever possible. Other limited empirical evidence suggests that consultants should be at least minimally in charge of the consultation process (Gutkin, 1996; Witt, 1990a). Consultees tend to view some degree of consultant dominance in which they follow the consultant's leads as being positive (Erchul & Chewning, 1990). Erchul and Chewning (1990) intimate that consultants may be more in control of their consultation relationships than they realize and that this control is positively perceived by consultees as indicating consultant competency. You may want to examine with your consultees the degree of your directiveness and their reaction to it during your supervised practice. For example, you may want to gain feedback from consultees regarding your questioning style (Hughes & DeForest, 1993). In collaboration, you will often be viewed as the expert in a certain area relative to the goals of helping the client system. For example, a school counselor might be viewed as the most knowledgeable about a child's capacity for learning.

EXAMPLES

The following two case studies are designed to show how the consultation and collaboration processes generally work. Although oversimplified, they will provide concrete examples to which you can continue to refer as you read and study the next five chapters. They represent idealized cases—for consultation and collaboration, like other helping relationships such as counseling, rarely proceed so smoothly—but, nonetheless, they provide a rough outline of how the processes work.

C A S E   3.1   Consultation

Assume that you are a school counselor who is going to act as a consultant. Your consultee is a schoolteacher and the client is a student of the teacher. You meet with the teacher, who discusses the behavior of the student, particularly the fact that the student rarely turns in homework. You help the teacher explore the problem and at the same time build rapport with him. You both agree that working on the homework problem is mutually agreeable, so you contract to meet three or four times to work on that problem. You agree to observe the student in the teacher's classroom and continue to use effective communication skills and gain the teacher's acceptance of you as a person he can trust. At this point, you have completed the entry stage.

You and the teacher now start to gather information on the student; together you examine the student's cumulative folder. The teacher keeps track of when homework is not turned in and the conditions surrounding that behavior. Based on the data, you note that the student does not turn in homework on Tuesdays and Fridays but does on the other school days. An interview with the student's parents reveals that they both attend school on Monday and Thursday nights and that the child is left with a babysitter. Based on this information, you and the teacher redefine the problem as lack of parental supervision on Monday and Thursday nights. You and the consultee set the goal of having the student turn in all homework every other Tuesday and Friday for the first month, and every Tuesday and Friday thereafter. When generating possible strategies you come up with several ideas, which

include the loss of recess time when homework is not turned in, rewards when homework is turned in, and the use of a parent–child contract for getting the homework done. You have now completed the diagnosis stage; you are ready to begin the implementation stage.

Weighing the pros and cons of each intervention, you and the teacher determine that the parent–child contract is the best alternative. You then formulate a plan that consists of obtaining parental cooperation and assisting in the formulation of a parent–child contract for getting homework completed on the nights the parents are not home. When the parents agree to the plan, you and the teacher assist them in carrying it out. Strategies for appropriately reinforcing both the child and parents are included. The parents carry out the plan effectively; based on your evaluation, the goal has been met. The third stage, implementation, has just been accomplished. Now you go on to the disengagement stage.

In this final stage, you have the teacher rate his satisfaction with your efforts to assist him during each of the previous three stages. You then lay the groundwork concerning the way he will carry on with the student after you cease consulting. You check in with the teacher every two weeks or so to see how things are going. A month or so after your last contact you follow up to make sure that the homework is still being turned in. Toward the end of the next grading period you again check in about the student's performance. Because everything is proceeding well, you and the teacher agree to terminate consultation.

You will recall the discussion of how to choose between consultation and collaboration from Chapter 1. You will frequently be faced with the decision to choose between consultation and collaboration as the service of choice in particular situation. Of particular note is that school-based professionals, because they are typically internal to the organization in which they provide services, may be better positioned to use collaboration as a primary service over consultation due to the fact that both parties can relatively easily implement a part of the overall plan designed for the client system.

MULTICULTURAL COMPETENCE USING THE GENERIC MODEL

Consideration of cultural issues should take place throughout consultation (Ingraham, 2000, 2003, 2004, 2008; Miranda, 2008). Clearly, the culture of the consultant, the consultee, and the client system are all aspects of the ecology dealt with in consultation (Cooper & Leong, 2008; Ortiz, 2006; Ramirez & Smith, 2007). Consultants need a perspective that facilitates their familiarity with and

---

C A S E   3.2   Collaboration

Assume that you are a school counselor who is going to act as a collaborator. Your fellow collaborator is a schoolteacher and the client is a student of the teacher. You meet with the teacher, who discusses the behavior of the student, particularly the fact that the student rarely turns in homework. You help the teacher explore the problem and at the same time build rapport with him. You both agree that working on the homework problem is mutually agreeable, so you contract to meet three or four times to work on that problem. You agree to observe the student in the teacher's classroom and continue to use effective communication skills and gain the teacher's acceptance of you as a person he can trust. At this point, you have completed the entry stage.

You and the teacher now start to gather information on the student; together you examine the student's cumulative folder. The teacher keeps track of when homework is not turned in and the conditions surrounding that behavior. Based on the data, you both note that the student does not turn in homework on Tuesdays and Fridays but does on the other school days. An interview with the student's parents reveals that they both attend school on Monday and Thursday nights and that the child is left with a babysitter. Based on this information you and the teacher redefine the problem as lack of parental supervision on Monday and Thursday nights. You and the teacher set the goal of having the student turn in all homework every other Tuesday and Friday for the first month, and every Tuesday and Friday thereafter. When generating possible strategies you come up with several ideas, which include the loss of recess time when homework is not turned in and the use of a parent–child contract for

getting the homework done. You have now completed the diagnosis stage; you are ready to begin the implementation stage.

Weighing the pros and cons of each intervention, you and the teacher determine that the parent–child contract is the best alternative. You then formulate a plan that consists of obtaining parental cooperation and assisting in the formulation of a parent–child contract for getting homework completed on the nights the parents are not home. When the parents agree to the plan, you and the teacher assist them in carrying it out. Strategies for appropriately reinforcing both the child and parents are included. You agree to counsel the child concerning the issues related to the child's lack of academic performance when the child is not under parental supervision. The teacher agrees to reinforce homework completion. The parents carry out the plan effectively; based on your evaluation, the goal has been met. In evaluating your work with the student, you determine that the goals have been met. The third stage, implementation, has just been accomplished. Now you go on to the disengagement stage.

In this final stage, you and the teacher rate your satisfaction with your respective efforts to assist one another. You then lay the groundwork concerning the way each of you will carry on with the student after you finish the collaboration process. You check in with each other every two weeks or so to see how things are going. A month or so after your last contact you follow up to make sure that the homework is still being turned in. Toward the end of the next grading period, you again check in about the student's performance. Because everything is proceeding well, you and the teacher agree to terminate.

---

sensitivity toward the cultural frame of reference of the consultee and client system's culture (Ramirez, Lepage, Kratochwill, & Duffy, 1998) while attending to the "personal culture" of the parties involved (Egan, 2010; Tomes, 2011).

It is critical to remember that consultants will need to implement the generic model with cultural sensitivity and competence as cultural issues impact all stages of consultation (Lopez & Truesdale, 2007). The generic model is designed to take consultees where they are and can be adapted to their style of problem management and cultural context. It is key to effective

implementation that the generic model be adapted with cultural competence in order to be relevant to the needs of consultees and their client systems.

CONSULTEE READINESS FOR CHANGE

As you implement the generic model, you will realize that not all consultees assume that they will have to change in some way to effectively help their client systems. Even those with the "Tell-me-what-to-do-and I-will-do-it" attitude frequently misconstrue the fact that they will need to change their behavior, and perhaps, even attitudes, to be effective with their client systems. The stages of change model originally developed by Prochaska and DiClemente (1984) can assist consultants to assess the consultee's stage of change and thus increase the likelihood of a successful consultation experience and minimize consultee resistance to consultation (see below). The first stage of change is precontemplation in which the consultee is unaware of the need to change on their part in order to effectively work with the client system. Consultants can move consultees toward more readiness to change by noting in the entry stage that doing things differently in order to assist the client system implies change on the consultee's part as well as the client system's. Consultees in the next stage, contemplation, are typically ambivalent about engaging in change. Consultants can assist consultees to do a "cost analysis." That is, guiding the consultee in determining how much effort it will take on the consultee's part to get the desired behaviors from the client system. The third stage of change, preparation, involves the consultee having the intention of trying to change his or her approach in dealing with the client system. Consultants can provide the usual support consultation provides as well as encouragement to gear the consultee toward more significant change in terms of dealing with the client system. The fourth stage, action, involves the consultee implementing the change with the client system with continued social support from the consultant. The fifth stage, maintenance, deals with the consultee successfully acquiring new behaviors that can be used with current and future client systems. This generalization can be enhanced through the evaluation of the plan and of the consultation process itself. Clearly, the success of the generic model is tied to consultee readiness for change. Successful consultants bear this fact in mind as they implement the generic model.

RESISTANCE TO CONSULTATION

No matter how many precautions consultants take to ease their physical and psychological entry into the system, some resistance to consultation is typical throughout the entire consultation process. Although such resistance is normal, this lack of cooperation with the process can present significant challenges to your consultation activities. *Resistance* is the failure of a consultee or organization to participate constructively in the consultation process (McGivern, Ray-Subramanian, & Auster, 2008; Moe & Perera-Diltz, 2009; Wickstrom & Witt, 1993). A related term, *reluctance*, when applied to consultation refers to the hesitancy of the consultee to engage in consultation (Egan, 2010). For example, teachers may be reluctant to participate in school-based consultation because they sense that to do so means more time and effort added to their already heavy and stressful workloads in a high accountability environment (Conoley, Conoley, & Reese, 2009).

Overcoming resistance involves accurately determining its source. A common mistake made by consultants is to assume that resistance is due to a negative attitude on the part of the consultee (D'Amato, Zafiris, McConnell, & Dean, 2011; Kratochwill, 2008; Kratochwill, Elliott, & Busse, 1995; O'Keefe & Medway, 1997; Watson & Robinson, 1996). Another perspective, for example, is that the consultee may not be able to effectively manage the environmental variables impacting upon the implementation of the intervention (Gutkin & Curtis, 2009). Consultants will need to differentiate resistance from lack of skill on the part of consultees to carry out interventions.

System-Level Resistance

When consultants enter organizations ready to initiate change, they frequently encounter a healthy systems-level resistance to such change (Block, 2000; Fuqua, Newman, & Dickman, 1999; Moe & Perera-Diltz, 2009).

This is an important survival mechanism that protects the system from outside threats. However, all organizations must adapt to change, and resistance can impede the progress of this adaptation. There are many variables that can promote resistance to consultation.

There are four classic sources of organizational resistance to consultation (Parsons & Meyers, 1984): the desire to keep things the way they are, the view of the consultant as an outsider, the rejection of anything new as nonnormative (a "we just don't do things that way around here" attitude), and the desire to protect one's own turf or vested interest ("silo mentality"). Resistance is common even in those organizations that want to change and that support consultation with appropriate degrees of money, time, and effort. In fact, the very title *consultant* can be threatening because it implies change. Because the organization's perception of the consultant's role early on in the consultation process is often unclear, resistance can be preempted by providing a clear picture at the outset of what the consultant is to accomplish (McLean, 2006). In addition, organizational resistance can be minimized when stakeholders understand the "why" and "how" of consultation and how it can help the organization better meet its mission (Sander, Sharkey, Olivarri, Tanigawa, & Mauseth, 2010). Obtaining support from the leadership of the organization for consultation also diminishes resistance (Kratochwill, 2008).

Nontraditional views of organizational resistance assume that resistance is present only to the degree that organizations are conceptualized in terms of power and conflict (Kress, Cimring, & Elias, 1998; Merron, 1993). In these cases, what is labeled *resistance* is regarded as simply the expression of alternative views of organizational events and a consultant's focusing on what is *wrong* in the organization.

Consultee Resistance

Whereas relatively little has been written about organizational resistance to consultation, a great deal has been written over the past few decades about consultee resistance (Dougherty, Dougherty, & Purcell, 1991; Erchul & Conoley, 1991; Gonzalez, Nelson, Gutkin, & Snwery, 2004; Hughes, 1983; Meyers & Yelich, 1989; Randolph & Graun, 1988;

Tingstrom, Little, & Stewart, 1990). When the consultation process is facing difficulty, it is not uncommon to attribute that difficulty to resistance in the consultee (Gonzalez et al., 2004).

In any helping relationship, resistance is both unavoidable and potentially helpful (Blom-Hoffman & Rose, 2007; Otani, 1989). Consultants need to be knowledgeable about the content of the resistance (Jeltova & Fish, 2005).

Consultants must manage resistance to maximize a positive consultation outcome (Blom-Hoffman & Rose, 2007; Brigman & Webb, 2008). From a behavioral viewpoint, resistance can arise from the consultee's aversion to the consultation outcome. Consultees may believe that the benefits of consultation are not worth the costs (e.g., it will take too much of their time) or that consultation will result in some form of punishment (e.g., criticism by one's supervisor) (Piersel & Gutkin, 1983). Therefore, to minimize resistance, the consultant should ensure that the cost of participating in consultation is at least matched by the benefits.

Cognitive dissonance theory can be used to analyze sources of consultee resistance (Hughes, 1983). Dissonance occurs when a person has concepts that are either not in accord with each other or illogical. For example, being a consultee and not liking it are dissonant concepts, and there is a strong likelihood that consultee resistance will ensue. Dissonance is minimized when a consultee buys into the consultation process. Ways to involve a consultee include keeping consultation a voluntary and peer relationship, showing how consultation can help but making no "guarantees," and making sure that the consultee puts forth some effort in the consultation process (Hughes, 1983). By involving the consultee in these ways, the consultant creates a relationship in which the consultee is more likely to cooperate.

Hughes and Falk (1981) examined resistance to consultation from the perspective of reactance theory, which suggests that when a person perceives that a freedom is taken away, he or she will try to restore it (Brehm, 1966; Hughes & Falk, 1981). One implication for consultants is to avoid the overuse of persuasion and recommendations, and instead provide consultees with choices whenever possible during consultation. In this way, consultees are most likely not to experience any infringement of their freedom. Dougherty et al. (1991) suggest that resistance can be due to a consultee's misconception concerning the nature of consultation, some dysfunction in the consultation relationship, fear related to the discomfort of disclosing need, or cognitive distortions that cause misunderstandings and lead to increased resistance. Kratochwill and Pittman (2002) indicate that resistance may be related to the consultee's perception of the acceptability of the intervention. In parent consultation, resistance on the part of parents in being consultees is their concern that they should be integral to dealing with any issues that their children may have rather than leaving it up to an outsider such as a mental health professional (Holcomb-McCoy, 2009; Holcomb-McCoy & Bryan, 2010). The bottom-line is that consultants need to be aware of consultee expectations for consultation and take them into account to minimize resistance (Tysinger, Tysinger, & Diamanduros, 2009).

Dealing Effectively with Resistance

There are several things consultants can do to minimize resistance:

- Create a strong relationship to build trust and alleviate fear.
- Demonstrate cultural competence and sensitivity.
- Collaborate whenever possible.
- Create conditions so that a consultation has a satisfying outcome and is worth the effort.
- Allow the consultee as many choices as possible.
- Throughout the process, point out how consultation might be helpful.
- Distribute the workload in consultation so that the consultee does his or her share.
- Give the consultee as much freedom as possible in all aspects of the process.
- Be clear about the nature of consultation from the outset.
- Challenge any cognitive distortions with specific disputing examples.

- Be as clear and specific as possible about what is expected of the consultee.
- Use examples to illustrate points.
- Try to minimize the new things a consultee has to learn.
- Link interventions to the consultee's explanation of the causes of the problem.
- Ensure that the consultee has the skills necessary to carry out the interventions.

Perhaps the best method of dealing with resistance is to prevent its occurrence in the first place through understanding and emphasizing referent power (Carlson, Dinkmeyer, & Johnson, 2008; Wickstrom & Witt, 1993), viewing some resistance as normal (Egan, 2010), and applying motivational interviewing (Blom-Hoffman & Rose, 2007). Understanding refers to the consultant's ability to comprehend and appreciate the consultee's views of events. Using referent power refers to consultant's attempt to use a collaborative and cooperative style in approaching the consultee. Motivation interviewing assists consultees in dealing with ambivalence-related resistance by allowing them to convince themselves that change is in order.

A Brief Example of Resistance to Consultation

As you consult with a mental health practitioner about a client, you increasingly note that the consultee avoids direct eye contact with you as he discusses his client. As you reflect on the consultation relationship, you note that you and the consultee are locked into a "Yes, but ..." kind of interaction in which you make suggestions regarding the case and he explains how none of them could possibly work with this client. You acknowledge the issue by noting that you are getting frustrated with what is going on and that you imagine the consultee is too. You suggest both starting anew by focusing in on what the consultee wants to have happen in the case and how both of you can collaborate to achieve it.

PERSONALIZING THE CONSULTATION AND COLLABORATION PROCESS

Discussing consultation and collaboration in terms of stages and phases tends to leave out the human side of the process. The skills and attitudes noted in Chapter 2 are essential for adequately implementing the generic model. As a consultant or collaborator, you are your best intervention (Bellman, 1990). That is, who you are as a person can affect the outcome of consultation or collaboration as much as what you do when you engage in these services. To include this human side, let's personalize the process of consultation and collaboration by showing the ways that you can "be there" for the people with whom you are working. I developed this idea after reading Gerard Egan's book *The Skilled Helper* (2010). Egan describes his counseling model as a series of steps for "being with" clients. Here is how you can be there for the people with whom you're working throughout the phases of the consultation process:

1. Ensure multicultural sensitivity and competence in your behavior.

2. Listen well at the outset and take the time to build rapport.

3. Assist in formulating a contract that will make explicit the expectations you have for each other.

4. Start the consultation/collaboration process on the consultee's or collaborator's turf as soon as possible.

5. Proactively attempt to gain acceptance, not only by the consultee or fellow collaborator, but also by the organization in which the service is being provided.

6. Do your best to determine what information should be gathered on the problem and how best to do it.

7. Attempt to be unbiased as you assist in analyzing and interpreting the gathered data.

8. Ensure that the goals you and the consultee or collaborator set are effective goals that have a good probability of being successfully accomplished.

9. Be as creative and sharp as you can be when it comes to generating possible interventions.

10. Assist in examining the pros and cons of each possible intervention you and the consultee or collaborator consider.

11. Collaborate in putting together the best possible plan and considering the available resources.

12. Be available, as a consultant, to monitor the progress that is being made and as a collaborator to fulfill your part of the plan.

13. Provide assistance and encouragement in evaluating the plan.

14. Ask for evaluations of yourself and your services.

15. Assist in planning what needs to be done regarding the consultation or collaboration after you have left the scene.

16. Avoid dependence by the consultee or fellow collaborator through a gradual reduction in your involvement and foster their independence through intermittent follow-ups.

17. Say goodbye professionally and personally and let go of the relationship when that is in everyone's best interest.

SUMMARY

The generic model consists of four stages—entry, diagnosis, implementation, and disengagement—and the four phases within each of those stages. The phases of the entry stage include exploring organizational needs, contracting, physically entering the system, and psychologically entering the system. In the diagnosis stage, the phases are gathering information, defining the problem, setting goals, and generating possible interventions. The implementation stage involves choosing an intervention, formulating a plan, implementing the plan, and evaluating the plan. The disengagement stage is made up of the following phases—evaluating the consultation process, planning postconsultation matters, reducing involvement and following up, and terminating.

Consultation and collaboration need to be practiced with cultural competence. This means that the consultant needs to have the knowledge, skills, and dispositions necessary to adapt the consultation or collaboration process to the cultural context in which these services are provided.

Resistance to consultation and collaboration is somewhat normal and common phenomenon. It is best handled by creating and maintaining a strong working relationship with consultees or fellow collaborators. Finally, implementing the generic model is not some rote, linear, or cognitive event. Rather, the model's implementation consists of a personalized helping relationship in which the intent to be of assistance is as important as the knowledge and skills necessary to be effective and successful.

SUGGESTIONS FOR EFFECTIVE PRACTICE

- Remember that consultation and collaboration are recursive processes.

- Accept resistance as normal and do not take it personally.

- Adapt the generic model to the cultural aspects of the consultee and the client system.

- Personalize the consultation and collaboration processes by "bringing who you are to what you do."

QUESTIONS FOR REFLECTION

1. What are the challenges in making consultees and fellow collaborators aware of the nature of the generic model?

2. You are a consultant using the generic model. How do you ensure that you implement it with cultural competence?

3. What can you do to minimize resistance?

4. What are some of the challenges you anticipate facing in personalizing the generic model when you are implementing it?

5. What is the "good news" and what is the "bad news" about consultation and collaboration both being recursive processes?

SUGGESTED SUPPLEMENTARY READINGS

Dougherty, A. M. (2014). Implications for effective practice. In A. M. Dougherty (Ed.), *Casebook of psychological consultation and collaboration* (6th ed.). Belmont, CA: Brooks/Cole Cengage. This chapter ties together important themes from seven case studies involving consultation and collaboration. Special attention is paid to the stages of the generic model and their implications.

Kratochwill, T. R. (2008). Best practices in school-based problem-solving consultation: Applications in prevention and intervention systems. In A. Thomas and J. Grimes (Eds.), *Best practices in school psychology* (5th ed., pp. 1673–1688). Bethesda, MD: National Association of School Psychologists. This work provides an up-to-date and succinct approach to performing consultation. It has a behavioral orientation, yet is broad enough to accommodate other theoretical perspectives.

4

✳

Entry Stage

J ust like a good novel, the consultation process should have a beginning, middle, and an end.

Frequently referred to as *start-up activities*, the entry stage can consist of for external consultants—one telephone call or several exploratory meetings—or, for an internal consultant, a first session with a consultee. Entry involves the initial contact the consultant has with the consultee.

Entry involves examining the consultation request, building a strong working relationship, and determining whether consultation should occur (French & Bell, 1999). Throughout this stage, the consultant and the organization contact person, or the consultant and an individual consultee, try to determine how advantageous consultation can be. The consultant should bear in mind that the success of the consultation depends in part on how well these start-up activities are accomplished. It is important to note that all consultants, whether internal or external, will have to "enter" each relationship they form with consultees.

The purpose of this chapter is to explain this beginning, or entry, stage of the consultation process. Entry, as both a distinct stage of consultation and a process in which the consultant begins to create relationships, is complex and consists of four phases: exploring organizational needs, contracting, physically entering the organization's system, and psychologically entering the system.

Here are five questions to consider as you read this chapter:

- In what ways is the entry stage a complex process? How do multicultural variables impact this stage?

- Why is the entry stage both a critical and delicate stage of consultation?

- How directive should a consultant be in guiding the course of consultation during the entry stage?

- "There is more to a contract than what is written on the paper." What are the implications of the preceding statement for consultants?
- How will the entry stage differ for external as opposed to internal consultants?

To get a feel for the entry stage, consider the following situation:

AN EXAMPLE OF ENTRY AT THE ORGANIZATION CLIENT-SYSTEM LEVEL

You are a professor at a state university. A former student, now director of advising at a nearby community college, telephones and wants to come and talk with you about enhancing the quality of advising services at the community college. You set up an appointment, which will take place in your office. During the appointment, you assist the advising director in exploring the advising office's specific needs in regard to enhancing the quality of advising. You ask the director to make up a wish list to stimulate preliminary exploration.

You ask what is going well and what is not going so well. You ask about the organizational environment in which advising occurs, and you ask for the advisors' views on the process of advising, its rewards, the level of administrative support for advising, and the advising director.

Based on this information, you agree to conduct two sessions with all the advisors. The first session is a workshop on effective advising, and the second a troubleshooting meeting with the advisors to help them feel more heard by the parties involved in coordinating advising services. You and the advising director sign a contract to that effect. The week before the workshop, you visit the community college and all of the workshop participants. You are supportive and ask them what things they would like to talk about. Next you arrange for the room at the community college in which the workshop is to occur. Then, when you open the first session, you ask the participants what they want and what they do not want out of the workshop.

AN EXAMPLE OF ENTRY AT THE INDIVIDUAL CLIENT-SYSTEM LEVEL

You are a school-based consultant contacted by a first year teacher for consultation regarding a child in the teacher's fourth-grade class. You briefly share social amenities and then explain to your consultee the nature of consultation and what it entails. You answer the teacher's questions regarding the process and then listen to the teacher's description of the problem. You are empathic, building trusting relationship with the consultee. Together you develop an informal contract to work together to assist the child, with the teacher taking on responsibility for implementing the intervention that you will later come up with. Throughout this process you continually try to psychologically enter the relationship by building rapport with the consultee. Finally, you make sure that the teacher knows that this is your permanent office and that you are available by request between sessions. You then set a next meeting with the consultee.

Entry is the general process by which the consultant enters the system in which consultation is to occur. The goals of entry include all stakeholders in the organization understanding consultation and coming to know the consultant (Gutkin & Curtis, 2009). You will recall that Chapter 2 discussed internal and external consultants. The scope of the entry stage often varies depending upon whether the consultant is internal or external.

External consultants typically have to deal with preentry and Phase One (exploring organizational needs) issues much more extensively and frequently than do internal consultants. For example, external consultants encounter issues related to on entering an organization for the first time every time they work with a new organization, even if the main focus of their work is on individual consultees.

Externals ask questions like: Have I prepared for the initial meeting? In today's Internet world (information superhighway), do I have baseline knowledge about the company or person(s) that I will come into contact (have I done my homework)? Am I comfortable with working with this group based on my expertise and/or their values? These questions are part of mental preparedness and the familiarization process. With this thoughtful preparation, entry becomes the execution of the plan that is based on the answers to the above questions.

Glidewell (1959), in a now classic article, defines entry by an external consultant as the attachment of a consultant to an existing social system through the creation of temporary membership in an organization for a person who is to help that system. This temporary membership is accomplished by creating relationships that assist in determining which functions a consultant should provide to best help the organization accomplish its ends.

Internal consultants typically deal with preentry issues related to the organization only when they begin their work for the first time in their employing organization or when significant organizational changes occur. For most internal consultants, entry involves creating and maintaining a relationship with an individual consultee, developing a contract (often informal and verbal) with him or her, working from their own established office or the consultee's work place, and maintaining the acceptance from current and prospective consultees. Internal consultants have to enter, in that each consultation situation is new to them. Even though internal consultants often work one-on-one with individual consultees, they will want to be aware and skillful in obtaining entry into a new organization for the first time. Through skillful entry, members of the organization will understand consultation processes, prospective consultees will have a sense of what consultation can do for them and their client systems, and the administrators in the organization will be knowledgeable so that they can sanction consultation as a desired service.

You will want to bear in mind that much of the material in this chapter is written from the

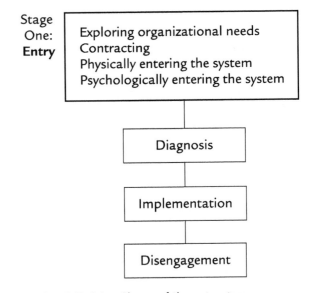

FIGURE 4.1   Phases of the entry stage

perspective of external consultants, although its contents will be very helpful to internal consultants entering the organization or dealing with an individual consultee in that organization for the first time. Figure 4.1 shows the four phases of the entry stage of consultation.

PHASE ONE: EXPLORING ORGANIZATIONAL NEEDS

Consultation typically begins when a representative of an organization contacts a consultant for the purpose of *exploring* the possibilities of initiating a consulting relationship. It is not unusual for an organization to contact a consultant without knowing the precise or even the appropriate reason why consultation is needed. In fact, the toughest aspect of entry is making a quick and accurate assessment of what is troubling the organization. Some authors (Conoley & Conoley, 1992) note that an organization rarely uses refined techniques to determine its need for a consultant, and frequently the organization has misidentified its problem. Therefore, consultants should be cautious about moving too quickly into planning implementation steps during the beginning of the entry process (Sperry, 2005).

Whether or not there is a firm grasp on what is needed in consultation, an organization usually contacts a consultant because it perceives it has a concern that cannot be solved within the organization or because there is an unfilled gap within the organization (Schein, 1988). In exploring organizational needs, the consultant must deal with certain issues (Cherniss, 1993; French & Bell, 1999); for example, whether the consultant appears to be the right person to help the organization and determining the things to focus on during consultation. Other issues include dealing with disagreements, for example, on the nature of the problem as well as issues related to whose interests are being served and the ramifications of that choice (Cherniss, 1993; Sperry, 2005). The process of considering these issues usually begins with an exploratory meeting referred to as the *first contact*.

First contact may be initiated by either party and usually involves the organization's contact person, perhaps some parties-at-interest (stakeholders), and the consultant. Ideally those involved should be knowledgeable about consultants and favorable toward their use (French & Bell, 1999). The initial meeting for exploring organizational needs typically occurs at the organization. The advantage for meeting at the organization is that it allows the consultant on-site observations of the organization and the ways its personnel interact.

Determining Whether Consultation Should Take Place

The primary decision to be made during the preliminary exploration of organizational needs is whether or not consultation should be undertaken. Over the years, six issues that relate to this decision have emerged (see Cherniss, 1993; Holtz & Zhan, 2004; McLean, 2006; Stroh & Johnson, 2006):

- the degree of congruence between the consultant and the consultee system (e.g., as regards value systems)
- the amount of resources the organization is willing to commit toward change (e.g., the

amount of administrative sanctioning for consultees' participation)

- the appropriateness of the consultee's or the organization's characteristics (e.g., the amount of flexibility within the organization with regard to the changes consultation may involve)
- the ways in which the organization perceives the need for change (e.g., the degree to which prospective consultees see consultation as important in meeting the organization's goals)
- mutual understanding of the expectations for consultation (e.g., the consultant and consultees being able to agree on how consultation should proceed and on desirable outcomes for all parties involved)
- agreement on who constitutes the consultee system, the client system, and parties-at-interest (e.g., the consultant agrees to consult only with the crisis intervention team in a mental health center regarding approaches in counseling their clients)

In the 1980s, Bell and Nadler (1985) developed four questions for discussion by the consultant and the organization's contact person or the consultee to determine whether or not consultation is necessary and worthwhile: Why am I here? Who are you? What is likely to happen? What will be the result? The degree to which the four questions are answered to the satisfaction of both the consultant and the contact person eventually determines the success of the preliminary exploration of the organization's needs. The importance of these questions has been corroborated (Stroh & Johnson, 2006).

The answers to these questions constitute the *task of familiarization*, during which consultants learn the ins and outs of the organization—for example, its history, mission, philosophy, and procedures (Caplan & Caplan, 1993). Another part of this task is determining what the organization has done so far to solve its perceived problems, to what degree these activities were successful, and what factors prevented them from being more successful (Mann, 1983; Strohn & Johnson, 2006). To determine this, the consultant conducts a "miniassessment" of the perceived problem (McLean, 2006).

Why Am I Here?

The question "Why am I here?" is important to contact person and consultant alike. From the contact person's perspective, this question concerns perceived need. From the consultant's perspective, the question involves assisting the consultee in defining an appropriate problem or concern and assessing whether the consultant is the right person for the job.

Who Are You?

The question "Who are you?" concerns defining the roles taken on by the consultant, contact person, and others involved in consultation. Answering this question entails identifying the roles and responsibilities of the consultant and the contact person. By discussing views, attitudes, and perceptions pertinent to organizational needs, values, and working styles, the consultant and contact person can determine the "goodness of fit" between the perceived needs and the consultant's abilities pertinent to those needs. In determining their respective roles, both consultant and contact person need to remember that they represent their respective organizations as well as themselves (Caplan & Caplan, 1993; Caplan, Caplan, & Erchul, 1994; Stroh & Johnson, 2006). The answer to this question also allows the consultant to have a better sense of cultural and ecological issues and how they might effectively be used in consultation (Meyers, Proctor, Graybill, & Meyers, 2009).

What Is Likely to Happen?

The third question, "What is likely to happen?", is really about expectations, means, and ends. What is the goal of consultation? How will the goal be accomplished? What are the desired outcomes? (see Stroh & Johnson, 2006). It is important for the consultant to deal with consultee expectations for consultation either formally or informally as these expectations can be related to consultation success (Rimehaug & Helmersberg, 2011; Roach, Kratochwill, & Frank, 2009; Tysinger, Tysinger, & Diamanduros, 2009). The consultant, for example, could assess consultee expectation by administering a questionnaire to the consultee and adapt accordingly. Consultee expectations could also be determined through informal means such as discussion of mutual expectations.

What Will Be the Result?

The fourth question is "What will be the result?" From the consultant's perspective, this concerns how the impact of consultation will be assessed and evaluated. From the contact person's perspective, the answer depends on how much change the consultation requires.

What Can Go Wrong?

The initial exploration of the organization's needs can go awry due to inadequacies in both the consultant's and the contact person's behavior.

What Ford (1979) noted long ago has been echoed by French and Bell (1999) and still holds today: A consultant can jeopardize the consultation relationship during the entry phase in several ways:

- fail to identify the real problem
- promise too much
- fail to specify consultant roles adequately
- fail to recognize a lack of competence with respect to the identified problem
- fail to adapt to the organization's particular problems and concerns

By bearing these potential pitfalls in mind and by monitoring their own behavior accordingly, consultants can frequently save the consultation process from difficulties. Consultees can also prevent entry from proceeding smoothly. The following are some of the many things a consultee or contact person can do during the entry phase to jeopardize the consultation relationship:

- fail to screen a prospective consultant properly
- neglect to clarify how the consultant intends to operate within the system
- fail to clarify specific expectations of the consultant's role and behavior

- fail to identify the organization's problem accurately
- fail to explain to the consultant how the organization's resource limitations might affect the potential consultation experience

Consultants must be aware of these potential pitfalls as they assist the organization's contact person in exploring the organization's needs. Perhaps the best way to prevent such pitfalls is by allotting sufficient time to develop a mutual understanding, which leads to open communication and discussions that are as specific and detailed as possible. Effective questioning by the consultant is particularly important in avoiding these pitfalls.

As you may have noted, all of the above questions asked at the organizational level are useful when meeting with an individual consultee during a first session concerning an issue the consultee is having with a client system. In order to determine if consultation should take place, the consultant and consultee together explore questions related to determining the consultee's views of the client system, getting to know each other, and ascertaining what will most likely happen during the consultation process and what to expect from it.

Two Brief Examples of Exploring Organizational Needs.

Example 1. A mental health consultant is approached by the members of a religious organization to help them develop a program for enhancing the self-esteem of its youth group members. The consultant meets with three members of the organization's governing board and the youth group leader. Together the group explores the possibilities of what such a program might look like, the history of the program's idea, and the consultant's comparable experience. The consultant is satisfied that she can assist, and the consultees believe that she can be of assistance. The resources necessary for program development are available, and everyone agrees on what is expected from the parties involved. The consultant agrees to draw up and submit a proposal and contract.

In summary, preliminary exploration of the organization's needs includes deciding who the consultees and client system will be, determining the consultant's role in the consultation process, and defining the organization's responsibility with regard to expectations about the consultant. Once this has been adequately accomplished and it is determined that consultation should occur, the information gathered in this phase can be used in contracting.

Example 2. (Note this example describes a consultant meeting with an individual consultee who is working with an individual client.) A school-based consultant meets with a teacher in the teacher's classroom. Although they are familiar with each other, the consultant and the teacher have not had a consulting relationship. They take the time to get to know each other by sharing family and professional information and so forth. They then discuss the client and issues that the teacher perceives. The consultant goes over the consultation process and what it entails, with the teacher asking question and making comments. Together they look at what changes, in general, the client system is expected to make. The consultant and consultee reach agreement on working together. The session then continues into the contracting phase.

PHASE TWO: CONTRACTING

With a decision that consultation is to take place, the consultant and the consultee or contact person begin to discuss and negotiate the terms of consultation. This activity begins the phase of *contracting*. A good contract not only provides mutual understanding of the consultation process and clarifies roles and responsibilities, but it can also provide legal protection for consultants (Remley, 1993; Remley & Herlihy, 2010) and is one method of obtaining informed consent (Rosenfield, 2008). For external consultants, contracts tend to be formal and written (see Figure 4.2). Contracting done by internal consultants with individual consultees can be very informal (see Figure 4.3). In a school-based

---

Mountain City School System, Mountain City, USA

Contract

This is a contract between the Mountain City School System, herein called the party of the first part, and L. G. Shandi, herein referred to as the party of the second part. This contract is entered into on the sixth day of February 2009 as follows: The party of the second part agrees to serve as a consultant between March 1, 2009, and December 31, 2009, by providing group case consultation regarding the students with whom the counselors and psychologists in the school system are working. Specifically, the party of the second part agrees to provide group case consultation services at the school system's central office from 1:00 p.m. until 4:00 p.m. on the first and third Monday of each month. The party of the second part further agrees to provide individual case consultation at any of the system's school upon request at a mutually agreeable time. The party of the second part agrees to use Bernie Thompson, Director of Psychological Services of the Mountain City School System, as the contact person for all matters pertaining to this consultation, including the possible use of additional consultants or the addition of other consultees.

The party of the first part agrees to pay the party of the second part a total of six thousand dollars ($6,000) plus expenses for travel and materials paid in nine equal monthly payments for the group case consultation sessions. In addition, the party of the first part will pay one hundred dollars ($100) plus travel and materials for each individual case consultation session for up to fifty individual sessions during the length of the contract with payment being on a monthly basis.

This contract is subject to renegotiation at any time, and either party is free to terminate it with twenty-four hours' notice if either determines the consultation progress to be unsatisfactory.

Signatures of appropriate parties indicated agreement to the terms of the contract.

For the Mountain City School System

_____

Party of the Second Part _____

Signature _____

Address _____

Date _____

F I G U R E 4.2   A Sample Contract

example, the contract can result from a discussion between a school counselor or school psychologist and a teacher regarding expectations, time commitment required, data gathering, and what will transpire in terms of the consultation process.

The Nature of Contracts

Every relationship is based on expectations, which, in the context of the consultation relationship, are usually made explicit in formal or informal contracts. For our purposes, the term *contract* has a variety of meanings when used in the helping professions. A contract in consultation is between the consultant and the organization and is typically an oral or written agreement that defines the parameters and character of the consultation relationship (Holtz & Zahn, 2004; McLean, 2006). The contract reflects and clarifies the shared understanding between consultant and consultee in three critical areas: what each expects from the relationship, how much time each will invest,

A school-based consultant and teacher have just started a consultation relationship and have reached agreement on working together. As the session then continues into the contracting phase the consultant and teacher develop mutual expectations about who will do what and when, the time commitment required (four sessions), data gathering and who will gather what data, and what will transpire in terms of the consultation process.

FIGURE 4.3 Informal verbal contract between internal consultant and individual consultee

and which ground rules the parties involved will follow. A contract should deal with informed consent (Thomas, 2010).

When adequately worded, a contract provides a general guide for the consultation process, clarifies the roles and expectations of the parties involved, and provides a form of self-protection for both the consultant and the organization (Caplan, Caplan, & Erchul, 1994; Sperry, 2005).

The contract can be oral, an exchange of letters, or a formal document. In collaboration, contracting is often informal, with the parties involved agreeing to take responsibility for the aspects of the case related to their area of expertise (Block, 2000). There is an increase in the use of contracts even by internal consultants (Stroh & Johnson, 2006).

The consultant will want to bear in mind, however, that a detailed written contract has the advantages of framing participants' roles and providing a focus for evaluating consultation services. Whatever form a contract takes, its particulars must be clear.

The specificity of a contract depends upon how precisely the problem will be defined. To the degree that the contract is structured and specific, the consultant's role will be relatively constant. To the degree that the contract is general and unstructured,

the consultant's role may vary and the more likely it is that the contract will be renegotiated during the consultation process (French & Bell, 1999). Since the matter of specificity can be an issue, it must be agreed upon when the contract is being drawn up. It is in the consultant's best interest to make the contract as specific as possible as it defines the ground rules for consultation (Remley & Herlihy, 2010; Rosenfield, 2008).

The stage of change in which the consultee's problem exists can be an important factor in developing the contract. There are typically four stages of change during which the consultee may seek help (Kurpius, Fuqua, & Rozecki, 1993): the *development* stage, as a problem begins; the *maintenance* stage, once a problem is established; the *declining* stage, when an existing problem begins to get worse; and the *crisis* stage, when the consultee is in dire need of immediate assistance. The consultant, through the use of judicious questioning, can determine the existing stage of change and create an appropriate contract (Kurpius et al., 1993).

A contract can have both formal and psychological aspects. The formal aspect of a contract covers such things as services to be rendered, type and amount of payment, and the length of consultation (French & Bell, 1999). The psychological aspect of a contract refers to what each party hopes to gain from the relationship. The "psychological contract" is based on interpersonal trust, which cannot be put in writing, and it reflects a collaborative effort between the consultant and the consultee concerning what each expects from the consultation process (Boss, 1993).

The Formal Aspects of a Contract

The formal aspects of contracting refer to the types of contracts used and their elements.

There are several types of contracts that can be used in consultation. For example, a contract may be a simple verbal working agreement or a written and detailed technical document. Contracts can vary to the agency in which consultation is to occur. A school district might well have a boiler-plate contract with type of service, dates, fees, and legal/disclaimer information, while state and federal agency contracts will have significantly more detail. Internal consultants often use verbal agreements. Whatever type of contract is used, its development should be a joint venture by all parties involved in the consultation (Armenakis, Burdg, & Metzger, 1989; Rosenfield, 2002). Two important aspects of contracts are mutual consent (i.e., all parties agree to it) and valid consideration (i.e., all parties get something out of it) (Block, 2000).

Elements of a Contract

To develop and maintain a good working relation-ship between the consultant and the organization or the consultant and an individual consultee, certain key issues pertinent to the consultation should be covered in the contract. A well-defined contract will minimize the possibilities of role conflicts, dual role relationships, and resistance—all of which can contaminate the consultation relationship. Consulta-tion contracts typically cover the following elements noted by Remley & Herlihy, 2010, p. 350:

- Clearly specify the work to be completed by the consultant.
- Describe in detail any work products expected from the consultant.
- Establish a time frame for the completion of the work.
- Establish lines of authority and the person to whom the consultant is responsible.
- Describe the compensation plan for the con-sultant and the method of payment.
- Specify any special agreements or contingency plans agreed upon by the parties.

Consultants will want to remember that the more complex the consultation, the more detailed the working agreement should be (Fuqua, Newman, Simpson, & Choi, 2012).

Figure 4.2 is a sample contract between a school system and a mental health (external) consultant who is going to provide case consultation to school counselors and school psychologists regarding stu-dents with whom they are providing services. This sample represents a relatively informal, simple con-tract that contains only those elements pertinent to the nature of the consultation. Figure 4.3 presents a summary of a verbal contract between an internal consultant and an individual consultee.

The Psychological Aspects
of a Contract

Contracting has psychological as well as formal aspects. The psychological aspect reflects a partner-ship in which the consultee's investment in the consultant's abilities is balanced by the consultant's investment in the opportunity to consult provided by the consultee (Bellman, 1990). The psychologi-cal aspects of a contract refer to the set of expecta-tions that govern the consultation relationship (Boss, 1993). These expectations are not always directly communicated, agreed upon, or written down; however, they are just as crucial to the con-sultation's success than a legal contract, and once broken they are difficult to repair (Rimehaug & Helmersberg, 2010). Therefore, early in the rela-tionship it is imperative that the consultant assess and shape any expectations deliberately or unwit-tingly withheld by the organization's contact person (Schein, 1988). In effect, the consultant must deter-mine what psychological and business needs are to be met through consultation. The psychological contract needs to be based on mutual honesty, real-ism, and interpersonal sensitivity (Boss, 1993; Block, 2000). Harrison (2004) points out that psy-chological contracts are likely to be rooted in fun-damental worldviews (p. 86). For example, "The psychological contracts operating between different genders and racioethnic groups will almost always be significant factors in any interactions that occur during the consulting process" (Harrison, 2004, p. 96). Clearly, cultural competence includes ensur-ing that the psychological contract excludes dimen-sions of bias and/or prejudice. The psychological contract is also very important in collaboration because each of the parties involved has some responsibility for directly helping the client system.

The following examples illustrate how psychological contracts can be broken:

Case Example 1. A consultant hired by a human service agency to assist in program development expected an office but was not provided one. The consultant's resulting resentment made it more difficult to focus objectively on the tasks to be accomplished.

A school-based consultant and teacher have just started a consultation relationship and have reached agreement on working together. As the session then continues into the contracting phase, the consultant and teacher develop mutual expectations about who will do what and when, the time commitment required (four sessions), data gathering and who will gather what data, and what will transpire in terms of the consultation process.

Case Example 2. A consultee, in this case a teacher, wanted to be reached by the consultant each day at school about a student. The teacher neither expressed this wish nor put it into the formal contract when the consultation relationship began. When the consultant innocently restricted communication with the teacher, the teacher felt snubbed and covertly began efforts to sabotage the consultant's activities.

In summary, if the consultant has effectively completed the preliminary exploration of an organization's needs or an individual consultant has done so with the perceived needs of an individual consultee, then the psychological aspects of contracting need less attention because mutual expectations have already been verbally expressed and agreed upon. The consultant's primary concern with regard to the psychological aspects of contracting is in involving the organization's contact person or an individual consultee in mutual development of the formal contract. To the degree that this involvement happens, the ground rules for the consultation process and mutual cooperation on future issues and problems will be established (Boss, 1993). Consultants will want to remember that as consultation proceeds, there may well be the need for renegotiating the contract.

Two Brief Examples of Contracting.

Example 1. The head of a group home for abused adolescents currently has five male and five female clients. The head has concerns about physical contact between clients and staff, and contacts you to consult about this matter. After an initial exploration of the organization's needs, you and the head develop a contract that will guide your consultation. You first agree to interview each of the three staff members and the head independently and then observe them discussing this issue in the next two staff meetings. You agree that all information you gather will be held confidential, set a fee, and put the contract in writing to be signed by both parties.

Example 2. You're a mental health consultant consulting with a substance abuse counselor in a for-profit agency. You have reached an agreement to work together and help the counselor deal with a 50-year-old male client suffering from chronic binge drinking. As the session then continues into the contracting phase, the consultant and counselor develop mutual expectations about who will do what and when. In this case the counselor understands that she will be responsible for carrying out any interventions, meet with the consultant for approximately three sessions, share in data gathering about the ecological context of the client as well as determining antecedents to the binge drinking, and agrees to participate fully in the consultation process as described. The consultant agrees to provide consultation services for the determined number of sessions and to provide clinical expertise.

PHASE THREE: PHYSICALLY ENTERING THE SYSTEM

Once a contract has been formalized, the consultant is ready to physically enter the system.

Physically entering the system begins when the consultant first comes into contact with the members of the organization (Gallessich, 1982) and where internal consultants sit down for the first time with individual consultees in a defined space at their workplace. Physical entry is different from psychological entry, which is the ongoing process by which the consultant achieves increasing acceptance by the members of the organization. This phase applies mostly to external consultants as internal consultants have usually already established the infrastructure for their work (McLean, 2006).

A very important feature of physically entering the system is the consultant's work site within the organization. Should the consultant be assigned a private office or meet in designated meeting rooms or the offices of other staff members? The reality of organizational life is that having one's own office is a sign of status and prestige. By providing the consultant with a temporary office, the organization makes a symbolic statement of strong support for the consultant, one that sanctions and demonstrates the administration's willingness to allocate the organizational resources needed to support the consultation process. Because site-based consultants and collaborators are frequently internal to the organization and are familiar with one another's work spaces, they have often already accomplished the task of physical entry.

Having an office and always being in it are two different things. When beginning the physical entry process, consultants should move about the work areas to begin building relationships with members of the organization. Consultees often feel most comfortable when the consultant is willing to meet them on their own turf. Thus, as soon as possible after entering the system, consultants should seek out everyone connected with the consultation. A specified time schedule that makes the consultant's comings and goings predictable is very useful in successfully accomplishing physical entry.

The consultant should proceed in a deliberate, cautious manner. Organizations are slow to change, and the consultant would do well to realize that appropriate physical entry will enhance the organizational members' acceptance so crucial to successful psychological entry. The consultant should adapt to the organization's schedules and thereby minimize any interruptions in the workday.

The consultant should remind the organization's contact person to inform the parties-at-interest of the consultant's upcoming entry into the organization. The members affected by consultation should be informed of the consultant's role and function, why that particular consultant was hired, what is to be accomplished within what time frame, and who is to be involved (Boss, 1993). McLean (2006) suggests accomplishing this communication by setting up a project management system by which the consultant's work can be tracked and a status reporting process for communicating with all stakeholders. Further, the work setting in which consultation services are to be delivered should be common knowledge (Schein, 1988, 1999). Such advance notification prepares the people involved for the consultant's entry. Finally, an open discussion concerning confidentiality and its limits are important, because it informs both administrators and consultees of what they can reveal to the consultant, and it can avoid problems later on.

Two Brief Examples of Physically Entering the System

Example 1. Reread the preceding brief Example 1 of contracting and assume you are the consultant in that example. Since the length of your consultancy is brief (three weeks or so), you realize that you do not need an office at the home. Yet you will need a place to conduct interviews with the staff and suggest to the head that you use one of the staff offices so that you will not become overly identified with the administration of the home. You then ask the head to discuss your coming at least a week in advance. At your first visit, you mingle with the staff and clients and try to get a feel for the atmosphere that permeates the group home.

Example 2. As an internal, school-based consultant you are consulting with a beginning teacher about one of the teacher's students. You conduct the first of four sessions in a teacher's classroom. During this session, you and the teacher decide to hold the remainder of the sessions in the classroom rather than in your office.

PHASE FOUR: PSYCHOLOGICALLY ENTERING THE SYSTEM

In actual practice, physical and psychological entry cannot be separated. *Psychological entry* refers to the gradual acceptance of the consultant by members of the organization in which consultation is being performed. Effective accomplishment of the first three phases of entry can enhance the consultant's acceptance by the organization. Internal consultants as well as collaborators internal to an organization frequently have already attained a general sense of psychological entry. Internal consultants must, however, achieve psychological entry with each individual consultee as each consultation situation is new.

In gaining psychological acceptance in an organization, the external consultant should consider the two levels of operation in any organization. The process level concerns how an organization does what it does (Schein, 1999), that is, how it makes major decisions. The second level involves the personal interactions among its members, for example, how peers are encouraged to support each other on the job to build the organization's morale. By quickly learning and adapting to the organization's norms, consultants can increase the probability of a successful outcome.

Consultants who achieve psychological entry relatively quickly can be said to be "working smart." Because they realize that organizations attempt to maintain a state of equilibrium and stability (Parsons, 1996), such consultants create the conditions in which only minimal stress is placed on the organizational personnel involved in the consultation. They follow existing rules, regulations, and communication channels, and they ask to be judged on their deeds rather than on what they say.

When consultants try too hard to be like their own stereotype of an organization's members, adverse effects can occur. For example, Deitz and Reese (1986) provided decades ago examples of how a mental health consultant tried to take on the jargon used by the members of the law enforcement agency in which he was consulting. Rather than being seen as "family" by the officers, the consultant was seen as an oddball who would never be trustworthy or deserving of respect. Clearly, psychological entry can be made more difficult if the consultant works too hard and overidentifies with consultees.

The consultant's acceptance by the organization can be enhanced by keeping matters pertinent to consultation as simple as possible. The consultant should describe consultation interventions in concrete and specific terms (McCarroll & Ursano, 2006), and changes in the organization's structure that result from consultation should be minimized. To effectively psychologically enter, the consultant must be perceived by the consultee as appreciating the consultee's role demands and stressors (Kelly, 1993).

Interpersonal Influence in Consultation

Social/Interpersonal Influence. Psychological acceptance can be accomplished through the use of social influence or the popular and broader terms *social/interpersonal influence* (Strong, 1968). Social influence is part of any helping relationship (Egan, 2010), and particularly in consultation (Gutkin & Curtis, 2009). There has been increased attention paid to this area in recent years, due in part to the fact that consultants in any setting spend most of their time working with other adults even when the clients targeted for assistance are children (Conoley, Conoley, & Reese, 2009; Gutkin, 1997). Consultation can be seen as a process of socially influencing consultees (Wilson, Erchul, & Raven, 2008). The trick is for consultants to impact the consultee in terms of gaining cooperation while maintaining a relationship among equals. The consultant develops a consultation alliance with the consultee that is typified by a strong interpersonal relationship that sets the stage of social influence (Conoley et al., 2009). As related to consultation, social influence theory states that the people affected by consultation are more open to influence to the degree that they view the consultant as being attractive, trustworthy, and competent. Increasingly, consultation in the human service professions has been recognized as an interpersonal influence process (Erchul, Raven, & Ray, 2001; Erchul, Raven, & Whichard, 2001; Noell et al., 2005; Wilson et al., 2008). Blom-Hoffman and Rose (2007) note the importance of "... knowingly weaving social influence into consultation" (p. 152). For example, a consultant uses interpersonal influence such as persuasion when directing the focus of the consultation process onto the problem-solving process and away from mere chitchat. In another example, a consultant attempts to influence a consultee's perception of a given client. Interpersonal influence should not be mistaken for controlling or manipulation, but rather is a tool to assist in problem solving and dealing with the relational aspects of consultation (O'Keefe & Medway, 1997). For example, interpersonal influence may help minimize resistance and may, in fact, help consultees believe they have the self-efficacy to implement the plan they are discussing with the consultant and subsequently enhance their commitment to follow through (Noell et al., 2005). Social influence does not diminish consultee responsibility for dealing effectively with the client system (Egan, 2010), but rather can enhance it (Blom-Hoffman & Rose, 2007; Getty & Erchul, 2009).

Consultants are seen as attractive when the people with whom they work perceive similarities between themselves and the consultant. They can increase their attractiveness by identifying with and manifesting as many of the organization's values as are congruent with their own. To this end, consultants can accept and abide by the organization's routines, use the terminology common within it, and abide by its dress codes.

Consultants are perceived as trustworthy when they demonstrate understanding, appropriate use of power, respect for confidentiality, and credibility. Consultants can create trustworthiness (Egan, 2010) by avoiding behaviors that imply ulterior

motives, using the power of social influence carefully, promoting the best interest of the consultee or the organization, and being realistic but optimistic about the ability of the consultee or organization to handle the demands of consultation.

Expertness is the perceived possession of specialized knowledge or skills to solve a problem (Short, Moore, & Williams, 1991). One method of enhancing perceived expertness is to cite one's experiences relative to the situation at hand.

One of the most valuable tools consultants have for obtaining acceptance is the effective use of questioning. During entry, it is better if consultants ask good questions about the system (to obtain some understanding of how organization's members perceive consultation) than if they rattle off what they already know about the consultee or the organization (Caplan & Caplan, 1993).

Consultants will not want to gain social influence at the expense of the consultee's need for self-responsibility (Egan, 2010). Consultants can become too accepted within the system.

Those who become too accepted risk losing their objectivity and having members of the system blindly accept what they say (Egan, 2010). On the other hand, if consultees feel pushed to accept the consultant's point of view, they might well become resistant. Thus, consultants should strive to obtain enough social influence to make the necessary impact while facilitating the consultee's reflectivity on the consultant's input. Ultimately, consultants' social influence may be as critical as their having skills and knowledge in determining the effectiveness of consultation (Erchul & Raven, 1997; Erchul et al., 2001, 2009; Martens, Kelly, & Diskin, 1996). For example, the increased emphasis on response to intervention suggests that attempts by consultants to influence consultees are legitimate (Getty & Erchul, 2009).

Models of Interpersonal Influence. Consultation involves either direct or indirect attempts to influence change in consultees. Some research suggests that social influence is a critical variable in consultation (Wilson et al., 2008). Consultants need to use some social influence strategies but avoid more ethically questionable coercive types (Wilson et al., 2008). Hence, I next explore two models related to attitude change, the Elaboration Likelihood Model (ELM) and French and Raven's bases of social power model, and discuss their significance with regard to working with consultees. You should note that an underlying assumption of this discussion is that any attempt to influence or change a consultee will be accomplished in an ethical and professional manner.

The ELM (Petty, Heesacker, & Hughes, 1997) offers a method to make sense of the antecedents and consequences of attitude change. Central to ELM is the idea that "attitude change can result from relatively thoughtful (central route) or non-thoughtful (peripheral route) processes" (Petty et al., 1997, p. 107).

Thoughtful processes include examining the underlying assumptions of the consultant's information. Nonthoughtful processes rely on the idea that the information makes the consultee pleased or the consultee simply acquiesces to consultant expertise (i.e., consultant-knows-best type of thinking). Nonthoughtful processes do not challenge the consultee to put any kind of rigor into thinking about what the consultant is saying. As you might guess, thoughtful attitude change is more likely to be permanent than that which is nonthoughtful.

The essence of this model is that consultants have a better chance of interpersonally influencing consultees when consultees have the motivation and the ability to think about the benefits of the data provided by the consultant and its underlying assumptions. On the other hand, if consultees are less involved, it is highly unlikely that they will change their attitudes and behavior in a way deemed desirable by the consultant. In other words, change is more likely when the consultee has internalized and accepted the consultant's message and is not simply being compliant at the time of the recommendation.

Ways to motivate consultees to consider information reflectively include making the information personally relevant to the consultee, restricting the focus to areas for which the consultee is accountable, ensuring that the consultee has an adequate amount of information, avoiding being forceful in delivering information, taking measures to be viewed as a credible source of information, and keeping a positive emotional atmosphere in the relationship. Ways to make sure that the consultee has the ability to think about the merits of the information include minimizing distractions when information is being considered, providing adequate time for processing the information, avoiding technical language, using written follow-ups to consultation sessions, and avoiding trying to consult during chance encounters.

In addition to motivating and facilitating consultee thought, it is important to create the conditions that will help the consultee think and feel favorably about the consultant's recommendations.

Two ways to accomplish this are to make the recommendations from the consultee's perspective (i.e., self-schemas) and to recommend an intervention that is congruent with the consultee's thinking about the problem. For example, a consultee with a humanistic bent has the client's problem explained from a humanistic perspective by the consultant.

As noted in Erchul and Raven (1997), French and Raven (1959) developed a typology that contains six bases of power that can be used for social influence. These bases, accompanied by examples, include:

- coercion—a consultee is fearful of confrontation by the consultant ("If I don't follow through with the plan, I will get confronted.")

- reward—a consultee views praise from the consultant as rewarding ("It feels good to be validated by the consultant.")

- legitimate—a consultee views the consultant's attempt to help as appropriate to the consultant's role ("It's right for the consultant to try to help me with this; it's part of the job.")

- expert—the consultant is viewed as being more expert in the consultee's opinion ("I should follow this recommendation. After all, the consultant knows more than I do.")

- referent—the consultant is viewed by the consultee as being similar ("Since we are all in this together, the least I can do is my part.")

- informational—the methods of persuasion by the consultant are viewed by the consultee as relevant ("I think I can really use these ideas to help my client.")

As you can note, each of the bases of power can be of use to consultants in their attempts to help their consultees. In addition, these bases of power can be used by all parties involved in collaboration, where the influence is more reciprocal than in consultation. Whatever the basis of power that is used in social influence, the method by which the power is exerted is critical to the success of the influence (Erchul & Raven, 1997). Consultants and collaborators will want to reflect upon available power bases and their mode of implementing in order to have maximum influence on their consultees. Some research (Erchul et al., 2001; Wilson et al., 2008) suggests that consultants prefer using informational, positive expert, and referent power bases, which are considered "soft," that is, they are subtle, indirect and noncoercive. Consultees tend to prefer informational, positive referent, and positive expert behavior from consultees. Subsequent research (Getty & Erchul, 2009) suggests that consultant gender may be an important variable in determining what influence strategies consultants select. In their study, the authors found that when consulting with female teachers, male consultants tended to use the exert mode of social influence, whereas female consultants did not. Riley-Tillman and Chafouleas (2003) discuss the process consultants go through to implement social influence on consultees.

Two Brief Examples of Psychologically Entering the System.

Example 1.   As a consultant you are preparing to conduct a workshop for teachers in an elementary school on indicators of child abuse. Before you conduct the workshop, you visit several of the teachers' rooms, introduce yourself, start to learn names, and begin building relationships. In your conversations you note that you were once a schoolteacher and a school counselor. You mention how serious the topic is and that hopefully a child or two can be saved from being victimized as a result of the workshop. You are friendly, professional, and yet genuine.

Example 2.   Continuing Example 1 from physically entering the system, as an internal, school-based consultant, you are consulting with a beginning teacher about one of the teacher's students. You conduct the first of four sessions in a teacher's classroom. You actively listen to the teacher's "story" about the client system and related issues in the classroom. You use effective attending skills, such as appropriate eye contact. You take multicultural contexts such as race into consideration. You respond with empathy, open-ended questions, paraphrasing, and clarification. Your consultee feels that you are knowledgeable and trustworthy. Together you and consultee start to become a team whose bond will grow over the period of the consultation.

MULTICULTURAL ASPECTS RELATED TO ENTRY

Consultants and collaborators will want to initiate the relationships by using "dynamic sizing," which is the ability to take into account cultural characteristics without stereotyping; and "culture-specific expertise," which is specific knowledge of the cultural groups with whom they work (Castillo, Quintana, & Zamarripa, 2000; Sue, 1998). The point is that consultants interact with consultees and their clients systems as individuals while maintaining cultural sensitivity and respect for differences in things such as communication styles (Egan, 2010).

People of differing cultural backgrounds can differ in the way they approach the consultation relationship. For example, an African American consultee may be primarily concerned about the interpersonal orientation of a white consultant, whereas a white consultee may be more interested in determining whether or not the consultant can be of assistance (i.e., instrumentally competent)

(Gibbs, 1980). Clearly, consultants and collaborators will want to be knowledgeable about culturally different groups (Castillo et al., 2000) and take that knowledge into consideration as they accomplish the entry stage. For example, consultants will want to bear in mind that the amount of information communicated by words versus by context varies among cultures. Clearly, communication and relationship building are essential to culturally skilled consultants.

Some consultees or collaborators from differing cultural backgrounds may view the consultant as the expert. Consequently, consultants will have to determine whether they wish to enter the relationship in this context or aim for a more nonhierarchical, collaborative relationship.

How consultants use their communication and interpersonal skills during consultation will, to a large extent, determine the success of consultation (Jackson & Hayes, 1993; Ramirez, Lepage, Kratochwill, & Duffy, 1998). One method consultants and collaborators can use to determine their suitability to work with consultees or fellow collaborators is to determine their level of comfort in dealing with any cultural or ethnic issues related to the problem being dealt with (Ingraham, 2003, 2004).

Awareness of cultural differences and how they might impact the consultative relationship should be considered before contracting. Some clues for how effective a consultant is being with a culturally different person can be gotten from the entry stage because demonstrated cultural awareness during entry is most likely positively related to positive outcomes (Duncan, 1995).

Culturally different consultees may perceive consultants in terms of interpersonal orientation (the ability to positively socially influence others) and instrumental orientation (the ability to be perceived as competent) (Gibbs, 1980).

Consultants should be aware that it is likely that minority consultees will make a commitment to the consultation process based upon their perception of the consultant's ability to relate and the consultant's familiarity with the meanings of specific nonverbal behaviors across cultures (Ortiz, Flanagan, & Dynda, 2008).

A FINAL NOTE ON ENTRY

Part of your work as a consultant will typically involve the work-related concerns of individual consultees. For example, you might consult with counselors in a community human service agency about their clients, with teachers concerning students about whom they have concerns, or with parents about issues regarding raising children. If you are going to be working with individual consultees within an organization, you will have to "enter" with each one, that is, explore their perceived needs that led to their requests for consultation. What Egan (2010) has written for helping relationships in general applies to consultation: Consultees may enter the consultation relationship with differing levels of progress on the problem; consultees have different style of approaching a given problem and awareness levels of their need to change in order to effectively help the client system, and external events can dictate movement among the stages of the model. It is important that you show that you are prepared to help in a way that will build and maintain rapport with the consultee.

You will have to develop a suitable contract with your consultees or fellow collaborators, be prepared to be willing to meet them on their own turf, and psychologically enter through building a good working relationship with them (Roach et al., 2009). In fact, some empirical evidence suggests that how well you can establish relationships with consultees is related to consultation success (Frank & Kratochwill, 2008; Gutkin & Curtis, 2009; Hughes & DeForest, 1993; Sheridan & Kratochwill, 2008). There is also support for the importance of a strong relationship from writers in the area of consultation theory such as Caplan and Caplan (1993). On the other hand, you have the potential to strongly affect consultees in their thinking (Granda, 1992)—you must successfully complete the entry stage not only with the organization, but with each consultee as well. You may have to orient the consultee to the consultation/collaboration process, engage him or her in a professional relationship, and understand the nature of the organization in which consultation occurs (Gutkin & Curtis, 2009; Larney, 2003).

C A S E   4.1   Entry for School Consultants

Maurice is a school-based consultant in a large, urban elementary school and frequently consults with many staff members, including the school's four administrators.

The administrators ask Maurice to assist them in developing a dropout prevention program. Although Maurice is internal to the school, he realizes that he is external to the problem and must go through the entry stage very carefully.

In a first meeting with the administrators, Maurice and the group explore the possibilities of his being a consultant for the program. Maurice wants to make sure that he can be of assistance as well as ensure that the administrators see him as someone who can be of help.

Together the group explores the underlying values concerning counseling that will guide the development of the program, how the program will be staffed, the kinds of resources that will be provided, and the flexibility available for fine-tuning the program. Maurice asks the administrators why they are interested in the program in the first place and what they think it will do for the school. He then interacts with the group concerning what they view his role to be in helping develop the program and, correspondingly, their own roles. Finally, the group discusses the limits of Maurice's involvement given his other duties in the school.

Based on this exploration, all agree that Maurice should be a consultant for the program's development.

Maurice suggests that a formal, written contract, although internal to the school, will help the parties involved stay on track with the project. He agrees to develop a contract for approval and submits one that describes the general goals related to the program's development, what roles he and the administrators will take on, a time frame, and a brief evaluation design for assessing the quality of the work accomplished through consultation.

In a brief meeting, Maurice and the administrators review and agree to the contract, as well as make sure everyone involved has the same set of expectations. To enhance physical and psychological entry, Maurice suggests a location for program development meetings, makes sure that he follows protocol in gaining access to the administrators, and acknowledges the fact that just because he is a consultant to the group does not make him an administrator or more important than any other staff member at the school.

Commentary

This case illustrates the importance of the maxim: You always have to enter. Even though Maurice was an internal consultant, he recognized that he was external to the problem and the consequent importance of appropriately entering. Notice that Maurice clarified his role very carefully and put things in writing. Even though he was functioning as an internal consultant, Maurice did not fall into the trap of making the consultation process so casual that it would be difficult to keep it on task and remain in a problem-solving mode.

The limited research on entry with individual consultees suggests that the consultant's knowledge is not as important to consultees as are the relationship-building activities of the consultant (Martens, Lewandowski, & Houk, 1989). This suggests that listening and clarifying are essential communication skills for the entry stage (Benn, Jones, & Rosenfield, 2008). There is additional attention being paid to the consultees' cognitive responses to the help they are receiving (Uhlemann, Lee, & Martin, 1994). In other words, consultees' perceptions about what is happening in the consultation relationship can be as important as what is actually happening. There is some research that suggests that there is a positive relationship between the degree to which consultants and consultees agree on the roles, process, and goals of consultation and consultee views of the successes of consultation (Tysinger et al., 2009). Therefore, as a practicing consultant you may well put a high priority on establishing solid working relationships with your consultees. In doing so, consultants will want to be aware that consultees may want a balance of directiveness and collaboration (Buysse, Schulte, Pierce, & Terry, 1994), and prefer some leadership from the consultant in determining the content of consultation (Gutkin, 1996).

CASE 4.2   **Entry for Community Consultants**

Marie, a mental health consultant operating out of a mental health satellite center, is contacted by Kristine, the director of a human resource development department of a local municipal government, to engage in some "train the trainer" consultation. She is interested in having her human resource development staff trained in consultation skills. During their first contact, Marie thoroughly explores what Kristine would like to accomplish in the training, shares her own related professional experiences as well as her values regarding consultation in general and training in particular, and asks Kristine about her views of training and consultants.

They discuss the human resource development department, its staff and mission, and how it is perceived by the rest of the organization. They also discuss the practical use of the consultation training to the department's staff and the resources that the department is willing to put into training. At the end of their discussion, both Marie and Kristine are positive about the prospect of working together. Before she agrees to become a consultant, Marie asks if she could have a brief meeting with the human resource development department's five staff members to inform them about the proposed consultation.

Marie meets with the staff for an hour, during which she gets to know the members in a leisurely fashion, briefly describes the proposed training and her own related professional experiences, and allows time for questions and discussion. At the end of the meeting, there is a consensus among group members that they are favorable about the training.

Marie contacts Kristine soon thereafter and clarifies the few issues that were raised in the meeting with the staff. Kristine mentions that the local municipal government has a form contract that is to be used by all departments when they hire consultants and that there was some flexibility in it for writing in items specific to a given consultation. Marie and Kristine agree to add a statement about the consultant's roles and the responsibilities of the director of the department.

Stopping by the human resource development office the day before the training sessions are to start, Marie makes a point of interacting with each of the participants and, with a couple of the participants, looks over the room in which the training is to be conducted. She provides a schedule for the training to the staff members as well as a couple of handouts on consulting ideas for human resource development specialists.

Commentary

It is of particular importance, as this case illustrates, for consultants to enter with each consultee as they enter the system. Marie wisely held a brief meeting with the consultees prior to beginning her training sessions with them. Notice how she also made personal contact with each of them on the day before the training. By taking the time to create relationships with consultees, consultants not only build trust and minimize resistance but they quickly move the consultation relationship to a partnership that allows for effective collaboration.

SUMMARY

The entry process in consultation is a critical stage. When successfully completed, it increases the probability that the entire consultation process will turn out successfully. The success of the entry process, whether at the organizational or individual level, relies heavily on the consultant's skills and how well these skills are used to accomplish the tasks of the entry stage. The most critical skills in the entry stage relate to exploring problems, contracting, relating, and communicating. By effectively

accomplishing the stage of entry, consultants not only set the stage for successful consultation, they also minimize the resistance that organizations and individual consultees can demonstrate.

Consultants should avoid the temptation to go quickly through the entry stage to get on with problem-solving activities. By effectively exploring the organization's or individual consultee's needs, the consultant can help it determine its priorities for consultation. A well-designed contract makes the expectations of everyone involved explicit and prevents misunderstandings regarding consultation later in the process. Effective physical entry makes consultants less intrusive as they join in the organization's activities. By taking the time necessary for building relationships and gaining acceptance, consultants can accomplish the difficult phase of psychological entry.

SUGGESTIONS FOR EFFECTIVE PRACTICE

- Remember the maxim: "You always have to enter."
- A contract is one of the best ways of documenting expectations.
- Consider resistance to be a normal part of the consultation and collaboration process.

- Make a deliberate effort to psychologically enter the system and create a relationship with *each* consultee even if you are internal to the setting in which consultation and collaboration occur.

QUESTIONS FOR REFLECTION

1. What do you think is meant by the phrase "You always have to enter"?

2. Why is it important for the consultant to obtain sanctions for performing consultation from the organization's upper echelon?

3. Recall a situation in which an outsider entered your classroom. What were your immediate reactions? Relate your feelings to how members of an organization must feel when they encounter a consultant for the first time.

4. What characteristics would you look for in an organization or a consultee before you would agree to consultation?

5. Under what circumstances can resistance in consultation be seen as normal?

6. How can the power attributed to the consultant due to expertise or trustworthiness be useful in ameliorating resistance?

7. What are the key points consultants should consider in assessing their performance during the entry phase?

8. How would you as a consultant go about accomplishing psychological entry? That is, how would you go about the task of building relationships with and gaining acceptance by staff members with whom you had no previous contact?

9. How would you go about the task of physically entering into consultation with an organization?

10. Under what circumstances do you think consultants should use formal contracts?

SUGGESTED SUPPLEMENTARY READINGS

If you are interested in reading in more depth and detail about the entry stage of consultation, here are some useful selected readings:

Cherniss, C. (1993). Preentry issues revisited. In R. T. Golembiewski (Ed.), *Handbook of organizational* *consultation* (pp. 113–118). New York: Marcel Dekker, Inc. Don't let the date on this article fool you. This is an excellent review of preentry issues. Two particular aspects of this article are dealing with conflict during preentry and choosing a primary focus.

Glidewell, J. C. (1959). The entry problem in consultation. *Journal of Social Issues, 15*(2), 51–59. This article is a classic and well worth reading. Glidewell was one of the first authors to promote the idea of the consultant as a person who temporarily attaches to a social system; he does an excellent job of pointing out that the process of entry can be accelerated or retarded by the perceptions of the members of the organization in which consultation is to occur.

Marks, E. S. (1995). *Entry strategies for school consultation.* New York: Guilford. Though somewhat dated, this text is dedicated to the nuts and bolts of helping consultants open the doors to effective consultation. The author emphasizes entry in school consultation, but consultants and collaborators in any setting will find useful information.

5

✳

Diagnosis Stage

C hapter 4 discussed the entry process, in which the consultant engages in a preliminary exploration of organizational needs or holds an exploratory meeting with an individual consultee, formulates a contract, and physically and psychologically enters the system or begins a relationship with an individual consultee. The stage following entry is called the diagnosis stage, which, like the entry stage, is very complex. The diagnosis stage has four phases, which are depicted in Figure 5.1: gathering information (which answers the question "What information do we need to find out where we are?"), defining the problem (which answers the question "Where are we?"), setting goals (which answers the question "Where do we want to be?"), and generating possible interventions (which answers the question "What are some things to do that might help us get there?").

As you read this chapter, consider these questions:

- How do the consultant and consultee determine what behaviors to analyze (positive and negative) in defining the problem?
- How do the consultant and consultee determine who should gather the data needed to define the problem?
- What factors should be considered in setting goals?
- How can a consultant assist a consultee in developing a set of possible interventions?
- In what ways is diagnosis an ongoing event?

Diagnosis is the identification of the forces underlying or precipitating the current way things are in a given situation. From another perspective, diagnosis is the "meaning or interpretation that is derived from assessment information when it is interpreted through the use of a diagnostic classification system" (Hohenshil, 1996, p. 65). It identifies "strengths, opportunities, and problem areas" (French & Bell,

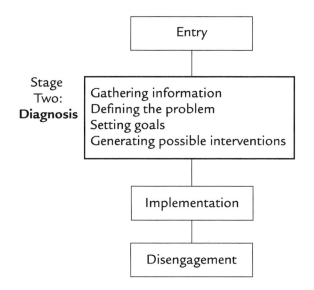

Stage
Two:
Diagnosis

Entry

Gathering information
Defining the problem
Setting goals
Generating possible interventions

Implementation

Disengagement

F I G U R E 5.1 Phases of the diagnosis stage

1999, p. 105). Diagnosis may pertain broadly to the present state of a client system, including the many positive forces giving rise to desirable outcomes, or may be narrower in the sense of focusing on the dysfunctional forces that are producing undesirable outcomes, or may focus on changes in the state of the client system over time (Harrison & Shirom, 1999). The terms *data* and *information* are used interchangeably in this discussion.

The nature of the diagnosis stage depends on the type of consultation being performed. But just as some kind of diagnosis, either formal or informal, is made in counseling and psychotherapy, so too is one made in consultation or collaboration. Although the term *diagnosis* is not attractive to all because of its medical model connotations, I use it to label this stage because of its broad-based connotations, which, for example, include problem identification. The term *diagnosis* simply captures the entire process of problem identification and goals setting. A mental health consultant working with a therapist may assist in diagnosing a client's problem and in prescribing a treatment plan. A behavioral consultant may examine the antecedents and consequences of students' selected classroom conduct with a teacher and then assist that teacher in designing behavioral strategies to change

that conduct. An organizational consultant may help an organization improve its efficiency by focusing diagnostic efforts, as necessary, on an individual, a group, a subsystem, or the organization as a whole. The process of diagnosis remains the same for all consultation, although the types of data gathered will depend on the type of consultation being performed. The bottom line is that diagnosis develops the foundation for, and is interdependent with, intervention and is a prerequisite for goal setting (Gutkin & Curtis, 2009).

What French, Bell, and Zawacki (1978) noted long ago still holds true today: Every consultant brings to and uses in the diagnostic process at least three theories. The first, descriptive and analytical in nature, is the theory by which the consultant attempts to understand the client system in terms of behavior and events surrounding them. In this view, for example, behaviors might be considered rather more critical than attitudes in understanding events. A second theory, one of change, consists of the consultant's views of how events influence one another and change. For example, one view of this theory might state that ecological context, not only people, determines change. Finally, consultants have diagnostic theories, which consist of a set of notions to determine what is dysfunctional or wrong (Sandoval, 2003). One example is the viewpoint that a problem must be a long-standing one in order to be severe. Another is a view based on the positive psychology movement that focuses on "what is going right" and related solutions (Gerstein, 2007). Consultants' theories of description-analysis, change, and dysfunction significantly affect which domains are examined and how a diagnosis is made. By being aware of their own theories, consultants can use them, along with those of their consultees, to accomplish accurate, effective diagnoses and avoid being unwittingly victimized by them during the diagnostic stage.

Assessment refers to the kind of information used in diagnosis (Hohenshil, 1996; Kamphaus, Reynolds, & Imperato-McCammon, 1999). Whatever the frame of reference for making a diagnosis, the data gathered must be relevant (Gutkin & Curtis, 2009). The kind of information used for diagnosis depends on a given consultation model's view of what must be examined to find out what is wrong. Three major areas or domains that consultants may examine in their diagnoses are consultee characteristics (e.g., pertinent knowledge and skill sets), client system characteristics (e.g., cultural factors), and environmental characteristics (e.g., degree of client resiliency, organizational climate).

Another important aspect of the diagnosis stage involves determining who constitutes the client system—an individual, a group, a subsystem, or the entire organization—for the nature of the client system affects diagnosis. As the client system increases in size, the complexity of the diagnostic stage usually increases as well: The more complex the diagnostic stage, the greater the need to use several methods to collect data from a larger group of people. Cataldo, Raelin, and Lambert (2009) look at diagnosis as a process of critical inquiry in which all areas of the organization are examined in terms of need for change so that an accurate diagnosis can be made. In addition, the increased emphasis on examining ecological factors as they impact the clients system's behavior underscores the importance of consultants being aware of and conducting ecological assessment, which can be invaluable in determining the client system (Ysseldyke, Lekwa, Klingbeil, & Cormier, 2012). Finally, the consultant's relationship with the consultee is critical to the successful completion of this stage. Unless the consultant is able to obtain accurate, pertinent information and assist consultees in translating this data into a list of viable possible interventions, then it is likely that the wrong problem will be solved.

Assume for the moment that you are the consultant described in the following examples.

AN EXAMPLE OF DIAGNOSIS AT THE ORGANIZATION CLIENT-SYSTEM LEVEL

You are a mental health professional in private practice with a caseload of clients, and you perform consultation with other therapists and human service organizations. The director of a county social service agency requests that you assist in resolving some of the agency's problems.

You have successfully completed the entry stage, and therefore, you have a rough idea of what the agency's problems are, have contracted with it, have gotten to know the staff, and are set up in the office of a part-time staff member. The director is concerned about the morale within the agency: People work behind closed doors, putdowns of clients are frequently heard, backlogs of paperwork are large, and little camaraderie is apparent. When consulting with the director, you agree to design and conduct a survey about what it is like to work in the agency. You agree to interview a random number of the staff about their personal views of their professional work site, and, based on the results of this information, you assist the director in determining related issues. You divide the problem into three smaller problems: morale, high caseloads, and little administrative support and encouragement.

You then assist the director in setting some goals to ameliorate these problems. You break these down further into more specific subgoals (e.g., more oral and written praise and support from the director for jobs well done). Once goals have been set, you and the director come up with a variety of intervention alternatives for meeting the set goals. As this example illustrates, consultants are sometimes asked to take on sole responsibility for determining the nature of a problem and take on the roles of information seeker and fact finder.

A critical part of diagnosis is determining that part of the organization in which the problem is located. How the consultant approaches the diagnostic stage depends on the purpose of consultation, the complexity of the problem, and the time available (Harrison & Shirom, 1999).

Tichy (1983) listed three types of organizational diagnoses based on complexity that are still valuable today:

- radar scan diagnosis (which involves a quick examination of the organization to locate problem areas)

- symptom-focused diagnosis (in which information is examined relative to known problem areas)
- in-depth diagnosis (which involves a systematic, detailed organizational analysis).

AN EXAMPLE OF DIAGNOSIS AT THE INDIVIDUAL CLIENT-SYSTEM LEVEL

You are a school-based consultant and have been approached by a teacher about a "misbehaving" student. The teacher is concerned about the child and wants consultation to provide some interventions to assist the student with challenging behaviors. Together, the consultant and teacher examine the teacher–student interactions that led to the misbehavior. They also examine the behavior itself by assessing it and then putting concrete behavioral definitions on the term *misbehavior*. They also look at ecological variables such as the student's family life that might contribute to his misbehavior. The consultant and consultee look at the classroom behavior of the teacher as well as other ecological factors related to the classroom such as peer behavior toward the student. They next identify the variables that seem to precipitate and continue the misbehavior. After developing target behaviors together, the consultant and consultee generate a set of possible interventions that could be designed to modify the student's behavior by providing alternative positive behaviors. For those ecological variables outside of the classroom such as those related to the student's home life, specific accommodations are determined and put into place. The consultant provides the teacher with information about evidence-based interventions. Finally, the consultant and teacher brainstorm a set of reliable and multiculturally sensitive interventions for possible use.

The above example considers a behavioral approach to change called *functional behavioral assessment* (FBA), often referred to as the "ABCs" (antecedents-behavior-consequences) of behavior.

In this process, the consultant and/or consultee gather data regarding the conditions (also called contingencies) that control a specific behavior (Daly, Martens, Skinner, & Noell, 2009). The idea is that by determining how antecedents and consequences surrounding a behavior in a given context interact with the behavior, the consultant and consultee can manipulate those antecedents and consequences to develop interventions tailored to the client system's specific problem (Crone, Hawken, & Bergstrom, 2007; Sheridan, 1993a; Watson, Steege, & Watson, 2011; Watson & Sterling-Turner, 2008). FBA can be useful when there are multiple sources of data from multiple sources and contexts. Figures 5.2 and 5.3 illustrate forms used in FBA as examples of interviewing and observation, respectively. For a detailed discussion of FBA, consult Daly et al. (2009) and Watson, Steege, and Turner (2011).

PHASE ONE: GATHERING INFORMATION

The Nature of Information Acquisition

Consultants will want to remember that, although the information gathered is critical, the method of gathering information and how that information is used is also important (French & Bell, 1999). For example, consultees will often face several problems at once and the consultant will want to help them sort through them to arrive at an agreed-upon problem. An accurate diagnosis requires accurate information (Gregory, Armenakis, Moates, Albritton, & Harris, 2007). Although data gathering does not cease during the consultation process, there is a formal time for the process of gathering information.

The first step is to conceptualize the problem. Some sense of the problem is obtained during the preliminary exploration of organizational needs or during the first session with an individual consultee. In either case, the results are, in part, determined by the model of consultation to be used, for each model has its own view of human behavior, of

Interviewer:
Date:
Student:
Respondent:
Title

_____

1. Describe the behavior of concern.

2. How often does the behavior occur? How long does it last? How intense is the behavior?

3. What is happening when the behavior occurs?

4. *When/where* is the behavior *most/least* likely to occur?

5. With whom is the behavior *most/least* likely to occur?

6. What conditions are most likely to precipitate ("set-off") the behavior?

7. How can you tell the behavior is about to start?

8. What usually happens after the behavior? Describe what happens according to adult(s), peers, and student responses.

9. What is the likely function (intent) of the behavior; that is, why do you think the student behaves this way? What does the student get or avoid?

10. What behavior(s) might serve the same function (see question 9) for the student that is appropriate within the social/environmental context?

11. What other information might contribute to creating an effective intervention plan (e.g., under what conditions does the behavior not occur)?

12. Who should be involved in planning and implementing the intervention plan?

F I G U R E 5.2   Interview form for functional assessment

SOURCE: Center for Effective Collaboration and Practice.

ABC Observation Form

Student Name: *Trish*   Observation Date: *10/5*

Observer: *Ms. Pasillas*   Time: *9:40–9:55 a.m.*

Activity: *Disruptive behavior on playground*   Class Period: *3*

ANTECEDENT	BEHAVIOR	CONSEQUENCE
Trish joins group of four girls playing catch.	*Trish waits for ball to be thrown to her. Trish yells "Throw it to me."*	*Girls do not throw ball to Trish. Girls throw ball to her, she misses it and another girl, Luanne, catches it and throws it to Sandy.*
Ball is again thrown to Karen.	*Trish yells "I said throw it to me you jerk!"*	
Karen begins to walk away with the ball.	*Trish runs up behind Karen and kicks her saying "Give it to me damn it."*	*Karen cries. Trish takes the ball.*

F I G U R E 5.3   Functional behavior assessment observation form

SOURCE: Center for Effective Collaboration and Practice.

what is necessary for change, and of what constitutes the client system. These factors in turn will determine the types of methods used to gather data (Meyers, Proctor, Graybill, & Meyers, 2009).

The consultant and the consultee must assign some parameters to the task of consultation before diagnosis (Gregory et al., 2007; Kratochwill, Sheridan, Carlson, & Lasecki, 1999) to help to define the scope of data gathering and assessment. To determine which intervention may have the best opportunity to be successful, relevant data should be gathered with minimal disruption to the natural environment and appropriately analyzed (Gutkin & Curtis, 2009). For example, in school-based consultation, client system behavior is often examined in terms of child's daily routine at school and/or home. In summary, the data collected should:

- be accurate in identifying what needs to be worked on

- be of assistance in determining possible interventions

- refined such that it can be accurately evaluated (Batsche, Castillo, Dixon, & Forde, 2008).

Depending on the model of consultation in use, consultants and their consultees can draw from several data sources: genetic data, current descriptive data, process data, interpretive data, consultee–client system relationship data, and client system behavior data (Bergan & Kratochwill, 1990; Caplan & Caplan, 1993).

- Genetic data: This type of data includes easily accessible, common information (e.g., an organization's role and mission statement) and historical information (e.g., a student's cumulative folder). (Example 1: A consultant might read the role and mission statement of a human service agency and decide to determine the degree to which the agency's members are aware of it.) (Example 2: A school counselor and teacher review a student's cumulative folder for clues in understanding the child's behavior.)

- Current descriptive data: As its name implies, this type of information describes a client system as it currently exists. (Example 1: A human service agency asks for a consultant's help with its internal communication problems. The consultant examines the agency's organizational structure as a prelude to determining how superiors and subordinates within the agency communicate with one another.) (Example 2: A consultant observes a student in the classroom to get a sense about possible ecological factors affecting the student's behavior.)

- Process data: Process data involve the organization's methods, including how decisions are made, and how meetings are conducted. (Example 1: A consultant acts as an observer at a crisis intervention team's staff meeting to determine who talks to whom about what.) (Example 2: A school psychologist observes the processes in which a teacher interacts with a child who misbehaves in class.)

- Interpretive data: This kind of information tends to be subjective and have emotional aspects to it. Interpretive data include members' attitudes, beliefs, and perceptions about the client system, its functioning, and relational characteristics. (Example 1: A consultant gathers information about how school counselors perceive the support given them by the teachers in their school.) (Example 2: A school-based consultant discusses with a teacher the teacher's perceptions of a group of students.)

- Consultee–client system relationship data: The dynamics between the consultee and the client system constitute this type of data, including the nature of interpersonal relationships, their direction, and how communication takes place. (Example 1: A consultant watches a videotape of a consultee providing therapy to a client to help the consultee work more effectively with the client.) (Example 2: A consultant observes an individualized education plan (IEP) meeting to ascertain the level of group functioning.)

- Client system behavior data: This type of information includes characteristics of the client system, such as level of intelligence, nature of the problem, levels of coping, the frequency of adaptive and maladaptive behaviors, and related environmental conditions. (Example 1: A school psychologist consulting with a school counselor administers an individual intelligence test to the counselor's client so as to suggest some effective helping strategies the counselor can use with that client.) (Example 2: An organizational consultant administers a leadership assessment instrument to a group of midlevel administrators in a human services agency.)

A great number of data sources are available to consultants, depending on the nature of consultation. For example, consultants working with consultees whose client system is an organization may want to examine genetic data (e.g., forms for writing up client reports from past years), current descriptive data (e.g., current forms for writing up client reports), process data (e.g., how the decision to use a given form for writing client reports was made), or interpretive data (e.g., the results of a survey that reveal how staff feel about the current form used to write up client reports). Consultants working with consultees who have individual clients tend to rely on consultee–client system relationship data (e.g., the theoretical approach the consultee is taking with the client) and client system behavior data (e.g., the nature of the client's behaviors with which the consultee is having difficulty) for purposes of classification (Kamphaus et al., 1999).

Whatever the type of data being gathered, it must be precise and meaningful. Imprecise data can intensify existing problems due to misdirected interventions (Stroh & Johnson, 2006). Data should also be selective, relevant, designed to answer pertinent questions, understandable (Gutkin & Curtis, 2009), and adequately defined (Kratochwill et al., 1999). Further, consultants will want to assure that their consultees engage in culturally sensitive diagnostic practices in order not to misdiagnosis or use unnecessary diagnoses with their client systems (see Hays, 2001; Miranda, 2008; White Kress, Eriksen, Rayle, & Ford, 2005). For example, in culturally sensitive assessment, the consultant focuses on the strengths of the clients system as well as its social supports. In addition, culturally sensitive assessment gathers data from multiple sources and encourages the assessor to be knowledgeable and experienced with the cultures of the consultee and the client system (Hays, 2001). If information gathering is well done at this stage, the method chosen may well be helpful in the evaluation process (McLean, 2006).

Scanning and the Ecological Process

Using the presenting problem as a starting point, it is a good idea for the consultant to scan the context in which the problem is thought to occur. *Scanning* is the process of looking at the big picture, including information about events, relationships, and forces impacting the client system (McLean, 2006). Scanning prevents a premature focus on the problem's more obvious major elements to the exclusion of other pertinent factors.

Scanning procedures can provide data for determining the validity of the problem, for identifying forces supporting or inhibiting effective change, and for detecting problems that are deeper than the ones identified in the preliminary exploration. In addition, scanning can prevent an a priori determination of the problem's nature and can counteract the consultant's professional and personal biases. For example, scanning could identify possible logistical issues in program implementation (Knotek, 2012).

Hypothetically, a consultant could scan the entire domain: consultee, client system, and environment; in practice, scanning must be cost effective. Therefore, consultants typically use their theories of description analysis, change, and dysfunction to scan these systems. To avoid biases, the consultant describes these theories and the results of scanning to the consultee, who can then add additional perspectives to the analysis of the diagnosis stage. Once the entire context of the problem has been scanned and the results of the scanning interpreted, the consultant and consultee are ready to focus on more specific data.

Recently, scanning has taken on increased importance for consultants. The emergence of ecological perspectives (Gutkin, 2012) and its related emphasis on the multiple contexts that impact the client system's behaviors as well as those behaviors themselves has led to a series of initiatives, including the nature of what is assessed in consultation related to advocacy, social justice, prevention, empowerment, systems–level interventions, and multicultural consultation. Thus, scanning can assist the consultant and consultee in avoiding the possible trap of concluding that only the characteristics of the client system's behavior needs to be examined and analyzed. The results of scanning also allow the consultant and consultee to engage in the aforementioned initiatives as pertinent. In one example, a school counselor and teacher determine that the teacher's classroom environment, and not a student in question, needs to change.

As it relates to assessment, the ecological perspective suggests that the consultant and consultee will examine external variables, that is, those beyond those in the client system itself. The focus is on the interactions of people and their environment. In a school-based consultation example, the consultant and consultee would examine the school, the home, and the school–home environments from both educational (e.g., quality of instruction and mental health (e.g., peer relationships) perspectives for influences on the client system's behavior (Ysseldyke et al., 2012). There are three basic assumptions when conducting environmental assessment (adapted from Ysseldyke et al., 2012):

- people and their environments are indivisible
- problems are not necessarily person-centered; they can be environmentally induced
- collaboration as a service is often a preferred approach in making assessments across environments.

In conducting ecological assessment, consultants and consultees tend to select procedures that tap multiple sources and tend to be nonintrusive to the environment(s) being assessed (Ysseldyke et al., 2012). Such procedures involve methods described below such as documents and records and observation.

Methods for Gathering Information

Data gathering can be done by the consultant, the consultee, or both. Confidentiality is often an ethical issue that arises when gathering information as confidential data needs to be protected and appropriate releases obtained as necessary. Confidentiality is covered in detail in Chapter 14.

It is often helpful for the consultant and consultee to employ multiple data-gathering methods to increase the reliability of the data. Using multiple sources of data can be important. Consider an example of a consultant separately interviewing a parent and a teacher about a child's behavior and receiving discrepant data in one example and corroborative data in another. Using multiple methods of data gathering can also be fruitful. Consider, for example, a teacher interview revealing a student being off task and disruptive, while another data-gathering method such as a reading assessment suggest, a skill deficiency that may be related to that same disruptive behavior while suggesting an inappropriate instructional level of reading. If time permits and conditions dictate, then consultants and consultees may want to consider it good practice, as time constraints permit, to gather data from multiple sources in multiple settings by multiple methods on multiple occasions.

Some authors (e.g., Noell & Witt, 1998) recommend a hybrid data collection strategy that involves both the consultant and the consultee. The information used in consultation is obtained by either unobtrusive or obtrusive data-gathering devices. Unobtrusive devices would disclose historical data (e.g., memos), external data (e.g., interviews with former teachers of a student), and observational data (e.g., observing a meeting in action). Unobtrusive measures are not likely to interrupt the normal flow of everyday activities or to be seen as threatening.

Obtrusive data-gathering activities include those that in some way ask for a reaction. Examples of this type of data gathering include questionnaires, surveys, and interviews.

From an organizational perspective, because these activities directly assess the organization through its members and may imply impending changes within the organization, they can be threatening and elicit resistance. When the client system is an individual, sensitivity to consultee and client system alike is essential.

Regardless of the method of data gathering used, the consultant can minimize resistance by ensuring that all appropriate personnel are informed of the data's anticipated uses.

Data can be soft such as subordinates' impressions of the organization's leadership, or hard, such as statistical data on the number of positive behaviors a student demonstrates. A general rule for data gathering is to move from less to more structured methods (Parsons & Meyers, 1984). For example, concerning the morale of an entire organization, it is best to gather general information first, such as a survey of a selected sample about the level of morale, and more specific information later, such as views concerning specific causes of the quality of morale. In another example, an informal unstructured interview with a teacher about a student would lead to a subsequent, more structured interview. Instruments and procedures used to gather data should, whenever possible, be designed to take into consideration the uniqueness of the consultation situation.

The methods used for gathering information in consultation depend on the nature of the client system and the perceived problem (Stroh & Johnson, 2006). A consultant working with a consultee who is a therapist experiencing difficulty with a case requires different information than would a consultant working with an organization suffering from poor morale. Nonetheless, the most common information-gathering methods used in consultation include examining documents and records; giving questionnaires, assessments, surveys, and interviews; and observation. There are some very specific models used. For example, there is a functional behavior assessment model used in school consultation, which can be used to gather information about antecedents, behaviors, and consequences to design interventions (Daly et al., 2009; Gresham, Watson, & Skinner, 2001).

Documents and Records.   Consultants and consultees sometimes erroneously assume that they have to collect all of the data needed to make a diagnosis. All organizations generate a wealth of information and keep some form of records, including numerical data and written communications (Harrison & Shirom, 1999). This information is often referred to as *secondary data* (McLean, 2006). Use of records is often considered unobtrusive because their examination does not interrupt the organization's normal flow of work. Records are frequently referred to as secondary data because the information in them has already been collected. However, records can be a strong method for use in assessing environmental factors that impact the client system's behavior.

The consultation party who is responsible for data collection searches these documents without the aid of any structure or procedure. Gallessich (1982) was among the first to note that a variety of documents supply the consultant with data for use in making a diagnosis: job descriptions, agency policies and manuals of operating procedures, historical records, annual reports, budgets, audits, personnel statistics, orientation procedures, promotion policies, program descriptions, grant proposals, client demographic profiles (e.g., student cumulative folders), surveys of client use of services, public information brochures, logs and appointment calendars, and case records.

By comparing an organization's current and past records and documents, the consultant may be able to identify trends and forces influencing the organization and can determine who corresponds in writing with whom, how critical information is disseminated throughout the agency, and so forth. By reviewing over time an individual's record such as a cumulative folder, the consultant and consultee may ascertain how a given student's problem developed. Reviewing relevant documents is a data-gathering technique that is frequently underused by consultants.

Examining records as an information-gathering technique has several strengths, including the use of existing information, cost efficiency, the wealth of relevant material, the provision of an historical context, and the data's credibility (McLean, 2006). Furthermore, the development of discourse analysis has created a methodology for interpreting records (MacNealy, 1999).

The use of documents as an information-gathering device also has weaknesses, among which are potential inaccuracy and incompleteness, limited availability, difficulties in data analysis, time consuming to review, and the possibility of increasing resistance among consultees (McLean, 2006). Records frequently can have little relation to reality. In addition, external consultants should rely on the consultee's assistance in determining the validity of existing data and in identifying which data might be diagnostically useful.

Questionnaires and Surveys. Questionnaires and surveys are actually self-administered interviews that allow for simultaneous collection of information from several sources. They can be extremely useful (Royse, 2011; Stroh & Johnson, 2006) and contribute to understanding the behavior of individuals and organizations and reveal possible targets for change (Westaby, 2006).

Standardized questionnaires are available either commercially or in research journals. Their validity and reliability have been demonstrated in the research literature. *Modified* questionnaires are usually standardized questionnaires that have been adapted in some way to meet specific needs of the data-gathering process. For example, a school counselor might adapt a questionnaire used in a mental health center for use in a school setting. When a questionnaire is *custom made*, it is developed by the consultant, often with the assistance of the consultee, for a specific purpose. Custom-made questionnaires require a substantial amount of time to construct and often lack high levels of validity and reliability. The type of questionnaire or survey a consultant chooses depends on the precise nature of the information needed to make an adequate diagnosis.

Most questionnaires and surveys use fixed responses for respondents' information about their attitudes, perceptions, or points of view. There are several advantages of using surveys and questionnaires as data-gathering techniques. They allow sampling of large numbers of people simultaneously, are cost effective, can be administered in a variety of formats, including Web-based, and can be used for a variety of purposes (Royse, 2011). Responses can be quickly and easily collated and statistically analyzed. Questionnaires and surveys are probably the most powerful data-gathering tools for yielding maximum information in the most efficient manner (McLean, 2006). They can be used to gather data for defining a problem, to provide clues about which data-gathering techniques (e.g., interviews) should be used subsequently, or in conjunction with interviews of a sample of the respondents.

Questionnaires and surveys also have disadvantages. They are nonempathic—the instrument does not interact with the respondent in a personal way—which can cause indifference toward the questionnaire on the part of the respondent. They lack adaptability; that is, they are prestructured. If some questions are inappropriate for some respondents, nothing can be done about it. They can also be difficult to interpret; different respondents may interpret the same question differently. The items on a given survey may not be tapping the most pertinent information (Westaby, 2006). Further, surveys and questionnaires can suffer from response bias, in which the respondent answers all items in a set way rather than each item on its own merit. Questionnaires can produce canned results and consultants frequently use them when direct human communication, such as interviews, is more appropriate.

Interviews. One of the frequently used ways to understand a client system or an organization is to ask the people in them what they think and feel (Stroh & Johnson, 2006). Such a technique, the interview, is another commonly used form of data gathering (Heppner, Kivlighan, & Wampold, 2008). Interviews allow increasing understanding of the client system and facilitate selection of an intervention (Beaver & Busse, 2000). Even though interviews are used in all phases of the diagnostic stage, the nature of the interviewing process will depend on the type of model from which the consultant operates, the issues the interviews are to explore, and the consultant's earlier observations (Beaver & Busse, 2000). Effective interviewing demands that the consultant be sufficiently skilled to note the interviewee's nonverbal and verbal behavior during the interview. Depending on how the interview is conducted, the consultant can uncover both positive and negative opinions and attitudes as well as information on a large number of relevant topics.

The interviewing process can be formal or informal, as can its setting, which can affect the type of information shared by the interviewee. Both groups and individuals can be interviewed, though interviewees are less likely to distort data in a group interview and also are less likely to share their true views and feelings (Greiner & Metzger, 1983). The process by which interviews take place is usually determined by such factors as cost and the data-gathering potential of the interviewing style.

Different types of interviews produce different types of responses from different people (Egan, 1985). There are three common types of interviews: unstructured, structured and open ended, and structured and fixed response.

Unstructured interviews are typically characterized by a minimal direction of their content by the interviewer (consultant) and allow for adapting the questions depending on the respondent (Heppner et al., 2008). *Structured and open-ended* interviews consist of a set of preselected questions that the consultant asks the interviewee. This type of interview is considered more flexible than procedures such as surveys and checklists. The interview structure depicted in Figure 5.2 illustrates a structured interview for use in analyzing student behavior using FBA. *Structured and fixed-response* interviews provide both predetermined questions and responses from which to choose. They allow for standardization and tend to have a high level of reliability (Beaver & Busse, 2000).

Interviews have several advantages (McKenna, Rosenfield, & Gravois, 2009). They are adaptive—the interviewing process can be modified depending

on the course of the interview. For example, if an interviewee provides an ambiguous response, the consultant can ask for clarification or an example of what the interviewee means. Interviews can be a source of detailed information on several topics and can provide rich sources of data about problems and their causes (Kratochwill et al., 1999). Furthermore, interviews allow the consultant to express empathy and understanding to the interviewee, and as a result, the interview process can be used to build rapport with some members of the organization.

Interviews also have their disadvantages. They are one of the most costly forms of data gathering in terms of both time and expense (Royse, 2011). The interviewee's responses can be affected by the consultant's biases to the degree that these biases dictate the types of questions asked.

Interviewee bias can also affect the data obtained because the consultant can record not only the interviewee's perceptions but also observations of the consultee's behavior (Beaver & Busse, 2000). Interviewees do not always accurately report on their own behavior (McKenna et al., 2009). Consequently, the results of interviews should be carefully validated. Two additional potential disadvantages of interviews are the inaccessibility of interviewees and the perceived threat that what interviewees say could somehow later be used against them. The reasons for interviewing and the uses made of the interview data should be made known to all parties-at-interest prior to the onset of the interviewing process.

Observation.   Data can be collected through observation—the deliberate viewing of events. It is used to gather objective features of behavior (Gresham et al., 2001; Gruman & Hoelzen, 2011; Heppner et al., 2008). There are two types of observation: naturalistic and systematic direct (Hintze, Volpe, & Shapiro, 2008). *Naturalistic observation* refers to observation within a particular environment, such as a classroom, without any specific behaviors being targeted for observation.

Systematic direct observation refers to using a standardized method to measure specific behaviors that have been operationally defined. This most obvious way to collect information puts the consultant in direct contact with the people, activities, and/or environment about which information is being collected (Ysseldyke et al., 2012). Observation is widely used to gather data and conducting ecological assessment, particularly in schools (Gruman & Hoelzen, 2011; Hintze et al., 2008). Consultants must make choices about what, when, and how much to observe; such choices lend observations structure that can range from a strictly defined to a general framework. The consultant's basic question regarding observation is, "How can the observation be structured so that meaningful and useful data can be collected?" The point is that direct observation "allows an outside observer to record data on the behavior of interest within the environment where the behavior is of concern" (Skinner, Dittmer, & Howell, 2000, p. 22). Systematic direct instruction can be laborious but advances in software and recording devices have lessened the burden on observers to collecting valid data. The three types of observation—structured, semistructured, and unstructured—differ in the degree to which observers watch and record the observations.

Structured observations typically use procedures or instruments that specify what type of behavior is to be observed and how it is to be recorded. For example, FBA uses several types of structured observation, such as observing specific behaviors over the time they start and stop, or their occurrence during specified time interval (Daly et al., 2009; Watson & Steege, 2003). Figure 5.3 illustrates a form used in a structured observation. *Semistructured* observations have relatively unstructured observations but highly structured recording. *Unstructured* observations have no strict guidelines for what is to be observed, what is to be recorded, or how recording should take place.

Observation has several advantages. It provides data on behavior rather than on reports of behavior and can note behaviors unrecognized by organization members or the client system. It can also be one of the more objective data-gathering methods; technology can allow for electronic data entry

during the observation process (Heppner et al., 2008). Observational data have strong face validity; that is, such data have concrete referents to back them up, whereas interviews and questionnaire data can be accused of being overly subjective. Further, this type of data is also current, whereas questionnaires generally sample respondents' past perceptions. Finally, observation, like interviewing, is adaptive: The consultant can adjust what is to be observed as the situation demands. For example, consultants can use observation to identify and prioritize target behaviors and indicate effective interventions (Skinner et al., 2000; Watson & Sterling-Turner, 2008).

Observation is not without its liabilities as a data-collection method (Gresham et al., 2001; McLean, 2006). Observation only gives information at one point in time. Like interviewing, observation is expensive. The coding and interpretation that must be applied to observational data is subject to observer bias, and the less structured the observation, the more likely observer bias will enter into the process. As is the case with questionnaires, sampling is also an issue in observation (Heppner et al., 2008). Observations require sampling with regard to people, time, space, and activities, and such intensive sampling can be costly in time and money. Finally, observation has the potential liability of observer effect. *Observer effect* is the impact observers have on the behavior of those being observed. For example, counselors being observed by a consultant may be more empathic than usual with clients simply because they are under observation. Therefore, training in observation is important (Kratochwill et al., 1999).

In summary, each data-collection method has its advantages and disadvantages. Consultants should consider using multiple and valid data-gathering methods as a way of both overcoming the liabilities of a given method and eliminating inaccurate or distorted data. Consultants should ensure that the information gathered is as valid and accurate as possible and have an agreement with the consultee as to how to integrate the data from multiple sources (MacMann et al., 1996).

Two Brief Examples of Gathering Information

Example 1. A counseling psychologist has contracted to assist a preschool program in determining how parents view its strengths and weaknesses. As the psychologist meets with the program director to develop a plan, they decide to gather survey and interview data from a random sample of half the parents (one-fourth of the selected group will be interviewed; the other three-quarters will be surveyed).The consultant agrees to develop a structured interview and develop a survey that is compatible with the interview. The consultee suggests that the consultant be responsible for conducting the interviews, while the consultee takes care of getting the surveys sent out and the results collated.

Example 2. A school-based consultant is consulting with a teacher regarding student misbehavior. They have already operationally defined misbehavior as the student gets in and out of his seat during important learning activities. Together they collect background information of the ecological context of the student to ensure that familial variables or multicultural issues and so forth are not precipitating the behavior. Behaviors are looked at in terms of frequency, intensity, and duration through interviewing the teacher and the student's family, and by observation of the student in the teacher's classroom.

PHASE TWO: DEFINING THE PROBLEM

After the data has been collected, it must be analyzed. An integral part of defining, also referred to as identifying, the problem is problem analysis which sets the stage for intervention. Analysis is "…the process of assessment and evaluation for identifying and understanding the causal and maintaining variables associated with a well-specified problem" (Christ, 2008, p. 159). As you might guess, if multiple methods and sources are used, interpreting will be complex and require time.

The importance of defining the problem cannot be overemphasized (Gutkin & Curtis, 2009). As a dynamic process, problem analysis assists the consultant and consultee to understand the characteristics of the problem, which then leads to identifying possible solutions and helps to understand what needs to be done, how it should be done, and by whom (Christ, 2008). If multiple problems are noted, then the consultant and consultee decide which to deal with first. This phase is quite critical because the task to be accomplished is defined and thus affects the rest of the consultation process (Gregory et al., 2007; Grier & Bradley-King, 2011; Kratochwill, 2008) and has long been linked to eventual success in consultation (Bergan & Tombari, 1976). Furthermore, an accurate definition of the problem determines what behaviors are associated with the problem (Christ, 2008). Since consultation can take on either a developmental or remedial perspective, it is important to establish which perspective is to be dealt with. Developmental consultation tends to have a broader, more general identified problem than does the remedial perspective (Kratochwill, 2008).

To define a problem, the consultant and the consultee should have a systematic, deliberate, and predetermined plan for analyzing the data using a variety of methods across a variety of domains from a variety of sources (Newell & Newell, 2011). This ensures clarity in the problem clarifying process. This also avoids slippery slopes and the possibility of unintended consequences. For example, from a behavioral perspective, the difference or "gap" between what the client system is expected to do and its actual performance is determined (Tilly, 2008). The consultant and consultee may engage in FBA (Daly et al., 2009) and examine the relationships among antecedents, behavior, and consequences. As another example, consultants can use "discrepancy analysis" (French & Bell, 1999) to determine difference between the current and desired situations. In addition, cultural competence needs to be shown (Newell, 2010b) and technician-like, insensitive diagnostic procedures avoided (Diller, 2007). When involved in the details of gathering information, it is easy to forget that the purpose of the collecting is to shed light on the problem (Heppner, Wampold, & Kivlighan, 2008; Newell & Newell, 2011). Thus, the consultant and consultee should consider working together as a team to thoroughly analyze a situation, interpret pertinent data, and choose the proper strategies that are likely to lead to the accomplishment of desired goals (Grier & Bradley-King, 2011). This is of particular importance when multiple methods of data are collected from multiple sources. In addition, there is some evidence to suggest that consultants who openly model the problem-solving process as they go through it create a road map that enhances consultee understanding and use of the process (Zins, 1993).

Historically, data analysis is made up of a conceptual model and a technical component (Nadler, 1977). The conceptual component—the diagnostic perspective described earlier—should have been agreed upon by the consultant and the consultee before data are gathered, as should the techniques for analysis. Analysis of the data may suggest new hypotheses concerning the problem that require collection of additional data and subsequent analysis.

As the consultant and consultee examine the data, a more complex conceptualization of the problem often occurs. Thus, consultants will want to take into account the problem-solving approach used by their consultee in examining the data. The analysis of the data may suggest more than one problem, in which case the consultant and the consultee should prioritize them in terms of importance (Zins & Erchul, 2002). Furthermore, how the consultee conceptualizes the problem might well influence the consultant's conceptualization. For example, cultural differences may influence both parties' perception of the problem (Nahari, Martines, & Marquez, 2007). As a result, when consulting in a multicultural context, consultants will want to engage the consultee in a detailed analysis to prevent misunderstandings and to take ecological factors such as organizational context into consideration (Newell, 2010b). For example, teacher–student interactions as well as individual student behaviors are examined.

During the significant amount of time spent on analyzing and interpreting data, the consultant and consultee determine how a broad range of factors affects the problem: how it develops over time, how past events are causing the present problem, or how future expectations are related (Batsche et al., 2008; Christ, 2008). Interpretation strongly impacts problem definition and may well be the most critical element on the diagnosis stage (Newell & Newell, 2011). A clear, specific problem statement with corresponding objectives is crucial in assuring that the correct problem is attached (Newell & Newell, 2011). Consultants have long been encouraged to frame their problem statements in language that is acceptable to the consultee (Dustin & Ehly, 1984). In addition, generating several alternative definitions of the problem is a good idea because then the consultant and consultee can choose the best one. Selection criteria could include:

- reasonability—the degree to which the definition seems logical to both consultant and consultee

- workability—the degree to which the definition seems practical and leads to new directions of action

- motivation—the degree to which the consultee will be willing to take action on the defined problem (Osterweil, 1988)

In addition, ignoring cultural variables in the problem identification stage could lead to misidentification of the problem (Miranda, 2008). Rushing to identify the problem and moving to problem solving prior to an adequate definition of the problem is a common pitfall in identifying the problem (Allen & Graden, 2002). A second problem is not adequately planning follow-up sessions and monitoring (Kratochwill, 2008). Finally, the consultant and consultee will want to be open to the fact that, as a recursive process, the problem definition may possibly change depending on what information and data gathering emerge in later points in the consultation process (Meyers et al., 2009).

Two Brief Examples of Defining the Problem

Example 1. A school administrator asks a school counselor for assistance in determining which programs the school's counseling department should implement. The counselor interviews a select group of administrators, teachers, parents, and students about the types of programs suitable for counseling department sponsorship. Based on these interviews, the department uses four surveys designed for and sent to a random sample of each group: administrators, parents, teachers, and students.

The counselor and administrator agree to conceptualize the data analysis based on the common themes that emerge from each of the four surveys. In addition, they agree to look for any program suggestions that are unique to any given set of responders. They ask themselves the following questions: Is there a consensus among the groups concerning the programs the counseling department should sponsor? What program suggestions are unique to each group? What are the implications of this information for planning programs? Survey items are tallied and their relative ranks determined for each of the four groups. A given program would be seriously considered if it is ranked in the top four in importance by two or more groups. The remainder of the data, though not given priority for the development of a particular program, is to be taken into account as the counseling department reviews its entire set of activities.

Example 2. You are a school-based consultant who has been working with a teacher about a student's misbehavior in the teacher's class. The "misbehavior" has been defined in measurable and observable terminology. Relevant ecological information such as family data has been explored. Possible target behaviors are then compiled. In general, defining the problem requires the consultant and consultee to interpret the analyzed data according to some mutually accepted conceptual scheme and determine the data's meanings and limitations. These efforts ideally result in both an appropriately defined problem and a cognitive map for the consultee's future use. Once the problem has been defined to the mutual satisfaction of consultant and consultee, the consultant facilitates a commitment from the consultee to act on it.

PHASE THREE: SETTING GOALS

Setting goals is an important phase in the diagnostic stage because consultation includes solutions and outcomes. Goals help to mobilize resources and motivate people (Egan, 2010). Consultants need to be experts in goal setting because often their consultees will not be (Egan, 1985). Goal setting focuses on which actions will effectively solve or ameliorate the identified problem or problems (Locke & Latham, 2002; Shapiro, 2008). From a behavioral perspective, a goal is the intended result from an intervention designed to change behavior (Christ, 2008). From another perspective, a goal sets the stage for closing the gap between "where we are" and "where we want to be" (French & Bell, 1999). Without setting goals, it is virtually impossible to effectively evaluate the consultation process (Newell, 2010a).

The Process of Setting Goals

Goal setting is the central point of the diagnostic process (Egan, 2006, 2010). Because choosing goals establishes what specific ends are to be accomplished (Shapiro, 2008), goal setting should not be rushed (Allen & Graden, 2002). If it is, inappropriate or poorly refined goals may be chosen.

Goal setting, then, is a process of shaping, a movement toward concreteness and specificity from a broader, more general perspective. If the problem is complex, the goal of resolving the problem will likely be complex, too (Egan, 1985).

The first step in goal setting is to determine the possible goals related to the problem. Once goal possibilities have been determined, the consultant and consultee engage in the following goal-setting steps (Locke & Latham, 2002):

1. Specify the task or objective.
2. Specify how the task or objective will be measured.
3. Specify the target or standard to be reached.
4. Specify the time span involved.
5. Prioritize possible goals.
6. Rate goals with respect to difficulty and importance.
7. Determine coordination requirements.

Based on these goal-setting steps, the consultant and consultee choose the most appropriate goal, which is then evaluated and adjusted in light of the characteristics of effective goals. It is important for consultants to promote self-efficacy in consultees when it comes to the consultee setting goals as well as solicit commitment from the consultee to pursue the accomplishment of goals (Locke & Latham, 2002).

Characteristics of Effective Goals

A *goal* is a specific outcome that is sought to solve or improve a problem; a *complex goal* is one that can be divided into subgoals. In the context of consultation, success is a complex goal that can be broken down into subgoals: success in each phase of each stage of consultation.

For the goal-setting process to be successful, goals should be written in clear, specific, behavioral terms (Upah, 2008), build upon existing strengths in the client system, and be useful in increasing the levels of those strengths for everyday life. Such specificity facilitates selecting appropriate interventions to solve the problem and evaluating those interventions. Specific goals allow the consultant and consultee to regulate and evaluate the effectiveness of interventions designed to meet those concrete goals. If, for example, a consultant and a consultee determine that the goal is improved morale, it would be insufficient until they specified what they meant by *morale* and *improved*. Similarly, a

goal for a student to "behave better" would be similarly insufficient.

Effective goals are verifiable in some way, preferably by measurement. They should be stated in terms of outcomes (Egan, 2010). Consultants and consultees must determine what should be measured, how it should be measured, and when measurement should take place.

Accomplishment of goals can be verified either quantitatively or qualitatively. Measures of quantity include volume and rate, whereas measures of quality include accuracy and novelty (Egan, 1985). Cost-effectiveness—whether the expense in meeting a goal was worth the benefits derived from accomplishing it—should also be taken into consideration in goal setting. Worthwhile goals are those that are meaningful to the people involved in achieving them; they are considered to be worth the effort required to accomplish them.

Three factors determine whether a goal is realistic: resources, control, and obstacles (Egan, 2010). The consultant and the consultee must determine the adequacy of available resources for accomplishing the goal. Thus, a mental health consultant whose consultee is a teacher may have to determine whether the school has the resources needed to help the teacher's student (client) who suffers from an emotional disturbance. The consultant should ensure that the consultee has some control over whether or not the goal is met, and the consultant and consultee must determine if the goal is adequate. In other words, the goal needs to be realistic and fit the developmental level of the client system.

Obstacles to the accomplishment of any goal must be expected, particularly if the goals are complex (Locke & Latham, 2002). Thus, for example, even though a consultant and consultee may have chosen as a goal the accomplishment of a treatment plan for the consultee's client, the client may not be willing to attend the number of counseling sessions required for effective implementation of the plan. The consultant and consultee should try to anticipate and neutralize any obstacles to the successful accomplishment of a goal.

Goals reflect the values of the people attempting to accomplish them (Egan, 2010), and they should conform to the values of the consultant, consultee, client system, and the organization.

Consultants may occasionally need to help consultees clarify their values so as to set effective goals. Furthermore, consultants may also need to reflect on their own values so that they do not inadvertently impose them on their consultees during this phase of the diagnostic process.

The consultant and consultee should determine who else needs to be informed about the goals.

Clear communication about goals to parties-at-interest (e.g., parents) is essential to receiving the cooperation crucial to the accomplishment of the goals, especially when the accomplished goals will affect many of the organization's members. In summary, goals are useful in that they:

- help to focus attention and action
- assist in mobilizing energy and effort
- provide an incentive to determine strategies to achieve them
- promote persistence when they are clear and specific (Egan, 2010; Locke & Latham, 2002).

Two Brief Examples of Setting Goals

Example 1. A social worker is consulting with the principal of a rural school on how to involve community agencies with the school more. In setting goals to accomplish this, the consultant engages the administrator in both brainstorming and scenario writing. They brainstorm on the types of organizations that could become more involved with the school and write scenarios depicting the nature of the involvement for each agency. Based on examining goal possibilities, the consultant and consultee determine that they will contact seven agencies within the next two months and sell them on the idea of becoming more involved with the school. Together they assess the feasibility of the goal, and the social worker agrees to coordinate attempts to accomplish the goal.

Example 2. Following up on the example from defining the problem, you are the same school-based consultant who has been working with a teacher about a student's misbehavior in the teacher's class. You are now ready to set goals (which can also be called "target behaviors" and can be accomplished to a certain level). For example, for the student in question, the target behaviors are getting out of the seat at inappropriate times. The consultant and consultee conduct a baseline of the target behaviors to establish a sense of what needs to be accomplished. The consultant and consultee conduct a baseline of the target behaviors to establish a sense of what needs to be accomplished. Together, they determine that the student's target behavior is to be in the seat at appropriate times 90 percent of the time within one month of implementing an intervention.

PHASE FOUR: GENERATING POSSIBLE INTERVENTIONS

Once the consultant and consultee have chosen an acceptable goal, they are ready to enter the last phase of the diagnosis stage—generating possible interventions, sometimes referred to as strategies, to accomplish the goal. In this important phase of consultation, the link between assessment and intervention is determined. Effective interventions are essential to consultation and collaboration (Upah, 2008). Like goal setting, generating possible interventions is a critical step in the diagnostic stage. Whereas the goal suggests what the consultant and consultee want to accomplish, interventions are things they can do to accomplish that goal. An *intervention* is a force that attempts to modify some outcome. In consultation, interventions are the actions or activities that, when put together in a systematic manner, make up a plan to achieve a goal.

It would be a mistake for the consultant to assume that because consultees know what goals they want to accomplish, they also know all of the ways to go about accomplishing them.

By discussing alternative interventions, consultants can ascertain both the consultee's knowledge of various types of interventions and what the consultee has tried so far to solve the problem.

Developing a broad array of interventions to choose from is related to consultee willingness to implement the selected intervention (Gresham & Lopez, 1996). At the same time, only interventions with demonstrated effectiveness should be seriously considered (Allen & Graden, 2002). Evidence-based interventions refer to those that are supported by research evidence (Auster, Feeney-Kettler, & Kratochwill, 2006). For example, some consultees may be used to employing interventions with which they are familiar, even though there is no empirical evidence or observed consistency that suggest that the interventions are effective. Consultants can encourage evidence practices and then support consultees in their implementation through providing training to the consultee, monitoring the implementation process, and providing assistance as needed to ensure treatment integrity.

Consultants can assist their consultees in generating possible interventions by using prompts (stimuli or reminders) that stimulate the consultee's creativity. These prompts include (Egan, 2006, 2010):

- *people* who might assist the consultee in achieving goals, such as resource people or role models (e.g., a program evaluator for a newly implemented program)
- *places* that might be more appropriate for implementing a plan (e.g., an off-campus location for a faculty retreat)
- *things* that may lead to an easier way of accomplishing a goal (e.g., computer technology for recording observational data)
- *organizations* that could sponsor or assist the consultee in some way (e.g., a community agency providing free substance-abuse services)
- *prepackaged programs* whose goals are similar to the consultee's (e.g., a social emotional learning (SEL) program for a school)

- *consultee resources* that can be used to a large degree to generate possible interventions (e.g., the consultee being the counselor for a client about whom a goal has been set)

Brainstorming is a powerful strategy that consultants can use to help consultees generate a list of possible interventions by using divergent and creative thinking (Curtis, Castillo, & Cohen, 2008; Egan, 2010). Such a technique assists the consultant and consultee to go beyond the usual consideration of only one or two alternatives in choosing an intervention. Whenever a consultee's work-related problem has some unknown factors and some uncertainty about the best way to solve it, it is appropriate to take the time necessary to generate and analyze a list of alternative interventions (Curtis et al., 2008). By following the rules of brainstorming, consultants can increase the probability that consultees will generate an adequate list of possible interventions. The rules of brainstorming include the following (Egan, 2010):

- Suspend judgments on strategies as they are being generated.
- Generate as many interventions as possible.
- Use piggybacking: using one person's idea to stimulate other ideas.
- Use creativity and novelty.
- Offer a few suggestions as a prime-the-pump technique.

Once the consultee understands the ground rules, the consultant and consultee brainstorm for an agreed-upon period (e.g., five minutes). The consultant and consultee should write down or record interventions as they come to mind. After the brainstorming period, the consultant and consultee reconsider and clarify each item to complete this list of possible interventions.

If the consultee is unfamiliar with the brainstorming process, the consultant should provide some practice sessions first. For example, the consultant and consultee could brainstorm ways people could stay dry after being caught out in the rain. Brainstorming does not replace the sound professional judgment of either the consultant or the consultee. Rather, it is simply a technique to enhance the quantity and quality of inputs into the decision-making process. Consultants should be aware that brainstorming is very demanding intellectually, because one must consider the future, examine complex situations, recall previous experiences, and use creativity. Froehle, Mullen, Pappas, Tracy, and Chait (1999) have utilized technology to expedite brainstorming interventions in organizational consultation.

Two Brief Examples of Generating Possible Interventions

Example 1. A consulting school psychologist and a high school counselor agree that their goal is to alleviate the test anxiety of an international student. To bring to mind possible interventions, the school psychologist asks the school counselor questions, including the following:

- "Who do you think can assist you in your work with this student?"

- "What do you think is the best setting for working with the student?"

- "What things such as CD-ROMs and booklets might be available for you to use?"

- "Are any organizations that work with international students available to be of help?"

- "Do you know of any companies who have prepackaged programs for test anxiety or for helping international students get acclimatized to American schools?"

- "What professional abilities do you have that you can use directly with the student?"

Example 2. Continuing on with Example 2 from above regarding setting goals, the consultant and consultee, having set goals for the student based on observation of the student's behavior, examine a variety of evidence-based interventions to implement with the student. Interventions related to manipulating antecedents as well as consequences are examined. The consultant and consultee look

at each intervention carefully to ensure that the nature of the consultee's style as well as the knowledge, skills, and dispositions of the teacher are taken into consideration in selecting an intervention. The main idea is to select an intervention or interventions for use in developing a behavior intervention plan for the student.

MULTICULTURAL ASPECTS RELATED TO DIAGNOSIS

Multicultural influences can impact the diagnosis stage (Ingraham, 2007, 2008; Jackson & Hayes, 1993; Lopez & Truesdell, 2007; Quintana, Castillo, & Zamarripa, 2000). Consultants will need to adapt accordingly to maximize the conditions for success (Ingraham, 2007, 2008; Ramirez, Lepage, Kratochwill, & Duffy, 1998). For example, a consultee's or fellow collaborator's view of the methods used for data gathering may be influenced by cultural variables such as context (Nahari et al., 2007; Ortiz, Flanagan, & Dynda, 2008; Sheridan, 2000). Consultees or fellow collaborators from high-context cultures may prefer interviewing or observational methods, whereas those from low-context cultures may prefer methods such as reading documents or conducting surveys.

Consultees of different cultural backgrounds may prefer a fluid definition of the problem, while others prefer a concrete and detailed process of defining the problem so that the major cause is concretely defined (Ramirez et al., 1998) or what the "problem" actually is (Sheridan, 2000). There can be cultural differences related to perceptions of what goals need to be set. Whereas, for example, one collaborator may view a whole family as the focal point of the goals, another collaborator may believe a particular member of the family should be the focus. Therefore, consultants need to ensure that goals and problems are defined with cultural context and sensitivity with input from both the consultee and the client system (Lopez & Truesdell, 2007; Nahari et al., 2007).

Cultural differences can play a part in determining what kinds of data are gathered and what

---

C A S E 5.1   **Diagnosis for School Consultants**

Geri is a school-based consultant who is working with a teacher concerning a child who has difficulty remaining in his classroom seat. During the diagnosis stage, Geri and the teacher decide that Geri should observe the child in the classroom on at least three different occasions and conduct an informal interview with him. During the observation, Geri is to observe the social conditions that surround the child's getting out of his seat as well as the antecedents and consequences of this behavior. In the interview, Geri is to inform the child that the teacher is concerned about his behavior. The teacher has asked Geri to talk to him about it and about his feelings toward the class, the teacher, his studies, and his own behavior.

Geri conducts the observations, interviews the child, and then meets again with the teacher. Together they determine that the child's behavior is most likely due to the attention he receives from his buddies for disturbing the class. Geri and the teacher discuss what is reasonable behavior for the child; the goal is for the child to decrease his inappropriate out-of-seat behavior by 50 percent the first month and 75 percent the second month. They decide on a second goal—for the child to increase the frequency of socially acceptable

classroom behaviors by 25 percent over a 3-month period. Geri and the teacher begin to brainstorm possible interventions, but don't evaluate any of the items at this time. They come up with interventions such as a change in the child's seat, a teacher contract with the child, a teacher face-to-face talk with the child, a parent conference that includes the child, a student assistant program, and a realignment of the entire structure of the classroom.

Commentary

Diagnosing the problem is a very important element in the consultation process. It is very easy for consultants and consultees to pay lip service to diagnostic procedures in organizations such as schools when there are numerous time constraints. Look at it this way: Would you prefer the physicians you see to perform cursory examinations (i.e., data-gathering procedures) on you? Certainly, you wouldn't because they might well be missing significant information related to your well-being. So too in consultation, it is better to ensure that you and the consultee have adequate data so that you have a higher probability of accurately defining the problem.

---

interventions are generated. Also, multicultural assessment is essential to prevent mistakes in identifying the problem. Consultees or fellow collaborators influenced by high cultural context may want to avoid interventions that they see as time bound, perceive to be overly structured, or view as exclusively dealing with authority figures. Furthermore, the cultural aspects of the client system are a variable in determining the types of interventions that

might be successful (Ortiz, 2006; Sheridan, 2000). In addition, collecting information about a culturally different client may necessitate multiple sources and contexts (Castillo, Quintana, & Zamarripa, 2000; Ortiz, 2006). Further, problem conceptualization needs to take into consideration not only cultural differences relative to the client system but also the culture of ecological factors like, for example, a school classroom (Newell, 2010b).

SUMMARY

Diagnosis is a critical stage in consultation. Indeed, if the wrong problem is defined, then the wrong problem is solved. During this stage, the consultant and consultee collaborate in gathering information by various means, in defining a problem from that information, in setting a goal

to resolve the problem, and then in generating some possible interventions to accomplish the goal. Diagnosis should not be rushed; consultants should encourage their consultees to remain patient and avoid the tendency to define the problem hastily.

C A S E   5.2   Diagnosis for Community Consultants[1]

Martin, a community consultant, was asked by a local hospital to assist in the development of a community AIDS prevention program. Martin's consultees are a community health practitioner, a hospital–community relations coordinator, and a physician with a strong interest in the prospective program.

At one of their first meetings, Martin brought up the idea that a lot of information needed to be gathered to get a focus on how the program might look. He noted that it would be valuable to determine the success of several existing AIDS and HIV education programs. The group reached a consensus that it would be foolish to try developing a program without proper study.

Their first task was to find out about as many of the existing programs as possible. Through Martin's facilitation, the group would review the literature, make calls to existing programs, and visit a few programs |that were close to the community. The physician agreed to call several programs, Martin and the hospital/community relations coordinator agreed to review the literature at a local university library, and the entire group agreed to make site visits to three existing programs.

As they reviewed all of the gathered information, one theme became quite evident: Many AIDS and HIV education programs were unsuccessful due to poor planning and lack of community involvement. Martin then helped the group define the problem in terms of the question "What is the best type of AIDS prevention program for this community?" Once the problem was defined, Martin and the group developed and prioritized a set of goals. In developing the goals by writing a scenario of what a quality program might look like, they realized that a quality program might be beyond the scope of the hospital's resources.

The prioritized goals were: start a publicity campaign to promote the need for an AIDS/HIV education program, develop a task force to promote and plan the program, develop targets for the programs within the community, and develop short- and long-term plans that demonstrate sensitivity to the social and cultural contexts of AIDS/HIV.

The following are some of the series of possible interventions they felt would help in meeting their goals: involve possible target group members in the development of the program; ask target group members to be part of the task force; include culturally relevant content and media in publicizing the need for the program; use community recognition to reward members who assist in the development of the program; and maintain the use of Martin as a consultant for developing short- and long-term plans.

Commentary

External scanning can be one of the most effective diagnostic procedures consultants, consultees, and collaborators employ. In your work as a consultant or collaborator, scanning will prevent you from working in a vacuum and from reinventing the wheel. The use of goal setting by writing desired scenarios can be an interesting process for the consultant and consultee to engage in.

Such scenarios provide a rich narrative that is often lacking from traditional goal-setting statements. Putting goals in priority order enables the consultant and consultee to remain aware of the most important tasks at hand while providing them with a map to guide their efforts.

Clearly, diagnosis involves more than figuring out what's the matter.

---

1. The idea for this case study came from the articles in the section entitled, "Special Feature: AIDS and HIV," *Journal of Counseling and Development,* 71(3): 1993, 259–309.

This stage of consultation requires that the consultant and consultee gather the appropriate, culturally sensitive information necessary for defining the problem. To do this effectively, the consultant and consultee need to know both what information they seek and the methods by which they are going to gather it. Because each method of data gathering has its advantages and disadvantages, the consultant and consultee must carefully weigh the pros and cons of each. Furthermore, they need to analyze the data using some valid method that is consistent with the goal of consultation. Both quantitative and qualitative methods can be used in assisting to define the problem.

Once the problem has been defined to the satisfaction of the parties involved, goal setting is initiated. Goal setting, like all phases of diagnosis, should be collaborative to enhance the likelihood that the consultee will obtain an effective set of diagnostic skills for future use.

Upon the completion of goal setting, the consultant and consultee generate a list of possible interventions. This is one of the more creative phases of diagnosis, and it is also one of the most difficult because consultees may experience conflict and uncertainty about having so many possible courses of action, especially if the majority of them appear to be equally effective in reaching a desired goal (Ashford & Cummings, 1983). Therefore, the consultant may need to assist the consultee in selecting some of the better alternatives. There is some evidence that such direction by the consultant is not a detriment to the consultation process (Houk & Lewandowski, 1996). Ultimately, the major goal of the consultant during this phase is to assist the consultee in developing an adequate number of possible interventions. Evidence-based interventions should be employed whenever possible.

The research on diagnosis is relatively sparse. There is some evidence about the frequency with which diagnostic models are used, but none on the relative effectiveness of different approaches to diagnosis. The research on providing consultees with feedback regarding the result of the data-gathering stage indicates that feedback is necessary and desired by consultees; as well, the response to such feedback is affected by how it is presented (Armenakis & Burdg, 1988).

Zins (1993) suggests that consultees be trained directly in problem-solving and intervention techniques, that consultants provide overt modeling of the problem-solving process for consultees, and that potential consultees receive direct training in problem solving prior to receiving consultation services as part of preservice training.

SUGGESTIONS FOR EFFECTIVE PRACTICE

- Remember that diagnosis can be an ongoing process and that numerous aspects of the problem may change as time goes on.
- Define the problem and related goals as specifically as you can.

- Use scanning as a tool to help deal with ecological and multicultural forces.
- Involve consultees and fellow collaborators as much as possible in the data-gathering process. Avoid the temptation to bypass the phase of generating possible interventions.

QUESTIONS FOR REFLECTION

1. What do you envision as the most difficult phase of diagnosis for you to function in? Why?
2. Which 10 skills are most needed by consultants to increase the chances that the diagnosis stage will be successful?
3. Consider your answer to the previous question: In which of these skills do you think most of your consultees will be deficient? Why?

4. What is the most practical way to scan a presenting problem? How would you determine what to scan? How would you scan for ecological and multicultural issues that could be impacting the problem?
5. How can you best teach consultees to enhance their skills in diagnosis?
6. Which methods of gathering information would you be most likely to use? Why?

7. Once the data have been collected, how does a consultant go about assisting a consultee in defining a problem?

8. Of the characteristics of effective goals mentioned in this chapter, which do you think are the most difficult to meet?

9. How would you assist a consultee in generating a list of several possible interventions while bearing in mind those that are evidence-based?

10. You have now read about the entry and diagnosis stages of consultation. In what ways does the diagnosis stage build on a successfully completed entry stage?

SUGGESTED SUPPLEMENTARY READING

Hohenshil, H. (1996). Editorial: Role of assessment and diagnosis in counseling. *Journal of Counseling and Development, 75,* 64–67. Although published almost two decades ago, this article presents a concise and valuable perspective on the role of assessment and diagnosis. Although it focuses on a counseling context, you will find a wealth of information to employ in consultation and collaboration.

6

✳

Implementation Stage

This chapter covers the implementation stage of consultation, which is composed of four phases: choosing an intervention, formulating a plan, implementing the plan, and evaluating the plan.

As you read through this chapter, here are some questions to consider:

- How does a consultant assist a consultee in choosing the most appropriate interventions from among those generated at the end of the diagnosis stage?
- What are the pros and cons of the various types of interventions?
- How do the consultant and consultee tailor the chosen plan to the organization in which it is to be implemented?
- What is the consultant's role in implementing the plan?
- How can the consultant and consultee determine the degree to which the plan was successful?

Consultants and collaborators assist their consultees and fellow collaborators in taking some action based upon the results of the diagnosis stage. "Taking action" in consultation is called the implementation stage. The consultant often functions as a resource person and trainer during this stage. It is important to note that consultants are accountable for the integrity of the treatment process, even though the consultee is implementing the intervention, even though both the consultee and the consultant have content expertise (Gutkin & Curtis, 2009). The various models of consultation conceptualize the implementation process differently and use different types of interventions. A mental health consultant might carefully determine whether the problem in consultation is due to consultee issues or to client issues before identifying and recommending possible interventions. A behavioral consultant might recommend some evidence-based interventions (EBIs) that appear to be beneficial to a given client and then choose along with the consultee an intervention that seems to be the one that is most likely to succeed. An organizational consultant might spend a lot of time determining the level of the organization at which to intervene and then facilitate a set of stakeholders and consultees in selecting an intervention appropriate to that level. A school-based consultant could provide the consultee, a teacher, with possible EBIs for assisting one of the teacher's students to enhance academic performance. Together the consultant and teacher select an intervention. Regardless of the model of consultation in use, the process of implementation remains the same.

AN EXAMPLE
OF IMPLEMENTATION
AT THE ORGANIZATION
CLIENT-SYSTEM LEVEL

A staff development coordinator in a human service organization has been working with a consultant on some of the organization's concerns about improving the quality of its work environment. The coordinator's immediate superior calls the coordinator in and asks what progress has been made with the consultant. The coordinator indicates that the problem has been identified, explored, and analyzed.

Furthermore, several prospective interventions have been identified. The supervisor then asks what the next steps will be. The staff development coordinator replies that a plan will be formulated and the logistics of implementing it worked out. The plan will then be put into action and evaluated. The supervisor then asks for a time frame within which all of this will occur.

This sequence of events is quite common in consultation. Often, people within the organization in which consultation is occurring have relatively little idea about how complex and time consuming effective consultation is. The staff development coordinator was in essence telling the supervisor that consultation had progressed to the implementation stage. She and the consultant had devised and were ready to choose among several possible interventions, formulate a plan, tailor it to the organization's needs, put it into action, and then evaluate the degree to which it worked.

AN EXAMPLE
OF IMPLEMENTATION
AT THE INDIVIDUAL
CLIENT-SYSTEM LEVEL

A school-based consultant and teacher have been working together to be able to help one of the teacher's students to be able to work effectively in small groups. The consultant and teacher have brainstormed a set of evidence-based and multiculturally sensitive interventions for possible use and use the next session to review each in terms of "goodness of fit" relative to the teacher's skill sets and values and the characteristics of the student and the student's behavior. Once the intervention is selected, the consultant briefly trains the teacher in related protocols for using the intervention. Then the consultant and teacher developed a plan for implementing the intervention. They determine who will do what and when and with what resources. In this case, the teacher asked for periodic observation by the consultant while the intervention was being delivered. The consultant monitored the plan implementation in this manner and provided feedback to the teacher throughout the time of the plan implementation. They then together evaluated the plan's implementation by reviewing data collected during implementation to determine the extent to which the results supported the accomplishment of the goals of the intervention. The data revealed a significant improvement in the frequency of behaviors related to effective small group work such as turn taking, complimenting others, staying on task, and so forth. Parent input indicated a sense of pride in the student for contributing to the group's project in significant ways.

Figure 6.1 illustrates the phases of the implementation stage. In choosing an intervention, the consultant and consultee answer the question

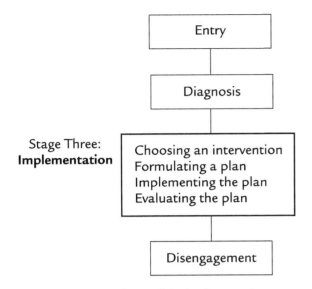

Stage Three:
Implementation

```
┌─────────────────────────┐
│          Entry          │
└─────────────────────────┘
            │
┌─────────────────────────┐
│        Diagnosis        │
└─────────────────────────┘
            │
┌─────────────────────────┐
│ Choosing an intervention │
│ Formulating a plan       │
│ Implementing the plan    │
│ Evaluating the plan      │
└─────────────────────────┘
            │
┌─────────────────────────┐
│      Disengagement       │
└─────────────────────────┘
```

F I G U R E   6.1   Phases of the implementation stage

"What are we going to do?" In formulating a plan, they answer the question "How are we going to do it?" They actively try to solve the problem in the phase of implementing the plan, and in evaluating the plan they ask "To what degree was the plan implementation successful?" As was the case in the entry and diagnosis stages, the implementation stage is critical in the consultation process: Imagine the difficulties that would be encountered if an inappropriate plan were chosen for a given problem. The consultant and consultee would come up with the wrong solution for the right problem. Or if a proper plan was chosen but the wrong interventions were used, the consultant and consultee might have the right solution put together in the wrong way.

In the implementation stage, the consultee provides direct service (intervention) to an individual client or to a client system with the consultant monitoring the consultee's implementation activities. The consultant and consultee will want to make sure that they have formulated an appropriate plan and that the consultee correctly implements it. Evaluating the plan is one of their highest priorities. Consider a situation in which the right plan, the right strategies, and correct implementation are

combined, but the consultant and consultee have failed to design an appropriate evaluation of the plan. In this situation, the consultant and consultee have no way of accurately determining the degree to which the plan actually worked.

The consultant may need to train the consultee in the interventions implemented during this stage; for example, a mental health consultant might need to train the consultee, a school counselor, in a specific procedure for assisting a child with school phobia. As in other stages in the consultation process, consultants take a collaborative approach whenever possible and avoid doing anything for consultees that they can do for themselves. In addition, the consultant typically relies on the consultee for information about the culture of the consultee's organization and the exact role of the consultee relative to the client system (Erchul & Schulte, 1993).

The implementation stage is important to the consultee because it represents some action on the problem that prompted the request for assistance in the first place. In this stage, the consultee makes some intervention with a client system and it assumes that this experience will have a preventive effect and the consultee will now possess useful skills for handling similar work-related concerns in the future.

PHASE ONE: CHOOSING AN INTERVENTION

Given adequate assessment, one of the most formidable challenges is to identify effective interventions prior to their implementation (Kratochwill & Shernoff, 2004; Noell, Roane, Van Der Heyden, Whitmarsh, & Gatti, 2000). The challenge is important because consultants and consultees, for better or worse, tend to rate the effectiveness of the entire consultation process based upon the effectiveness of the intervention (Newell, 2010a). Since there are often a large number of interventions available (Gutkin & Curtis, 2009), consultants may need to deal with the fact that the consultee may be overwhelmed because all of the interventions appear feasible. Often, one of the tasks of the consultant is to ensure that the intervention selected is effective given the situation of the client system (Snyder, Quirk, & Dematteo, 2011). The selection of interventions needs to be linked to assessing those interventions (Christ, 2008). Furthermore, consultees may prefer interventions that they are familiar with, they think are easy to implement, are the most practical (Martens & Ardoin, 2002), and for which they perceive that they have the necessary knowledge and skills (Egan, 2010).

In addition, there has been a great deal of attention in the school consultation literature to EBIs. Consultants will need to consider what evidence there is when considering a given intervention and share that evidence with their consultees. These are interventions that have research support for their effectiveness (Kratochwill, 2008). The issue of *empirically supported interventions* (ESI), also often referred to as *evidence-based interventions* (Cox, 2005; Gibbs, 2003; Guli, 2005), has come to the forefront in the consultation/collaboration literature, particularly in school-based consultation (Graden, 2004; Stoiber & Kratochwill, 2000; Wilkinson, 2005). School reforms—such as those dictated by the No Child Left Behind Act (NCLB), developments in the field of special education, and gap between research and practice—have all stressed the importance of evidence-based activities (Kratochwill & Shernoff, 2004; Merrell, Ervin, & Gimpel, 2006). These developments have risen, not without implementation issues (Kratochwill & Shernoff, 2004), from the idea that scientific inquiry should guide practice. For community consultants, the health care delivery system and its focus on accountability in the United States and other countries has led to an emphasis on EBIs . Depending on the consultee's skill level related to implementing the intervention, the consultant should be prepared to provide indirect training (e.g., didactic instruction) or direct training (e.g., modeling) (Sterling-Turner, Watson, & Moore, 2002). The main idea is that by having a catalog of EBI, consultants can be linked to research in their practice. This practice, of course, puts the consultant in the expert mode. The major strategies

for introducing EBI include: developing a practice–research network, promoting research on the efficacy of EBIs, establishing guidelines for implementation and evaluation of EBIs by practitioners (Kratochwill & Shernoff, 2004). EBI is not without controversy. For a pertinent discussion, see Egan (2010).

Therefore, the first phase of the implementation stage involves selecting one or more interventions that have a high probability of success. As noted above, one way to accomplish this is to make sure that all of the interventions under consideration have research to back their efficacy; that is, they are evidence-based (Barnett, VanDerHeyden, & Witt, 2007; Hoard & Shepard, 2005; Sheridan et al., 2009; Theodore et al., 2009). EBIs are validated either by research and/or data-based decision making (Stoiber & Vanderwood, 2008).

Kratochwill (2008) notes that there are several aspects to evidence-based practice:

- The endorsement by a legitimate group that an intervention is evidence-based.

- Use of a manual related to the interventions' implementation.

- Ensure the consultee's competency to deliver the implementation.

- Document treatment integrity.

- Use of an evaluation that determines outcomes are due to the intervention.

- High-quality monitoring throughout the intervention period.

By virtue of their training, consultants are in an excellent position to assist consultees to select, understand, and implement EBI. However, consultants and consultees can be quite variable when it comes to selecting interventions (Newell, 2010a). In addition to examining current research, consultants take into consideration the context in which the consultee and client system interact in determining how to proceed in selecting an intervention; that is, they use clinical judgment and consider multicultural variables (Gutkin, 2009; Wesley & Buysse, 2006). For example, does the consultee find the intervention attractive to use? In another example, are there characteristics of the client system that require additional attention to multicultural aspects?

As noted, consultants will want to be aware of the cultural limitations of and possible ecological issues related to EBI and make related adaptations (Li & Vazquez-Nuttall, 2009; Meyers, Proctor, Graybill, & Meyers, 2009; Ysseldyke, Lekwa, Klingbeil, & Cormier, 2012). Other ways involve addressing the social factors that bear upon the problem (Farmer, 2000), considering the costs and benefits of the intervention (Topping & Ehly, 2001), reviewing potential crucial consequences of the alternatives (Egan, 2010), and developing an intervention that readily fits into the consultee's other responsibilities (Allen & Graden, 2002; Noell & Witt, 1998).

In addition, consultants should remember that knowing about a wide range of potential interventions is not enough. As Elliott and Busse (1993) note: Consultants must also "be sensitive to the skills and perceptions of their consultees and be able to clearly communicate treatment procedures so that they are implemented with integrity" (p. 194).

Although proposed over three decades ago by Janis and Mann (1977), one still effective procedure the consultant can still use in helping a consultee choose among possible interventions is decision consultation. Although developed for use in counseling and psychotherapy, this procedure is useful for ensuring that the consultee goes through the process of choosing an intervention in an appropriate manner. The process of *decision consultation*, which is based on effective decision making, consists of eight questions consultants can ask consultees. Decision consultation can be looked at as a type of balance-sheet method for choosing an intervention (Egan, 2010). The following questions are adaptations of those developed by Janis and Mann (1977, p. 371):

- To what degree has the consultee developed a wide range of alternative interventions?
- To what degree has the consultee considered the objectives and related values of the possible interventions?

- To what degree has the consultee weighed the potential negative consequences, risks, and potential payoffs of each intervention?
- To what degree has the consultee searched for new information relative to each intervention?
- To what degree has the consultee processed the consultant's comments about potential positive and negative factors related to the interventions?
- To what degree has the consultee made a final determination of the interventions' potential positive and negative consequences, as well as the driving and inhibiting forces that affect their implementation?
- To what degree does the consultee have the capacity to successfully execute the chosen intervention?
- Which interventions have been set aside for use in contingency plans?

By engaging the consultee in the pursuit of answers to these questions, the consultant can help the consultee be a true partner in making a reasonably effective choice of interventions and can ascertain not only the degree to which the implementation appears satisfactory to the consultee, but also whether any adaptation of the intervention by the consultee will negatively affect its impact.

The use of this process helps to ensure that the intervention selected is logically related to the information gathered and is congruent with the reasons the problem is believed to exist (Allen & Graden, 2002). In addition, the process involved in this kind of assistance can "rub off" and have a preventive effect on the consultee, who can then be more effective in choosing interventions for similar problems in the future.

By engaging in decision consultation, the consultant can increase the probability that the consultee will follow through with the agreed-upon intervention. Some research suggests that consultees do not always follow through on the intervention they are supposed to implement. Later in this chapter, you will read about the concept of treatment integrity and the way to enhance consultee commitment to interventions. Whether consultees will accept an intervention appears to be a function of their perception of the fit between the problem and the intervention, their beliefs about the intervention (e.g., humaneness, consultee self-competence, consultees' beliefs about their professional responsibilities regarding the problem), the level of difficulty in implementing it (Erchul & Chewning, 1990; Theodore et al., 2009), the quality of the consultant–consultee relationship (Conoley, Conoley, Ivey, & Scheel, 1991), the consultee's values (Egan, 2010), and its compatibilities with behavioral routines in the consultee's work setting (Gutkin & Curtis, 2009). Therefore, the consultant should address these considerations when developing a rationale for an intervention.

In addition, in selecting an intervention, the consultant and consultee should examine the following questions (Gutkin & Curtis, 2009):

- Do they believe that the intervention will really work?

- Can the consultee implement the intervention with high levels of treatment integrity?

- Does the consultee see it as part of his or her duties to carry out the intervention?

- Is the intervention in line with the consultee's perception of what needs to be done?

- Does the intervention fit relatively easily with the consultee's routine?

Being able to explain a wide variety of interventions from several different perspectives is a very desirable skill for consultants (Conoley et al., 1991), and it helps to avoid considering a limited number of interventions due to bias or favored interventions.

Consultants should be aware of potential obstacles to the successful completion of this phase. First, the consultee and consultant must process a tremendous amount of information in selecting the intervention. Second, it is difficult to predict realistically the specific outcomes of various interventions due to the possibility of unforeseen events and potential human error (Lentz, Allen, & Erhardt, 1996). Therefore, the consultant should consider having the consultee keep a consistent, detailed set of

notes concerning alternative interventions (to facilitate discussion about the possible impacts of given interventions). One possible method of maintaining such a record is to use a balance-sheet method that deals with the acceptability and unacceptability of benefits and costs of various interventions (Egan, 2010). The process of supporting the intervention should also be taken into consideration. In other words, the technical components need to be blended together with an ecological understanding of the problem setting (Lentz et al., 1996; Ysseldyke et al., 2012). There are some additional guidelines that can assist consultants and consultees in choosing an adequate intervention (Gutkin & Curtis, 2009; Zins & Erchul, 2002):

- Try to use positive interventions first.

- Avoid complex and intrusive interventions.

- If the consultee is to learn a new skill, incorporate it into daily routines as much as possible.

- Promote interventions that require the least amount of time.

- In addition to empirical research on the intervention, rely on the consultee variables discussed previously.

Types of Interventions

You are hungry, so you decide to go to a restaurant that offers a smorgasbord. As you walk through the smorgasbord, you have a difficult time selecting from among the offerings because they all look so good. You decide to choose one item that is representative of each of the four food groups. So you choose one meat, one dairy product, one cereal product, and one green vegetable—and then you proceed to enjoy your meal. You have, in effect, just classified all of your possible food choices into four categories and then chosen from each of them. By categorizing your options, you made your decision about what to eat much easier.

Indeed, consultants and consultees have a smorgasbord of interventions available to them. There are, for example, reference guides for assisting in intervention selection (Sink, 2011a).

Therefore, consultants typically categorize all the possible interventions that might be put together in a plan, which expedites the decision-making process. In dealing with a problem situation, an intervention can be a single task, a series of related tasks, or a series of unrelated tasks organized around a common theme. One or more interventions can be put together systematically into a plan that is tailored to the unique problem that has been identified.

Effective consultants have a large number of interventions in their repertoire to most effectively assist their consultees. Such expertise allows the consultant flexibility in combining programs to meet the goals of consultation. Do you know about the carpenters who could only use hammers? They saw every problem as a nail to be hit. Consultants who do not have knowledge of, and skill in, many types of interventions tend to conceptualize solutions in terms of what they know how to do instead of what is really needed.

A useful device for obtaining a broad perspective on interventions is a classification system. A categorization of interventions based on primary target groups is a convenient one and is used in the following discussion. The target group is usually the client system. A classification scheme developed by French and Bell (1999) includes the following targets: individuals, dyads/triads, teams and groups, intergroup relations, and the total organization. Though developed for interventions in organizational consultation, this scheme can easily make up a generic classification system useful to all consultants. A classification system is of increasing importance for consultants due to the renewed emphasis on prevention, multicultural context, ecological factors, social justice, systems-level interventions, and multitiered models of intervention such as response to intervention (RTI).

Individual Interventions

Individual interventions can apply in a variety of consultation settings. A common example is when a consultant assists a counselor, psychologist, or social worker with an individual case. Many individual-based school-based consultations involve

the academic and/or behavioral interventions described below.

Academic Interventions. For many school-based consultants, student academic problems are the most common source for consultation (Bramlett, Murphy, Johnson, & Wallingsford, 2002). Academic difficulties can be caused by a variety of variables, including student behavior (Noell, 2002; Noell & Witt, 1998). In some cases, students don't have the academic skills to learn. In others, students have the appropriate academic skills but still don't learn adequately, thus suggesting a disability or an inadequate learning environment.

Academic interventions typically include those related to student's learning behaviors, teachers' instructional behaviors, and instructional materials and practices (Berninger, Fayol, & Alston-Abel, 2011; Elliott, Busse, & Shapiro, 1999; Kampwirth, 2006). Among the academic interventions with strong empirical support are: school-home notes (e.g., daily report cards); providing students with constructive feedback on their performance, training students in self-management techniques, peer tutoring, and cooperative learning (Elliott et al., 1999); as well as other instructional principles such as pacing (Kratochwill, 2008).

Behavioral Interventions. Consultants have a broad array of interventions available to assist consultees in changing the behavior of the client system. However, detailed discussion of behavioral interventions is beyond the scope of this text. For a detailed discussion see Akin-Little, Little, Braym, and Kehle (2009). From a school-based perspective, problem behavior can result from lack of knowledge or skills, the fact that the problem behavior is more rewarding than nonproblem behavior, and that problem behavior is a way to avoid the demands of things like school work (Martens & Ardoin, 2002). Interventions should then be designed using positive behavioral support in such a way that appropriate behavior is rewarded. For example, a student can be reinforced with praise from a teacher for engaging in a new behavior

(Martens & Ardoin, 2002). Kampwirth (2006) lists commonly used behavior-related interventions in schools:

1. general preventative techniques (e.g., classroom rules);

2. contingency management and contracting;

3. noncontingency interventions (e.g., modeling appropriate behavior);

4. social skills training; and

5. conferencing.

It is important to note that individual interventions may be part of a systems-level, multitiered approach that targets individuals with identified problems, individuals considered at risk, and the remainder of the population as a whole. For example, an entire school develops and implements a multitiered RTI program.

Client-Centered Case Consultation. In client-centered consultation, the consultee presents a case in which a client has issues that are causing the consultee some difficulty. The primary goal of this type of consultation is to develop a plan to help the client.

Consultee-Centered Case Consultation. This intervention is another approach to the mental health consultation model and is given in-depth coverage in Chapter 9. Consultee-focused interventions are used when the consultee is experiencing a work-related problem due to a lack of objectivity or confidence or a lack of knowledge or skill in problem solving and decision making (Caplan & Caplan, 1993; Caplan & Caplan-Moskovich, 2004; Knotek & Sandoval, 2003).

Dyadic and Triadic Interventions

Sometimes consultants are called on to make interventions that are most effective with groups of two (dyads) or groups of three (triads) consultees. Interventions aimed at these small groups are limited but popular due to frequent use of dyadic and triadic work groups in human service organizations. Some of the types of interventions that are useful with individuals can be used to increase effectiveness of dyads and triads and are hence consultee-centered.

Third-Party Peacemaking. Conflict, common in most organizations, usually stems from parties' different perspectives on the same events. Consultants will frequently be called upon to deal with conflict management (French & Bell, 1999; McLean, 2006). Differences between two consultees can be effectively dealt with in a variety of ways, including third-party peacemaking (Golembiewski & Rauschenberg, 1993), an intervention unique to dyads and triads, which is used to resolve interpersonal conflict.

The consultant guides a process in which two parties directly confront one another and use conflict resolution techniques, such as those developed by Fisher, Ury, and Patton (1991), or Walton (1987). The term *third party* refers to the consultant, who presumably is skilled and objective in terms of the conflict's resolution or management. The consultant is interested in improving the conditions and the manner in which the conflicting parties manage the conflict.

Interventions for Groups and Teams

Organizations make extensive use of teams and groups, and consultants and collaborators frequently are called on to make interventions to enhance the effectiveness of an intact group or team. The most common group or team intervention is the education/ training approach, which is covered extensively in Chapter 11. Other interventions are described here.

Team Building. A team is a group of individuals working together in a coordinated effort. There is increasing attention being paid to developing leadership teams through team building (Rawlings, 2000), particularly in the area of cross-cultural team building, which includes cross-cultural training (McLean, 2006). Team building is the process by which a team's individuals attempt to improve the group's functioning through analyzing and evaluating their interactions (French & Bell, 1999). The term *team building* came about because selected interventions lead to increases in team cohesiveness and effectiveness. Note that the consultant is not a member of the team with which he or she is working.

During team building, the consultant acts as a facilitator and a collaborator. The consultant typically interviews each team member individually, examining the strengths and weaknesses of the team. The strengths and weaknesses are grouped and presented to the team for prioritization.

The team then analyzes the selected issues and sets an action plan to effectively deal with them. The consultant follows up periodically to determine if the expected results have been achieved. Special attention is paid to how the team's various members use power.

Nominal Group Technique. The nominal group technique (NGT) was originally developed by Delbecq, Van de Ven, and Gustafson (1986). The NGT is a group problem-solving process designed specifically for engendering the members' involvement and creativity. Its purpose is to involve groups in determining solutions to issues and problems.

The NGT is based on two assumptions: that all group members need only the proper encouragement to induce them to express their ideas, and that the exchange of ideas and group decision making contribute to greater acceptance of decisions by the individuals involved.

The NGT is a structured problem-solving meeting with a "one person, one vote" orientation; superiors and subordinates all have equal status in the NGT. The technique yields a large quantity of high-quality, specific ideas and encourages independent thinking by participants.

The process is highly motivating, and participants experience the satisfaction of task accomplishment, as well as the social reinforcement of having worked effectively together. The consultant acts as a facilitator of the problem-solving process, as well as a taskmaster who ensures that the steps of the NGT process are completed (Sandland & Dougherty, 1985).

Quality Circles. Quality circles are small problem-solving groups (French & Bell, 1999) whose members are typically from the same work area. The groups meet for one to two hours per week to discuss concerns, investigate the sources of those concerns, make recommendations, and take authorized corrective action. A primary purpose of these circles is to enhance product quality. The sharing of information is essential in quality circles (Kovach, 1998). According to one of the early writers in this area (Dewar, 1980), the objective of quality circles is to improve work quality, productivity, and motivation.

The consultant's primary role with regard to quality circles is educating and training potential members and administrators in the ways quality circles work. Consultants may want to recommend that quality circle participants are highly rewarded because of the stress of participation (Jennings, 1988). The quality circle concept has expanded to include quality improvement teams. The primary difference is that quality circles tend to focus on one task or issue, whereas quality improvement teams tend to be more permanent and focus on issues related to quality as those issues emerge.

Interventions for Use Between Groups

Human service organizations are made up of several groups that interact with and affect one another. One group frequently experiences tension or conflict with one or more other groups within the same organization. Consultants can assist groups to relate more effectively by using strategies designed to alleviate group conflict. Two or more interdependent groups are put together as a single unit and engage in joint activities (French & Bell, 1999).

The two major types of intergroup interventions—team building and organizational mirroring—work because the group interactions are structured to maintain control (French & Bell, 1999). All information is shared between groups: There are no secrets and the consultant engenders a spirit of constructive problem solving (French & Bell, 1999).

Organizational Mirroring.   When the increased effectiveness of three or more groups is desired, including reducing conflict (McLean, 2006), organizational mirroring is frequently used (French & Bell, 1999). In this technique, one group, called the host group, receives feedback from other groups about the ways it is perceived; the technique's goal is to change the host group. To keep the number of participants manageable, representatives of each of the groups (rather than the entire membership of each group) are involved. As in intergroup team building, the consultant acts as the process's facilitator, enforcer of norms, and coordinator. As an example, a consultant might lead while a group of school counselors (host team) receives feedback from select groups of administrators and staff on their perceptions of the counseling department's programs.

Interventions for the Entire Organization

Interventions that attempt to enhance an entire organization's effectiveness are called organizational interventions. They are often also referred to as systems-level interventions. School-based professionals are increasingly being called upon to consult regarding the development and implementation of system-level interventions such as positive behavioral intervention supports (PBIS) and RTI, as well as prevention programs such as those related to social emotional learning (SEL) and antibullying (see Chapter 12).

Consultants who intervene at the organizational level must be experts in systems theory, prevention, and ecology.

Total Quality Management.   Total quality management (TQM) is a combination of many of the interventions discussed in this chapter. Also called total quality improvement, this model, along with its offshoot, Six Sigma, emphasizes teams, a focus on service, measurement of objectives, and a major emphasis on continuous training (David & Strang, 2006; McLean, 2006). Major concepts include "customer focus, reduction of variability, continuous improvement and employee participation" (David & Strang, 2006, p. 216). The role of the consultant is to assist with the training in any of the methods or in providing instruction in total quality philosophy. For example, a school-based consultant might work with a group of teachers on implementing total quality concepts into their classroom instruction.

Survey Feedback/Action Research.   Survey feedback/action research owes much of its development to the social psychologist Kurt Lewin (1945, 1951). It is a problem-solving intervention designed to systematically collect data about some system (through surveys and/or interviews), analyze the data, and feed results back to appropriate personnel in workshop settings (French & Bell, 1999). The problem is diagnosed and action steps are planned during the workshop meetings. One underlying assumption of this approach is that whatever discrepancies are noted from interpreting the data will create the motivation to change things (French & Bell, 1999). Another underlying assumption is that ongoing feedback is necessary to keep the organization on course in terms of its role and mission. Survey feedback/action research takes on a cyclical approach: research, data collection, feedback, planning, action, and evaluation (McLean, 2006). Depending on the outcome of evaluation, the process may be repeated. For an interesting approach to action research, see Dahir and Stone (2009).

Capacity Building.   *Capacity building* is a generic term for interventions designed to ensure that members of the organization have the knowledge, skills, and attitudes necessary for the organization's optimal functions. There are two forms of capacity building: general and innovation-specific (Anderson-Butcher et al., 2010). General capacity building focuses on things such as working in teams and relationship building. Innovation-specific capacity building focuses on the unique knowledge, skills, and attitudes necessary for a specific innovation being implemented. For example, a school system adopting a positive behavior supports (PBS) program will require mastery of terminology, program techniques, and coordination issues.

Strategic Planning.   Strategic planning is a futuristic and visionary intervention process that helps organizations deal better with the future (Fuqua & Kurpius, 1993; Kormanski & Eschbach, 1997). It emphasizes process over product, separates vision from the steps to accomplish that vision, sees change as a positive force, involves as many people in the organization as possible, is long term by nature, and takes into consideration the needs and security of the people involved in the planning (Demers, 2007; Fuqua & Kurpius, 1993). The process typically involves goal development, environmental analysis, strategy development, strategy evaluation, strategy implementation, and strategic control. It often employs SWOT (strengths, weaknesses, opportunities, threats) (McLean, 2006). The main roles of the consultant are to make sure everyone involved understands the process (e.g., how to engage in internal and external scanning) and to guide the consultees in determining where they want the organization to go and how they are going to get there, as well as in developing specific action and monitoring plans. Strategic planning has been increasingly used in educational settings (Knoff, 2008).

A final note on choosing an intervention: You have just read about several interventions. It is important for consultants and collaborators not to take a "cookbook" approach to choosing an intervention. Employing the criteria of convenience and popularity do not necessarily end up with an EBI that directly deals with the problem with a high probability of success. Consideration of cultural context is essential for adapting the intervention to the client system.

Because choosing an intervention varies somewhat in consultation and collaboration, below I provide an example of choosing an intervention in each using the same scenario.

Two Brief Examples of Choosing an Intervention in Consultation

Example 1. Ellen, the head of a community agency serving developmentally disabled adults, has been consulting with Lisa, a mental health worker specializing in consulting to management. Ellen is feeling all of the pressures associated with being placed in charge of an important program. The diagnosis has pointed to Ellen's deficiency in management training. Lisa and Ellen discuss the large array of interventions that could be made in this situation, and select several interventions that seem likely to be successful. Lisa leads Ellen through the decision consultation by asking her eight questions related to her concern about lack of management skills. Based on outcomes to these questions and a determination of Ellen's beliefs about the possible interventions, Lisa and Ellen choose a general intervention, shadow consultation, in which Lisa will follow Ellen at work for three days and then provide feedback on possible management skills Ellen may want to pursue as part of her professional development plan.

Example 2. A school-based consultant and consultee have generated possible interventions and are now ready to select one. The intervention will be aimed at a student in the teacher's (consultee) classroom. All of the interventions are evidence-based. The consultant and consultee then engage in decision consultation to determine the best approach for the given situation and its context. The teacher wanted an intervention that dealt with antecedes (e.g., talking while the teacher is talking), the behavior (e.g., being on task), and consequences (e.g., a star) while making a minimal intrusion into the daily classroom routine. Together the consultant and consultee came up with three different interventions—self-monitoring, proximity control, and token economy—that could be incorporated into a plan.

A Brief Example of Choosing an Intervention in Collaboration

Ellen, the head of a community agency serving developmentally disabled adults, has been collaborating with Lisa, a mental health worker in the agency specializing in consulting to management. Ellen is feeling all of the pressures associated with being placed in charge of an important program.

Lisa is concerned that she needs to be more effective in her work of providing more effective services to the management of the agency. The diagnosis has pointed to Ellen's deficiency in management training and Lisa's lack of a systematic plan for assisting management. Lisa and Ellen discuss the large array of interventions that could be made in this situation and select several interventions that seem likely to be successful.

Together, Lisa and Ellen engage in decision consultation by asking and answering the eight questions related to their concerns. Based on outcomes to these questions and a determination of their beliefs about the possible interventions, Lisa and Ellen choose a general intervention, shadow consultation, in which Lisa will follow Ellen at work for three days, and then provide feedback on possible management skills Ellen may want to pursue as part of her professional development plan. They also choose a focus group approach through which Lisa will determine more effective approaches for her providing her services. Ellen, who has expertise in conducting focus groups, agrees to help monitor Lisa's progress.

PHASE TWO:
FORMULATING A PLAN

Once the consultant and consultee have been able to decide on one or more interventions that have a high probability of helping meet the goal that has been developed, they begin formulating a plan. A *plan* refers to a detailed step-by-step method for doing something and is formulated beforehand (Upah, 2008). In many instances, formulating a plan refers to joining the pieces of the interventions into a sequence and generating appropriate time lines (Egan, 2010).

In other words, the consultant and consultee construct an overall game plan (French & Bell, 1999). It is critical in this planning phase that the consultant emphasize the collaborative nature of consultation to ensure that the consultee has a ready-made commitment to the plan (Erchul & Chewning, 1990). It is usually best for the consultant and consultee to formulate a few possible plans and then choose the plan that appears to have the highest probability of succeeding.

Good plans shape successful consultation outcomes. When formulating a plan, the consultant and consultee should consider the what (objectives), the where (locale of the implementation), the when (time frame), the how (methods, procedures, sequence), and the who (who is responsible for which elements) (Upah, 2008). In doing so, the consultant and consultee can plan more effectively.

Plan formulation is a complex activity that requires time to accomplish adequately. The consultant and consultee first determine the plan's objectives, choose its procedures, and establish the time frame in which it is to be carried out. Next, they assign responsibility for carrying out each part of the plan. Each step is scrutinized again and adjusted as necessary. Finally, they assess the plan in terms of its feasibility, cost effectiveness, and capability of succeeding.

Consultants and consultees should adhere to several principles of formulating plans (Egan, 1985). Plans should be clearly linked to the established goals; a connection must exist between what the consultant and consultee want to accomplish and how they are going to accomplish it. A variety of plans to accomplish set goals should be constructed and examined. Brainstorming is a helpful procedure for generating a variety of plans. Plans should be evaluated in terms of the criteria of effectiveness, efficiency, and ability to meet human needs. Steps in plans should be viewed as subgoals and measures taken to see that the subgoals meet the criteria of effective goals. Plans should have reasonable time frames for completion and be sufficiently detailed. Finally, plans should be examined in terms of their feasibility as contingency plans. It is a good practice to have a "Plan B."

Once plans have been formulated, the consultant and consultee choose a plan. One common way of choosing the best plan is *force-field analysis*, a method of determining the driving and restraining forces affecting the accomplishment of a goal (Egan, 2010; Lopez-Baez & Paylo, 2009). Restraining forces inhibit movement toward a plan's successful implementation and driving forces support the plan's successful outcome. Force-field analysis helps consultees gain perspective on possible plans' pitfalls and strong points, and such awareness allows consultees to adapt plans to the specific settings in which clients are being served.

In using force-field analysis, the consultant has the consultee review each plan that has been generated. For each plan, the major restraining and driving forces, identified by brainstorming, are listed and examined in detail. Depending on the plan, one or more restraining and driving forces over which the consultee has some control are identified for modification. The consultee and consultant then brainstorm ways to minimize the selected restraining forces and maximize the selected driving forces for each of the plans. They look at the relative weights of the restraining and driving forces, and those plans whose restraining forces outweigh their driving forces are discarded. From the remaining plans, one plan and a backup contingency plan are chosen. Specific adaptations of the plan to the unique needs of the client or client system are worked out.

In addition to using techniques such as force-field analysis, the consultant and consultee can work together to create a checklist to avoid the following pitfalls, which frequently contribute to the failure of plans (Egan, 2010):

- trying to accomplish too much
- formulating too large a plan
- overanalyzing the plan, which causes disinterest and resistance
- underanalyzing the plan and failing to anticipate pertinent problems
- failing to consider the plan's system-wide impact
- inadequately defining the plan's desired outcomes
- failing to consider the human-side factors

As a final safeguard, the consultant and consultee may want to "walk through" the process one time to see who is affected in what ways by the plan.

In summary, to choose a plan, the consultant helps the consultee consider each plan's comprehensiveness and positive and negative consequences, as well as the adequacy of the consultee's information about each plan. The consultant checks out the acceptability of the treatment by helping the consultee make a judgment of the appropriateness and likely effectiveness of the selected intervention (Meyers et al., 2009).

High treatment acceptability indicates a high level of willingness to proceed with the intervention in the situation at hand, making it more likely that the consultee will both stick with the intervention and implement it appropriately (Meyers, Truscott, Meyers, Varjas, & Collins, 2008; Kratochwill & Stoiber, 2000a). Furthermore, the consultant helps the consultee integrate the consultant's input regarding the plans and makes a final check of each plan's potential positive and negative consequences. The plan builds upon the natural interaction between the consultee and the client system and the realities of the environment in which the plan is to be carried out (Lentz et al., 1996). Plans can keep the consultee from being overwhelmed and uncover unanticipated obstacles. Finally, the consultant assesses the consultee's capacity to carry out plans and develop contingencies successfully.

Two Brief Examples of Plan Formulation in Consultation

Example 1. A school counselor is consulting with a school principal about the most appropriate type of in-school suspension program that demonstrates multicultural competence and a focus on both academics and behavior. They develop three possible plans for operating the program: a punitive approach, a "time-out" approach, and a counseling approach. The pros and cons of each approach are weighed, and the consultant makes sure that the administrator possesses adequate knowledge of, and the basis for, each plan. The consultant's input into the various plans is clarified and a force-field analysis is applied to each. Together they decide that the in-school suspension plan with a counseling focus is the best plan; the "time-out" approach is chosen as a contingency.

Example 2. Following Example 2 from Two Brief Examples of Choosing an Intervention above: Together the consultant and consultee have selected three different interventions—self-monitoring, proximity control, and token economy—that are to be incorporated into a plan. The consultant and teacher develop a clear description for implementing the plan, create methods for ensuring that the interventions are implemented as planned, settle on how to monitor the plan's implementation, and determine an evaluation strategy.

A Brief Example of Plan Formulation in Collaboration

A school counselor and a school principal are collaborating about the most appropriate type of in-school suspension program. They develop three possible plans for operating the program: a punitive approach, a "timeout" approach, and a counseling approach. The pros and cons of each approach are weighed, and the school counselor makes sure that the administrator possesses adequate knowledge of, and the basis for, each plan. The administrator ensures that the school counselor is aware of how to deal with the organizational dynamics of program implementation. A force-field analysis is applied to each possibility. Together they decide that the in-school suspension plan with a counseling focus is the best plan; the "time-out" approach is chosen as a contingency. They agree to implement the program by each taking on a variety of responsibilities.

As these examples clearly illustrate, good planning is essential to successful consultation and collaboration, yet it is very easy to neglect. Because every plan has its advantages, disadvantages, and possible glitches, there is no one best plan, but rather one that has the highest probability of succeeding.

PHASE THREE: IMPLEMENTING THE PLAN

Now that the consultant and consultee have narrowed the possibilities and formulated a plan, they are ready to implement the plan. The plan designed in the previous phase is now put into operation, and the focus of consultation turns to making sure that the plan is followed in such a way that it achieves the desired results.

Although putting a plan into action seems quite straightforward on the surface, it is actually a very complex process; planning needs to involve strategies for effective implementation (Ervin & Erhardt, 2000; Riley-Tillman & Chafouleas, 2003). This phase dictates that consensus needs to be reached on items such as the roles taken and the timing of any monitoring by the consultant (Kratochwill, 2008). For example, the consultant and consultee should engage in role analysis (Golembiewski, 1993a) to ascertain who is responsible for the tasks involved, while recognizing that each brings unique skills to the problem-solving process (Lentz et al., 1996). Furthermore, the consultant should discuss with the consultee the fact that events sometimes get in the way of the plan's implementation and that most often this is due to factors in the complex real-life environment in which all interventions must eventually be made.

The consultant can increase the probability of successful plan implementation by providing logistical and tactical assistance. *Logistics* refers to the provision of resources in a timely manner. *Tactics* is the art of adapting a plan (program) to the immediate situation (Egan, 2010), possibly on short notice. Therefore, consultants should consider maintaining contact with consultees during the implementation phase.

Consultant availability can be a critical factor in the success of an intervention, because of the reliance on the consultee (who may not be as well trained as the consultant) to carry out the intervention. By monitoring the consultee's implementation of the intervention, the consultant is, in effect, providing a quality control mechanism to the process (Tilly, 2008). Careful monitoring by the consultant will help to ensure that the consultee has or acquires the skills necessary for reflective implementation. It will also provide the contact necessary to prohibit consultees who think they have the necessary skills from implementing a procedure, which, in actuality, they lack the ability to implement (Caplan, Caplan, & Erchul, 1994).

Because the consultant and consultee made plans jointly, it is reasonable to assume that the consultee may welcome contact with the consultant during implementation (Conoley & Conoley, 1992). Such contact can be in the form of technical assistance (e.g., plan revision) or emotional and cognitive support (e.g., encouraging the consultee to take risks). For example, the consultant may engage in the functional outcome analysis (FOA) in order to evaluate and/or monitor interventions (Noell & Gresham, 1993) or provide support concerning an RTI initiative (Barnett et al., 2007). In collaboration, of course, both parties are responsible for some aspect of the implementation of the plan. As a result, they will provide the necessary support to one another during the implementation.

Some consultants monitor the consultee's intervention efforts through a series of brief interviews and/or observations of the consultee during the implementation process (Bergan & Kratochwill, 1990). Such contact allows consultants to gather data from the consultee concerning the effectiveness of the intervention; this data can range from a description of the consultee's and client's behavior during the intervention to measurements of changes in the client. A note of caution: During the implementation phase, the consultant must exercise care to prevent excessive dependency in some consultees who may inadvertently rely too heavily on the consultant's expertise (French & Bell, 1999). For example, a school counselor consulting with a teacher might judiciously use questions to stimulate the teacher to take more responsibility for implementing the plan. In another example, a consultant would suggest that the consultee take partial responsibility for assessing treatment integrity. As a final

example, in collaboration, the monitoring is typically accomplished through team meeting in which team members report on their progress and receive input from the others.

There are some principles of effective implementation that I have extracted from the work of Egan (2010) with counseling clients and I have applied them to consultation and collaboration:

- develop a strong commitment to specific interventions to accomplish goals
- ensure that consultees don't jump on the first implementation thought of
- assist consultees who are subject to inertia
- engage in force-field analysis
- identify benefits for persisting with the intervention

Treatment Integrity

Choosing a proper intervention and formulating an effective plan do not guarantee successful implementation. Consultees may not carry out a carefully designed plan effectively (Noell et al., 2005; Sheridan et al., 2009, 2012; Wilkinson, 2006) and, in fact, many don't. An improperly implemented intervention, even though it has empirical support, can damage the consultation process. Treatment integrity has typically been presumed but not assessed (Hagermoser Sanetti & Kratochwill, 2009). Consequently, treatment integrity is important in drawing conclusions about the intervention's success (Hagermoser Sanetti & Kratochwill, 2009). Consultation intervention can go awry for many reasons, thus negatively impacting treatment integrity (Sheridan et al., 2009):

- they are implemented in a naturalistic environment, not controlled settings
- real-life events (e.g., how the consultee feels at the time implementation) can comprise the intervention's integrity
- consultees are typically not highly trained in interventions

- ecological variables can impact the intervention for better or worse
- in behavioral interventions, the high level of specificity makes it a challenge to develop adequate assessment tools to assess the intervention's integrity

Treatment integrity, sometimes referred to as treatment fidelity, in its simplest form refers to the degree to which the intervention is implemented as intended (Ruby, Crosby-Cooper, & Vanderwood, 2011; Wesley et al., 2010; Wilkinson, 2006). There is a great deal of confusion in the literature regarding defining treatment integrity as it is a complex variable. Hagermoser Sanetti and Kratochwill (2009) define treatment integrity as "… the extent to which essential intervention components are delivered in a comprehensive and consistent manner by an interventionist trained to deliver the intervention" (p. 448). Treatment integrity has received increasing attention in the literature (Hagermoser Sanetti & Kratochwill, 2009, 2011; McLeod, Southam-Gerow, & Weisz, 2009) and is critical to evidence-based practice and RTI initiatives (Schulte, Easton, & Parker, 2009).

In consultation, treatment integrity has two dimensions (Noell, 2008). The first dimension focuses on how effectively the consultee carries out the intervention. This has been the traditional focus on treatment integrity in consultation. The second dimension, which is receiving increased attention in the literature, is consultation procedural integrity (CPI) referring to how well the consultant carries out consultation process in which the intervention is embedded (Hagermoser Sanetti & Fallon, 2011; Schulte et al., 2009). For example, assessment looks at how well the consultant supports the consultee's implementation (Wesley et al., 2010). Both dimensions can be affected by contextual variables such as cultural diversity (Wesley et al., 2010).

High levels of treatment integrity strengthen the cause and effect relationship between the intervention and evaluated outcomes (McKenna, Rosenfield, & Gravois, 2009). It is important to assess treatment integrity effectively (Sheridan et al., 2009). A variety of techniques are available from questionnaires and observation to the more rigorous single case design (Barnett, Hawkins, R., & Lentz, 2011). The method selected is a function of the nature of the decisions to be made as a result of the intervention. An example of a high-risk decision would entail classification for special education, whereas an example of a low-risk one would involve a morale boosting program in an organization.

Effectively implemented interventions are used with the proper frequency, used consistently, and used with sufficient intensity (Riley-Tillman & Chafouleas, 2003). If the intervention is a program, for example, then many issues can arise in the implementation (Larson & Samdal, 2007). Finally, most interventions are adapted to their cultural and/or organizational context when they are implemented (Hagermoser Sanetti & Kratochwill, 2009). As a result, treatment integrity is often looked at in terms of what adaptations need to be made to increase the probability of successful outcomes.

In recent years, there has been a significant amount of research conducted on treatment integrity (see, e.g., Noell, 2008; Sheridan et al., 2009). One reason for the lack of implementing interventions as designed is the cost incurred by the consultees during the phase of implementation (Noell & Gresham, 1993). There are two types of costs in implementing interventions: objective (e.g., time) and subjective (e.g., inconvenience). So, too, there are two types of benefits: objective (e.g., a change in the client system's behavior) and subjective (e.g., a sense of accomplishment).

Interventions that are complex and time consuming are particularly at-risk. To help reduce this cost, consultants can train and coach consultees to use interventions (Hagermoser Sanetti & Kratochwill, 2009; Noell & Witt, 1998; Roach, Kratochwill, & Frank, 2009) and follow up with performance-based feedback on intervention implementation (Hagermoser Sanetti & Kratochwill, 2009; Noell et al., 2005; Roach et al., 2009). Assessing intervention costs allows consultants to help consultees determine the conditions under which interventions are implemented and maintained with minimal adverse by-products so that the benefits outweigh the costs (Gresham & Noell, 1993).

One method of assessing the cost-benefit ratio for interventions is *functional outcome analysis* (FOA) (Gresham & Noell, 1993). In short, FOA determines the amount of effort required to accomplish a desired outcome, and answers the question: "How much does it cost to get the desired change in the client system?" Recently, methods for assessing treatment integrity have received attention. Interviews, observation and monitoring of implementation, training in the intervention, and use of scripted intervention plans can assess treatment integrity (Hagermoser Sanetti & Kratochwill, 2009, 2011; Upah, 2008). Hagermoser Sanetti and Kratochwill (2011), for example, found that consultees were quite accurate when relating their treatment integrity by using a daily rating system that assessed the integrity of their treatment on a step-by-step basis.

Treatment integrity is likely enhanced by choosing high-probability interventions and promoting correct implementation. High-probability interventions are those that focus on key behaviors, are empirically supported, and are acceptable to the consultee. Interventions should be relatively easy to implement, be positive, perceived to be effective, and fit easily into the consultee's routine (Riley-Tillman & Chafouleas, 2003). Promotion of correct implementation of interventions involves things such as the social influence of the consultant on the consultee (Wilson, Erchul, & Raven, 2008), treatment manuals and guided practice in monitoring of the implementation (Martens & Ardoin, 2002) as well performance feedback during follow-up (Codding & Smyth, 2008; Dufrene et al., 2012; Gueldner & Merrell, 2011; Hagermoser Sanetti & Kratochwill, 2009; Noell et al., 2005), and the addition of a treatment monitoring interview to the consultation process (Wilkinson, 2006). There is limited evidence that a collaborative approach to consultation, rather than an expert-driven approach, results in greater treatment integrity (Kelleher, Riley-Tillman, & Power,

2008). Perhaps the bottom line in promoting the practice of assessing treatment integrity is create the time to do it, secure administrative support in the organization for valuing it, and stressing to all stakeholders its importance (Hagermoser Sanetti & Kratochwill, 2009).

Collaborators and consultants are also involved in program implementation aimed at part of or an entire organization. Such implementation brings its own treatment integrity issues (Gueldner & Merrell, 2011; Henderson, MacKay, & Peterson-Badali, 2010; Wesley et al., 2010). Programs cannot be poorly implemented and expected to work (Durlak, 2009). When the intervention is an evidence-based program, for example, an antibullying program in a middle school, treatment integrity also involves issues related to adapting the program to the applied setting, in this case the cultural context of the school. Imagine the difference between implementing an evidence-based antibullying program in a rural elementary school versus a large urban high school in a low socioeconomic setting.

Social validity, an aspect of treatment integrity, refers to the notion that the parties involved agree to the value of the intervention (Gresham & Vanderwood, 2008). It involves the social significance of goals, the social acceptability of the procedures, and the social importance of effects (Gresham & Lopez, 1996). Consultees are more likely to follow through on an intervention if they see the goals of consultation as socially significant and worth the cost of meeting them.

Treatment acceptability refers to the concept that the parties involved believe that the intervention is in line with their value systems and their perceptions of what it takes to help the client system. Treatment acceptability basically denotes the relative perceived effectiveness, feasibility, and comfort level of the consultee relative to the implementation (Easton & Erchul, 2011). Assessing treatment acceptability in consultees at the outset of the intervention and during its implementation is essential to the successful implementation of an intervention (Meyers et al., 2008; Roach et al., 2009; Yetter, 2010). If consultees view the intervention and the plan to implement it as acceptable, then they are more likely to be willing to self-monitor or be monitored by the consultant (Easton & Erchul, 2011; Erhardt, Barnett, Lentz, Stollar, & Reifin, 1996). They are also more likely to proceed with the implementation as planned and increase the likelihood of accomplishing treatment integrity (Noell et al., 2005; Schulte et al., 2009; Tysinger, Tysinger, & Diamanduros, 2009; Yetter, 2010). But even though a treatment is highly acceptable to a consultee, other factors such as the amount of time necessary to implement the treatment (Briesch & Chafouleas, 2009); and how (e.g., self-report), when (e.g., weekly), and by whom (e.g., school-based consultant) the implementation will be monitored need to be considered (Easton & Erchul, 2011). When dealing with large numbers of people in organizational consultation or on teams, consultants will want to assure "group treatment acceptability" by ensuring that organization members see the intervention as: (1) existing within the parameters of their roles, and (2) tailored to the specific needs of the organization (Truscott, Cosgrove, Meyers, & Eidle-Barkman, 2000; Yetter, 2010). Not all interventions developed by the consultant and consultee are viewed as equally acceptable. Acceptable interventions usually are simple, time effective, and free of jargon; they also tend to deal with a severe situation, and involve something that the consultee is knowledgeable about (Gresham & Lopez, 1996). Questionnaires are typically used to assess treatment acceptability. More recently, focus groups, observation, and other qualitative measures have been used (Finn & Sladeczek, 2001) as well as self-report measures determined by the consultee (Easton & Erchul, 2011). It is important to remember that treatment acceptability is quite distinct from treatment integrity (McNamara, Rasheed, & Delamatre, 2008). For an interesting study regarding treatment acceptability, consult Cowan and Sheridan (2003).

Social importance refers to the consultees' view that the intended changes are important to long-term functioning of the client system (Gresham, 2011). The quantity and quality of changes in the client system determine to a large extent the social importance of the intervention. Consultees are more likely to follow through with plans when they view the intervention as making significant differences in the life of the client system.

Two Brief Examples of Implementing the Plan in Consultation

Example 1. Lyhne is an external consultant whose consultee is the manager of a small oil refinery. The consultee was particularly interested in publically supporting a recently implemented antibullying program at the refinery. A plan was established for having the manager be more present to employees while sending messages about the importance of a civil workplace environment for all members of the organization. The manager became a "cheerleader" regarding bullying/mobbing prevention in particular and for enhancing the positive climate of the refinery in general. The manager started to become more visible and holding forums with each department to update employees to events effecting the organization as well as noting the importance to the organization and its employees of everyone getting along and working together. The manager began to send monthly emails to employees that cited the importance of strong team work and civility among the refinery's members. Lyhne and the manager developed a treatment integrity checklist that the manager would complete at intervals during the implementation period.

Example 2. Mary, a school consultant, is assisting Louise, a third-grade teacher, in helping a student diagnosed as having test-taking anxiety. The plan they have devised together involves a cognitive behavioral approach that focuses on the child's "self-talk." The teacher instructs the child in a variation of stress inoculation training. As the child is applying this strategy during an exam, he starts saying aloud the coping phrases that were to be said silently. Mary, who had been monitoring Louise's implementation of the plan, assists Louise in revising the procedures for instructing the child in stress inoculation training procedures. At the same time, Mary is quite cautious in avoiding the creation of any dependency on her by Louise.

A Brief Example of Implementing the Plan in Collaboration

Mary, a school counselor, and Louise, a third-grade teacher, are collaborating together to help a student diagnosed as having test-taking anxiety. The plan they have devised together involves a cognitive behavioral approach that focuses on the child's "self-talk." The teacher instructs the child in a variation of stress inoculation training. As the child is applying this strategy during an exam, he starts saying aloud the coping phrases that were to be said silently. Mary provides individual counseling to the child in terms of stress management procedures the child can use. Mary, who had been monitoring Louise's implementation of the plan, assists Louise in revising the procedures for instructing the child in stress inoculation training procedures. At the same time, Louise assists Mary in understanding the various strategies that might help Mary's work with this particular child.

PHASE FOUR: EVALUATING THE PLAN

After the plan has been implemented, it must also be evaluated. In this phase, the following questions are asked: "Was the plan implemented as intended?" and "To what degree were the plan's goals met?" Evaluating the plan is a part of a larger evaluation effort that assesses the effectiveness of the entire consultation process, which is covered in Chapter 7. As it relates to the plan implementation, *evaluation* refers to the collection of data/information about the implementation to determine its effectiveness in meeting the specified goals (Upah, 2008). Both the plan itself and how it was carried out need to be evaluated (Hagermoser Sanetti & Fallon, 2011). The goal of plan evaluation is to review data collected during implementation to determine the extent to which the client system had met the goals of the intervention, the overall effectiveness of the intervention, and the acceptability of the intervention to the consultee. If the

evaluation suggests that the plan has been successfully implemented to an appropriate degree, the consultation proceeds to the disengagement phase. If the analysis finds that the plan was not successfully implemented to the degree sought, the consultant and consultee determine the source of the implementation challenges. Based upon this determination, the consultation relationship will revert back to a previous phase, for example, defining the problem, and then proceed from there.

Evaluation of the plan within consultation frequently involves two foci: implementation evaluation and outcome evaluation. In many cases, evaluation of these processes is not conducted as part of consultation (Hagermoser Sanetti & Fallon, 2011; Newell, 2010a). First, implementation evaluation determines whether the implementation occurred as originally planned, what problems and/or variations were encountered in the implementation, and how these problems/variations affected the outcomes (Hagermoser Sanetti & Fallon, 2011). You will remember in the discussion of the third phase of this stage—the actual implementation of the plan—that we discussed such items as tactics and unforeseen glitches that might occur, as well as treatment integrity. Implementation evaluation reviews these items in case the consultant and the consultee choose to develop alternative plans and strategies.

Second, outcome evaluation determines whether, and the degree to which, the goals of the plan have been achieved in terms of changes in the client system. Questions to answer include: "To what degree was the plan successfully implemented as indicated by changes in the client system?", "What are the next steps that need to be taken to achieve the target behaviors of the client system?", and "How can the glitches that occurred be eliminated?" If the plan did not meet its goals for the behavior of the client system, the evaluation may shed some light on reasons why. In this case, the consultant and consultee can revisit the problem and determine the subsequent phases that need to be repeated in the problem-solving process.

Evaluation of the plan is frequently considered to be out of the realm of expertise of the typical consultant and consultee. However, consultants are increasingly being held accountable for the quality of their services. They must at least be able to evaluate their own interventions, and they should also assist in evaluating their consultees' plans. This can be accomplished by determining ahead of time what needs to be measured and how, what resources are available to assist with evaluation, and what decisions will be made based on the evaluation (Hagermoser Sanetti & Fallon, 2011).

There are an adequate number of well-researched methods to measure the costs and benefits, either objective or subjective, of interventions (Barnett et al., 2007). Further, the purpose of the intervention can impact how rigorous the evaluation needs to be (Barnett et al., 2011). Whereas an RTI process that determines possible special education classification requires rigorous evaluation, the evaluation of intervention with therapist's client may well need to be less rigorous because the stakes are not as high. In any case, EBIs are often a preferred starting point as consultants and consultees can review related studies prior to selecting an intervention. Research results also suggest possible evaluation methods for the intervention at hand.

Outcomes can be measured in terms of what happened to the client or client system as a result of some plan. The consultant and consultee have a variety of instruments and techniques available for this purpose, but basically there are three ways to evaluate a plan's outcome: individualized goal attainment measures, standardized outcome assessment devices, and consumer satisfaction surveys.

Individualized goal attainment measures are "techniques whereby the efficacy of services is measured according to criteria that have been specifically tailored to the needs, capacities, and aspirations of the person(s) receiving services" (Anderson, Frieden, & Murphy, 1977, p. 293).

One example is concrete goal setting used with goal-oriented progress notes. Ideally, the consultant and consultee have already performed concrete goal setting during the diagnosis stage of consultation. Plan evaluation then becomes a simple procedure of determining the degree to which each goal was accomplished. For example, if the plan called for the client to reduce the number of cigarettes smoked from 40 to 6 a day, then it is relatively easy to monitor the degree to which this goal is being met.

Measurement of individualized goal attainment is often accomplished through goal attainment scaling (GAS) (Kirst-Ashman & Hull, 2012; Sladeczek, Elliott, Kratochwill, Robertson-Mjaanes, & Stoiber, 2001). In this technique, the dimensions representing desired changes in client behavior are scaled (e.g., from 1 = minimally attained to 5 = totally attained), expected levels of attainment are set, and scores are determined at the end of the plan's implementation. As Sladeczek and others (2001) note: GAS "involves (a) the selection of the target behavior … (b) an objective description of the desired intervention outcome, and the development of three to five descriptions of the target behavior … that increasingly approximate the desired outcome" (p. 46). These authors note that GAS is individualized, personalized, inexpensive, and nonintrusive. The approach is very flexible and is easy for stakeholders to understand (Kirst-Ashman & Hull, 2012).

Standardized outcome assessment devices measure the accomplishment of goals through some norm- or criterion-referenced device. Checklists and ratings scales are typically used in consultation. For example, if a consultee assessed a client's career maturity on a standardized instrument and later retested the client on the same measure, the client's progress toward the goal of increased career maturity could be ascertained by the differences between the scores. Be aware that there are two issues in considering standardized measures. First, the measures selected should be appropriate for use with the client system and for clinical purposes. Second, the measures should be sensitive enough to measure the desired changes in the client system.

Consumer satisfaction surveys attempt to assess the opinions and attitudes of the client or client system regarding the services and effects of the plan provided to them. These data, typically gathered through an interview or questionnaire, can be, without adequate precaution, quite subjective and of questionable validity if used as the only indicator of the plan's success. Consumer satisfaction surveys also can be helpful in determining the consultee's satisfaction with the specific of the consultation plan that was implemented (Kirst-Ashman & Hull, 2012).

For a more in-depth and step-by-step discussion of evaluation methods in consultation, see the section entitled "Evaluating the Consultation Process" in Chapter 7.

Two Brief Examples of Evaluating the Plan

Example 1. Yvonne, a community projects consultant, is working with Ashley, the head of an Upward Bound program, concerning the implementation of personal counseling to the program's teenage participants. Their efforts over several sessions have given birth to and implemented a personal counseling program. They are now at the stage of evaluating its success. Because they conducted ongoing evaluations of the program, Yvonne and Ashley have a sense of its success. The goal attainment measures they developed for each of the program's 20 participants show that the average participant benefited from the program to a level of 4.1 on a 5-point scale. On a standardized problem checklist, the students also reported fewer concerns after counseling. Student satisfaction surveys showed that they preferred group counseling over individual counseling, although the latter was also of benefit.

Example 2. Mortia, a school-based consultant, has been working with a teacher-consultee, Leigh, with a student in Leigh's classroom. The goals were to decrease off-task behavior to three incidences per week in math and to increase Leigh's ratings of the student's group project skills to three (out of five) during the next grading period (six weeks). Stickers were given intermittently by the teacher for on-task behaviors during math class, and the teacher used praise for specific positive group behaviors (e.g., taking turns, contributing pertinent ideas) demonstrated by the student. The teacher then filled out the rating scale scoring the student's positive group skills on a weekly basis. Measures are taken along the way to ensure treatment feasibility and treatment integrity as well as to modify plan if necessary.

At the end of the sixth week, the plan was evaluated for a final time with the result that the student had met both goals. The interventions were stopped and measures on the student behaviors taken again after three weeks.

MULTICULTURAL ASPECTS RELATED TO IMPLEMENTATION

Cultural differences can influence the perception of how interventions are selected and implemented. For example, interventions focusing on the use of groups may be preferred and the time required for implementing an intervention may not be highly valued by some cultural groups. The cultural views and expectations of the parties involved should be considered when selecting and planning for an intervention (Jackson & Hayes, 1993; Lopez & Truesdell, 2007) as well as modifying one (Ingraham, 2000, 2003, 2007, 2008), as these might well affect how the intervention is perceived and implemented. Also, assessment devices need to be culturally fair and appropriate for the setting in which they are used. Collaborators will want to make sure that the team doesn't attempt to divvy out the responsibility for various aspects to individuals, but rather they will want to keep more of a team approach to implementation.

When a plan is being formulated, differences in opinion about the importance or necessity of a time frame for the plan's implementation can exist. In addition, people with some cultural backgrounds will prefer collaboration to consultation based on their views of interdependence.

In terms of evaluation of the plan, input from consultees or fellow collaborators is critical so that the perspectives of different cultures are considered. People from high-context cultures, for example, may approach evaluation of the plan in a quite different manner, relying more on a constructivist model. For example, efficiency—a must in a plan in a traditional low-context culture—may not be of particular interest to a person from a high-context culture.

CASE 6.1   Implementation for School Consultants

Barbara, a human service professional working in a large urban secondary school, is consulting with Shirley, who is the school's chief administrator. Both have spent time in the business world prior to entering education and are familiar with "total quality management" (TQM) programs.

Shirley is very interested in implementing quality management concepts throughout the school. At this point in the consultation, they are ready to choose from several goals and a long list of possible interventions to get the program into place.

To obtain the support of the entire staff, Barbara and Shirley have thought of numerous ways to help them freely buy into learning and utilizing TQM concepts. Ideas ranged from having the district superintendent make an announcement that the school would implement the program to having a series of departmental meetings led by heads in which teachers as well as staff from other departments could freely discuss the proposal.

To develop school-wide ownership of the program, Barbara and Shirley tested each intervention using decision consultation questions to assess how the intervention would fit the environment of the school, the kinds of resources and personnel necessary to do an adequate implementation, and the glitches that might occur if the intervention was put into place.

They decided that a grassroots approach to getting the program accepted is probably the best plan since the school district had a history of imposing new programs on schools without their input. Thus, how they attempted to get the program accepted was the most important step. First they decided that Shirley would hold a school-wide faculty meeting to present the program as a possibility along with her personal

recommendation as chief administrator. However, she would also make it clear that she was not going to force the program on the school. She would discuss her rationale for wanting the program, what it would do for the school, and also what it would cost in terms of staff behavior.

Department heads would then be taken on a one-day retreat during which the program would be discussed and debated. The heads would then use regularly scheduled departmental meetings to discuss and debate the program with staff. Shirley would hold another regular faculty meeting dedicated to the TQM idea and have open discussions about it.

Shirley put the plan into action and frequently used Barbara as a resource. She bounced ideas off Barbara concerning ways to approach certain resistant department heads. After the plan was implemented, Shirley conducted an anonymous survey of the staff's views of the program and how they had been approached about it. The survey's results were very positive, and Barbara and Shirley took the next step toward implementing the program.

Commentary

Decision consultation is an excellent method for selecting an intervention given the context in which it is to be implemented. This case shows, through decision consultation, how the history of prior program implementation in the school affected what intervention was selected and how that intervention was implemented. Note also the importance of consultants "staying online" while the consultee implements the intervention.

Similarly, whether or not the plan was executed in a timely fashion may not be nearly as relevant as the social impact the plan will have. Even the preferred model of evaluation itself may be framed in a social consensus, constructivist model rather than the traditional positivist, empirical model so frequently employed in consultation and collaboration.

SUMMARY

The implementation stage of consultation consists of choosing an intervention, formulating a plan, implementing the plan, and evaluating the plan. In this stage, the consultant provides the consultee with practical assistance to meet the goals set to help the client or client system.

C A S E   6.2   Implementation for Community Consultants

Roy is a mental health consultant who has been working with Robbie, a counselor for a residential summer program for academically gifted students at a small state university. Robbie is working on his master's degree in counseling at the university. During their second session, Roy and Robbie have gotten to the point of generating several possible interventions for helping Zachary, one of the program's students.

Zachary has been having a series of interpersonal conflicts with many of the other academically gifted students in the program. It appears that he offends his peers by playing the game "Who's most gifted?" During their third session, Roy helps Robbie select an intervention to help Zachary. Through use of decision consultation, they choose individual counseling with Zachary as the best approach. Robbie has the counseling skills, and he and Zachary have a good working relationship already established. Robbie's beliefs about individual counseling seem congruent with making it the method used and Zachary's needs for some skills in dealing with his peers would be accomplished by this method. Robbie realizes that Zachary would probably benefit most from being in a counseling group with his peers but strongly believes that Zachary is not ready to be in such a group. Robbie designates the group as a possible contingency plan in case the individual counseling relationship falls through.

In formulating a plan, Roy and Robbie decide that both supportive and behavioral approaches are needed to help Zachary. A supportive approach would help him to not feel singled out or considered sick in some way, while the behavioral approach could help him quickly learn some interpersonal skills to enjoy and benefit from the summer program. Roy and Robbie determine that the best way to evaluate the success of counseling will be the self-report of Zachary as well as Robbie's observations of Zachary and his peers during the next three weeks of the program.

In deciding to be tactful, yet honest, with Zachary, Robbie invites him to become involved in counseling.

Robbie hopes to get Zachary excited about their project in which Zachary can design his own methods for relating more effectively to his peers.

As they conduct a brief force-field analysis on the plan, the only loose end that emerges is the possible rejection of Zachary by his peers in spite of any constructive changes he might make. Roy helps Robbie choose an initial target group of Zachary's peers for him to try his new skills with first. The target group will be students with whom Zachary has had no known conflicts.

After success with these students, Robbie could help Zachary target those students with whom he has had some difficulties. Robbie then implements the plan with Zachary. Robbie consults with Roy over the next two weeks about behavioral rehearsal procedures and methods of giving specific feedback. As the summer program ended, Robbie notices Zachary being more positive about his peers and less in need of being the best at everything.

Zachary's peers seem to make less of a big deal about Zachary to the degree that Zachary made less of a big deal about himself. They accept him as one of them.

Commentary

The development of a contingency plan is an important part of the planning process. Without a contingency plan, consultees are left in a "sink or swim" predicament if the primary plan falls through. Force-field analysis teases out possible glitches in a plan and enables the consultant and consultee to better align the plan with its goals. Force-field analysis procedures enabled Robbie and Roy to refine their plan to accommodate Zachary's situation. Notice also the importance of Robbie's staying in touch with Roy during Roy's work with Zachary in terms of behavioral rehearsal.

A vast number of interventions are available for use in plans. Interventions can be categorized in a variety of ways, but classification by target level is the most common. Decision consultation is an effective method for selecting an appropriate intervention. As a consultant, your role in interventions can range from that of facilitator to that of trainer/educator. Make sure that you have the expertise in a variety of interventions, while keeping abreast of the development of those that are evidence-based and multiculturally sensitive. Once the appropriate intervention or interventions are chosen, consultants help consultees formulate and choose an appropriate plan.

During plan implementation, the consultant provides the consultee with tactical assistance and also monitors his or her procedures. Treatment integrity is also taken into consideration and monitored.

After the plan has been implemented, evaluation is performed to assess the degree to which it was effective in realizing its goals in terms of changes in the client system's behavior. If the plan is considered to have worked satisfactorily, consultation moves to its next stage—disengagement. If not, then the consultant and consultee analyze the data and determine the subsequent phases that need to be repeated in the problem-solving process.

As in entry and diagnosis, the research on the implementation stage is quite limited. Research on developing a plan suggests that consultees who feel empowered by the consultant and that they can have a positive impact regarding plan implementation are more willing to take responsibility for the planning process, as opposed to those who feel their efforts may have no impact.

A final note on the implementation stage: Many consultants report that they do not engage in evaluation of the plan; when they do, consultee verbal reports about the client system are more about the source of the evaluation rather than observations of actual client system behavior (Bramlett et al., 2002). Evaluation of the plan also creates a mechanism for feedback to researchers on the application of ESI (Stoiber & Kratochwill, 2000a). It is important to remember that evaluation is essential to determine the effects of consultation and that it should be integral to your practice.

SUGGESTIONS FOR EFFECTIVE PRACTICE

- Ensure that consultees and fellow collaborators have the skills and an acceptant attitude toward the interventions being considered.

- Focus on evidence-based and multiculturally sensitive interventions.

- Have a plan that is the result of the input of all stakeholders.

- Have a monitoring mechanism in place that will examine the progress the plan is making as well as its treatment integrity.

- Avoid the temptation to disregard evaluation of the plan.

QUESTIONS FOR REFLECTION

1. What is unique about the consultant's behavior during the implementation stage?

2. How would you as a consultant help a consultee choose an appropriate intervention that is both evidence-based and multiculturally sensitive?

3. Look over the interventions discussed in this chapter. How many of them could be used at more than one level?

4. Which of the interventions for individuals have the most danger of turning from consultation into counseling or psychotherapy? Why?

5. Which of the interventions described in this chapter could be most effectively implemented by a group of consultants rather than by one alone? Why?

6. What are some ways in which consultants can learn new interventions?

7. Under what circumstances would you monitor a consultee's implementation of a plan to ensure treatment integrity?

8. What kinds of tactical assistance might most consultees require during plan implementation?

9. What are the basic differences between plan evaluation and evaluation of the process of consultation?

10. What should the consultant and consultee do if the evaluation of the plan indicates that little success in meeting the plan's goal was achieved?

SUGGESTED SUPPLEMENTARY READINGS

French, W. L., & Bell, C. H., Jr. (1999). *Organization development: Behavior science interventions for organization improvement* (6th ed.). Englewood Cliffs, NJ: Prentice-Hall. This text provides an interesting and practical overview of various interventions available to consultants. Of particular interest is the authors' discussion of the various ways in which interventions can be categorized. This book has become more or less a classic for those who work as organizational consultants. Still, this book has a tremendous amount of information that consultants in any setting will find invaluable.

The What Works Clearinghouse (WWC): http://ies.ed .gov/ncee/wwc/.

This website is an excellent resource for information about evidence-based best practices on a variety of education topics such as student behavior and academic achievement. The site is sponsored by the U.S. Department of Education's Institute of Education Sciences.

http://www.campbellcollaboration.org/

The Campbell Collaboration (C2) helps people make well-informed decisions by preparing, maintaining, and disseminating systematic reviews in education, crime and justice, and social welfare. The Campbell Collaboration is an international research network that produces systematic reviews of the effects of social interventions. Campbell is based on voluntary cooperation among researchers of a variety of backgrounds. Campbell's strategic and policy-making body is its steering group. A number of coordinating groups are responsible for the production, scientific merit, and relevance of our systematic reviews.

7

✳

Disengagement Stage

If the entry stage is characterized by the question "Hello, what would you like to change?," then the disengagement stage is characterized by the question "What do we need to take care of before we say goodbye?" In effect, the disengagement stage winds down what was started up in the entry stage. Disengagement refers to the ending of the consultation or collaboration relationship.

The purpose of this chapter is to discuss and explore the disengagement stage, during which the consultant and consultee evaluate the consultation process, make plans for maintaining the effects of consultation after the process is over, go through a period of reduced contact, make provisions for follow-up, and terminate the consultation process itself. Figure 7.1 illustrates the phases of disengagement.

As you are reading the chapter, here are some questions to consider:

1. When does the process of disengagement really begin?
2. What issues need to be taken into consideration during postconsultation planning?
3. What are the basic differences between evaluating the process of consultation and evaluating the plan in the implementation stage?
4. How would you arrange for follow-up with a consultee organization?
5. What effect does the length of time the consultant has spent with the consultee or organization have on what the consultant should do during the disengagement stage?

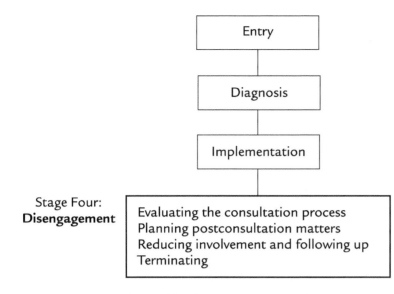

FIGURE 7.1 Phases of the disengagement stage

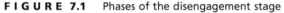

AN EXAMPLE OF DISENGAGEMENT AT THE ORGANIZATION CLIENT-SYSTEM LEVEL

Haley is an external consultant working with selected team of stakeholders to implement a school resiliency program. A multitiered program has been implemented. Evaluation data demonstrate that the goals of the program for students with issues, students at risk, and the student body as whole were adequately met. Evaluation of the consultation process itself involved surveys and interviews with selected stakeholders that included levels of satisfaction with the program as well as opinions about suggested program modifications. The data were then analyzed against a database containing the same surveys and interview results from similar schools from across the nation. The data suggest that the program is fairly successful when compared to national averages. Postconsultation planning involved the team considering the feasibility of suggested program modifications, continued monitoring of program data, and the use of Haley in

follow-up with the team. Haley provided a consultation session to the implementation team every three months for one year for the purpose of adjusting the existing program and considering possible program modifications the team was considering. At the end of the follow-up year, Haley and the team agreed to terminate consultation as the program's evaluation data continued to be positive.

AN EXAMPLE OF DISENGAGEMENT AT THE INDIVIDUAL CLIENT-SYSTEM LEVEL

You have worked very closely with a certain consultee on one of the consultee's cases. When you enter the disengagement stage, you first evaluate the consultation process. The evaluation showed that the consultee's satisfaction with the consultant, the consultation process, and its outcomes was high. The evaluation data were collected by the consultant by interviewing the consultee as well as having the consultee complete a consultation evaluation checklist developed by the consultant. Postconsultation planning related to modifying the treatment plan and the agreement for one more consultation session to identify methods the consultee could use to help the client maintain the gains made in counseling. After that final session, the consultant and consultee agreed to periodic follow-up by the consultant. They mutually agreed that the goals of consultation had been met and terminated the relationship.

Once the consultant and consultee have evaluated the plan, they must decide whether to continue or discontinue consultation. The length and complexity of the consultation or collaboration process can complicate this decision (Dougherty, Tack, Fullam, & Hammer, 1996). The decision to end consultation occurs when the consultant and consultee agree that the consultation process has adequately met the goals that were set for the client system. On the other hand, the decision to continue with consultation most often results from an evaluation with subsequent analysis that indicates that the goal was not met satisfactorily (Brack, Jones, Smith, White, & Brack, 1993). The consultant and consultee usually return to the end of the diagnostic stage and generate other possible interventions; occasionally, they may need to redefine the problem. In some other cases, consultation may start over because the consultee has an additional work-related concern about which consultation is desired. In these cases, the consultation process typically reverts to the entry stage.

Consider the following situation: You are a consultant who for two years has been working with a human service organization for an average of four hours a week. You have worked with several individual consultees, have done a lot of team building and organizational-level interventions, and have had your own office space and clerical assistance. Leaving would not be as simple as packing your briefcase and walking out the door. What would you need to accomplish before you left? To whom would you say goodbye? How would you help the system plan to maintain the benefits of consultation after you have gone? How would

you evaluate the process of consultation? What arrangements for follow-up would you make?

PHASE ONE: EVALUATING THE CONSULTATION PROCESS

The Role of Evaluation

As it relates to consultation, evaluation might be defined as the systematic collection of information about the activities and outcomes of consultation for the purpose of making judgments and decisions about how consultation is proceeding and/or the effects it is having (Patton, 1986). Evaluation involves some form of measurement and is helpful to understand if the goals of consultation have been met and if the consultee is more likely to be effective with similar cases in the future (Knotek, 2004). The idea is to determine what is to be measured and how. Then measure it. Then interpret the results in light of the goals that were set.

Lack of agreement in the field on definitions of consultation and collaboration make accurate evaluation difficult (Pryzwansky, 2003). Consultants may well need expertise in quantitative methods in order to document outcomes well and qualitative assessments methods in order to adequately take cultural variables into account (Rogers, 2000). In addition, consultants often do not do a good job of evaluating their services (Gibbons & Silberglitt, 2008; McLean, 2006). Conducting an effective evaluation can be difficult and time consuming. With that said, a properly performed evaluation can provide the consultant with a quality control device, a learning device, legal protection, and a marketing tool (Kelley, 1981).

When evaluating consultation or collaboration outcomes, the parties involved will want to evaluate both instrumental and expressive elements (Chowanec, 1993; O'Driscoll & Eubanks, 1992). *Instrumental performance* refers to how well the party providing assistance did in helping to solve the situation presented. *Expressive performance* refers to the people-side of the relationship and deals with the level of comfortability of the parties involved. The bottom line is this: To enhance their performance, consultants should consider evaluating not only what they did, but the way the consultee perceived their behavior.

Because the evaluation process is not always easy to perform, it is not unusual for consultants to consult others about how to evaluate both their services and the consultation process itself.

Still, consultants and consultees should realize that they do not need to be experts in evaluation or research to adequately perform the practical evaluations required in consultation. Whereas merely going through the motions of evaluation is professionally inexcusable, a simple, yet credible, evaluation can be very informative (Caplan & Caplan, 1993). Consultants need to be aware that at the opposite extreme, they can spend so much of their time evaluating the consultation process that its human side can get lost in the volume of information collected and interpreted. Basically, they need to identify what to measure and find a way to collect appropriate data in an evaluation (Gibbons & Silberglitt, 2008).

Pertinent evaluation information should be provided to the consultant, the consultee, administrators of the organization in which consultation has occurred, and (in some cases) the client. The consultant should take measures to see that the results of evaluation are not used in the following covert and inappropriate ways: for protection of an ineffective consultee or program, to avoid decision making, as a public relations tool, or for getting rid of an effective but unpopular consultee or program.

Consultants and consultees need two primary skills to perform evaluation effectively: the ability to identify the consequences of their actions, and the ability to compare results to some standard. Although these skills were identified in the context of counseling clients on skills they need to change their behavior effectively (Egan, 2010), they are certainly needed by the consultant and consultee as well.

Deciding who should conduct the consultation evaluation is difficult, and perhaps the best rule of thumb is: it depends. The consultant and consultee will usually make this decision during the contracting stage. In some cases, the consultant helps the consultee gather and make sense of the data; in other cases, the consultee gathers the data, and the consultant assists in its interpretation; in still other instances, someone other than the consultee (e.g., the organization's contact person) conducts some aspects of the evaluation. Some organizations even have special departments to evaluate services like consultation. So long as the people who perform the evaluation are qualified to do so and have no conflict of interest, it probably does not matter who conducts given aspects of it. Regardless of who performs it, consultants are responsible for arranging an evaluation of their services.

Frequently, consultation is evaluated only at the end of the process, but evaluation is an *ongoing* process that should be performed throughout the consultation process.

Three steps are common to all evaluation processes: formation of criteria, assessment of attainment of the criteria, and utilization of results.

Formation of criteria refers to the creation or designation of the criteria (frequently goals) that will be used to assess those aspects of consultation under evaluation (Anderson, Frieden, & Murphy, 1977). Decades ago, Lippitt (1969) noted that developing evaluation criteria is one of the most difficult problems facing consultants. Systematically assessing the degree to which criteria have been met involves determining what, how, and by whom information is to be gathered, as well as how it is to be analyzed. Utilization of results involves disseminating the results to appropriate parties, often for some form of decision making. For example, an organization might use the results of consultee satisfaction surveys to decide whether or not to retain a particular consultant.

Consultation is typically evaluated by examining pertinent data gathered from observations, questionnaires, surveys, interviews, and the organization's documents. The use of a multi-method approach to evaluation, which provides more than one perspective on the results obtained, may add information valuable in interpreting the data and can reduce response bias. The use of devices for gathering data is discussed in Chapter 5.

When evaluating consultation, it is appropriate to gather data from the client system, the consultee, the consultant, and other parties-at-interest. To make evaluation manageable, the consultant and consultee should determine during the formation of the contract which kinds of evaluative information should be gathered from which parties. Consultants may want to evaluate three general consultation topics: the plan that was carried out in the implementation stage, the overall effects of consultation and the consultant's behaviors, and the efficacy of certain stages and phases along the way. The decision concerning which topics to evaluate depends on the type of evaluation, the nature of the problem, and the level at which consultation occurs. For example, an organizational consultant might be interested in evaluating the impact of consultation on total organizational effectiveness, participants' attitudes toward the change process itself, or the efficacy of a specific intervention. It is very important that the consultant, consultee, and (if necessary) other parties-at-interest plan what is to be evaluated, how evaluation is to occur, and who is going to perform it and when. Such planning prevents evaluation procedures from becoming overwhelming.

The following questions provide a starting point for identifying the many things that can be evaluated at the end of consultation:

- To what degree has behavior in the client or client system changed in the desired direction?

- To what degree was the consultant able to enter the system psychologically?

- In what ways has the organization changed as a result of consultation?

- To what degree have the goals established in the contract been met?

- To what degree have established timetables been met?

- How successfully has a given intervention been carried out?

- How effectively has the consultant established an effective working relationship with the consultee?

- To what degree has consultation been worth the cost in time, effort, and money?

Specific items that can in some way be evaluated:

- consultee preference for given models of consultation

- initial planning of the consultation process

- quantity and quality of consultee reports about the work-related problem

- progress made relative to each consultation stage

- organizational variables that affect the consultant process

- consultant behaviors at each consultation stage

- consultee behaviors throughout the consultation process

- client behaviors throughout the consultation process

- interpersonal behaviors of the consultant and consultee

- consultee satisfaction with consultation

- the degree to which goals are being attained

- adequacy of each consultation contact

- institutionalization of change

Changes in behavior are looked for in the client or client system, but consultees can also be examined for such changes. For example, an evaluator could look for a reduction in the number of physically aggressive behaviors by a student (client) or an increase in the number of open-ended questions a consultee asks a client.

Cost effectiveness is a judgment call: Were the costs in the terms of time and resources needed for consultation worth the returns? Thus, the administrator of a human service agency might calculate how much time and resources it took to have a consultant help to reorganize the agency and compare those costs with the perceived benefits of the consultation. Attitudes and opinions about benefits of the consultation can range from indexes of consultee satisfaction with the consultant to views about the overall success of the consultation.

Consultation evaluation can be viewed throughout the consultation process, and/or it can be considered once it has run its course. Just as the consultant is continually entering the system, continually diagnosing, and continually intervening, so too should he or she be continually evaluating. The evaluation performed along the way by the consultant and consultee is referred to as *formative evaluation*. The question answered by formative evaluation is "Is consultation working?" (Upah, 2008). In other words, formative evaluation can be used as a method of monitoring (Kirst-Ashman & Hull, 2012). The process of consultation is evaluated without respect to the ultimate product. For example, a consultant and a consultee might use formative evaluation to investigate the degree of success of the diagnosis stage.

When the consultant and consultee evaluate the effects of the consultation process at its conclusion, such an evaluation is referred to as a *summative evaluation*. Its role is to determine the effects of consultation outcomes; it sums things up at the end of the process and evaluates the product. Summative evaluation assesses impact (Kirst-Ashman & Hull, 2012). For example, the consultant and consultee might decide to assess a training program's effect on the participants' morale. Whether the evaluation is formative or summative, consultants will want to realize that there are real-world obstacles like time limitations that can make the process challenging (Newell, 2010a).

Formative Evaluation

One of the best ways to conduct formative evaluation in consultation is to perform evaluations at the end of each phase (Curtis, Castillo, & Cohen, 2008). Such evaluations will assist the consultant and consultee in determining whether to stick to the current course of consultation or to modify the process (Gibbons & Silberglitt, 2008). Frequent formative evaluation has been linked to consultation success (Noell & Witt, 1998). Formative evaluation allows for feedback along the way on processes and outcomes (Egan, 2010). Evaluation can be formal (e.g., using written surveys or performing observations and monitoring on some combination of consultant, consultee, and client behaviors) or informal (e.g., a discussion between the consultant and the consultee or other parties-at-interest concerning how a given phase has progressed).

Human service professionals are familiar with and traditionally positive toward the use of surveys. Thus, consultants may want to develop questionnaires and surveys related to each of the phases of the consultation process. Sample evaluation questions for the phases of each stage of the consultation process are provided later in this chapter. These questions can be helpful in developing a frame of reference, whether evaluation is conducted by surveys, observations, interviews, or the examination of records.

Formative Evaluation Across the Consultation Process.   Certain useful questions can be asked in the various stages of consultation; the answers obtained are helpful in evaluating each stage to make decisions concerning the progress and subsequent direction of consultation.

The following questions are adapted from an evaluation form developed by Parsons and Meyers (1984):

- How many contacts have been made with the consultee?
- What is the average length of the contacts?
- What is the average length of time between contacts?
- What progress has been made so far?
- What issues have come up that still need to be handled?
- Who needs to be apprised of what has been done so far?
- What does the consultee think about what has happened to date?
- To what degree is the consultee satisfied about what has happened?
- What does the consultee think about the consultant's style?

- What details need to be worked out?
- What does the consultant think about what has happened so far?
- To what degree is the consultant satisfied with what has happened?
- What are the consultant's impressions of the consultee?
- Are there any changes needed in the way the consultation is being conducted?

As noted earlier, it is useful for consultants to evaluate their effectiveness at the end of each phase of the consultation process. In the following section, I provide questions that may be asked during each phase of the entry stage. Consultants can convert these questions into surveys or checklists, use them for directing observations, or develop them as a basis for interviewing. Figure 7.2 is an example of a survey for use in the formative evaluation of the exploration of organizational needs, whereas Figure 7.3 is a sample checklist for evaluating the contracting phase of the entry stage. The following example of formative evaluation of the entry process can easily be extended to each of the other stages; the consultant simply evaluates each phase of the current stage before moving on to the next stage.

Directions: Please rate each item according to the five-point scale listed by circling the number that most accurately expresses your opinion on the following statements:

5 = strongly agree	2 = disagree
4 = agree	1 = strongly disagree
3 = undecided	

1. The level of congruency between the consultant's abilities and the consultee system's needs was adequately determined.

    5   4   3   2   1

2. The amount of resources the organization was willing to commit to consultation was adequately defined.

    5   4   3   2   1

3. The identification and clarification of the need for change was adequately accomplished.

    5   4   3   2   1

4. The organization's readiness for change was adequately explored and defined.

    5   4   3   2   1

5. The potential of the parties involved for working together was adequately explored.

    5   4   3   2   1

6. Role expectations for those involved were made clear.

    5   4   3   2   1

7. The roles of the consultee and client system were adequately defined.

    5   4   3   2   1

FIGURE 7.2   Sample survey for evaluating the exploration of organizational needs

Directions: Please place a check mark on the line under the appropriate response.

	Yes	No
1. Were the professional expectations of the parties involved spelled out in the contract?	____	____
2. Were the personal expectations of the parties involved made explicit?	____	____
3. Were the conditions under which each party involved would invest time and other resources adequately defined?	____	____
4. Were the ground rules under which the parties involved would operate specified clearly?	____	____
5. Were the boundaries of consultation defined?	____	____
6. Was the nature of the contract reviewed with all appropriate parties?	____	____
7. Were arrangements made for the periodic review and evaluation of consultation?	____	____

FIGURE 7.3   Sample checklist for evaluating the contracting phase

Formative Evaluation of the Entry Stage.   In the entry stage, the consultation process progressed through the phases of exploring organizational needs, contracting, physically entering the system, and psychologically entering the system. The consultant and consultee can evaluate each of these phases as a guide for conducting subsequent consultation phases.

Exploring Organizational Needs.   Some questions used in formative evaluation during this phase include:

- To what degree was the level of congruence between the consultant's abilities and consultee system's needs determined?

- Was the amount of resources the organization was willing to commit to consultation adequately defined?

- To what extent was the identification and clarification of the need for change accomplished?

- How well was the organization's readiness for change explored and defined?

- How well was the potential for working together explored by the parties involved?

- To what degree were role expectations made clear?

- How well were the roles of consultee and client defined?

Contracting.   The questions that can be asked about contracting are more specific than those for the previous phase:

- How effectively were the professional expectations of the parties involved spelled out in the contract?

- To what degree were the personal expectations of the parties involved made explicit?

- Were the amount of time and other resources each party would invest, the times they would invest them, and the costs of those investments adequately defined?

- How precisely specified were the ground rules under which the parties involved would operate?

- How well were the boundaries of consultation defined?
- To what degree was the nature of the contract reviewed with the appropriate parties?
- Were arrangements made for the periodic review and evaluation of consultation?

Physically Entering the System.   Evaluation of the physical entry into consultation is relatively straight-forward. Some questions useful in evaluating this phase include:

- Is the selected work site conducive to effective consultation? Is the selected work site strategically located?
- Is the consultant appropriately balancing the amount of time spent at the work site with the time spent moving throughout the organization?
- To what degree does the consultant adapt the schedule for consultation activities to the regular schedule of the organization?
- To what degree have the parties affected by consultation been informed about the nature of consultation, its purpose, and its time frame?

Psychologically Entering the System.   Even though psychological entry cannot be divorced from physical entry, its aspects can be evaluated by the judicious selection of questions. Some questions that can be used in evaluating this phase include:

- To what degree has consultation placed minimal stress on the parties involved?
- To what degree has consultation placed minimal stress on the organization's structure and processes?
- To what degree has the consultant developed social influence within the organization?
- How effectively has the consultant obtained some sanction for consultation from the organization's top-level administrators?

- How effectively has the consultant built strong professional relationships with all parties affected by consultation?

In summary, evaluation of the entry stage—as with any of the other stages—is best applied to each of its phases. The consultant and consultee must agree on the most appropriate methods of evaluation and must limit the number of events that will be evaluated.

Two Brief Examples of Formative Evaluation in the Consultation Process

Example 1. Monica, a mental health consultant, has been consulting with Wendell, the director of a community council on aging program, on a "Remi-niscences on Life" program series the council has been holding once a month in the community services center in a small rural town. The program was designed to bring seniors of the community together to recall wholesome reminiscences of their life experiences and share them with youth volunteers who were being trained by the council on aging to work with the elderly. Monica and Wendell came up with an evaluation scheme for evaluating the program prior to its inception. After five program sessions, they evaluated the program by means of a survey with the 12 seniors participating in the program, the program's two other staff members besides the director, and the 24 youth to whom the seniors had been sharing their reminiscences. After they conducted the evaluation, Monica and Wendell decide to "evaluate the evaluation." They determined that perhaps they should have spent more time on interviewing the participants and less time on surveying. Although the program's staff members had no complaints about the evaluation, some of the seniors had trouble seeing and said they couldn't read the survey very well. Several of the youth said it was hard to take the survey seriously and that they found it to be an unwanted demand on their time. As Monica and Wendell examined the results, they determined that a structured interview approach to evaluating the program would lend the most valid data. The seniors would appreciate the time given to them by a program member one-on-one, and the youth would be offered not only time to speak about how they felt, but also some coupons for free pizza. Monica and Wendell concluded that although the evaluation plan was appropriately linked to the goals of the program, the data-gathering methods were not adequately chosen or implemented. In addition, more methods of data collection like a combination of interviews, observation, and surveys were in order.

Example 2. Skyler, a first-year school-based professional consulting with a teacher, wanted to ensure that the consultee perceived that the entry stage was truly beneficial. Before moving on to the diagnosis stage, Skyler and the teacher jointly evaluated the entry stage. They decided to use an informal approach that consisted of several questions that Skyler had drawn up. They met after school in the teacher's classroom for around 20 minutes to discuss the questions. The questions related to questions revolved around the effectiveness of how they got started in the relationship, how mutual expectations were set, how things were going, the strength of their relationship, and the comfort level of their meeting space. The only change that came about was that Skyler and the consultee decided that they should slow the process down some and not try to accomplish too much in a given session.

The Use of Qualitative Methods in Consultation

Qualitative evaluation is an umbrella for the many methods in which data can be interpreted from a qualitative perspective (Carter & Morrow, 2007; Hays & Wood, 2011; Meyers, Truscott, Meyers, Varjas, & Collins, 2008). Excellent resources include: *The Qualitative Research Experience* (Padgett, 2004), *The SAGE Handbook of Qualitative Research* (Denzin & Lincoln, 2011), and *Handbook of Mixed Methods in Social and Behavioral Research* (Tashakkori & Teddlie, 2003).

Qualitative evaluation often focuses on the nature of the experiences people have had (Kirst-Ashman & Hull, 2012). It does not deal with cause–effect relationships, but rather is often layered on top of quantitative techniques. While the quantitative approach can get at cause and effect, the qualitative approach can help to explain why the cause and effect relationship exists, for whom it exists, and how to sustain any effects that were observed. Concepts such as constructivism, empowerment, multicultural issues, and ecology are common areas for investigation using qualitative methods (Meyers et al., 2008).There is increasing acceptance of qualitative methods as being rigorous and having credible results (Berrios & Lucca, 2006; Haverkamp, Morrow, & Ponterotto, 2005; Royse, 2011; Sander et al., 2010) and they are increasingly being used along side of quantitative methods (Ponterotto, 2005). Qualitative evaluation methods can extend consultants' ability to effectively evaluate their efforts (Denton, Hasbrouck, & Sekaquaptewa, 2003; Polkinghorne & Gribbons, 1999) and assess the impact of cultural and organization context (Sander et al., 2010). Qualitative evaluation is sometimes considered more of an attitude of inquiry that uses particular types of procedures (Athanasiou, Geil, Hazel, & Copeland, 2002; Hays & Wood, 2011). Qualitative evaluation methods include those such as the case study and the self-evaluation. Data for these methods include transcripts of interviews, notes from observations, descriptions from appropriate stakeholders, and scores from assessment instruments. Qualitative evaluation deals with specific situations and is directly related to decision making. In addition, qualitative methods are increasingly being considered to answer questions related to consultation processes (Sander et al., 2010). The first three methods discussed—triangulation, member checking, and recursive analysis—are particularly helpful to consultants and consultees in enhancing the trustworthiness of any findings and minimizing any bias.

Triangulation. Triangulation is an approach in which multiple methods and/or sources of data are put together to validate a given explanation of a situation (Hays & Wood, 2011; Lincoln & Guba, 1985; Royse, 2011; Tashakkori & Teddlie, 2003). Data are examined across sources to look for consistencies in patterns (Goldstein & Harris, 2000; Plummer, 2011).

Member Checks.   Member checks involve a process by which the original data and evaluation scheme are fed back to the participants for their evaluation (Lincoln & Guba, 1985; Truscott, Cosgrove, Meyers, & Eidle-Barkman, 2000). This method is used to increase the credibility of collected data (Goldstein & Harris, 2000). You might view this method as a specialized focus group.

Recursive Data Collection.   This is the method in which multiple data sets are collected over time and analyzed to try to verify previous findings (Meyers, Proctor, Graybill, & Meyers, 2009; Truscott et al., 2000). An example would be following a student's behavioral adjustment over several years of schooling.

Case Study Method.   A case study is an example of a qualitative evaluation method in which the focus is on an individual, a group of individuals, or an organization, and a broad range of data sources are obtained from the naturalistic setting. The main strength of case studies is depth, which includes richness, detail, and an understanding of context (Flyvbjerg, 2011). Case studies have "a unique strength in providing a format to understand the dynamics of a situation, linking context, processes, and outcomes" (Pryzwansky & Noblit, 1990, p. 297). This method allows for the observation and understanding of the complexities that make up consultation and collaboration (Newell, 2010a). Case studies can be valuable in evaluating multicultural consultation (Ingraham, 2008).

Narrative in nature, case studies are often conducted under naturalistic conditions (Flyvbjerg, 2011). The case study method typically uses observation as a data-gathering tool (McNamara, Rasheed, & Delamatre, 2008). The case study method can be used to monitor and/or analyze the effects of consultation on the consultee and/or the client system (Pryzwansky & Noblit, 1990); for example, a consultant might conduct a case study on the effects of quality circles on job satisfaction in

a community service agency. Although it is descriptive in nature, the case study method does not excuse the consultant and consultee from identifying specific and behaviorally defined goals at the outset of consultation (Bergan & Kratochwill, 1990; MacNealy, 1999). It does, however, permit application of consultation evaluation to an individual consultee and/or client with a minimum of statistical work, even though they require detailed data collection (Pryzwansky & Noblit, 1990).

The case study can provide insight into previously unsuspected relationships affecting consultation. The case study is, however, very susceptible to bias and use of this method requires careful judgments about the efficacy of consultation. Because of its uncontrolled nature, consultants and consultees can have only limited confidence about the cause of any observed effects (Barlow, Hayes, & Nelson-Gray, 1999) and any generalizability (MacNealy, 1999). On the other hand, Lincoln and Guba (1985) point out mechanisms of dealing with bias and Flyvbjerg (2011) notes that case studies can compliment quantitative studies. To the degree that a case study is comprehensive, it can be quite time consuming. Case studies are often viewed as lower-level evaluation tools, but they are increasingly showing value as a method to evaluate multicultural consultation (Ingraham, 2008).

Focus Groups.   Focus groups are both an intervention and a qualitative research data source (Kamberelis & Dimitriadis, 2011; Tashakkori & Teddlie, 2003). They usually consist of 7–10 members who are chosen due to their relationship to the topic under consideration, led by a moderator. Although the consultant selects the topics that will be focused on, the objective is to determine the consultees' perspectives on these topics. The reactions of the consultees guide the direction the focus group takes (Heppner, Kivlighan, & Wampold, 2008). Focus groups allow consultants to observe group process and, if it is in the consultation plan, intervene in the ongoing group dynamics.

They also act as a source of rich data about selected topics and provide a detailed data bank from which to draw conclusions. Focus groups have the advantage of providing a wealth of information but the disadvantage of producing data that are difficult to analyze (Marshall & Rossman, 1995). Focus groups can be used for a variety of purposes, such as determining workers' beliefs about diversity management in their work settings (Russell-Chapin & Stoner, 1995) and evaluating programs for children and families (Nabors, Ramos, & Weist, 2001). They go beyond interviews in that members interact with one another, which adds richness to the data collected (Royse, 2011).

Ethnographic Interviews. This data-gathering method assumes that the evaluator is familiar with, and understands, the unit such as an organization so that the reports of members of the unit are meaningful. The main premise is that the evaluator adequately understands the frame of reference of the persons providing data (Hays & Wood, 2011; Meyers et al., 2008; Truscott et al., 2000). There are two types of ethnographic interviews: casual and systematic (Macnealy, 1999). Casual interviews are very similar to the unstructured interviews discussed in Chapter 5 of this text. Systematic interviews are very similar as the structured interviews described in the same chapter. This method can be particularly useful if the consultant is charged with dealing with cultural issues within a group or organization.

Summative Evaluation

Summative evaluation refers to the evaluation of outcomes or products; indeed, it is often referred to as *product evaluation* (Royse, 2011). It assesses how well consultation worked (Upah, 2008).

Consultants and consultees use summative evaluation to determine if the objectives of consultation were met (Gibbons & Silberglitt, 2008). In some circumstances, consultants can benefit from consulting with experts in evaluation concerning the design of summative evaluation procedures. Evaluation methods in consultation and collaboration are typically based on research design. Evaluation methods can be quantitative, qualitative, or a mixture of both. These methods are not opposed to each other; they are merely different (Polkinghorne & Gribbons, 1999). These methods can all provide

valid information (Berrios & Lucca, 2006; Padgett, 2004; Tashakkori & Teddlie, 2003).

An exhaustive treatment of the many possible designs used in summative evaluation is beyond the scope of this book. Excellent resources already available to consultants and consultees can provide guidance in designing evaluations of the consultation process; they include *Research Design in Counseling* (Heppner et al., 2008), *Single Case Experimental Designs: Strategies for Studying Behavioral Change* (Barlow, Nock, & Hersen, 2009), *Single-Case Research Designs* (Kazdin, 2011), *The Scientist Practitioner* (Barlow et al., 1999), and *Experimental and Quasi-Experimental Designs for Generalized Causal Inference* (Shadish, Cook, & Campbell, 2002).

The Use of Quantitative Methods in Summative Evaluation

The Pre-Post Method. The pre-post method attempts to assess changes that result from consultation by measuring variables related to desired changes before and after the consultation process. For example, a consultant might measure an organization's morale before and after an intervention designed to improve it. The advantages of this method are that it is relatively simple and requires a minimum of time to perform.

The pre-post method is particularly valuable when the variables being measured are specific and observable. Because there is no control group, however, this method is of limited value.

Changes that were sought and achieved may not be directly attributable to consultation because of other factors—such as changes in the organization and life experiences—that may just as well explain the results. Still, this method is a step above nonstandardized observation and anecdotal accounts in that it provides more useful information and more conclusive evidence.

The Group Comparison Method. The group comparison method adds clout to the evaluation by including a comparison or control group, which strengthens the evaluation's validity; a group that received consultation services is compared with a group that did not receive such services. This method is recommended to empirically validate interventions (Heppner et al., 2008; Stoiber & Kratochwill, 2000). This method allows the consultant and consultee to be more confident that any changes found in the measurement are specifically attributable to consultation itself and not to extraneous variables. For example, a consultant might train half of an agency's crisis intervention team in cognitive therapy strategies for crisis situations. The other half of the team, which would receive no training, would be used as a control group. The performance of both groups is assessed and compared on selected criteria.

Sometimes consultants use a no-contact control group or an attention-only control group.

In using a *no-contact control group*, the only contact with the group occurs during the assessment of the dependent variables (measures of the factors to be changed by consultation). In an *attention-only control group*, the assessment of the dependent variables is made and the group is informed of the nature of consultation services without receiving these services directly.

Attention-only control groups are useful in that they eliminate the possibility that the attention paid to the consultees and/or clients, not consultation itself, led to differences in the dependent variables. Several potential problems can be associated with the group comparison method of evaluation: management of the control groups, developmental complexity of the experimental design, and required statistical knowledge beyond the expertise of consultant and consultee.

The group comparison method is particularly useful in a follow-up assessment using the same measurements taken in posttesting. Because of the complexity of the group comparison method, it is a desirable, but relatively infrequently used, method of consultation evaluation (McLean, 2006).

Single-Case Method. The single-case method involves "… observing repeated patterns of behavior under repeated and alternated baseline and experimental conditions. If a behavior pattern under the baseline condition systematically differs from a behavior pattern under the experimental

condition, then one can conclude that differences in these behavior patterns are not caused by chance" (Gresham & Vanderwood, 2008, p. 68). The time-series method involves establishing a series of measures on one or more individuals on one or more given variables such that there is little variation over time (Barlow et al., 1999). The primary difference between this method and the group comparison and pre-post methods is that the time-series method uses more frequent assessments of designated variables. The effects of intervention are then assessed in terms of the variability of their level of occurrence, and possible trends (Barlow et al., 2009; Kazdin, 2011). Thus, pertinent information can be gathered on a measurement's changes over time (Barlow et al., 2009). Single-case experimental designs in which the client system is assessed before, during, and after the intervention are increasingly popular (Brown-Chidsey, Steege, & Mace, 2008). As an example, a consultant and consultee might make a series of observations on how an imagery program affects a client's eating behavior at breakfast, lunch, and dinner.

Multiple baseline designs are an example of the time-series method. Multiple baselining reduces the effects of random influences on behavior change by replicating the change obtained in one period with that in subsequent periods; each subsequent period serves as a control for the earlier period (Barlow et al., 1999; Brown-Chidsey et al., 2008). Time-series methods are most effective when it is likely that a large number of variables are affecting the outcome of consultation.

The Use of Mixed Methods
in the Evaluation of Consultation

There is a trend in using a mix of quantitative and qualitative methods (Creswell, 2011; Teddlie & Tashakkori, 2011) and some support for the single-case methodology for which some of the quantitative methods described above are appropriate (Bangert & Baumberger, 2005; Gresham & Vanderwood, 2008). The self-report method described below is one common mixed-methods approach to evaluation.

Self-Report Assessment Method. The self-report assessment method is frequently used at the end of the consultation process to evaluate the effects of consultation. This method makes use of such instruments as rating scales, surveys, checklists, and questionnaires, which can be developed by the consultant and consultee or are available in some standardized form. When using assessment and evaluation instruments for any purpose, the consultant will want to bear several important points in mind (Cooper & O'Conner, 1993): first, develop a specific connection between the goals of consultation and the instruments chosen; second, consider using a combination of assessment instruments that reflect hard, soft, and qualitative methods; third, use repeated measures; and fourth, inform consultees of the limitations of any instruments used, which is an ethical obligation.

In summative evaluation, self-assessment can be used in all of the previously mentioned methods, including a postconsultation assessment measure. The method tends to lack rigor in terms of experimental design and can easily provide inaccurate results if the precision of the instruments used is inadequate. However, this is a very common method of evaluating consultation, and its use has been enhanced by significant improvements in the development of questionnaires and surveys (e.g., see Oher, 1993). The self-report method is particularly appropriate for evaluating consultation in terms of consultee satisfaction, consultant satisfaction, and perceived consultant effectiveness.

In summary, the evaluation of consultation effects can move the consultant and the consultee into the realm of experimental design, which may require more sophistication in this area and/or statistics than the consultant and consultee possess. Under such circumstances, they must either seek outside assistance or develop a suitable evaluation method that is within their levels of expertise. Because of the time, effort, and expense that outcome evaluation can require, the evaluation plan used must be cost-effective. The consultant must ensure that evaluation results are described completely and accurately and are disseminated to the appropriate parties, such as the consultee, organization contact person, administrators, and other appropriate parties-at-interest.

A Brief Example of Summative Evaluation in the Consultation Process

Bonnie has been consulting with Dorothy concerning a "Back on Your Feet" program at a local shelter for battered women. Half of the women in the shelter have agreed to be trained in a program designed to help them reestablish themselves as independently functioning members of the community. The other half were promised the same training provided that the evaluation of the training was positive. After three months, the group comparison method was used in the evaluation.

Differences were found between the experimental group and the control group on several measures ranging from personality inventories and interviews to survey results and the impressions of the experimental group's counselors regarding the effectiveness of the training. Results of the evaluation suggested that the training might well benefit the women. The control group was immediately provided with the training.

PHASE TWO: PLANNING POSTCONSULTATION/ POSTCOLLABORATION MATTERS

Consultants can increase the chances that the benefits of consultation will be maintained after their departure by engaging their consultees in effective postconsultation planning. Plans for this purpose rely heavily on the resources available to the consultee. In collaboration, this phase involves all of the collaborators "getting on the same page" with regard to what activities, if any, they will be engaging in after the collaborators stop formally meeting about the client system in question. The result is often referred to as a maintenance plan (Watson & Sterling-Turner, 2008).

To accomplish this, the consultant and consultee can effectively plan postconsultation procedures by following many of the procedures used in the phase of the implementation stage that concerns formulating a plan (Racine Gilles, Kratochwill, Felt, Schienebeck, & Vaccarello, 2011). You may want to review the planning process in Chapter 6, including determining objectives, establishing procedures, defining steps, assigning responsibilities, and testing for feasibility, cost effectiveness, and capabilities. A classic technique called *force-field analysis* (Lewin, 1951) is a useful technique in assessing the forces that may aid or impede the accomplishment of plans. With the proper planning, then, the consultant can help the consultee effectively follow through to maintain the results of consultation.

Because one goal of consultation is generalization to similar current and future cases, prevention is of primary concern during the phase of postconsultation matters. Consultants can most likely increase the generalization of skills across situations by explicitly discussing the case at hand in terms of how to use it in future appropriate situations. One way to accomplish this would be for the consultant and consultee to come up with possible future scenarios that resemble the case at hand and discuss "lessons learned" and those lessons might apply to those scenarios.

Two Brief Examples of Planning Postconsultation Matters

Example 1. An external consultant has been working with an organization to reduce violence in its workplace. After the evaluation of the program indicated its success, the consultant engaged the implementation team in the postconsultation planning. The planning involved the team's monitoring the organization's ongoing evaluation of the program, a plan for making program adjustments based on the periodic evaluations, and follow-up by the consultant with the team.

Example 2. A marriage and family therapist has been consulting with a counseling psychologist who is working with a couple on enhancing their relationship. The family therapist has assisted the consultee in using therapeutic metaphors with the couple. Consultation has proceeded effectively. Together the consultant and consultee formulate a plan for how the consultee will proceed with the couple after consultation has ended. Part of the plan to enhance their emotional intimacy involves helping them write their own metaphors.

PHASE THREE: REDUCING INVOLVEMENT AND FOLLOWING UP

Once the consultant and consultee have formulated postconsultation plans to the satisfaction of the parties involved, the consultant initiates a period of reduced involvement and enacts any agreed-upon follow-up procedures.

Reducing Involvement

Reduced involvement refers to the gradual reduction in the consultant's contact with the consultee, which effectively prevents abrupt termination. Reducing involvement is typically less critical for internal consultants in that they typically have close proximity to the consultee at the workplace. Fox external consultants, intermittent contact can actually empower the consultee who will begin to pick up the slack left by the consultant's declining involvement. The reduced involvement reinforces independence in the consultee. In collaboration, reducing involvement refers to the gradual reduction of contact of the collaborators with one another.

One method proved effective in reducing involvement is called *fading*, a lessening of contact and involvement with the consultee. For example, if an internal consultant has been meeting with a consultee on a weekly basis, contact might be faded to once every two weeks, then to once every three weeks, and so on. Similarly, the external consultant's visits to the organization are reduced over time. However reduced involvement is accomplished, it should be negotiated, for then it is clear to everyone involved that reduced involvement does not mean *no* involvement (Schein, 1999). For example, consultees may still need emotional support, practical feedback, and/or technical assistance (Athanasiou et al., 2002), thus necessitating some contact rather than termination.

No matter how reducing involvement is conducted, one of its major focuses is on how the gains made during consultation will be maintained. For example, the consultee may continue treatment for a specified time period and then gradually withdraw the intervention and assess related outcomes.

Two Brief Examples of Reducing Involvement

Example 1. An external consultant has been facilitating the adoption of a response to intervention (RTI) program in an urban middle school. As the program's implementation becomes complete, the consultant reduces involvement with the implementation team who now takes complete responsibility for all implementation procedures. The consultant, instead of meeting weekly with the implementation team, agrees to two more sessions but on a monthly basis.

Example 2. A school counselor has been meeting weekly with a teacher regarding some classroom management problems the teacher has been having. As a result of consultation, the teacher has made great strides in eliciting appropriate behavior from the students. The consultant has helped the teacher plan how the class will be managed for the entire term and how data on the students' behavior will be collected. To reduce the consultant's involvement, the consultant and consultee set two final meetings

at three-week intervals before terminating the consultation.

Following Up

Although follow-up can be a critical phase, it is often not conducted (Gutkin & Curtis, 2009; Zins & Erchul, 2002). Planning follow-up procedures can reduce the stress that comes with winding down consultation. Follow-up develops a sense of how the benefits resulting from consultation are being maintained. It helps to deal with things like "quirks" in the implementation, unanticipated resources that are needed to be successful, unanticipated issues such as the nature of consultee communication with the client system, the need for gathering and interpreting additional data, the need to check the "goodness of fit" between the intervention and the environment in which it is being implemented, needed consultee support and reinforcement, and provide for the professional development of the parties involved (Gutkin & Curtis, 2009) as well as increase treatment integrity (Riley-Tillman & Chafouleas, 2003).

Follow-up refers to the process of periodically determining how well the results of consultation are being maintained over time and how effectively the consultee is implementing postconsultation planning. In the language of behavioral consultation, the term *monitoring* is often used (Kratochwill, 2008; Noell & Witt, 1998) when the consultant follows up. Follow-up provides the consultee with a regular "check up" (Kelley, 1981). For example, follow-up can help to determine if certain target behaviors have been generalized or if a certain behavior has been maintained by the client system (Kratochwill, Sheridan, Carlson, & Lasecki, 1999). Follow-up is important because it provides some indication of consultant availability, an opportunity to modify plans that have not been effectively carried out, some assistance while promoting independence on the part of the consultee and the organization, some prevention of future problems, review the skills the consultee has learned from consultation and how to apply them in the future (Kelley, 1981; Watson &

Sterling-Turner, 2008), as well as an opportunity to celebrate successes. Follow-up procedures for external consultants are typically defined in their contracts. On the other hand, there has been some criticism that follow-up is generally not well done by internal consultants (Zins & Erchul, 2002) and that how follow-up is conducted can make a difference in the level of the integrity with which interventions continue to be applied (Noell et al., 2005; Theodore et al., 2009).

According to recent research, when done properly and effectively, follow-up often includes performance feedback to the consultee (Noell et al., 2005; Watson & Sterling-Turner, 2008). Performance feedback involves monitoring the implementation and then sharing with the consultee, in a structured manner, specific information of the level of treatment integrity and client performance (Noell et al., 2005). There is evidence that performance feedback leads to superior treatment implementation and child behavioral outcomes whereas simply talking about the implementation does not (Noell et al., 2005). When properly accomplished by both internal and external consultants, reduced involvement and follow-up fill a gap between postconsultation planning and termination.

Two Brief Examples of Follow-Up

Example 1. A human resource development specialist has been training volunteers who work with incarcerates in a rehabilitation program. Three months after the training has concluded, the specialist calls the program director to check on how the volunteers are doing according to a format agreed on during postconsultation planning.

Example 2. Montana, a school-based consultant, has reached the point of follow-up in a consultation relationship. Montana and the consultee, a teacher, decide that follow-up is critical because of the consultee's lack of experience in implementing an evidence-based intervention. Although, the consultee's implementation has shown treatment integrity, there is concern over making adjustments to the implementation procedures if the consultee deems them necessary. Montana, as an internal

consultant, agrees to follow up with the consultee on a weekly basis for the next four weeks, which coincides with the school's next grading period.

PHASE FOUR: TERMINATING

Termination is one of those aspects of consultation that has received minimal attention in the literature (Lopez, 2007). Like any helping relationship, consultation requires closure; termination provides that closure in a formal, ritualistic manner. Termination formally ends a process and ideally leads to a sense of satisfaction with whatever has been accomplished. It also provides an appropriate time for celebrating whatever successes have been achieved. However, the termination process has received relatively little attention in the consultation literature (Dougherty et al., 1996; Stroh & Johnson, 2006).

Termination is often a critical element in the consultation process. It involves loss in that a relationship is ending (Neukrug, 2012). If performed properly, it can lead to subsequent requests for consultation for internal consultants such as school counselors and school psychologists (Dougherty et al., 1996). If performed inappropriately, it can result in dissatisfaction on the part of the consultee. Inappropriate termination can affect the manner in which previous postconsultation planning and subsequent consultation experiences are perceived. As a result, poor termination could adversely impact the consultee's follow-through with postconsultation plans and even prevent a consultee from seeking assistance with a new case or program. Examples of inappropriate termination procedures include a unilateral decision (by either the consultant or consultee) to terminate, abrupt termination, indefinite retention of consultation (with no formal end point), and unnecessary extension of the consultation process by any of the parties involved.

Abrupt termination is a shock and can be a distraction (French & Bell, 1999). Conversely, unnecessary extension of consultation is a particular danger to consultants in private practice and to consultants internal to the organization who feel they must always have something to do. As the termination process is begun, consultants should maintain awareness of their need to be needed and avoid engendering dependence (Huckabay, 2002). A lingering consultation prevents the human side of termination from receiving adequate consideration.

A meeting that concludes postconsultation planning is an excellent time to deal with any unresolved issues before the consultant or collaborator's formal departure, and such a ritual can set the termination process in motion. A formal review of the consultant's final report is one proven method of effectively accomplishing termination (Gilmore, 1993); a debriefing conversation on lessons learned is another (McLean, 2006), as is a brief last follow-up visit. In these instances, participants can discuss the progress made in consultation relative to the contract and stated goals of the consultation, and a clearly defined point of termination is obvious. Finally, discussing future possibilities for consulting is another way of easing the stress of termination.

Two Brief Examples of Terminating

Example 1. Sherill, a school-based consultant, has worked with several teachers for a period of four semesters on managing work-related stress. The stress management program was now being phased out, and it was time for Sherill to terminate the consultation relationships she formed. At the last meeting of the group, Sherill gave her work phone number to each participant and conducted a brief discussion in which each member responded to the question, "What have I learned from this experience?" Sherill then provided a light snack over which each group member sent every other member a "telegram."

Example 2. Dakota, a doctoral-level clinical mental health counselor, is wrapping up a three-session consultation relationship with a consultee, a master's level clinical mental health counselor, about a particularly difficult client of the therapist. In their final session, the two discuss future possibilities for consultation while providing closure on the case at hand.

MULTICULTURAL ASPECTS RELATED TO DISENGAGEMENT

Multicultural influences can have a strong effect on the disengagement stage, and particularly the evaluation of the consultation process (Lopez & Truesdell, 2007). For example, the cultural experiences of some consultees or collaborators may suggest that the evaluation be informed by general questions and would therefore bring into question the suitability of checklists or questionnaires.

Just as in evaluating the consultation plan, consultants and collaborators should be cautious about assuming what kind of evaluation process is to be conducted and what kind is acceptable to consultees of differing cultural backgrounds (Sheridan, 2000). Cultural differences can relate to perceptions of what needs to be accomplished during postconsultation and postcollaboration planning. Whereas, for example, the consultant may judge the progress to date as time to begin withdrawing from the relationship, the consultee may have a perception that there needs to be increased collaborative activity, including additional monitoring (Ramirez, Lepage, Kratochwill, & Duffy, 1998).

The cultural experiences of the parties involved can influence follow-up. For example, some fellow collaborators may desire frequent follow-up contacts, not due to dependency, but to their view of proper social professional relationships. The critical nature of termination becomes even more apparent when consultants and collaborators take cultural experiences into consideration (Lopez & Truesdell, 2007). Depending on one's cultural experiences, the termination process may be considered as one that should be rather drawn out. For example, the rituals of some cultures suggest that consultants terminate with an approach that involves a series of brief meetings. To ignore cultural differences in disengagement is to risk jeopardizing the current relationship as well as future consultations and is ethically questionable.

C A S E 7.1   Disengagement for School Consultants

Rosie, a school-based human service consultant, has been working with Wilma, a fourth-grade teacher, about a boy named Leo in Wilma's class. Leo had become increasingly withdrawn over the first grading period of the academic year and Wilma had contacted Rosie for consultation. The two professionals evaluated the plan they had put into motion and determined that Leo's level of participation in class activities had increased dramatically thanks to an increase in group activities initiated by Wilma as well as the special attention she provided him.

As they wound down the consultation process, Rosie and Wilma reviewed their work together and shared their perceptions of the experience. Rosie engaged Wilma in a reflective discussion of each stage of consultation they went through. By use of selected questions, Rosie and Wilma concluded that although the majority of the process went quite smoothly, they had some difficulties in actually defining how Leo's withdrawing behavior manifested itself. They determined that Wilma saw Leo as more withdrawn than Rosie did and that these different perceptions led to some difficulties in defining the problem. Wilma agreed that the quick manner with which Leo responded to her interventions suggested that perhaps she had misconstrued his behavior.

Rosie and Wilma reviewed the results of pre- and postconsultation measures, which included a behavior checklist and observational data they had both filled out on Leo periodically. Rosie discussed how she had analyzed the data statistically and cautioned Wilma about the limitations of the data. The two then focused their discussion on whether the results obtained with Leo were worth the cost of having

Wilma work with him in the classroom rather than having him sent for individual and group counseling. Wilma admitted that at first she wanted Rosie to take Leo and "fix" him so that she wouldn't have to continually prod him to get involved in classroom life. She had to admit that she was pleasantly surprised with the quick progress that Leo had made.

Rosie and Wilma then changed the focus of their meeting to discuss the kinds of behaviors that Wilma would engage in after consultation was completed to keep the gains Leo had made. They agreed that informal contacts with Leo as well as verbal reinforcement for social interactions should be continued on an intermittent level.

Rosie agreed to check in with Wilma at two-week intervals for a month, after which they would terminate their relationship. During the next academic year, Wilma contacted Rosie again for assistance with two other students she was concerned about.

Commentary
Evaluation of the plan is essential to having the parties involved believe in the process. Notice the effort Rosie made to ensure that Wilma had a thorough understanding of the nature of Leo's behavior change. Notice further how this might well be linked to Wilma's seeking additional consultation with Rosie about different students the next school year. Part of disengagement is planning postconsultation procedures with the consultee.

In this case, Rosie and Wilma made plans to assist Leo in maintaining the progress he had made.

SUMMARY

Disengagement in the consultation process involves a sense of letting go on both professional and personal levels. Its four phases include evaluating the consultation process, planning postconsultation matters, reducing involvement and following up, and terminating. Disengagement, which should be differentiated from termination, should not be rushed; it should be a well-planned and well-executed procedure.

Evaluation of consultation is frequently done poorly and as a result does not provide any consultation participants a chance to examine how effectively they have managed the process or how they have grown by participating. Therefore, consultants should be ready to assist their consultees in evaluating consultation and should ensure that evaluation of their own services is part of the overall evaluation procedure.

C A S E   7.2   Disengagement for Community Consultants

Hernando, a hospital social worker, has been an internal consultant to a long-term care team at a community hospital. The team consists of an activity therapist, a patient advocate, the charge nurse, the director of physical therapy, and a part-time social worker. The twofold problem of staff and patient morale led to the consultation.

With its 55 beds typically filled, the long-term care program was continually experiencing severe stress, and the problem was considered to be significant. Hernando's reputation throughout the hospital led to his being asked to consult. For the past three months, he had worked intensely with the team members, who in turn took the resulting ideas to their units for review and decision making.

Consultation had resulted in a complex plan of interventions that was evaluated and determined to be fairly successful. The primary changes for staff included flexible work scheduling and a stress management group.

Improved caregiving to patients included getting them fed and taken to bathroom facilities within proper time frames. In addition, significant changes to the activities program made it more appealing to the patients.

To begin winding down the consultation process, Hernando requested a special two-hour meeting with the team, during which he and the group evaluated the consultation process. Hernando asked the group for face-to-face as well as written feedback in the form of a consultee satisfaction survey he had developed for his work at the hospital. Hernando provided his observations of what had transpired and how effective he thought the process had been. The group discussed what had happened as a result of the consultation and how much these changes had cost—the group agreed that the changes had been somewhat painful. They noted that, at first, there was a tendency for the different work groups assigned to the program to feel severely understaffed and to believe that this was causing the problems.

Only after discussions with the different shifts—led by Hernando and the appropriate team member—did any kind of group ownership of the problems begin to emerge.

Only then were goals set and implemented. The group of consultees and Hernando decided that he should follow up with them during the next two months to work out any glitches. The team would continue to take responsibility for monitoring the impact of the recent changes. Six months after the beginning of the consultation, Hernando followed up with the team one last time. Since things were continuing to go smoothly and the morale of the staff and patients alike was improved, Hernando and the team officially terminated their intense, yet successful, relationship.

Commentary

Evaluating the consultation process is good business on the part of consultants. In this case, Hernando, through a face-to-face evaluation process, allowed the consultees to express their deeper feelings about the consultation process and most likely created the conditions for the consultees to communicate more genuinely among themselves in the future. Follow-up procedures, such as those implemented by Hernando, demonstrate the consultant's commitment to the consultee as well as provide opportunities for refining any postconsultation planning.

In postconsultation planning, the consultant asks the consultee, "How are you going to follow through after I am gone?" This planning process places increased responsibility on the consultee and the organization to make effective use of the products of consultation. Postconsultation planning is an appropriate time for consultees to express their concerns about the consultant's leaving and for the consultant to encourage them to realize that they have the abilities to follow through.

The egos and self-esteem of everyone involved in consultation are affected during reduced involvement. Being needed as a consultant is gratifying, and thus, it is sometimes difficult to let others follow through on what the consultant has been instrumental in accomplishing.

The consultant can more effectively reduce involvement by remembering that one goal of consultation is to help the consultee continue to function without the consultant as well as being as empowering and facilitative as possible during the entire process. Consultants can take pride in being instrumental in enabling consultees to use the new skills they have learned.

During follow-up, the consultant takes on a troubleshooting role in which help is provided to the consultee or organization on an as-needed basis. It is important to define what is meant by "as-needed" so that dependence is not fostered.

Termination is the formal ending of the consultation process. Saying goodbye is not always easy. Consequently, formal termination does not always occur or may be done in a stiff, artificial manner. By being perceived as fair, competent, human, and effective, consultants can take leave with an enhanced reputation, which can be intrinsically satisfying and earn them subsequent consultation opportunities. You should bear in mind that very little of the consultation/collaboration literature related to stages has focused on the disengagement stage.

In sum, consultants and collaborators can minimize problems during disengagement by accurately timing its initiation, by developing proper postconsultation/collaboration planning, by properly reducing involvement, and by following up and planning a formal time to terminate (Dougherty et al., 1996).

SUGGESTIONS FOR EFFECTIVE PRACTICE

- Design all evaluation procedures prior to carrying out the plan.
- Remember that formative evaluation can be as valuable as summative evaluation.
- Use fading procedures for reducing involvement.

- Bear in mind that follow-up procedures, although frequently neglected, help to sustain gains made by the consultee or fellow collaborators.
- Ensure for a culturally competent termination.

QUESTIONS FOR REFLECTION

1. How does the term *disengagement* differ from the term *termination*?

2. In what ways is disengagement a winding down of the consultation process?

3. For what purposes can evaluation of the effects of consultation be used?

4. As a consultant, when in the consultation process would you start to plan evaluation procedures?

5. How does a consultant proceed in determining what events to evaluate?

6. How would you handle evaluation of consultation if both you and your consultee lacked the expertise to perform sophisticated evaluation procedures?

7. What kinds of things should be accomplished in postconsultation planning?

8. What is the major difference between reduced involvement and follow-up?

9. How would you go about the process of terminating the consultation process in a culturally competent manner?

10. What does the following statement mean: The consultant begins termination upon entry into the consultation process?

SUGGESTED SUPPLEMENTARY READINGS

Dougherty, A. M., Tack, F. E., Fullam, C. B., & Hammer, L. A. (1996). Disengagement: A neglected aspect of the consultation process. *Journal of Educational and Psychological Consultation, 7,* 259–274. This article, still one of the few on the topic, examines and summarizes the existing literature on disengagement in consultation. The authors describe the stage of disengagement, identify important stage-specific consultant skills and roles, examine relevant psychological dynamics, and suggest how to avoid pitfalls during this stage. The authors conclude with recommendations for further study.

Heppner, P. P., Wampold, B. E., & Kivlighan, D. M. (2008). *Research design in counseling* (3rd ed.). Belmont, CA: Thomson Brooks/Cole. This book provides invaluable evaluation information for consultants, whether or not they are trained as professional counselors. I recommend this as a handbook to help consultants determine how to evaluate the effects of consultation. Even though the book's focus is on research, its concepts are easily translatable into evaluation procedures. Chapter 11, "Qualitative Research," and Chapter 19, "Design Issues Related to Process Research," should be of high interest to consultants. I strongly recommend this book to consultants who believe their evaluation skills need a boost.

8

✳

Pragmatic Issues of Working Within an Organization

There are a variety of pragmatic issues that you will encounter in your practice of consultation. In addition, all consultation occurs in some organizational context, which contains complex forces that affect, for better or worse, the consultation process (Lewis, Lewis, Daniels, & D'Andrea, 2011; Truscott, Cosgrove, Meyers, & Eidle-Barkman, 2000). This chapter discusses both the pragmatic issues related to consultation and the nature of organizations in which consultation occurs. The chapter provides coverage of important topics such as systems theory, ecological variables, social justice, and time constraints.

As you read this chapter, consider the following questions:

- How can you cope with the time constraints imposed upon you by the structure and culture of the organization for which you are consulting?

- If organizations are so complex, how can a consultant or group of consultants accomplish real changes in them?

- Why do you think that systems theory is gaining increasing importance in the eyes of consultants and collaborators?

- What do you see as the main components of a multiculturally sensitive organization?

- How does an ecological view of consultation change the view of the client system?

An organization is a complex social system that interacts with its environment and is, therefore, subject to influences from without and within. It is important for consultants to be familiar with the technical and social forces as well as structures that will impinge on the consultation environment so that they can help to ensure consultation success (Knoff, 2008). Organizational factors and related pragmatic issues about which consultants may want to be knowledgeable include: recent changes in organizations and our society, the influence of organizational theory on the consultation process, the importance on an ecological perspective, the nature of organizational change, the impact of organizational culture, multicultural competence in organizations, issues in assessment, social justice, and time constraints.

TWO CASE EXAMPLES

Consider this situation:

In your job as chief administrator of a large human service agency, you notice an excessive turnover rate in two of your organization's six departments. You have made several unsuccessful attempts to rectify the problem; you know what is wrong, but you don't know how to fix it. As a last resort, you decide to call in a consultant. In preparing for the first meeting with the consultant, what exactly would you tell him or her about your organization, the people in it, the problem, and the solutions you've tried? Where would you suggest the consultant begin to try to help? If you were the consultant in this situation, what information would you want to know? What values and biases about "how to fix things" would you bring into the consultation setting? Which personnel would you want to interview? How would you go about solving the problem? How would you know whether or not consultation had been successful? The answers to these and many other important questions depend on how well you (the consultant) and the human service agency's administrator understand the nature of organizations.

Now consider a second situation:

You are a school-based consultant in a middle school that serves 600 students. Although there are clinical mental health counselors and psychologists available for students with serious mental health issues, you are expected to provide, among other things, counseling services, group guidance, and consultation and collaboration services. How would you go about trying to effectively manage your time so that you would have adequate time for consultation and collaboration services? How would you go about obtaining staff administrative support for delivering these services?

RECENT CHANGES IN SOCIETY AND ORGANIZATIONS

Some understanding of recent changes in society and organizations provides consultants a framework for being more effective in assisting the organizations with which they consult. In the new millennium, basic societal change has affected new workers: There has been a diminishing percentage of young people entering the work force; new workers are less skilled than those of previous generations; and women and minorities continue to make up a very large proportion of the workforce and will make up even more (Leong & Huang, 2008). Issues in the workplace (Cooper & Leong, 2008; Lewis et al., 2011) that have continued into the 21st century include those related to dependent care, substance abuse, AIDS, feminization of the workforce, stress (e.g., violence in the workplace), advances in technology, the creation of a "flat world" and global economy, workplace bullying, a realignment of the world's economy, the economic downturn, and cultural diversity. Additional issues have resulted from the "... rapidly changing culture, race and ethnicity mix of workers, managers, customers, and services ..." (Cooper & Leong, 2008, p. 133). The effects of catastrophic events such as September 11, 2001, the tragedy at Virginia Tech, and Hurricane Katrina have tested the way American society goes about its business by making the incomprehensible comprehensible. The events have changed the nature of the workplace in terms of dealing with terrorist threats or attacks and tragic events (Knotek, 2006; McCarroll & Ursano, 2006; Stock, 2007). In addition, there is a widespread view that the ethical climate of organizations has deteriorated over the years, leading to public distrust of corporations (Fuqua & Newman, 2009).

Within the helping professions, the ever-changing make up of our society has dictated the necessity of ensuring cultural competence in the work of consultants and collaborators. As a result, advocacy, social justice initiatives, multicultural factors, prevention, empowerment, systems-level interventions, and an ecological perspective on consultation and collaboration all have emerged as significant elements related to effective practice.

In addition to societal changes and those involving the helping professions, organizations themselves are changing. Organizations, including human service organizations, have been going through several changes (Lewis et al., 2011). Organizations have been experiencing change at an increasingly rapid pace. The economic downturn has led to budget cuts and a reduction in service provision. Organizations have become more complex; the number of specialized people performing different tasks has increased. This increased complexity and diversification makes it much more difficult for an organization to have a common purpose and makes coordination difficult for management.

Implications for Consultants

Consultants, both internal (including school-based) and external, will be increasingly called upon to assist organizations and their members manage and cope with the aforementioned changes (Lewis et al., 2011). Organizations are likely to want help in the following areas that impact organizational culture and climate: focusing more on the human side of management, becoming adaptive and resilient, being culturally competent, resolving the human resource problems caused by budget reductions, and providing training in effective communication regarding the impact of change (Cooper & Leong, 2008; Lewis et al., 2011). Increases in workplace violence as well as the increased possibility of terrorist attacks and natural disasters have created a need for consultants who can assess the risk of workplace violence, review and update crisis management plans, and work with members of the organization's crisis management team and others

to prepare for when violence occurs (Stock, 2007), as well as provide consultative services during crises and disasters (Halpern & Tramontin, 2007; McCarroll & Ursano, 2006). As examples, consultants can work with organizations to develop or improve crisis management plans, increase social cohesiveness to minimize the psychological impact related to a trauma in the workplace (McCarroll & Uranus, 2006), and conduct postcrisis audits (Simola, 2005). Because many of these organization needs are related to the human factor, consultants from the helping professions will find themselves increasingly involved in work with schools as well as the traditional areas of public and nonprofit organizations.

Organizations are increasingly looking at multitiered change initiatives that focus on the entire membership of the organization, those at risk for a given set of issues, and those who exhibit manifestations of a given set of issues. As a result, regardless of whether they are internal or external, consultants will need to be competent in assessing ecological variables (Ysseldyke, Lekwa, Klingbeil, & Cormier, 2012), and knowledgeable about systems-level interventions, adapting consultation to multicultural contexts, advocating for the disenfranchised stakeholders when necessary, focusing on empowering consultees whenever possible, being involved in multitiered interventions, taking on a preventive focus as a matter of practice, and promoting social justice as a matter of course.

THE INFLUENCE OF ORGANIZATIONAL THEORY

Consultants develop a broad perspective on the nature of organizational forces by considering each organization with which (externals) or in which (internals) they work, relative to some organizational theory. The consultant's organizational theory is the glue that holds together events into a meaningful form. This theory is, of course, contextualized to the organization at hand.

Organizations' day-to-day functioning are guided by the particular theories of organization their members adhere to. By being aware of such theories, both internal and external consultants will understand the ways things are done in a particular organization, how that organization functions, and, as importantly, the way the forces that impact that organization are interpreted (Kirst-Ashman & Hull, 2012). Further, the theory on which an organization is based affects the way processes such as consultation and collaboration are performed.

Historically speaking, *organizational theory* is the study of the structures and processes of organizations and the behavior of groups and individuals within them. Because they attempt to explain these complex entities and how they are best designed, most theories must simplify organizations; how this is accomplished depends on which factors are considered relevant. The following overview of two important and common organizational theories highlights the different perspectives from which organizations can be studied. I particularly believe that a view of the bureaucratic model and the systems model provide a contrast for consultants to consider as they analyze organizations (Lewis et al., 2011).

The Bureaucratic Model

Before the turn of the century, organizations were considered individual entities, such as church, government, and so forth. With the rise of capitalism in the late 19th century, organizations came to be viewed as a *class of collectivities* (French & Bell, 1999). The classical model of organizations came into vogue near the beginning of the 20th century and was epitomized by Max Weber's model of bureaucracy. This model is considered a "machine" theory. *Machine theory* is a generic term that implies that each organization is built according to the blueprint derived from its purpose, just as each machine is built according to a set of specifications.

Weber designed the bureaucratic model as the ideal of organizational effectiveness. Its principles, which are "means to ends" in nature, emphasize the structure of the organization over the human element (Lewis et al., 2011). Rules and regulations are important and provide order and continuity. Jobs are analyzed in terms of what is required to do them effectively, and the most highly qualified people are placed in them. Communication patterns are vertical rather than horizontal, with each unit under the direct control of a higher unit. Emphasis is placed on the written record, with all decisions, acts, and regulations written down (Lewis et al., 2011).

According to this bureaucratic theory, organizations were meant to be efficient, effective, and equitable. However, the potentially counterproductive elements in this model can lead to red tape, rigidity, apathy, and resistance to change.

Implications for Consultants

Consultants encountering an organization emphasizing bureaucratic values will want to be sensitive to the lines of authority, the dedication to the written word, and the importance of rules and regulations. They should be on the lookout for apathy/morale issues, views of leadership among the organization members, concern over confidentiality, and the nature of the informal power structure.

The classical models of organizational theory, such as the bureaucratic model, emphasize specialization of tasks, standardized role performance, uniformity of function, and avoidance of duplication (Katz & Kahn, 1990). These models are inadequate in that they do not provide for interaction between the organization and its environment and thus deny the organization a means to change (Lewis et al., 2011). Consultants may need to assist bureaucratic organizations in examining systems theory concepts to better align the organization to deal proactively and productively with change.

Open Systems Organizational Theory

One of the most popular models of organizational theory is systems theory, which provides a broadly based perspective on organizations developed from attempts to understand biological events

(Adelman & Taylor, 2007; Curtis, Castillo, & Cohen, 2008). Systems theory is integral to the consultation-related activities of professionals in the helping professions (Lewis et al., 2011). Systems theory is related to ecological theory and as a result can be useful in promoting the preventive aspects of consultation, including empowerment of individuals and groups, implementation of prevention programs, and support for social justice and cultural-competence issues.

A *system* can be defined as "an orderly combination of parts that interact to produce a desired outcome or product" (Curtis et al., 2008, p. 888). The idea is to understand interdependencies, multiple causes, and multiple effects (Forman & Selman, 2011). Systems theory is noted for focusing on continuous assessment and the resulting adjustments to the internal and external environments (Kirst-Ashman & Hull, 2012). In systems theory, *organizations* can be defined as "dynamic entities continually interacting with their environment, changing and adapting to develop congruence between people, process, structure, and external environment" (Beer, 1980, p. 15). According to systems theory, everything is interrelated and interdependent (Li & Vazquez-Nuttall, 2009). The interaction among the subsystems of the organization and the organization and its environment operate under reciprocal influence (Forman & Selman, 2011). When applied to organizational members' and consultants' behavior in organizations, systems theory suggests that events impact and are impacted by whatever transpires. There are two types of systems: closed and open. Closed systems are not affected by their environments: They have a finite amount of energy, and when that energy is used up, the system runs down. Open systems, in contrast, have permeable boundaries and can obtain energy from and send energy back to the environment. Organizations can be viewed as open systems (French & Bell, 1999). Open systems have an input-throughput-output mechanism. These three systems must work well together for an organization to work effectively.

The systems view of organizations identifies four components: a framework (pattern of activities), goals, methods and operations, and people.

The systems theory of organizations assumes that organizations are open systems; they are not isolated, closed entities, but instead are subject to internal and external influences (Curtis et al., 2008; Lewis et al., 2011). Systems theory considers the organization to be a totality, and it directly examines the interrelationships among an organization's subsystems and between the organization and its environment.

The most fundamental property of a system is the interdependence among its parts (Curtis et al., 2008; Forman & Selman, 2011). The systems approach is helpful in conceptualizing the multidimensional parts of a system as an integrated whole and it assumes that an organization is more than the sum of its parts. Organizations (and the people within them) are seen as adaptive and as social systems operating within larger environments (Lewis et al., 2011).

Characteristics of Systems

When viewed as open systems, organizations have nine characteristics (Henning-Stout, 1993; Kirst-Ashman & Hull, 2012):

1. *Importation of energy.* No social structure is self-sufficient: The organization must draw new energy from other organizations, from the material environment, and from people such as consultants.

2. *The throughput.* Energy is transformed as it goes through the organization. In a human service organization, throughput can be service to clients, training of existing personnel, addition of new staff, and so forth.

3. *The output.* The organization exports some product into the environment, such as some new service to the client system.

4. *Systems are cycles of events.* Organizations have an input-throughput-output cycle; the output product supplied to the environment provides energy for repetition of the cycle.

5. *Negative entropy.* Entropy is the degradation process of all organisms toward death or disorganization. Organizations can arrest this

entropy by importing more energy than they expend. This process of energy storage is called negative entropy.

6. *Information input, negative feedback, and the coding process.* Information input can give the organization signals about the environment and the organization's relationship to it. One type of information input is negative feedback, which allows the organization to stay on its chosen course or, if necessary, change course. The reception of inputs into the organization is selective; that is, the organization can attend to only so many inputs, and those inputs are the only ones among many that the organization tunes in. This selective mechanism is called coding, and the coding procedures of an organization are determined by its functions. (For example, if a mental health center learns that the community would fund a dropout prevention program, it might make plans to develop and implement such a program.)

7. *The steady state and dynamic homeostasis.* The importation of energy can maintain constancy in the flow of energy such that an organization is characterized by a steady state. Dynamic homeostasis refers to the basic preservation of the system's character. In preserving its character, the organization must import more energy than it exports. In adapting to its environment, an organization moves toward assimilating the external resources considered necessary for survival. Hence, organizations attempt to grow both quantitatively and qualitatively over time.

8. *Differentiation.* Organizations move in the direction of differentiation and elaboration: Roles within the organization become specialized and the number of such roles tends to increase. (For example, a mental health center might differentiate from a single team to a crisis-intervention team, a substance-abuse team, and any number of other specialized teams.)

9. *Equifinality.* The principle of equifinality proposes that organizations can reach the same end

by different means: This is the "there's more than one way to skin a cat" principle. (For example, a single human service organization might use any of several methods to improve its public relations image.)

Subsystems Within the Organization

A subsystem is a smaller system contained in the major system (Kirst-Ashman & Hull, 2012). The subsystems of an organization are integrated by means of the norms, roles, and values present within the system (Sue, 2008). Role behavior is sanctioned by norms that are justified by values. Historically, five subsystems within organizations are built around the organization's norms, roles, and values (Katz & Kahn, 1990):

- the technological or production subsystem
- the support subsystem
- the maintenance subsystem
- the adaptive subsystem
- the managerial subsystem

The *technological subsystem* is concerned with the quantity and quality of the work accomplished within the organization. For example, in a counseling center, the direct delivery of services to the client system—the throughput—constitutes the technological subsystem. Organizations are often classified according to the type of product they provide, and the products of human service organizations are the clients they serve. (More precisely stated, the product of human service agencies is "better" people.) The technological subsystem is responsible for the input-throughput-output cycle.

The *support subsystem* is concerned with the procurement of inputs, the disposal of outputs, and the maintenance of an environment favorable to the organization. For example, a university might seek funding (procurement of inputs) for a counseling program for learning-disabled college students. Upon termination of the program, a written report is submitted to the funding agency (disposal of outputs), and the program is widely publicized to attract students and strengthen its public image (maintenance of a favorable environment).

The *maintenance subsystem* is concerned with connecting people within the organization to their roles. It is not concerned with the material being worked on (typically the client system in human service organizations), but rather with the equipment used to get the work done. In human service organizations, this concern relates to getting people who work for the organization into their proper roles: patterned human behavior. This subsystem integrates people into the system through recruitment, socialization, training, rewarding, and sanctioning, and it is concerned with input with respect to maintenance (e.g., recruitment of personnel).

The *adaptive subsystem* helps an organization exist in a changing environment. It is specifically concerned with sensing and interpreting important changes in the external environment. Functions such as long-range planning, research and development, and market research are part of the adaptive subsystem.

The *managerial subsystem* controls, coordinates, and directs the other subsystems of the organization and adjusts the total system to its environment. There are two major types of managerial subsystems: regulatory mechanisms and the authority structure.

Regulatory mechanisms gather and interpret data about the organization's input-throughput-output cycle and give feedback to the system about its output in relation to its input. In a human service organization, a follow-up study of clients' perceived benefits from the organization would be an example of a regulatory mechanism.

Organizations must have a defined and established decision-making framework called the *authority structure*. This structure describes the organization of the managerial system with regard to the positions at which decisions are made and the routes through which they are implemented.

Implications for Consultants

Because of the current popularity of the systems view, I have provided extensive coverage of the implications of this perspective. As you will note from the above

discussion, consultation using systems theory is quite complex (Rimehaug & Helmersberg, 2010). One obvious implication is that consultants need to be prepared to develop systems-level interventions to promote organizational change that benefits all stakeholders (Forman & Selman, 2011). O'Neill and Trickett (1982, pp. 4–5) have pointed out six implications that still hold today for consultants taking on a systems view of organizations:

- Consultation is an activity designed to intervene in the social context.

- An important source of knowledge includes understanding the social context where consultation is occurring.

- Cultural and institutional diversity is a positively valued fact of life for the consultant.

- Consultation interventions should be matched to the organization within which consultation occurs.

- Priority should be given to predicting the side effects of consultation.

- Interventions should be designed in such a way that the organization's resources are managed and preserved.

In addition, just as each person is unique and special, so too is every system (Curtis et al., 2008; Lewis et al., 2011). Consultants need to take a fresh perspective each time they enter a new consultation setting. They need to view behavior from a systems perspective, remembering that everything is connected to everything else, and use collaborative procedures (McLean, 2006). Furthermore, because the effects of consultation can go far beyond those intended, consultants should ensure that communication flows smoothly and accurately throughout the subsystems of an organization. You no doubt have heard horror stories about organizations such as schools or mental health centers in which the staff in one area was totally unaware of what the staff in other areas was doing and planning, even though they would be affected by those decisions.

Consultants need to understand systems well and will want to ensure that their consultees do also. This is important because lack of understanding of systems is related, among other things, to ineffective program implementation (Forman & Selman, 2011). Other implications of systems theory for consultants include helping an organization maintain focus on its core mission, promoting the use of feedback as a self-regulating mechanism to expedite change, fostering ecologically focused assessment procedures that go beyond the client system itself, and using preventive as well as remedial interventions. From a systems theory perspective, the community is viewed as both a possible target for consultation and collaboration as well as a force impacting the organization (Lewis et al., 2011). For example, cross-systems changes can occur between a school and a child welfare agency (Anderson-Butcher et al., 2010).

The goal of consultation using systems theory can be a change in the *microsystem* (i.e., the closest social elements of the defined client system such as a client's family), the *mesosystem* (i.e., the near but not immediate influences, such as the general influence of family and friends), and the *exosystem* (i.e., the most remote factors, such as ethical and legal procedures; see Kurpius, Brack, Brack, & Dunn, 1993, pp. 416–417). Finally, the *macrosystem* entails things like customs and laws that influence the microsystem, the mesosystem, and the exosystem. Conceptualizing at these levels permits the consultant to design interventions at multiple levels. Effective consultants using systems theory will take into account the relationships between the problem at hand and systems variables, including those related to culture (Harris, 2007; Schein, 2010). The interaction between the client system and the environmental context (i.e., the various systems levels) will be assessed in consultation to assist in the determination of whether the change efforts should target the client system or the context in which the client system resides (Li & Vazquez-Nuttall, 2009; Meyers, Meyers, Graybill, Proctor, & Huddleston, 2012).

The bottom line is that consultation based on systems theory has as its goal an increase in the level of problem-solving expertise of the system in the long run. While the immediate goal is to assist the system with a specified problem, the ultimate goal is to assist the system to be a more effective problem solver on its own. As a result of this perspective, the use of training in problem-solving activities for consultees is strongly encouraged. Likewise, a strategic long-term plan for system change is essential (O'Connell, 2008) so that stakeholders do not expect immediate change and small "wins" related to long-term change can be celebrated (Anderson-Butcher et al., 2010). Even with all of its merits, the systems approach can be challenging to all involved. As a result, planning related to organizational communication, communication with outside entities, and internal consultation among stakeholders is essential (Lewis et al., 2011).

Now that we have examined the bureaucratic and systems theories of organizations, it should be clear that when consultants enter an organization, they regard it and analyze it based on some theory. The more you are aware of that theory, the more you will know what you are looking for, what you are likely to overlook, and how forces within the organization can affect the client system for better or worse; you will also be in a better position to understand how your consultees view their organizations and the concomitant implications this has for your consultation.

Will you see the organization relative to the bureaucratic theory and assume that the members of the organization need to be controlled by certain highly regulated structures? Will you adopt the position of the systems theorists and look at the interdependencies and interrelationships among the organization's subsystems to understand the organization? Will you take a systemic approach that analyzes the context as well as the client system itself? Whatever questions you ask, the variety of organizational theories available to consultants suggests that consultants should take a flexible view in analyzing organizations.

The Ecological Perspective

Models of consultation are increasingly examining the human–environment interface, which has led to greater emphasis on human ecology (Gutkin, 2012; Sheridan & Kratochwill, 2008). Termed the *ecological approach*, this view emphasizes that behavior is a function of the interaction of the characteristics of the environment and the characteristics of the individual (Gutkin, 2009; Kloos et al., 1998). The main point is that human behavior is produced by the impact of several interacting systems, making the context of behavior very important (Newell, 2010b). As a result, behavior needs to be examined in its given context (Durlak, 2009); interventions therefore need to focus on realigning the fit between environment and the individual by changing either one or both. For consultation, this trend implies less emphasis on case-oriented, "medical" models and more on those concerned with systems, ecology, and prevention (Erchul, 2011; Newell, 2010b). Both individual client system variables and contextual variables are examined and dealt with. For example, when an ecological perspective is employed in school consultation, the consultant deals with "… school, family, community, peer group, society" (Nastasi & Varjas, 2008, p. 1353). In another example, a school-based professional consults with teacher–parent pairs to ensure that both school and home environments are aligned in assisting a child.

Proponents of the ecological perspective suggest that a great deal of consultation fails to consider its environmental context. For example, whereas consultants typically realize that consulting in a school is vastly different from consulting in a hospital's human resource development department, they rarely consider that one school differs vastly from another (Kelly, 1987). Consider a second example in which a consultant helps a therapist effectively assist a client, but the client returns because he or she is unable to fit into the community.

What Gutkin and Curtis (2009) note about consultants using an ecological approach in a behavioral consultation context is perhaps true for all models of consultation employing an ecological approach: "… consultants work with their consultees to identify manipulate relevant person-environment relationships to improve, eliminate, and/or prevent identified problems" (p. 661). A strong conclusion is that frequently it is the environment, not the client system, that needs to change.

The ecological perspective is often contrasted with the medical model, which examines problems as residing in the individual (Gutkin, 2009). For example, whereas the ecological model might look at a student's classroom behavior in terms of the interaction of the classroom environment and the student to determine what needed to be changed, the medical model would examine the student in terms of what needs to be changed in the student with minimal attention being paid to the environment as impacting the problem at hand (Gutkin, 2009, 2012). As Jason, Pokorny, Ji, and Kunz (2005) note: "The ecological perspective helps school and community consultants consider and work with the broader social systems and institutions within the community that reflect community norms and ultimately people's lives" (p. 207). Gutkin (2009) echoes this statement with a school-based example: "Developing effective school-, home-, or community-based treatment plans requires detailed information about teachers and the classroom environments in which they work, parents and the nature of the home environments in which they live, and community leaders and the array of community programs they offer" (p. 475). Two guiding principles for the consultant and consultee include: the client system is a part of a functioning social system and disturbances are not things inside the individual but are discordances in the system. The term *discordance* refers to the differences between the individual's abilities and the demands of the environment (Conoley & Haynes, 1992).

A major point of the ecological perspective is that both the promotion of environmental "wellness" factors that lead to individual self-esteem and competence and the effort to lower the incidence of environmental stressors on individuals that may lead to negative outcomes (Meyers, Proctor, Graybill, & Meyers, 2009). Clearly, given this context, the ecological perspective is closely related to prevention. In addition, the ecological approach also provides a framework when consultants serve as agents of social justice (Li & Vazquez-Nuttall, 2009). Hence, consultants are increasingly moving toward adopting an ecological perspective, which, in many cases, leads into the area of systems-level consultation.

Advantages of the ecological framework include:

- a more accurate perspective on how humans behave

- an increase in the number of possible interventions

- environmental forces are more easily changed than the characteristics of an individual

- the major social support systems for the client system are engaged in the change effort

- making the environments in which a person lives may produce longer lasting changes than simply trying to change only the individual

- neutralizing to a degree the shortage of mental health specialists in American society by involving significant others of the client system in changing the client system's environment (Gutkin, 2009).

Whether aimed at the micro-, meso-, exo-, or macro-level, ecological consultation modifies the environment in order to create more productive person–environment interactions.

The ecosystem, the interacting systems related to the individual and their environment, in particular, provides the important context for understanding human behavior. The ecological perspective provides consultants and consultees with ways of making changes within a given system, which results in individuals being better empowered while adapting to the system as appropriate.

The ecological perspective suggests that a strong consultation relationship and shifts in consultee attitudes are insufficient to effect change (Kelly, 1983). Rather, consultation should also take into account the resources within the environment to promote the well-being of the parties involved. As noted above, prevention is a key goal of the ecological perspective. The setting often constitutes the client system in this perspective and is usually some combination of an organization, the community at large, school, family, and

their interrelationships. Interventions often are "aimed at developing long-term adaptive processes for the betterment of the setting and its members" (Trickett, 1986, p. 189) as well as for immediate benefit. Interventions and strategies for any model of consultation can be used when appropriate.

The ecological perspective is often applied by community psychologists in a variety of community settings, including schools (Trickett & Rowe, 2012). From this context, consultation is successful when the organization or community is able to locate and develop its own resources, which are then linked to external resources (Kelly, 1987). From this perspective, to think ecologically is to consider how people, settings, and events can become resources for positive developments in individuals and total organizations, as well as how these resources can be managed and conserved (Trickett, Kelly, & Vincent, 1984). This model assumes that consultee power is needed to effect true change—for example, in reducing the constraints due to social structure and processes within a given system. If we were to make assumptions about the ecological nature of consultation as it is currently put into practice, we might well agree with the assumptions about community counseling put forth by Lewis and others (2011): Environmental contexts can be influential for better or worse on people; individuals are more resilient than they are typically given credit for; attention to multicultural factors are central; and individual and community development are linked. Further, the site in which consultation occurs is not the target of change; rather, the target is the system itself (Trickett & Rowe, 2012). The people, setting, and events become positive forces for change.

There are potential advantages to adopting an ecological perspective in consultation (Gutkin, 2012):

- allowing for focusing on groups as well as individuals

- promoting prevention

- creating more potential human resources in promoting change

- expanding treatment targets beyond the individual

As you might have surmised, this approach to consultation is very demanding and can be quite time consuming. The ecological perspective is just that—a perspective. It does not attempt to be a model of consultation. Therefore, it is up to consultants to interpret the principles of this perspective as guidelines for effective practice. For example, they focus more on educating within person–environment settings than curing an individual. They could focus on helping the client system function on a day-to-day basis and help significant others adapt the client system's environment accordingly (Gutkin, 2009). Consultants would shift away for diagnosing the client system toward critically examining the client system–environmental interface and designing, along with their consultees, appropriate interventions.

Case Example of the Ecological Approach to Consultation. A community psychologist was consulting with a family service center concerned about its work environment. By coming from an ecological perspective, the consultant had a lot of leeway in how she might proceed.

Realizing that each family service center is a unique setting, the consultant investigated how the people at the center interfaced with their work setting.

She reviewed the history of the center, observed the people in their work environment, and conducted interviews to determine how newly hired people were oriented and how employees were acknowledged during the everyday course of events. The consultant provided a survey that assessed the workers' views of their real and ideal work settings. In noting discrepancies between the real and the ideal, she found that employees had issues with the degree of autonomy they felt, the amount of work-related stress they experienced, and the quality of communication with supervisors. Areas of strength included reward for productivity, acknowledgment for effort, and opportunities for professional development.

Based on her findings, the consultant and staff engaged in a variety of interventions to enhance the center's quality of life. First, they capitalized on informal elements of the center.

People were encouraged to take breaks together, flexible work scheduling was introduced, and a staff volleyball team was formed. Quality circle problem-solving groups with participation at all levels of the center were created. Finally, a community advisory group for the center was created and an internal network was formed to smooth the flow of communication. These empowering interventions were designed to prevent the center from experiencing major problems.

The consultant's final report noted that assisting the center from an ecological perspective would have been much more difficult if the director had not been supportive of change.

Further, it appeared that the center staff were now involved in daily operation of the center to a degree that they could be self-supporting.

ORGANIZATIONAL CHANGE

Consultants, both internal and external, frequently are called upon to facilitate processes that lead to organizational change. With the increasing call for systems level interventions, a thorough understanding of organizations will become a necessity for both internal and external consultants whether they are community- or school-based. The following discussion incorporates current thinking about effective organizations and the principles of organizational change.

Approaches to Change

All organizations change in response to pressure from internal and/or external forces; this change can be deliberate or accidental (Demers, 2007). Most organizations, including schools, are not adept at making changes. Depending on how well an organization monitors its internal and external environments and considers systems-level and ecological variables, change may be either well planned or forced through a crisis situation. In addition, change is best approached within an organization by courting the members and other stakeholders (e.g., parents in a school-based setting) who are open to considering change and by addressing members' levels of concern in an ongoing manner throughout the change process (Curtis et al., 2008).

When an organization senses the need for change, it looks for new directions to proceed. A major mistake organizations can make is in determining that any change that is made is positive. Nothing could be further from the truth. Change needs to be well planned and executed.

From both philosophical and historical perspectives, there are three classical views of planned change: the empirical-rational approach, the normative-reeducative approach, and the power-coercive approach (Chin & Benne, 1985). Although conceptualized decades ago, these views of change remain current and influential in planned change initiatives.

The *empirical-rational approach* assumes that people are rational by nature and will follow their rational self-interests once these are made known. Thus, any proposed changes are presumed to be congruent with the self-interests of the organization and its members. Because the organization and its members presumably are rational and motivated by self-interest, changes will be adopted only if they can be rationally justified and gains are evident. In other words, according to this approach, changes in cognitions produce changes in behavior. This approach's credibility is based on scientific research and the process of educating people for change.

The *normative-reeducative approach* does not deny the role of rationality in change but points out that change is supported by sociocultural norms based on attitudes and values. Change involves a shift in those attitudes and values away from old patterns and a commitment to new patterns. This approach views people as social by nature; their shifts in emotion about something will bring about change. This position holds that change is not only intellectual; it also involves feelings and attitudes.

The *power-coercive approach* to change focuses on the ingredients of power and the ways it is used in bringing about change. This approach relies on the use of political, economic, and moral sanctions in the exercise of power; it assumes that externally based sanctions are necessary for change to occur. Most consultant activities related to organizational change involve the normative-reeducative category, although some activities may be a combination of normative-reeducative and empirical-rational approaches (French & Bell, 1999). A major implication for consultants is that the involvement of internal stakeholders within from all levels of the organization as well as that of external stakeholders is essential in determining the nature and course of change in an organization. As a result, the data gathering functions are critical in developing change strategies from the very beginning when change is first being discussed to the very end of the change process (Curtis et al., 2008).

The Nature of Organizational Change

Change is a part of the daily routine of any organization; it can be precipitated by internal or external forces and can be planned or unplanned. If these forces are adequately monitored, then change can occur in a planned and systematic way. If these forces are not adequately monitored, crises ensue and the organization is forced to cope in a less orderly, less effective manner. Pressure to change can be strong and can demand great adaptability from an organization. Nonprofit organizations frequently have a more difficult time coping with, and planning for, change because they are not subject to the marketplace forces that act on for-profit organizations.

Efforts to achieve change must be responsive to organization–environmental interfaces; it is no longer practical to improve internal effectiveness without explicit attention to the relationship between an organization and its environment.

Real organizational change will not take place and be maintained unless the following three conditions exist:

1. There must be a sufficiently high level of dissatisfaction with the status quo to mobilize energy toward some change.

2. Leaders must have some vision of the desired result of change.

3. Leaders must envision and communicate some practical first steps toward this desired result if energy to begin change is to be mobilized.

Implications for Consultants

Consultants from the helping professions in any setting generally consult with the purpose of achieving change in an organization or on the part of an individual or group of consultees within that organization. Clearly, to be most effective, consultants must be familiar with many models for conceptualizing organizational change and understand how change is viewed in the organization in which they are consulting (Fuqua & Kurpius, 1993).

Consultants are well-advised to buy into the method of change typically used by the organization prior to recommending or implementing their own views. Because change is such a sensitive issue for people, consultants should minimize the stress of change whether for an individual or an entire organization. They will also want to ensure that ideas for change are integrated into the organization that changes are conducted by members of the organization with top-level sanctioning and involvement, and that change strategies are well planned and implemented. They will note that change is more than what administrators of the organization desire; rather it is a function of how the groups of individuals in the organization interact to make change an emergent and collective process. Consultants will need to develop an operational view of organizational effectiveness, which can help the consultant and consultee develop a framework for effective change. By using such activities, consultants will better understand the change process within an organization and can thereby minimize resistance and enhance the probabilities that their efforts will be successful. Leaders of the organization may well call upon consultants to train selected stakeholders in the model selected to create change, such as response to intervention or positive behavioral supports so that the change

process can go as orderly as possible (Curtis et al., 2008).

Finally, consultants will want to be familiar with different types of leadership styles, that is, how leaders interact with other members of the organization to assist the organization in meeting its mission (Lewis et al., 2011). Consultants will want to ensure that they as leaders, or when consulting with organizational leadership, promote vision, leadership knowledge, and skills related to the organization, and support the welfare of both the organization and its members.

DEALING WITH
ORGANIZATIONAL CULTURE

Organizational culture has a large impact on individual and group behavior (Schein, 2004, 2010). Although the term *organizational culture* is not well-defined, the concept is important for consultants to be aware of in terms of designing and implementing successful strategies (Schein, 1990b, 2004, 2010). The forces in an organization that are derived from its culture are powerful and complex. Members of the organization need to understand them so that they can adequately deal with them (Schein, 2010). I have dedicated extensive coverage to organizational culture because of its potential to significantly impact the behavior and effectiveness of an organization.

Culture can be defined as "a pattern of shared basic assumptions that was learned by a group as it solved its problems of external adaptation and internal regulation, that has worked well enough to be considered valid and therefore, to be taught to new members as the correct way to perceive, think, and feel in relation to those problems" (Schein, 2004, p. 17). Manifestations of the organization's culture include climate, group norms, roles, systems, politics, and values.

The culture is maintained by the socialization of members new to the organization. Successful organizations have the following cultural attributes: uniqueness in their philosophy, a focus by management on maintaining the philosophy, deliberate attempts to integrate the philosophy throughout the organization, and involvement by all staff in communicating and reinforcing an organization-wide view of events and decisions (Lundberg, 1993; Schein, 2010).

Consultants need to have a sense of how an organization defines itself in terms of its culture (Schein, 2010). In addition, different segments of an organization may define themselves in terms of culture differently than does the entire organization. For example, school teachers may have a different organizational culture than school administrators. You might say that organizational culture gives a particular organization its "personality" (Kirst-Ashman & Hull, 2012).

Consider the situation in which you are a consultant asked to conduct professional development experience for junior high school teachers on the characteristics of the middle school child. Although the administrative unit sees this as an important step in moving the school toward a middle school concept, the teachers might see the training as another unnecessary imposition on valuable time and another set of expectations without any subsequent reward. You can readily see that the intervention would not likely be successful without the consultant's understanding of how the two units within the school tend to view the use of the consultant's training.

What does a consultant look for when attempting to understand an organization's culture? According to Schein (1990b, 2004, 2010), culture manifests itself in terms of the interaction of artifacts, values, and basic underlying assumptions. *Artifacts* refer to relatively superficial things such as dress code, annual reports, role and mission statements, and the various interpersonal rituals people engage in. Consultants may intervene at this level by helping the organization reorganize the way people problem solve (e.g., by setting up quality circles). *Values* refer to the espoused ways people think and feel in the organization. Consultants can intervene at this level by conducting team-building exercises among various subgroups within an organization (e.g., between teachers and support

personnel). *Basic underlying assumptions* refer to those views of the organization that are taken for granted and are unconscious. A basic implication for consultants is that interaction with members of the organization is essential to get to these assumptions. Another implication is that getting to the underlying assumptions of the organization can assist the consultant in suggesting the right type of interventions. Consultants can intervene at this level through leading exploratory groups in which consultants raise focused questions and consultees volunteer to analyze their deep-seated views of the organization.

Implications for Consultants

By having the skills to understand an organization's culture, consultants are better able to get a feel for an organization's history, current behavior, and future aspirations (Schein, 1990b, 1999, 2004, 2010), which will help them determine how to approach consultation and in particular select the best interventions. This is particularly important for external consultants who may well have to function as a "student" of the organization's culture. By understanding an organization's culture, consultants will be better able to help the organization deal with the sets of problems with which organizations most often need assistance: dealing with its environment and internally integrating daily functions and the ability to adapt (Schein, 2010).

By understanding an organization's culture, consultants are better able to manage the cultural forces that impact their consultation and to help an organization change in constructive ways. For example, they can promote their consultation and collaboration services in the framework of "how things are done" and fitting these services into the routines of the organization (Welch, 2000). In addition, they and their consultees might well attain a better understanding of the behavior of the organization, which can be linked to effective change within the organization. Knowledge of culture is essential when consultants are asked to help clarify individual roles within the organization, restructure for accommodating change, develop the management function within the organization (Lewis, Lewis, & Souflee, 1991), and understand how contextual variables shape behavior within the organization (Schein, 2010).

THE CULTURALLY COMPETENT ORGANIZATION

As the changing demographics of our society have reached the workplace, the need for diversity awareness and skill has grown (Cooper & Leong, 2008). Diversity is receiving increased attention in organizations (Egan, 2010). We are beyond looking at diversity in organizations in terms of legal compliance and human rights protection and seeing it as a value-added opportunity to maximize the potential of the organization (Arredondo, Tovar-Blank, & Parham, 2008; Cox, 2001; Hoffman et al., 2006; Holcomb-McCoy & Coker, 2009). As Hogan (2012) notes: "Cultural awareness, coupled with the skills needed to interact successfully with people of diverse cultural backgrounds living and working in the same place, is called *diversity competence*, *cultural competence*, or *cultural diversity competence*" (p. 1). Hogan goes on to note that: "Culturally competent organizations have congruent structures, policies, programs, protocols, and processes that enable the entire system to work with culturally diverse people" (p. 1). Culturally competent organizations are proactive in responding to the constant diversity-related, economic, political, and social conditions. These organizations have a sense of open-mindedness and a commitment to continuous learning (Arredondo, 1996). Culturally competent organizations have the ability to identify the organization's needs; increase awareness, understanding, and skills of all employees; implement a strategic plan; effectively monitor progress in becoming a strategic organization (Hogan, 2007); and allow for how diversity can impact services such as coaching (Thomas, 2006) and consultation (Knotek, 2012). From a human service organization's perspective, the bottom line is that a culturally

competent organization can effectively provide services cross-culturally (Diller, 2007; Lewis et al., 2011) and they can do that by dealing with issues such as: "… questions of access, equal opportunity, cultural competence, bias, conflict management, climate and cultural changes, and over multicultural organizational development" (Romney, 2008, p. 141).

Diversity competence is promoted in organizations by ensuring cultural awareness throughout the organization, recruiting culturally diverse employees, providing career development opportunities for all employees, creating working conditions conducive to the needs of all employees, and monitoring the change process related to cultural issues (Hogan, 2007; Washburn, Manley, & Holiwski, 2003). As Lum (2011) notes about cultural competence in organizations, "The culturally competent agency has the attitudes, practices, and policies that demonstrate respect for different cultures and people by seeking advice and consultation from ethnic communities and by being committed to incorporating these practices into the organization." (p. 26). Lum notes further that culturally competent organizations "… value diversity, have the capacity for cultural self-assessment, be conscious of the dynamics of cultural interaction, institutionalize cultural knowledge, and develop programs and services that promote diversity between and within cultures" (p. 11). As Sue (2008, p. 159) notes: "… multicultural organizations are sensitive to creating and maintaining a validating, supportive, and responsive environment."

Management, of course, plays a major part in developing and maintaining a culturally responsive organization. There are models of diversity management (e.g., Arredondo, 1996) that attempt to develop the organization in a diversity-sensitive manner while encouraging organizational-level change and employee empowerment. The goal for consultants is to help to develop and maintain an organization that is culturally competent in its functioning through a variety of interventions at different levels within the organization. The implementation of diversity into an organization's programs, policies, and practices is essential to the organization's well-being (Sue, 2008). There is some empirical evidence that organizations with multiculturally competent mission statements and multicultural training tend to have employees who perceive themselves to be multiculturally competent (Darnell & Kupermine, 2006). See Knotek (2012) for a case illustration illustrating a school as a culturally responsive organization.

SOCIAL JUSTICE

Professional organizations in the helping professions have increasingly incorporated social justice into best practice. Social justice is progressively influencing the work of consultants and collaborators (Lewis et al., 2011; Shriberg & Fenning, 2009; Toporek, Gerstein, Fouad, Roysircar, & Israel, 2006). Consultation, for example, has been found to be an appropriate service for social justice advocacy through consultant activities such as functional behavior analysis, systems-level organization consultation, collaboration, and impacting policy (Baker, Robichaud, Westforth Dietrich, Wells, & Schreck., 2009; Moe, Perera-Diltz, & Sepulveda, 2010).

Mental health professionals realize that they must move beyond one-on-one helping and assist with ecological and systems interventions that promote positive human development (Ivey, Ivey, & Zalaquett, 2012; Toporek, Lewis, & Crethar, 2009) and remove barriers such as equal opportunity for all organizational members (Dixon, Tucker, & Clark, 2010; Sue, 2008). From a school perspective, social justice strives to create a socially just educational environment by removing barriers to learning (Meyers et al., 2012). Consultation, when looked at from a multicultural perspective, can promote the reorganization of organizations such as schools so that their practices become more socially just in their cultures (Dixon et al., 2010; Holcomb-McCoy & Bryan, 2010; Holcomb-McCoy & Coker, 2009). This often puts consultants and collaborators in the advocacy role for changing the status quo by eliminating counterproductive environmental forces and expanding productive

ones (Holcomb-McCoy & Coker, 2009; Williams & Greenleaf, 2012). In a school, for example, consultants engage in social justice initiatives when they act "… to meet the needs of individuals and groups who are the most vulnerable and disenfranchised in schools" (Shriberg & Fenning, 2009, p. 1). When consultants and collaborators work from a social justice perspective, they typically take a systems-level view and consider the organization as the client system, rather than an individual within that organization. They help organizations to: "… not discriminate, and they work to include, empower, and promote individuals and groups who have been discriminated against" (Romney, 2008, p. 152). They also assist in facilitating dialogues on diversity issues (Sue, 2008). For example, a school-based consultant will advocate for the equal treatment of all students (Tomes, 2011). The organization and its community is examined for its justness and equitable treatment and appropriate access of individuals (Lewis et al., 2011; Ratts & Hutchins, 2009).The idea is that by changing the system for the better, the forces that caused individual client issues will be remediated and future similar problems prevented (Ivey et al., 2012). As a result, the well-being of the individual and those in the entire organization are supported (Clare, 2009). When engaging in social justice issues, consultants and collaboration frequently use the advocate role mentioned in Chapter 2 and take a prevention orientation (Speight & Vera, 2009). Collaboration, for example, is emerging as a best practice for dealing with social issues related to working with clients (Lopez-Baez & Paylo, 2009). Collaboration can also be an effective tool for school counselors to use in addressing the diversity of needs of students and their environments (Dahir & Stone, 2012; Woodward & Davis, 2009). School counselors, for example, are particularly suited to promote social justice to eliminate inequities such as the achievement gap (Dahir & Stone, 2009, 2012). School counselors, in another example, can foster interventions and other activities that reduce educational barriers and promote appropriate learning expectations for all students. Because of their unique expertise, mental health professionals can often take a leadership role in community collaboration when tackling systems-level issues in organizations that are related to social justice (Toporek et al., 2009). Consultation has been involved in the promotion of social justice by consulting directly with school personnel (Davidson, Waldo, & Adams, 2006). In addition to advocacy, consultants can promote and facilitate social justice through empowerment of individuals, families, and groups so that they can have the ability to better their situations (Pearrow & Pollack, 2009). Concomitantly, consultants need to facilitate the responsiveness of the members of the organization to empowerment initiatives.

From a social justice perspective, consultants are encouraged to promote social justice, increase their own multicultural effectiveness, consider the contextual elements around the organization such as social, cultural, and economic, be aware of organization-specific social justice issues when consulting, ensure fair relationships among all stakeholders involved in activities, and advocate for equitable treatment of all members of the organization and other stakeholders (Li & Vazquez-Nuttall, 2009).

TIME CONSTRAINTS

One of the biggest issues you will face in work as a consultant or collaborator is finding the time to perform it adequately (Bryan & Griffin, 2010; Gottlieb, 2006; Harris, 2007; Mellin, 2009; Mellin, Anderson-Butcher, & Bronstein, 2011). Whether you work in a school, a clinic, an agency, a business, or industry setting, you will be challenged to cope with time constraints. Part of the time-constraint issue involves the mindset by many consultees that consultants are professionals to whom a problem is given to be fixed. In this mindset, consultees frequently see themselves functioning mainly as referral sources for the consultant. Some managers, for example, do not see their role as collaborating with the consultant and then implementing the recommendation, but rather view the consultant as one who can come up with a traditional training intervention that should fix the

problem. Managers often think, "If employees are not motivated, then come up with a training application that will get them motivated and then implement it." Rarely will the consultant hear: "Help me figure out what *I* can do to help motivate my employees." Involving consultees in more collaborative approaches frequently entails educating them about the nature of consultation and training them in problem-solving procedures. Administrators and supervisors who sanction consultation as a desired activity in the organization also legitimatize the use of time for consultation purposes.

In some organizations, the use of consultants is considered a professional growth activity that is rewarded during the annual review process. An even more critical issue is the severe time constraints faced in most organizations.

Increasingly, organization members are being asked to do more with less. This makes time an even more precious commodity in organizations. As a result, school-based, as well as external, consultants will need to take the risk of consulting on the run (e.g., discreetly in the hallway of a school) and keep initial attempts to establish consultation simple and time efficient (Bramlett & Murphy, 1998).

Methods to create time for effective consultation include scheduling meetings in advance as much as possible, doing as much data gathering as possible early on in the consultation process, and training prospective consultees in the problem-solving process prior to consultation. In schools, teachers can be given more time to be consultees by being given release time, having teacher aides assigned to them, and by using some team meeting times for consultation.

Another possible method of dealing with time constraints is to have an "entry presentation" at a faculty meeting that orients teachers to consultation and allows the consultant to begin entry on a group basis. Training consultees directly in selected interventions is another effective method of dealing with time constraints.

Indirect ways for finding time to consult and collaborate include publicly articulating the rationale for consultation/collaboration, having

---

C A S E   8.1   **Organizational Concepts for School Consultants**

Sharon is a school-based consultant who has transferred to an elementary school after 15 years of working in a middle school. The central office of the school system has recently mandated that each school must develop a wellness program for its staff and students within the first nine weeks of school. Sharon's principal has assigned her the task of designing the program. Because Sharon is new to the school, she decides that she must carefully do her homework to design an effective program. It's an opportunity for her to learn about her new work environment and get a project done at the same time. Yet Sharon is disconcerted by the nagging question of why the principal would give a new staff person a project like this.

As Sharon began to familiarize herself with students, staff, and the physical plant of the school, she found out many interesting things. The school was run in a very business-like manner. Sharon was expected to develop her proposal and send it directly to the principal without discussing it with anyone. She was to schedule a weekly 15-minute appointment with the principal in his office to update him on her progress. She found out that rules and regulations were of paramount importance to the principal. Staff had to sign in and out of school, and a high priority was put on keeping detailed records. Teachers appeared to be very friendly with one another and the "informal power structure" of the school kept up the morale of teachers and staff alike. It was obvious to Sharon that there was a rather large communication gap between the faculty and administration. The principal was highly respected, yet seen as overly concerned with the mechanics of running the school at the expense of its "human side." The students dreaded going to his office but typically liked their teachers.

Sharon felt the principal gave her the job because of her qualifications and because he didn't want to take time away from any teacher's instructional obligations. To the principal, the teachers' job was to teach. Similarly, ancillary personnel like Sharon were to do ancillary tasks. Sharon was very

used to the middle school concept. What she found out as she began developing her project shocked her; she would have to be careful not to let her own values about how the school should be run interfere with her project and her attitude toward the principal. Sharon sensed that the values of the teaching staff were basically those related to a humanistic view of education, whereas the administration valued "getting the job done." A deeper underlying assumption appeared to be "the administrators are the bosses, let them do their thing, but don't let them get in the way of our doing our thing." "Like two ships passing in the night and not noticing each other," thought Sharon.

The wellness program would mean some changes, which in this school meant in a somewhat autocratic top-down manner. She also noted that the informal power structure of the school supplemented the principal's authority and got things done in a less legalistic and more personal manner. In reflecting on how to proceed with developing her proposal, Sharon made a list of as many of the school's organizational characteristics as she could come up with and then looked at them in terms of force-field analysis.

Commentary

As experienced consultants will tell you, there is more to organizational change than appears on the surface. Wisely, Sharon took the time to analyze the organizational context in which her project was to take shape. She further had the insight to look at the development of her project in terms of both the formal and informal power structures in the school, thus increasing the chances of having a politically correct, yet user-friendly, program. Notice her attempt to creatively use a force-field analysis of her school's characteristics to guide her planning. This case clearly illustrates the importance of consultants being aware of the organizational forces that impact their practice and the importance of taking these forces into consideration in their attempts to be of service.

---

leadership participate in these activities, defining staff roles to include consultation/collaboration, creating a schedule that allows time for these activities, providing occasional additional time for these

activities during the work day, and providing incentives for engaging in these activities. Ferguson (2006) adds the Adlerian concept of encouragement and mutual respect as time-tested strategies for

---

CASE 8.2   Organizational Concepts for Community Consultants

Ward is a counseling psychologist asked by a hospital-based hospice program to provide consultation services to its staff. Because the program had been in existence only a few years and Ward had limited experiences with the hospice staff, he decided to proceed cautiously in developing his consultation for the staff. Part of his approach was to ensure that he first studied the organization in which he was going to consult before proceeding further.

He had been introduced at a staff meeting and the director of the program had taken Ward around the unit for a day introducing him to the staff members on an individual basis. Ward then spent three days orienting himself to the hospice program: He observed and interacted, paid attention to a variety of aspects of the program's culture, and noted that the staff dress code was less rigid than that of the rest of the hospital, that families were encouraged to visit their loved ones at any time and were warmly seen by the staff as participants in the care of their loved ones, and that there was a sense of camaraderie among the staff as being special people serving a higher need of society.

As Ward tried to determine the theoretical nature of the problems, he constantly kept in mind the influence of his lengthy experience in the military as a psychologist.

With this perspective in mind, he noted that the hospice program was designed with a human relations approach. The people in the program held frequent team meetings, program decisions were made through consensus-seeking meetings, and the program director acted as a buffer against the strong bureaucratic element of the hospital at large. Staff stated and the patients concurred that teamwork was important and that interdependence was more valued than independence.

Although they were not espoused as values, the program seemed to work on the underlying principles that satisfied staff members contribute more compassionately to patient welfare and that people and love were more important than rules and regulations. In interviewing staff, patients, and the patients' families, Ward determined that changes in the program were based often on a normative-reeducative basis and on a shared approach involving people from all levels of the program, including patients' families. Based on what he had learned about the hospice program, Ward set about to develop a proposal that would outline a consultation program suitable for the type of "mini-organization" the hospice program seemed to be.

Commentary

Ward, as any perceptive external consultant would, took the time to analyze the organization in which he was going to work. Notice that Ward investigated the manifestations of the organization's culture by noting indicators such as employee dress and attitudes. Ward also attempted to grasp the "philosophy" of change in the hospice unit in order to make sure that he could minimize resistance to his consultative efforts. Finally, notice how Ward attempted to design a program with the unique characteristics of the organization in mind.

---

expediting motivation on the part of consultees and hence effective use of time.

Perhaps the best solution to dealing with time constraints is to have the consultation process unfold in a series of short meetings that meet the schedules of the parties involved. Rather than leaving important elements of the process out and using a bare-bones approach, distributing the process out allows for a quality experience and increases the probabilities of a successful outcome.

The use of technology-assisted consultation to deal with issues of time is also a possibility. The use of technology permits contact between face-to-face sessions or as substitute for them, expands the availability of services in a timely fashion, and makes contact easier (Walz, 2007). Some evidence from the counseling literature that may have relevance to consultation suggests that consultees might, just as counseling clients, see work over the telephone as convenient, accessible, and giving them more control in the process (Reese, Conoley, & Brossart, 2006). The same might be said for vehicles such as Voice Over Internet Protocol and instant messaging.

SUMMARY

Whether they are internal or external to organizations or in an educational or community setting, consultants will need a basic understanding of organizations and organizational context to maximize their effectiveness.

How consultants view the broad range of organizational theories—from those that emphasize organizational structure to those that emphasize the human side of organizations—determines how they think organizational change should occur. Because the process of change within organizations is very complex, consultants can use a variety of approaches and many methods to assist organizations in the process. Consultants will want to study an organization's culture to understand it well enough to implement change effectively. Systems and ecological perspectives are becoming increasingly popular as consultants increasingly work to change environments as well as individuals. The emphasis on prevention, social justice, empowerment, and multicultural issues continue to promote broad, environmental view of issues when consultation occurs.

SUGGESTIONS FOR EFFECTIVE PRACTICE

- Consider the culture of the organization in which consultation or collaboration is occurring in deciding how to proceed.
- Be able to clearly articulate your view of organizations as part of your professional development as a consultant.

- Have a sense of organizational change procedures in the organization in which you are delivering services.
- Ensure multicultural competence in all aspects of your practice.
- Use systems-level and ecological perspectives when appropriate.

QUESTIONS FOR REFLECTION

1. Do you think that most members of a typical organization could explain how their organization really operates? Why or why not?

2. What is organizational theory and how is it useful?

3. Why is a firm understanding of ecological and systems theory important for a consultant?

4. Why should a consultant have a "personal" theory of organizations that is carried into the consultation process?

5. How could a consultant teach members of an organization about their own organization?

6. What are the advantages for consultants of the systems model of organizational theory?

7. You are hired as a consultant to a human services organization. As you enter the organization for the first time, what types of things and activities would you look for? How would you find out more about these things and activities?

8. What are some of the ways that the adaptive subsystem of an organization can monitor its internal and external environments?

9. Which approach to change do you hold to most firmly: the rational-empirical, the normative-educative, or the power-coercive? Why?

10. Why is promoting understanding of cultural competency in an organization essential?

SUGGESTED SUPPLEMENTARY READING

James, R. K., & Crews, W. (2014). Systems consultation: Working with a metropolitan police department. In A. M. Dougherty (Ed.), *Casebook of psychological consultation and collaboration* (6th ed.). Belmont, CA: Brooks/Cole Cengage. This case presents a very complex systems-change organizational consultation. One strong merit of this case is how the consultants were able to minimize conflict among the organizations, all of which had different agendas.

Journal of Educational and Psychological Consultation. (2012). Special issue: Ecological approaches to mental health and educational services for children and adolescents. *Journal of Educational and Psychological Consultation, 22*, 1–157. This special issue provides a wealth of information on ecological psychology as it relates to consultation and collaboration. Although the focus of this special issue is school-based, consultants from all areas will find valuable material to inform their practice.

Sherlock, J. J., & Smith, K. (2014). Process consultation in a workplace setting. In A. M. Dougherty (Ed.), *Casebook of psychological consultation and collaboration* (6th ed.). Belmont, CA: Brooks/Cole Cengage. This case study, which is very intricate, deals with how process consultation can be used by members of the helping professions in even the most delicate situations in organizations, including executive coaching.

✳

Models of Consultation
and Collaboration

The purpose of Part III is to consider some popular models of consultation. These models include mental health, behavioral, and organizational consultation. The name associated with a given model of consultation serves to identify its primary focus. In the chapters in this part of the book, you will be reading about how each model is defined and implemented. *Mental health consultation* focuses on the implications of consultants' mental health-related programs and their work with consultees. Mental health consultation was originally influenced by psychodynamic theory, and then later by Adlerian psychology as well as the work of person-centered psychology (Kennedy, Frederickson, & Monsen, 2008). *Behavioral consultation* focuses on specific changes in clients, client systems, and/or consultees. It is very popular in schools. *Organizational consultation* tends to consider the entire organization to be the client system. I discuss these models separately, all the while noting the rapidly disappearing differences among them. Since most models of collaboration are the same as for consultation, I discuss them in the appropriate chapter. Four emerging theories of consultation include those based on Gestalt (Melnick, 2003), rational emotive therapy consultation (Bernard & DiGiuseppe, 2000), feminist consultation (Hoffman et al., 2006), solution-focused consultation (Kahn, 2000), and situation consultation (Rimehaug and Helmersberg, 2010). Because the development of these approaches to consultation is currently limited, they are not covered in detail in this text.

Finally, although progress is being made, traditional models of consultation do not adequately deal with cultural issues (Ingraham, 2007). That progress includes the idea that cultural perspectives can be a significant aspect of the use of any model of consultation as long as they are managed with cultural competence (Ingraham, 2008). As a result, I mention the multicultural aspects of each model as well as provide thorough coverage of a multicultural consultation model in the chapter dedicated to school consultation and collaboration.

In Chapter 9, mental health consultation and collaboration are reviewed. Chapter 10 examines behavioral consultation and collaboration. In Chapter 11, organizational consultation and its three primary types—purchase of expertise, doctor–patient, and process consultation—are analyzed.

Because the context in which consultation occurs is important (Ingraham, 2007; Zins & Erchul, 2002) and a great deal of consultation and collaboration occur in school settings, Chapter 12 surveys school-based consultation with teachers, parents, administrators, and community agencies. Chapter 13 provides you with the opportunity to review a case study in order to obtain a realistic depiction of what occurs during consultation and collaboration as various types of the consultation models are used in the same organization described in the case. Following the case study, the chapter then presents typescripts of school-based consultation and school-based collaboration using similar cases. These examples will help to link theory to practice.

9

✳

Mental Health Consultation and Collaboration

It is difficult to promote the mental health of society in a preventative way, but mental health consultation attempts to do just that. Consider the difficulty: How would you promote the unique mental health needs of each of the numerous subgroups in our culture? In this chapter, we'll consider the historical development of the mental health consultation model and examine Caplan's model (Caplan, 1970; Caplan & Caplan, 1993) of mental health consultation as well as current modifications that have evolved from his original ideas.

This model is included both because of its historical and practical utility and because Caplan is considered to be the one person who put consultation on the human services landscape.

Included are the approaches the model can take, their respective goals, the consultant's role, the consultee's experience in consultation, and the techniques and procedures used. This chapter will examine a relatively new professional role called *mental health collaboration*. Finally, we will cover some contributions and criticisms of the model and cite some trends in mental health consultation that have led to modifications of Caplan's original model. You should note that a great deal of the literature is written from the perspective of an external consultant. However, mental health services delivered by internal consultants and collaborators are on the increase.

As you read this chapter, consider the following questions:

- What might be some of the multicultural issues surrounding mental health consultation?

- What difference would it make if a mental health consultant's primary goal in working with a human service worker was to make him or her a better worker in general, rather than to help the client under discussion?

- What are the basic differences between mental health collaboration and mental health consultation?

- How would a consultant best determine the reasons that a human service worker or administrator is having difficulties with a work-related problem?

- Are there really differences between work-related and personal problems? If so, what are they?

Mental health consultation has provided the foundation for the development of consultation as service delivery approach (Henning-Stout, 1993). Mental health consultation is based on the idea that society's mental health can be promoted through the efforts of consultants who work with human service personnel (e.g., counselors) or with administrators of human service programs (e.g., the director of a factory's employee assistance program). It started with consultants providing consultation services to community mental health workers (Racine Gilles, Kratochwill, Felt, Schienebeck, & Vaccarello, 2011). Over the years, mental health consultation has expanded the type of consultee worked with to include teachers, parents, and paraprofessionals. The recipients of the consultant's efforts are the "primary agents in preventing mental disorders in a population" (Caplan, 1993b, p. 41). If the consultant can enhance the effectiveness of the consultee, some emotional problems will be reduced, making referral to an expert unnecessary (Meyers, Brent, Flaherty, & Modafferi, 1993). More precisely, mental health consultants assist their consultees with specific work-related problems, such as a difficult case or glitches in a mental health-related program. An important goal of mental health consultation is not only to help consultees cope with their specific work-related problems, but also to have a preventive effect by improving their general level of functioning so that they can be even more effective in the future. As Caplan, Caplan, and Erchul (1994) note, writers in the field need to "underscore the importance of mental health consultation *in the service of primary prevention*" (p. 6).

Mental health consultation has been used in mental health settings, schools (Doll, Spies, & Champion, 2012), nursing homes (Meeks, 1996), hospices (Lindberg, 1996), religious settings (Maloney, 1991), medical settings (Quirk, Strosahl, Kreilkamp, & Erdberg, 1995), police hostage negotiation teams (Butler, Leitenberg, & Fuselier, 1993), community residences for people with developmental disabilities (Hyman, 1993), employee assistance programs (Shosh, 1996), postsecondary education settings (Amada, 1993), youth shelters (Grigsby, 1992), the postwar theater (Garland, 1993), and a variety of other settings.

It has been used for many purposes, including assistance with cases, organizational change, and diversity training, as well as in delivering mental health programs in schools (Doll et al., 2012).

HISTORICAL BACKGROUND

Mental health consultation is a part of the community mental health concept that asserts that services should be available as needed within the community and should be integrated with other human services. Mental health consultation began in the late 1940s with the passage of the federal Mental Health Act of 1946, which created the National Institute of Mental Health (NIMH) and provided states federal moneys for the purpose of supporting mental health services. Public acceptance for community-based mental health services increased in the 1950s; the idea that mental health services were limited to treating severely disturbed individuals in residential treatment centers waned. In 1963, Congress passed the Community Mental Health Centers Act, which provided federal funds for the construction of mental health facilities in local communities and called for consultation and education services to the community.

The concept of the prevention of mental illness became very important both because there was a large discrepancy between the need for services and the ability to meet those needs (Caplan & Caplan, 1993) and also because the efficacy of psychotherapy in treating mental illness was under criticism. The ability of local mental health centers to provide preventative services thus became one of the criteria for being considered for these federal funds.

Consultation services were seen as one type of preventative service to public and private human service professionals, who would become more effective as they attempted to meet the mental health needs of their clientele. Consultation was to be a method for helping non–mental health professionals to learn the mental health skills necessary to assist those people for whom they had professional responsibility (Watson & Robinson, 1996). Consultation was to promote social support systems for all members in the community and thereby have the preventive effect of promoting the psychological well-being of the members of the community as well as reducing the incidence of mental health issues among the community's populace.

A trend that paralleled public and federal interest in preventative services was a shift in the conceptualization of consultation. Before 1950, consultation in agencies was considered to be an extension of clinical psychiatric consultation. In other words, consultation was viewed in terms of the medical consultation model: The psychiatrist examines the patient, makes a diagnosis, and prescribes treatment to the professional in charge. Two trends emerged around 1950 to change this view: Professionals other than psychiatrists came to be viewed as legitimate consultants, and it became clear that problems in treating cases could be due, not only to a lack of knowledge or skills on the part of those in charge of treatment, but also to the consultee's personal concerns or to organizational factors present in the consultee's work site. A few articles incorporating these trends began to appear in the early 1950s, and evidence increased substantially in the mid-1950s.

Around this time, Gerald Caplan arrived on the scene. A psychiatrist by training, Caplan's name has become synonymous with mental health consultation. In fact, mental health consultation is frequently referred to as the *Caplanian model*. He is often credited with "discovering" the usefulness of mental health consultation and describing its various forms.

Caplan attempted to incorporate and apply the ideas of public health in his consultation model. By improving a community's ability to create resources for the promotion of mental health, the prevalence of mental illness would be diminished. By having consultants work with consultees to serve their clients better, mental health would be promoted more widely than possible by a mental health practitioner working individually (Kelly, 1987). For example, if a mental health consultant helped a group of three teachers raise the self-esteem of the students in their classrooms, the consultant, by working directly with three people, would indirectly affect the lives of over 90 students in a relatively short time. Contrast this with the idea of having the practitioner work individually with all 90 students or even work in each of the three different classrooms, one at a time. Clearly, consultation could be a time-saving and efficient mode for promoting mental health.

Caplan's 1970 book, *The Theory and Practice of Mental Health Consultation*, reflects his experiences as a consultant and his research in consultation. Caplan relates that his interest in mental health consultation began around 1949, when he was a member of a team of psychiatrists, social workers, and psychologists at a child guidance center in Israel. Part of the team's duties was to attend to the mental health needs of over 16,000 immigrant children who were cared for in about 100 residential centers.

Referrals to the team far outweighed its ability to provide direct services to the children (Knotek, Kaniuka, & Ellingsen, 2008). The operation of the team under these circumstances led to five discoveries by Caplan. First, the caretakers seemed to have a very restrictive perception of possible management strategies. Second, many of them had very stereotypic perceptions of the children and their difficulties. Third, they were frequently quite upset, and their personal concerns affected their ability to be objective about the children with whom they were working. Fourth, their narrow perceptions, stereotypic attitudes, and personal issues could be ameliorated by particular consultant attitudes and interventions. Finally, the team could learn a substantial amount of relevant information about the children and caretakers by visiting the institution, rather than by bringing the caretakers and children to the team's central office. Out of Caplan's experiences in Israel, the basic rudiments of his model began to take shape. Consultation could be viewed as working with another person to help a client. Consultation typically would take place on the consultee's turf, and the consultee's perceptions of the client would be the basis for consultation.

The consultant would need to be especially observant of the consultee's perceptions and would look for possible distortions, stereotypes, and personal issues that might adversely affect working with the client. The consultant would be objective yet sympathetic and would focus on the client as a person with problems, not as a problem who happens to be a person. When the team members working with the children were treated in this way, they seemed to be able to return to their duties with renewed enthusiasm and a broader perspective on working with clients (Caplan et al., 1994).

After his experiences in Israel, Caplan continued to develop his model of consultation at Harvard's Schools of Public Health and Medicine, where he began to use the term *mental health consultation*. He formally developed the concept of the consultation as a collaborative relationship among equals. The idea that consultation need not occur in a crisis situation, but could also be used for preventative measures, also emerged as did techniques of group consultation. Through Caplan's efforts, mental health consultation became conceptualized as a "method whereby a small group of mental health specialists would guide and support ... non–mental-health-specialist caregivers, such as doctors, nurses, teachers, clergymen, and welfare workers, in mastering the cognitive and

emotional challenges of ... their traditional duties" (Caplan, 1993b, p. 45). Professionals in the human service professions were now able, through consultation, to work at a systems level. Caplan continued updating his views over the years (Caplan, 1974, 1977), including a revision of his first text, entitled *Mental Health Consultation and Collaboration* (Caplan & Caplan, 1993, 1999).

Mental health consultation has expanded over the years in spite of federal spending cutbacks.

Most models remain adaptations of Caplan's, although the theoretical bases underlying these adaptations vary. There has been a move away from the psychodynamic orientation toward other approaches; that is, mental health consultants are free to conceptualize their consultees, clients, and the dynamics of the organizations in which they work from any number of perspectives and approaches. In addition, mental health consultants now regularly consult with other mental health professionals, parents, and paraprofessionals as well as non–mental health professionals such as teachers.

MENTAL HEALTH CONSULTATION DEFINED

Case Example

Consider this relatively simple form of mental health consultation:

You are a social worker who consults with psychiatric nurses concerning approaches to counsel the relatives of Alzheimer's disease victims. One of your consultees is having difficulty with a family of a certain patient. As you listen to the consultee describe the case, you get the impression that the patient's "Jekyll and Hyde" personality is keeping the family off balance. You suggest that the nurse teach the family some self-talk strategies they can use when the patient is acting out. You refer the nurse to several sources of information on self-talk strategies and agree to provide the consultee a training session on these strategies.

This example erroneously suggests a relatively simple definition of mental health consultation.

Various attempts have been made to define mental health consultation. The most consistently recognized definition of mental health consultation is from Caplan and Caplan (1993), who describe it as

> a process of interaction between two professional persons—the consultant, who is a specialist, and the consultee, who invokes the consultant's help in regard to a current work problem with which he is having some difficulty and which he has decided is within the other's area of specialized competence. The work problem involves the management or treatment of one or more clients of the consultee, or the planning or implementation of a program to cater to such clients. (p. 1)

Subsequent attempts at defining mental health consultation (e.g., Hodges & Cooper, 1983; Mannino, MacLennan, & Shore, 1975) elaborated on the type of help the consultant provides while holding to the basic ideas in Caplan's definition. Notice this emphasis in the following definition by MacLennan, Quinn, and Schroeder (1975, cited in Bloom, 1984, p. 155):

> Mental health consultation is the provision of technical assistance by an expert to individual and agency caregivers related to the mental health dimension of their work. Such assistance is directed to specific work-related problems, is advisory in nature, and the consultant has no direct responsibility for its acceptance or implementation. This definition suggests that the consultant will function as a technical expert in an advisory capacity.

Hodges and Cooper (1983) in the 1980s expanded on Caplan's definition by adding some of the specific role behaviors the consultant uses in helping consultees:

> Community mental health consultation can be defined as the process by which a mental health professional interacts with community-based professionals and other service providers (the consultees) to supply information, skill training, and individual process change or system change in order to help the consultee or the system better serve the mental health needs of the people in the community. (pp. 19–20)

In summary, mental health consultation is a process in which a mental health professional interacts with a consultee and assists him or her with the mental health aspects of a work-related problem that concerns either a client or a program. The consultant uses knowledge and skills to assist the consultee with the specific concern and, in addition, attempts to improve the consultee's ability to function in the future. The consultee has the freedom to choose whether or not to apply the assistance provided in consultation and remains responsible for the client or the program. The bottom line is that the consultant serves to assist the consultee with the psychological elements of a current work-related or caregiving problem related to a specific client or program (Erchul & Schulte, 1993).

KEY CONCEPTS OF MENTAL HEALTH CONSULTATION

Basic Characteristics

From Caplan's point of view, mental health consultation has several basic characteristics, awareness of which is essential for understanding his view. (The following list is adapted with permission of Waveland Press, Inc. from Caplan & Caplan, *Mental Health Consultation and Collaboration*, pp. 21–23. Long Grove, IL; Waveland Press, Inc. [reissued 1999]. All rights reserved. Reprinted by permission of the publisher.)

1.   Mental health consultation is a method used by two professionals in respect to a lay client or a program for such clients.

2. The consultee's work problem must be defined by him or her as being mental health related, such as a mental disorder or personality idiosyncrasy of the client, the need to promote mental health in the client, or interpersonal aspects of the work situation. The consultant must have expert knowledge in these areas.

3. The consultant has neither administrative responsibility for the consultee's work nor professional responsibility for the outcome of the client's case. She or he is under no compulsion to modify the consultee's conduct of the case.

4. The consultee is under no compulsion to accept the consultant's ideas or suggestions.

5. The basic relationship between the two is coordinate; there is no built-in hierarchy or authority–subordinate tension, which in our culture potentiates the influence of ideas. The consultees' freedom to accept or reject what the consultant says enables them to take quickly as their own any ideas that appeal to them in their current situation.

6. The coordinate relationship is fostered by the consultant's membership (typically) in another profession and his or her arrival into the consultee's institution from the outside.

7. The coordinate relationship is further supported by the fact that consultation is usually given as a short series of interviews—two or three on average, which take place intermittently in response to consultees' awareness of their current need for help with a work problem. The relationship in individual consultation is not maintained and dependence is not fostered by continuing contact. In group consultation there may be regular meetings, but dependence is reduced by peer support.

8. Consultation is expected to continue indefinitely, for consultees can be expected to encounter unusual work problems throughout their careers. Increasing competence and sophistication of consultees in their own profession improves the likelihood of their recognizing mental health complications and asking for consultation.

9. Consultants have no predetermined body of information that they intend to impart to a particular consultee. They respond only to the segment of the consultee's problems that the consultee exposes in the current work difficulty. The consultant does not seek to remedy other areas of inadequacy in the consultee but instead expects other issues to be raised in future consultation.

10. The twin goals of consultation are to help consultees improve their handling or understanding of the current work difficulty and through this to increase their capacity to master future problems of a similar type.

11. The aim of consultation is to improve consultees' job performance, not their sense of well-being. It is envisaged, however, that, because the two are linked, consultees' feelings of personal worth will probably be increased by successful consultation, as will their capacity to deal in a reality-based socially acceptable way with certain life difficulties. In other words, successful consultation may have the secondary effect of being therapeutic to consultees.

12. Consultation does not focus overtly on personal problems and feelings of consultees.

It respects their privacy. The consultant does not allow discussion of personal and private material in the consultation interview. This does not mean that consultants disregard the feelings of the consultee. They are particularly sensitive to the feelings and to the disturbance of task functioning produced by personal problems. They deal with personal problems, however, in a special way, such as by discussing problems in the context in which they relate to the client's case and the work setting.

13. Consultation is usually one of the professional functions of a specialist—even if he is titled *consultant*. He should use the consultation method only when it is appropriate. At other times he should use different methods. Sometimes the demands of the situation will cause

him to put aside his consultation. For instance, if he gets information during a consultation interview that leads him to judge that the consultee's actions are seriously endangering the client (e.g., failing to prevent a suicide or to pursue treatment for a dangerous psychosis), he should set aside his consultant role and revert to the basic role of a psychiatrist, psychologist, or social worker. He will then give advice or take action that the consultee is not free to reject. This destroys the coordinate relationship and interrupts the consultation contact in favor of a higher goal. Such dramatic occasions are rare, but the possibility demonstrates the realistic limits of this method.

14. Finally, it is worth emphasizing that mental health consultation is a method of communication between a mental health specialist and other professionals. It does not denote a new profession, merely a special way in which existing professionals may operate.

These characteristics represent the basis for the practice of mental health consultation from Caplan's perspective. Although the consultant is the expert, the relationship is an equal one. The nature of the consultant–consultee relationship is crucial: The consultant assists with work-related problems only and does not deal directly with the consultee's personal concerns. The consultee's work problems may be viewed from a psychodynamic perspective, and the goal of consultation is to enhance the consultee's current and future ability to function professionally. The consultant does not take any supervisory authority over the consultee's actions and has no responsibility for the client/program (Caplan, 1993a). Further, it is essential that the consultant take organizational influences into account when conducting consultation (Conoley & Wright, 1993).

Psychodynamic Orientation

The original Caplanian model used a psychodynamic approach to consultation, for, as a trained psychiatrist, Caplan was heavily influenced by the work of Sigmund Freud. The Caplan model relies on an intrapsychic view of behavior change; this psychodynamic orientation makes the Caplan model one of the most complex consultation models (Conoley & Conoley, 1992). A detailed discussion of the psychodynamic approach is beyond the scope of this book. Those interested in reviewing Freud and his modifiers should consult a good text on theories of counseling and psychotherapy, such as Corey's *Theory and Practice of Counseling and Psychotherapy* (2009). A brief review of psychodynamic perspective follows. The *psychodynamic approach* fosters the concept that our behavior is a product of unconscious motivation and that most of our personal issues result from early childhood experiences. These issues often lead to inner conflicts that affect our behavior and cause us problems. Because these inner conflicts are usually unconscious, we are often unaware of the causes of our behavior. True behavioral change must deal with these unresolved conflicts from the past; merely dealing with the behavioral manifestations of a person's problems only results in the emergence of another problem because the core problem has not been adequately addressed. This phenomenon is often referred to as symptom substitution.

Not every difficulty a consultee has with a case or program is due to inner conflict. A difficulty might stem from a lack of appropriate professional knowledge about some aspect of the case. But from Caplan's perspective, when the consultee's inner conflicts are causing problems with a case or program, they must in some way be addressed to ensure the consultee's adequate functioning with the current case and with similar cases in the future. Changing overt behaviors will only provide temporary change. Because the consultant does not provide psychotherapy to the consultee, the consultee's inner conflicts must be dealt with indirectly.

In his later writings (e.g., Caplan et al., 1994), Caplan has stressed the importance of taking into consideration not just the psychodynamics of the individuals involved but also those forces operating in the organizations (e.g., environmental factors) represented by the consultant and consultee in addition to those in the community itself. Hence, Caplan's thought has evolved into one that takes into consideration the larger systems context of consultation.

Transfer of Effect

Transfer of effect refers to the concept that what is learned in one situation should be usable in similar, future situations, which is central to the Caplanian model. Prevention has always been an important element in mental health consultation, most likely due to Caplan's background in preventive psychiatry public health. The premise was that psychiatry had the capability to assist communities by providing preventive interventions in the community. These interventions would have a preventive effect, thus reducing the frequency of occurrence of mental health problems within the community while bolstering its psychological well-being.

Consultee-centered consultation improves the consultee's capacity to function effectively and to benefit current clients as well as similar ones in the future. By listening to the consultee's perceptions of the client or program and extrapolating the pertinent information concerning the consultee's difficulty, the consultant by indirect means can help the consultee be more objective. In addition, by retaining responsibility for the case or program, the consultee is set up for optimal learning and generalization to future cases (Erchul & Schulte, 1993).

Types of Consultation

The manner in which mental health consultation is conceptualized is a critical factor in terms of how it is practiced. The consultant should have a system to anticipate what is likely to happen in each consultation situation and to identify effective strategies with which to approach the consultation. To accomplish this end, Caplan (1970) devised a classification system with two major divisions.

The first concerns whether the consultant *focuses on a case* (e.g., a client at a halfway house) or *focuses on an administrative problem* dealing with a mental health–related program (e.g., helping a health science teacher implement a unit on substance abuse).

The second division concerns whether the consultant's primary goal is "giving a specialized opinion and recommendation for a solution" (Caplan, 1970, p. 32) (e.g., observing a client and recommending a specific therapeutic technique) or "attempting to improve the problem-solving capacity of the consultees and leaving them to work out their own way of solving it" (Caplan, 1970, p. 32) (e.g., helping a parole officer be more objective about a case with a parolee). The goal is thus to change either the *client* (or program) or the *consultee*.

These two divisions make up four types of consultation: *client-centered case consultation, consultee-centered case consultation, program-centered administrative consultation,* and *consultee-centered administrative consultation* (Caplan & Caplan, 1993). This classification formed the early organization of consultation types, and most reconceptualizations of types are summaries of Caplan's work.

Each of the four types of consultation has a different level of intervention, an identifiable target, and an identifiable goal (Bloom, 1984). Table 9.1 presents Caplan and Caplan's (1993) classification as defined by these three factors.

THE CONSULTATION PROCESS

Next we'll examine these four types of mental health consultation in terms of their goals, the consultant's function and role, the consultee's experience in consultation, and the use of consultation techniques and procedures. Because of its unique nature and its impact on the development of mental health consultation, consultee-centered case consultation is covered in more depth than are the other three types.

The Client-Centered Case Consultation Process

Consultation Goals. Client-centered case consultation is the most commonly used form of mental health consultation. It typifies what most human service professionals think of when they hear the

T A B L E   9.1   Caplan and Caplan's Consultation Classification in Terms of Level, Target, and Goal

	CLIENT-CENTERED CASE	CONSULTEE-CENTERED CASE	PROGRAM-CENTERED ADMINISTRATIVE	CONSULTEE CENTERED ADMINISTRATIVE
Level	Case	Case	Administrative	Administrative
Target	Client	Consultee	Program	Consultee
Goal	Behavioral change in client	Enhanced consultee performance in delivering services to clients	More effective delivery of program	Enhanced consultee performance in programming

word *consultation*. The consultant is viewed as an expert or specialist who can diagnose and recommend an intervention. It is prescriptive in nature (Hylander, 2012). This type of consultation can serve certain purposes (Raines & Dibble, 2011). First, the absence of clinical supervision in many settings, such as schools, indicates the necessity of having case consultants available. Second, consultants can provide specialized expertise on demanding cases. Third, in some cases, mental health professionals, for whatever reason, are simply having difficulty with a given case and require consultation from a person who is current in the research related to the issues with the client. Fourth, mental health professionals may request consultation regarding any ethical and/or legal issues they encounter in their casework. Finally, a consultant may be needed by those professionals who have just experienced a difficult situation such as a law suit or adverse client outcome.

In this type of consultation, the consultee presents a case in which a client has mental health problems that are causing the consultee some difficulty. The primary goal of this type of consultation is to develop a plan to help the client. Secondarily, the consultee is better able to handle similar cases alone in the future as a result of contact with the consultant. However, only limited educational benefit to the consultee is expected from this type of consultation because the consultant spends very little time with the consultee. From a school-based consultation example, client-centered case consultation would have the consultant assist with a student who is having academic difficulties by having the consultant diagnose the situation and make

related recommendations to the referring teacher (Snyder, Quirk, & Dematteo, 2011).

Consultant Function and Roles.   The consultant functions primarily as an expert in assessing the situation, diagnosing the client, and making recommendations for the consultee's use in the case. Specifically, the consultant builds a relationship with the consultee (in ways previously discussed); assesses the client's difficulty by gathering information from the client (e.g., observation, interviewing formal assessment) and other sources; assesses the consultee's strengths, weaknesses, and work setting by visiting the consultee at work; and files a written report, usually a letter or a case record, which should (if possible) be reviewed in a meeting with the consultee. In this way, the consultant can improve the consultee's functioning in similar cases in the future. It is the consultee's responsibility to use the written report and the conference with the consultant in dealing with the case. In other words, the consultee takes the consultant's report and develops and implements a plan of action. Finally, the consultant plans for a follow-up session with the consultee.

Consultee Experience in Consultation.   Consultees in client-centered case consultation focus on providing the consultant with as much pertinent information and professional opinion as possible regarding the case, such as the consultee's role relative to the client system and any constraints that have been laid upon the consultee.

Even though the consultant is likely to observe, interview, or test the client, the consultant wants to know how the consultee views the case. The consultee, then, is not only a link between the consultant and client but also a professional collaborator who knows the client better than the consultant and knows best how to deal with the client within the consultee institution.

The consultee's primary responsibility is to adapt and carry out the consultant's recommendations, but the consultee is free to accept or reject any or all of them. The consultee may require the assistance of the consultant in implementing a given recommendation but must ask for such assistance. Finally, the consultee participates in a scheduled follow-up session with the consultant.

Application: Consultant Techniques and Procedures.   It is not unusual for a written note to accompany a consultee's request for consultation, and it is best for the consultant to respond to the consultee with some form of personal contact so as to build a relationship, clarify what the consultee desires from the consultant, and obtain more information on the client.

In assessing the client, the consultant has two basic questions: Should the client be referred for specialized treatment? What can the consultee do to help the client in the consultee's work setting? These are answered by listening to the consultee (and perhaps the client and his or her significant others when applicable [see Karg & Wiens (2005) for interviewing suggestions]).

It is quite risky to provide client-centered case consultation in the consultant's office. Without assessing the consultee and the consultee's work setting, the consultant can rely only on the client's report about the consultee and the work setting. Because the consultant needs to know about the strengths and weaknesses of the consultee and the consultee institution to make effective and realistic recommendations, the consultant should visit and perform consultation in the consultee institution.

One of the consultant's major tasks in client-centered case consultation is writing a report for the consultee. This report, typically supplemented by a face-to-face meeting with the consultee to clarify the report and answer questions related to it, should be written in language appropriate to the consultee's institution, should be practical, and should avoid condescending terminology.

The main body of the report should focus on how the client is or is not coping in major areas of life and include some recommendations as to how the consultee can facilitate improved client functioning in appropriate areas.

A Sample of a Consultant's Written Report.   The following is a portion of a consultant's report prepared by a counselor working with a teacher having difficulty with Dana, a third-grade student who steals from other children in the classroom: The stealing behavior is most likely caused by Dana's need for security. The objects taken are usually food (e.g., snacks) or school supplies (e.g., pencils). The fact that Dana makes little attempt not to get caught perhaps suggests that there is the perception on her part of too little attention. Stealing objects thus helps Dana feel more secure and get attention.

I recommend that the teacher make a deliberate attempt to praise Dana throughout the school day for appropriate classroom behaviors. In addition, she could be assigned some classroom responsibilities (e.g., erasing the board) and then be reinforced for acting responsibly. Dana's security might be increased if the teacher frequently communicated to her that she belongs in the classroom and that the teacher takes care of all children in the classroom. Such verbalizations can reduce insecurity. Implementation of the consultant's recommendations is the consultee's prerogative because he or she has responsibility for the case. However, the consultant can help determine whether the consultee has the knowledge and skills required to perform the suggested interventions. Such a judgment is best achieved by having a history of sustained contact with the consultee so that an assessment of consultee strengths and weaknesses is possible before the formulation of recommendations.

Follow-up by the consultant is crucial: It provides the consultant a rough evaluation of the effects of consultation; it provides feedback on how the consultant's interventions affected the consultee in the case under discussion, which could be useful to the consultant in improving future interventions; and it conveys consultant interest to the consultee and improves their relationship so that the consultee may actively seek additional consultation about the current or some other case.

Case Example of Client-Centered Case Consultation. Tracy is a resident psychologist consulting with Kim, an activity therapist, concerning a patient in a residential psychiatric hospital. The therapist reports that the patient, a 15-year-old, refuses to engage in any activity therapy. The client shows up on time but just sits and watches as the other patients engage in the therapy.

Tracy observes the patient in several hospital settings, including activity therapy, and interviews the patient's primary therapist concerning the case. She determines that the patient appears to have few friends at the hospital but is friendly and approachable. She also concludes that Kim has the ability and motivation to assist the patient to begin participation in activity therapy.

Tracy writes a brief report suggesting a "buddy system" for the patient. Kim would implement the program, in which one or two higher functioning patients could become friends with and accompany the patient to the activity therapy group, where they could perform the activities together. Tracy shares this recommendation in a final consultation session with Kim, who agrees to the recommendation, and takes steps to implement the program. Tracy follows up after two weeks to monitor the intervention.

The Consultee-Centered Case Consultation Process

Consultation Goals. Consultee-centered case consultation not only fosters client change but it also promotes consultee professional development (Knotek et al., 2008). Consultee-centered case consultation developed from Caplan's view of primary prevention (Calderon, Subotnik, Knotek, Rayhack, & Gorgia, 2007; Gutkin & Curtis, 2009). The idea is that consultee-centered consultation

promotes "… consultees' professional development within and through the consultation process" (Calderon et al., 2007, p. 351) by changing consultee's conceptualizations of the case. Consultee-centered consultation is nonprescriptive in nature and its purpose is to foster conceptual change on the part of the consultee regarding the client system (Hylander, 2012). The bottom line in this approach is that the behaviors of the consultee significantly impact the difficulty experienced in working with the clientsystem (Pryzwansky, 2011). When the consultant supports the resulting consultee reconceptualization, the client system will be more effectively assisted by the consultee. The primary goal of consultee-centered case consultation is improvement of the consultee's ability to work effectively with a particular case as well as with similar cases in the future. "In consultee-centered case consultation the consultant's primary focus is upon elucidating and remedying the shortcomings in the consultee's professional functioning that are responsible for his difficulties with the case with which he is seeking help" (Caplan & Caplan, 1993, p. 101). Improvement of the client is the secondary goal (Gravois, Groff, & Rosenfield, 2009). As in client-centered case consultation, the case is the focus of discussion, although usually the consultant does not see the client because the goal is to help the consultee. The consultant helps the consultee by focusing on his or her subjective view of the case.

Consultant Function and Roles. In consultee-centered case consultation, the consultant plays the roles of detective, expert, and educator. In the role of detective, the consultant seeks out the consultee's cognitive and emotional problems through active listening and judicious questioning. The consultant discusses the case with the consultee in the role of an expert mental health professional. As an educator, the consultant provides the consultee the information and/or training needed to solve problems with this and similar cases in the future. Thus, the consultant builds a relationship with the consultee, assesses his or her problem with the case, and intervenes to alleviate the problem.

The consultant asks the consultee to discuss the case, and the remainder of the consultation relationship involves such discussions. The consultant, however, is more directive than in client-centered case consultation in that the consultee is asked to discuss selected aspects of the case, which provides the consultant information about the consultee's work difficulty. As the consultee discusses the case, the consultant categorizes the consultee's work difficulty as a lack of knowledge, skill, confidence, or professional objectivity. The consultant intervenes to resolve the consultee's particular work problem. The so-called "grist for the mill" in consultation comes from the consultee's "subjectively determined story" (Caplan & Caplan, 1993, p. 101), not from the real facts about the case.

Consultee Experience in Consultation. In consultee-centered case consultation, the consultee's task is to enter into the consultation relationship and discuss a case that is causing difficulty. Under the consultant's guidance, the consultee elaborates on the particulars of the case. When the consultant makes interventions to assist the consultee, it is up to the consultee to implement those recommendations, which often include ways the consultee can improve professional functioning. The consultee maintains full responsibility for the case under discussion.

During the initial stages of consultation, the consultee may have a very narrow view of the case. Indeed, consultees often do not know why they are having difficulty with cases. In responding to the consultant's judicious questioning, the consultee's perceptions of the case are enriched and broadened so that the "cognitive grasp and emotional mastery" (Caplan & Caplan, 1993, p. 101) of the particulars of the case are increased.

Application: Consultation Techniques and Procedures. There are four approaches to consultee-centered case consultation, one for each of the four reasons that consultees may have difficulty with cases: lack of knowledge, skill, self-confidence, and professional objectivity. Now we'll consider each of these four approaches, which can be performed individually or in groups.

Lack of Knowledge. When the difficulty with a case is due to lack of knowledge, the consultee might not have sufficient understanding of the client's problem, some important client characteristics, or both. According to Caplan, the consultee may lack either factual or theoretical knowledge needed to deal effectively with the case. The consultant imparts the missing knowledge to the consultee in a manner conducive to the consultee's success in the case under discussion as well as for possible similar cases in the future. It is very important that the consultant provide this information without violating the coordinating nature of the relationship, a task best accomplished by capitalizing on the consultee's motivation to learn information relevant to the case at hand. The consultee's education results from applying the needed knowledge to the current case, which also maintains the desired consultant–consultee relationship.

Lack of Skill. The consultee may well have the knowledge required to understand a case but lacks only the skill to intervene effectively. In this situation, the consultant should avoid the temptation to supervise the consultee's conduct of the case.

Procedurally, the consultant and the consultee conduct a joint appraisal of the case: They explore the problems, what the consultee has tried so far to help the client, and what the consultee could yet do to resolve the issue. Such a procedure broadens the consultee's perspective on the case, provides a broader context for perceiving subsequent similar cases, maintains the coordinate nature of the relationship, and preserves the consultee's self-esteem. The consultant determines the degree of the consultee's skill deficit, describes what skills are needed to deal effectively with the case, and explores with the consultee the means to get the appropriate skills training within the consultee institution. If such training is not available within the consultee institution, the consultant can provide the training.

Lack of Self-Confidence. Lack of self-confidence can cause confusion and uncertainty about how to handle a case. It can result from consultee inexperience (e.g., being assigned a particular client problem for the first time or being a beginner on the job) or be a generalized trait within the consultee that manifests itself in reduced on-the-job functioning.

The goal of the consultant is to provide support and encouragement by fostering hope, confidence, and courage by affirming the consultee's strengths and capabilities. Reassurance, which damages the nonhierarchical nature of the relationship, should be avoided. The consultant's second goal is to help the consultee find a peer support group within the consultee institution.

Lack of Professional Objectivity.   The consultant considers lack of objectivity only after lack of knowledge and lack of skill are eliminated (Erchul, 1993a). Lack of objectivity is the most common problem among consultees who work in institutions that have a knowledgeable, skilled staff and a supervisory system; hence, most consultee-centered case consultations are of this type. The consultee's lack of professional objectivity is a defective judgment—an inability to maintain an appropriate professional distance. The consultee's role functioning, perceptions, and judgments are impaired by subjective factors that make him or her unable to apply existing knowledge and skills to the case effectively.

By the time the consultee seeks out consultation, confusion, frustration, incompetence, and declining self-esteem are often evident and can cause a lack of professional poise. The coordinate nature of the consultant–consultee relationship is in greatest jeopardy in consultee-centered case consultation because the consultant appears to be in control of personal issues in the professional setting, whereas the consultee is not. Therefore, the consultant should *indirectly* help the consultee recapture professional objectivity by discussing the client, the consultant, or some fictitious client in a story or parable (Knotek, 2012). The consultee's problem should not be dealt with directly. The consultee's confidence and poise must be maintained (Caplan, 1993b).

Lack of objectivity in even the most knowledgeable and skilled consultees can result from five somewhat connected reasons: direct personal involvement, simple identification, transference,

characterological distortions, and theme interference (Caplan & Caplan, 1993).

When a consultee loses professional objectivity due to *direct personal involvement*, the relationship changes from a professional to a personal one. An obvious example is when a consultee falls in love with a client. Because of the emotional nature of personal relationships, objectivity is lost. Professionals should keep a certain distance from their clients to maintain objectivity, and personal involvement alters the balance of that relationship by causing the consultee to be either too close or too distant from the client. Consultees are frequently unaware of their personal involvement with their clients and do not realize they are fulfilling their own personal needs at the expense of those of the client.

Simple identification occurs when the consultee does not merely empathize with but instead identifies with the client (or some person in the client's life) and loses the sense of neutrality so essential to maintaining objectivity. The consultee identifies with some real characteristic of the client (or person in the client's life), such as race, gender, or some behavior pattern the consultee considers idiosyncratic. For example, a consultee who is a minister might overidentify with a client who is also a minister.

The client is then described in a positive, sympathetic manner, while others in the case are viewed in derogatory terms. The consultant can relatively easily identify simple identification because of the obvious similarities between the consultee and some person in the case.

A *transference* distortion occurs when the consultee transfers onto the client feelings and attitudes from key relationships in the past. Once the consultee's predetermined attitudes and feelings are imposed on the client and objectivity is lost, the consultee is unable to assess the client's real situation. For example, a consultee who has difficulty with authority figures due to her childhood relationship with her mother might have difficulty dealing with a client who is the head of a large company. The transference relationship tends to be repeated over time in similar cases.

Minor disturbances in consultees, often referred to as *characterological distortions* of perceptions and behavior, can cause consultees to lose their professional objectivity. Caplan defines these distortions as personality problems most people have that interfere with the effective delivery of human services to the client. To illustrate this point, Caplan (1970) tells of a teacher, with a tendency toward sexually acting out, who anxiously attributed harmful sexual behaviors to several of her students that a consultant later described as quite normal.

Caplan's concept of *theme interference* is a special type of transference reaction that causes consultees to lose their professional objectivity. Theme interference becomes apparent to a consultant when the consultee is "blocked" from progressing with a case for no explicable reason.

For example, a consultee who has difficulty dealing with anger might impose this trait on the client, in effect saying, "Unless this client deals with his anger during our sessions together, no progress can be made in this case." For some reason, the consultee has identified with some aspect of the client's case.

According to Caplan and Caplan (1993), theme interference develops in the following manner: "A conflict related to actual life experiences or to fantasies in the consultee that have not been satisfactorily resolved is apt to persist in his preconscious or unconscious as an emotionally toned cognitive constellation which we call a 'theme'" (p. 122). The theme is a recurring symbol of an unresolved problem and has a preemptory quality. When suffering from theme interference, the consultee sees the case as being hopeless and makes several inappropriate problem-solving efforts (Erchul & Schulte, 1993). Themes generally repeat themselves, carry a negative emotional valence, and take the form of a syllogism. This syllogism has two statements that constitute a prejudicial stereotyped notion and are perceived by the consultee to be linked in such a way that they are inseparable: an "initial category" followed by an "inevitable outcome."

The initial category is a statement that signifies the condition that was characteristic of the original unresolved problem in the consultee's life. In reality, the client may or may not fit the stereotype, but still the consultee applies the stereotype to the client. The stereotype is imposed when consultees form their impressions of the client; certain pieces of information are put together and the initial category is formed. Placing the client in the initial category leads to expectations that are typified in the inevitable outcome, which is a rigid assumption that the worst-case scenario will occur.

When put together, the initial category and inevitable outcome take the following form: If A (initial category) happens to anyone, then B (inevitable outcome) must occur. One example might be, "If my client doesn't deal with his anger, we will never make any progress in therapy." In such cases, the consultant must assume that the consultee has a problem in dealing with anger and that the client may or may not have the same problem.

The problem with theme interference is that, by losing objectivity, the consultee is unable to see that there are many possible outcomes to any problem and that several possible interventions are available to achieve those outcomes. This lack of objectivity causes inconsistent, sometimes panicky behavior in the consultee, and the subsequent lack of progress in the case reaffirms the belief in the inevitable outcome. Thus, a vicious cycle develops. There is, however, one source of consolation for the consultee: The inevitable outcome happens to the client, not the consultee. Theme interference tends to recur as long as the theme is manifest.

There are two basic methods the mental health consultant can use to relieve theme interference in consultees. These methods are subtle and designed to "alter the emotional theme underlying the lack of objectivity" (Henning-Stout, 1993, p. 21). First, the consultant helps the consultee reassess the cues in the client's case that led to placement in the incorrect category in the first place. Such a reevaluation helps the consultee see that the original perceptions were erroneous and return to professional objectivity because the inevitable outcome is no longer pertinent. Caplan and Caplan (1993) label this technique *unlinking* (p. 125) because it unlinks the client from the consultee's theme.

Whereas unlinking attempts to invalidate the initial category, the second approach, called *theme interference reduction*, attempts to invalidate the inevitable outcome. The consultant invalidates the "If A, then B" syllogism by helping the consultee reexamine the evidence on which the inevitability of the outcome is based. The consultee is then able to view the previously inevitable outcome as merely one of an array of possible outcomes (and not necessarily a very likely one at that). The influence of the consultee's theme then begins to wane.

Theme interference reduction affects the consultee on both cognitive and affective levels. Theme interference reduction techniques neither exacerbate resistance nor cause a loss of face because the consultant accepts the consultee's view of the initial category: The consultant does not try to deal with the consultee's inner conflicts directly but rather through their discussion of the case. When properly carried out, theme interference reduction helps consultees by lowering their level of tension, raising their level of objectivity, weakening the theme, and reducing the likelihood that the theme will be displaced on subsequent cases.

Several techniques are effective in theme interference reduction, and all of them have the following steps occurring over a three- or four-week period: assessment of the theme, the consultant's intervention, and ending and follow-up (Caplan & Caplan, 1993). The expression of intense feelings by the consultee is permitted as long as the consultee expresses feelings about the case and does not believe that the feelings are about him- or herself (Caplan, 1993b). Part of the consultant's job is to help the consultee feel safe while expressing emotionally sensitive material.

In assessing the theme, the consultant examines the consultee institution, the affective and cognitive reactions of the consultee to the case, indications of an initial category and inevitable outcome, and the possibility that there is more than one theme. Once the existence of theme interference has been established, the consultant can make one or more of the following interventions (Caplan & Caplan, 1993):

- verbal focus on the client
- verbal focus on an alternative object—the parable
- nonverbal focus on the case
- nonverbal focus on the consultation relationship

A *verbal focus on the client* is the most commonly used technique in theme interference reduction. The consultant discusses with the consultee the evidence for the inevitable outcome by examining in significant detail the facts concerning the case, by which the so-called inevitable outcome is seen instead as one possible outcome among many others. The likelihood of the inevitable outcome's occurrence is explored specifically and in depth to ensure that the consultee does not consider the consultant to be prejudiced against that outcome. By such a thorough examination, the consultee realizes that the inevitable outcome is not even among the most likely outcomes. For example, when a consultee thinks a client must deal with the issue of avoidance of competition, a consultant might help the consultee consider several other therapeutic approaches to pursue with the client.

Parables are used when the consultant thinks it important to create greater distance between the consultee's growing awareness of the theme and its connection to the personal issues in his or her life. It must be remembered that consultation is not psychotherapy; the consultee's personal issues are not to be discussed, even though they may be affecting the case. Once the consultant identifies the initial category and the inevitable outcome and decides that the case under consideration is not a good vehicle to break the connection between the two, a verbal focus on an alternative object is often used.

In using a parable, the consultant artistically creates a believable story concerning the identified theme but uses a fictitious client in a fictitious case (Caplan & Caplan-Moskovich, 2004; Mang, 2004). The details of the current case are used as a springboard for creating the anecdote, but details are changed significantly so that only basic similarities to the client and consultee remain. Discussion of the fictitious case then results in the realization that the so-called inevitable outcome was only one of many possible outcomes and that the fictitious case did indeed have a different outcome. Thus, for example, when a consultee suggests that a client must agree to assertive training to overcome shyness, the consultant might relate a story about a fictitious client who overcame shyness by going through a cognitive behavioral form of counseling.

Because the consultee is likely to consider the consultant a role model, the ways the consultant responds nonverbally to the consultee's anxieties about the case can be a very powerful tool in theme interference reduction. When the consultant uses a *nonverbal focus on the case*, the consultant's nonverbal behavior demonstrates to the consultee in a relaxed state free of anxiety that the consultant is not really worried that the inevitable outcome must occur. This technique works only if the consultee perceives that the consultant has dealt with the case seriously and thoroughly and has appreciated both the consultee's concern for urgent action and the client's situation. In a simple example, when a consultee nervously relates the specifics of a case, the consultant would maintain a calm demeanor.

A *nonverbal focus on the consultation relationship* is needed when the consultee transfers themes not onto a case but onto the consultant, particularly when the consultation relationship is well developed and contains emotional connections between the two parties. If the consultee transfers a theme by ascribing a certain role to the consultant and then plays the complementary role, the consultant needs to show the usual acceptance of the initial category and then invalidate the inevitable outcome through discussion of the case. However, the expectation of the inevitable outcome should be dealt with in a nonverbal manner, that is, by remaining calm, objective, and free from anxiety. By staying "cool, calm, and collected" both about the case and the transference occurring in the consultation relationship itself, the consultant is working on both planes simultaneously. For example,

when a consultee suggests that the consultant should be as upset about the case as the consultee is, the consultant shows appreciation for his or her view but remains calm about what is happening in the consultation session.

Innovations in Consultee-Centered Consultation

Consultee-centered consultation has received a great deal of attention and development in the first two decades of the new millennium (Hylander, 2003, 2012). Consultee-centered consultation has evolved over time beyond Caplan's original conceptualization, with factors such as constructivist theory creating the need for a new definition. This new definition has two important components. First, the consultant assists the consultee to "… pinpoint critical information and then consider multiple views about well-being, development, intrapersonal, interpersonal, and organizational effectiveness appropriate to the consultee's work setting. Ultimately, the consultee may reframe his or her prior conceptualization of the work problem" (Knotek & Sandoval, 2003, p. 245). The second point deals with the goal of consultee-centered consultation, which is "… the joint development of a new way of conceptualizing the work problem so that the repertoire of the consultee is expanded.… As the problem is jointly reconsidered, new ways of approaching the problem may lead to acquiring new means to address the work dilemma" (Knotek & Sandoval, 2003, p. 245). As a result, the working relationship between the consultee and the client system is improved (Calderon et al., 2007; Sandoval, 2003).

Knotek and Sandoval (2003) point out the significance of these changes to the definition of consultee-centered consultation. First, rather than a psychodynamic orientation, the process employs a constructivist approach that emphasizes cognition and constructing *conceptual change*, that is, how the consultee (and often the consultant) understands and views the problem (Sander, Sharkey, Olivarri, Tanigawa, & Mauseth, 2010; Sandoval, 1996, 2004). Second, the consultee-centered consultation now encompasses more than mental health consultation (e.g., instructional consultation) and can occur in a variety of settings beyond mental health clinics such as schools (Caplan & Caplan-Moskovich, 2004; Knotek et al., 2008). A third change noted by Hylander (2012) is that the focus is not really on the consultee him- or herself, but on the consultee's "… representation and presentation of the problem with the client" (p. 31). The consultee's presentation is how the consultee thinks, feels, and is considering action.

In the new consultee-centered consultation, consultants build strong relationships with consultees and help them tell their stories about their experiences with their clients. Through judicious questioning, the consultants determine their consultees' conceptualization of the problem and their efforts to date in resolving the problem (Sandoval, 2003). Consultants then share their view of the problem with consultees and make their thinking transparent and explicit. By explaining their views and their rationale for reconceptualizing the problem, consultants help consultees to begin to think differently about the client system. At this point, consultants often point out anomalous (e.g., atypical) data that may cause dissonance for the consultee that can lead to richer and deeper thinking on the part of the consultee. This leads to a mutual reconstruction of the focus of consultation and answering why the client system is behaving in a particular manner (Knotek, 2012). The consultee now has a neutral, not biased, conceptualization of the problem. The dynamics of the consultant move through confirming the consultee's original views, then shift to being neutral by asking judicious questions, and then change to professionally challenging the consultee to look at other possible views. Typically, because the consultee has moved from the original conceptualization and representation, resistance does not occur.

Caplan and Caplan-Moskovich (2004) have modified consultee-centered consultation to include a range of techniques that consultants can use given the specific consultation situation. They have also made the point that theoretical conceptualizations beyond psychodynamic theory are legitimate for the consultant to use.

Case Example of Consultee-Centered Case Consultation. A mental health consultant is working with a social worker whose caseload consists primarily of indigent families. The consultee brings up a case about the members of a particular family the consultee thinks are "just plain lazy" and are becoming more so because of the welfare they are receiving. The consultee notes that the middle class is the ultimate loser. The consultant listens carefully to the consultee's subjective view of the case, notes the consultee's defective judgment, and determines that the consultee's difficulty in working effectively with the family is due to theme interference. The consultee views hard work and effort as vehicles for achievement. The theme interference takes the form of the syllogism: Unless the family overcomes its laziness (initial category), family members will never amount to much (inevitable outcome). The consultant notes that the consultee appears to be fixated on the "laziness" of the family.

In attempts to reduce the theme interference, the consultant calls this case a tough one and suggests that three consultation sessions over a three-week period might help alleviate the problem. During the consultation sessions, the consultant listens and reacts calmly to the consultee's frustrations concerning the case. The consultant then describes two cases involving "lazy" families in which therapeutic benefits were attained, even though the families remained "lazy." As a result of these fictitious case examples, the consultee feels more comfortable about working on the case and begins to consider alternative approaches to it, such as training in child-rearing practices. The consultant agrees to follow up at a later date concerning the consultee's progress with the case.

The Program-Centered Administrative Consultation Process

Consultation Goals. In program-centered administrative consultation, the consultant, acting as an expert diagnostician, comes into an organization and consults with an administrator with regard to the mental health aspects of some program or the internal functioning of the organization. The consultant enters the organization, assesses and defines the problem, and makes a written report that includes a series of recommendations. It is up to the consultee to adapt the consultant's report and implement it within the organizational setting. Consider this example based on an article by Petti, Cornely, and McIntyre (1993): The mental health unit of a university medical center was asked to conduct an assessment of a mental health program for at-risk children and adolescents in a rural county. The scope of the consultation was to evaluate the services of the local mental health center to the county, examine independent service providers as supplements to the programs of the local mental health agency, and recommend scope of services for at-risk children and adolescents. The consultation resulted in a five-year plan developed by the mental health center in conjunction with representatives from the county. A follow-up study after the implementation of the five-year plan indicated separate service units for children and adolescents and a successful mechanism for coordinating services by all mental health providers in the county. In another example, Cowles and Washburn (2005) describe a consultation on program design of intensive management units in juvenile correctional facilities.

The specific goals of program-centered administrative consultation depend on the nature of the consultation request and could include recommendations to deal with problems in program development, organizational planning, or program functioning. A secondary goal is that the consultee will learn to deal more effectively with similar program problems and issues in the future. Just as client-centered case consultation makes recommendations for working with a given client, administrative-centered program consultation makes recommendations for an administrative plan of action. As with client-centered consultation, a minimum of time is spent in direct contact with the consultee. The goals of program-centered administrative consultation are met in a relatively brief time, generally ranging from several hours to a few days. The consultant is seen as an expert who comes in, assesses the situation accurately, and writes knowledgeable recommendations.

Consultant Function and Roles.   The consultant needs sufficient data-collecting, action planning, and communication skills to be able to make findings and present recommendations in a form understandable to the principal consultee and other members of the consultee institution. The consultant should be a content expert, that is, have a thorough knowledge of the problem area in which the program administrator (principal consultee) requests assistance. The consultant also should be knowledgeable and experienced in organizational theory and practice, program development, fiscal policy, administrative procedure, and personnel management.

It may be advantageous for an organization to hire a mental health consultant, rather than a generic management consultant of the purchase of expertise type in the chapter on organizational consultation, because he or she can assist more effectively with the mental health aspects of a program.

The consultant must be particularly careful to create effective relationships with staff members of the consultee institution because their help might be needed in gathering data. For example, the consultant may obtain significant amounts of information from individual and group interviews with staff, including information about the internal and external forces working on the organization.

The consultant must consider two issues when performing program-centered administrative consultation. The first concerns being responsible for collecting and analyzing the data required to solve the problem and make recommendations. Therefore, the consultant must do more than merely help the organization's staff determine what data they want to collect since they may lack the knowledge, skill, and confidence necessary to make that determination. Because the consultant bears responsibility for the content of the assessment and the recommendations, the amount, type, and timing of data collection should ultimately be based on his or her expert knowledge and objectivity.

The second issue relates to the consultant's authority with the organization's staff members affected by the consultation. In program-centered administrative consultation, the consultee is the administrator who requested the consultant. This administrator, like any consultee, needs a coordinate relationship with the consultant and is free to accept or reject any or all of the consultant's report and recommendations. The consultant's relationship to the administrator's subordinates, however, is not coordinate. Therefore, in this type of consultation, the sanctioning process should guarantee that the consultant's requests for information and cooperation will be honored by all involved. A final note on the consultant's role: Consultants should work to ensure that any changes are responsive and respecting of all stakeholders and designed for the unique characteristics of the program's setting (Knotek, 2012).

Consultee Experience in Consultation

The consultee in program-centered administrative consultation is the program administrator who expedites the hiring of the consultant in the first place. (This may or may not be the person who initially contacts the consultant.) The administrator should be the principal consultee because of the power of that position to both sanction the consultation and ensure that the consultant's recommendations are carried out at the end of consultation.

The consultee's task is to meet with the consultant to discuss the main reasons the consultant is being hired, any strategies for clarifying the problem that involve some of the organization's staff, and the time frame for consultation, as well as to select methods of approving the consultant's activities throughout the organization.

Because the consultant needs considerable knowledge about the organization to determine which data to collect and to make realistic recommendations, the administrator should make available as much information as possible concerning the organization's nature and methods of operation. The administrator also produces a rank-ordered list of administrative problems about which the consultant's assistance is being requested.

During the consultation, the consultee should have as much contact with the consultant as the consultant deems necessary and should complete two primary tasks: to provide the consultant an ongoing broad view of the organization and the interactive nature of its subsystems, and to react to the consultant's tentative findings so that he or she can modify the recommendations at key times during the consultation process.

After the consultant's report has been filed, the consultee is responsible for the degree to which the recommendations are accepted and implemented. Finally, during follow-up the consultee is expected to assist the consultant in assessing the impact of consultation.

Application: Consultant Techniques and Procedures. How does the consultant proceed in program-centered administrative consultation? In the beginning of consultation, needs are explored, the contract is negotiated, the administrator is identified as the principal consultee, and the approximate amount of time the consultant and the consultee will spend together is established.

In obtaining an overview of the problems and their ramifications, the consultant makes a rapid initial assessment of the consultee institution's structure and culture and the nature of its problems. At this stage, the consultant is interested in forming general impressions and hunches that will provide a procedural blueprint for the remainder of the consultation.

Once the principal problems are identified, the consultant must gather additional information to shed light on them and to formulate potential solutions. Data are gathered by conducting formal and informal interviews with both individuals and groups, by observing the behavior of the organization's members in their routine work patterns, and occasionally by using questionnaires.

Based on the information gathered, the consultant begins to develop interim recommendations, which are then provided to the principal consultee and other authorized parties-at-interest.

The consultant incorporates the reactions received into progressively more detailed, complex, and sophisticated recommendations.

During assessment and the reformulation of interim recommendations, the consultant should maintain as much contact with the primary consultee as is feasible. Such contact provides the consultant with reactions from the organization's administration, maintains the consultee's interest in the consultation, and increases the likelihood that some of the consultant's skills will "rub off" on the consultee.

By progressively modifying the recommendations made to solve the problem, the consultant has used a collaborative approach. The final recommendations should have both a short-term and a long-term focus and should detail procedures required to implement the recommendations.

Because the consultant's report is typically distributed widely and throughout several levels in the consultee institution, it should be written in a formal style and should cover the issues and problems investigated well enough to be understandable to parties-at-interest who had no direct contact with the consultant. It is up to the principal consultee to determine which, if any, of the recommendations will be implemented.

Finally, the consultant should set up a follow-up schedule before terminating the consultation and should arrange to receive the results of the implementation of the recommendations.

Case Example of Program-Centered Administrative Consultation. Marilyn, a mental health consultant, is working with an administrator, the head counselor, and the dropout prevention coordinator of a large urban secondary school. The focus of consultation is the school's dropout prevention program. The dropout rate for the school is one of the highest in the state and is still increasing in spite of the dropout prevention program, which has been in existence for three years. Marilyn has been asked to make recommendations to improve the program. Before the onset of consultation, Marilyn made a thorough study of the dropout prevention programs in the state.

She spent one day in the school to get a feel for a typical school day and during the next week conducted in-depth interviews with the administrator, the head counselor, and the dropout prevention coordinator about their perceptions of the program.

A few "high-rise" students and some teachers were also interviewed. The results of these interviews led Marilyn to conclude that the program was viewed as a stigma by virtually everyone except the school's principal and the program coordinator. The program coordinator was viewed as being inadequately trained for the job, as having an easy job, and as not being sensitive enough to the needs of the students in the program.

Based on these findings, the consultant made some interim recommendations for changing the program's image and for getting the coordinator additional training. These recommendations were shared with the appropriate staff members and were modified according to their input. The following is part of the consultant's final written report:

> Problem 1.1. The image of the dropout prevention program is poor among students and many staff members. The interviews conducted by the consultant suggest that most students view the dropout prevention program as "not a cool place to be." Students in general perceive students associated with the program as rejects. The school counselors see the program as a "dumping ground" for students who are having a difficult time adjusting to school. The teachers tend to think of the program as one more "non-academic" activity at school. The administration and dropout prevention coordinator see the program as being adequate.
>
> The following suggestion is made: The administration of the school should appoint a Dropout Prevention Program Advisory Committee with representatives from the administration, the program, students, the counseling department, and teachers. The dropout prevention coordinator would present the committee an annual plan for working with potential dropouts as well as methods of promoting the program's image throughout the school. Special attention needs to be paid to student views of the program.

The consultant followed up three months later and found that the school was actively engaged in carrying out these recommendations. The dropout prevention coordinator was enrolled on a part-time basis in a master's degree program in counseling.

The Consultee-Centered Administrative Consultation Process

Consultation Goals.   Consultee-centered administrative consultation is the most complicated, interesting, and demanding type of consultation. The consultant is hired to work with an organization's administrative-level personnel to help solve problems in personnel management or the implementation of organizational policy. It moves beyond the specific program dealt with in program-centered administrative consultation to broader issues such as leadership (Meyers, Meyers, Graybill, Proctor, & Huddleston, 2012; Meyers, Proctor, Graybill, & Meyers, 2009). The goal is to enhance the professional competency of an administrative staff (Erchul & Schulte, 1993). The consultant gathers information from within the organization to identify its problems and help consultees overcome them. The consultant can work with an individual, although most often there is more than one consultee.

The primary goal of consultee-centered administrative consultation is an increased level of consultees' professional functioning with regard to program development and organization, so they help the institution accomplish its mission in the future—this form of consultation is educative in nature (Mendoza, 1993). A secondary goal is producing positive program change.

Consultant Function and Roles.   In consultee-centered administrative consultation, the consultant may work with one or more administrators referred to as *principal consultees*. The consultation is expected to be long-term, ranging from a few months to more than a year.

Depending on the size of the consultee institution and the nature of the requested consultation, more than one consultant may be used. The consultant needs the same skills required for program-centered administrative consultation, including expertise in group consultation and specialized knowledge of social systems, administrative procedures, and organizational theory.

In particular, the consultant must be able to understand how these skills relate to individuals and subgroups within the consultee institution, as well as to how the institution relates to the broader community. A final skill needed is the ability to scan the entire organization and make quick judgments about portions of the organization to examine in more depth.

Upon determining who the consultees are, the consultant enters the organization, performs relationship-building activities, studies the social system of the institution, plans an intervention, intervenes at the individual, group, or organization level, and then evaluates and follows up.

The consultant is more or less "free to roam" through the organization and assists in defining problems and gathering data. Consultants present ideas to consultees and encourage them to discuss and act on them.

Recent trends in consultee-centered administrative consultation suggest that consultants should focus on trying to achieve lasting organizational change (Caplan et al., 1994). This can be accomplished by attempting to reduce stressors in the organization, by assisting in developing programs that deal with crises that may arise, and by creating mechanisms such as employee assistance programs (EAPs) that permit individuals to seek psychological assistance on an easily accessible basis. Another trend is the renewed emphasis on ecological variables and their relationship to prevention. Here the focus includes "mental health environments" (Ysseldyke, Lekwa, Klingbeil, & Cormier, 2012, p. 23). This trend focuses on examining and assessing mental health–related ecological forces in an organization and assisting consultees to diminish negative forces and promote enabling forces that lead to the well-being of members of the organization. An example is a consultant working with school administrators to improve school climate.

Consultee Experience in Consultation. The principal consultee in this type of consultation is the administrator who hired the consultant. This administrator has the job of helping the consultant decide whether additional forms of consultation are required, whether there are to be other consultees, and how they are to be involved in the consultation process. As in consultation of any kind, the principal consultee negotiates the contract, assists in getting sanctions from the top administrator, and provides the consultant logistical support for studying the organization's social structure.

The consultee must determine the extent of contact with the consultant and arrange meetings at which the consultant can present findings to all consultees involved. It is important that consultees know from the start that the consultant will discuss the findings with them for their consideration and input. Although the primary focus of consultation is on organizational problems, an important goal is for consultees to use the consultant's input to further develop their own skills. As in all consultation, the consultees take the consultant's contributions and do with them as they see fit.

Application: Consultant Techniques and Proceures. The beginnings of consultation are the same as in the other types of mental health consultation and more or less follow the entry procedures discussed in Chapter 4. The consultant in consultee-centered administrative consultation, however, has two unique problems at the onset of consultation. The first is determining who, in addition to the administrator, will be consultees. The administrators may want the consultant to have contact with subordinates so that they can inform the consultant about the organization. The consultant would then use this information while consulting with the administrator. However, the administrator may want the consultant to consult with the subordinates concerning issues and problems within the organization. Whichever is the case, it is very important for the consultant to be sure that everyone involved is aware of the nature of the consultant's role.

The second problem is to ensure both that members of the consultee institution understand that the consultant is an agent of change who can move freely within the organization and that the threat they perceive in the consultant's position of power is minimized. Members of the organization may suspect that the consultant is a spy for the administrator, an agent who will use psychological influence to get them to do what the administrator wants, or an outsider who wants to mold the institution into some preconceived form. This perceived threat can be minimized by building proper relationships, including maintaining coordinate relationships, communicating openly, and proceeding cautiously when introducing interventions.

As the consultant studies the organization's social system, problems and issues are identified and then presented to the consultees concerned. The consultant's intervention is a neutral one that is restricted to "increasing the range and depth of their [consultees'] understanding of the issues and to augmenting their emotional capacity to use such knowledge productively. It is then up to them to work out solutions in the light of their own personal and role-related choices" (Caplan & Caplan, 1993, p. 272). The most effective way for the consultant to remain neutral is to keep in mind the consultation processes of collecting information, making a consultation plan, and intervening to implement the plan.

Data collection has more constraints in consultee-centered administrative consultation than it does in program-centered consultation. First, staff participation in data collection is voluntary, even though it is administratively authorized. Second, because the people from whom the consultant is collecting data are potential consultees, relationship building must be accomplished as well. Third, although consultants have the freedom to collect data about any aspect of the organization, they would do well to focus on issues that are both important to the staff and related to changes the staff would like to make.

In planning the intervention, the consultant should avoid the temptation to intervene too quickly and should review the findings, set some goals, and determine how these goals are to be met. Each intervention has a time limit, should be related to a problem the consultee thinks is important, and targets an individual, a group, or an organization.

As in all types of consultation, the consultant schedules a follow-up session in which to evaluate. If the consultation is ongoing, the consultant is then free to move on to another problem.

Case Example of Consultee-Centered Administrative Consultation.   A community counselor was consulting with the staff of a community mental health center that was working with an increasing number of clients with special problems, including AIDS. A former staff member had, in fact, recently contracted the disease. The staff members seemed familiar with the controversies surrounding AIDS, but were ill at ease about such problems because of denial of the disease by some patients. The consultant decided to use a consultee-centered approach but did not focus directly on the AIDS issue until some consultees brought it up. Once the subject was broached, the consultant attempted to extend the consultees' knowledge of denial in some AIDS patients.

The consultant met with the group of consultees for four sessions to discuss coping with client denial and shared information on the feelings helpers often have when working with chronically ill patients. After the four sessions, the consultant evaluated the consultation process with the principal consultee and arranged for a follow-up in six months.

Modifications of the Caplanian Model

Caplan and Caplan updated the ideas expressed in *The Theory and Practice of Mental Health Consultation* in a text entitled *Mental Health Consultation and Collaboration* (1993, 1999). The vast majority of Caplan's original ideas remain the same, though several have been expanded.

In addition to developing the concept of collaboration as an alternative to consultation, Caplan and Caplan have modified the earlier model in some

relatively minor ways. For example, they more strongly support consultation with groups of consultees so that members can assist one another. The support that group members can provide one another allows the consultant to maintain a peer relationship with the consultees. Finally, mental health consultation is now seen as a viable option in schools.

The consultant roles—mediator and conciliator—have been advocated by Caplan and Caplan for use in specific situations such as helping divorcing parents safeguard their children's rights and form a collaborative relationship for dealing with the children as parents.

Some of Caplan and Caplan's techniques such as theme interference reduction have received criticism for being manipulative in nature. For example, Henning-Stout (1993) recommends referral to other mental health professionals in case of loss of professional objectivity. However, Caplan and Caplan (1993) argue that the intention of the consultant is what determines whether or not the manipulation is unethical and that the consultant and the manipulator both try to note the other person's weaknesses—the manipulator to undermine the person, the consultant to help the consultee overcome those weaknesses. Thus, they conclude that if the consultee knew about the benign nature of the consultant's manipulations, he or she would judge the manipulation as positive. Furthermore, Caplan and Caplan suggest that when consultees seek consultation, they are giving tacit or explicit consent for any interventions, including benign manipulation. These authors also conclude that not every consultee is suitable for consultee-centered consultation and that, in such cases, consultants should move to a client-centered method that excludes any manipulation. They also note that many of the principles and basic techniques of mental health consultation are quite appropriate for use by consultants outside of the mental health field.

Caplan has made greater contributions to mental health consultation than anyone. Due to his efforts, mental health consultation had developed into an important service delivery system. His contributions include but are not limited to: focusing on the consultee as well as the client system in the consultation process; developing consultation theory; maintaining a nonhierarchical relationship with the consultee; promoting of indirect techniques; and creating a categorization scheme for the types of consultation and advocating a systems view of consultation (Erchul, 2009).

COLLABORATION FROM A MENTAL HEALTH PERSPECTIVE

As you are aware, Caplan developed his model of consultation in the context of an external consultant who becomes a temporary member of the consultee organization. As increasing numbers of mental health professionals such as school psychologists and school counselors were hired in the schools and started providing consultation services, there were some strong effects on Caplan's original consultation model. These effects included the idea that it would be more difficult for the consultee to reject the consultant's recommendations; that the level of expertise of the consultant would make a nonhierarchical relationship impossible; and that an in-house mental health expert would, under normal circumstances, be expected to participate in the intervention and thereby would be responsible to some degree for the outcomes of the case (Caplan et al., 1994). As a result, Caplan and Caplan (1993) have expanded the concept of *collaboration* into a process complementary to, but different from, consultation.

Collaboration does not take away from consultation but adds to it (Erchul, 1993a). The difference is this: In collaboration, the mental health practitioner determines which cases to discuss, takes responsibility for the mental health outcomes of the case, and typically joins in the treatment of the client and seeks changes in the host organization that will benefit the clients; in consultation, the consultee chooses which case to discuss, remains responsible for the outcomes of the case and makes any interventions, and does not seek changes in the host institution unless asked to do so.

Caplan and Caplan (1993) make the distinction between collaboration and consultation in this way:

> The essential difference between *collaboration* and *consultation*, as I use the terms, is this: In *collaboration*, the mental health specialist joins the care-giving team inside the community institution, such as a school system or a general hospital, and accepts responsibility for the mental health outcome of its cases. The specialist may fulfill his or her mission by ensuring that the other team members deal effectively with the clients, in line with his or her assessment of their needs, or else he or she may undertake to implement part or all of the diagnostic and remedial plan him- or herself. (p. 46)

As you can see, in collaboration, the collaborating specialist takes primary responsibility for the mental health outcome of the case or program and equal responsibility for the overall outcome of the case or program (Caplan et al., 1994).

The major implication of Caplan and Caplan's recent ideas for practicing consultants seems to be the necessity for members of the helping professions to determine at the outset of the helping relationship whether consultation or collaboration is in order. This determination can be made by assessing the skill level of the consultee: If high, then perhaps consultation is in order; if not, then the consultee can either be trained to manage the case and then consulted with, or the human service professional can suggest a collaborative relationship and take part in the treatment. On the other hand, the counselor or psychologist may want to consider collaborating in all cases and programs by the very fact of being an in-house professional.

Mental health collaboration can be particularly suitable for school-based professionals (Caplan et al., 1994). Caplan and Caplan (1993) use the terms *collaborating professional* and *collaborating specialist* to describe the counselor or psychologist in a school providing collaboration. For example, a school-based mental health professional might consult with a teacher about classroom management procedures for an acting-out student while collaborating with the teacher by providing counseling services to the student to help reduce the behavior. As this example demonstrates, there is no inherent conflict between collaboration and consultation. In addition, as this example suggests, the mental health professional is responsible for certain aspects (helping the student adjust to the situation behaviorally) of the case, as is the teacher (making sure appropriate academic learning occurs). Caplan's (1993b) last writings strongly suggest that mental health collaboration should replace consultation as the method of choice by mental health workers who are staff members of an organization. At the same time, Caplan cautions about ignoring the differences between human service and for-profit organizations when considering mental health collaboration. Table 9.2 summarizes the differences between mental health consultation and mental health collaboration.

MULTICULTURAL ASPECTS RELATED TO MENTAL HEALTH CONSULTATION

Just as organizational consultation offers more than one type of consultation, so too does mental heath consultation. Caplan's client-centered case model allows for minimal disclosure on the part of the consultee. Consultee-centered case consultation is suitable for consultees wanting assistance from a

TABLE 9.2   **Mental Health Consultation and Mental Health Collaboration Contrasted on Key Dimensions**

DIMENSION	MENTAL HEALTH CONSULTATION	MENTAL HEALTH COLLABORATION
Location of consultant's home base	External to the organization	Internal to the organization
Type of psychological service	Generally indirect with little or no client contact	Combines indirect and direct services, and includes client contact
Consultant–consultee relationship	Assumes a coordinate and nonhierarchical relationship	Acknowledges status and role differences within the organization and thus the likelihood of a hierarchical relationship
Consultee participation	Assumes voluntary participation	Assumes voluntary participation, but acknowledges the possibility of forced participation
Interpersonal working relationship	Often dyadic, involving consultant and consultee	Generally team based, involving several collaborators
Confidentiality of communications within relationship	Assumes confidentiality to exist, with limits of confidentiality (if any) specified during initial contracting	Does not automatically assume confidentiality, given organization realities and pragmatic need to share relevant information among team members
Consultee freedom to accept or reject consultant advice	Yes	Not assumed to be true, as collaborator's expertise in his or her specialty area is generally deferred to by team
Consultant responsibility for case/program outcome	No	Shares equal responsibility for overall outcome, and primary responsibility for mental health aspects of case or program

Source: From Caplan, G. R., Caplan, R. B., and Erchul, W. P. (1994). Caplanian mental health consultation: Historical background and current status. *Consulting Psychology Journal, 46,* p. 7. © 1994 by the Educational Publishing Foundation and Division of Consulting Psychology. Reprinted with permission.

knowledgeable authority figure. Ingraham (2003, 2004, 2007, 2008) points out that consultee-centered consultation can be effectively used in multicultural consultation to help consultees construct culturally sensitive understandings of problems. Consultants use a variety of methods, including reframing, self-disclosure, and impartation of knowledge (Ingraham, 2007). The focus of both of these types of consultation on the case (and not the consultee) makes them safe for consultees from cultural groups that do not value self-disclosure. Caplan's model is flexible enough to account for other worldviews due to the coordinate, nonhierarchical relationship between consultant and consultee (Harrison, 2004). As a result, mental health consultation may be seen as desirable by disenfranchised groups. The move toward eclecticism on the part of mental health consultation allows for a broad conceptualization of the problem and a wealth of interventions for assisting the client system. The increased breadth and flexibility that has emerged in mental health consultation has created the conditions that allow for sensitivity toward cultural variables and modifications of the process to meet the needs of culturally diverse groups. The ability to focus on mental health environments sets the stage for ecological assessment (Gutkin, 2012) that can lead to effectively dealing with multicultural issues, including those related to social justice. Harrison (2004) noted one criticism: The concept of theme interference and its related issues of control over one's psychodynamic issues may be discrepant from the worldview of groups such as Native Americans and Alaska Americans, women, and racioethnic minorities.

Trends

In addition to the significant innovations in client-centered case consultation mentioned above, several trends have occurred in mental health consultation since Caplan published his inaugural work on consultation in 1970. It is to his credit that many of these trends involve adaptations of his model, such as reconsideration of who may qualify as a consultee, and innovations in methods of working with consultees.

One trend, described earlier in this chapter, is the move toward using collaboration when internal consultants need to take some direct responsibility for part of the plan to help the client system. This is a rather dramatic move away from traditional consultation, in which the consultee maintains responsibility for the outcome of the plan. The concept of reciprocal consultation, which is implicit in collaboration, is not well developed in Caplan's writings. Rather than focusing on how professionals working with the same client system can consult with one another about the client system, Caplan's writings emphasize each professional implementing a part of a mutually agreed-upon plan.

Another trend in mental health consultation is the continued inclusion of nonprofessionals as consultees. Parents, volunteers (e.g., hospice workers), and paraprofessionals (e.g., mental health technicians) all work with people in ways that can loosely be described as providing human services. Consultants can help these workers deal more effectively with the people they serve by using essentially the same methods used with professionals. However, Caplan's consultee-centered model does not apply to parents because it is unlikely that they can be objective about their children. Over the years, experts in the field of mental health consultation have modified Caplan's original formulations.

The issue of whether or not the consultant should directly confront consultee defenses has received some attention. Some authors (Dougherty, Tack, Fullam, & Hammer, 1996; Parsons, 1996) take a positive view of such confrontation. These authors disagree with Caplan's contention that direct confrontation takes away a consultee's defenses and that the time available in consultation for providing defensive coping strategies is too short. Proponents of direct confrontation argue that it is time effective, much less dangerous than Caplan implies, and does not diminish self-esteem.

Theme interference reduction has also been modified. Heller and Monahan years ago (1983) reconceived theme interference as being due to stereotypes and produced a method for alleviating these stereotypes without having to focus on manipulating the consultee or on the psychodynamic influence that

---

C A S E   9.1   Mental Health Consultation for School Consultants

---

Micheline is a school counselor assigned to a large urban junior high school. The school has been experiencing an increase in gang behavior along with an alarming increase in the number of students bringing weapons to campus. Micheline was asked by representatives from a group of language arts teachers to consult with them on stress management.

In a meeting with the teachers, it was apparent to Micheline that they were experiencing a great deal of stress over possible violence in the classroom. Teachers noted that the increase in stress had begun to affect the quality of the group's communication adversely, had increased the number of teacher leave days, and had led many of the teachers to leave school at the earliest possible moment after student dismissal. The teachers related their concerns that the school administration had neither taken a strong enough stand with the gangs nor implemented adequate security procedures to prevent weapons on campus. Having discussed the matter with the principal and been told that the procedures for making the school secure were appropriate, adequate, and approved by the local superintendent's office, the teachers concluded that their only recourse was to create a self-help group to cope with the ongoing stress.

Micheline agreed to meet with the group for one hour after school once every two weeks with the focus being to form a peer support group and to train the teachers in stress management strategies. The first two meetings dealt with the nature of peer support groups among teachers and subsequent meetings were divided between stress management training and dealing with issues individual teachers raised.

Micheline began to feel that the teachers tended to look at her as the ultimate authority in the group instead of focusing on how to help one another, perhaps because she was training the group. In bringing up her concern, she was very surprised at the reaction: Several of the teachers felt that although they were in a support group, Micheline would be the one who would be the leader and the expert, while others wondered why Micheline kept the group focused on work issues even when some members brought up very personal issues.

On hearing this feedback, Micheline suggested that she and the group renegotiate her role and had each member write down and then read what he or she expected from the group and from Micheline. As it turned out, most members wanted Micheline to be more active and directive. There was also a trend among the members to discuss how to make their classrooms more secure from gang activity and weapons.

Micheline agreed to the group's request, moving away from stress management training and toward teachers' concerns about particular students with regard to gang behavior or potential violence. She acted as a resource on gang behavior and ways of minimizing violence in the classroom. The group's evaluation of the consultation experience reflected a very positive attitude toward Micheline's role as a resource person. The evaluation also indicated that the teachers felt very supportive of one another, even though the concept of a direct support group had been abandoned.

Commentary

Regardless of the initial contract and expectations of the parties involved in consultation, things change. Micheline showed both flexibility and resiliency in her work with the group as indicated by her willingness to renegotiate the nature of role with the group members. This case also brings out another very important point about mental health consultation: Even though the consultant can make group-focused interventions such as stress management training, it is typical for individual consultees to want assistance with their own agendas—in this case, strategies for dealing with particular students.

---

originated the theme interference reduction methods. Theme interference can be reconceptualized in terms of irrational beliefs and corrected using the principles of Rational Emotive Therapy (RET) developed by Albert Ellis (Harrison, 2004).

Group consultation has received positive attention because of its cost-effectiveness and the realization that it may be as effective as individual consultation, particularly in promoting innovation.

Drum and Valdese (1988) long ago developed a system for determining levels of client system needs and the degree to which advocacy is appropriate for each level. Advocacy consultation can also be linked to network-building consultation in which human service consultants work with community groups, schools, and/or agencies for the purposes of sharing information, promoting linkages, and developing a unified response to mental health issues that arise (Dahir & Stone, 2012; Lewis, Lewis, Daniels, & D'Andrea, 2011; Li & Vazquez-Nuttall, 2009; Lopez-Baez & Paylo, 2009). For example, a mental health professional might proactively assist a small rural community in developing a network for assisting the community's AIDS patients. Advocacy can also be involved in grassroots consultation, in which mental health consultants assist groups and/or agencies in dealing with issues that have mental health implications for them or their community. For example, a mental health worker might help neighborhood groups develop strategies for keeping drug pushers out of their neighborhood. Advocacy is now reemerging as an important role for consultants, particularly in social justice situations.

Mental health consultants are getting more involved in staff development. Mental health consultants are also increasingly working with different types of support groups for families with special needs, parents, teachers, and other workers. For example, consultants assist support groups for families of the mentally ill, families being served by hospice, teachers under stress, and organizations wanting to become more culturally competent. This trend capitalizes on the increasing popularity of the mutual help movement. In addition, there is a demand for mental health consultants to increase their skills in helping groups organize, recruit members, and make themselves known to the larger community (Werner & Tyler, 1993).

Another trend is the increasing amount of mental health consultation performed in medical settings (Sears, Rudisill, & Mason-Sears, 2006). For example, a mental health consultant may be asked to assist a physician concerning a patient's unwillingness to take medication. In another example, administrators of nursing homes often rely on mental health consultants to assist with issues residents present such as depression, combative behavior, and confusion (Crose & Kixmiller, 1994). Mental health consultants are increasingly being asked to conduct organizational consultations in medical settings, for example, in the areas of program development or communication between hospital departments.

The amount of technical assistance mental health consultants provide to agencies is also increasing (Lewis et al., 2011). Such assistance frequently takes the form of outreach consultation and involves the direct dissemination of knowledge and skills to human service agencies. For example, mental health consultants are increasingly being called on to assist in programs that lead to independent living, are designed to decrease psychiatric hospitalization, and whose objectives are to increase the number of clients served by human service agencies. In another example, mental health consultants may serve as key members of the multidisciplinary team with hospice organizations (Lindberg, 1996).

The onset of managed care has also impacted mental health consultation. Having to "do more with less" has created opportunities, particularly for psychologists, in providing consultation such as that based on personality assessment to other therapists and clients' families (Quirk et al., 1995; Sears et al., 2006). Increasingly, psychologists are marketing themselves and the clinical utility of their assessment skills with organizations such as health maintenance organizations.

There has been an increase in the involvement of personnel from counseling and psychological services centers in postsecondary education settings to participate in consultation with other units in the educational institution (Knotek, 2006; Silverman, 1993). Consultants provide guidance on retention efforts, students in academic difficulty, relationships between culturally different groups, and issues surrounding fraternities and sororities.

While mental health consultation has not been used to a large degree in schools (Knotek et al., 2008), there is a trend for mental health consultant to work with schools and school systems using a public health model which focuses on prevention (Hughes, Lloyd, & Buss, 2008; Nastasi, 2004). These mental health services will be based in the school and focus on health, promotion of wellness, and competence at the class or school level, thus moving away for a "deficit" model (Doll et al., 2012; Ysseldyke et al., 2012). Mental health consultants are also working with teachers in consultative and coaching relationships to

---

C A S E 9.2   Mental Health Consultation for Community Consultants

The consultee, Clover, is a family resource coordinator for a New Start program for low-income single mothers. The program provides support in such areas as finding work; raising children; developing budgets; personal, career, and family counseling; and advocacy. The program helps women set and meet goals that lead to self-sufficiency. Clover is a support person for the women and maintains contact with them over a two-year period. She was having some difficulties in helping one client meet her program goals and had asked Della, a community counselor with a local mental health center, to consult. Clover had made several home visits with the client, who avoided any significant discussion of her problems and had difficulty being assertive—this was a trait Clover wanted the woman to deal with. The woman also had difficulty with minor bouts of depression and exhibited self-esteem issues. Clover had asked Della for assistance in building stronger rapport with the client and for methods to motivate her to work on her goals.

Della took time during the first session to build rapport with Clover, and then asked how she had proceeded with the case so far—in particular what interventions had already been implemented to resolve the problems. In looking for any lack of skill, confidence, or objectivity in Clover, Della determined that client-centered case consultation was appropriate. Clover admitted that she had resorted to persuasion and a few gentle confrontations. In looking over the client's written goals and history, Della wanted more data so she could further determine Clover's strengths and limitations in managing the case and better assess the client's difficulties. She asked Clover to contact the client for a home visit and for permission to go along.

During the home visit Della took a low profile, observing Clover and the client as Clover again went over the client's goals and the lack of progress being made toward them. As Della drove back with Clover to her office, they discussed what happened during the home visit. Della questioned Clover about alternative approaches to focusing directly on the client's goals. Della mentioned that she saw the client as reluctant rather than resistant. Perhaps taking the first step toward accomplishing her goals was just too much for the client.

Della then wrote a detailed report that contained recommendations on how Clover might manage the case, a brief analysis of the client including her lack of any type of social support system, and the conclusion that such a support system should be the primary goal for Clover to help the client develop. Della listed several interventions that she knew Clover was familiar with or could obtain resources for, among which were peer counseling, a singles support group, strength bombardment, and goal-attainment scaling.

Della met with Clover one more time to go over the report and encouraged her to follow through. They agreed to meet in a month to discuss Clover's progress with her client, and Della encouraged her to call if any glitches showed up in the plan.

Commentary

This case illustrates the skill of determining which type of mental health consultation to employ. Notice that this decision, although not irrevocable, did guide Della in her work with Clover. If Della had determined that consultee-centered case consultation was in order, she would have proceeded in a very different manner. Notice that Della was not reluctant to share her expertise with Clover and that she based her recommendations on direct observation of the client. Such observations are time consuming and raise the issue of whether alternative ways of observing through audio or videotapes are as legitimate as direct observation. This case also highlights the importance of assessing the consultee's skills to ensure that the consultant's recommendations are doable.

---

enhance student well-being and teacher efficacy (Cappella et al., 2012). In addition, Caplan's preventive approach is affecting schools with the emergence of positive behavioral supports and response to intervention.

Finally, there is a trend for consultation to look beyond the problem-solving paradigm, as well as increasing support for the concept of empowering consultees, with the consultant taking on the role of resource person (Lewis et al., 2011). For example, a consultant may act as a resource person for assisting the administrators of a domestic-violence program and the administrators of a substance-abuse program communicate more effectively. In all actuality, this is what consultants who take on a collaborative mode do when they are with a very skillful consultee. There is a corresponding move away from the problem-solving approach, which places the consultant in the expert mode.

CONCLUSIONS

Mental health consultation has contributed significantly to the psychological well-being of our society. First, it has made possible increased and better delivery of human services to client systems through the use of a pyramid structure in which consultants assist consultees working with clients or programs. Thus, a relatively large segment of the population can be served by a relatively small number of professionals. Second, it has promoted mental health and has helped to create positive public attitudes concerning the delivery of human services. A significant portion of our society now views mental health as everyone's business. Third, it has allowed untold thousands of human service professionals to improve and refine their skills, which has benefited the clients with whom they work. Fourth, mental health consultation has taught us a hard lesson in regard to our fast-paced society: namely, unhurried and systematic reflection increases the consultee's awareness of the range of options available, counteracts premature and emotionally based closure, and reestablishes a state of equilibrium (Caplan et al., 1994). This position has tempered the tendency on the part of consultants to give in to the time constraints placed on them and their consultees' efforts in organizations, such as schools, where a quick fix is often considered better than nothing. Finally, it has reemphasized the notion that personal issues can affect our work lives for better or worse. Indeed, human service professionals may bear the following dictum in mind throughout their careers: Physician heal thyself.

Even though there is no doubt that mental health consultation has had a broad and positive impact, it is not without criticism. One basic criticism is that even though mental health consultation has been defined, it has been done so more in terms of what consultants do, than in terms of what the concept itself means. This has led to some controversy over the boundaries of consultation. Long ago, Mazade (1983) contended that the boundaries of mental health consultation are too broad: Until there is a better definition of mental health consultation and a more consistent set of expectations concerning what mental health consultants do, research and attempts to define relevant and irrelevant delivery of services to consultees will suffer.

Bloom (1984) related several criticisms of mental health consultation that are, unfortunately, still all too true today. First, because mental health consultation focuses on clients and their issues, consultees seek new cases rather than perform preventative measures. Hence, mental health case consultation may work at cross-purposes with primary prevention. Second, the value of consultation is limited when the individual consultee (instead of the consultee institution) is the target for change. Third, mental health consultation can erroneously assume that consultees are not functioning effectively with their cases and programs when in fact they are. Caplan and Caplan (1993) have also recently made this criticism.

Most of the criticisms of mental health consultation have been directed at Caplan's model (1970). For example, some authors criticize Caplan for creating a model that only works in an ideal situation that is rarely, if ever, obtained. Caplan's model has also been described as elitist, a vestige of a time when consultees had limited training in their field and few well-trained consultants were available to assist them. A more preventative perspective would characterize consultee-centered case consultation, for example, as the development of knowledge, skill, confidence, or objectivity in the consultee (Knotek, 2003, 2004; Meyers et al., 1993). As it stands, the model has a deficit perspective in that it assumes there is something wrong with the consultee. Hence, the model focuses on problem solving rather than prevention and has thus not developed a larger plan to assist communities in creating structures that prevent mental illness (Trickett & Rowe, 2012). Although Caplan views his model as preventative, there is a limited amount actually written about prevention in his writing regarding consultation.

Caplan also possibly underestimates the amount of time needed to build relationships with individual consultees, particularly in consultee-centered approaches to consultation. Even the psychodynamic assumptions underlying theme interference reduction have been questioned, and theme reduction techniques have been criticized as being manipulative and unsupported by research. Henning-Stout (1993) and even Caplan (1993a) himself have suggested that Caplan was perhaps too preoccupied with theme interference reduction when he developed his model.

Furthermore, consultants who are also therapists may have much more difficulty than Caplan suggests in avoiding direct therapeutic interventions to consultees who are too emotionally involved in their cases. The transfer of effect, discussed earlier as a key concept, has been increasingly questioned; only minimal research supports this concept's existence. Caplan's view of a coordinate, nonhierarchical relationship is criticized because consultants, particularly in consultee-centered case consultation, do not always act as if the relationship were equal. Finally, mental health consultation remains the least empirically researched model of consultation (Knotek et al., 2008).

SUMMARY

In traditional mental health consultation, a mental health expert (consultant) helps a human service worker or administrator (consultee) with a work-related problem. The approach is historically identified with Gerald Caplan (1970, 1974, 1977; see also Caplan & Caplan, 1993, 1999; Caplan & Caplan-Moskovich, 2004) and has its origins in the psychodynamic school of psychotherapy. This model stresses the importance of the consultant–consultee relationship and emphasizes enabling consultees to apply what they learned in consultation to similar situations in the future.

The combination of two levels of mental health consultation (case and administrative) with two possible targets (the client or program and the consultee) produces the four types of mental health consultation: client-centered case, consultee-centered case, program-centered administrative, and consultee-centered administrative. Consultees can have work-related concerns due to a lack of knowledge, skill, confidence, or objectivity. Depending on the type of consultation and the nature of the consultee's difficulty, consultants have at their disposal a broad array of techniques, including the most innovative and controversial of these techniques—theme interference reduction. All of these approaches to mental health consultation share the common goals of helping the consultee be more effective in the present and the future and benefiting the client or program.

SUGGESTIONS FOR EFFECTIVE PRACTICE

- Listen to how the consultees describe the situation for which they requested assistance as a guide to determine whether to use client-centered or consultee-centered consultation.

- Avoid using techniques like theme interference reduction unless you have been trained and directly supervised in their use.

- Be willing to demonstrate effective role modeling on the problem-solving process for consultees.

- Consider the increasing importance of administrative consultation, even though the primary work you will do will be case consultation.

- Don't do for consultees and fellow collaborators what they can do for themselves.

QUESTIONS FOR REFLECTION

1. How did the psychodynamic perspective influence Caplan?

2. Do you believe that the transfer of effect really takes place in mental health consultation? On what do you base your belief?

3. What does Caplan mean when he describes the consultation relationship as coordinate and nonhierarchical?

4. What are three basic differences between program-centered administrative consultation and consultee-centered administrative consultation?

5. To what extent do you agree that mental health collaboration is the service of choice for in-house mental health practitioners?

6. What ethical issues are raised by the use of techniques for reducing theme interference?

7. Is manipulation ever a legitimate consultant intervention? Why or why not?

8. Which of Caplan's four types of consultation would you feel most comfortable using? Why?

9. How would you go about practicing mental health consultation and collaboration in a multiculturally competent way?

10. What does the ecological perspective add to mental health consultation?

SUGGESTED SUPPLEMENTARY READINGS

If you are interested in more detail and depth about mental health consultation, the following selected readings are recommended:

Caplan, G. (1970). *The theory and practice of mental health consultation*. New York: Basic Books. This classic on mental health consultation was the primary source for this chapter and presents a nice blend of theoretical and practical aspects. Of particular interest is Caplan's discussion of consultee-centered case consultation. Many of today's mental health professionals have used Caplan's ideas as a basis for developing their own particular style and approach to consultation.

Caplan, G., & Caplan, R. B. (1999). *Mental health consultation and collaboration*. Prospect Heights, IL: Waveland. (Original work published in 1993). The first part of this text is a reprint of the majority of Caplan's 1970 text. The latter part is filled with

Caplan and Caplan's ideas on mental health collaboration and methodological and technical issues. New material includes discussion of the significance of manipulation, when to use consultation, and key modifications in Caplan's theory since 1970. The ideas and case studies on collaboration are quite informative.

Tack, F. E., & Morrow, D. F. (2014). Mental health case consultation. In A. M. Dougherty (Ed.), *Casebook of psychological consultation and collaboration* (6th ed.). Belmont, CA: Brooks/Cole Cengage. The authors present a challenging case in which a mental health consultant assists an HIV/AIDS service organization counselor with a case that involves death and dying issues associated with counseling people with end-stage Acquired Immune Deficiency Syndrome and the behavioral inconsistencies inherent in the transition from living to dying.

10

✳

Behavioral Consultation and Collaboration

Behavioral consultation emerged as an alternative to mental health and organizational consultation, is very popular in school settings, and is well researched (Andersen et al., 2010). In 1977, John Bergan introduced behavioral consultation as a way to provide more service to larger numbers of clients (Watson, Sterling, & McCade, 1997). Behavioral consultation evolved from the behavioral paradigm based on positivism (Henning-Stout, 1993). A fundamental assumption is that behavior is acquired as a result of the interaction of the individual with the environment (Sheridan & Kratochwill, 2008). Behavioral consultation is a very popular approach to consultation that applies behavioral technology to the consultation process (Elliott & Busse, 1993) and is most likely the most frequently used model of consultation (Andersen et al., 2010; Anton-LaHart & Rosenfield, 2004). The expanding application of behavioral technology to mental health and educational concerns has led to behavioral consultation's immense popularity. While behavioral consultants specialize in this approach, all consultants make at least occasional use of behavioral approaches to consultation. In essence, the consultant in this model assists the consultee to be specific about behaviors to be changed. This allows for focused behavioral assessment that leads to the determination of the contingencies controlling the behavior, thus permitting the development of specific interventions to accomplish behavior change.

A consultant functioning within this framework needs to be skilled in behavioral theory and practice (Kratochwill, 2008; Kratochwill & Bergan, 1990) and should become familiar with the work of such leaders in behavioral psychology as B. F. Skinner and Albert Bandura. Because behavioral consultation places heavy emphasis on assessment and evaluation, you may want to review the various methodologies for data collection described in Chapter 5, the discussion of treatment integrity covered in Chapter 6, and the various evaluation methods described in Chapter 7.

The purpose of this chapter is to present three models of behavioral consultation suggested by Vernberg and Reppucci (1986) and, most recently, Kratochwill (2008). In *behavioral case consultation*, the consultant helps as consultees apply behavioral principles to a case. *Behavioral technology training* teaches specific behavioral technology skills to consultees. *Behavioral system consultation* analyzes and modifies an organization's processes and structures using behavioral technology principles. Because of its popularity, I provide the majority of the coverage to case consultation.

As you read this chapter, consider the following questions:

- What makes behavioral consultation "behavioral"?

- What unique ethical issues, if any, might arise from the use of behavioral consultation?

- Is this model's emphasis on measurement an asset or a liability?

- To what extent do you agree that an ecological perspective increases the complexity of behavioral assessment?

- What special skills does a behavioral consultant need?

Case Example

The following is an example of behavioral consultation:

You are a schoolteacher who asks a school counselor to consult with you concerning one of your students who causes disturbances by talking at inappropriate times throughout the school day. The counselor asks you to describe exactly those behaviors you consider to be "inappropriate" as well as your and the child's behaviors immediately before and after the undesirable behavior occurs. Based on your description and direct observations of the child, the school counselor leads you through a problem-solving process to eliminate the child's inappropriate behavior. Strategies that you can implement and appropriate positive behavioral supports are discussed. You agree to implement the program, and the school counselor agrees to help you measure the subsequent frequency of the child's inappropriate behavior.

Chances are excellent that the school counselor in this example was using a model of behavioral consultation. Behavioral consultation is based on behavioral psychology, which has had a tremendous influence on all areas of human services. Behavioral psychology applies theory and research findings to behavior change techniques in systematic, problem-solving procedures (Gmeinder & Kratochwill, 1998). It stresses the principles of learning in understanding how behavior is acquired and changed. Behavioral models of consultation are based on the idea that because most behavior is learned, it can be unlearned and new behavior can take its place. The result of consultation is some change in behavior in the consultee and/or the client system. Therefore, the principles of behavior change are combined with indirect service by the consultant to form the basis for consultation.

When the behavioral consultant uses principles of learning to help consultees bring about desired changes in themselves or their clients, these principles are translated into empirically validated behavioral methods, often referred to as evidence-based interventions. Two key aspects of this type of consultation are a focus on *behavior change* and an extensive use of the *scientific method*.

Behavioral consultation can be used in a variety of settings, including mental health centers, schools, and other human service organizations. In addition to its wide applicability, behavioral consultation is one of the most frequently practiced forms of consultation (Kratochwill, 2008). It is, for example, the most frequently reported method for working with other professionals in school settings.

HISTORICAL BACKGROUND

Behavioral consultation has its roots in behavior therapy: It developed out of experimental psychology, which encompasses not only operant and classical conditioning but also social, developmental, and cognitive psychology.

In the early 1900s, John Watson founded the behavioral school of psychology, which shunned covert events such as cognitions and restricted the parameters of psychology to observable behaviors only. As behaviorism became a strong force in experimental psychology, it was applied to the study of people's personal problems (Lutzker & Martin, 1981). Behaviorism strongly influenced operant conditioning, classical conditioning, modeling, behavioral ecology, and cognitive-behavior modification.

In the 1940s, behaviorism became the dominating force in psychology under the guidance of Harvard psychologist B. F. Skinner. In developing the concept of operant conditioning, Skinner researched such principles of behavior change as reinforcement, punishment, and shaping, as well as their applications to humans (Skinner, 1953). From the 1950s through today, many behaviorists have applied learning theory in developing treatment techniques for a variety of personal problems.

Psychotherapists such as Wolpe, Lazarus, and Eysenck were pioneers in applying the Pavlovian model of classical conditioning to the treatment of human psychological disorders. Until the 1960s, behavior therapy was based primarily on the learning principles known as operant and classical conditioning. In the late 1960s, Albert Bandura popularized modeling, a powerful social learning theory based on observation and imitation of certain behaviors (modeling) under conditions of reinforcement (Bandura, 1977, 1982). His views related to internal, cognitive events as influencing human behavioral as well as external, environmental events set the stage for cognitive-behavioral interventions and have been incorporated into behavioral consultation.

In the 1970s and early 1980s, behavioral ecology (Willems, 1974) and systems theory (Morasky, 1982) began to receive attention. In behavioral ecology, people are considered a part of a multilayered ecological environment. The settings in which people behave are interactive, and a change in behavior for one setting could affect behavior in another setting. For example, the assertiveness behaviors a client learns in the workplace may produce different results when used in the home.

In the mid-1970s, the cognitive-behavioral therapy movement became popular. This movement asserts that what we think or say to ourselves can affect our behavior for better or worse and that there is a connection between what a human thinks and whether or not a personal problem is likely to develop. Donald Meichenbaum (1977, 1985), a leader in this field, has shown that changing self-statements in an appropriate way can lead to desirable behavior change. For example, people who instruct themselves to cope with perceived stress are more likely to be able to manage it effectively than are people who engage in self-talk that expresses doubt in their ability to deal with stress.

The behavior therapy movement has grown to include nationwide societies such as the Association for the Advancement of Behavior Therapy (AABT). At the same time, this growth and expansion have produced such diversity that it is more accurate to speak of multiple behavior therapies rather than one, and consequently behavior therapy has become a difficult concept to define. The unifying factor underlying behavioral therapies is their derivation from experimentally established principles and procedures and the focus on the importance of learning and the careful assessment of behavior (Kazdin, 2001).

As the effectiveness of behavioral therapy became increasingly apparent, there occurred a parallel increase in requests from human service providers for assistance in the design and implementation of behavior change programs. Hence, the role of the behavioral therapist or counselor was expanded to include that of behavioral consultant. Behavioral consultation was first practiced in organizations that require high levels of client control, such as state mental hospitals (Gallessich, 1985; Martens & DiGennaro, 2008). As behavior therapy came to be used in a variety of settings, behavioral consultation was increasingly used in mental health centers, schools, and other human service organizations. Most of the consultation provided by behavioral consultants consists of casework; that is, the consultant helps a consultee apply behavioral principles to a specific problem so as to help a client or group of clients. Recently, there has been a movement to call behavioral consultation *problem-solving consultation* to reflect the increasing diversity of approaches that extend behavioral consultation (Kratochwill, 2008).

Bergan's (1977) text was the first definitive expression of behavioral case consultation. Bergan's model was an extension of D'Zurilla and Goldfried's (1971) model of behavior therapy (Martens & DiGennaro, 2008). Although this model tended to focus on interventions that relied on behavior modification, it has expanded to include interventions from diverse theoretical origins (Kratochwill, 2008). The influence of behavioral ecology and behavioral training models in the 1970s broadened the role of today's behavioral consultant to include behavioral system consultation and training in behavioral technology.

Proponents of behavioral consultation tend to lead the way in designing and conducting research related to consultation with most of the focus being on school-based consultation. In fact, behavioral consultation has done much to establish consultation itself as a legitimate service for human service professionals.

BEHAVIORAL
CONSULTATION DEFINED

Behavioral consultation "encompasses a wide variety of activities conducted in a broad range of settings with diverse populations" (Vernberg & Reppucci, 1986, p. 65). It is most likely the most widely practiced form of consultation (Racine Gilles, Kratochwill, Felt, Schienebeck, & Vaccarello, 2011). Because the conceptual framework that underlies behavioral consultation (behavior therapy)

has become diffuse, behavioral consultation does not possess a central theory of consultation. According to Keller (1981), "Behavioral consultation is based upon a theory of change that is derived from a broad-based social learning model encompassing diverse streams of psychological and social science research and theory" (p. 64). When all these factors are taken into consideration, defining behavioral consultation clearly becomes a difficult task.

In its broadest sense, behavioral consultation is a problem-solving process that has its foundation in behavioral theory (Kratochwill, 2008; Martens & DiGennaro, 2008). According to Keller (1981), behavioral consultation involves a "relationship whereby services consistent with a behavioral orientation are provided to a client through the mediation of important others in that client's environment, that is, indirect service" (p. 65). Note that this actually defines behavioral case consultation because its major emphasis is on helping a consultee help a client. Keller's (1981) definition reflects a traditional classification scheme: Mental health consultation focuses on the consultee so that the client will be helped; behavioral consultation focuses on the client so that the client can be helped; and organizational consultation focuses on helping the system so that the client system can function better. In a school-based example, a school-based consultant and teacher select and implement interventions to assist student learning and behavioral change (Snyder, Quirk, & Dematteo, 2011).

Four characteristics typify behavioral consultation of any form (Kratochwill, 2008; Vernberg & Reppucci, 1986):

- the use of indirect service delivery models

- a reliance on behavioral technology principles to design, implement, and assess consultative interventions

- a diversity of intervention goals ranging from solving problematic situations to enhancing competence to empowering

- changes aimed at various targets (e.g., individuals, groups, organizations, and communities) in different settings (i.e., from single settings to multiple settings)

In effect, these characteristics broaden behavioral consultation from a case-oriented concept to one that includes the training and system forms of consultation.

Combining Keller's (1981) definition with ideas suggested by Vernberg and Reppucci (1986) produces the following definition of behavioral consultation that is still used today: a relationship whereby services consistent with a behavioral orientation are provided either indirectly to a client or a system (through the mediation of important others in the client's environment or of those charged with the system's well-being) or directly by training consultees to enhance their skills with clients or systems.

Such a definition is consistent with eight characteristics or assumptions that typify behavioral consultation and account for its uniqueness (Henning-Stout, 1993):

- All behaviors are learned.
- The establishment, maintenance, and change of social behavior can be explained through observation of functional interactions of the individual, his or her behavior, and the environment.
- Assessment, intervention, and evaluation of the intervention's effectiveness are directly linked.
- Behaviors of focus must be observable, measurable, and quantifiable.
- Environmental antecedents provide powerful points for initiating change.
- Because learning histories vary, intervention is necessarily idiosyncratic.
- Understanding and intervening with any behavior are guided and modified according to systematically collected data reflecting the frequency, intensity, or duration of that behavior.
- For one person's behavior to be changed, behaviors in other individuals interacting within the environment of focus must also be modified. (pp. 25–26)

Recent additional characteristics include a problem-solving orientation, emphasis on a collegial relationship, and a focus on a structured interview process (Bergan & Kratochwill, 1990; Kratochwill, 2008; Sheridan, Kratochwill, & Bergan, 1996). For example, emphasis on the collegial relationship focuses on the idea that the behavioral consultant is a content expert and the consultee is an expert on the situation at hand. These characteristics and assumptions reflect behavioral consultation's emphasis on quantification and measurement, as well as its perspective regarding how behavior is learned and changed.

All three forms of behavioral consultation tend to follow a set problem-solving sequence (Kratochwill, 2008):

1. description of the problem in behavioral terms
2. a functional analysis of the problem's antecedents and consequences
3. selection of a target behavior(s)
4. generation of behavioral objectives
5. design and implementation of a behavior change plan
6. evaluation of the process

Behavioral consultation typically requires three consultant–consultee sessions called "interviews." Both problem solving and applied behavior analysis (ABA) are emphasized in this model (Martens & DiGennaro, 2008).

It might occur to some that the behavioral technology training form of consultation does not fit this sequence perfectly. In this form of consultation, the implementation step of the sequence consists of the training sessions. (Steps 1 through 4 will already have been accomplished prior to the training.)

KEY CONCEPTS OF BEHAVIORAL CONSULTATION

Next we'll discuss the following key concepts of behavioral consultation: its scientific view of behavior, its emphasis on current influences on behavior, and the principles of behavior change.

An understanding of these key concepts will help clarify why behavioral consultation proceeds as it does.

Scientific View of Behavior

Behavioral consultation, like the behavior therapy that spawned it, is grounded in a scientific view of human behavior, which implies the use of a systematic and structured approach to the delivery of human services such as consultation. Because knowledge obtained from empirical research is valued so highly by behavioral consultants, such research is subjected to scientific validation, or, in other words, is put to the scientific test. Such evaluation and subsequent validation are essential to the advancement of behavioral consultation beyond its current state of practice (Vernberg & Reppucci, 1986). The emphasis on scientific investigation also leads behavioral consultants to use empirically validated consultation interventions because they believe that such a method of operation increases the likelihood that consultation will be successful (Bergan & Kratochwill, 1990).

Emphasis on Current Influences on Behavior

Behavioral consultation focuses on current behavior as well (Kazdin, 2001). For the most part, behavioral consultation takes the position that because certain current behaviors constitute the problem in a particular situation, behavioral consultation should focus on those behaviors. Behavioral consultation, as Bergan (1977) notes, "defines problems presented in consultation as being outside the skin of the client" (p. 26). It is the description of behavior, not the description of a person, that is essential (Gresham, Watson, & Skinner, 2001). Thus, by the standards of behavioral consultation, it is better to describe a client's hitting behavior in terms of its environmental antecedents and consequences than to describe the client as aggressive.

By focusing on current behaviors, behavioral consultation is better able to discriminate between existing and desired behavior and allow for an operational definition of the problem (Bergan & Kratochwill, 1990). Such discrimination allows for defining the goals of consultation in behavioral terms as well as the creation of sophisticated data collection (Watson & Sterling-Turner, 2008). The consultant and consultee can mutually determine what behaviors currently exist and what alternative behaviors are desired; they then set behavioral goals, which create the conditions for more rigorous evaluation of the effects of consultation. Past behavior is viewed as important only to the degree that it assists in present interventions. As a result, behavioral consultants do little to help consultees or the consultees' clients gain insight into their problems or concerns. Rather, they concentrate on directive and active treatment of current behavior (Kazdin, 2001).

Principles of Behavior Change

Behavioral consultation assumes that behavior is lawful (i.e., orderly, following a set of rules) and that changing the consequences of behavior by using the principles of learning produces a change in behavior (Kazdin, 2001). The consultant helps the consultee select these principles for use in the problem-solving process (Bergan & Kratochwill, 1990).

Behavior consultants use such principles as reinforcement, punishment, extinction, shaping, and modeling in the behavior change process. The consultant uses these principles to examine and understand the client's behavior, to examine the consultee's behavior, and to determine how to proceed with the course of consultation (Bergan & Kratochwill, 1990). These principles can also be used by consultees in their own work with clients.

There has been a trend to use *social learning theory* to integrate different learning paradigms. Social learning theory uses various learning models to explain behavior while emphasizing the context of events, human social development, and internal perceptions of events. Social learning theory's major contribution is its recognition of multiple influences (e.g., cognitions and the environment) on behavior,

T A B L E 10.1   Common Behavioral Methods

METHOD	PROCESS
Positive reinforcement	To increase the occurrence of desirable behavior, the application of positive conditions (praise, attention, privilege, tokens) if the subject's performance warrants it
Negative reinforcement	The removal of an aversive condition if the subject engages in desirable behavior
Punishment	To decrease the occurrence of undesirable behavior, the application of aversive conditions depending on the subject's performance
Extinction	Eliminating an undesirable behavior by terminating the conditions that reinforce the subject's performance
Ignoring	Eliminating the subject's undesirable behavior through inattention to it
Shaping	Changing the subject's undesirable behavior through the positive reinforcement of successive approximations of the desirable behavior
Differential reinforcement	Increasing the subject's performance of desirable behaviors through the selective reinforcement of desirable behaviors and ignoring the undesirable behaviors
Environmental cues	Environmental stimuli that prompt the subject's behavior
Inadvertent reinforcement	Inadvertently or unintentionally reinforcing the subject's behavior by creating conditions that have an effect opposite of that anticipated
Contingency contracting	The process of formalizing an agreement that specifies the behavioral conditions or plans associated with behavioral change
Behavioral rehearsal	An educational learning process in which subjects practice new, adaptive behavior in a controlled setting

Source: From Wallace, W. A. & Hall, D. L. (1996). *Psychological consultation: Perspectives and applications*, Table 1, p. 77. Copyright 1996 by Brooks/Cole-Thomson, Pacific Grove, CA. Reprinted with permission.

while at the same time offering a framework for explaining behavior (Kazdin, 2001). For an excellent, detailed introduction to the principles of behavior, consult Kanfer and Goldstein's *Helping People Change* (1991) or Kazdin's *Behavior Modification in Applied Settings* (2001). Table 10.1 illustrates common techniques based on the principles of behavior change.

THE CONSULTATION PROCESS

Behavioral consultation can take three forms: behavioral case consultation, behavioral technology training, and behavioral system consultation. All three forms have the following characteristics: indirect service to the client system, use of behavioral technology principles throughout the consultation process, a problem-solving orientation, and empirical validation of interventions (Vernberg & Reppucci, 1986).

Next we'll examine each of the three forms of behavioral consultation in terms of goals, the consultant's function and role, the consultee's experience in consultation, and the use of consultation techniques and procedures.

Behavioral Case Consultation

In *behavioral case consultation*, a consultant provides direct, behavior-based service to a consultee concerning the management of a client or group of clients assigned to the consultee. To be effective, behavioral consultation requires an effective analysis of the problem and related intervention, and an effective implementation of the intervention (Noell & Witt, 1998). Most case approaches to behavioral consultation (e.g., Bergan

& Kratochwill, 1990) still rely heavily on operant conditioning. However, more recent models use a variety of models such as the social learning theory developed by Bandura (1977, 1982), which includes the prototype for ecological assessment. By far the most comprehensive approach to behavioral case consultation is that of Bergan and Kratochwill (1990); indeed, most other models are basic variations of Bergan's original model (1977). In behavioral case consultation, behaviors are operationally defined; concrete goals are set; data, including environmental data, are collected; interventions are developed based on the data collection; and decisions are made from a data-based model.

Behavioral case consultation consists of a series of four stages that provide form and focus to the problem solving engaged in by the consultant and consultee (Kratochwill, 2008). These four stages deal with identifying the problem, analyzing it, implementing a treatment, and evaluating the treatment.

The challenge of behavioral consultation is to "select treatment strategies from a pool of potentially effective strategies that can be … managed by people who have not had specific training in behavioral change methods" (Elliott & Busse, 1993, p. 180). As Sheridan (2000) notes: "Compared to other forms of consultation, behavioral consultation is characterized by (a) the use of a standard four-stage problem-solving process, (b) adherence to behavioral assessment, (c) reliance on behavioral intervention strategies, and (d) evaluation of outcomes based upon behavioral analysis and related methodologies" (p. 344). In a nutshell, this model consists of identifying the problem, analyzing it, intervening to treat the problem and evaluating the treatment—all from a behavioral context.

Consultation Goals.   In behavioral case consultation, the consultee presents a work-related concern with a client to the consultant, who uses his or her expertise in the principles of learning to *manage the consultee's management of the case*; that is, to help the consultee make positive changes in the client's

environment (Feld, Bergan, & Stone, 1987) and therefore in the client's behavior. Recently, some authorities on behavioral consultation (e.g., Bergan & Kratochwill, 1990) have suggested that a second, complementary goal is to effect change in the consultee.

Consultant Function and Roles.   Behavioral consultants use a systematic problem-solving process to assist consultees with their clients (Bergan & Kratochwill, 1990). Behavioral consultants frequently act as experts to ensure that the stages of problem identification, problem analysis, plan implementation, and problem evaluation occur and are adequately accomplished.

Although the consultant is called on to provide expertise, most behavioral consultants take a collaborative approach to the consultation relationship (Racine Gilles et al., 2011). In this context, the consultant is also a "student" in learning from the consultee about the client system and takes a collaborative approach when possible. The consultant takes steps to build rapport with the consultee as a basis for an effective consultation experience for the participants. Even though the content and process of consultation are under the consultant's control, the consultee is encouraged to become involved in content- and process-related decision making to the degree his or her knowledge and skill in the behavioral approach permit. That said, the behavioral consultant is typically more in control of the relationship than a consultant coming from a mental health perspective. The consultant helps the consultee determine the best course of action in the case and suggests an array of choices from which he or she can choose. Because the consultee is the primary instrument of change in the client, the consultant avoids dictating the consultee's behavior.

The consultant provides knowledge concerning those principles of learning pertinent to the case and whatever knowledge is needed to help the consultee accomplish each of the consultation stages. In some cases, the consultant must train the consultee in the use of strategies based on principles of learning (Watson & Sterling-Turner, 2008).

However, Bergan's model does not emphasize consultee training to a great degree. To ensure that the stages of consultation occur and are successfully accomplished, the consultant guides the consultee's behavior through the use of selected types of verbalizations.

Thus, the consultant makes sure that problem identification occurs, but the consultee controls the process whereby identification of the problem occurs. The consultant must inform the consultee about the use of this form of management at the outset of consultation and be satisfied that he or she is seeking services voluntarily. Management of the consultation process by using verbal skills in structuring the consultant–consultee interaction is therefore the major task of the consultant.

Verbal Interaction Techniques. Because consultation can be reduced to a series of verbal interactions between the consultant and the consultee, these interactions must not be left to chance (Andersen et al., 2010; Bergan & Kratochwill, 1990). The consultant controls not only his or her own verbalizations, but also those of the consultee. There is some evidence that consultant verbalizations are related to successful consultation outcomes (Busse, Kratochwill, & Elliott, 1999). There is some empirical support that the content of the consultee's responses tends to match that of the consultant's questions, thus providing the consultant with a tremendous amount of influence in controlling all

aspects of the consultation process (Turco & Skinner, 1991).

There is also evidence to suggest that consultants with high-dominance scores on personality inventories are perceived as more effective by consultees (Erchul et al., 1999). The consultant does not attempt to control the specific content of the consultee's verbalizations during consultation, but rather attempts to encourage him or her to produce the various types of verbalizations needed to achieve the task at hand in the consultation process.

Bergan produced a classification system to assist consultants in controlling the verbalizations in consultation (see Table 10.2). Verbal interchanges can be classified in terms of message source, content, process, and control. Judicious use of this classification system can enable the consultant to successfully guide the consultee through the consultation process.

Message Source. The message source simply indicates whether the verbalization comes from the consultant or the consultee.

Message Content. Message content refers to what the consultant and the consultee discuss. The consultant usually controls the content of verbalizations in consultation, which includes seven subcategories: background/environment, behavior setting, behavior, individual characteristics, observation, plan, and other. The verbalizations that occur in behavioral

T A B L E 10.2   Classification of Verbal Interchanges

MESSAGE SOURCE	MESSAGE CONTENT	MESSAGE PROCESS	MESSAGE CONTROL
Consultant	Background/environment	Specification	Elicitor
Consultee	Behavior-setting	Evaluation	Emitter
	Behavior	Inference	
	Individual characteristics	Summarization	
	Observation	Validation	
	Plan		
	Other		

case consultation are to be controlled by the consultant because what is talked about in consultation directly relates to the course and degree of success of the consultation. By determining what to discuss and when, the consultant can help the consultee work with the client more efficiently and effectively.

The background/environment content consists of verbalizations that concern historical factors or current environmental factors related to the behavior under discussion and might affect the client's behavior. For example, if the major focus of consultation is the client's adjustment at work, a consultant might ask for information on a client's home life or for a developmental history of the client's problem.

Behavior-setting verbalizations, which are among the most frequently used by behavioral consultants, are used to analyze the client's behavior so that appropriate plans to change that behavior can be made. These verbalizations concern the antecedent, consequent, and sequential conditions in the immediate environment that affect the client's behavior. Antecedent conditions occur just before the behaviors under discussion. Thus, the consultant might ask the consultee to describe exactly what happens just before the client's behavior occurs. Consequent conditions occur just after and may reinforce the behavior in question; they reflect the patterns of antecedents and consequences or the timing of the client's behavior. For example, sequential conditions can become clear when the consultant asks about the events leading up to the client's behavior, when and how frequently the behavior tends to occur, and any special conditions that may be pertinent.

Behavior verbalizations allow precise specification of client behaviors so that they can be measured and discussed. Such verbalizations can also help identify which environmental factors affecting the client's behavior should be investigated. Verbalizations of this type include descriptions of the client's thoughts, feelings, overt behaviors, and their intensity, as well as discussions of written records concerning the client's behavior (e.g., baseline behavior graphs). As an example, the consultant

and consultee might discuss a client's written autobiographical statement, or the consultant might ask the consultee to describe as specifically as possible what happens when the client engages in a problem behavior.

The *individual characteristics* of verbalizations describe the unique features or traits of the client. They can help determine what is unique about the client and how that uniqueness is related to the client's problem. Consultant–consultee discussion of clients' attributes and traits can range from basic matters like age and weight to more complex personality characteristics and handicaps. For example, the consultant and the consultee might discuss the age, weight, and shyness of a teenage boy as it relates to his being the "class clown."

Often the consultant–consultee interaction produces a decision to obtain more information or data about the client's behavior. Verbalizations in this *observation* subcategory are related to documenting client behaviors. For example, a consultee might determine that data should be collected to compare the number of negative self-references a client makes in group therapy with those made during individual therapy. In another example, a consultant might help a consultee determine the best way to record observations of a client's behavior.

The *plan* subcategory is broad and consists of those verbalizations related to attempts to solve the consultee's problems. Planning in this context typically refers either to general strategies for the consultee to consider or the tactics for intervening with some specific strategy. However, any verbalization about a plan—how it should be implemented, how it should be evaluated, or how well it worked—falls under this category. For example, the consultant and consultee might plan a strategy called a *token economy system* to help a child stay on task when doing schoolwork, or discuss how well such a plan worked.

No classification can be fully comprehensive and concise, and in fact, consultants and consultees make many other kinds of verbalizations during consultation. Therefore, a catchall subcategory, *other* verbalizations, is used for those not appropriate to the other six subcategories. For example, the consultant and consultee might "talk about the weather" or make statements only indirectly related to client behavior or to the consultation process.

Message Process.   Consultants control not only the things that are talked about but also the way in which they are discussed—the message process, in other words. Consultant–consultee verbal exchanges can be categorized by type of verbal process. As noted by Bergan (1977), "The message-process category classifies verbal messages in accordance with the kinds of speaker actions they describe vis-à-vis the content of conversation" (p. 38). Process, then, refers to the type of verbal action conveyed in a message. The five message-process subcategories are specification, evaluation, inference, summarization, and validation.

Specification verbalizations ask for some detail or description concerning one of the content subcategories. Information about some behavior's background, setting, nature, or occurrence could be specified. This subcategory is used when more precision or detail is needed to assist the consultee. For example, a consultant might ask a consultee to specify exactly how an intervention will be implemented or to describe the consequences of a given client behavior.

Evaluation verbalizations involve some sort of value judgment or reveal emotions and attitudes about a topic. For example, a consultee might judge a plan to be ineffective, or a consultant might praise the consultee's behavior in implementing a selected strategy.

Inference verbalizations concern making and playing hunches as compared with acting on known fact. Such verbalizations are frequently used to predict the effects of certain interventions on the client's behavior or to demonstrate the set of assumptions under which the consultant and consultee are acting. For example, a consultant might think or feel a certain plan will be effective and might tell this to a consultee, or a consultee might surmise that a client is acting out because of some kind of inappropriate child-rearing practice.

Summarization verbalizations are reviews or summaries of previously discussed information that can help the consultant and consultee remember what has been discussed previously, keep them focused on the task at hand, and provide a review of what has been agreed on. For example, a consultant might review what has been accomplished during a given consultation interview or ask a consultee to review his or her perceptions of the client's problems.

Validation verbalizations give or ask for a yes or a no response concerning the facts at hand and are used primarily to develop and maintain consensus between the consultant and consultee concerning each stage in the consultation process. They can be used at any time to make sure that the consultant and consultee are on the same wavelength. For example, a consultee might review some implementation strategy and ask the consultant if he or she agrees about it, or a consultant might ask if there is agreement on the kind of observation that needs to be performed on a client's behavior. There is some evidence that the use of validating statements by the consultant early on in the consultation relationship may encourage consultees to more prematurely through the consultation process (Martens, Lewandowski, & Houk, 1989).

Thus, there are five message processes that can describe what is occurring in each of the content subcategories. Consider the content subcategory "plan." By using each of the processes, the plan could be specified, evaluated, inferred about, summarized, or validated. The consultant, then, should know not only what to talk about, but the way in which it should be talked about.

Message Control.   The consultant is charged with guiding the consultee through a successful consultation experience and must control the consultee's verbal behavior to do so. To this end, the consultant must determine not only what (content) and how things are to be discussed (process) but also who is going to talk about them (control). In effect, the consultant uses message control to either give input or to get input from the consultee. (The consultee can also use message control for the same purpose.) In message control behavior, the speaker's verbiage is classified in terms of whether or not it will have a direct effect on the receiver's response.

If a direct verbal response is intended (and is thus considered controlling), the message is called an *elicitor*. If the message is not intended to obtain a direct response (and thus does not control the receiver's response), it is termed an *emitter*. Elicitors usually take the form of either direct or indirect questions that ask the consultee to engage in specification, evaluation, inference, summarization, or validation in one of the message content subcategories. The consultant could ask the consultee to use a verbal process about the conditions affecting the client's behavior, the behavior itself, related observations, or pertinent plans. There is some evidence that specificity when questioning consultees is related to the effectiveness of consultation (Bergan & Kratochwill, 1990). Four examples of elicitors and their classifications in terms of content and process follow:

- A consultant asks a consultee to describe the most problematic situation about the client's behavior (behavior-specification).

- A consultant asks a consultee to validate a plan that is to be implemented (plan-validation).

- A consultant asks a consultee how he or she feels about making a series of observations of a client's behavior (observation-evaluation).

- A consultant asks a consultee for some hunches on why the client is acting in a certain way (background/environment-inference).

An emitter does not call for a reaction from the listener. When consultants use emitters, they provide both content and process information to consultees without attempting to control the consultee's response. Emitters usually take the form of declarative statements. Consider the following examples of emitters and their classifications according to content and process:

- A consultant summarizes the individual characteristics of a client for the consultee (individual characteristics-summarization).

- A consultant summarizes for the consultee some plan they have agreed to use to help the client (plan-summarization).

- A consultant makes a statement agreeing with the consultee regarding the consequences of a given client behavior (behavior setting-validation).

- A consultant shares hunches with the consultee about suspected traits and habits that the client might have (individual characteristics-inference).

In summary, the behavioral consultant controls the verbal communication in consultation so as to help the consultee use the consultation process with maximum effectiveness and efficiency by controlling who should talk, what should be discussed, and how the discussion should proceed.

Consultee Experience in Consultation. The consultee is expected to work with the consultant toward the successful completion of the consultation process and to be actively involved in the problem-solving process (Martens & DiGennaro, 2008).

As in other forms of case consultation, such as Caplan's (1970) client-centered case consultation, the consultee is a link between the consultant and the client. The consultee's four primary duties in the consultation process are to specify or describe, evaluate or decide, provide direct services to the client, and monitor the client's actions. The consultee should describe as specifically as possible the details of the case and the nature of the work-related problem. The consultee should respond to the consultant's prompts and probes as accurately as possible and provide him or her with the most comprehensive, detailed picture of the work-related concern possible. The consultee's role as evaluator or decision maker reflects the peer nature of all consultation: The consultant may make a recommendation concerning a case, but it is the consultee's task to determine what to do with that recommendation. Bergan (1977) relates an example of this consultee role in noting that the consultant might help the consultee select a method for measuring client behavior, but the consultee would have to evaluate that measurement's effectiveness in achieving desired outcomes.

Of course, a primary role of the consultee is to continue to work with the client. Such work can include performing a particular caregiving role relative to the client (e.g., teacher to student or counselor to client) and collecting data regarding the client's behavior. Frequently, the consultee's work with the client will be adaptations of the consultant's recommendations. A critical part of the consultee's work with the client involves the client in the selection of the goals and processes of consultation; this is frequently accomplished by having the consultee discuss with the client what the consultant and consultee are considering.

Application: Consultant Techniques and Procedures. Both types of behavioral case consultation—developmental and problem centered—concern changes in client behavior (Bergan, 1977). Developmental consultation deals with more or less long-term behavior change, whereas problem-centered consultation deals with problems that call for immediate attention (e.g., crises). Most of the literature on behavioral case consultation refers to developmental consultation because it is by far the most extensively used, and thus our discussion of behavioral case consultation will be limited to developmental consultation.

There are four stages to the behavioral consultation process (Bergan & Kratochwill, 1990; Erchul et al., 2009). The first stage consists of the *Problem Identification Interview* (PII) during which the consultant focuses on "the specification of a problem by emphasizing the selection and definition of a target behavior and by the determination of baseline data collection procedures" (Kratochwill, Elliott, & Busse, 1995, p. 87). Problem analysis and plan implementation are dealt with through the *Problem Analysis Interview*. The objectives of this interview "are to validate the problem through examination of baseline data, analyze the problem and related variable ... and develop an intervention plan" (Kratochwill et al., 1995, p. 88).

The third stage, plan implementation, involves selecting and implementing an intervention (Kratochwill, 2008). The consultant is "on call" (often through some combination of observation, email, text, or phone) as the consultee implements

the plan. The fourth stage of consultation, plan evaluation, is accomplished through the *Treatment Evaluation Interview* (TEI), during which the consultant and consultee assess the degree of success in meeting the plan's goals. There are typically three to four sessions between the consultant and the consultee in this model.

Problem Identification Stage. This stage provides the momentum for the entire consultation process (Kratochwill et al., 1995). The term *problem identification* sounds quite simple, but from a behavioral perspective, defining the problem can be a complex and difficult matter. This stage is crucial; what occurs here will determine the direction that consultation takes and affects whether or not consultation will be successful (Kratochwill, 2008). In fact, this stage is considered the most critical because its outcome is the formulation and implementation of a plan (Kratochwill et al., 1995). Bergan and Tombari (1976) found years ago that if the problem identification stage was not successfully completed, the entire consultation process might be irreversibly damaged.

During the problem identification process, the consultant helps the consultee accomplish the following steps:

1. Designate the general and specific client performance goals to be achieved in consultation.

2. Determine how to measure the designated goals.

3. Assess current client performance in terms of the designated goals.

4. Examine the results of the assessment.

5. Discern the discrepancies between current and desired client performance.

These steps are accomplished by two consultant-led interviews, the first a PII in which Steps 1 and 2 are accomplished. Step 3 is accomplished by the consultee. The second is a follow-up interview in which Steps 4 and 5 are accomplished. The problem identification stage ends once the discrepancy between current and desired client behavior has been specified (Bergan & Kratochwill, 1990).

In the problem identification stage, the consultant uses more elicitors than emitters—more specifications, validations, and summarizations than inferences and evaluations—and more verbalizations in the behavior, behavior setting, and observation categories than in other content categories.

When successfully accomplished, the problem identification stage results in a well-specified problem defined by the discrepancy between current performance (as measured by collected data, including baseline data) and desired performance (as indicated by stated goals) (Kratochwill, 2008). Successful problem identification sets the stage for problem analysis.

Problem Analysis Stage.   In this stage, the consultant determines the conditions that maintain the client's problem behavior and formulates a plan to alleviate that behavior. The consultant jointly pursues these two tasks with the consultee. There is some research that suggests that consultees prefer that consultants take the lead in recommending evidence-based interventions from which the consultee can choose (Erchul et al., 2009).

This stage can thus be divided into two phases that contain a total of five steps:

Phase One: Problem Analysis

Step 1. Choose a procedure for analyzing the problem.

Step 2. Conduct a conditions and/or skills analysis.

Phase Two: Plan Formulation

Step 3. Develop plan strategies.

Step 4. Develop plan tactics.

Step 5. Establish procedures for assessing the plan's effectiveness.

These steps are accomplished by means of one or more interviews, during which the client's problem behavior is examined from one of two perspectives: internal and external conditions related to the behavior, or a skills deficit in the client. The consultant and consultee must first decide whether to conduct an analysis of the conditions surrounding the behavior, the skills of the client, or both. Bergan

and Kratochwill (1990) suggest that a conditions analysis be performed if the problem behavior tends to be variable over conditions; if the problem behavior remains constant over conditions, then a skills analysis is recommended, as is the case when increased self-direction on the part of the client is desired. Once the consultant and consultee decide on which type of analysis to perform, Step 1 is accomplished.

In Step 2, conducting an analysis of the problem, the consultant and consultee work together to determine what conditions and/or skills need to be changed to resolve the client's problem successfully.

Consultation next enters Step 3, developing plan strategies, during which a systematic course of action to use with the client is developed. The consultant usually starts out by suggesting a broad strategy that seems promising based on the conditions or skills analysis performed earlier. In general, the consultant and consultee determine which principles of learning should be used and convert them into strategies to help the client. For example, a consultant might suggest using positive reinforcement as a strategy to change the client's behavior, but allow the consultee flexibility in its use. Or the consultant might suggest assessing the view of the client with whom the consultee is working to ascertain what types of reinforcement are most attractive (Damon, Riley-Tillman, & Fiorello, 2008).

In Step 4, the consultant and consultee consider the tactics involved in implementing the strategy, and in Step 5 they establish procedures for determining the plan's effectiveness. If a conditions analysis was performed, then those same techniques are used for assessment purposes. If a skills analysis was performed, then methods for measuring skill acquisition need to be used. Bergan and Kratochwill (1990) suggest that items used in the skills analysis should be adapted to measure skill acquisition. Once assessment procedures have been established, consultation moves to the plan implementation stage. The bottom line is that the consultant and consultee develop a plan that is acceptable both objectively (i.e., empirically sound) and subjectively (i.e., mutually acceptable) (Sheridan et al., 1996).

In the problem analysis stage, as in the earlier problem identification stage, the consultant uses more elicitors than emitters and more specifications, validations, and summarizations than inferences and evaluations. Whereas the problem identification stage has a balance of verbalizations in the behavior, behavior setting, and observation subcategories, the problem analysis stage has a balance of verbalizations in the behavior, behavior setting, and plan subcategories. The problem analysis stage builds naturally on the problem identification stage (Altschaefl, 2014; Kratochwill, 2008; Kratochwill et al., 1995).

Plan Implementation Stage. The result of successful problem analysis is a plan designed to assist the client system. In this stage, what was planned during the problem analysis stage is put into effect. Good planning does not necessarily lead to good implementation, and thus the consultant's task is to ensure adequate implementation. To this end, the consultant guides the consultee in accomplishing two steps of this stage: preparing for and carrying out the implementation. This stage is different from the previous two stages in that there is no formal interview between the consultant and the consultee.

In preparing for plan implementation, roles related to the implementation are assigned, required materials are gathered, and skills necessary for implementation are affirmed. The consultee generally takes the roles of the plan implementation director, plan executor, and observer of client behavior. The consultant is responsible for determining the need for training and providing it to the consultee (or a designee of the consultee) so they can adequately perform these roles. Training can be very time consuming, so any plans should take the strengths of consultees into consideration (Kratochwill, 2008). Often, the consultant trains the consultee in techniques like those in Table 10.1. Once the appropriate roles have been assigned and arrangements for use of materials made, the consultant and consultee implement the plan, during which the consultee attempts to help the client with the consultant's guidance. Plans should be time efficient, have few restrictions, and carry a low level of risk to the client system (Kratochwill et al., 1995). The consultant is available to assist with any revisions to the plan that become necessary as the implementation

proceeds. Revisions in the plan may be called for if the consultee is having difficulty in implementing the plan as intended (e.g., there are issues with treatment integrity). A second reason for revision is that the client system is not making adequate progress toward the goals set.

Treatment Evaluation Stage. Behavioral case consultation stresses evaluation of consultation more than any other model of consultation. Considerable time is spent evaluating the goals of consultation and the effectiveness of the plan, which determines what happens next in the consultation process.

The problem evaluation stage has three steps: evaluating goal attainment, evaluating plan effectiveness, and postimplementation planning (Altschaefl, 2014; Bergan & Kratochwill, 1990; Kratochwill, 2008). In reality, plan evaluation is often not as rigorous as that used in research, but nonetheless there needs to be adequate support to verify outcomes. For example, outcome criteria should involve measures of the degree to which desired behaviors were demonstrated over time, such as with single case study designs (Kratochwill et al., 1995).

Goal attainment is assessed by determining whether the client's behavior change adequately meets previously set standards. Recall that the problem was defined in terms of a discrepancy between current and desired levels of behavior. In evaluation, the degree to which desired and observed behaviors coincide is judged in order to determine whether the goals of consultation have been met. There are three possibilities in terms of goal attainment: no progress, some progress, and accomplishment. If there has been no progress, the consultant typically suggests a return to the problem analysis stage, or perhaps to the goal identification step within the problem identification stage. In some situations, consultation may be terminated and replaced by another type of service. If there is some progress in goal attainment, the consultant usually suggests a return to the problem analysis stage. On occasion, the consultant might suggest a return to the problem identification stage to reexamine goals; on rare occasions, he or she might recommend termination. If the goals have been accomplished, the consultant and consultee then proceed to evaluate the plan's effectiveness.

Behavioral consultants believe that even though the goals of consultation have been achieved, an appropriate design must be used in evaluating the plan so as to demonstrate that the plan was indeed responsible for the success of consultation. Plan evaluation has no direct bearing on the case, but it can be used in solving similar concerns in the future. Plan effectiveness is determined by applying an appropriate evaluation design that states when client behaviors are to be measured and when plan implementations are made relative to those measurements. Interested readers can consult Bergan and Kratochwill (1990) for a discussion on evaluation design; a detailed discussion of this subject is beyond the scope of this book.

Step 3 in problem evaluation is postimplementation planning. The consultant and consultee design a plan for use after consultation has formally been terminated. Such a plan prevents the problem from recurring and provides a way for the consultee to reestablish contact should the problem behavior return to undesirable levels. Sometimes this plan is left intact and maintained, especially when it is relatively easy to implement and when there is some likelihood that the client's behavior would return were the plan eliminated.

The implementation of a new plan often occurs when it is determined that it is equally effective as, but more convenient than, the first plan. Moving from tangible to nontangible reinforcers is a common example of this type of strategy. Finally, a program can be removed once it has been determined that it is no longer needed to maintain the performance levels desired of the client. Whatever the postimplementation plan, behavioral consultants suggest that consultees continue to monitor client behavior for some period of time.

When the goals of consultation and the implementation plan have been evaluated and postimplementation plans made, consultation is terminated. During this stage, the consultant uses a balance of elicitors and emitters; more specifications, summarizations, validations, and inferences (instead of evaluations); and more verbalizations in the behavior, plan, and observation subcategories. On occasion, the consultant may want to formally communicate the results of an intervention program to a consultee. Figure 10.1 illustrates the format for such a report.

An Example of Behavioral Case Consultation

A counselor working as a mental health consultant assists a family therapist with a family. The consultant has expertise concerning runaway youths. Two of the family's three teenagers have run away. The family therapist wants to consult with the counselor before using certain interventions with the family.

Together, the consultant and consultee define what is meant by "running away" behavior. They functionally analyze the behavior in terms of what occurs before and after its occurrence (Martens & DiGennaro, 2008), and then devise a plan based on rewarding responsible behavior that has the goal of decreasing the target behavior. The consultee then implements the strategy with the family and evaluates it at its conclusion.

Behavioral Technology Training

This approach to behavioral consultation is used when consultees seek to increase general usage of behavioral technology principles when working with clients. Behavior technology training can also be incorporated into behavior case consultation when necessary (Watson, Steege, & Watson, 2011; Watson & Sterling-Turner, 2008). Behavioral technology training is an indirect service because the consultees use their new learning with their client systems. It is basically a form of consultee-centered consultation with an emphasis on providing training for consultees in consultation-related matters (Racine Gilles et al., 2011). The consultant has indirectly affected those client systems through the intermediary of the consultee who is applying the newly learned skills (Sheridan & Kratochwill, 2008). Consultees

I.   Background Information
     A. Demographic Information on the Child
     B. Ecological Context of the Problem

II. Problem Definition
     A. Referral Problem
     B. Target Behavior
     C. Desired Outcome Behaviors
     D. Critical Setting/Situations for Change
     E. Preliminary Functional Analysis

III. Problem Analysis
     A. Description of Assessment or Data Recording Procedures
     B. Rationale for Use of Data Collection Procedures
     C. Presentation and Discussion of Data

IV. Intervention Plan
     A. Basic Design
     B. Contingencies
     C. Criterion for Contingencies
     D. Acceptability of Interventions to Teacher/Parent and Child
     E. Personnel Involved in Intervention Implementation
     F. Setting and Time
     G. Resources
     H. Procedures for Promoting New Behaviors
     I. Procedures for Increasing Existing Behaviors
     J. Procedures for Reducing Interfering Problem Behaviors
     K. Procedures for Facilitating Generalizations
     L. Treatment Integrity Checks

V.   Plan Evaluation
     A. Change in Behavior via Direct Observation
     B. Change in Teacher/Parent Performance Ratings
     C. Mainstreamed Peer Comparison
     D. Outcome Interview with Significant Adults
     E. Intervention Side Effects

VI. Summary and Recommendations
     A. Summary and Results Obtained
     B. Discussion of Effectiveness
     C. Suggestions for Increasing Program Effectiveness
     D. Suggestions for Future Follow-Up

F I G U R E 10.1   Outline for writing a behavioral consultation case report

SOURCE: From Kratochwill, T. R., Elliott, S. N., and P. Carrington Rotto (1995). In A. Thomas and J. Grimes (Eds.), *Best practices in school psychology* (3rd ed., pp. 519–537). Washington, DC: National Association of School of Psychologists. Copyright 1995 by the National Association of School Psychologists. Reprinted with permission.

tend to be professionals such as teachers, or caregivers such as parents (Kratochwill, 2008; Kratochwill and Pittman, 2002). Consultants train consultees in general behavioral principles or specific behavioral technology skills (Watson & Robinson, 1996; Watson & Sterling-Turner, 2008) or both (Barnett, Hawkins, & Lentz, 2011; Elliott & Busse, 1993; Racine Gilles et al., 2011). For example, Kratochwill and Pittman (2002) note: "One common format for technology training is teacher skill development that focuses on teaching specific information such as assessment techniques, discipline or child management tactics, the process of consultation, or a combination." (p. 79). Technology training with parents can also cover a broad array of topics. Behavioral technology training can be formal or informal and be given to individuals (e.g., in training a therapist to perform systematic desensitization) or groups (e.g., in training special education teachers in token economy procedures).

Behavioral technology training has several justifications for its existence (Kratochwill, 2008; Watson & Sterling-Turner, 2008). Consultees who use behavioral technology are frequently successful. An understanding of behavioral technology increases the likelihood that behavioral programs will be implemented appropriately. Consultees who understand behavioral technology are likely to generalize it to new situations and thus enhance all aspects of their lives. Behavioral technology training is cost-effective and efficient.

The goal of behavioral technology training is increased consultee competence in the use of general and/or specific behavioral technology procedures. The consultant functions as a resource person and trainer. The consultee is a trainee expected to apply learned procedures with appropriate work-related concerns. As is the case in most types of education/training consultation, the steps involved are conducting a needs assessment, planning the training, performing it, and evaluating it. Behavioral technology training usually consists of behavior modification procedures and, more recently, a variety of other behaviorally derived methods. It has been provided to a variety of human service professions, especially schoolteachers.

Problems encountered in evaluation of behavioral technology training revolve around whether it is generalized to settings beyond the training and whether consultees continue to use the results of training in intended environments (Elliott & Busse, 1993). Consultants who use behavioral technology training must decide what form of this training is best for which type of consultee and under what conditions. Behavioral technology training can be a particularly important intervention in the schools, though some authors (e.g., Rosenfield, 2008) suggest that teachers tend not to use its interventions in the classroom, or, if they do, they give up on them early before the desired outcomes have developed. This happens because: (1) teachers using behavioral technology are responsible for solutions to the problem, though not for the child's problem, (2) teachers' working knowledge of behavioral technology is limited, and (3) the underlying assumptions of behavioral technology may be at odds with teachers' explanations of human conduct. Rosenfield (1985) cites an example in which an elementary school teacher gave up on a successful classroom management project agreed to in consultation because her aide didn't like it. Clearly, technology training for consultees can be linked to success in other consultative experiences due to the increased knowledge and skills bases.

Implications for Consultants.   Rosenfield (1985) has made some suggestions for consultants regarding behavioral technology training, which still hold true today. They should be seen as resources for classroom practice and need to encourage teachers to be resource persons among themselves. Teachers should be encouraged to use techniques that allow them to put some of themselves into the implementation. It is very important that they understand the underlying assumptions of behavioral technology since they frequently modify the consultant's suggestions and must do so constructively. Consultants need to be available to teachers since some research suggests that teachers turn to resources that are convenient. Other research suggests that teachers are not well trained in behavioral interventions as they relate to instruction (Crone, Hawken, & Bergstrom, 2007).

Because the language of the behavior approach can still cause a clash of values, consultants need to choose meaningful and acceptable words in behavioral technology training. Time should be provided at the outset of training for discussion and experiential learning related to values regarding behavioral technology.

Teachers need to be in control of the use of behavioral technology and see interventions as congruent with their values. Consultants need to actively promote their suggestions rather than thinking teachers will use them because they think they will work. Behavioral consultants are advised to develop behavioral technology training with the consultee's frame of reference in mind. When working with teachers, the consultant should plan the training with their daily routine and classroom life in mind.

Watson and Sterling-Turner (2008) present an interesting approach in which they incorporate behavioral technology training (via direct instructional methods) into traditional behavioral case consultation.

An Example of Behavioral Technology Training

A school counselor acting as a consultant conducts a three-session workshop for teachers on "Catching Students Being Good." The workshop focuses on effectively using the principles of extinction and positive reinforcement and covers an overview of the concepts and what to expect in using them, situations from the classroom that illustrate how the principles can be used effectively, and general rules for using these kinds of reinforcement. The teachers then practice using the principles in comparable classroom situations and receive feedback on their performances as well as hints for remembering to use the principles in the classroom. Finally, the consultant agrees to observe each teacher applying the principles in the classroom and to provide feedback.

Behavioral System Consultation

In behavioral system consultation, behavioral technology principles are applied to a social system (Lewis & Newcomer, 2002; Williams, 2000). Intervening with behavioral interventions at the systems level is on the increase as efforts are made through consultation to affect the quality of life in social systems through prevention in consultation. Consultants use behavioral technology principles to analyze and change interactions among the various subsystems of a larger social system, such as a school or university mental health center or between two or more interactive systems. For example, a behavioral consultant might interact with the staff at a substance-abuse clinic and the staff at a halfway house for substance abusers to assure proper coordination of treatment efforts. The goal of behavioral system consultation is to enhance the efficiency and effectiveness of a system in terms of its stated functions and to focus on the process and structure of the system itself (Curtis & Stollar, 1996), whereas behavioral case consultation focuses on an individual client within a system. The positive behavioral support movement, for example, can include systems-level consultation/collaboration for its implementation (Minke & Anderson, 2005).

Behavioral system consultation is influenced by the research and theory of ecology and systems theory. The primary goal of behavioral system consultation is to help a social system function more effectively in terms of its stated mission. A combination of individual, group, and system-wide interventions can accomplish this goal, the last of these being the most prevalent. The system itself is the client, and the people with whom the consultant works are the consultees. For example, in a school setting, the classroom is the client system, not an individual student.

Consultees' increased future functioning relative to their job duties within the system can be a secondary goal. As in the other types of behavioral consultation, the consultant acts as an expert, but in behavior system consultation, the consultant must specifically be an expert in systems theory and ecology. The consultant guides the consultee(s) through a systematic problem-solving process and ensures that the steps of system definition, assessment, intervention, and evaluation are accomplished. Even though the consultant is an expert in behavioral technology, systems, and ecology, the nature of the consultation relationship is collaborative; consultees participate to the degree their skills and knowledge permit and can also be trained in behavioral technology, systems theory, and ecology as they relate to the organization.

The consultee's most important function is that of decision maker. Although the consultee and consultant are peers, in the end it is the consultee who decides how consultation is to proceed. The consultee is charged with providing the consultant with fully accurate information, which can include descriptions of the problem or of the system's parameters, suggestions for gathering data, or feedback on the feasibility of possible interventions.

In system definition, the consultant and consultee gather information about the behavior of members of the system relative to the system's goals and structures. There are the two steps of defining the system structure and defining the system process. In determining the *structure* of a system, the consultant and consultee or the collaborators define the system's parameters with regard to time and space, including such variables as physical setting and boundaries (e.g., where the system is located), environmental design (e.g., the system's physical plant), number of system members (i.e., demographic data), and policies and procedures (e.g., rules and regulations).

In determining the *process* of a system, the consultant and consultee or the collaborators define the system's parameters in terms of the behavior of the system's members, including such variables as assessment functions (i.e., how behavior of various systems' groups will be measured), intervention functions (i.e., how the system tries to change on its own), evaluation functions (i.e., how the quality of the system's functions is determined), and communications functions (i.e., who talks to whom, in what manner, and how often).

Once the system's structural and process factors are known, it is time to assess the system in terms of those factors. Assessment is a joint effort of the consultant and consultee or the collaborators to gather appropriate information concerning the interrelationships among identified structures and processes using direct observation, interviews, and appropriate standardized instruments. Based on the system's structural and process limitations, the parties involved can then decide which parts of the system are operating adequately and which are not. The consultant and consultee use three steps in system intervention to eliminate structural and process limitations: They prioritize system needs, specify behavioral outcomes goals, and design and implement intervention programs. Examples are school-based consultants being involved in the selection and implementation of a positive behavioral interventions and support (PBIS) program in a school (Curtis & Van Horne, 2014) and consultants working with various community groups to provide higher quality or service to the mentally ill (James & Crews, 2014).

In system evaluation, the consultant and the consultee evaluate the intervention program operations and system change. In evaluating the operations of the intervention program, the parties involved determine whether the program was implemented in the way intended and with the results expected. This in turn helps to determine which activities were responsible for the outcome and to modify the program for future use.

An Example of Behavioral System Consultation

A professor from one of the helping professions from a university is consulting with a human service agency about enhancing its effectiveness. The consultant and the designated consultee first define the system in terms of its structure and process. Although the first of these is easy, it takes them quite a bit longer to define the system's process. They examine each of the agency's subsystems (e.g., the technological subsystem, which consists of the caseworkers) in terms of how communication takes place, how the behavior of the subsystem is measured and evaluated, and how the subsystem attempts to solve its own problems.

After defining the system, the consultant guides the consultee in assessing the interaction between the identified structural and process factors. They determine that part of the system's limitations is due to poor "top-down" communication and lack of adequate autonomy for the agency's caseworkers. In intervening to rectify the matter, they identify poor "top-down" communication as the most important problem. They set the objective of having a regular weekly staff meeting in which all participants are allowed to submit agenda items and all important information is discussed. In addition, the final 10 minutes of each meeting is allocated for discussion of any topic that an individual wants to bring up. The consultant and consultee generate three possible programs, weigh their advantages and disadvantages, and decide that the consultant will be a participant/observer at the first meeting and will provide feedback to the group.

Based on this feedback, the group will decide how to modify procedures for conducting subsequent staff meetings. Following this intervention, the consultee agrees to monitor staff meetings on a regular basis to make sure the desired changes in "top-down" communication indeed occur. The changes in the system are evaluated six months later by surveying the staff and providing the information to the appropriate decision makers.

CONJOINT BEHAVIORAL CONSULTATION

There is a trend in behavioral consultation in schools to use parents and teachers as conjoint consultees (Auster, Feeney-Kettler, & Kratochwill, 2006; Pryzwansky, 2011; Sheridan, 2000; Sheridan & Kratochwill, 2008; Sheridan et al., 2012). This model is termed *conjoint behavioral consultation*

(CBC). As an extension of behavioral consultation, CBC consists of involvement of teacher–parent pairs who together (simultaneously rather than individually) serve as consultees (Sheridan, 1997, 2000) and both school and home settings are considered and their resources combined (Grissom, Erchul & Sheridan, 2003; Holcomb-McCoy, 2009; Sheridan, Clarke, Knoche, & Edwards, 2006). The process parallels that of behavioral case consultation (Guli, 2005) while taking into consideration ecological factors (Kratochwill, 2008). The literature on school–family partnerships has heavily influenced the development of CBC (Sheridan & Kratochwill, 2008). Designed to bridge the gap between the school and the home and maximize the spread of effects from one setting to another, CBC emphasizes continuous data collection and programming between the school, home, and community (Sheridan, Warnes, Woods, Blevins, Magee, & Ellis, 2009). This approach has been a logical step in attempting to link the significant settings in a student's life such as home, school, and primary community arenas and their reciprocal influence (Auster et al., 2006; Kratochwill, 2008). CBC has the added benefit of distributing the consultee workload across the teacher and parents (Conoley, Conoley, & Reese, 2009).

CBC is defined as "a strength-based cross-system problem-solving and decision-making model wherein parents, teachers and other caregivers or service providers work as partners and share responsibility for promoting positive and consistent outcomes related to a child's academic, behavioral, and social-emotional development" (Sheridan & Kratochwill, 2008, p. 25). It basically follows the same steps as in behavioral consultation. Although the addition of more consultees complicates this approach, the benefits can be more than worth the costs. For example, this approach can expedite change across the home and school settings as well as assist consultees to better manage similar situations in the future (Sheridan & Kratochwill, 2008).

The concepts of CBC are compatible with culturally competent practice. Sheridan and Kratochwill (2008) recommend the following practices to maximize CBC's effectiveness with diverse families:

- practice cultural sensitivity
- build trusting relationships
- address diversity issues directly
- enhance communication
- implement a family-centered approach. (p. 81)

This approach has built up strong empirical support (Gutkin, 2009; Sheridan et al., 2009, 2012) and some empirical validity (Auster et al., 2006; Guli, 2005; Sheridan, Eagle, Cowan, & Mickelson, 2001; Sheridan, Eagle, & Doll, 2006). Research has primarily been conducted in terms of outcomes, communication processes, and social validation (e.g., viewed as an accepted practice by professionals) (Sheridan & Kratochwill, 2008). In one example, there is some evidence that parents and teachers prefer CBC over parallel, one-on-one consultation for each party (Freer & Watson, 1999). In another example, there is growing evidence that this model accommodates multicultural variables that affect the consultation process (Guli, 2005; Sheridan, 2000; Sheridan et al., 2006). Research on this model is promising (Guli, 2005; Sheridan & Kratochwill, 2008; Sheridan et al., 2012; Wilkinson, 2005).

CBC serves the two goals of bridging the gap between the home and the school and maximizing the potential of treatment effects in both places. CBC and ecological assessment can be quite complementary (Ysseldyke, Lekwa, Klingbeil, & Cormier, 2012). One trend is to use CBC in pediatric school psychology (Sheridan et al., 2009). This version of CBC allows for collaboration across school, family, and health-related systems, which results in unique information from each system being shared in terms of developing a consistent approach to assisting the client system. Pediatric-oriented mental health professionals are often called upon to coordinate consultation efforts. Another trend is the use of CBC by teams such as those that deal with prereferral to

special education issues (Sheridan & Kratochwill, 2008; Sheridan et al., 2012). Instead of teacher–parent pairs, a team including parents is formed. A final trend is the use of CBC with Head Start programs (Sheridan & Kratochwill, 2008). CBC consultants, for example, can observe families and use resulting identified strengths to meet the goals of consultation.

COLLABORATION FROM A BEHAVIORAL PERSPECTIVE

Very little has been written about behavioral collaboration as distinct from behavioral consultation. This is most likely due to the fact that much of behavioral consultation is practiced in the schools and many of the professionals in the typical school are not familiar with the intricacies of implementing behavioral interventions to the degree that treatment integrity can be ensured. As a result, the consultant often has no choice but to take on an expert mode of consultation.

The use of behavioral collaboration can be increased in three important ways. First, organizations can make effective use of behavioral technology training for their members. To the degree that other professionals can become skilled in behavioral interventions and accept their use as methods of choice, behavioral collaboration can become a frequently used service. Second, use of collaborative teams can be increased with the mental professional maintaining and using their expertise on the team, while other team members have expertise in other important ways, such as client-system data, knowledge of the community, and so forth. Third, members of the helping progressions can provide direct service to the client system while providing consultation to the consultee. In that way, the professional is taking some specific as well as general responsibility for the outcome of the case. At the individual- to school-wide level of intervention, behavioral collaboration

---

C A S E   10.1   **Behavioral Collaboration for School Consultants**

Monica is a school-based consultant in an inner-city elementary school. She has received extensive training in behavioral case consultation and cognitive-behavioral interventions. Her consultee is Jose, a 5th-grade math/science teacher. Jose has participated in some behavioral technology training sessions in the recent past.

In their first two meetings, Monica and Jose engaged in problem identification and analysis. Jose reported that he was having difficulties with four aggressive boys in one of his classes. Jose was concerned that the children in his class were not learning enough because of the time he had to spend "keeping his thumbs on" the boys, who exhibited verbal and physical forms of aggression to their classmates and each other. Jose was worried about the harm they were causing. He felt that they were well on their way to dropping out, and he wanted to do everything he could to keep them in school.

For one week, Monica had Jose write down his descriptions of exactly what the boys did when they were "verbally and physically aggressive." In the meantime, she observed the boys in Jose's classroom on three different days and did the same thing. Based on a comparison of their notes, they came to a consensus on operationalizing the behaviors that were problematic. In their analysis they examined the boys' behavior, the classroom conditions, and Jose's behavior at the time the undesirable behaviors were emitted. It was found that Jose used proximity control and appropriate verbal responses to the boys when they were acting out, as well as the "assertive discipline" techniques that were prescribed school wide. In analyzing the boys' behavior, they came to the conclusion that their verbal and physical aggression was due to poor anger coping techniques. The boys came to math class right after a physical education class, whose focus was competitive sports. The boys seemed to be angry when they or their teammates didn't do particularly well in competition.

The physical education teacher wanted nothing to do with the attempt to help the boys and said, "If they can't cut it now, they never will." So Monica and Jose determined that the boys needed training in anger-coping skills but also, and most importantly, the ability to demonstrate the newly learned skills in Jose's classroom. So Monica agreed to counsel the boys using a cognitive-behavioral and coping skills approach to anger control. As far as the consultation process with Jose went, he agreed to monitor the boys' behavior in the classroom and cue them when necessary to implement their newly learned skills. When they effectively used their coping skills, Jose would reward the boys with tokens that could be used to "buy" a variety of items Jose had for rewarding good conduct and academic achievement.

Jose implemented his monitoring program at the same time Monica began the coping-skills training. Jose's charts showed slow but steady decreases in the boys' verbal and physical aggression. He contacted Monica on a couple of occasions to make sure that he was accurately identifying the boys' attempts to use their coping skills. After Monica had finished the training group, she met with Jose one more time to plan how he was going to fade the cueing and reward system over the semester.

Commentary

Notice how this case nicely illustrates collaboration using a behavioral model. Both Monica and Jose own a piece of the helping "pie." At the same time, Monica uses her expertise to assist Jose in developing a token economy program for the boys. She also follows up with him periodically to help him with the details of the program. This case shows how consultants, through collaboration, can serve the client system directly while assisting a fellow collaborator to work more effectively with that same client system.

---

can be an effective tool for implementing PBIS programming (Curtis & Van Horne, 2014; Minke & Anderson, 2005). As a caution, experts in behavioral interventions will want to ensure that they minimize their expertise to the degree allowable to allow for an equal relationship among the collaborators while maximizing benefits to the client system.

MULTICULTURAL ASPECTS RELATED TO BEHAVIORAL CONSULTATION

The known effects of cultural issues on behavioral and CBC are limited but promising (Ingraham, 2008; Sheridan, 2000; Sheridan & Kratochwill,

---

C A S E   10.2   Behavioral Consultations for Community Consultants

The consultee is a qualified mental retardation specialist with Washington County Citizens for Persons with Disabilities, an organization that operates a six-resident intermediate care facility for the mentally retarded (ICF-MR). As a qualified professional, the consultee is responsible for ensuring that "active treatment" is provided for each resident in accordance with state and federal regulations governing ICF-MR group homes. The consultant was asked to help the consultee develop an appropriate program for each demonstrated need.

The 30-year-old client, Ms. Jones, has been demonstrating aggressive behaviors: striking other home members and some of the staff, particularly a female staff member. The consultee wanted assistance in developing a behavior program to increase Ms. Jones's positive social behavior and reduce her unacceptable behaviors in a nonrestrictive manner that would not violate her client rights.

The consultant built rapport with the consultee during the first session as they discussed Ms. Jones. They defined *striking* as hitting out at another and *socially appropriate behavior* as smiling at others, being next to others without striking, talking to others about routine matters, and engaging in social activities while following any rules.

The consultant then observed the client for five consecutive days at 15-minute intervals for one hour each in the morning and the evening during social activities. A graph of the incidence of striking behavior showed that Ms. Jones tended to strike out at others in the evening during social activities. Her socially appropriate behavior index was fairly average during other times. The consultant and the consultee agreed that it would be important to create a reinforcement program for Ms. Jones so as to increase the number of socially appropriate behaviors during the evening hours.

During the next session, they discussed Ms. Jones's strengths and skills as well as environmental conditions that might be influencing her striking-out behavior. By applying their mutual knowledge bases to the problem, they agreed that Ms. Jones tended to sit by Mr. Smith. Whenever she was not sitting by Mr. Smith in the evenings, she tended to strike at another group member, typically another female. She did not have a history of striking at Mr. Smith.

Based on this and other observations, the consultant and consultee developed a program that involved a type of "time out" procedure in which Ms. Jones would be escorted to her room any time she attempted to strike anyone. She would then be free to leave her room and join in social activities after a 10-minute period. Ms. Jones was also rewarded with additional activity therapy time when she fulfilled the token economy procedures indicated in her treatment plan. The program called for a 90-percent decrease in the striking behavior and a 30-percent increase in socially acceptable behaviors.

The program was approved by the Human Rights Committee and was signed by the client's guardian. The consultee implemented the program with the consultant being "on call" for any monitoring that was needed. It was obvious that within one month of implementing the plan, Ms. Jones had almost totally stopped her striking-out behavior and had significantly increased the frequency of her socially acceptable behaviors.

Further data and information were gathered and analyzed. Every indication was that the plan was a success. In a final interview, the consultant and consultee reviewed the case. Both were pleased with Ms. Jones's success, but they still wondered what part Mr. Smith had played in influencing her behavior.

Commentary

This case illustrates the use of behavioral consultation in a somewhat delicate situation. The case also demonstrates one of the premises of behavioral consultation, namely, that the cause of a behavior does not necessarily have to be understood to effectively change that behavior. Notice how the consultant and consultee worked together in reinforcing the appropriate target behaviors exhibited by Ms. Jones while at the same time enforcing consequences for inappropriate behavior. Clearly, behavioral consultation focuses on assessing and operationalizing behavior prior to intervening. This strength of behavior consultation suggests to consultants the critical nature of knowing what it is that is to be changed through an intervention.

2008). However, behavioral consultation, being Eurocentric-based with its focus on environmental events, may be appealing to cultural groups that do not freely express feelings, value linear thinking, or want concrete and predictable outcomes. Because some cultural groups value the nature of the relationship more than the expertise of the consultant, behavioral consultants may want to look at how to build effective relationships prior to consultation (Sheridan, 2000) and develop collaborative procedures within the consultation relationship (Sheridan et al., 2006). Groups that value independence and individual accomplishment may see value in this approach. Part of behavioral consultation's assessment procedures take into account social and cultural environments, thus setting the stage for modification of interventions due to the cultural context. Behavioral consultation's focus on monitoring and follow-up may be welcomed by those from cultural groups that perceive themselves to be disenfranchised. Consultants are cautioned to be careful with the jargon-laden terminology or time-focused strategies that can be a turnoff to some cultural groups (Sheridan, 2000). Further, the model's control of the process of consultation by the consultant can be an issue for some cultural groups (Harrison, 2004; Hoffman et al., 2006). The bottom line is that for maximum effectiveness, "… addressing racial/cultural issues and modifying the consultation process in response to those issues are major barriers that must be overcome …" (Newell, 2010b, p. 100).

TRENDS

The major trends in behavioral consultation are linked to developments in behavior therapy and behavioral psychology and research on behavioral consultation itself; findings in these areas are quickly incorporated into the practices of behavioral consultants.

A major trend in the field is the expansion of behavioral consultation to include behavioral system and behavioral technology training approaches. These approaches have allowed the field to move beyond traditional case consultation (see Williams, 2000). Kratochwill (2008) suggests substituting the term "problem-solving consultation" for behavioral consultation to allow for these expansions and for a more eclectic approach to interventions.

There has been a trend for researchers to recommend adding an additional interview in the behavioral consultation paradigm (Easton & Erchul, 2011; Wilkinson, 2006). The focus of this structured interview would be on determining what, if any, challenges there are related to the implementation and how to deal with them.

Instead of relying solely on the current abilities of the consultee, consultants now are taking increasing responsibility for assessment and are teaching intervention procedures to consultees (Martens & DiGennaro, 2008). An implication is that having consultees change their behavior is as important as helping the client system change. As a result, direct behavioral consultation (Ervin & Erhardt, 2000; Martens & DiGennaro, 2008; Sterling-Turner et al., 2002; Watson & Sterling-Turner, 2008), as a variation of behavioral consultation, has been receiving increasing attention. This model differs from traditional behavioral case consultation in that the consultant does not exclusively use indirect instruction (e.g., didacticism) in teaching consultees the skills necessary to effectively implement interventions. Rather, the consultant uses direct instructional methods such as role playing, modeling, and coaching. Consultees are taught data-collection methods and interventions by the consultant and data is collected on consultees' behavior and they are provided with performance feedback (Dufrene et al., 2012; Martens & DiGennaro, 2008; Watson & Sterling-Turner, 2008). There is a tendency to include more ABA techniques than in behavioral consultation (Kazdin, 2011; Noell & Witt, 1998). One implication of this trend is that there will be more emphasis on direct techniques for assessing behavior, such as observation, and less on the recollections gotten through interviews.

Another trend is treatment validation consultation (Andersen et al., 2010), which adds technological innovation and ABA to traditional behavioral consultation. In this model, the consultant assesses the client system prior to meeting with the consultee, which is one method of being time efficient.

Curriculum-based assessment (CBA) and other assessments are also employed. This method is substituted for relying on the verbal report of the consultee regarding the client system's behavior.

Behavioral consultants are increasingly engaging in PBIS programs (Lewis & Newcomer, 2002; Luiselli, 2002; Martens & Ardoin, 2002). PBIS is an approach to intervention that uses positive, individualized support to promote positive and socially important behavior change. Functional behavioral assessment is utilized. Frequently used in schools, positive behavior support is used at the school system, classroom, and individual levels; those who implement this model want it to encompass all levels. The idea is to create a system for optimizing the capacity of schools for addressing behavioral issues using evidence-based and culturally appropriate interventions (Minke & Anderson, 2005; Sugai et al., 2000).

Another trend in behavioral consultation is an increased tendency to include other forms of behavioral technology in addition to those based on operant conditioning, classical conditioning, and observational learning in both behavioral and academic interventions (Kratochwill, 2008). The cognitive-behavioral and behavioral ecology movements have made strong headway and now have a place in all behavioral consultation approaches. Cognitive-behavioral theory has greatly expanded the number of potential interventions available to consultants and permits more flexibility in developing plans (Allen, 2011; Lochman, Lampron, Gemmer, Harris, & Wyckoff, 1989). Hughes, Hasbrouck, Serdahl, Heidgerken, and McHaney (2001) report the development of Responsive Systems Consultation (RSC) as an alternative to CBC. RSC emphasizes a larger menu of interventions and a greater focus on improving client relationships with significant others than does CBC. Problems seen as being located in the client system are reframed as products of the interactions of the client system and the interpersonal contexts in which the client system behaves (Denton, Hasbrouck, & Sekaquaptewa, 2003). All interventions can have a systemic effect, even though they are "responsive" to the individual client. In school consultation, authors such as Gutkin and

Curtis (2009) have suggested changing the name of behavioral consultation to *ecobehavioral consultation* in order to expand its parameters to include distal environmental events such as parental pressures affecting the consultation process. Behavioral consultants are becoming increasingly aware that the success of any approach to behavioral consultation is in part determined by the environment in which consultation occurs (Dickinson & Bradshaw, 1992; Kratochwill & Pittman, 2002). As ecological assessment is becoming more prevalent, behavioral consultation is also considered as a tool for effectively implementing response-to-intervention procedures (Reschly & Bergstrom, 2009) as well as other multitiered interventions as the selection and implementation of social emotional learning programs and strategic planning.

In terms of the consultant–consultee relationship, behavioral consultants are devoting more attention to the development of relationships based on rapport with their consultees and the consultee variables that may affect the success of consultation (Kratochwill, 2008; Rosenfield, 1991, 2002). Treatment acceptability by consultees is receiving more varied attention in behavioral consultation (Easton & Erchul, 2011). Treatment acceptability goes beyond the treatment itself to how the consultant will be involved in monitoring the implementation by the consultee.

Behavioral consultation and CBC, in particular, places more attention on multicultural variables (Sheridan, 2000; Sheridan & Kratochwill, 2008). Issues such as trust, acknowledgement of diversity, use of jargon, and even the effect of interpreters are under examination. More attention is being placed on the potential impact of multicultural variables during all stages of the consultation process (Sheridan, 2000).

Finally, from a school-based consultation perspective, the related state and federal mandates regarding consultation as well as the ascension of evidence-based interventions suggest that behavioral consultation may need to be adjusted in terms of certain considerations such as voluntary participation, consultee privilege to ignore consultant recommendations, and absolute confidentiality (Martens & DiGennaro, 2008). That said, these same mandates suggest strong support for the focus of behavioral consultation and collaboration.

CONCLUSIONS

The major contribution of behavioral consultation has been its emphasis on approaching consultation in a systematic, structured, and researchable way. Members of the helping professions can be taught to perform behavioral consultation in a straightforward, step-by-step manner, which has reinforced the view that consultation is a sequential process made up of identifiable stages. There is considerable evidence that behavioral consultation is effective (Erchul & Schulte, 1996; Kratochwill & Pittman, 2002; Martens & DiGennaro, 2008). It has been applied in a variety of settings, most notably, in schools.

A second major contribution of behavioral consultation, its emphasis on specifics, has contributed to more effective methods in setting the goals of consultation, gathering data on the perceived problem, and most importantly, in evaluating the effects of consultation. Behavioral consultation's emphasis on specifics and measurement has encouraged consultants to be more accountable for their consultation efforts. Further, behavioral consultation's emphasis on specifics has allowed it to have the most research activity and empirical support among consultation models (Martens & DiGennaro, 2008).

Behavioral consultation has also emphasized treatment acceptability, treatment integrity, and treatment evaluation (Kratochwill, 2008). More than any other model, behavioral consultation has focused on ensuring that consultees implement plans that they believe are satisfactory, that they are skilled to accomplish, and that they, along with the consultant, agree need to be rigorously evaluated. Another contribution of behavioral consultation is the training of consultants in techniques from behavioral and cognitive-behavioral approaches to counseling and psychotherapy. Hence, schoolteachers are frequently able to use behavior modification procedures, and many counselors can use stress inoculation training (Martens & DiGennaro, 2008).

Behavioral consultation strongly supports the use of evidence-based interventions in the consultation process and is increasingly promoting the use of both person-centered and ecological-centered assessment.

Behavioral consultation is not without its limitations and criticisms. Limitations include problems surrounding problem identification (Kratochwill & Van Someren, 1995) and the need for even more focus on ecological and systems-level perspectives. Other criticisms pointed out by Watson and Sterling-Turner (2008) include that assumptions held in behavioral consultation, such as it is cost-effective relative to direct service, better accomplished when a collaborative, rather than expert, stance is taken, and effective in allowing the consultee to apply the learning from consultation to future situations, are not empirically supported. Another major criticism is that behavioral consultation does not adequately take into account consultees' thoughts and feelings regarding the use of behavioral principles with clients (Hughes, 2000). Many times consultees have reservations about using behavioral interventions with clients because of perceived technical problems or manipulative behavioral procedures and because of concerns about their ability to implement the required procedures. Researchers have begun to address this issue by exploring consultee reactions to consultant language (e.g., the use of jargon) and consultee involvement in selecting interventions as they relate to consultee acceptability of suggested interventions (Rhoades & Kratochwill, 1992; Sheridan, 1992). There have also been writings aimed specifically at the use of relational variables in the context of behavioral consultation (Kratochwill, 2008).

Behavioral consultation is often criticized for the difficulties involved in applying behavioral procedures in real life or in natural environments (Kazdin, 2001; Witt, Gresham, & Noell, 1996a). For example, it is one thing to help a teacher make a plan to control the behavior of a seventh-grade boy but quite another to implement the program in a classroom with 36 students.

Some consultants' neglect of a collaborative approach to consultation is frequently cited as a criticism of behavioral consultation. Because some work-related problems can be addressed simply by using behavioral interventions, some behavioral consultants adopt the role of expert and perform most of the consultation tasks except the intervention. The long-term positive effects on the consultee's future performance are likely to be negligible as a result. A closely related criticism is that some behavioral consultants rely too much on pet interventions (e.g., tangible reinforcers) when designing intervention programs with their consultees.

Some authors challenge some of the fundamental assumptions of behavioral consultation, such as that talking to consultees is adequate to get them to change their behavior and empower them to generalize the problem-solving skills learned in consultation to similar situations in the future (Witt et al., 1996a, 1996b).

Finally, Andersen et al. (2010) point the following limitations: more or less exclusive focus on consultee verbal reporting, the necessity of long interviews before selecting an intervention, and not capitalizing on current technological advances in treatment planning.

With some exceptions, several of these criticisms suggest that the shortcomings of behavioral consultation result from inadequacies of practicing behavioral consultants rather than from the failings of consultation approach. As with the other models of consultation covered in this text, the remedy to this situation may well be better training and a refinement of approaches to behavioral consultation.

SUMMARY

Behavioral consultation is a process in which a consultant uses the principles of learning to assist one or more consultees having a work-related problem with a client or client system. Behavioral consultation owes its heritage primarily to behavior therapy and behavioral psychology. The boundaries of behavioral consultation tend to expand in direct relationship to advances in these two areas.

The result of all behavioral consultation is a change in behavior in the client, the consultee, or both that is accomplished through a systematic problem-solving process. The consultant–consultee relationship is a collaborative one in which the consultant is an expert who guides the consultee through the consultation process using the principles of learning.

Behavioral consultation can be performed in case, training, or system approaches. In the case approach, by far the most common, the consultant helps the consultee manage a client's case. Behavioral technology training consultation involves preparing the consultee in the use of general and/or specific behavioral principles for future use with clients and client systems. This approach is often incorporated into case consultation. In the system approach, a system or some part of it is modified through use of behavioral principles. The systems approach is increasingly becoming popular as consultation interventions are increasingly becoming multitiered or systems-level based.

The basic assumptions of behavioral consultation are that behavior can be viewed scientifically, overt and current behavior is the focus of change, and behavior is lawful and subject to systematic change. Among the procedures advocated by behavioral consultants are use of direct assessment, operationalization of goals, objective measurement of target behaviors, and evaluation of both the goals of consultation and the consultation plan. Behavior consultation has been successfully applied in a variety of settings but is most frequently used when there are high levels of client or system control. It is the most researched model of consultation (Kratochwill, 2008).

SUGGESTIONS FOR EFFECTIVE PRACTICE

- Avoid behavioral jargon at all times.
- Note the importance of relational issues.
- Consider training prospective consultees in behavioral interventions as part of their staff development training.

- Make the goals of consultation and collaboration as concrete and specific as possible.
- Recall the importance of evaluation of the plan and the consultation process.

QUESTIONS FOR REFLECTION

1. Could any individual behavioral consultant incorporate the findings from operant conditioning, classical conditioning, observational learning, the cognitive-behavioral movement, and behavioral ecology into the practice of consultation? Justify your answer.

2. What are the essential characteristics of any approach to behavioral consultation?

3. To what degree are the underlying assumptions of each of the influences on behavioral consultation compatible with each other?

4. When would you, as a behavioral consultant, incorporate punishment into a treatment plan? Justify your answer.

5. How can a consultant using the behavioral case consultation approach avoid manipulating and excessively controlling the consultee's verbal behavior?

6. Which of the three subcategories of verbalizations would an organizational process consultant employ most frequently? How would this compare with a consultant employing behavioral case consultation?

7. Which of the three subcategories of verbalizations would a mental health consultant using consultee-centered case consultation employ most frequently? How would this compare with a consultant using behavioral case consultation?

8. What strengths does behavioral ecology add to behavioral system consultation?

9. What do you believe are some important elements in providing behavioral consultation in a culturally competent manner?

10. When you consider both the contributions and criticisms of behavioral consultation, what conclusions do you draw?

SUGGESTED SUPPLEMENTARY READINGS

Those further interested in behavioral consultation should consult the following suggested readings:

Altschaefl, M. R. (2014). Problem-solving (behavioral) consultation: School-based applications. In A. M. Dougherty (Ed.), *Casebook of psychological consultation and collaboration* (6th ed.). Belmont, CA: Brooks/ Cole Cengage. This case study illustrates, in a cogent manner, the use of behavioral consultation in a school setting. In this case study, a school

psychologist consults with a fourth-grade teacher about one of the teacher's students with behavioral issues.

Bergan, J. R., & Kratochwill, T. R. (1990). *Behavioral consultation and therapy.* New York: Plenum. This text is, in effect, a second edition of Bergan's classic text *Behavioral Consultation* (1977). This is "the book" on behavioral case consultation. Although the authors assume consultants will be working in a school setting, readers can easily apply the ideas in the text to any human service setting. The authors devote at least a full chapter to each of the four stages of behavioral consultation, and extensive treatment of verbal interaction techniques is also provided. A case study section is provided to demonstrate precisely how a behavioral consultant would proceed. The major difference in this text from Bergan's (1977) text is the addition of a chapter on methodological and conceptual issues in behavioral consultation outcome research. Be advised that this book is laborious reading but well worth the effort.

Kratochwill, T. R., & Bergan, J. R. (1990). *Behavioral consultation in applied settings: An individual guide.* NewYork: Plenum. This guide is a fine resource for those who want to better understand the basics of behavioral case consultation but who do not desire the in-depth discussion presented in the Bergan and Kratochwill text just described. It provides summaries of each of the stages of the behavioral case

consultation model as developed by Kratochwill and Bergan, as well as exercises at the end of each chapter to help readers assess their understanding of the material.

Sheridan, S. M., & Kratochwill, T. R. (2008). *Conjoint behavioral consultation* (2nd ed.). New York: Springer. This model involves an expansion of traditional behavioral consultation to include conjoint consultation with parents and teachers. This is an excellent resource for those interested in consulting with both parents and teachers from a well-researched behavioral perspective. http://www.pbis.org /english/. The Technical Assistance Center on Positive Behavioral Interventions and Supports (PBIS) has been established by the Office of Special Education Programs, a division of the U.S. Department of Education, to give schools capacity-building information and technical assistance for identifying, adapting, and sustaining effective school-wide disciplinary practices. This is an excellent site for information on PBIS.

11

✳

Organizational Consultation and Collaboration

Given your basic familiarity with organizations and the ways they operate, we'll now examine how consultants operate within organizations. Why do consultants work in organizations? As Bellman (1990) has noted, "In this imperfect world full of imperfect people, we try to get things done through large, imperfect organizations—organizations of our own creation" (p. 69). Consequently, the main goal of organizational consultation is improvement in the organization's effectiveness, and this can take many forms and utilize a multitude of methods. A basic premise is that healthy organizations create healthy experiences for members of the organization and organizational consultation can assist organizations in becoming and remaining healthy (Gutkin & Curtis, 2009). Organizational consultation typically emphasizes data gathering, problem identification, and organizational well-being (Truscott, Cosgrove, Meyers, & Eidle-Barkman, 2000; Zins & Erchul, 2002). Many types of organizational consultation originated in business and industry settings, whereas the mental health movement influenced others. There is currently an increasing emphasis on organizational consultation in school settings (Meyers, Meyers, Graybill, Proctor, & Huddleston, 2012).

In this chapter, we'll consider the historical development of organizational consultation and define some important terms. Then we'll examine a few of its key concepts, drawing from the discussion of the preceding chapter. We'll consider three specific models of organizational consultation: purchase of expertise, doctor–patient, and process consultation (Schein, 1969, 1987, 1999, 2006). In discussing the expertise model, we'll focus on education/training and program approaches. In the doctor–patient model, diagnosis is emphasized. In the section on process consultation, Schein's model is explored.

For each of these approaches, we'll examine the goals, roles, and functions of the consultant and the consultee's experience in consultation. We'll explore some applications of organizational consultation by discussing its techniques and procedures, and we'll note some contributions and criticisms of this kind of consultation.

Here are some questions to consider as you read this chapter:

- Why is consulting with organizations more complex than consulting with individuals?

- Who or what makes up the client system in organizational consultation?

- How can a consultant evaluate the effects of organizational consultation when the process is so complex?

- How does multicultural competence relate to the practice of organizational consultation?

- What are the basic differences among the various approaches to organizational consultation?

Case Example

Consider the following example, which covers just one of several approaches to organizational consultation:

You are a human service professional who is asked to consult with a rehabilitation center staff. The center, which serves as a counseling facility for incarcerates nearing eligibility for parole, is having staff conflicts that are adversely affecting the success of its programs. The center's head administrator asks you to sit in on three of the regularly scheduled weekly staff meetings and provide the staff feedback concerning how they might resolve their conflicts. As you observe the meetings, you take notes on such things as what and how things are said, as well as who talks to whom. You provide feedback to the staff at a special meeting and then help the group process that feedback. As a result,

three areas of conflict are identified: some staff members are perceived as being too hard on the clients, some staff members are perceived as being too soft on the clients, and the center has no evaluation system in place to determine whether it really helps its clients. You agree to spend an additional session with the staff to help them resolve their conflicts and to help a select group of staff develop procedures for evaluating the effectiveness of the center's services.

Organizations are groups of people put together for a particular purpose. Each of these complex entities has goals and objectives. When they have difficulty meeting their goals and objectives, organizations frequently seek the help of consultants. Organizational consultation is based on the concept that an organization can be made to function more effectively through the efforts of one or more consultants who work with some (or possibly all) members of the organization. Thus, the organization itself or one of its parts becomes the client system and the members are the consultees.

Counselors, psychologists, and other members of the helping professions, through their specialized training, are particularly suited to provide organizational consultation (Lewis, Lewis, Daniels, & D'Andrea, 2011). Increasingly, professionals who provide consultation (either internal or external) are being asked to assist with organization-wide concerns and issues. Consider a school counselor or school psychologist who assists a group consisting of seventh-grade teachers and parents to decrease the number of incidents of school violence. Or for example, a school counselor and school psychologist might be asked to develop a multitiered intervention assistance program that provides teachers with methods to meet the academic and behavioral needs of their students (Curtis, Castillo, & Cohen, 2008).

Organizational consultants can fulfill the following functions (Schein, 1987, p. 20):

- provide information that is not otherwise available

- analyze information with sophisticated tools not available to clients or their subordinates

- diagnose complex organizational and business problems

- train clients or their subordinates to use diagnostic models that help them make better decisions

- listen and give support, comfort, and counsel during troubled times

- help implement difficult or unpopular decisions

- reward and punish certain kinds of behaviors (by using status as an "outsider" as a special source of authority)

- transmit information either up the normal chain of command or laterally as needed

- make decisions and give directives on how to proceed if for some reason line management cannot do so; and take responsibility for decisions, allay anxiety that may attend the uncertainties of consultation, and in other ways provide the emotional strength to help others through difficult situations

HISTORICAL BACKGROUND

Organizational consultation first emerged in the 1890s in industrial settings. Consultants, experts who focused on manufacturing productivity, were called on to fix production problems. In open systems terminology, the early organizational consultants dealt with the technological subsystem of the organization. At the outset of organizational consultation, consultants combined industrial engineering with time and motion studies and were often referred to as management engineers.

During World War I, organizational consultants frequently were considered efficiency experts; they were concerned with functions such as input–output ratios and the relationships between humans and tools. During the 1920s, organizational consultation expanded into other subsystems of industrial organizations, particularly management and maintenance.

The Great Depression created a crisis in which many businesses, industrial and nonindustrial alike, were forced to fight for survival. This financial crisis

produced conditions conducive to a new consultant activity: helping "sick" organizations. Although *sick* referred to finances during the Great Depression, the term has since come to refer to any aspect of an organization considered to be problematic.

With the advent of field theory and group dynamics research as well as the call to improve work conditions during the 1940s and 1950s, psychology entered business settings, and motivation and leadership studies became quite popular (French & Bell, 1999). Organizations, therefore, no longer needed to be sick to benefit from the assistance of a consultant; rather, healthy organizations could become more efficient and effective in meeting their goals by obtaining consultant services in motivation and leadership. Thus, consultants became increasingly involved in serving organizations in such matters as lines of authority, types of leadership, and the distribution of labor (Gallessich, 1982).

The national attention given to the concept of mental health and the emergence of mental health consultation (Caplan, 1970) began to influence not only human service organizations, but business and industrial organizations as well. Greater emphasis was placed on the psychological well-being of the worker on the job. Organizational leaders began to realize that satisfied workers were crucial to effective and productive organizations. Coincident to the national emphasis on mental health was the emergence of organization development.

Organization development is the application of the behavioral sciences to an organization's internal workings to increase its efficiency, effectiveness, and its ability to change (McLean, 2006). Organization development has strongly influenced organizational consultation (Meyers, Proctor, Graybill, & Meyers, 2009). The organization development effort focuses "on the characteristics of the workplace as a whole, with the consultant attempting to use a variety of interventions that can integrate organizational and individual needs" (Lewis & Lewis, 1986, p. 202).

Organizational consultation developed under the influences of applied behavioral science and managerial science (Shultz, 1984): From behavioral science came laboratory training methods, the use of the survey research and feedback method, and autonomous work groups; from managerial science came quantitative analysis of business activities, particularly managerial decision making (French & Bell, 1999).

The laboratory training methods are a series of experimental activities that focus on developing skills for more effective organizational functioning. Development occurs in a laboratory setting in which group members experiment with new behaviors and are given feedback. The new behaviors are then supposedly transferred to the work site.

In the survey research and feedback method, results of surveys about the organization are conveyed to the respondents to further pinpoint problem areas and to generate discussion. Such discussions are intended to improve relationships among the participants and help solve identified problems.

The Tavistock Institute of London developed a psychoanalytic theory of groups that influenced organization development (French & Bell, 1999). Much of this institute's work focused on study groups formed to examine how participants dealt with issues such as authority, leadership, and norms. Participants were to take their newly acquired knowledge and apply it in their own organizations. In 1969, Edgar Schein wrote a landmark text entitled *Process Consultation*. This text strongly influenced the human side of organizational consultation and gave great momentum to legitimizing organizational consultation in all types of organizations, including educational institutions.

Schein emphasized focusing on process events such as leadership style and balancing individual needs and organizational goals (Kormanski & Eschbach, 1997). Later, Blake and Mouton (1983) and others developed their famous "consulcube," which helped consultants determine the nature of the problem, the target of change, and the type of intervention.

Managerial science, which accompanied the development of management as a profession (Katz & Kahn, 1990), focuses on finances and quantitative analysis of all aspects of management. Unlike applied behavioral science, managerial science focuses almost exclusively on the tangible and the quantitative.

Organization development influenced another field called human resource development (HRD), which developed during World War II out of military and industrial organizations' needs for competent personnel (French & Bell, 1999). The philosophical framework of HRD is the development of human potential. Whereas organizational consultation focuses on the workplace as an entity, HRD focuses on the individuals within the organization. HRD consists of the learning experiences "that are organized, for a specified time, and designed to bring about the possibility of behavioral change" (Nadler, 1980, p. 5). HRD gained recognition when the American Society of Training and Development (ASTD) emerged and promoted HRD nationally. HRD can take place in educational as well as business and human service settings.

A current trend in organizations is to provide counseling for employees on the work site through, for example, employee assistance programs (Hopko & Hopko, 2003). This trend has led many counselors in organizational settings to become increasingly involved in organizational consultation activities.

The emergence of organization development and HRD has given legitimacy to using either internal consultants (when present) or outside consultants (whenever internal ones are absent or unskilled in the area of service for which consultation is needed). This point of view exemplifies the philosophy that satisfied workers make productive employees and that democratically run organizations based on relationships lead to organizational success. Later, Deming's TQM (Total Quality Management) concepts influenced organizational consultation in all settings. This movement gave legitimacy to the concept of *continuous improvement* in all organizations, irrespective of their mission.

Recently, multicultural organizational consultation (MOC) has emerged as one method of supporting organizations in dealing with issues of diversity (Cooper & Leong, 2008; Sue, 2008). Another development is the increasing use of organizational consultation in schools to deal with the impact of federal legislation, high-stakes testing, and other factors (Meyers et al., 2012). Consequently, organizational consultation has been related to renewing organizations, multitiered interventions, empowerment, social justice, multicultural competence, prevention, and the renewed emphasis on systems and ecological perspectives.

ORGANIZATIONAL CONSULTATION DEFINED

In spite of the many attempts to define it, there is no agreement on a single definition of organizational consultation. What is clear is that there are many types of such consultation, and how it is performed depends on the theoretical orientation of the consultant, the nature of the organization, and the nature of the problem for which consultation is sought (Lewis & Lewis, 1986). Organizational consultation attempts to both solve organizational problems and strengthen the overall well-being of the organization (Meyers et al., 2009). In one example, a team of school-based consultants works with a group of administrators to implement a school-wide response to intervention (RTI) program (Snyder, Quirk, & Dematteo, 2011).

A synthesis of the literature on organizational consultation suggests the following generic definition: Organizational consultation is the process in which a professional, functioning either internally or externally to an organization, provides assistance of a technical, diagnostic/prescriptive, or facilitative nature to an individual or group from that organization, or to the entire organization itself to enhance the organization's ability to engage in productive change and maintain or enhance its effectiveness in some designated way.

Some confusion surrounds the terms *consultee* and *client system* in organizational consultation. Consultees are those people in the organization with whom the consultant works; frequently they are mid- to high-level managers or those who provide direct services to clients. In the organizational

consultation literature, the term *client* often refers to the consultee, particularly when the discussion concerns those in the organization with whom the consultant is working. With respect to organizational consultation in this text, the term *consultees* refers to those with whom the consultant works directly; the *client system* is always the organization or some part of it. From this conceptualization, the concept of consultation as indirect service is preserved due to the assumption that the job of the consultee in organizational consultation is to use the benefits of consultation to directly enhance the effectiveness and/or efficiency of the client system, that is, the organization.

KEY CONCEPTS IN ORGANIZATIONAL CONSULTATION

We have discussed most of the key concepts concerning organizational consultation in earlier chapters. However, two are sufficiently important to highlight: the organization as client, and the fact that process is as important as content.

The Organization as the Client System

The client system in organizational consultation is the organization or some part of it. However, defining the client system can at times be challenging (Fuqua, Newman, Simpson, & Choi, 2012). In any case, the goal of organizational consultation is to enhance the overall effectiveness of the organization, making the organization the client system. This can be a hard concept to grasp because many consultants are used to viewing the client system as either an individual or a relatively small group. The more complex the organization, the more complex the client system becomes. Organizations are systems made up of interactive and interdependent parts; consulting with one part of the organization can affect all of its parts. Organizations are made up of people, each of whom possesses a unique set of attitudes, values, beliefs, and behaviors. Individuals in an organization are affected not only by these attributes of their coworkers, but also by the social relationships and supports that exist within the organization. When consultants provide services to one part of the organization, the potential impact on other parts must be considered.

Among the concepts important to understanding the complexity of the organization as the client system is the principle of *synergy*, which states that the whole of a set of products is greater than the sum of its parts. When buildings, offices, people, and equipment are put together in a certain way, they become more than the sum of their parts (organizations). This concept makes understanding organizations even more complex, thus suggesting a systems perspective. Such a perspective allows the system (the organization itself) or one or more of its subsystems to be the target of change. By viewing the entire organization as the client system, consultants will understand the complexity of the potential ramifications of their interventions, including prevention, and avoid oversimplified consultation methods.

Process Is as Important as Content

An important underlying assumption of organizational consultation is that process is as important as content; that is, *how* something is done can be as important as *what* is done. In one example, how a consultee carries out a given intervention is as important as the nature of the intervention itself. As a result of the importance of process variables, consultants will often examine processes and procedures in which organizations engage (Meyers et al., 2009). For example, how people communicate with one another in an organization is as important as what they communicate, and if organizations only conduct person-centered assessment as opposed to ecological assessment, such processes could miss important environmental variables that influence given problems within the organization. If we think of the problem to be solved as the content, then the process can be thought of as the method by which the problem is defined and

solved (Schein, 1978, 1999). There is even a specific kind of consultation, called *process consultation*, which focuses on the process of organizational behavior as it relates to its content.

In organizations, process factors are distinguished from structural factors, such as departments and lines of authority. These structures coordinate and control tasks in an efficient and timely manner (Jerrell & Jerrell, 1981), but they are surrounded by process factors, such as informal relationships, traditions, and culture (Meyers et al., 2009; Schein, 1987, 1999). Further, how people perceive a structure (e.g., their job's role) determines how they relate to others within the organization and how they act in that role (Schein, 1988). Only when its members are smoothly interacting with one another can the organization be functioning effectively. Consultants often help organizations become aware of the interactions between process factors and their members to assist them in functioning at optimal levels (Golembiewski, 1993b).

Process and content are often subtly related. There can be a connection between an organization's problem and how the problem is being worked on. Consider how one school could implement a positive behavioral interventions program quite smoothly while another, similar school's attempts at implementing the same program is fraught with teacher and staff resistance. Consultants frequently have the difficult task of deciding whether or not to focus on the interaction between process and content.

EDGAR SCHEIN'S MODELS OF CONSULTATION

Whereas Blake and Mouton (1983) originally developed a broad conceptual framework for organizational consultation, more specific conceptualizations such as those of Schein (1988, 1999, 2006) have been developed.

Schein conceived three models of consultation: the purchase of expertise model, the doctor–patient model, and the process model. Both the purchase of expertise and the doctor–patient models are versions of "expert" consultation (Schein, 1987, 1999). They focus on what needs to be done. In the *purchase of expertise model*, the consultee "purchases" a consultant who can provide expertise (knowledge or skill) to solve a previously determined problem. For example, a school psychologist could be an expert on data-based decision making. In the *doctor–patient model*, the consultee "purchases" the consultant's ability to both diagnose a problem and prescribe an appropriate set of solutions for it. For example, a school counselor could consult regarding evidence-based interventions. The consultee retains control of defining the problem in the purchase of expertise model but not in the doctor–patient model. In the purchase of expertise model, the consultee has already identified the solution (what the consultant does), whereas in the doctor–patient model, neither the problem nor the solution is defined prior to consultation.

The *process model* views consultation as a "set of activities on the part of the consultant which help the [consultee] to perceive, understand, and act upon process events which occur in the [consultee's] environment" (Schein, 1988, p. 11). It focuses on *how* problems are solved. In process consultation, the consultee "purchases" the consultant's ability to help the consultee focus on process (as opposed to content) events; this approach focuses on the processes by which problems are solved rather than on the content of problems. In one example, an external mental health consultant consults regarding the process of implementing a social emotional learning (SEL) program.

There are two versions of the process model: the catalyst version and facilitator version. The *catalyst* version of process consultation occurs when the consultant does not know the solution to some problem but can help the consultee formulate his or her own solution. The *facilitator* version occurs when the consultant may have ideas (content) about solutions but withholds them to help the consultee clear up his or her own dilemma by going through the problem-solving process. Effective consultants use the version of process consultation that is most appropriate to the circumstances (Schein, 1987).

There is some evidence that consultee readiness and the amount of time available for consultation relate to the choice of Schein's models (Stayer & Dillard, 1986). Consultees with low readiness and little time may want and be best suited for the purchase of expertise model. Consultees with high readiness and sufficient time might be more suitable for process consultation. Schein's models of consultation are compared with one another in Table 11.1, which is adapted from O'Connell (1990).

Schein's models form the basis of the following discussion of organizational consultation. First, education/training consultation and program consultation are discussed as examples of the purchase of expertise model. Next, the process of diagnosis is given special attention in the discussion of the doctor–patient model, and then the process model of consultation is considered last.

TABLE 11.1   Schein's Models Compared

	EXPERT	DOCTOR	PROCESS CONSULTANT
Defines problem	Consultee	Consultant	Consultee with consultant
Suggests an intervention	Consultant	Consultant	Consultee with consultant
Major responsibility for work in consultation	Consultant	Consultant	Consultee
Consultee learns more effective problem solving	No	No	Yes

The Purchase of Expertise Model

When consultees request help from consultants, they frequently are seeking some form of expertise, which can take the form of the knowledge or skill to fix a predetermined problem (Leong & Huang, 2008). Some combination of information, methods, tools, and support is provided to the consultee (Lawson, 1998). The essence of this model is that the consultee knows what the problem is, what needs to be done to solve it, and who can be of help. The consultee is in effect saying to the consultant, "Here's the problem; fix it." This model is by nature very content oriented. The consultant functions as a content expert (Schein, 1990c). For example, a consultant leads a school system to assess and improve its crisis management plan.

For the purchase of expertise model to be effective, four basic assumptions must be met (Schein, 1987, 1988, 1999). The consultee must have made a correct diagnosis of the problem, chosen the right consultant, correctly communicated the problem, and thought through and accepted the consequences of consultation. If the consultee has not made the correct diagnosis, the entire consultation will be invalid: The right consultant may have been chosen, but the wrong problem will be solved.

If it becomes apparent that consultation is solving the wrong problem, the consultant is under no obligation to assist the consultee in making a new diagnosis. It's the consultee's responsibility to ensure that the consultant has the skills and abilities to meet the consultee's needs and to correctly communicate the nature of the problem. By using effective communication skills such as clarifying responses, the consultant can assist the consultee in expressing the perceived problem in such a way that both parties agree about its exact nature. However, ultimately it is the consultee's responsibility to correctly communicate the problem. Inherent in the purchase of expertise model is the assumption that the consultee has thought through the consequences of consultation.

Things happen when consultation takes place; a change in one part of an organization often affects other parts. Sometimes consultees are not fully aware of the potential long- and short-term impact of consultation. For example, polishing the communication skills of mid-level managers might have the unwanted impact of making them too assertive in trying to improve the entire organization. From the outset, effective consultants help the consultee think through the consequences a consultant's activities could have.

In summary, the purchase of expertise model is often appropriate when a problem has been well defined, such as when a consultant can provide specific information or training or when a glitch arises in a human service program. It works best when the consultee has ascertained the consultant's suitability for the job and has thoroughly thought through the consequences of consultation. Two of the most common forms of purchase of expertise consultation provided by human service consultants are education/training consultation and program consultation. This is not to say, however, that they are necessarily the most effective methods of organizational consultation. What it does say is that consultants may include in their direct service to consultees' activities such as education and training, which can benefit the consultees' effectiveness with the client system.

Education/Training Consultation.   The education/training approach is the most frequently used kind of purchase of expertise consultation. It is considered indirect service in that consultees use their acquired skills with their respective client systems (Sheridan & Kratochwill, 2008). Education/training consultation is but one method of assisting organizations to change and should not be viewed as a stand-alone experience distinct from other organizational change initiatives (Arredondo, 1996). The use of consultants in education/training is often referred to as *staff development* or *professional development activities*. Recent changes in organizations have dictated an increased need for education/training consultation (Arredondo, 1996). Consultants provide education/training services in any number of settings, and topics range from motivation techniques and classroom discipline to substance-abuse prevention and effective parenting. In one example, Adlerian-focused consultants conduct a workshop for teachers on the purposive nature of student misbehavior (Carlson, Dinkmeyer, & Johnson, 2008). In another example, a workshop on sexual harassment is led by consultants (Barak, 1994). The reason for this type of consultation is the facilitation of change or improvement in an organization or one of its subsystems. Education/training consultation can occur in a group or on an individualized basis for a variety of purposes.

As its name suggests, this approach emphasizes the two most common roles of the consultant: educator and trainer. In this type of consultation, the consultant shares expert knowledge and/or skills by some education means, such as a lecture on motivation, or through some kind of on-the-job training, such as a workshop on techniques for motivating supervisors.

Consultation Goals. The primary goal of the education/training consultation is the increased effectiveness of the organization that results from the consultee's improved professional functioning in the area(s) on which education and/or training focuses. The idea is that consultees will learn new knowledge and/or skills related to their job duties or, in the case of parents and guardians, something related to their caregiving responsibilities. When consultation is educative in nature, some form of information is being provided; when the consultant acts as trainer, however, the learning is usually experiential and focuses on skill acquisition.

Whether a consultant uses an educational or a training approach depends on whether the goal of consultation is to affect cognitive learning or to change attitudes and behaviors (Arredondo, 1996). In an example affecting cognitive learning, a consultant might provide a junior high school faculty an in-service program on the differences between a junior high school and a middle school. In an experiential learning situation, a consultant might have mid-level managers practice different types of strategies to strengthen their leadership skills.

Education and training can also be combined in consultation. For example, a group of ministers might first be taught the characteristics of depression by a mental health consultant and then participate in supervised counseling sessions in which they attempt to detect these characteristics by role-playing. A school-based consultant can both educate and train a consultee in behavioral interventions. Whether the consultant emphasizes education, training, or both depends primarily on what the consultee perceives the problem and its solution to be.

Consultant Function and Roles. The consultant in education/training consultation functions as an expert who possesses information or skills that the consultee needs and transmits that knowledge in one or more of the roles of advisor, educator, trainer, or technical expert. The consultant's function is to provide the information and/or the training that best matches a consultee's interests and needs (Conoley & Conoley, 1992) and is designed in the context of the particular workplace with emphasis on workplace goals (Cox, 2001).

In addition to assisting in needs assessment and in planning and implementing education/training interventions, the consultant also assists in the evaluation of consultation. Although many organizations have standard evaluation forms to help in this task, many consultants prefer to use their own forms, which can be specifically tailored to any particular evaluation.

The purpose of evaluation is to determine whether consultees have learned the appropriate knowledge and/or skills required for the intervention in use. Lippitt and Lippitt (1986) were the first to define the critical skills needed to function effectively as a consultant in education/training consultation:

- assessing the training needs related to the problem
- developing and stating measurable objectives for learning experiences
- understanding the learning and change process
- designing a learning experience

- planning and designing educational events
- going beyond traditional training and using heuristic laboratory methods
- using multiple learning stimuli, including multimedia presentations
- functioning as a group teacher or trainer
- helping others learn how to learn

Consultants should remember that they also have a commitment to the organization and should consider any ecological and systems variables related to the training that might impact the organization.

The Consultee's Experience in Consultation. The major role of the consultee is to be a good learner. Consultees are expected to learn the knowledge or skills they are taught, adapt them if necessary, and use them on the job to contribute to the organization's overall effectiveness. Consultees accomplish these tasks by giving the consultant honest and accurate information during needs assessment, being cooperative and motivated learners during the education/training process, and attempting to implement their new knowledge on the job. As learners, consultees also take on the collaborator role in providing formative feedback and related recommendations regarding the training experience throughout its duration.

During the needs assessment, the consultee is interviewed (or fills out a survey form) to identify topics for education/training, to give opinions on the nature of the problems of concern during the consultation, and to provide some idea of his or her willingness to participate in the consultation.

Most consultants agree that if consultees must be coerced, however subtly, to participate, positive benefits will probably not accrue from consultation. If consultee participation is voluntary, cooperation and motivation can be enhanced during consultation by providing special incentives for participating. Consultees can also be taught to understand that consultation is a process, to know how to initiate consultation, to understand that the timing of a request for consultation can affect both the process and the outcome, and to

determine when to choose consultation from among the available services. Consultees can be encouraged to implement what they have learned by education/training methodologies that help them to personalize the material. It is one thing to listen to a lecture on management styles; it is another to be asked to consider how the different management styles match or contrast with a consultee's own style. Responding to consultees' perceived needs during the entire consultation process is an effective way to maximize the likelihood that consultees will follow through on consultation activities. However, as in all forms of consultation, it is ultimately up to consultees to decide whether or not they'll use the information and/or training received.

Application: Consultant Techniques and Procedure. The education/training model consists of four steps: developing the needs assessment, planning the education/training activities, conducting the activities, and performing an evaluation.

Either the consultant—the organization's contact person—or both conduct the needs assessment, which identifies the content of education/training sessions and occasionally the problems that consultation can help ameliorate. Needs assessments help identify discrepancies between "what is" and "what is desired" (McLean, 2006). Through the use of interviews, needs assessment can obtain in-depth information and opinions. This method is comprehensive, but it is very expensive and time consuming. In other cases, needs are assessed through questionnaires, which are cost effective and provide information that is relatively easy to collate. However, questionnaires frequently lack depth, and the framing of questions can affect the kinds of responses obtained. Needs assessment also includes an examination of what resources are available to meet the identified needs (Nagle & Gagnon, 2008). An example of a needs assessment form is provided in Figure 11.1.

Once a needs assessment is conducted, the consultant then plans the education/training in line with best practice such as taking into consideration the nature of adult learning.

Our organization has set aside the week of April 10 for staff development training. Your frank and candid responses to the following items will assist the training division in arranging for training and development activities that coincide with your needs. In the next few weeks, we will collate your responses and put them into a questionnaire that will help us to formulate specific training needs and activities. Please answer the following questions carefully and return them to the training division by the end of this week. All responses will be kept anonymous. Thank you for your participation.

1. I would benefit from knowing more about the following recent trends in my field:
2. I would benefit from discussing the following current issues in my field:
3. I would like to know more about the following new skills areas that are currently receiving much attention in my field:
4. List the needs within your part of the organization that you think staff development should address.
5. List the needs within the entire organization that you think staff development should address.
6. Add any suggestions you think are relevant to the week of staff development.

FIGURE 11.1   A sample needs assessment form

In performing the education/training, the consultant should attempt to use methods that are appropriate to the consultees' characteristics and the objectives of the consultation. Many education/training consultants use designs that incorporate methodologies such as lectures, media and materials, structured laboratory experiences, small group discussions, behavioral role modeling, movement, and feedback. Depending on the nature of the education/training experience, consultants and consultees may also have programs, including those that are research-based, available with manuals.

How consultees respond to the consultant at the outset of education/training also affects the ultimate success of the consultation. Consultants using this type of consultation should consider the culture of the organization and permit participation by the consultees in all aspects of the education/training.

During *evaluation* of the education/training, consultants often use questionnaires and pre- and postintervention measures of pertinent material. Evaluation is typically made in terms of participant reactions, participant learning, behavior/skill

acquisition, and organizational impact. Evaluations of education/training interventions include feedback loops that allow continuous adaptation of procedures and methods for measuring the impact of education/training on the entire organization. In evaluation of education/training, it is often effective to focus on *impact* rather than *change* given the often short-term nature of the experience. Chapters 6 and 7 of this book cover related points on evaluation in more detail and depth.

Case Example of Education/Training Consultation. A human service professor at a university was asked by the director of personnel services of a large school district to conduct some workshops for the district's school counselors and psychologists. When the consultant asked the director what kinds of workshops were desired, the director responded with: "You know, some of that new counseling stuff." The consultant advocated the use of a needs assessment instrument to give prospective participants input about the nature of the workshops, and the director agreed to gather the information by using a form developed by the consultant.

The needs assessment revealed that the participants desired information and training for dealing with AIDS, teenage pregnancy, and date rape. The consultant planned the activities by developing behavioral objectives to be accomplished through a variety of methods. A balance was struck between providing information and skills training. The consultant also took the needs of adult learners into consideration during the planning process.

One workshop was held on each topic. Additional input from the participants was obtained at the beginning of the first workshop. Several methods were used during the workshops, and a good working climate was developed and maintained throughout the workshops. At the conclusion of each workshop, the participants evaluated the consultant, the workshop content, and the usefulness of the session. The consultant's views concerning the workshop and its effects on the participants were sent to the personnel services director in a written report.

Program Consultation. Most human service organizations have programs that frequently require programmatic consultative services. Community-based consultants frequently engage in this type of consultation (Staton et al., 2007; Wesley & Buysse, 2006) as do schools (Ball, Pierson, & McIntosh, 2011; Elias & Leverett, 2011). Program consultation is a form of purchase of expertise consultation in which the organization in some way uses the consultant to help plan a new program or revise or deal with factors that affect an existing program. For example, program consultation can be used for "… promoting innovation, best practices, and systems level change in schools" (Godber, 2008, p. 2202). Program consultation is unique in that it is restricted to a specific program and its goals. Human service consultants, internal and external, are increasingly being asked to engage in program consultation. For example, the increasing focus on systems-level change, multitiered programs, and prevention in schools makes program consultation

particularly attractive to school-based consultants for the purpose of assisting with the implementation of school improvement efforts and their evaluation (Godber, 2008).

In program consultation, the organization "purchases" some kind of technical assistance from an internal or external consultant. Clearly, the consultant will need to have expertise in the area for which consultation is sought (Meyers et al., 2009). The organization perceives a need with respect to the program and hires a consultant to help fulfill that need. For example, a consultant might help to design an evaluation assessing whether a program has met its goals; indeed, evaluation is the primary reason consultants are asked to assist with programs. In this example, the consultant serves as a data coach (Godber, 2008). Even though program consultation does not typically require any new skills on the part of the consultant, it clearly demonstrates how consultants, both external and internal, can work with organizations to meet their goals (Elias & Leverett, 2011).

Program consultation is becoming increasingly popular due to human service organizations and schools' increased emphasis on programs, the increasingly complex technology related to programs, and the trend toward cost effectiveness and accountability in organizations (Lewis et al., 2011; Sears, Rudisill, & Mason-Sears, 2006). In addition, the professional standards of organizations in which consultants work demand that evaluation of programs be performed. School reform programs as well as prevention programs are often the focus of consultants working with schools. For example, many schools are implementing SEL programs and other prevention programs to promote a positive school climate (Elias & Leverett, 2011). Outside consultants frequently use program consultation as a way to "get their feet in the door" of an organization and eventually perform other types of consultation. Internal consultants are also called on to assist in program evaluation (Ball et al., 2011; Godber, 2008; Staton et al., 2007), for example, by helping to determine which programs fit best in the local environment. Internal and external consultants can work together on program consultation initiatives (Elias & Leverett, 2011). Program evaluation is critical as it sheds light on program strengths and weaknesses, provides a sense of why things happened as they did, and provides feedback for improvement (Royse, 2011; Zins, Elias, Greenberg, & Pruett, 2000).

The primary goal of program consultation is to provide an organization technical assistance so that a given program is successful. Consultation services can be provided for any aspect of a program, including development and evaluation. There is increasing emphasis, particularly with school-based programs on evidence-based programs. Consultants can be of assistance in selecting evidence-based programs as well as adapting to the local organizational context (Elias & Leverett, 2011). Consultation is usually requested for some skill or knowledge that the organization neither possesses nor has time to use. Because program evaluation is the most frequently requested form of program consultation, we'll focus now on how program evaluation consultation is performed. Program evaluation is a systematic set of data collection and analysis activities. It involves "… determining the worth or values of actions directed toward specific goals as a means of assessing credibility" (Staton et al., 2007, p. 389). The results of program evaluation are typically used for program improvement, accountability, or assessment related to program continuation.

Consultation Goals. The goal of program evaluation is to improve current decision making and outcomes in the program being evaluated (Ball et al., 2011). As a result, the effort, effectiveness, and adequacy of a program can be improved (Kirst-Ashman & Hull, 2012). Organizations want to know if their programs are meeting their goals and objectives in a cost–effective manner (Royse, 2011). When they are not sure how best to determine this, organizations frequently turn to program consultants who evaluate with a variety of methods and then transmit their findings to the organization so that program decisions can be made. For example, a consultant might assist in evaluating

the effects of an employee assistance program in a large textile firm.

A secondary goal of evaluation in program consultation is increasing the consultee's ability to evaluate current and subsequent (similar) programs. If this goal is part of the consultation, the consultant might also function in the education/training consultation model described earlier in this chapter; in this case, the consultant "gives away" the very skills that led to the need for consultation in the first place. Such a process helps to build a "culture of evaluation" in the organization (Godber, 2008; Rosen, Young, & Norris, 2006).

Consultant Function and Roles. In this model, consultants act as objective experts in program development and evaluation: they provide accurate, timely, and useful information to decision makers so that the program can be run more effectively. The consultant, as a technical expert, conducts exploratory meetings with consultees to determine the needs of program evaluation, develops a program evaluation design, obtains consultee feedback on the design, and redesigns the evaluation (Rosen et al., 2006). Often, the consultant has been involved in the evaluation design from the onset of the program. The use of qualitative evaluation strategies has increased, as has the inclusion of all stakeholders in the evaluation process (Arredondo, 1996). The consultant then carries out the evaluation by collecting and analyzing data and filing a report. The process of designing a program evaluation can be very time consuming; much of the consultant's time is spent in preparation and planning. In models such as that proposed by Lusky and Hayes (2001), which view program evaluation as a gradual process, the success of one phase depends upon the success of the prior phase. Qualitative methods of program evaluation are becoming increasingly popular (Royse, 2011).

Consultee Experience in Consultation. The consultee's primary role in this model is to provide the consultant with as much accurate information as possible, which is critical in the initial stages of program evaluation because the consultant needs as much information as possible to develop the appropriate design. Therefore, the consultee must make a commitment to spend whatever time and effort are required to be interviewed or to react to the consultant's progress in formulating a suitable evaluation design. Top-level administrators should champion the consultees' participation so that they are encouraged to become fully engaged.

Application: Consultant Techniques and Procedures. Four steps in program consultation focus on evaluation: hold ongoing meetings with consultees to design the evaluation, collect data, evaluate it, and write a final report.

After program evaluation has been requested, the consultant, whether internal or external, completes the entry stage as in any other consultation situation. Once the consultant is involved, issues such as who will gather the data, who will interpret the data, how the data will be presented, and to whom it is presented are determined. The consultant and the consultees are then ready to develop the program evaluation design, which involves a series of meetings with the consultees.

The participants try to identify what decisions are to be made, determine who the stakeholders are, and discuss how the program evaluation will tie into the decisions to be made, and how those decisions will affect the organization (Kirst-Ashman & Hull, 2012; Rosen et al., 2006).

Evaluative methods can involve retrospective monitoring or naturalistic monitoring (Illback et al., 1999) and can include qualitative methods. In retrospective monitoring, "self report information is obtained from program managers and staff about the extent to which the program has been operationalized" (Illback et al., 1999, p. 917). In naturalistic monitoring, the evaluator examines the program processes directly. Outcome methods include goal-attainment scaling (see Chapter 6). The success of the evaluation will depend upon the degree of congruence among the program, the evaluation scheme, and the setting of the program.

The consultant and consultees meet as necessary until both consultant and consultees are confident that all parties have an appropriate understanding of what is to occur and why. From all of this information, the participants begin to put together an evaluation design that dictates the who, what, where, and when of the evaluation procedure.

Regardless of the model of evaluation used, there are four traditional evaluation standards to bear in mind: accuracy, utility, feasibility, and propriety (Matuszek, 1981). Accuracy standards relate to the methodological soundness of the evaluation. Utility standards relate to the concept that evaluation should have some practical application. Feasibility standards deal with whether the evaluation design is appropriate for the program in the first place. Propriety standards relate to any ethical or legal issues that are connected to the evaluation. Participants will also want to include qualitative methods of evaluation such as periodic discussions with program developers as well as program participants as a source of data about program implementation, and not rely exclusively on quantitative indicators (Domitrovich & Greenberg, 2000; Forneris, Danish, & Fries, 2009). Once the consultant and consultees have put together the program evaluation design, a final review is held with the consultees and parties-at-interest. Any needed modifications in the design are made at this time.

The consultant and consultees are now ready to carry out the design. Data are collected and analyzed according to the design plan. After the data have been analyzed, the consultant writes and presents a formal report so that appropriate action can be taken. The consultant will ensure that stakeholders are frequently involved in making use of the evaluation results (Illback et al., 1999).

Case Example of Program Consultation. Pat, a psychologist in private practice, is selected by a human service agency to help evaluate its Big Brother Big Sister program, which has been in operation for three years. Although the agency thinks that the program is "doing okay," there appears to be a high turnover rate among its volunteers. Pat has had considerable experience with program evaluation and has worked with volunteer programs in the past.

He starts out by holding a meeting with the program's staff to design an evaluation. Four other meetings are held to make sure that the parties involved are in agreement about what is going on and that the evaluation is proceeding smoothly. Pat and the program staff then collect information on the volunteers and the children in the program, including how long volunteers tend to stay with the program. Methods are determined for assessing the program's impact on the children. Pat then analyzes the collected data and presents a report to the program staff. Among other things, the data show that volunteers last an average of nine months, receive little recognition or encouragement from the agency, and are not sure what is expected from them.

Pat recommends a training program for the volunteers, more personal contact with the volunteers by the program's staff, and some form of recognition for service as a volunteer. The program's impact on the children was deemed to be positive. Parents reported that volunteers gave their children additional, desirable adult role models and helped "keep the kids off the streets." The children liked the program because they "got to do a lot of extra things that were fun."

The Doctor–Patient Model

Even though both internal and external consultants typically engage the consultee in diagnosing the problem, sometimes consultees know something is wrong but don't know what it is. When consultation is requested, the consultant is given the power to make a diagnosis and prescribe a solution (Leong & Huang, 2008). It is as if the consultee says, "I don't know what's wrong. Find out and tell me how I can fix it." In the doctor–patient model, another type of expert consultation, the consultee is "purchasing" the consultant's expertise in diagnosing and prescribing. Schein (1990c) points out that the consultant's role in the doctor–patient model differs from that in the purchase of expertise model because "it empowers the consultant to dig into the workings of the organization and to combine information

gathering expertise with knowledge of organizations such that a deeper and consultee-relevant diagnosis can be reached" (p. 264).

For the doctor–patient model to be effective, the following assumptions must be met (Schein, 1987, 1988):

- The diagnostic process itself is seen as helpful and not disruptive.

- The consultee has correctly interpreted the organization's symptoms and has located the "sick" area.

- The person or group defined as "sick" will provide the information needed to make a valid diagnosis; that is, they will neither hide data nor exaggerate symptoms.

- The consultee understands and will correctly interpret the diagnosis provided by the consultant and will implement whatever prescription is offered.

- The consultee can remain effective after the consultant leaves.

The very act of asking a consultant to perform a diagnosis is an intervention, and the consultant should make sure that the consultee is aware of this. If the consultee is unaware that diagnosis is an intervention or does not explain the consultant's presence adequately, then the consultant's efforts can meet considerable resistance that can adversely affect the results of consultation.

Because both organizations and individuals are very complex, faith that the consultee has correctly interpreted the symptoms or behaviors and knows where the client system is "sick" is a very large assumption. Consultees can easily misconstrue and misjudge events concerning their work. In addition, consultees and consultants can easily get caught in a cycle of incorrect diagnoses due to the consultee's desire for help and the consultant's desire to give it.

The doctor–patient model assumes that consultees and other members of the organization are straightforward and honest with the consultant about their perceptions of the organization's problems. The nature of this honesty is a function of the organizational climate: If the climate is one of mistrust, then the consultant is not likely to get the real story; if the climate is one of trust, the consultees and other organization members are likely to tell the consultant everything and may even exaggerate the problem. The consultant also needs to be cautious about creating dependence among consultees.

What will happen if the consultee doesn't like the consultant's diagnosis? Even if the diagnosis is accepted, what guarantees are there that the prescription is going to be implemented?

It may not be accurate to assume that the consultee will accept diagnosis and prescription and remain effective after the consultant leaves— especially if the consultee did not learn any problem-solving skills during the consultation. If a similar problem arises for the consultee in the future, the consultant will have to be called in again.

Clearly, the relationship between the consultant and consultee is critical in the doctor–patient model of consultation. The consultant must be able to gain the trust of the consultee so that open communication can occur. If the consultee trusts the consultant, then real issues helpful to the diagnosis are more likely to emerge. In addition, if the consultant is able to create an effective relationship with the consultee and develop professional credibility, the prescription provided to the consultee also has more credibility.

In summary, the doctor–patient model works best when the consultee is willing to use a consultant, has observed and described the symptoms accurately, does not have the ability to perform the diagnosis and prescription, and is willing to follow through on the consultant's recommendations. A possible drawback of this model is that consultees might not enhance their problem-solving skills and may become dependent on the consultant. Because many ideas in the doctor–patient model, including diagnosis, are covered in Chapter 5, only a brief overview of this model is given now.

Consultation Goals. The consultant's primary goal in the doctor–patient model is to define the organization's problem and to recommend realistic interventions to ameliorate that problem.

Enhancing the consultee's diagnostic skills is not a goal in this model.

Consultant Functions and Roles. The consultant functions as an expert who enters the system, interviews consultees and parties-at-interest, collects data, makes a diagnosis, and recommends a solution. The consultant may well be hired to implement the solution, in which case he or she would change to the purchase of expertise model. Whereas the latter model demands content expertise on the part of the consultant, the doctor–patient model demands expertise in diagnostic and prescriptive skills.

Consulting skills that are critical to the doctor–patient model include:

- diagnostic skills
- a broad repertoire of prescriptive skills
- an in-depth knowledge of organizational theory
- the ability to "read" organizations
- data collection skills
- data interpretation skills
- human relations skills

Consultee Experience in Consultation. The main task of the consultee is to be a good "patient"—that is, to tell the consultant in as honest, objective, and accurate a way as possible the areas in which the organization has problems. The consultee should realize that the very act of using a consultant will affect the organization in some way. The consultee's tasks also include assisting the consultant in gathering additional data, ensuring that the consultant's diagnosis is fully and accurately understood, and advocating that the consultant's prescription be implemented.

Application: Consultant Techniques and Procedures. In the doctor–patient model, consultants enter the system as they would in any other consultation model. The major step in this model is to determine how best to go about making a diagnosis which is based on the situation. The method used to diagnose the organization's problems should obtain information about how its people see the organization's internal processes (Beer, 1980). It is crucial for the consultant to ensure that people involved in the diagnosis feel free to express their true thoughts, opinions, and feelings.

After the data have been gathered, the consultant analyzes it and formulates a diagnosis. The diagnosis defines problems in the organization in terms that the consultee can both understand and utilize.

The consultant typically follows one of three paths after making the diagnosis (Schein, 1990c): The consultant shares the diagnosis with the consultee as the basis for collaborating on finding a solution, shares the diagnosis and ends the consultation relationship, or makes recommendations and then helps implement them. In the latter case, the consultant then moves from the doctor–patient model to the purchase of expertise model.

Usually the consultant determines what is best for the consultee to do about the problem. However, consultants cannot necessarily help consultees make a commitment to change; they can only prescribe some solutions that the organization is capable of carrying out and tailor them to the unique aspects of the organization. Generalized prescriptions are rarely successful because they fail to consider the uniqueness of each organization.

Case Example of Doctor–Patient Consultation. A counselor in a community counseling center was asked to be an internal consultant to improve the center's effectiveness in delivering services to its clients. She was chosen because of her effective diagnostic skills, her solid working knowledge of organizations, and her trustworthiness. The consultant was given "free run" of the center and was charged with defining the center's problem areas and prescribing some ways to effectively manage them. She began by informing all staff members of the nature of consultation. Interviews and surveys were used to gather data from the center's administration and staff and from former clients. Complete confidentiality was guaranteed to all involved. Information was sought on such factors

as interpersonal relationships, views of the center's organizational climate, and the center's role and mission. Based on the analysis of the data, the consultant concluded that there was little consensus concerning the center's overall role and mission, which led to a lack of understanding of how the center was run and what the staff and administration were supposed to do. In turn, this lack of understanding led to inadequacies in the area of program development.

The consultant prescribed a review and subsequent modification of the center's role and mission statement. Furthermore, she recommended development of a five-year strategic plan based on the modified role and mission statement and suggested that all employees be involved in each of these activities.

The Process Model

Schein (1990c) points out that failure to involve the consultee in the diagnosis may lead him or her to misdiagnose the problems inadvertently. This led Schein (1987, 1988, 1999) to formulate his model of process consultation. Process consultation is based on the supposition that "… the primary goal of the consultant is to help the organization to help itself" (Leong & Huang, 2008, p. 171). The basic difference between this model and the purchase of expertise and doctor–patient models is that the consultant's expertise includes skills to involve the consultee in defining the problem, to form a team with the consultee, and to ensure that the consultation process focuses on the consultee's needs. It is a very empowering form of consultation. The consultant's expertise lies in making individual consultees as well as groups of consultees more effective problem-solvers in the future, potentially having a strong preventive effect (McLean, 2006; Meyers et al., 2009). The main point is that process consultant assists the organization in defining and solving its own problems (Leong & Huang, 2008). Process consultation may be in order when a consultant is needed to supplement the consultee's problem-solving skills—the consultee knows something is wrong and wants to figure out what that is, and what to do about it (Meyers et al., 2009).

Process consultation can be defined as guidance provided to some group by an individual "trained in group dynamics and organization development" (Kormanski & Eschbach, 1997, p. 137).

Process consultation is what the consultant does to help the consultee identify, understand, and change the process events that occur within an organization (Schein, 1978, 1999). The focus of consultation is not on the content of the problem, but rather on the process by which problems are solved. The consultee "owns" the problem (and continues to own it throughout the consultation process) and "purchases" the consultant's expertise in handling process events. Process consultation is designed to help consultees examine and deal with human and social events as they relate to problems the consultee tries to solve.

Process consultation is based on the premise that often things in an organization can be changed only if the consultee is involved in diagnosing the problem and generating solutions. Because of the complexity of problems in organizations and the consultees' familiarity with them, consultees' input into the diagnosis is crucial. In addition, advice given by consultants can be counterproductive in that it can cause resistance, power struggles, and resentment.

The relationship between the consultant and the consultee is extremely important. The consultant must create an environment of trust and credibility and help the consultee feel safe enough to own the problem and work on it throughout the consultation process. Such tasks demand empathy, respect, and genuineness on the part of the consultant. Process consultation works best when the following assumptions are met (Schein, 1987):

- The consultee is distressed somehow but does not know the source of the distress or what to do about it.

- The consultee does not know either what kind of assistance might be available or which consultant could provide the help needed.

- The nature of the problem is such that the consultee not only needs help in figuring out

what is wrong but would benefit from participation in the diagnostic process.

- The consultee has "constructive intent," is motivated by goals and values that the consultant can accept, and has some capacity to enter into a helping relationship.

- The consultee is ultimately the only one who knows what form of intervention will work best in the situation.

- The consultee is capable of learning how to diagnose and solve his or her own organizational problems. (pp. 32–33)

In a nutshell, process consultation assumes that consultees must acquire and maintain ownership of their problems, that they do not fully understand these problems, and that they can learn to design and manage change on their own (Ledford, 1990).

The process consultation model is most applicable when a consultee with some problem-solving ability is willing to learn how to work out solutions without seeking content assistance or giving the problem to the consultant for diagnosis. By focusing on the *how* rather than the *what* of problem solving, the consultant and consultee work together, enabling the consultee to solve current concerns and similar ones in the future. Schein (1990c) admits that the need for content experts will increase in the future but that their services will not be well-utilized unless their efforts are combined with process consultation.

Consultation Goals.   The primary goal of process consultation is to help consultees gain insight into the everyday events occurring within the organization. It attempts to teach consultees to act on those events and become more adept at identifying and modifying them in ways that achieve their goals (Schein, 1987). If the consultant and consultee are successful, the ultimate goal of increasing the organization's overall effectiveness is also met.

Consultant Functions and Roles.   The primary roles played by the process consultant are facilitator, catalyst, and co-diagnostician. The consultant collaborates with the consultee such that consultation becomes a joint effort. The consultant creates a peer and equal relationship with the consultee (Puuitio, Kykyri, & Wahlstrom, 2008; Saltzman, 2011). It is essential that the consultee feels supported by the consultant on the problem-solving effort (Lambrechts, Grieten, Bouwen, & Corthouts, 2009). Rather than providing content expertise, the consultant facilitates consultees' process of self-discovery and self-exploration so that they are able to use their skills in identifying and addressing the problems at hand.

The consultant must be an expert in processes that occur at the individual, interpersonal, and intergroup levels; content expertise in the consultee's institution's area of perceived difficulty is not required. The consultant helps the consultee obtain insight into the everyday human activities in an organization (e.g., who talks to whom about what), which are viewed as critical to the appropriate diagnosis of an organizational problem (Schein, 1988, 1999). The process consultant provides less structure and direct input than would a consultant operating in either the purchase of expertise or doctor-patient models. At the same time, the consultant uses "humble and critical inquiry" by which consultant makes no assumptions in order to get to the notions about what the consultee really wants (Cataldo, Raelin, & Lambert, 2009; Lambrechts, Bouwen, Grieten, Huybrechts, & Schein, 2011; Saltzman, 2011). In addition to creating a climate conducive to consultee exploration and input, the process consultant assists in gathering data about the relationships within the organization and members' perceptions of organizational processes. The consultant then assists the consultee in making a diagnosis using these data, and process-oriented interventions such as agenda setting and feedback are made by the consultant and/or the consultee. Finally, the consultant helps the consultee evaluate the consultation by looking for changes in values, targeted behaviors, and any other areas that were the focus of consultation. Once the evaluation has been concluded, the consultant reduces involvement and terminates the consultation.

Consultee Experience in Consultation. The consultee—a person or persons within the organization—senses that something is not quite right in the organization, that things could be better, and that he or she wants them to improve. The consultee uses the consultant to translate vague feelings and perceptions into concrete actions to enhance the overall effectiveness of the organization.

The major role of the consultee in this model is that of an active collaborator and teammate (Meyers et al., 2009). The consultee is assumed to have some problem-solving skills and be knowledgeable about his or her organization. The consultee provides the content of the consultation and participates in the processes at issue as the consultee's process skills dictate. The consultee then discusses content issues and the nature of the perceived problems, sets goals, and attempts to make plans for action (Schein, 2010). The consultation process itself helps the consultee define diagnostic steps that lead to action plans or organizational change (Schein, 2010).

Application: Consultant Techniques and Procedures. The premise of process consultation is that organizations are merely networks of people. If these networks are not functioning effectively, there will be extreme difficulty in accomplishing the tasks of the organization. Process consultation attempts to enhance the overall functioning of the organization by helping the consultee change values and develop skills. In effect, the consultee's development is accomplished when the consultant models the desired values and skills. During this process, the consultee begins to take more and more responsibility for the diagnosis and implementation of procedures. As the desired skills and values become more evident in the consultee's behavior, the consultant gradually disengages from consultation.

There are seven overlapping steps to process consultation (Schein, 1988):

1. making initial contact with the consultee organization

2. defining the relationship, formal contacting, and creating a psychological contract

3. selecting a setting and method of work

4. gathering data and making a diagnosis

5. intervening

6. reducing involvement

7. terminating

The process consultant spends a significant amount of time building relationships with consultees and assumes that, without trust, the consultee will not deal with the basic issues that are concerning the organization and therefore consultation will not likely be successful. In addition to developing trust, the consultant selects a work site close to "where the action is." By being able to observe the real work of the organization, he or she is able to ask the right kinds of questions to help consultees explore things such as organizational culture and values. Process consultation assumes that the organization's problems are typically due to communication and the organization's processes rather than the organization's structures (Leong & Huang, 2008).

The process consultant favors the use of interventions that maximize opportunities for consultee–consultant interactions. Consequently, observation, informal interviews, and group discussions are used frequently by process consultants. The process consultant considers data gathering to be a crucial process that should be conducted in a manner consistent with the consultee's values. Further, the process consultant believes that plans for gathering data should be general in nature because the only way to determine how to proceed is to use experiences resulting from initial data-gathering strategies.

As process consultation proceeds, the consultant can intervene in a variety of ways. Schein has categorized these in terms of their tactical goals—exploration, diagnosis, action alternatives, and confrontation—because the process consultant usually moves through these interventions in that order as the consultation process unfolds. The consultant uses exploratory questions to stimulate the consultee's thinking and to determine his or her views. Diagnostic interventions are used to involve the consultee in the diagnostic process, action alternatives help convince the consultee that something can be done about the situation, and confrontational interventions are used to test the consultee's motivation and willingness to act.

Regarding evaluation, the process consultant determines what outcomes might occur as a result of consultation and how they are to be measured. As its ultimate goal, process consultation attempts to improve organizational performance by changing values and interpersonal skills in key personnel.

Case Example of Process Consultation. A group of teachers at a secondary school were unsatisfied with the general quality of communication between the staff and students and wanted to improve the communication efforts of the staff as a whole. They asked Gene, the school counselor, to sit in at their meetings and act as a "sounding board," which he agreed to do.

Time at the end of each meeting was allocated for Gene to give feedback to the group. He was also asked to help the group stay on task and get through the problem-solving process. During the consultation, Gene provided feedback to the group on its problem-solving skills, challenged it to define its goals more precisely, and suggested that group members develop specific ways to evaluate their attempts to communicate better. All in all, he helped the group members become more effective problem solvers. Finally, Gene provided feedback on the group's ways of gathering information from students and the types of interventions it developed for improving communication. When everyone involved was satisfied with the way things were going, Gene reduced involvement with the group and attended only every third meeting.

COLLABORATION FROM AN ORGANIZATIONAL PERSPECTIVE

The aim of organizational collaboration is the same as organizational consultation: the enhanced functioning of the organization. As organizations have become complex, collaboration across

---

C A S E   11.1   Organizational Consultation for School Consultants

---

Doris is a middle school consultant who was asked by the administration of her school to work with one of its interdisciplinary teams. The team consisted of a social studies teacher, a math teacher, a science teacher, and a language arts teacher.

The team leader had been complaining to the administration that certain team members consistently go "around" her rather than "through" her when communicating with the principal. This was in spite of the fact that the principal had reminded the other team members of proper protocol.

As Doris was determining how to approach the team, she realized that part of the problem was the principal's high level of approachability. The principal met with Doris and the team and asked them to work together on resolving the apparent problem the team was having. The principal mentioned that the team may want to use Doris for building some procedures for communicating outside of the team.

Doris started out by meeting with the team during its planning session. As she heard the intensity of the feelings among the team members, she decided that process consultation was in order. It was obvious to Doris that *how* things were being said was just as important as *what* was being said.

Doris suggested: (1) that the team knew it had a problem in internal and external communication (the team members, including the leader, agreed), (2) that the members were in the best position to determine how to resolve these issues, and (3) that they engage in a collaborative effort that would help them solve not only their current concern but similar ones in the future. She and the team agreed to meet for three sessions during the next month.

In playing the roles of facilitator and catalyst, Doris raised questions for exploration and helped the team look closely at itself and its communication processes. She raised the issue of authority when it appeared that there were differences in whether the team leader was "in charge" or a "group spokesperson." The team felt awkward as it attempted to be humane, yet honest. The teachers had worked together for over 10 years but only recently had been placed together as a team.

At the close of the third session when Doris asked the team to evaluate her, themselves, and the progress that had been made, the members generally acknowledged that as an objective and facilitative person, she had been of great assistance in helping them help themselves. Though they had initially been defensive and looked for blame rather than taking responsibility for the problems they were experiencing, the members had come to agreement about the role of team leader, resolved their authority issue, and improved their communication in terms of concreteness and authenticity. Doris followed up in one last meeting a month later.

Commentary

Doris demonstrated some excellent skills in determining which approach to organizational consultation she might take. She noted the significant amount of emotion surrounding the team's functioning and accurately determined that process consultation, with its more interpersonal focus, was an appropriate method to start out with. She also astutely determined that if the goal was to get the team to collaborate more effectively, then the approach to consultation should be one, like process consultation, that places people in a position of collaborating to solve their problems.

---

elements of the organization has almost become an essential component of organizations' everyday routine (Rawlings, 2000). Because of the tremendous increase in "in-house" human service professionals, such as HRD specialists, organizations are uniquely poised to maximize the benefits of collaboration. Structures such as self-directed work teams, quality circles, project management teams, and the increasing number of types teams used in schools all lend themselves to having the human service professional function as a collaborator. In organizations where collaboration is relatively new, human service professionals, including school-based professionals, can train members of the organization in problem-solving skills and team functioning. The human service professional can then participate as a collaborator and take responsibility for the outcome of some aspects of the project, as well as providing consultation to and receiving it from fellow collaborators.

C A S E   11.2   Organizational Consultation for Community Consultants

The general manager of the local branch of AME Telephone Company contacted the local mental health agency for the purpose of developing and implementing a professional outplacement counseling program. The company was undergoing a downsizing mandated by its parent company. The general manager informed the director of the mental health agency that the parent company had made funds available for the purpose of counseling displaced workers. The manager noted that almost half of the unit's 56 workers were going to be laid off.

Maria, a community mental health consultant, was assigned to explore the possibilities of the agency working with the telephone company. Using the principles of program consultation, she spent a great deal of time with the manager discussing the nature of the telephone company, which was a typical bureaucracy, like many other telephone and utility companies she had worked with over the past 20 years. Everyone had their assigned duties and did them well. The general manager was aware of the bureaucratic structure and attempted to ensure adequate morale by having an upbeat newsletter and recognition of birthdays. He also used a personal touch by getting out and about the divisions of the company and he knew each employee by name.

After she had a feel for the organization and made some conclusions as to its nature, Maria informed the manager about some general principles of outplacement counseling and the possible structures that such a program could take on. She noted the importance of the program on the morale of those employees remaining with the company, as well as the goodwill the program could develop with the departing employees. Maria and the manager discussed the positive impact that an outplacement program could have not only on the local unit but on the parent company's national reputation. Any outplacement program has three phases: preparing the company to make terminations, helping those employees who are terminated find new jobs, and assisting remaining employees to feel secure.

As Maria and the general manager roughed out an outline that Maria could develop into a program proposal, they concluded that the general manager himself should undergo some training in

effective termination, determined that severance packages should be discussed with the employees being terminated prior to the offering of outplacement services, and discussed the nature of outplacement counseling services needed by the employees. Since the company was in a moderately rural area, many of the employees' families had lived in the area for generations. Hence, part of the counseling process would encourage employees to discuss their feelings concerning termination, myths, and realities about finances, career counseling, and placement.

Maria and the manager discussed outplacement concepts that seemed particularly applicable to the employees being terminated at the telephone company: job hunts within and outside the local community; "creating your own job" strategies; and assessment of a candidate's aptitudes and skills. Finally, they determined what the outplacement counseling program could do for the remaining company employees and addressed occupational wellness.

Based on their discussion, Maria developed a proposal for the program and submitted it to the mental health agency director and the telephone company general manager for approval. The program included a detailed blueprint for how the program was to be implemented and an extensive evaluation procedure that included input from all employees as well as placement success data.

Commentary

Maria did an excellent job of being thorough in her approach to program consultation. Instead of plugging in a canned program, she analyzed the organization and considered some of its unique aspects. Notice how she educated the general manager and made him part of the intervention. Maria also looked at the outplacement counseling program from the perspective of the entire company by including something for the remaining employees. Such systemic thinking enhances the probability of successful program implementation.

The idea for this case study came from an article by Siobhan McGowan (1993) entitled "Employees, Managers Work It Out after Layoffs" in *Guidepost*, 35(10), 1, 10.

Because of its collaborative nature, the process consultation model may be the easiest to adapt to collaboration. Human services professionals will need to adapt the purchase of expertise and doctor–patient models to include a method for empowering fellow collaborators who can use their own expertise to a greater degree and develop a shared vision.

The emergence of the internal consultant role also has implications for collaboration in organizations (Caplan, Caplan, & Erchul, 1994). Managers, for example, may find it more suitable to have some responsibility for some part of a plan, rather than be seen as a person trying to consult with a subordinate, thereby walking the thin line between supervision and consultation (Caplan et al., 1994). Finally, although leaders of organizations see the need for collaboration, they sometimes have difficulty building the capacity for it (Rawlings, 2000). One method of building such capacity involves developing a shared vision, a shared understanding, and shared goals (Rawlings, 2000). Organizational collaboration has received more attention in the literature and has been used more frequently by all types of organizations. It is now common practice in schools; for example, used in implementing RTI initiatives.

MULTICULTURAL ASPECTS RELATED TO ORGANIZATIONAL CONSULTATION

Without question, organizational consultants need to be multiculturally competent (Meyers et al., 2009). Schein's typology sets the stage for the effective practice of multicultural consultation. Those cultural groups that prefer structured, expert-based consultation should find the purchase of expertise model attractive. Its focus on problem-solving and content expertise allows consultees the security of having a knowledgeable and skilled person leading the consultation process. The purchase of expertise model demands little in terms of self-disclosure or expression of feeling. For those cultural groups that prefer assistance in problem definition and determining interventions and desire an expert, the doctor–patient model will be attractive. For those who prefer a nonhierarchical relationship, the purchase of expertise model may not be attractive. By its focus on diagnosis, the doctor–patient model can readily take cultural variables into consideration. Like the purchase of expertise model, the doctor–patient model demands limited self-disclosure.

For those groups that value the nature of the relationship, process consultation is an attractive model. Its focus on understanding the interpersonal process as an aspect of problem definition creates the necessity for a strong relationship between the consultant and the consultee. For cultural groups with strong self-determination needs, this model allows for them to bring and use their own personal resources in the consultation process. Process consultation can be viewed as empowering to disenfranchised groups.

MOC has emerged as a promising form of organizational consultation (Cooper & Leong, 2008). Its purpose is to assist organizations in becoming multiculturally competent. Characteristics of MOC include assisting organizations to have a conceptual framework that relates to the enhancement of diversity in the organization, advocating for social justness in the sociopolitical/power elements of the organization, having the consultant culturally competent, developing social forces that enhance diversity, and facilitating dialogues about diversity-related issues (Sue, 2008). For Sue (2008), MOC involves multicultural organizational development (MOD) by which the organization, through consultation, becomes more effective and adaptive by the appropriate use of diversity. For example, with the rise of coaching as a subset of consultation, coaching across diversity lines will require more attention in the future (Thomas, 2006). MOC can include all three types of Schein's models.

Another model with multicultural emphasis is that developed by Leong and Huang (2008). These authors have adapted Schein's process consultation model to include multicultural elements such as culture-specific variables like interactions between organization members of different cultures. The inclusion of these elements may well lead to more accurate and culturally sensitive diagnosis, problem identification, and implementation.

TRENDS

The major trends in organizational consulting are linked to several societal factors: the impact of living and working in an information society; the ever-increasing pace of change in all aspects of life; the growing awareness that quality change requires systemic thinking; the realization that change can be successfully accomplished only through social influence (Schein, 2006; Truscott et al., 2000); and increasing internationalization and diversity within organizations (Leong & Huang, 2008; Rawlings, 2000; Sue, 2008). Note, for example, the models of organizational consultation described above that focus on multicultural issues. These factors have created the following general trends in organizational consulting: a continued reliance on computer hardware and software, a primary consideration of the effects of organizational culture and diversity on consultation efforts when selecting interventions, and the willingness and ability of organizational consultants to "wear many hats" when they provide services. For example, as diversity continues to increase in the work force, consultants will need to be increasingly sensitive to workplace diversity issues related to organizational infrastructure, job satisfaction, relationships among staff, and work productivity (Sears et al., 2006; Sue, 2008).

One trend in organizational consultation is the tendency to combine process consultation with the purchase of expertise and doctor–patient models (Schein, 1990c). Schein (1990c) suggests that such combinations involve consultees at more significant levels in the consultation process and enhance the probability of success in consultation. By combining process consultation with other forms, the consultant ensures that the consultee is appropriately invested in the process, the appropriate problems are being worked on, the diagnosis is relevant and clear to pertinent parties, and the solutions generated are appropriate for the organizational context and culture (Rockwood, 1993; Schein, 1990c, 1999). Further, since consultation is a helping relationship, focus on process events such as the dynamics of communication is essential (Schein, 1999).

There has been an increase in consultants acting as coaches to mangers and administrators (Davison & Gasiorowski, 2006). As you most likely know, the term *coaching* is increasingly being used the organizational consultation literature. Yet, there is very little in the literature that speaks to agreement on the definition of the term and very little empirical evidence about its effectiveness. Recently, Schein (2006, 2010) has suggested that coaching is a subset of consultation. Regardless of the coaching situation, consultation skills such as the ability to move easily among the expert, doctor–patient, and process roles is essential (Schein, 2006, p. 24).

One trend in education/training consultation has been the emergence of performance consultation (Schein, 2010). Performance consultation assumes that solutions proposed by education/training approaches often miss the mark because what are really needed are solutions that are based on *performance*. Performance consultation assumes that the focus should not be on skill acquisition because much of the research on training suggests that trainees do not follow through after the training. While the education/training approach focuses on training activities and experiences, performance consultation teaches the skills and knowledge related to specific job performance. In short, performance consultation makes the shift from what consultees need to learn to what they must do.

There has been increased involvement of organizational consultants in schools (Merrell, Ervin, & Gimpel, 2006; Meyers et al., 2012). Consultants have been asked to assist in addressing a variety of issues such as those posed by the No Child Left Behind Act, response to intervention (RTI), positive behavioral interventions and supports (PBIS), SEL programs, and the achievement gap between majority and minority students. In addition, the use of multitiered interventions and the focus on important topics like prevention, systems-level thinking, ecological variables, social justice, multicultural issues, and empowerment of all stakeholders have all promoted the use of organizational consultation.

As noted above, another trend is the emergence of MOC as consultation is being sought for assistance with diversity issues within the organization. Diversity consultation recognizes the increasing diversity in the workplace and the importance of managing diverse work environments. Diversity consultation is used to deal with issues related to awareness, sociopolitical implications, open dialogue, cultural competence, and cultural norms (Cooper & Leong, 2008; Sue, 2008; Thomas, 2006). Consultants will need the attitudes and skills related to diversity in order to practice effective and competent multicultural consultation (Cooper, Wilson-Stark, Peterson, O'Roark, & Pennington, 2008; Sue, 2008).

There is an increasing emphasis placed on determining how and when to apply models of organizational consultation. For example, Carson and Lowman (2002) discuss the implications of individual-level variables on organizational consultation. Fuqua and Kurpius (1993) have developed seven principles for assisting consultants in determining how best to select from among consultation models. These still hold today.

1. Consultants should select models congruent with the perceived needs of consultees and the organization.

2. Consultants should clearly articulate to consultees which model is being used.

3. The major goal in model selection should be expanding consultees' conceptual framework.

4. The model should allow consultees to generalize from the enhanced conceptual framework after the consultant exits.

5. The most powerful implementations will involve development of the consultees.

6. There is more positive power in sharing the application of models with consultees.

7. The application of multiple models will more likely lead to consultation success than will applying a single model.

Consultants are increasingly being called upon to provide service in crisis and disaster situations (Gottlieb, 2006; McCarroll & Ursano, 2006; Stock, 2007). Organizations use consultants to review or create crisis management plans and to train organizational personnel in how to react to crises/disasters and related events such as workplace violence. The idea is for the consultant to help the organization "… to plan pre-event interventions to minimize post-event consequences (McCarroll & Ursano, 2007, p. 193).

CONCLUSIONS

Because organizational consultation encompasses a variety of approaches, it is difficult to assess its major contributions. It has, however, clearly contributed to improving workplace conditions (e.g., through process consultation) and helping organizations become more diverse and accountable (e.g., through program consultation).

Organizational consultation has emphasized the interconnectedness between meeting human needs and organizational structure. The specialized types of consultation available in organizational consultation have increased. Organizational consultation's concept of the organization-as-client has helped organizations understand the importance of organizational culture; indeed, most organizations now realize that organizational culture strongly influences much individual behavior (French & Bell, 1999). Organizational consultation has also demonstrated that working with groups of consultees can be a cost-effective way to meet workers' needs and increase organizational effectiveness.

Organizational consultation considers the complexity of issues that arise in any setting. Systems theory and an ecological perspective permit complexities to be defined in manageable ways that become amenable to consultation.

The criticisms of organizational consultation are frequently those directed at organization development; for example, that it has not fulfilled its early promise to integrate or systematize its interventions. The following criticisms were adapted from a critique of organizational consultation noted by Gallessich (1982, pp. 221–222) several years ago. Unfortunately, they are still true today:

- It is too preoccupied with interpersonal process to the detriment of problem-related factors such as budgeting and technology.

- Its interventions are often "band-aids on an open wound" and hence are not effective in solving many organizational problems in the long run. (For example, there is an overreliance on the use of workshops to solve identified concerns.)

- Its results are often "cosmetic" or only involve "fine-tuning."

- Its consultants sometimes perform "dirty work" or "spy" for managers and other administrators.

- Its consultants sometimes produce such grand designs that their interventions in effect are worse than the organization's problems were in the first place.

- Its consultants sometimes try to apply methods of business and industry when providing organizational consultation to human service agencies.

There are yet other criticisms of organizational consultation. Some organizational consultants rely on one or two pet interventions, particularly education/training, and some cannot always take into account administrators' deeply rooted assumptions about administration and personnel—assumptions that may differ from those held by the consultant. Hence, there is at the outset of consultation tremendous potential for resistance that may never be overcome.

Schein (1987, 1988) noted that the purchase of expertise and doctor–patient models are limited because they rely on basic assumptions that are rarely met in practice. Therefore, they are at best superficial and, at worst, counterproductive.

These criticisms reflect more the imperfections of practicing organizational consultants than imperfections in the models and their principles. Accordingly, better training procedures for organizational consultants are as likely to produce improvements, as would refinements in organizational consultation models.

SUMMARY

Organizational consultation encompasses many types of consultation performed by consultants, internal or external, to organizations. Consultants function as technical experts, diagnosticians, or process experts. Regardless of the role, organizational consultation is predicated on the notion that an organization can

increase its overall effectiveness through consultation. The organization itself, or one of its parts, is the client, and consultees are people in the organization with whom the consultant works.

Organizations suffer because their personnel lack the knowledge, skills, or values to function at optimal levels of effectiveness. Organizational consultants, armed with a broad repertoire of techniques grounded in organizational theory, attempt to help consultees deal with the complexities of organizational life and enhance effectiveness. Consulting with organizations is a little like feeding a hungry animal: in living its life, the organization uses up energy and becomes hungry. If it doesn't get some food (consultation), it cannot function optimally and will eventually starve to death.

SUGGESTIONS FOR EFFECTIVE PRACTICE

- Be able to determine if you should be using the purchase of expertise, doctor–patient, or process model of consultation.

- Remember that your ultimate goal in organizational consultation is to assist the entire organization in some way.

- Use the dictum that *how* you do what you do is as important as *what* you do.

- Strive to take multicultural variables within the organization into account as you consult.

QUESTIONS FOR REFLECTION

1. What historical forces led to the development of organizational consultation?

2. How can an organization be a client?

3. Differentiate among the purchase of expertise, doctor–patient, and process models of consultation.

4. Why are the purchase of expertise and doctor–patient models particularly limited?

5. Explain how both education/training and program consultation are examples of purchase of expertise consultation.

6. Why is program evaluation the most common function of the program consultant?

7. Process consultation aims for changes in values and skills of the consultees involved. How are these values and skills related to organizational effectiveness?

8. Is it really possible for a consultant to produce an accurate diagnosis of an organization's problem? Why or why not?

9. Why do so few consultees follow through on the prescriptions made by organizational consultants?

10. How can multicultural issues be dealt with at the organizational level?

SUGGESTED SUPPLEMENTARY READINGS

If you are interested in organizational consultation, you may want to read some of the following resources:

McCarroll, J. E., & Ursano, R. J. (2006). Consultation to groups, organizations, and communities. In E. C. Ritchie, P. J. Watson & M. J. Friedman (Eds.), *Interventions following mass violence and disasters:* *Strategies for mental health practice* (pp. 193–205). New York: Guilford.

Robertson, P., Deck, M. D., & Isenhour, G. E. (2014). Education/training consultation with school personnel. In A. M. Dougherty (Ed.), *Casebook of psychological consultation and collaboration* (6th ed.). Belmont, CA: Brooks/Cole Cengage. This case study adeptly illustrates the factors and related issues in providing education/training consultation in a school setting. Of particular note in this case is the section implications for effective practice.

Schein, E. H. (1988). *Process consultation: Its role in organization development*, Volume 1 (2nd ed.). Reading, MA: Addison-Wesley. This classic text is a must for anyone interested in consulting with organizations. Schein discusses process consultation in detail and in relation to the purchase of expertise and doctor–patient models.

Schein, E. H. (1999). *Process consultation revisited: Building the helping relationship*. Reading, MA: Addison-Wesley. Another classic, this is Schein's latest contribution to the field of process consultation. Of particular interest is Schein's discussion of consultation as a helping relationship. Its business and industry orientation should not diminish the wealth of applicable information in this book for human service consultants and collaborators.

12

✳

School-Based Consultation and Collaboration

S chools are different from organizations related to human services delivery, or business and industry settings. Because the context in which consultation and collaboration occur is important (Zins & Erchul, 2002), I dedicate an entire chapter to these services in a school context. For example, the use of consultation in school settings has grown over the last decade due to the addition of programs such as response to intervention (RTI) (Erchul, 2011). Even though you may never work in a school, it is highly likely that you will collaborate or consult with school personnel. Awareness of and skills in consultation and collaboration in the context of a school are essential for all human service professionals.

A great deal of consultation and collaboration occurs in schools, resulting in a time-efficient and cost-effective way to affect the well-being of students in a variety of ways, including academic achievement (ASCA, 2005) and behavioral and social-emotional development (Nastasi & Varjas, 2008; Sheridan, Warnes, Woods, Blevins, Magee, & Ellis, 2009). For example, 80 percent of school counselors consult with administrators, teachers, and parents (Perera-Diltz, Moe, & Mason, 2011). This chapter surveys the scope of school consultation and collaboration. I will briefly discuss their history and examine the nature of consulting with administrators, including how school consultants can use organization development consultation with their administrators. In addition, this chapter surveys methods of consulting and collaborating with teachers. Adlerian consultation and instructional consultation are included in this discussion. From there, this chapter discusses consulting and collaborating with parents, including parent case consultation and home–school collaboration. After a discussion of interagency collaboration and school partnerships, I examine some practical issues, including those surrounding multicultural school consultation, special education, RTI, a systems view of schools, prevention, and time constraints. Finally, the chapter concludes with a discussion of school consultation and collaboration in the 21st century.

Here are some questions to consider as you read this chapter:

- In what ways is consultation in the school different from that in the community?

- How would you, as a consultant or collaborator working in a school context, ensure that you are practicing in a multiculturally competent manner?

- What special factors does a consultant have to take into consideration when consulting or collaborating with parents?

- What special ethical issues does interagency collaboration in the schools raise?

- How can collaboration be viewed as the service of choice over consultation for school-based human service professionals to provide?

RATIONALE FOR SCHOOL-BASED CONSULTATION AND COLLABORATION

The incidences of mental health, behavioral, and academic issues in school-aged youth has skyrocketed in the last three decades (Gutkin, 2009). Interest in school-based consultation and collaboration to help address these problems has increased commensurately (Gutkin & Curtis, 2009; Kanel, 2007). The increasing number of societal problems that school-aged youth encounter is increasing the need for mental health services, including consultation and collaboration (Allen, 2011; Gutkin, 2009).

Up to 20 percent of youth in the United States suffer from mental health issues with barely over one-fourth receiving appropriate care (Greenberg et al., 2003).

Revisions to the Individuals with Disabilities Education Act (IDEA; Pub. L. 108-446, 2004) (Wilczynski, Mandal, & Fusilier, 2000), school violence, the No Child Left Behind Act (NCLB), emphases on school reform and restructuring (Adelman & Taylor, 2007), as well as increased school accountability and high-stakes testing (Braden & Tayrose, 2008) have all led to an increased importance for consultation and collaboration in school settings. In addition, because administrators, parents, and other school support personnel affect the learning climate of the school, they are appropriate persons for consultative assistance.

School-based and non-school-based mental health professionals are increasingly called upon to assist with the organizational change necessitated by school improvement initiatives and the increasing popularity of the ecological model (Gutkin, 2009, 2012).

Because schools represent a microcosm of community life, they are excellent settings for consultation and collaboration. By working with the adults in a student's life space, consultants, paradoxically, are best able to indirectly influence the well-being of that student (Kennedy, Frederickson, & Monsen, 2008). In other words, school-aged youth are best served when consultants work with those adults who "control" those students' environments (Gutkin, 2009, 2012). Further, the corresponding decreases in economic resources and the increasing number of social issues school-age youth exhibit make consultation and collaboration, particularly involving other community agencies, viable services to affect the success of students (Mellin, 2009). Mental health professionals—internal and external to school settings—consult and collaborate regularly with teachers, administrators, and parents/guardians who are often the first ones to note issues students may be having (Doll, Spies, & Champion, 2012; Keys, Bemak, Carpenter, & King-Sears, 1998; Kratochwill & Pittman, 2002; Studer, 2005). School-based personnel such as school counselors and school psychologists foster relationships through consultation and collaboration to promote the academic achievement and psychological well-being of students (Baker, Robichaud, Westforth Dietrich, Wells, & Schreck, 2009; Manz, Mautone, & Martin, 2009).

The pressure on schools to perform better has also added impetus to the use of consultation and collaboration. As Truscott et al. (2012) note, "... public education provides tremendous opportunities for school-based consultation (SBC) and effective professional development because the needs of schools are great, pressure to change practices is building, and current school improvement efforts have not been particularly effective" (p. 64).

To be effective, mental health/human service consultants—internal and external—should be aware of the educational, social, and emotional needs of children. They must understand how to communicate with teachers, administrators, and parents; and they must be aware of the forces operating in the local building, at the school system level, and in the community at large. By working effectively with other professionals at school and with parents/guardians, school-based human service professionals can positively impact the lives of large numbers of children (Cohen, Linker & Stutts, 2006) and can help resolve concerns, prevent future problems, and provide developmental strategies. In addition, by providing these services, counselors and psychologists can broaden the scope of their influence in the school (Dougherty, 1992b).

Consultation and collaboration can occur as primary prevention (e.g., enhancing the school climate), secondary prevention (e.g., working with school administrators in developing programs for students at risk for teenage pregnancy), and tertiary prevention (e.g., consulting with a teacher about a child who is having difficulty in the classroom). Increasing attention has been given to providing primary prevention services to those who have basic responsibility for students (teachers, administrators, and parents) that can positively affect school and home climates.

The actual way in which consultation and collaboration occur varies according to the model being employed. Keys et al. (1998) made some important clarifications regarding the distinction between consultation and collaboration. The problem-solving process in collaboration and consultation are essentially the same. What varies is that, in collaboration, there is an emphasis on shared expertise throughout the entire process (Keys et al., 1998). The "triadic-dependent relationship" style of consultation is known as the "expert" mode of consultation. In the "collaborative dependent" style, the consultant functions not only as an expert but also as a facilitator and educator. The consultee, however, still depends on the expertise of the consultant. The consultant educates the consultee about the problem-solving process and together they collaborate to identify and solve a problem. In other words, even though the consultants take on a collaborative role, they are still "in charge" of the process.

When mental health/human service professionals are involved with staff development, parent groups, intervention teams, and program development, and when they are used as resources on a variety of topics, they are engaging in consultation or collaboration (see Pellitteri, 2000; Safran & Safran, 2001). As a means by which psychological services are delivered in a school, consultation is an indirect service to students and attempts to help others work more effectively with students.

Collaboration combines indirect and direct services to students. Thus, students are the ultimate beneficiaries of the consultant's services, and both the direct and ultimate beneficiaries of collaboration.

Case Example of School-Based Consultation

Consider this example:

You are a school counselor who is asked by a teacher to help him "increase the motivation to learn" of an academically gifted junior who is failing the teacher's chemistry class. You and the teacher discuss in detail his concern. You develop a plan in which you will interview the student about his lack of achievement and report back to the teacher. The teacher agrees to observe the student's behavior in the classroom and search for any possible clues. You both agree to meet during the teacher's planning period to share your experiences and develop the next steps.

Commentary

This example is just one of a variety of ways in which school-based human service professionals consult. It is important to remember that all you have read about in this text so far is applicable to school consultation.

As noted above, the underlying premise for school consultation is that, by helping the significant others of students such as teachers and parents make appropriate changes, consultants can contribute to substantive, positive outcomes for students (Gutkin & Curtis, 2009). Through consultation, the consultant has the potential to positively affect more students through intermediaries (i.e., consultees) than would be the case working with individual students. Thus, consultants have the ability to significantly impact the mental health and development of children by improving the skills and knowledge of parents and those professionals who work with children at school.

Case Example of School-Based Collaboration

Now consider this example:

You are a school counselor who asks a teacher to collaborate in order to "increase the motivation to learn" of an academically gifted junior who is failing the teacher's chemistry class. You and the teacher discuss in detail his concern. Together, you develop a plan in which you will interview the student about his lack of achievement and report back to the teacher. The teacher agrees to observe the student's behavior in the classroom and search for any possible clues. You both agree to meet during the teacher's planning period to share your experiences and develop the next steps. After you both engage in these tasks, you develop a plan that allows both of you to take responsibility for some aspect of the case.

Commentary

This example provides a description of the basic rudiments of school-based collaboration. Notice how it differs from the example of SBC in which the teacher took all of the responsibility for the implementation of the plan. School-based collaboration allows for individual expertise to be used in a team situation. It builds relationships for other problem-solving activities such as consultation, maximizes productivity, and requires shared accountability (Mellin, Anderson-Butcher, & Bronstein, 2011; Petri, 2010). Collaboration activities are typified by a cooperative relationship. The activities are cooperative in that the relationship is one among equals, given possible differences in expertise and need, with each partner having different contributions to make (Ysseldyke, Burns, & Rosenfield, 2009). The activities are accomplished through a partnership in that the distribution of labor involved is specified and agreed upon. Collaboration emphasizes shared accountability for outcomes and a shared responsibility for participation and decision making.

Collaboration is particularly appropriate for multidisciplinary team conferences. At these meetings, professionals and sometimes parents attempt to develop an appropriate educational and/or behavioral plan for a student. As early as the mid-1980s, Zins and Curtis (1984) suggested the importance of having all parties at such meetings skilled in consultation to overcome the possible shortcomings of these types of meetings. Collaboration, like an effective team, works best when the leadership of the process is shared over time. School-based counselors and psychologists may well want to consider using collaboration whenever possible (Caplan & Caplan, 1993; Pryzwansky, 2011; Sink, 2011b).

HISTORICAL BACKGROUND

The history of what is now called school-based consultation and collaboration dates back to the 1920s. As early as 1925, school psychologists' functions were described in a way that would today be considered similar to consultation (Bramlett & Murphy, 1998; Merrell, Ervin, & Gimpel, 2006). These included contributing to the study of children with learning problems and developing a mental hygiene program in the school (French, 1990).

But it was during the 1950s that the term *consultation* began to be used regularly as part of the consultant's functioning. Subsequent federal legislation over the decades would provide a strong impetus for the use of consultation in school settings. The 1954 Thayer Conference all but made consultation a part of the school psychologist's role. In the early 1960s, some school psychology researchers (see Lambert, 2000) wrote about school psychology being a suitable profession for the practice of school-based mental health consultation.

Cottingham (1956) was among the first to recognize the need for special assistance for teachers by school-based counselors, which provided the basis for the consultation role in the elementary school. The rationale was that by acting as consultants, school-based human service professionals could assist the school in developing a climate conducive to student growth and development, hence creating an avenue by which all students could be affected. When school-based human service workers delivered only direct services such as individual and group counseling, their impact on the school climate was limited since it was virtually impossible to reach all children in the school (Dinkmeyer & Carlson, 1973).

Impetus for consulting with parents came from the work of Faust (1968), who noted that students' relationships with their parents could affect their learning ability at school. Therefore, Faust (1968) strongly advocated consulting with parents but cautioned school personnel against using the "brush fire" (p. 86) approach in dealing with crises that teachers and administrators have with parents. He advocated the idea of parent training groups as well as consulting with parents about their individual children. Faust (1968), however, gave priority to consulting with school personnel such as teachers and administrators over consulting with parents. Because of efficiency, he suggested that the most

important form of consulting was with groups of teachers, not only with regard to student behavior but also concerning curriculum development and classroom activities. Faust was also one of the first to call for counselors to engage in in-service programs for school personnel. For the school counseling profession, there was some initial resistance to consultation as some writers thought that it would take away from the school counselor's time with students (Myrick, 2003).

In 1966, a report by the Joint Committee on the Elementary School Counselor (ACES/ASCA, 1966) made consulting an official role for school counselors along with counseling and coordination. The literature on consultation for school counselors was very limited at this time. Kahnweiler (1979) reported locating 12 articles on consultation in counseling journals written between 1964 and 1968. By 1972, however, there had been articles published for counselors on topics such as Adlerian consultation, behavioral consultation, in-service programs for teachers, and parent consultation.

Fullmer and Bernard (1972) and Dinkmeyer and Caldwell (1970) also advocated the role of school consultant as one who could provide in-service education to teachers on open communication and the wise use of tests, as well as on assisting work groups. Fullmer and Bernard were among the first to note that when consultation is successful, the consultant is made obsolete while at the same time increasing the long-term possibilities of the enhancement of the consultation role. These authors strongly advocated the use of group consultation.

Dinkmeyer and Carlson's (1973) text *Consulting: Facilitating Human Potential and Change Processes* advocated that school consultants be active change agents for improving the organizational climate of the school, thus expanding the concept of school consultant to include organizational consultation.

In 1975, the passage of Public Law 94-142 supported the use of consultation by school-based consultants regarding students with special needs. Subsequent federal and state legislation supported the use of consultation and collaboration as a viable method of indirect service in the schools. Hence, consultation was to be an effective way to assist regular education teacher with children who had special needs (Martens & Ardion, 2002). The 1990s and the first decade of the new millennium saw increased attention to collaboration an important service. The IDEA and NCLB legislations impacted special and regular education in ways that fostered consultation and collaboration on school-based professionals. Today, consultation and collaboration are important services provided by school-based consultants, even though questions remain about how well they are trained to deliver these services (Newman, 2012). As American society becomes even more culturally diverse, social and economic problems remain, and federal and state legislation affecting the expectations of schools continues, the demand for these services in the school will increase even more.

CONSULTING AND COLLABORATING WITH SCHOOL ADMINISTRATORS

A school's leadership is a powerful force in determining the extent to which consultation and collaboration are considered acceptable services (Bryan & Griffin, 2010; Raforth & Foriska, 2006). Therefore, it is important that school psychologists and school counselors not only inform administrators about, but actually engage them, in these services (Paisley & Milsom, 2007; Ysseldyke et al., 2009). Consultants will want to remember that administrator support and acceptance of programs is essential for change to occur (Knotek, 2012; McDougal, Clonan, & Martens, 2000; Meyers, Proctor, Graybill, & Meyers, 2009). Administrators have priorities and pressures for which they may actively seek consultation or collaboration (Dahir & Stone, 2012; Hughes, 2000); for example, system-level changes like implementing a school-wide positive behavioral support (PBS) program (McKevitt & Braaksma, 2008). In another example, administrators may seek consultation and collaboration services in

assessing the readiness for, and subsequently implementing, school-wide preventions programs such as those related to positive student behavior and academic achievement as well as forging partnerships between the school, community agencies, and parents.

School-based consultants can consult with school administrators in a variety of ways. They frequently meet with principals to discuss particular children that have come to the principal's attention. For example, a consultant may use a client-centered case approach with a principal who is trying to decide whether or not to suspend a student from school. A consultant may use a consultee-centered consultation by assisting an administrator to reconceptualize an issue and plan accordingly (Calderon, Subotnik, Knotek, Rayhack, & Gorgia, 2007). For example, a consultant could facilitate awareness in the school administrators of the benefits of engaging community partners in school improvement programs that look to alter academic and nonacademic barriers to school success through capacity-building innovations (Anderson-Butcher et al., 2010; Bryan & Griffin, 2010). Examples of innovations reported by these authors include: expanded use of multiple data sources; the development of new and expanded family and community partnerships; development of enhanced systems and structures; and enriched program and service delivery. Consultants support these innovations through technical assistance, facilitation, professional development, and ongoing support for initiatives such as revising roles and responsibilities of personnel.

Principals often request consultation regarding programs that operate in the school (Jacob & Hartshorne, 2007; Van Velsor, 2009) like playground practices and behavioral discipline (Doll & Cummings, 2008). In one additional example, a school-based consultant using consultee-centered administrative consultation facilitates increased awareness in a school administrator about how school policies have the potential to block systemic change initiatives (Sander, Sharkey, Olivarri, Tanigawa, & Mauseth, 2010). In one further example, school consultants may be asked to evaluate their own in-school consultation programs or programs that involve cultural diversity (Pena, 1996), school reform (Colbert, Vernon-Jones, & Pransky, 2006), institutionalize classroom-based group interventions (Robinson & Elias, 1993), gifted education (Calderon et al., 2007), and systemic change (Adelman & Taylor, 2007, 2008; Anderson-Butcher et al., 2010; Moe & Perera-Diltz, 2009).

Other topics for which administrators seek consultation include: school violence, substance abuse programs, positive behavioral interventions and support, RTI, high-stakes testing, data-based decision making, professional development, planning for crisis situations, and professional competence issues (Blader & Gallagher, 2001; Jacob & Hartshorne, 2007; Ysseldyke et al., 2009). Administrators typically are concerned about the potential for disruptive behavior. As a result, they frequently seek consultation on ways to manage behavior at the school, classroom, and individual levels (Luiselli, 2002; Sugai et al., 2000). In these cases, consultants may have to assist administrators in developing programs that deal possible stereotypes of certain groups of students like adjudicated youth (Sander et al., 2010). When consulting with administrators about programs, consultants will want to ensure that the following factors are addressed: how the program will be introduced; how stakeholders will be engaged; how previous research affects program implementation; and program resources will be prioritized (Rotheram-Borus, Bickford, & Milburn, 2001). Furthermore, school-based professionals will want to work closely with administrators in incorporating primary prevention programs into the school setting; for example, prereferral intervention teams and problem-solving teams (Bahr & Kovaleski, 2006; Raforth & Foriska, 2006) or in working to prevent school violence (Larson, 2008). Principals frequently request school consultants to co-consult with external consultants when human services are the focus of the external consultants' assistance. Such collaboration can enhance the effectiveness of the external consultants' services. As in other contexts, when human service professionals collaborate with administrators, they take on responsibility for some of the outcome.

There is a move toward increased organization development consultation on the part of school-based consultants (Dougherty & Dougherty, 1991; Meyers, Meyers, Graybill, Proctor, & Huddleston, 2012; Meyers et al., 2009) because school administrators increasingly want assistance with goals that involve the entire school (Anderson-Butcher, Lawson, Iachini, Bean, Flaspohler, & Zullig, 2010). Since case consultation and program consultation are covered elsewhere in this text, I will focus here on organization development consultation.

School Consultation and Organization Development Change

Schools, with increased forces—internal and external—requiring organizational-level change, are increasingly looking to consultation and collaboration services as tools to accomplish these necessary and challenging changes (Cowan, 2007; Flaspohler, 2007; Hazel, 2007; Meyers et al., 2012). There is increased focus on organizational consultation in schools, including programs, groups of consultees, entire schools, and even school districts (D'Amato, Zafiris, McConnell, & Dean, 2011; Merrell et al., 2006; Zins & Erchul, 2002). The main idea is that by making the school more effective as an organization in some way, the student population of the school (and other members of the school) will be positively affected.

Organizational development consultation is a specialized from of organization consultation that involves a series of planned and sustained efforts to apply the principles of behavioral science to improve the functioning of the school. Consultation from an organization development perspective, as its name implies, is not an event of itself but a process of changing the system (Cummings & Worley, 2009; Racine Gilles, Kratochwill, Felt, Schienebeck, & Vaccarello, 2011). There is some empirical evidence to support its use in schools (Conoley, Conoley, & Reese, 2009; Meyers et al., 2009; Racine Gilles et al., 2011). School counselors and school psychologists are being called upon to assist in implementing system-wide programs related to school reform that are driven by their central offices (Colbert et al., 2006; Knoff, 2008; Paisley & Milsom, 2007) and engage in consultation regarding the development of crisis intervention teams for responses to issues like school violence (Bramlett, Murphy, Johnson, & Wallingsford, 2002; Gutkin & Curtis, 2009), the implementation of positive psychology into the mainstream of the school (Akin-Little, Little & Delligatti, 2004), instructional consultation (IC) (Knotek, 2012), the creation of a safe school climate for all students (Sherblom & Bahr, 2008), and the development of needs assessment procedures for determining where changes are needed (Nagle & Gagnon, 2008). These initiatives can include developing a collaboration program in each school, building assistance teams, determining the necessary processes for systems monitoring, assisting with strategic plans (Adelman & Taylor, 2007, 2008), and providing ongoing staff development. Three examples of current popular programs whose implementation could greatly benefit from consultation with an organizational development perspective include RTI, PBS, and the advancement of evidence-based interventions (EBI) (Racine Gilles et al., 2011). The goal is ongoing school renewal through the creation of a culture of change, teacher professionalism, and high expectations (Raforth & Foriska, 2006). As you can imagine, this type of consultation can be challenging to pull off due to the challenges of coordinating efforts in complex organizations such as schools (Moe & Perera-Diltz, 2009; Racine Gilles et al., 2011).

The impetus for consultation from an organization development perspective in the schools has come from the school reform movement (Curtis, Castillo, & Cohen, 2008), a renewed emphasis on public health principles in mental health (Hazel, 2007), and the realization that often what appears to be a child-focused problem is merely a symptom of a building or systems problem (Knoff, 2008). Merrell et al. (2006) and Greenberg et al. (2003) note issues that have an impact that necessitates organizational-level change: preparing for an increasingly diverse student population; advances in technology; and the increasing severity and complexity of student needs. This approach appreciates and uses the unique characteristics of the school in the change process (Curtis et al., 2008). In spite of the recent attention organization development has been receiving, its application to schools is not new (see, e.g., Illback & Zins, 1993; Meyers et al., 2009, 2012).

Organization development is a systematic process, using the principles and methods of behavioral science, to increase the effectiveness of organizations, such as a school (Harris, 2007). Increasingly, consultation from an organization development perspective in the schools is taking on an ecological perspective (Meyers et al., 2012). The change that is targeted must reflect the complexity of the school that is being changed (Zins & Illback, 1995).

Organization development as it relates to consultation usually starts with the administrator of the school who involves the school-based consultant and other professionals in the change process (Meyers et al., 2009). Such consultation is a way of making carefully planned, predictable changes in the school (Elliott & Busse, 1993). Its goal is to enhance the school's effectiveness by helping school personnel understand and effectively act on problems and move toward self-renewal.

This type of consultation can be long-term, lasting for several years. As a result, it can be quite time consuming (Larney, 2003). On the other hand, targeted change for a school may simply involve the implementation of a single program and not take a long time (Meyers et al., 2009). One of the first steps in using organization development in consultation is to train the stakeholders and gatekeepers in problem solving (Curtis et al., 2008; Knoff, 2008).

Examples of areas which could benefit from this type of consultation include developing a team to enhance school climate, creating a task force to creating and promoting effective problem-solving teams (Raforth & Foriska, 2006), IC (Knotek, 2012), and sustaining innovations (Adelman & Taylor, 2003, 2007).

When school-based consultants use an organization development approach, they generally adopt the systems approach, which allows them to observe and intervene in the school's subsystems (Curtis et al., 2008). For example, there may be a rift between teachers (the technological subsystem) and counselors (the supportive subsystem) concerning "pulling out" students for counseling services during class time. Consultation of this type attempts to help these subsystems function more smoothly together by promoting a culture that fosters collaboration and strong working relationships among stakeholders (Racine Gilles et al., 2011). This view keeps in mind the school's ability to manage change and differences among cultural groups (Harris, 2007). For example, if the cultural diversity of a school's student body is increasing, the school-based consultant may be placed in charge of a school-wide program to accommodate this change. Finally, consultation looks to the satisfaction of school personnel, since satisfied workers are productive workers. The school-based consultant operating from this perspective might well monitor the school's morale, climate, and multitiered intervention programs as indicators of whether change is necessary.

Consultation from an organization development view follows the steps presented in the generic model in Chapters 3 through 7, and its primary interventions include process observation and feedback, training, and survey feedback. The typical targets are the school's structure (e.g., policies), processes (e.g., ways of planning), behavior (e.g., roles of personnel), and capacity building (Nastasi, 2004). In another example, school-based consultants can assist their organizations to deal with unintended outcomes of school reform and high-stakes testing, such as focusing the curriculum exclusively on tested subjects and dealing with repeated poor performance on the part of many students (Braden & Tayrose, 2008). School-based consultants typically ensure that programs related to organizational change are acceptable to stakeholders so that they can be more effectively institutionalized (McDougal et al., 2000). When human service/mental health professionals collaborate from an organization development framework, they take on responsibility for some aspect of the outcome.

A Brief Example of Organization Development Consultation. Wes is a school-based consultant with training in organization development. His school is rapidly undergoing changes in the cultural diversity of its student body, for which his principal has asked for assistance in developing a plan to help the school adjust. Wes begins by assessing the degree to which the school is adjusting to the change and compares his findings with the desired state of affairs. He surveys the staff and conducts structured interviews with randomly selected teachers and support personnel.

Wes draws two conclusions as a result: The entire school staff is not well trained in multicultural education and has unrealistic fears of increased violence and vandalism at the school.

Wes creates and submits to the principal a plan involving an in-service program on multicultural education, visitations by staff to schools experiencing cultural diversity, and the development of a special committee to develop ongoing plans for adjustment and monitoring progress.

CONSULTING AND COLLABORATING WITH TEACHERS

Consultation and collaboration are effective tools for assisting teachers to solve current problems and prevent future ones (Cook & Friend, 2010; Dahir & Stone, 2012). Teachers typically receive consultation regarding the academic, behavioral, and social-emotional behavior of students (Tysinger, Tysinger, & Diamanduros, 2009). In SBC, consultants "… work strategically to address both student presenting issues and consultee behavior and cognition" (Truscott & Albritton, 2011, p. 170).

Interest on the part of teachers in consultation and collaboration depends on many factors. Traditionally, school counselors and psychologists have worked with teachers to establish interventions in the regular classroom as a way to reduce special education placements (Kratochwill, 2008). These efforts have led to increased consultation and collaboration activities with personnel such as special education teachers, teachers of children with behavioral disorders, and teachers in charge of programs for preschool children. School-based consultants have assisted teachers with both academically and behaviorally challenged children as well as those with less severe concerns. More recently, school psychologists and counselors have engaged in collaboration with teachers as a method of providing service to students and their families. Hughes (2000) points to the bottom line for teachers in need of consultation: "Teachers typically have a student in their classroom for a limited period of time and are interested in interventions that offer quick results. Teachers are also interested in decreasing behaviors that interfere with smooth functioning of the classroom and that they experience as personally stressful" (p. 323).

School consultation and collaboration can be effective and efficient ways to help teachers enhance their professional skills and to generalize the effects of psychoeducational interventions (Caplan & Caplan, 1993). Consultants can use social dynamic information to support the direct interventions of teachers; for example, in determining how the peer group and the classroom support undesirable behavior (Farmer, 2000). Consultation has benefited teachers in a variety of areas, such as conducting effective parent conferences, managing student behavior, choosing instructional methodologies, and meeting the unique needs of children of military personnel.

The nature of the consultation relationship and its influence on the teacher determine whether or not the teacher is going to follow through with the consultant's recommendations and implement the interventions (Hagermoser Sanetti & Kratochwill, 2009; Sheridan et al., 2009). Interventions should be as teacher-friendly as possible (Theodore et al., 2009). The bottom line is that teacher expectations for consultation have become the ultimate criterion for consultation success (Tysinger et al., 2009). There is some evidence that the number of teachers who are willing to engage is increased by: the consultant being based in the school; consultation

services being offered rather than waiting for requests; the teachers perceiving that the consultant has excellent problem-solving skills; and the teachers perceiving that they themselves have good problem-solving skills (Stenger, Tollefson, & Fine, 1992). School-based consultants should be viewed as assessable and informed by teachers who are potential consultees. This can be accomplished through actions such as using technology to promote consultation/collaboration services and for teachers to make contact and being part of the social mainstream of the school (Dahir & Stone, 2012). Part of that availability means providing ongoing brief consultation sessions on the phone, via email, or in the hall (Roach, Kratochwill, & Frank, 2009).

Consultants may need to dedicate time to training teachers to effectively implement interventions (Hershfeldt, Pell, Sechrest, Pas, & Bradshaw, 2012; Martens & DiGennaro, 2008; Watson & Sterling-Turner, 2008). Consulting with high school teachers may vary from that with elementary teachers (Gray, Gutkin, & Riley, 2001). Because high school students have more than one teacher a day, consultants at this level are more likely to engage in group consultation.

One way to conceptualize school-based interventions is through a matrix of change agents and intervention categories (Lentz, Allen, & Erhardt, 1996). Change agents include students themselves, peers, the home, the teacher, and other school adults. The general category of intervention includes: contingency-based (e.g., praise after task completion); antecedent-based (e.g., changing prompts); teaching academic skills; teaching learning strategies; teaching appropriate social behaviors; and teaching coping or problem-solving strategies (e.g., personal problem-solving strategies).

On the other hand, in collaboration, in which most parties are providing direct service and have responsibility for part of the outcome, the issue becomes getting everyone "on board" with what needs to happen and time factors (Burns, Wiley, & Viglietta, 2008). In one model of collaboration called the *inclusion* model, school counselors actually carry out their direct service in the teacher's classroom (Clark & Breman, 2009). The teacher is also responsible for some aspects of any interventions. This model allows for ease of collaboration and is alternative to the traditional pullout model, which is increasingly being challenged by the time constraints imposed by the high-stakes accountability schools are now facing.

There are a variety of models from which school consultants and their consultees can choose. Popular models such as education/training consultation, behavioral consultation, and mental health consultation have already been discussed elsewhere in this text. I have chosen two other models that are popular in school consultation to discuss in this chapter: Adlerian consultation (Dinkmeyer, 2006; Dinkmeyer & Carlson, 1973; Dinkmeyer, Pew, & Dinkmeyer, 1979) and IC (Pryzwansky, 2011; Rosenfield, 2008).

Adlerian Consultation

Adlerian consultation with teachers is based on the works of Alfred Adler's individual psychology (Brigman & Webb, 2008; Carlson et al., 2008). The major proponents of Adlerian consultation in schools have been Don Dinkmeyer, Jon Carlson, and their colleagues. This discussion is based on writings by Carlson, Watts, and Maniacci (2006), Dinkmeyer (2006), Dinkmeyer and Carlson (2001), and Kottman (1995). Adlerian school consultation is based on several assumptions:

- Teachers cannot take responsibility for student behavior.

- Teachers should be more involved with encouragement than with praise.

- Teachers cannot always prevent failure on the part of students.

- Teachers need to try to meet the affective as well as the cognitive needs of students more effectively.

- The consultant talks directly to the teacher about their problem with the child as opposed to talking about the child exclusively.

- The consultee is to learn new skills to facilitate change.

Case Consultation.   How consultation proceeds with an individual teacher depends on his or her perceived needs, but usually a collaborative mode is employed (Brigman & Webb, 2008; Carlson et al., 2006, 2008). The Adlerian approach does not employ a traditional diagnostic-prescriptive-remedial model but a more collaborative model that maximizes the consultee as a resource for determining how consultation should proceed (Brigman & Webb, 2008). In case consultations, Adlerian consultants frequently use a detailed referral form, which the teacher fills out prior to the first consultation session and which provides the consultation a beginning point. In addition to using the referral form, the consultant asks the teacher to tell his or her story in such a way that the dynamics of the teacher–student relationship are evident (Dinkmeyer, 2006; Kottman, 1995). As the teacher relates his or her beliefs about the child's behavior, the consultant tunes into the teacher's feelings so as to further understand the possible goal of the student's behavior (Carlson et al., 2008).

The consultant may also observe the child in the teacher's classroom. The consultant and teacher then make a tentative hypothesis about the goal of the child's behavior and discuss possible alternatives from which the teacher may choose (Brigman & Webb, 2008). The alternatives are based on the realization that to change the student's behavior, the teacher must change his or her own behavior first. A recent trend in Adlerian consultation involves the use of narratives and anecdotes to assist with the consultation process (Mortola & Carlson, 2003). Advice-giving is avoided and is replaced by a process that integrates new skills with the consultee's belief system.

Adlerian consultation follows the following steps (Carlson et al., 2006, pp. 253–254):

1. Establish the tone.

2. Get a specific description of the problem.

3. Get a second specific example and clarify the goal of misbehavior and the teacher's troubling belief.

4. Review the guidelines for reaching the goal.

5. Solicit tentative solutions.

6. Attain closure.

A Brief Example of Adlerian Case Consultation.
Alfred, a school-based consultant, is working with Howard, a middle school teacher who has voluntarily sought out consultation regarding a seventh-grader who seems to be rapidly becoming the class clown. Howard has completed and submitted the referral form. Alfred establishes rapport with Howard and together they get specific examples of the student's behavior and then determine Howard's feelings and reactions to the behavior. Howard reports that he is mostly annoyed because constantly reprimanding the boy gets in the way of his teaching the class. The consultant observes the student in class and conducts a diagnostic interview with him. In the meantime, Howard is keeping a record of the boy's acting-out behavior.

Alfred and Howard then hold a planning session and determine that the boy's primary goal is attention. They develop a plan in which Howard changes how he responds to the student.

Alfred agrees to follow up with Howard within a week.

C-Group. Consultants often work with teachers in groups (Carlson et al., 2008). The C-group is a group Adlerian consultation method so named because each of the forces operant in the group begins with the letter C. These forces include consultation, collaboration, clarification, confrontation, cohesion, commitment, changes, concern, caring, confidentiality, and communication (Dinkmeyer & Carlson, 2001). The C-group is an alternative to traditional staff development training in which ideas about behavior are disseminated. The group is both didactic and experiential.

The typical group consists of four to six teachers and the consultant. It meets once a week for about an hour and has a life of about six to eight sessions. It is based on the rationale that most problems are interpersonal in nature, classroom, and

otherwise, and that these problems are best solved in an open, safe group setting. Teachers present problems they are having with individual students and the group discusses them.

The purposes of the consultation group are to help teachers understand patterns of student behaviors and ways to improve those patterns, as well as to provide teachers with an arena in which they can openly communicate, understand the practical application of Adlerian ideas about human behavior, and experience the rewards of group learning.

Outcomes for teachers include the satisfaction of sharing similar concerns, acquiring more effective ways of dealing with student misbehavior, understanding their interpersonal relations better, and learning about how to lead classroom discussions concerning affective topics.

A Brief Example of a C-Group. Loretta is a school consultant leading a C-group for a group of six elementary school teachers. The first meeting has all of the teachers sharing something about themselves with Loretta pointing out similarities in their concerns and building rapport among the teachers. In subsequent meetings, Loretta shares Adler's ideas on the purposive nature of human behavior, which gives the group a common ground for approaching their concerns. She also encourages the members to share anecdotes and helps them identify and share their feelings as they relate to such anecdotes. The concept of discouragement is discussed as well as practical methods of working with misbehavior. Loretta maintains control over the group's process by keeping it focused and encourages the teachers to help one another with their concerns about students. During the group meeting, Loretta passes out a variety of handouts on Adler's ideas on children. The group then applies this information to the children they are seeking to help.

Instructional Consultation

Instructional consultation (IC) (Lopez & Truesdell, 2007; Pryzwansky, 2011; Rosenfield, 1987, 1992, 2004, 2008) is an important model for helping teachers modify their instructional behavior and more effectively create a learning environment for students. Rosenfield (2008, p. 1655) defines IC as an "... early intervention, stage-based problem-solving process based on consultee-centered consultation principles. The purpose is to enhance teacher capacity to use data-based decision making and evidenced-based interventions to address student academic and behavioral concerns in the classroom." IC frequently involves modifying the teacher' beliefs and understanding about the student and situation (Benn, Jones, & Rosenfield, 2008) and also deals with ecological and person-centered variables (Rosenfield, 2008). The goal of IC is to increase student and staff performance regarding student academic and behavioral issues (McKenna, Rosenfield, & Gravois, 2009). Gravois and Rosenfield (2006, p. 45) note: "The model is based on the premise that quality instructional and management programming, matched to a student's assessed entry skills, increases student success, reduces behavioral difficulties, and avoids the need for special education evaluation and placement." Consultation can be provided by an individual consultant or interdisciplinary school-wide team (Racine Gilles et al., 2011).

IC, mental health consultation, and behavioral consultation all have some basic common elements (Rosenfield, 2002, 2004, 2008). As a form of consultee-centered consultation, the success of IC is dependent on the quality of the consultant–consultee relationship and the degree to which suggested interventions are carried out and followed up. An ecological approach is taken rather than exclusively looking at a problem strictly inside of the student. Three ecological components make up the instructional triangle and are assessed: (a) current competencies and skill sets of the student; (b) the tasks expected to be accomplished by the student; and (c) the teacher's management and instructional behavior (Racine Gilles et al., 2011).

IC is a collaborative process in which a problem is identified and interventions are selected and made (Tysinger et al., 2009). Since the planned

interventions typically require that the consultee change his or her instructional style, a strong consultant–consultee relationship based on trust and mutual sharing is essential. A strong focus is placed on defining the problem in specific, measurable terms, and decisions are data driven (Wizda, 2004).

The most common roles of the instructional consultant appear to be those of collaborator and educational trainer but may also include being an advocate for a particular instructional technique or service for a given student. The consultant often functions as a fact finder and observes and collects data to define the problem more clearly. The consultant may assess the student's learning, the teacher's instructional style, and the teaching–learning process. The consultant attempts to collaborate whenever possible but is obviously an expert as far as instructional improvement goes.

Prior to accepting consultees, the consultant suggests a referral process within the school. With the process in place, teachers will be informed of the nature of consultation and its collaborative intent and nonsupervisory nature. They will also understand that they are in control of how the problems presented will be solved and that the consultant will function as a resource person. The consultant clearly informs the consultee about the consultation process and its potential benefits. The consultee needs to enter the consultation relationship with an expectation of success, a nondefensive attitude, the motivation to discuss the problem situation openly, and a willingness to make changes. It is helpful if the consultee is knowledgeable about or willing to be trained in problem-solving strategies.

The consultation procedure includes the following steps: contracting, problem identification, intervention and planning design, implementation, evaluation, and follow-up (McKenna et al., 2009; Rosenfield, 2008).

The problem is identified in terms of the student behaviors that concern the teacher and the learning environment in which the student resides. Clarifying the problem at this stage requires strong communication skills from consultant and consultee. This stage often ends with a reconceptualization of the problem that focuses on the problem as the result of the interaction of instruction, the learning task, and student skills rather than merely as a deficit in the student (Knotek, Rosenfield, Gravois, & Babinski, 2003). From a multicultural perspective, reconceptualization can occur relative to the influence of cultural differences on student learning, the cultural sensitivity of classroom management practices, and views of the academic progress of diverse students (Ingraham, 2008; Lopez & Truesdell, 2007). In addition, the problem is often conceptualized as an instructional mismatch rather than an internal deficit in the student.

The consultant often learns the teacher's instructional goals and plans prior to making objective and systematic observations of the student and the learning environment as a step in problem identification. The consultant's findings are discussed soon after the observation. Data collection and interpretation often lead to a reconceptualization of the data.

As the assessment of the problem is curriculum based, the consultant must understand the scope and sequence of the material as well as the teacher's attitudes about the curriculum. For example, is the teacher being driven to complete the coverage of certain material at the expense of mastery by the student? This assessment provides a basis for planning intervention strategies.

The consultant and teacher refine the problem, discuss alternatives, and brainstorm possible interventions that will improve the management of the student (e.g., time on task) and the management of learning (e.g., instructional style). From the list of available strategies, the teacher selects ones that are feasible from the point of view of time, resources, and classroom structure.

As these strategies are put into place, the consultant monitors the process on a regular basis and helps make modifications as necessary. Based on the results, the consultant and consultee will then terminate the relationship. The consultant typically makes and submits a complete write-up of the consultation experience.

Knotek, Babinski, and Rogers (2002) summarize IC by noting that the "… traits of reframing the etiology of the problem, the collection of data to confirm or disconfirm ideas, the iterative brainstorming, and the generation of alternative hypotheses, resulted in a process of orderly reflection that supported the construction of new understandings of and approaches to the workplace problem" (p. 325).

Recent developments in this model include the concept of IC teams and ecological perspectives (Gravois, Groff, & Rosenfield, 2009; Gravois & Rosenfield, 2006; Rosenfield, 2002, 2008). Like any other innovation, IC teams should be implemented with care by being adapted to local norms (Knotek, 2012). These teams, using a systemic and ecological perspective, can have the impact of changing the school culture to be more accepting of a collaborative, problem-solving focus and can create a shift to arranging systemic variables from a traditional view, which looks for deficits in a given student. IC takes organizational factors like local norms and cultural context into consideration (Knotek, 2012). In this process, individual members of teams consult one-on-one with a teacher rather than having the teacher work with the entire team as a unit (McKenna et al., 2009).

There is a trend in conducting IC with Limited English Proficient (LEP) students and their families by using school interpreters (Lopez, 2000; Lopez & Truesdell, 2007). As diversity increases in the classroom so do the instructional tasks of the teacher (Ingraham, 2007, 2008). The limited research on the use of interpreters in this way suggest that the pace of consultation will be slowed, the accuracy of communication will need to be monitored, and that the use of the interpreter may effect how rapport with the family and student will be developed (Lopez, 2000). IC is also an effective service in targeting English Language Learners' (ELL) language instructional needs in non-bilingual settings as the consultant can provide background materials, modeling, and intervention scripts (Lopez, 2006).

Lopez and Truesdell (2007, p. 79) list important aspects of multicultural IC:

- the relationship between the consultee's and students' cultural backgrounds as they relate to classroom expectations
- expectations of parents relative to the focus of consultation
- issues related to cross-cultural communication
- mutual determined agreement on the nature of collaborative efforts within consultation
- cultural responsive during consultation
- impact of system-wide factors on student needs

Another trend in IC is the use of curriculum-based assessment (CBA) (Burns, 2004; Wizda, 2004). CBA is a method that, in a systematic way, analyzes the instructional needs of a student and then designs instruction for optimal achievement (Burns, 2004; Gravois & Gickling, 2008). The idea is that academic problems are viewed as a mismatch between student skill level and how and/or what the student is being taught. Assessment is used repeatedly to help determine what and/or how the student should be taught (Gravois & Gickling, 2008) and a scale has been designed to assess the treatment integrity of IC and is promising (McKenna et al., 2009). The referring teacher's skills are developed so that they can be used effectively with similar students in the future (Wizda, 2004). One other recent development is that the language used in IC has moved to the forefront and the actual words used in the consultation relationship are considered to be the subject of study in IC in order to maximize the effectiveness of consultation (Rosenfield, 2004). Consultants may need to instruct teachers in assessment techniques as well as behaviorally oriented instructional strategies (Begeny, 2006).

A Brief Example of Instructional Consultation[1]. Wilma is a fourth-grade teacher, who has recently had a new student, Maria, enter her room from another school district. School records indicated that her attendance over the past three years had been erratic. Wilma had placed Maria in the slower reading group. Maria is a quiet, unassuming child who appears to listen to directions in class but has not been able to complete classroom work assigned to her, especially in reading. She stays at her seat for about five minutes during independent work time and then begins to move around the room. Because Wilma has had such a small amount of written work from Maria, she has little information to help her discover Maria's reading level, and there are no test scores in her school records to indicate past in-situational evaluations. Wilma feels this child would be better served by more individual attention and that she should be removed from her classroom for at least a part of the day for special services. Wilma has no assistant and states that she cannot slow the progress of the class for this one student.

Wilma came to the first meeting with the consultant convinced that moving the child from the classroom was the best option. After listening carefully to Wilma's explanation of the problem, the consultant presented the advantages of working together to identify specific areas of concern in Maria's academic performance.

Although Wilma was still unsure she could comfortably commit the extra time needed to help Maria, she was willing to work with the consultant to define Maria's reading problem more fully. Wilma and the consultant agreed to two classroom visits for the consultant and a follow-up meeting. The observations were planned to systematically assess Maria's reading performance level as well as her interactive patterns with the teacher, other students, and the classroom environment as a whole. The consultant and teacher discussed the instruction that would be taking place on observation days and the objectives Wilma planned to achieve. The consultant planned to review the scope and sequence expectations of fourth-grade reading materials so that she could more adequately determine Maria's instructional level.

After the classroom observations, the consultant and Wilma discussed what the consultant had learned from observing Maria, the classroom environment, Wilma's relationship with Maria, and the

---

[1]The author would like to thank Carole Williford for this case study.

performance of the other children with respect to Maria. From this information, they refined the instructional problem to be addressed. The consultant agreed to assess Maria's current reading instructional level formally, and permission forms for this were sent to Maria's parents.

Once these data were collected, Wilma and the consultant met once more to determine how best to meet Maria's reading needs. They brainstormed potential approaches—from peer teaching to classroom volunteer parents—and Wilma chose the best alternative. They plan step-by-step intervention strategies and agree to talk by phone weekly to make any needed modifications in the interventions. Once Wilma is satisfied with Maria's progress, they will agree to terminate. The consultant will document the consultation through a written report to the teacher, and the school and consultation will end.

A Final Note on Consultation with Teachers. There is, in my opinion, a bottom line for effectively consulting with teachers. When consultants work with teachers, it is very important that teachers do not view consultation as a process with the following underlying message: How can I (the consultant) help you do your job better without my having to do anything myself? For consultation with teachers to be effective, teachers need to perceive the consultation process as an enterprise with an equitable workload distribution that requires minimal time, all the while being optimally helpful. Further, it is critical that teachers perceive that their input into the problem-solving process is valued. As you might guess, collaboration may well often be the service of choice for work with teachers. For example, school-based counselors and psychologists might well recommend collaboration when dealing with teachers on students' homework completion issues (Margolis, McCabe, & Alber, 2004). That said, I also agree with Erchul et al. (2009) that (1) different actions are called for both consultant and teacher at different points in the process, and (2) an understanding of both the teacher's point of view of the problem at the outset and the use of

consultant influence later on to ensure treatment acceptability and treatment integrity may be very important.

CONSULTING AND COLLABORATING WITH PARENTS/GUARDIANS/ EXTENDED FAMILIES

Please note that in this chapter when I use the term *parent*, I include the terms *single parent*, *guardian*, and *extended families* to enhance readability. That said, much of the literature in consultation and collaboration ignores the importance that caregivers other than parents play in the lives of children.

Consulting and collaborating with parents has received increasing attention (Hughes, Hasbrouck, Serdahl, Heidgerken, & McHaney, 2001; Reschly & Christenson, 2012). School-based consultants will want to make sure that all parents are aware of consultation and collaboration services and feel welcome to use them (Dahir & Stone, 2012). At the same time, school-based consultants may want to redefine their job roles to include more parent consultation and collaboration (Epstein & Van Voorhis, 2010). You may want to review conjoint behavioral consultation (CBC) in the behavioral consultation chapter as it actively involves parents.

Because families influence a student's academic, social, and behavioral competencies, consultation and collaboration with families are essential and has been on the rise (Dahir & Stone, 2012; Manz et al., 2009; Reschly & Christenson, 2012). The need for parental consultation and collaboration has been well stated by Riley (1996): "Thirty years of research make it clear: Parents and families are pivotal to children's learning" (p. 480). The benefits of partnerships between parents and schools, such as those in consultation and collaboration, have been demonstrated time and again (Amatea, Daniels, Bringman, & Vandiver, 2004; Miller & Kraft, 2008; Sheridan & Kratochwill, 2008).

School-based consultation and collaboration can be keys to parent involvement on a broader scale (Finello, 2011). There are great numbers of parents who are confused about their roles and relationships with their children (Kottman, 1995). Changes in many societies have increased the stress levels of parenting significantly. From an ecological perspective, the family and school are both very powerful forces in influencing the learning and development of children. This implies that human service professionals in the schools are expected to have significant contact with parents, largely through consultation and collaboration. For example, school-based consultants can use parent consultation as an adjunct to counseling students (Athanasiou, 2001). Some authors (e.g., Weiss, 1996) suggest that it is best for mental health/ human services professionals to assume that all parents are interested in their child's welfare and try to involve even those who consistently reject invitations for involvement.

Research has shown that parent consultation can be effective in assisting with school-based behavioral and emotional problems of students (Cohen et al., 2006; Golden & Cook, 2010) but research with ethnic minorities is sparse (Guli, 2005). Consultation with parents typically involves a problem-solving process in which the parent is the consultee. Parent consultation usually takes the form of either direct case consultation about a given child but can also involve advocacy consultation (Dahir & Stone, 2009, 2012; Tomes, 2011). See Chapter 10, which is on behavioral consultation, in this text for coverage of CBC (Sheridan & Kratochwill, 2008) that includes consulting with parents as well as educational personnel.

There is no "one" eclectic model of parent consultation or collaboration. As a consultant or collaborator, you need to be aware of the models in the literature and then form your own personal model. These approaches to working with parents look similar, but are different. Sheridan (1993b) points out some of these differences. These approaches vary in terms of the breadth of information provided (with parent education being highest), the depth of skill development (with parent consultation being the highest), the specificity of skill/knowledge imparted (with parent consultation being the highest), and individuality of focus (with parent consultation being the highest).

Due to collaboration's emphasis on mutual accountability for outcomes and the resulting engagement of all of the collaborators, parents may more likely become involved when they are offered this service (Finello, 2011). In this manner, parents become instigators of change rather than the target of change. They have the type of relationship, one of equals, that builds trust. Even if human services professionals are gearing their efforts toward the psychological well-being of the child, it is best to link these efforts to the academic achievement of the child as the academic success of their children is a top priority of parents.

Finally, as school-based professionals know, the diversity of the settings in which children are raised is considerable and varies by race (Carlson, 2006; Holcomb-McCoy, 2009). Consequently, consultants and collaborators will bear in mind that both the culture of the client system and the other participants in the consultation process will influence the events that transpire (Holcomb-McCoy, 2009).

Parent Case Consultation

Parents may seek out consultation for a variety of reasons ranging from concern over their child's moving into or out of the school to worries about their child's academic, emotional, or social behavior. There are many approaches to parent case consultation, among the more popular of which are the Adlerian (Brigman & Webb, 2008; Holcomb-McCoy, 2009; Holcomb-McCoy & Bryan, 2010), behavioral (Kratochwill, 2008), and mental health approaches. Behavioral consultation is the most popular and the behaviorally based CBC (Sheridan, Clarke, Knoche, & Edwards, 2006; Sheridan & Kratochwill, 2008) is rapidly gaining popularity (Guli, 2005; Holcomb-McCoy & Bryan, 2010). There has been some application of family therapy and solutions-based models to parent consultation (Nicoll, 1992; Sommers-Flanagan, 2007). A newer model entitled values-based parent consultation has emerged (Nelson, Amio, Prilleltensky, & Nickels, 2010). This model focuses on power sharing among consultants from the formal sector and parents and community members. Regardless of the model used, a positive consultation experience can promote increased positive involvement by parents in the school life of their child and improve family relationships (Kottman, 1995; Sheridan, 1993b). A rule of thumb is to ensure monitored two-way communication and provide parents with support and viable options for interventions and allow them to select the ones with the highest likelihood of success as they see it. You should note that there is increasing empirical research that supports the efficacy of parent consultation. Buerkle, Whitehouse, and Christenson (2009) point out that consultants can assist schools in developing partnerships with families by ensuring that appropriate procedures and processes such as shared responsibility and parent empowerment are in place for quality parent–school interactions. They can also consult with families about issues of individual students.

A Brief Example of Parent Case Consultation Using a Generic Model.   Sunny is a school consultant who has been approached by a parent named Mardy. Recently tested for the academically gifted program at her school, Mardy's daughter had failed to meet the program's criteria and was concerned that she would lose her friends, many of whom were already in the program. Mardy was worried about how she had taken the news.

Sunny quickly established with Mardy that they would be collaborating. Sunny assessed the parent's feelings about her daughter not being included in the program. Mardy noted that she just didn't meet the program's criteria and that that was okay. Mardy was not disappointed in her child or the school but wanted advice on how to help her daughter deal with this "defeat." Sunny provided Mardy with some information on how children take such setbacks and discussed the family dynamics that had occurred since the child had not made the program.

Mardy confessed that so far her strategy for helping had amounted to reassurance. Sunny and Mardy agreed that Mardy would use active listening with her daughter about the situation.

In addition, Mardy would increase the time spent with her daughter doing special things, like going horseback riding, and would have her daughter invite some of her girlfriends to their house for a stay over. Sunny helped Mardy put all of these activities into a plan and followed up by phone two weeks later to assist her with any loose ends.

Home–School Collaboration

It is important to distinguish parent involvement, which is typically a one-way flow of information from the school to the parent, from home-collaboration, sometimes referred to as home–school partnerships or school–family partnerships, which is a two-way communication effort based on joint efforts to assist the child (Epstein & Van Voorhis, 2010; Miller & Kraft, 2008; Sheridan et al., 2012). Home–school collaboration has taken on a new importance as a result of federal legislation regarding students with disabilities (Cook & Friend, 2010). In spite of the need, parents often have low levels of involvement and collaboration in the schools (Esler, Godber, & Christenson, 2008; Manz et al., 2009). However, school-based professionals such as counselors and psychologists can be an important influence in creating the conditions for home–school collaboration (ASCA, 2005; Bryan & Griffin, 2010; Epstein & Van Voorhis, 2010). For example, family–school teams can be developed to collaborate in enhancing student achievement (Conoley & Conoley, 2010; Nastasi, 2005; Paisley & Milsom, 2007).

From an ecological perspective, it is often helpful to think of the school and parents together rather than only separately (Reschly & Christenson, 2012). The goal is to "… produce positive and productive interactions of home, school, and community to produce the best results for students" (Epstein & Van Voorhis, 2010, p. 2). In home–school collaboration, the goal is to create effective and mutually valued partnerships between school-based professionals and parents to enhance student learning and well-being (Buerkle et al., 2009; Nahari, Martines, & Marquez, 2007; Sheridan et al., 2009). Home–school collaboration involves both supporting parents, including attempts to empower them, as well as gaining parental support for the school's efforts to effectively serve students (Minke & Anderson, 2005; Raines & Dibble, 2011). For example, parent involvement is related to dropout prevention (White & Kelly, 2010). Home–school collaboration is "… the relationship between families and schools where parents and educators work together to promote the academic and social development of children" (Cox, 2005, p. 473). Through culturally competent and individualized collaboration, parents are not on their own, but have the assistance of a trained professional who is willing to partner with and provide assistance to their child (Buerkle et al., 2009). In addition, home–school collaboration allows parents to exercise their roles, rights, and responsibilities related to their child's welfare (Raines & Dibble, 2011).

School personnel can learn detailed information about the child and the family and engage parents in jointly defined goals (Bryan & Griffin, 2010; Finello, 2011). Consequently, the reciprocal influences of home and school on student learning is maximized (Buerkle et al., 2009).

According to Esler et al. (2008), basic considerations in home–school collaboration include:

- a preventive, problem-solving approach
- both educators and families are critical in socializing learners
- broad opportunities for parent participation are essential
- building relationships with parents can take time and effort

In collaborating with parents, school-based professionals will want to ensure that parents are true partners, are viewed as experts on their children, and have responsibility for some of the outcomes related to the shared goals of collaboration and are developed as resources in their child's education (Griffin & Galassi, 2010; Holcomb-McCoy & Bryan, 2010). School-based professionals will take into account language differences when collaborating with parents and ensure that parents are equal partners in collaboration efforts and treated in a culturally sensitive manner (Bryan & Griffin, 2010; Nahari et al., 2007). It is also important to keep a solutions-oriented perspective during collaboration to help the parent remain focused on behavior change.

Barriers and openings to collaboration exist for culturally and linguistically diverse (CLD) families for children classified as special education (Olivos, Gallagher, & Aguilar, 2010) and can exist for students of any classification. Barriers include the fact that the scope of parental collaboration is usually defined by the school without input from parents; the relative isolation in which CLD families live; CLD families may not be considered as equal stakeholders in their child's education; and that educators may not be aware of possible bias they have when dealing with CLD families. Openings include: informal social supports for student and family and the development of parity between the school and the parents.

Recent trends in collaboration with parents include an emphasis on ecological perspectives that underscore the importance of several levels of ecological influence that need to be considered when collaborative efforts to assist students are initiated (Reschly & Christenson, 2012). One important issue that works against parental collaboration is the lack of time available for this activity on the part of parents and school professionals (Manz et al., 2009). There is empirical support that home–school collaboration is effective in positively effecting the social, academic, and behavioral domain of students (Buerkle et al., 2009; Reschly & Christenson, 2012).

A Brief Example of Parent Collaboration.   Kyrie is a school psychologist who is collaborating with a parent, Shameika, regarding her child Al. Shameika has initiated the collaboration due to her concern that Al, a sixth grader, is falling in with a peer group that Shameika believes is inappropriate for Al. Kyrie and Shameika create a collaboration based on shared responsibility with a solution-based focus. Kyrie agrees to invite Al to a group she is forming in which the students discuss interpersonal relationships with their peers. Shameika agrees to work with Al on broadening the number of extracurricular activities in which he engages, thus setting the stage for new and more appropriate peer relationships.

Together they develop a plan along with a timeline. Shameika details for Kyrie some of Al's behaviors at home to assist her in working with Al in the group. Kyrie suggests some ways for Shameika to get Al involved in additional extracurricular activities in ways that Al would feel he had some say. Kyrie gets Al's permission to discuss in general what they talk about in the group. The two adults communicate regularly over the phone on the progress they are making. In time, Al gets involved in extracurricular activities that have more desirable peer groups. The skills he has learned in the group allows him to relate better to his peers. Kyrie and Shameika agree to follow up regularly with each other to monitor Al's progress.

Cross-Cultural Considerations When Working with Parents

By the year 2020, it is estimated that the number of school-age children that will come from minority groups is over 50 percent. Consultants and collaborators will increasingly be called upon to work in culturally diverse situations (Arra, 2010; Dahir & Stone, 2012; Moore-Thomas & Day-Vines, 2010) by addressing the developmental needs of an increasing number of students from culturally diverse backgrounds (Portman, 2009; Simcox, Nuijens, & Lee, 2006; Suarez-Orozco, Onaga, & Lardemelle, 2010). Culture directly influences the family in a significant manner (Ortiz, Flanagan, & Dynda, 2008; Sheridan, 2000). As a result, school counselors and psychologists will want to remember that, with the increasing diversity in many societies, including that of the United States, they will also encounter issues related to cultural and linguistic diversity when working

with parents (Steen & Noguera, 2010; Suarez-Orozco et al., 2010). Clearly, cultural issues can amplify the complexity of consultation and collaboration (Clare, 2009; Minke & Anderson, 2005; Nastasi, 2006; Ramirez & Smith, 2007). For example, consultants will need to remember that some cultural groups view achievement in terms of the individual, while others view it through group cooperation. This difference can impact the way a consultant works with parents about the school-related issues their child is facing (Diller, 2007). At the same time, consultants will want to exercise caution in making any kind of generalizations regarding any characteristics of a given culture. There is diversity within culturally diverse groups (i.e., individual differences) and it needs to be taken into account (Clare, 2009; Nastasi, 2006; Nastasi, Varjas, Bernstein, & Jaysena, 2000; Ramirez & Smith, 2007). For example, variables such as socioeconomic status and geographic location influence and shape a family's values (Ortiz et al., 2008).

Increasing numbers of non–English-speaking families with children, radical changes in the structure of families, and increased number of families in poverty have all led to challenges in creating and maintaining school–family relations, including opportunities for consultation and collaboration (Buerkle et al., 2009). In addition, children today are less likely to reside with both biological parents and this fact varies significantly by race (Carlson, 2006). Many issues are made even more complex due to the relationship between high poverty and lack of parental school involvement (Manz et al., 2009) and a lack of knowledge on the school's part regarding parent priorities (Miller & Kraft, 2008; Tomes, 2011). In one example, Tomes (2011) points out that American Indian families might assign certain family duties to extended family members. Thus, having appreciation for and valuing of cultural differences is essential for culturally responsive practice, as is realizing that there are significant differences among cultures in communication styles (Knotek, 2012; Li & Vazquez-Nuttall, 2009; Lopez & Truesdell, 2007). In addition, as Jeltova and Fish (2005, p. 18) note: "There is now acknowledgement that parents may be biological, adoptive, step, or foster, that they may be single or in a couple, and that they may be married, divorced, widowed, remarried, or in a partnership, gay, straight, or transgender."

So what can consultants and collaborators do to ensure culturally competent practice in cross-cultural situations? There is little research that identifies evidence-based practices for such situations (Carlson, 2006), yet there is some important literature emerging (Buerkle et al., 2009).

Consultants can work to ensure that schools are responsive and attentive to removing any barriers nonmainstream parents encounter in their attempts to obtain a quality education for their children and instead welcome their input and active participation and contributions (Li & Vazquez-Nuttall, 2009). Consultants will also want to involve parents by taking on the collaborative role to tap their knowledge base and expertise on their children as method of consulting with cultural competence (Moore-Thomas & Day-Vines, 2010; Tomes, 2011).

When consulting with parents in cross-cultural situations, consultants will want to consider the impact of culture on children's academic achievement, children's behavior, modes of parental communication and expectations, and the family system itself (Brown, 1997; Minke, 2006; Steen & Noguera, 2010). The impact of culture on variables such as these can be accounted for by doing the following things when consulting (Moseley-Howard, 1995, pp. 343–344):

- Remain aware of the systemic impact upon the child.

- Evaluate the cultural milieu of the child and the degree of acculturation.

- Evaluate strengths of the culture of origin and its adaptive characteristics.

- Focus on development/readiness and all aspects of cognitive style.

- Be aware of characteristics influenced by culture that may have an impact on assessment and intervention results.

Nastasi (2005) suggests that the focus for consultants should be on "… (a) empowering parents to navigate the public education system, (b) effectively integrating cultural considerations into consultation and intervention efforts, and (c) educating both families and school personnel" (pp. 114–115). For example, school-based consultants can assist parents in developing relationships with school personnel who typically come from the mainstream culture. In another example, they can focus on nonmainstream students' strengths, engage in culturally sensitive communication, and demonstrate a culturally sensitive understanding and valuing of parents' coping strategies in activities such as conducting parent support and empowerment groups (Lott, 2003; Lott & Rogers, 2005; Steen & Noguera, 2010).

In addition, there are six dimensions of racial/ethnic variability that consultants should be knowledgeable about: notions of kinship, roles and status, sex-role socialization, language, religion/spirituality, and ethnic identity (Lee, 1995). Lee points out that in their consultative function, school-based professionals can bridge potential gaps between the school and parents through "incorporation of the inherent strengths of families and communities into the educational process" (p. 13) and by promoting the use of cultural diversity as a way to enhance the soundness of the education of students. Lott and Rogers (2005) echo these points. Consultants can use systemic strategies related to promoting collaboration between the school and culturally diverse families such as recommending staff development to increase cultural competency among school staff and facilitating the creation of parent support groups (Li & Vazquez-Nuttall, 2009). In addition, consultants can help parents more effectively take on the role of advocacy as it relates to getting their children appropriate services (Sander et al., 2010).

Holcomb-McCoy (2009) and Holcomb-McCoy and Bryan (2010) discuss an emerging framework for parent consultation that involves advocacy and empowerment that leads to a more supportive, culturally responsive climate at school. Consultation in this form considers and deals with any existing cultural differences and acknowledges the interdependence of parents and their environmental contexts. Holcomb-McCoy and Bryan (2010, p. 262) note: "that any attempt to understand and assist consultees and clients with culturally diverse and historically oppressed backgrounds necessitates an understanding of societal issues that the consultee and client face every day. In relation to this environmental aspect of consultation, it becomes critical for consultants to understand how parents of varying cultural backgrounds may approach and perceive the consultation process." Holcomb-McCoy and Bryan posit that empowerment and advocacy may well often be called for in the parent consultation process. Consultants can empower parents by:

- acknowledging the power difference between the consultant and the consultee;

- purposefully minimizing the use of their expert role;

- ensuring that the consultee is a co-expert in the consultation process;

- engaging parents in examining how their group membership has impacted their life situation (e.g., sociocultural factors and oppression); and

- assisting parents to build upon their strengths and, as a result, develop the knowledge base, skill sets, and personal power to recognize and deal with their problems.

Advocacy in consultation can be accomplished by helping parents to raise important issues, actively engage other stakeholders, and challenge the status quo.

The interested reader is referred to the following articles on the best practices for considering cultural factors in working with nonmainstream families: general considerations (Lott & Rogers, 2005); gay, lesbian, bisexual, and transgender families (Jeltova & Fish, 2005); families in poverty (Guishard et al., 2005); African American parents (Griffin, 2011; Koonce & Harper, 2005); bilingual families (Ochoa & Rhodes, 2005); Latinos (LaRoche & Shriberg, 2004); and migrant families (Clare, Jimenez, & McClendon, 2005).

INTERAGENCY COLLABORATION AND SCHOOL–COMMUNITY PARTNERSHIPS

As noted in Chapter 1, interdisciplinary collaboration is receiving increased attention in the collaboration literature (Cappella et al., 2012; Griffin & Farris, 2010; Mellin, 2009). Agencies such as the school, health services, social services, the child evaluation center, family services organizations, and often the family itself collaborate together to assist selected children and their families (Rimehaug & Helmersberg, 2010; Staton et al., 2007; Sulkowski, Wingfield, Jones, & Coulter, 2011). Such collaborations can promote community mental health reform (Bryan, 2010) as well as develop systems-level programs that promote student success and well-being (Schellenberg & Grothaus, 2011; Steen & Noguera, 2010). Interagency collaboration and school–community partnerships can be effective in improving access to services for citizens as well as to meet their complex needs (Henderson, MacKay, & Peterson-Badali, 2010; Nastasi & Varjas, 2008). One example is a community fire service organization and mental health professionals implementing a program for at-risk youth regarding fire starting (Henderson et al., 2010). In another example, both external and internal consultants can assist with increasing behavioral and academic performance of students in classrooms where there is low emotional involvement between the teacher and students (Cappella et al., 2012).

The need for effective prevention programs serving at-risk youths and their families has increased (Hughes, Lloyd, & Buss, 2008; Strein & Koehler, 2008). This has involved a shift from single-setting practice to school/community-based and -linked interagency service (Bemak et al., 2005; Cohen et al., 2006; Lewis, Lewis, Daniels, & D'Andrea, 2011; Mellin et al., 2011). Counselors in school and community settings can be instrumental in developing and maintaining mental health programs for today's youth. Because school counselors and school psychologists have a primary responsibility for addressing the social and personal needs of students, they are thereby involved in school–community collaboration (Bryan, 2010; Portman, 2009; Walker, Shenker, & Hoover-Oempsey, 2010). They will work on interagency teams to plan, coordinate, evaluate, and provide direct services to students and their families. In addition to working together to assist students and their families, school-based professionals work with human service agency personnel to provide primary and secondary prevention programs in the school or in the community such as those related to bully proofing the school and developing programs for students at risk. As with other forms of collaboration, interagency collaboration requires cultural competence (Armstrong & Evans, 2010; Lewis et al., 2011; Manz et al., 2009; Staton et al., 2007). For example, school and community consultants working on health and educational issues for migrant families will need to be knowledgeable about the cultural values of these families (Clare et al., 2005). In another example, school-based professionals can collaborate with agency personnel in community asset mapping, which results in a current list of community resources to assist students and their families (Griffin & Farris, 2010).

The rationale for interagency collaboration and school–community partnerships, in the case of students, is that the social and/or educational problems of a child affect all aspects of his or her life such as the home and school. Such collaboration is often considered a best practice in helping children and their families as it is increasingly evident that one professional cannot adequately address in isolation the necessary issues for effectively assisting a family (Epstein & Van Voorhis, 2010; Mellin et al., 2011). The shared responsibility for the case shifts the focus from what the school can do to what the community should do to provide services (Portman, 2009).

Whereas more traditional expert modes of consultation were adequate in the past, the complexity of the problems faced by today's youths and their parents suggest that a more collaborative approach may be in order. "School-linked and school-based programs, with services located either at the school or in the community, offer a promising model for service delivery, and collaborative planning between schools and community has become critical to the success of such efforts" (Keys et al., 1998, p. 123). In one example, there are a variety of ways in which school and medical agencies can engage in collaboration. These include: prevention and health promotion; plans for crises; coordination of medical services in the school; and hospital-based education (Shaw & Brown, 2011; Shaw & Woo, 2008).

Collaboration has become increasingly popular, as school and community agencies have understood the fragmentation of at-risk youth services (Dedrick & Greenbaum, 2011). Consultants must develop multifaceted programs for at-risk youth and their families because the problems faced by these groups are multicausal and must be solved by addressing a larger context: there is no single answer to such problems (Cummings et al., 2004b; Keys et al., 1998; Lerner, 1995).

Although school and community counselors and psychologists provide case-related services on a regular basis, collaborative efforts with outside agencies are relatively new. The emergence of approaches to providing mental health services such as the systems of care approach promote interagency collaboration for providing services (Armstrong & Evans, 2010; Dedrick & Greenbaum, 2011). These efforts have come about as schools and agencies have realized that no one person or no one organization can solve the complex issues and problems that need to be dealt with; hence service integration has been introduced among schools and agencies. In collaboration, there are multiple experts who come together to "jointly identify problems to be addressed … to determine strategies and the role each person plays in implementing these strategies to carry out their roles interdependently, and to monitor progress" (Keys et al., 1998, p. 124). Both school and community consultants, in order to use collaboration effectively, must see themselves as connected to a broader community (Epstein & Van Voorhis, 2010; Koonce & Harper, 2005).

Interdisciplinary collaboration involves the pooling of expertise by a variety of professionals to assist a client system using shared decision making and intervention. For example, school-based personnel can function within collaborative teams in capacities such as making interventions at school, monitoring overall progress at school and home, and making suggestions to community-based mental health professionals. The client system may be a child, a child and family, or the entire school (Epstein & Van Voorhis, 2010; Suarez-Orozco et al., 2010; Walker et al., 2010). The goal of interdisciplinary collaboration is the melding of the expertise of the collaborators to assist the client system, whether it is an individual, a group, or an organization (in this case, the school). The shared responsibility necessitates solid agreement on the roles and responsibilities of individual collaborators (Henderson et al., 2010; Mellin et al., 2011). You can imagine the complexity of this collaboration effort with different agencies with different mission statements and procedures for providing services. Further, the collaborating professionals will want to recognize that their team will have a distinct "personality" that will impact how the team will function (Garrett, 1998). Finally, there can easily be issues with treatment integrity when several professionals are involved in the implementation procedures (Henderson et al., 2010).

Eagle, Dowd-Eagle, and Sheridan (2008) note two categories of school–community partnerships: school-linked and school-based. School-linked partnerships include those in which community services are linked to the school (e.g., a community mental health referral system). School-based partnerships are those which are housed within the physical structure of the school.

A popular model of interdisciplinary collaboration (Bronstein, 2003, cited in Mellin, 2009) points out five elements to interdisciplinary collaboration:

1. interdependence
2. progress in the collaboration involves building interventions with the contributions of each collaborator
3. flexibility in the collaborative process to accommodate power sharing and role adaptation

4. collective ownership of goals
5. discussion of progress and feedback to fellow collaborators

Teams are often used to ensure that collaboration services are delivered in a timely, efficient, and integrated manner. To deliver services of this level of quality, the collaborating team needs to ensure commitment from all parties, encourage time-saving approaches to effective communication, have strong leadership, have an understanding of the culture of the collaborating agencies, engage in serious preplanning, commit adequate resources, and minimize turf issues (Cohen et al., 2006; Petri, 2010; Sulkowski et al., 2011).

In order to maximize the probability that an effective plan will be designed and implemented, the collaborating professionals will want to meet soon after the child and his or her family have been identified as needing services. By having several professionals as well as the family itself involved in planning and implementing the interventions that are part of the plan, a broad knowledge base is applied to the plan. On the other hand, it is essential that each collaborating professional recognize the philosophical orientation, service limitations, and mission of the other agencies involved as part of the collaborating team (Sulkowski et al., 2011; Swenson, Randall, Henggeier, & Ward, 2000).

By having an awareness of boundary issues, collaborating professionals can be prepared to implement their "piece of the pie" without doing anything counterproductive to the efforts of other collaborating professionals or duplicating services (Tseng, Liu, & Wang, 2011). These issues highlight the importance of developing interagency policies that provide for a broad-based and comprehensive delivery system (Armstrong & Evans, 2010).

The collaborating professionals will usually select a team facilitator, frequently a school counselor or school psychologist, who will convene meetings, ensure documentation of meeting discussions, and make sure that progress on the individual collaborator's work with the family is discussed during meetings. The team facilitator will make sure that the plan is made and carried out with adjustments made as necessary.

Further, the team facilitator has the responsibility to make sure an evaluation of the plan is made and shared. The facilitator has the collaborating professionals develop some kind of form that will enable the team to monitor the plan. For example, the plan will have the following sections: the problem identified along with the date of identification, a description of the goal developed to deal with the problem, a description of the intervention used to meet the goal along with a notation of which collaborating professionals were to do what and by when, followed by a section describing the outcome of the intervention. Interagency collaboration can take time in terms of being out of the school building and the amount of paperwork necessary. Ways to minimize the constraints of time include rotating team meeting sites and using technology to store, retrieve, and communicate information (Cohen et al., 2006). Collaboration involves trade-offs. School personnel have to give up some power in order to get the benefits of community responsibility.

When working with families, it is important to empower the family so that there is not a hierarchical difference between the family and the school (Short & Talley, 1999). When collaborating with parents, every attempt should be made to provide them with maximum input into meaningful participation in the collaboration team's work with them and their child (Friend & Cook, 1996). This type of group consensus seeking on how to proceed and follow up can increase the chances of success. Consistent use of language among various agencies, even to the point of developing a common brochure describing services, can minimize misunderstanding by parents as well as some school personnel (Ikeda, Tilly, Stumme, Volmer, & Allison, 1996).

Due to managed care, a trend in interagency collaboration includes increased involvement of health care service agencies with school and community integrated planning and service provision as well as increased attention to policy issues (Armstrong & Evans, 2010). When professionals in these settings look across their settings and

circumstances, they will be able to define concerns and generate solutions in a joint manner (Hellkamp, 1996), often using strategic planning (Knoff, 1996). Such strategic planning emphasis will determine who will provide services, how they will be provided, and whether health care reform will determine the provision of services (e.g., a certain limit on the number of sessions a family may have that insurance will pay for).

The limited research on interagency consultation suggests that shared physical space, mechanisms for both formal and informal communication, team coordination, organizational support, and collaborative decision making all contribute to success (Cohen et al., 2006).

MULTICULTURAL SCHOOL CONSULTATION

Multicultural school consultation, also sometimes referred to as cross-cultural consultation, has grown rapidly. It borrows some concepts from mental health consultation such as the reasons for consultee challenges with cases and the use of reconceptualization of client issues as in consultee-centered consultation. However, multicultural school consultation has its own unique identity. The increasing diversity of all stakeholders related to schools dictates that consultation and collaboration services need to be multiculturally competent (D'Amato et al., 2011; Gutkin & Curtis, 2009; Holcomb-McCoy, 2009; Holcomb-McCoy & Bryan, 2010). "Ethnic and linguistic minority children constitute the most rapidly growing segment of the youth population of the United States. Over 60% of the population of the United States is predicted to be culturally or linguistically diverse by 2050" (Li & Vazquez-Nuttall, 2009). There are a large number of other diverse populations such as the lesbian, bisexual, and gay (LBG) population in schools (Sherblom & Bahr, 2008). These demographic changes that are reflected in the students in schools impact the delivery of consultation and collaboration (Merrell et al., 2006; Portman, 2009).

School-based consultants as well as community consultants working in school settings (Lewis et al., 2011; Tomes, 2011) will increasingly be called upon to work with school personnel and parents to meet the needs of these students and will want to engage in culturally responsive practice (Arra, 2010; Knotek, 2012; Li & Vazquez-Nuttall, 2009). This calls for multicultural competence on the part of mental health professionals (Ivey, Ivey, & Zalaquett, 2012; Miranda, 2008), including exhibiting respect for diversity and having a thorough examination of potential biases and cultural knowledge (Holcomb-McCoy, 2009). Multicultural consultation can be an effective service for promoting cultural competence and therefore student success (Ingraham, 2000, 2007, 2008). *Multicultural school consultation* is an approach to consultation that takes into account how cultural issues affect the consultation process and how related adaptations can be implemented at the individual, group, or system-wide levels (Ingraham, 2000, 2007, 2008; Rogers, 2000). Multicultural consultation "… seeks to facilitate greater understanding of the diverse meanings different individuals attach to the purposes and practices of organizations" (Holcomb-McCoy & Coker, 2009, p. 177). For example, a school psychologist or school counselor determines how a student's cultural background impacts that student's learning and consults with the student's teacher accordingly (Miranda, 2008; Tomes, 2011). Multicultural consultation is more a way of looking at consultation than a distinct model. This model tends to focus on teachers and parents as they are in a critical position to affect student achievement and well-being. Ingraham (2000) points out several components of multicultural school consultation:

- domains for consultant learning and development (e.g., understanding the cultural context for consultation)
- domains of consultee learning and development (e.g., avoiding overemphasis on culture)
- cultural variations in the consultation constellation (e.g., taking into account cultural

differences among the consultant, consultee, and client system)
- contextual and power influences (e.g., minimizing power differentials between the consultant and the consultee)
- hypothesized methods for supporting consultee and client success (e.g., using consultation methods matched with the consultee's style)

Taken together, these dimensions provide a framework for dealing with the multicultural issues that arise in consultation and collaboration. Within this framework, consultants take into account both individual differences and cultural issues so as not to overemphasize cultural variables; that culture goes beyond characteristics such as race and language. For example, this framework helps to avoid *intervention paralysis*, the inability to determine an intervention due to uncertainty in how to select culturally appropriate interventions and *reactive dominance*, whereby consultees impose their own typical patterns of thinking/behaving because they are out of their comfort zones in a multicultural context (Ingraham, 2000). Through multicultural consultation, teachers' knowledge, skills, confidence, and objectivity are increased so that they can deal more effectively with the changing cultural landscape of schools.

Lopez and Truesdell (2007, pp. 75–79) cite six underlying principles that facilitate framing multicultural consultation:

- Consultants are sensitive to cultural differences.
- Consultants and consultees acquire knowledge about their clients' cultural backgrounds.
- Consultants are mindful of cultural differences in communication.
- Cultural differences influence interpersonal relationships between consultants and consultees.
- Multicultural issues are addressed throughout every stage of the consultation process.
- Consultants acknowledge how systemic issues impact the cultural context of consultation.

Holcomb-McCoy and Coker (2009, p. 177) add the following awarenesses as necessary for effective multicultural consultation to occur:

- The language that the participants in consultation use may conflict.

- Culture, gender, race, and class shape the experiences consultation participants have.

- Social/economic barriers may impact the participants' perceptions and expectations of consultation.

- Cultural, linguistic, and gender differences mediate the quality of the experiences different groups receive.

There is some evidence that modifications to traditional consultation approaches when consulting with teachers and parents of culturally diverse background is important; these modifications may vary by culture (Holcomb-McCoy, 2009; Ingraham, 2007, 2008; Tarver Behring, Cabello, Kushida, & Murguia, 2000) and can use advocacy as a role (Holcomb-McCoy & Coker, 2009). As a result, consultants must balance between providing new information to parents and creating relationships with parents that takes into account the sociocultural context of the family (Holcomb-McCoy & Bryan, 2010). In other words, consultants must balance their expertise with parent empowerment as well as the consideration of psychosocial forces such as adaptive coping systems that involve extended families in problem solving while at the same time being aware of preconceived notions regarding the cultural attributes of the parent-as-consultee (Holcomb-McCoy, 2009; Holcomb-McCoy & Bryan, 2010). As Merrell et al. (2006) note: We "… must adopt practices and service delivery models that reduce bias, meet individual needs, and result in better outcomes for all children and their families" (p. 59). Multicultural consultation has increasing empirical support for its effectiveness but more is needed (Ingraham, 2008). Other research suggests that consultants/collaborators take into account parental views of "parent involvement" when implementing programs (Minke & Anderson, 2005).

PRACTICAL MATTERS

There are a variety of practical matters that currently face school-based psychologists, counselors, and external consultants in their consultation and collaboration activities due to the school setting. For example, effective consultation takes time, yet the time constraints in schools are myriad. The areas around which these issues revolve are addressed next.

Consultation/Collaboration and Special Education

Federal legislation, advances in the field of special education, and the national organizations related to school-based professionals have all contributed to increasing the opportunities for consultation and collaboration in areas related to special education (Trolley, Haas, & Patti, 2009). As a result, school-based professionals such as school counselors and school psychologists will increasingly be involved in individual and group consultation as well as collaboration related to assisting students with disabilities. This dictates an awareness of special education literature, including classifications as well as assessment methods and related ethical, professional, and legal issues. School-based consultants and collaborators will engage in collaborative services with other students support professionals, serve on multidisciplinary teams, be members of individual education plan (IEP) teams, provide advocacy for students to receive necessary services from the school and community, consult regarding RTI and PBS programs, assist with providing transition consultation as students move from grade to grade and from school to school. School-based consultants and collaborators also work directly with teachers, administrators, and parents in ensuring that the needs of children with disabilities are met.

Response to Intervention (RTI)

The RTI model is receiving increasing attention and widespread use in school settings when addressing academic, behavioral, and socioemotional issues in all students (Forman & Selman, 2011; Gruman & Hoelzen, 2011). It is often seen as an alternative to traditional special education assessment. RTI is a systemic intervention and change, so consultants are often needed in its implementation (Ball, Pierson, & McIntosh, 2011; Froiland, 2011; Gresham, 2011). RTI is "… a data-based process to establish, implement, and evaluate interventions that are designed to improve human services outcomes" (Reschly & Bergstrom, 2009, p. 434). The RTI framework "… uses a multitiered model of intervention that involves universal, targeted, and intensive levels of intervention in an attempt to address problems school-wide" (Allen, 2011, p. 218). Each tier is focused on a specific level of intervention assessment and exactness (Reschly & Bergstrom, 2009) and, as a result, has a preventive, ecological component (Greenwood & Kim, 2012; Gutkin, 2009; Reschly & Christenson, 2012). RTI can positively impact the quality of interventions delivered in school settings, for example, interventions for struggling learners. The model uses evidence-based intervention delivered in a timely fashion with treatment integrity (Hagermoser Sanetti & Kratochwill, 2009). RTI uses "… data-based decision making as a basis for modifying, titrating, or changing the nature of interventions" (Gresham, 2006, p. 526). In other words, assessment is seen as needing to be related to the selection of interventions and their evaluation. RTI requires intervention at multiple levels to address both the organizational and individual needs (Cowan, 2007; Reschly & Bergstrom, 2009; Schellenberg & Grothaus, 2011).

RTI developed from applied behavioral analysis and provides a history of interventions, their impact, and guides problem solving. RTI is most commonly used to address students' academic and behavior concerns while increasingly a multitiered system of interventions is often integrated with RTI (Hagermoser Sanetti, & Fallon, 2011; Sulkowski et al., 2011). It is important to remember that RTI and consultation are both problem-solving activities but not one and the same. Some differences include:

- Consultation focuses on the teacher–consultee, while RTI focuses on the student client.
- Consultants can be internal or external to the school, whereas the professionals implementing RTI are school-based.
- Consultation is less likely to be team-based like RTI.
- Consultation focuses on more areas and can be more general than RTI.
- Participation in consultation is voluntary, while participation in RTI may not be (Erchul, 2011).

Consultation is consistent with the type of RTI that has a systematic problem-solving approach, focuses on prevention, and uses data-based practices (Erchul, 2011; Gruman & Hoelzen, 2011; Kratochwill, 2008). Consultation about RTI typically revolves around topics such as implementation of programs like a Tier 1 program related to student engagement, or a Tier 2 action like consulting with teachers and parents on goals set for a child at risk, or a Tier 3 action such as serving on an interagency collaboration team (Gruman & Hoelzen, 2011), troubleshooting, modifications, and evaluation (Greenwood & Kim, 2012).

Consultation/collaboration related to RTI can be categorized into tiers: Tier 1 aims at the entire student body, Tier 2 involves the at-risk student population (5–10 percent of students), and Tier 3 targets students who require intensive intervention (1–5 percent of students) (Sulkowski et al., 2011).

RTI includes attempts to measure the integrity of the intervention, particularly at the individual level (Barnett, Hawkins, & Lentz, 2011). Ecological conditions addressed by consultation can include (Greenwood & Kim, 2012):

- school-wide implementation
- multiple levels of support
- evidence-based interventions
- formative evaluation
- movement of students across tiers as needed

The controversy over traditional assessment and RTI (Barnett, VanDerHeyden, & Witt, 2007;

Clare, 2009; Willis & Dumont, 2006) continues to influence consultant behavior. For example, there is some question of the culturally sensitive appropriateness and quality of interventions for some populations in one or more of the tiers of the RTI model (Li & Vazquez-Nuttall, 2009). School-based consultants can provide support in both content and process issues in assuring that interventions are appropriate and implemented with integrity (Meyers et al., 2012). RTI also creates a venue which leads to engaged partnerships with families (Reschly & Christenson, 2012). Finally, RTI allows for school-based counselors and psychologists to consult on the unique implementation of school-wide RTI programs as a way of providing responsive service based on research-based practices, data-based decision making, CBA, and program evaluation (Ryan, Kaffenberger, & Carroll, 2011).

Systems View of the School

School-based consultants will be increasingly called to provide system-level services (Conyne & Mazza, 2007; Hojnoski, 2007; Merrell et al., 2006; Paisley & Milsom, 2007) such as assessing readiness for change, as well as to encourage and sustain changes (Adelman & Taylor, 2007). A systems view of schools is a useful framework for understanding the organizational context of consultation and collaboration, and may actually assist in promoting the development of children, organizational change (Meyers et al., 2012; Reschly & Christenson, 2012), the promotion of social justice (Bidell, 2011; Li & Vazquez-Nuttall, 2009; Schmidt, Glass, & Wooten, 2011; Williams & Greenleaf, 2012), the development of leadership skills among consultants (Forman & Selman, 2011), and the responsiveness to cultural differences (Tomes, 2011). Because individual interventions are often not adequate in dealing with issues related to the educational and psychological well-being of students, multitiered services and systemic interventions are often necessary (Bryan, 2010; Meyers et al., 2012).

A systems view allows for capacity building within schools that includes the development of supportive environments for all stakeholders (Forman & Selman, 2011; Meyers et al., 2012). By taking a systems view of the school, consultants and collaborators can take on leadership roles aimed at maximizing the academic achievement and well-being of all students (Harris, 2007; Moe & Perera-Diltz, 2009; Neukrug, 2012), including ensuring a safe, caring, and inviting environment for all (Forman & Selman, 2011). As Sheridan and Kratochwill (2008) note, "Children and youth exist in multiple contexts that both separately and together affect their functioning. These contexts include immediate settings of classrooms, home environments, peer groups, neighborhoods and other important ecological settings. They also include the interconnected relationships among settings and individuals who participate in these settings" (p. 1). A systems view of schools allows for the use of ecological and preventive perspectives and their related interventions and can reflect a postmodernism point of view. For example, when looked at from an ecological perspective, school mental health services can be better linked to student academic success by assessing not only a given student but also the "... adequacy of supports within the nested tiers of influence within and around schools and classrooms" (Doll et al., 2012, p. 56).

In addition, in a systems view, consultants take on a broad framework for consultation because of the complexity of organizational factors and how they can be changed (Harris, 2007). For example, consultation is viewed as a recursive process whose direction can change based on continuous data gathering as well as one that engages all stakeholders (Meyers et al., 2012). Consultants and consultees can intervene at several ecological levels, including the individual client level. In terms of consultation and collaboration, a systems perspective takes the focus off of a reactive approach for dealing with the issues of individual students to a broader approach that promotes prevention and the well-being of all students. This focus on prevention moves consultation service delivery to include working with administrators and community organizations as well as influencing public policy (Ysseldyke et al., 2009). The *American School*

Counselor National Model: A Framework for School Counselor Programs (ASCA, 2005) promotes school counselors as leaders for systemic change initiatives in schools. The increased focus on improving the entire school through prevention and social justice initiatives implies increased collaboration among school-based and community groups (Mellin et al., 2011). Dahir and Stone (2009, p. 18) add that "… school counselors can initiate, develop, lead, and coordinate programs that can contribute to systemic change and improved learning success for every student." It also allows for a multilevel service delivery model that can include individuals, classrooms, and the entire school. Increasingly, interdisciplinary collaboration is focusing on systemic change (Mellin, 2009).

System-level change demands that all aspects of education be examined in terms of multiple levels and be based on multiple partnerships among stakeholders (Kratochwill, 2008; Manz, 2007; O'Connell, 2008). As a result, all students receive services that match their needs (Hojnoski, 2007; Portman, 2009). The idea is that the consultant will use existing structures and processes within the school to target, initiate, and maintain system-level changes (Hoffman et al., 2006; Jeltova & Fish, 2005), including evaluating and sustaining change initiatives (Stoiber & Vanderwood, 2008; Taylor & Dymnicki, 2007). Consultants help to accomplish how schools can realize desired changes (Adelman & Taylor, 2007). This view allows for issues related to student learning and behavior to be viewed beyond the student and more from the perspective of environmental context. In a systems view of consultation, the student is examined in the context of school and family units.

These units and their interaction (e.g., teacher attitudes, parent child-rearing practices, communication patterns between parents and the school) then become eligible for attention and modification. Individual change can be facilitated when the wider system that directly interrelates with the student is considered.

Systems theory assumes the school to be the target for consultation intervention; to consult with a teacher represents a linear view of the child being responsible for negative behavior, and the teacher for correcting it. This may reinforce in the teacher's mind that the child, not the system, has the problem. One concern is that not all teachers are comfortable with systems approaches; some want more concrete ways of approaching perceived problems. In addition, many school consultants have not been trained in systems methods. Finally, the systems view typically dictates that consultants examine the child in interaction with a variety of levels of the ecosystem such as home, school, and community, thus complicating the nature of the consultation relationship (Hoffman et al., 2006; Reschly & Christenson, 2012).

Developing a Framework for Prevention and Intervention

Prevention programs are seeing a resurgence in schools (Strein & Koehler, 2008) and many of them have been designated as evidence-based (Forman & Selman, 2011). Community mental health professionals, for example, have increasingly become involved in prevention programs in schools (Lewis et al., 2011). School counselors, in another example, increasingly are viewing their professional identity as involving prevention (Mellin et al., 2011). The Council for Accreditation of Counseling and Related Educational Programs (CACREP) (2009) has supported an increased focus on prevention activities as integral to any counselor's role. The *School Psychology: A Blueprint for Training and Practice III* (Ysseldyke et al., 2006) also promotes prevention on the part of school psychologists. The idea is to provide a more prevention-oriented model of consultation in addition to the common case models typically used (Hojnoski, 2007; Hughes et al., 2008). In that way, both personal behaviors and environmental forces are taken into consideration (Lewis et al., 2011). Further, a focus of prevention is to build capacities in systems (e.g., a school or other organization) so that the overall development of members of that system in areas such as mental health, social skills, and health is optimized relative to the mission of the system (Meyers et al., 2009;

Ysseldyke et al., 2009). By maximizing the supportive capacities of systems, all members of those systems have their growth supported (Meyers, Roach, & Meyers, 2009; Sander et al., 2010). Mental health professionals, however, still find it difficult to take time away from remedial activities to focus on prevention activities (Ball et al., 2011; Hughes et al., 2008; Stoiber & Vanderwood, 2008). Further, there is some concern that school-based consultants may be experiencing a research to practice gap in prevention programs (McAdams, Shillingford, & Trice-Black, 2011).

You will recall from Chapter 1 that school-based interventions have increasingly become categorized within a three-tiered model that matches resource intensity with problem intensity (Strein & Koehler, 2008). Interventions include: Tier 1: *universal* (target: the entire population); Tier 2: *selective* (target: a segment of the population which is at risk); and Tier 3: *indicated* (target: students who need individualized and intense intervention). Each of the three tiers provides significant opportunities for consultation (Racine Gilles et al., 2011).

Consultation at the universal level can be used to "... ensure that schools have incorporated and can sustain effective, research-based practices that often involve environmental and instructional redesign" (Racine Gilles et al., 2011, p. 674). Consultation at this level is often conducted by a team of consultants with key stakeholders, such as teachers, with the client system consisting of the entire school. Consultation at the selected level can have the desirable outcome of accurate analysis and understanding of school-wide data that sheds light on what programs are working or not working for some students. Consultation then focuses on identifying students, for whom universal interventions are not working, setting goals with consultees for those students, and recommending EBI to meet the identified needs (Racine Gilles et al., 2011). When it is determined that neither Tier 1 nor Tier 2 interventions are working with a given student, consultation at Tier 3 focuses on specific individualized EBI, with behavioral case-centered

consultation and community-based resources often being employed (Racine Gilles et al., 2011).

One popular type of a prevention program is social and emotional learning (SEL), which is a process by which students "... become socially and emotionally intelligent" (Van Velsor, 2009, p. 51). SEL can provide an integrated, preventive framework for programs dealing with students' social, academic, and behavioral needs (Van Velsor, 2009; Zins, Bloodworth, Weissberg, & Walberg, 2004, 2007). SEL assists schools to see that social, emotional, and academic development need to be looked at together, are for all students, and are thus all part of the school's responsibility (Forman & Selman, 2011; Manz, 2007; Van Velsor, 2009). For example, SEL is related to dropout prevention (White & Kelly, 2010). Greenberg et al. (2003) note that "... school-based prevention and youth development interventions are most beneficial when they simultaneously enhance students' personal and social assets, as well as improve the quality of the environments in which students are educated" (p. 467). School-based consultants are especially qualified to assist with such prevention efforts (Gueldner & Merrell, 2011). Consultants can assist in ensuring that environmental supports exist for participants to use the skills learned and particularly in ensuring that these programs are contextualized to the school in which they are being placed, have accurately interpreted evaluation data, and that they contain elements that promote SEL such as self-management, communication skills, conflict resolution, and study habits (Carlson, 2007; Elias & Leverett, 2011; Meyers et al., 2009).

SEL programs do not yet have a strong research base due to the complexity of their implementation and measurement (Tanyu, 2007), but that research base is growing. That said, successful implementation of SEL programs requires a view of schools as multilevel systems, an understanding that human dynamics are involved in program implementation and maintenance, the empowerment of the people involved, the development of polices that support implementation (Elias & Leverett, 2011), and a focus on treatment integrity (Gueldner & Merrell, 2011).

Prevention efforts can be related to responding to traumatizing events such as acts of terrorism by working with schools and families on resiliency training and preparedness (Alpert & Duckworth Smith, 2003). In another example, health promotion in schools can be conducted through collaborative programming by medical professionals and school-based consultants (Shaw, Glaser, & Ouimet, 2011). Consultee-centered, program, education/ training, and organizational consultation and collaboration are methods to accomplish this (Meyers, 2002; Meyers, Meyers, & Grogg, 2004). For example, a school-based consultant may help to develop a team of stakeholders to collaborate together in coordinating a program related to school attendance. In another example, consultants can provide education/training consultation regarding mental health promotion and the public health model to school personnel and parents (Nastasi, 2004). In yet another example, a school and community consultants work together on a prevention program involving community members to restrict access to tobacco among school-aged youth (Jason, Pokorny, Ji, & Kunz, 2005). There is a growing body of evidence that prevention programs can be effective (Metropolitan Area Child Study Research Group, 2007; Strein & Koehler, 2008). Other research suggests that consultees adapt prevention programs to their perceived needs when implementing them and that implementation of intervention programs is difficult (Larson & Samdal, 2007).

Prevention programs have their own set of challenges. Schools in which there is an existing acceptance of consultation and collaboration have a head start in effectively implementing prevention programs (Strein & Koehler, 2008). For those that do not, the challenges include getting stakeholders on board and adequately trained to implement the program; facilitating schools to choose from among programs that have evidence that they work; making sure that the efforts are implemented with cultural competence; and ensuring that prevention programs are integrated into the curriculum (Durlak, 2009). Consultants can assist in both selecting evidence-based programs and ensuring their integration into the mainstream of the school.

Time Constraints

Time constraints are a large and real issue for conducting effective consultation and collaboration. A limitation of school consultation and collaboration is that both take time to do well (Ball et al., 2011; Manz et al., 2009; Mellin, 2009; Mellin et al., 2011; Meyers et al., 2009). Because the direct service to the client system is distributed across all collaborators, I am of the opinion that collaboration is the most desirable way to proceed in such cases as the amount of time spent by the parties involved may be reduced. With increasing accountability in schools, there is very little free time at school for the people who work there, so it can be difficult for counselors and psychologists to engage teachers and administrators in these services, let alone parents who must often take time off from work to come to the school for any reason. The school environment can encourage engagement in short consultations and collaborative efforts (Davis, 2005).

Caplan and Caplan (1993) have stressed the importance of "orderly and unhurried reflection during consultation discussions" (p. 43). On the other hand, counselors and psychologists need to find strategies to effectively cope with the very real-time constraints placed upon consultation and collaboration during the school day. Effective time management on the part of school professionals is one obvious help in creating time for consultation and collaboration. Recent research has supported that collaboration is valued by school personnel and that adequate time is found to conduct it (Welch & Tulbert, 2000). Consultants can likely have more positive impact on the consultation process by using their limited time to observe and assess the problem, and then model and coach, rather than by just talking to the consultee (Watson & Sterling-Turner, 2008) and assisting student assistance teams to run efficiently (Doll, Haack, Kosse, Osterloh, Siemers, & Pray, 2005).

Five other strategies include: early release/ late arrival of students, use of substitutes, teaching strategies that free up personnel (Friend & Cook, 1996), use of the telephone and/or other technologies such as VoIP and e-mail (Florell, 2011; Kruger et al., 2001; Reese, Conoley, & Brossart, 2006) for accomplishing some of the tasks related to consultation and collaboration, engaging in peer consultation, and the use of group methods as appropriate. For example, various technologies can be used for gathering information, researching possible interventions, monitoring interventions, and follow-up, as well as for creating a record of the consultation process (Florell, 2011).

Another more challenging option is to adjust the school culture so that consultation and collaboration are seen as systematic, organized activities through which the school psychologist or school counselor provides assistance (Fall, 1995). For example, school-based mental health professionals can use an inclusion-type model of collaboration and provide direct service in the teacher's classroom, thus avoiding having to use the pullout model (Clark & Breman, 2009).

SCHOOL CONSULTATION IN THE 21ST CENTURY

What trends are occurring in school consultation in the second decade of the new millennium?

What areas of need will school personnel and parents calling for assistance from school consultants have? I will next describe some of the ways that you, as a school consultant/collaborator, may be using your skills. Merrell et al. (2006) have pointed out trends in school psychology (and, in this author's opinion, there are similar trends in school counseling and school social work) that will impact the delivery of school-based consultation and collaboration. Consultation and collaboration will:

1. focus more on positively impacting all students in addition to those with major concerns;

2. develop culturally sensitive interventions that apply to increasing demographic changes in the school population;

3. engage in system-level initiatives (e.g., entire school) in addition to those that are individual-related; and

4. use date-driven decision making to select and evaluate interventions.

The ecological perspective will increasingly be employed when examining school issues, whether those issues be related to individual students, selected groups of students, or all students (Gutkin, 2012). This perspective will create more focus on systems issues, social justice, prevention, and empowerment of stakeholders such as parents. In another example, ecological and systems factors will continue to be incorporated into RTI consultation/collaboration procedures (Greenwood & Kim, 2012; Reschly & Christenson, 2012).

The use of the telephone, texting, the Web, and e-mail to accomplish some tasks (i.e., follow-up) is on the increase. These methods help to save time but may also have disadvantages when compared to face-to-face contact.

The use of consultation and collaboration teams will continue to increase (Gravois et al., 2009; Truscott et al., 2012). In a case management model, the consultation team is made up of a variety of school and community personnel. When consultation is requested by a teacher, a member of the team volunteers to be the lead consultant and engages the teacher in one-on-one consultation, focuses on the teacher's professional development, and is known as the case manager. The case manager accesses the team on an as-needed basis and is accountable to the team. The use of the team approach bolsters the knowledge and skills of the individual team members and facilitates the acceptance of consultation as an indirect service in the school. Truscott et al. (2012) have developed a consultation program called exceptional performance learning (EPL) using learning communities of teachers, case studies, and ongoing formative assessment and it can be considered a form of consultee-centered consultation.

Schools are dramatically expanding their services to prekindergarten children. Public education is being offered to children at risk from birth onward and to all 3- and 4-year-olds (Fine & Kontos, 1992; Steen & Noguera, 2010). Therefore, school-based consultants will increasingly be asked to offer services to the significant others of prekindergarten children (Bacon & Dougherty, 1992; Sheridan et al., 2006; Wesley et al., 2010), including interventions related to RTI (Barnett et al., 2007) and prevention programs (Lehman, Salaway, Bagnato, Grom, & Willard, 2011). Further, consultants will increase their work as liaisons between school systems and early childhood settings (Hojnoski & Missal, 2006).

The role of consultants and collaborators in gifted education is receiving increasing attention, particularly in relation to cross-disciplinary perspectives (Culross, 2007; Knotek, Kovac, & Bostwick, 2011; Peterson, 2007). At the systems level, for example, consultants will increasingly raise the awareness of other school personnel about the academic and emotional needs of gifted students, assist with the selection and interpretation of assessments of giftedness, promote increased educational services to cultural and ethnic groups in gifted programs, and promote a preventive and wellness focus to consultation (Knotek et al., 2011; Ouyang & Conoley, 2007). Consultee-centered consultation is also a potential role for consultants when working on issues in gifted education at both the systems and individual levels (Calderon et al., 2007). At the systems level, consultants can facilitate administrator's rethinking of gifted education and then support the administrator's implementation of related changes. At the individual level, consultants can assist in facilitating the knowledge and skills of school personnel and parents as they relate to gifted education.

School-based consultants will help their schools create a positive climate with regard to the school reform movement's continuing impact on public education (Colbert et al., 2006; Steen & Noguera, 2010). School-based consultants have increasingly been called on to help schools deal with four major concerns related to school reform: children at risk, reintegration of special students, school–community integration of services, and restructuring of schools (Curtis et al., 2008; Ponton & Duba, 2009). In addition to their typical consultation practice, school-based consultants will be involved in projects designed to promote collegiality in the school, support SEL through prevention programs (Portman, 2009; Van Velsor, 2009; Zins et al., 2007), develop programs for students at risk as academic standards are increased, create study skills programs, and ensure that the socioaffective domain is included in any curriculum planning. Other areas in which consultation and collaboration will be needed include: quality assurance, parent involvement (Walker et al., 2010), supporting teacher competence, providing itinerant consultation in early childhood education (Harris & Klein, 2004), and developing peer–teacher consultation groups (Blase & Blase, 2006).

The infusion of positive psychology to increase the well-being of the individuals in the school through mental health and behavioral consultation is also receiving more attention (Akin-Little et al., 2004; Foster & Lloyd, 2007; Larson & Samdal, 2007; Love, 2007). Consultants will increasingly translate the findings of positive psychology into interventions that focus on "what is going right" with the client system, and on its strengths.

In a related initiative, the PBS movement (Barnett et al., 2007; Carr, 2007; Curtis & Van Horne, 2014; Sugai, Horner, & McIntosh, 2008) will continue to provide an approach that allows consultants to help develop support and interventions (behavioral and/or academic) at the individual, classroom, or school-levels (Cowan, 2007). PBS is an applied science which employs a preventative and positive influence approach that attempts to develop a climate in a school that promotes positive behavior in all students (Hagermoser Sanetti & Simonsen, 2011; McKevitt & Braaksma, 2008). Maintaining effective practices is emphasized. The focus can be on both problem behavior and problem environments. Similar to RTI, PBS utilizes a tier system and emphasizes primary, secondary, and tertiary prevention. Functional behavioral assessment (FBA) is often used in PBS. Students receiving PBS learn about themselves, social skills, and community-building skills. PBS implementation often requires organizational consultation (Meyers et al., 2012). For an excellent case study on collaboration and PBS, consult Curtis and Van Horne (2014).

In a related trend, consultants will increasingly be using a community vision that emphasizes fulfillment rather than a therapeutic vision when working in interagency collaboration with regard to transitioning students with disabilities to community life (Michaels & Lopez, 2005). This will involve a person-centered, strength-based orientation rather than a deficit-based orientation (Smith & Nevin, 2005).

The multiple issues brought about by high-stakes testing, such as teacher burnout, will be fertile areas for consultation. With the significant rate of turnover in school personnel—such as the 50 percent of teachers who leave before completing five years of service—and the "aging" of school faculties, school-based consultants will increasingly be called upon to facilitate teacher support groups through a variety of models, including consultee-centered consultation (Babinsky & Rogers, 1998). Collaboration as a service will not only increase in frequency but will also occur in the classroom with the mental health professional providing direct service there (Clark & Breman, 2009).

In their work with prevention programs, school-based consultants will increasingly be involved in helping to determine research-based practices and program accountability, advocating for programs that view the school and its surrounding community as the unit of change, providing research-based training programs in preventive techniques for stakeholders, looking at prevention more from a public health perspective (Gutkin, 2009; Trickett & Rowe, 2012), focusing on positive psychology (e.g., subjective well-being) (Seligman & Csikszentmihalyi, 2000), and functioning as part of the support systems to keep programs going (Graden, 2004; Greenberg et al., 2003; Lehman et al., 2011; Meyers et al., 2004; Nastasi, 2004). For example, by taking a public health perspective, consultants can engage in organizational consultation that builds an infrastructure for sustained and institutionalized problem solving (Nastasi, 2004) and work to promote an ecological perspective that focuses on the entire school (Meyers et al., 2012; Trickett & Rowe, 2012).

School-based consultants are increasingly called on to act as organizational consultants during a disaster or national crisis (Costello, Phelps, & Wilczenski, 1994; Halpern & Tramontin, 2007; Studer, 2005) as well as local ones such as school violence. Events such as 9/11 and Hurricane Katrina have sensitized schools to the reaction of students to disastrous events. School-based consultants help schools develop crisis plans. They train and work with teachers, parents, and other mental health colleagues concerning appropriate crisis intervention, coordination of the response to the crisis, and engagement in postcrisis debriefing activities. From a developmental perspective, school-based consultants can promote resiliency and coping skills of students through SEL (Burnham, 2009).

School-based consultants may well be called upon to serve as "cultural mediators" between the school and the community (Portman, 2009). In this role, consultants will consult with community leaders, agencies, and other mental health professionals in areas such as social justice issues (Dixon, Tucker, & Clark, 2010), advocacy, improvement and integration of educational and community services, and systems-level interventions.

Finally, school-based consultants will be increasingly called upon to promote children's health and collaborate with medical/health professionals to meet children's health needs (Truscott & Albritton, 2011; Steen & Noguera, 2010; Sulkowski et al., 2011), since the number of children with physical and mental health needs continues to increase. This means that there will be an increase in the number of schools that employ a collaborative team model and/or a systems model to deal with student health issues as well as the promotion of wellness for entire schools (Doll et al., 2012; Shaw & Woo, 2008; Shaw et al., 2011). Both of these models require "... proactive, integrated and cost-efficient

---

C A S E   12.1   Consultation for School Consultants[1]

Dr. Purdy, a professor of counseling in a southeastern university, was asked by the principal of a local elementary school, Mrs. Abdujaparov, to provide consulting services. Principal Abdujaparov explained that they were just beginning the process of developing a school-wide PBS program and knew that Dr. Purdy had assisted other schools in successfully implementing similar programs. Within the next several weeks, Dr. Purdy and the principal met and discussed the consulting fee and the team's tentative implementation timeline, then arranged suitable regular meeting times for the rest of the academic year.

Before the first meeting with the PBS leadership team, Dr. Purdy researched different aspects of the school, including: its geographic location, academic status, the percentage of students on free or reduced lunch, the number of teachers with advanced degrees and/or national certification, and the last four years of disciplinary reports. He also spoke informally with two different parents he knew who had children attending that particular school.

In the first meeting, after introducing himself and explaining his experience with PBS, he spent the rest of the hour getting to know the team, including their hopes and hesitations regarding the implementation of PBS, and finished the day by taking a tour of the school. In subsequent meetings, Dr. Purdy found that the team was exceptionally spirited and talkative and would often veer off on tangents about different problem areas within the school (e.g., buses, cafeteria). At first, Dr. Purdy allowed the team some leeway when they strayed from the topic, but as the weeks progressed, he began speaking up more quickly, often summarizing the teacher's complaint and finding ways to integrate the complaint into the PBS planning process. In time, other team members began modeling Dr. Purdy's style of redirecting and the meetings became more productive. The majority of the detail work was delegated to different team members to be completed between meetings, and Dr. Purdy regularly provided feedback to questions, mainly through e-mail.

Shortly after the initial meetings began, Dr. Purdy asked if he could attend the next full faculty and staff meeting where the PBS process was going to be introduced. During this meeting, he took special care to inform all faculty and staff that their feedback was welcome and needed, and that no final approval or implementation would take place without their knowledge.

As expected, it took a full academic year for all aspects of PBS to be implemented. Throughout the process, Dr. Purdy assisted the team in many ways: he collaborated with team members to determine efficient ways to implement PBS procedures while keeping all staff abreast of developments; he wrote brief articles in the school's monthly newsletter highlighting favorable outcomes other schools had experienced after establishing their PBS plans; he attended several parent–teacher organization (PTO) meetings to discuss the benefits of PBS and highlight their progress; and he assisted the team in analyzing the data so that problem areas could be addressed. With all procedures in place, Dr. Purdy ended his involvement in the project but assured the team that he was available for future consulting if needed.

Commentary

In this example, Dr. Purdy was wise to keep the stakeholders abreast of the PBS implementation process through faculty and PTO meetings and newsletter articles because nothing compromises consultation quicker than to impose one's expertise on a reluctant staff. This is not to say that every stakeholder will welcome changes with open arms; some resistance is to be expected, but people are much more willing to accept reorganization when they feel they have had opportunities for providing input into the process. Thus, it is vital to the success of consultation to make the process as transparent and collaborative as possible.

---

[1] The author would like to thank Russ Curtis for this case study.

---

strategies" to be successful (DuPaul, 2011, p. 168). Some authors (e.g., Phelps, 2011; Shaw et al., 2011) have suggested a new role of medical liaison for school-based consultants. Among other things, the liaison's function would be as follows:

- serve as the primary case manager

- understand and communicate the systemic needs and the information requirements of the different agencies involved

- reduce any conflicts that occur

- serve as a point person for the program (Shaw et al., 2011)

SUGGESTIONS FOR EFFECTIVE PRACTICE

- As you plan the work in your practice, deliberately take into consideration the very real-time constraints that school personnel face.

- Remember that many, if not most, of the students you will serve will not come from intact families.

- Bear in mind the importance of cultural diversity in your practice of school consultation and collaboration.

- Remember that schools are among the slowest of organizations to change.

QUESTIONS FOR REFLECTION

1. What strikes you as most notable about the history of school-based consultation?

2. To what degree do you see organizational consultation as a viable option when consulting with school administrators?

3. Do you see any possible pitfalls in consulting with school administrators who may also be your immediate superiors?

4. To what degree can Adlerian case consultation be used effectively at the elementary, middle, and secondary school levels?

5. Why is the Adlerian C-group a good alternative to traditional in-service programs for teachers?

6. Do you think that most school-based consultants are adequately trained in the

teaching–learning process to employ instructional consultation effectively? Why?

7. What are some special factors consultants need to take into account when consulting with parents in cross-cultural situations?

8. Which of the pragmatic issues covered in this chapter has the most relevance to your practice as a consultant?

9. What changes are going to impact how school-based consultants deliver their services in the 21st century?

10. To what degree can the mental health and behavioral models discussed in earlier chapters be implemented in a school setting?

SUGGESTED SUPPLEMENTARY READINGS

Gutkin, T. B., & Curtis, M. J. (2009). School-based consultation: The science and practice of indirect service delivery. In C. R. Reynolds and T. B. Gutkin (Eds.), *The handbook of school psychology* (4th ed., pp. 591–635). Hoboken, NJ: Wiley. This chapter covers a variety of topics on school-based consultation, including its characteristics, rationale for services, major approaches, and contemporary and future issues. Broad in scope, consultants will find a wealth of useful information in this chapter.

Ingraham, C. L. (2000). Consultation through a multicultural lens: Multicultural and crosscultural

consultation in schools. *School Psychology Review, 29,* 320–343. This article offers a model of consultation called Multicultural School Consultation. The article offers a conceptual framework for multicultural consultation and makes suggestions for future research. Read this article to get grounded in the foundations of consultation from a multicultural perspective.

Kottman, T., & Dougherty, A. M. (2014). Adlerian case consultation with a teacher. In A. M. Dougherty (Ed.), *Casebook of psychological consultation and collaboration* (6th ed.). Belmont, CA: Brooks/Cole

Cengage. This case study presents an interesting situation in which a school counselor consults with a somewhat resistant teacher consultee on recalcitrant students in the teacher's class.

Ortiz, S. O., Flanagan, D. P., & Dynda, A. M. (2008). Best practices in working with culturally diverse children and families. In A. Thomas and J. Grimes (Eds.), *Best practices in school psychology* (5th ed., pp. 1721–1738). Bethesda, MD: National Association of School Psychologists. This is an excellent article that provides a wealth of information for consultants who work with culturally diverse populations. The authors apply their views on multicultural helping to families in a very practical way.

13

✳

Case Study Illustrations of Consultation and Collaboration

The purpose of this chapter is to provide links between theory and practice and to illustrate the effective practice of consultation and collaboration. The chapter provides a case study of a human services agency to which the various types of mental health, behavioral, organizational, and ecological consultation are applied in some fashion. Recall that some approaches deal with the entire organization as the client system (e.g., process consultation), whereas some work with consultees who are delivering direct services to clients (e.g., client-centered case mental health consultation). Therefore, strict comparison among the various approaches to the models of consultation and collaboration is not possible because these different approaches are used to accomplish different results.

Following the case study, we will illustrate and compare school-based consultation and collaboration by using transcripts of two cases—one involving consultation, the other collaboration—that both deal with the same problem situation and context. As you read these two transcripts, you will detect the subtle differences in the processes involved in consultation and collaboration. I have embedded consultant/consultee and collaborator reflections within the transcripts to aid you in this process.

Consider the following questions as you read through this chapter:

- Are the various approaches to consultation and collaboration more alike than they are different?
- Based on the case studies in this chapter, are there any skills that consultants need that are common to all the approaches discussed?

- How can you use this chapter to help you develop your own personal model of consultation and collaboration?

- Which of the different models seem most attractive to you personally?

- In what ways would you apply the approaches presented in this chapter differently than the author did?

DEVELOPING A PERSONAL MODEL OF CONSULTATION AND COLLABORATION

Illustrations of each approach to consultation and collaboration in more or less the same context can provide you several learning experiences, including:

- a real-life feel for how the approaches work

- a deeper understanding of how the approaches converge and diverge in theory and practice

- an opportunity to begin developing personal preferences for some approaches over others. In addition, the studies are a basis for forming your own personal model of consultation and collaboration, a lifelong process of development based on your professional and personal experiences.

The keys to a useful personal model of these services are fourfold:

1. Know your own values about life in general and these services in particular.

2. Know your personal and professional strengths and limitations.

3. Know and be able to practice as many approaches to consultation and collaboration as possible.

4. Know what the organizations you are serving, whether you are internal or external to that organization, really need from you before you start.

THE CASE: ACME HUMAN SERVICES CENTER

This section describes a fictitious organization, Acme Counseling and Psychological Services Center, in terms of its environment, people, structure, and activities, and the data concerning the organization that were gathered in various ways from various sources. To demonstrate the many approaches to consultation, we will assume this human service organization delivers direct services to clients. Assume that, for each approach, the consultant has all the data mentioned for Acme. Assume also that the contact persons in the organization know what kind of consultation is needed. (In reality, this happens only occasionally; thus, the overall context in which each consultation model is illustrated is somewhat unrealistic. However, the given illustration of each consultation approach will be very realistic.) Each approach to consultation is discussed in terms of its goals, the consultant's role and function, the consultee's experience in consultation, and the application of the approach.

Assume that you are equally talented in each of the approaches to mental health, behavioral, organizational, and ecological consultation. Assume further that you are contacted by a human service organization—Acme Counseling and Psychological Services Center—and asked to perform, in turn, each approach to consultation. You would be asked to perform the client-centered case, consultee-centered case, program-centered administrative, and consultee-centered administrative approaches to mental health consultation. You would next be asked to provide the behavioral case, behavioral technology training, and behavioral system approaches to behavioral consultation. You would then be asked to perform the education/training, program, doctor–patient, and process approaches to organizational consultation. Finally, you would conduct ecological consultation in a generic form.

You would need to ask yourself several questions before proceeding with each approach:

- What assumptions do I need to make according to the approach I am about to use?

- What are the goals of the approach I am about to use?

- What consultant roles and functions will be demanded of me?

- What will my consultees experience during the consultation process?

- In specific terms, how will I go about applying this particular approach?

- What, if any, are the issues related to multi-cultural competence in consulting from this approach?

A Description of the Organization

Acme Counseling and Psychological Services Center (The Center) is a private institution that provides a variety of counseling and psychological services in a wide portion of a rural southeastern state. The Center is located in a city with a population of 90,000 and provides services to many of the small surrounding communities. The population base is 60 percent white, 30 percent African American, and 10 percent other minorities, including Latinos and Asian Americans. Textiles, furniture manufacturing, automobile assembly, and agriculture are the main industries of the area, which has been labeled economically depressed. There is a high unemployment rate and a moderate crime rate.

Referendums for civic improvements such as schools and recreation centers are continually voted down by the populace. A four-year university in the area provides a variety of cultural, recreational, and social events. The casual observer would note the presence of modern churches, parks, music and drama organizations, and library facilities.

In competition with the Center, which has been in operation for 10 years under the same director, are two other small private practice corporations, a small number of individuals in private practice, and a local community mental health center that has been in existence for 30 years and has recently been told to divest itself of direct service programs. The Center has a professional staff of 15: one psychiatrist, one nurse, two doctoral-level psychologists, two doctoral-level counselors, two master's-level school psychologists, two master's-level counselors, two master's-level clinical psychologists, and three master's-level social workers. Two clerical staff members and one mental health technician also work there.

To provide community-based services, the Center offers a variety of outpatient programs.

Its clients are referred by schools, physicians, juvenile and adult court systems, the social services department, and occasionally the local mental health center. The basic realm of services is divided into several categories, including adult mental health services, child and adolescent mental health services, substance-abuse services, community consultation services, and employee-assistance program services. Plans for providing consultation to positive behavioral support (PBS) and response to intervention (RTI) programs are being developed.

The Center has no written role and mission statement. Its founder, a psychiatrist, feels that its mission is to help citizens develop and maintain an adequate level of social and personal well-being and dignity. Dramatic growth over the past four years due to the addition of the substance-abuse and employee-assistance programs has led to a doubling of the organization's income and the hiring of five additional staff during that time.

The Organization's Problems

When the director of the organization last reviewed its progress, she listed problems that had emerged so that steps could be taken to solve them. She thought that such a procedure would help the organization maintain and perhaps enhance its financial position. As she reflected on the past four years, she listed the following problems:

- an increase in referrals of cocaine-related substance abusers with no true "experts" on the staff to handle them

- a lack of knowledge about how to evaluate the effectiveness of the employee-assistance programs

- increasing concern over the deteriorating relationship between the staffs of the child and adolescent program and the adult program

- too much of the decision-making responsibility in the hands of one leader for an increasingly complex organization

- insufficient time for program heads to consult on cases

- a lack of definite direction in the substance-abuse program

- an increase in the number of "acting out" adolescents as clients

- an increase in requests from schools for assistance with PBS and RTI programs

- the need for each program to clarify its own specific goals and objectives

- a growing concern over staff morale in general

Although the agency director knew that she had a few staff members who could function as internal consultants, she felt that objectivity was at a premium and thus determined that it was most likely best to seek consultation from an external consultant for each of the problem areas. The director, herself a well-known consultant in the area, was easily able to identify an effective type of consultation that would be likely to solve each problem.

Because the staff had no true experts in cocaine-related substance abuse, an education/ training organizational consultation was selected. The inability to evaluate the employee-assistance programs could be resolved through program evaluation consultation. Because the deterioration of the relationships between the two staffs was a mystery as far as the director was concerned, a doctor–patient type of organizational consultation was in order. The centralization of leadership in an increasingly complex organization called for a review of how decisions are made and what other possibilities existed, and thus, a process form of organizational consultation seemed appropriate.

Because program heads were increasingly taxed with other duties, they had little time to consult with the psychologists, counselors, and social workers who provided direct services to clients; client-centered and possibly consultee-centered case mental health consultation seemed correct for this problem. The lack of definite direction in the substance-abuse program called for either program-centered administrative or consultee-centered administrative mental health consultation. The increasing number of requests from schools for assistance with PBS and RTI required training the agency's staff, so behavioral technology training consultation was needed. Each program could formulate its own specific goals and objectives with the assistance of behavioral system consultation. Finally, the increasing number of "acting out" adolescents clearly required behavioral case consultation.

Existing Data on the Organization

The organization's internal environment is frantically paced: Everyone seems so busy that there is little time for social interaction at work. Office doors remain closed during the day, even when clients are not being seen. Paperwork appears to be backlogged in spite of computer-assisted office support and electronic databases. A trained observer would label the environment as somewhat unstable and heterogeneous.

The organization's personnel are cordial with one another, yet relationships tend to be superficial. Efficiency and productivity are high but come at a price, for little discussion occurs relative to the direction the Center should take. Although personnel feel secure about their jobs, it is evident that morale and a sense of teamwork are declining. The competition between the child and adolescent program and the adult program has caused some intense (but suppressed) negative feelings between some program members.

The organization is bureaucratic: The Center director makes all decisions and only infrequently consults with program directors. Lines of communication follow a vertical chain of command, and thus, the ideas of many of the therapists are not solicited. Employees were hired for specific purposes and are to work only to achieve those purposes. The rules of the organization, although explicitly stated in a manual, are never discussed. The director keeps a complete but disorganized set of records.

Change occurs at the Center in a "top-down" fashion. Typically, members are informed of changes through memoranda, although the nature of changes is described without any rationale. Clearly, there is the assumption that each change will be acceptable and willingly carried out without discussion.

The Center does not place adequate emphasis on the personal or professional growth of its staff. It assumes that talented people have been hired and that they will take care of their own professional and personal needs. No attempts are made to include employees in the emotional "ownership" of the Center. An environment that nurtures employee growth is lacking, and networking is not used as a supplement to the director's leadership.

As a whole, the organization is in some trouble. Although the Center and the demand for diversified services are growing rapidly, it is run as if it were still a small operation with a simple mission. The organization is still doing what it does well, but the price it is paying has alerted the director to the need for consultation.

THE APPROACHES TO CONSULTATION AND COLLABORATION

In each of the approaches illustrated in this section, you can assume that the consultant engages in all the appropriate behaviors expected of a highly professional, competent consultant.

Most approaches to consultation adhere to some version of the generic model previously discussed. You can also assume that the consultant proceeds in the same sequence as the generic

model. Thus, a good working relationship is established, a problem defined, a contract agreed upon, and entry accomplished. For the sake of brevity, I do not describe these basics of effective consultation behavior in each illustration. Rather, I attempt to provide the essence of each approach so that you can make appropriate comparisons and contrasts.

Mental Health Consultation

Client-Centered Case Approach.   Client-centered case consultation does not deal with issues that may be residing within the consultee. Rather, the contract specifies that I, as a mental health consultant, examine the consultee's client concerning some professional matter and write a report that includes recommendations. I operate in a fashion analogous to the doctor–patient approach to organizational consultation except that the diagnosis and prescription are based on data concerning a client, not some aspect of the organization.

My focus is on the client, and my aim is to advise the consultee on how to "fix" some problem concerning the client under consideration. I examine the client, make some form of assessment and diagnosis, and provide the consultee with a report containing suggestions and recommendations to help the client. I spend very little time with the consultee.

A counselor from the Center seeks my help in determining how to go about getting a mother and teenage daughter to communicate openly during their counseling sessions. I function as an expert in parent–child interactions and use my expertise in diagnosing the causes of toxic relationships and in prescribing remedies for improving them. The counselor is to provide me with as much pertinent information as possible regarding the difficulties the clients are having in communicating with each other in general and in the counseling sessions in particular. She gathers additional information on the client's family and relates it to me and is responsible for reading my report and determining whether to implement the recommendations I make.

I meet with the counselor for one session at the Center, during which I build a relationship with her and get a feel for her perceptions of the particulars of the work-related problem. I assess her general abilities as she discusses the case and consider the strengths and weaknesses of the Center. As I do this, I come to the realization that my consultee is likely to get very little individual or group supervision on this case because of the very busy state of affairs at the Center. I realize that I need to devise a plan that is short term and well within the counselor's level of expertise. My assessment is that she is a talented professional but has had relatively little experience in helping parents and children work through communication difficulties during the counseling process.

Next I interview the mother and daughter, first together and then separately. My talk with the mother reveals that she had found out about and told her husband about a sexual experience of their daughter. I pursue this topic in terms of the current state of affairs in the mother–daughter relationship.

Based on all the information I have gathered, I write up a report for the counselor and discuss it with her at our final meeting. After telling her that she is under no obligation to follow through on my recommendations, I proceed to share them with her. I suggest that she see the mother and daughter on an individual basis for two or three sessions to get to know each of them better and to develop a more trusting relationship with each. This would create the conditions that enable the mother and daughter to communicate more effectively in subsequent sessions together. I also suggest that she utilize a nondirective, person-centered counseling style for the purpose of enhancing the relationship between the mother and daughter. These recommendations are well within the professional competencies of the counselor and have a high probability of being successful. No special training is necessary, nor were there any increased demands for supervision. As a final step, I arrange for a follow-up session in about six weeks.

Consultee-Centered Case Approach.   In applying consultee-centered case consultation, my primary goal is to improve the ability of my consultee to work more effectively with the current client and with similar clients in the future. I am retained as a consultant because no one at the Center has sufficient time for routine consultation. I am available to all staff. The case at hand involves a psychologist with a female client who, in the words of the psychologist, "has a lot of anger inside of her that she needs to express." As I listen, I develop a strong hunch that some of the unresolved needs of the consultee are blocking his effectiveness in the case. I play the roles of detective, expert, and educator in this approach to mental health consultation. I determine what emotional and cognitive factors within the consultee are blocking progress in the case and give the consultee specific information he can use to help the client.

While discussing the case, the consultee mentions how much anger the client has and how important it is for the client to deal with that anger. He discusses the case with some emotion, even a sense of desperation. He knows that I am going to make some recommendation to him, but he seems driven to convince me that I should recommend that anger be the central focus of the therapy.

As a matter of procedure, I do not interview or examine the client, but proceed by listening to my consultee's subjective view of the case. I determine that he is suffering from a lack of professional objectivity and that there is little available supervisory assistance from members of the Center. In deciding to make some interventions designed to help the consultee regain more professional objectivity, I ask him specific, detailed questions about the client's anger and the therapy interventions that have been used thus far, since I'm more interested in his version of the case than I am in the actual facts of the case. I'm hoping that by discussing the client's need to express anger, the consultee will develop a broader, more objective perspective on the case.

I determine that theme interference is causing the lack of objectivity. It is as if the consultee is saying, "Unless she deals with the repressed anger in our therapy sessions, we will never make progress in therapy." He cannot see that there are several ways to help the client besides helping her get in touch with and express her anger. I attempt to use theme interference reduction through a combination of techniques.

First, I keep the discussion on the client and remain calm in discussing the case. In addition, I remain very calm and objective about my relationship with the consultee. Finally, I tell him a parable about a former client of mine who was similar to his. The client in my story never dealt with her repressed anger but still benefited tremendously from therapy. As I discuss the story, I notice a sense of reduced tension in the consultee about the case. He seems more objective and hopeful, and I close the session by calmly scheduling a follow-up meeting. I express continued hopefulness and interest in the progress of the case.

Program-Centered Administrative Approach.
When applying program-centered administrative consultation, I work with the Center's director and the head of the substance-abuse program, both of whom want to develop a sense of direction for the program. My specific goal is to help them develop that sense of direction and therefore fix the program. My general goals are to enhance the overall functioning of the program and increase the program development skills of the director and the program head.

My role is that of an expert familiar with substance-abuse programs and how they operate.

I collect information on the program and how it works, analyze that information, and recommend some solutions. I use my expertise in organizational theory to determine how to collect the information I need. My consultees discuss with me why they hired me in the first place and what they think they want from consultation. They point out some of the organization's idiosyncrasies and make suggestions about which staff I should contact in gathering information on the program.

The administrators help me develop a timetable for consultation and the methods by which they will sanction my work throughout the Center. They provide me with as much information about the organization as possible, respond openly to my questions, and then develop a list of their reasons

why the substance-abuse program has a lack of direction. Finally, they wish me good luck and let me know that they are available any time I have questions or need anything. They realize that they will have limited contact with me. The program concerns treatment, not prevention.

In concentrating on management and giving some attention to program accomplishments, I examine agency records on unemployment rates, arrests for drug use and possession, and substance-use driving offenses. I interview key staff and administrators and find out that no one uses the information. Further, there are no records on the types of substances clients are abusing. No outcomes are recorded as a part of the program's objectives. Counselors and therapists in the program see clients as part of their caseloads but have little input into the overall workings of the program.

I proceed through the stages of formulating a simplistic solution, first becoming very confused about the entire situation and then getting a firm grasp of the consultation problem. Based on this information, I develop a set of tentative recommendations, which I feed back to all parties involved irrespective of their ranks within the organization. Based on the reactions I get, I modify those recommendations. The final list of recommendations looks something like this:

- Use available data to determine community needs relative to substance abuse and, based on current staff, modify the program.

- Set objectives and develop a philosophy for the program.

- Point out that alcohol and cocaine abuse are on the rise in the community and that treatment of these illnesses could become the central focus of the program.

- Keep detailed databases that include the records of the contacts personnel have with substance-abuse cases.

These recommendations and the report that contains them are distributed to the appropriate people at the Center. It is up to the director to determine if and how my recommendations are to be implemented. I then set up a follow-up session to occur six months from the date of the report's distribution.

Consultee-Centered Administrative Approach. As a consultant applying consultee-centered administrative consultation, I am involved in the most complex and demanding type of mental health consultation. I am asked to work with the director and the head of the substance-abuse program regarding the program's lack of direction. The difference between this consultation and the example just described under program-centered mental health consultation is that its main goal is to enhance the consultee's program development and maintenance skills, and its secondary goal is to improve specific programs.

My role is that of both expert and facilitator. I expect consultation to take a long time because I involve the consultees in every step along the way to help them improve their skills in developing plans and strategies related to the successful running of the substance-abuse program. I need the skills of knowing about organizations, how they are best managed, and how they change for the better. I also need the skill of "reading" an organization to pinpoint possible problem areas. I move about the Center as if I were a member and try to understand it from the employees' perspective. Because my role is complex, I need to make sure that the administrator lets everyone involved know precisely what my role is to be.

The director and program head are involved with me as much as possible in this collaborative effort. They lay the groundwork for my presence within the organization and provide the necessary sanctions. They arrange times for me to meet with everyone involved in the substance-abuse program so that I can present my findings.

As I begin to "float" through the Center, I make sure that no one regards me as a "spy" for the director. I want everyone in the program to see me as a helper, not a threat to their security. I am careful to build trusting relationships not only with the director and program head but with all members of the program. The consultees know that their skills will be enhanced by gathering and discussing the data; I therefore get them to uncover what is needed to give the program a sense of direction. I help them use group meetings, interviews, and questionnaires as data collection devices and then help them discuss the data in meetings involving the entire program staff. As the consultees discuss the information, I notice that they incorrectly think they know what is happening in the program and where it is going. In helping them be more objective in analyzing the data, I point out some key factors: There is no philosophy surrounding the program; there are no written objectives and goals for the program. My observations increase their objectivity. In being very patient and in trying not to force my ideas on them, I take a relatively nondirective stance and ask them what they think various kinds of data mean.

Through my efforts, the director and program head realize that if the substance-abuse program had a well-defined sense of direction—complete with philosophy, goals, objectives, and a strategic plan for the next five years—then a great deal of stress would be alleviated for all the parties involved. The director then appoints the head of the substance-abuse program to chair a committee charged with developing such direction. It consists entirely of substance-abuse program employees, who are paid an honorarium beyond their normal salaries for their work. I agree to "coach" the program head in effective ways to run this committee and to help him try out new leadership styles and techniques as the committee attempts to fulfill its charge.

Behavioral Consultation

Case Approach.   As in client-centered case mental health consultation, my main objective in behavioral case consultation is to assist the consultee with a work-related problem in a given case. The difference between the two approaches is that in behavioral case consultation my work is within a behavioral framework. I work as a consultant in the Center and am available one day a week. My consultee is a master's level social worker at the Center whose client is a schoolteacher who wants to overcome his fear of flying in airplanes. I am an expert in behavioral technology and its application to counseling/therapy. I keep that role of expert throughout the consultation process, although I collaborate whenever possible with the consultee. Although I control the process of consultation, the consultee determines the best course of action to take in regard to the case. I provide knowledge concerning the learning principles related to phobias about flying and make sure that all the stages of the consultation process are successfully accomplished.

As my link to the client, the consultee provides me with as much specific information as possible concerning the case. I lead her through the stages of problem identification, problem analysis, plan implementation, and problem evaluation. We verify that a phobia about flying in airplanes exists and determine that the client does not possess "free floating" anxiety, but only a few situation-specific anxieties. Our goal is to have the client actually ride in an airplane with minimal anxiety, and we determine that this can be easily measured by having the client use a checklist during the flight and by intermittently taking his pulse rate.

I illustrate how the process of classical conditioning has probably occurred and created the client's phobia. The consultee and I then examine how this conditioning maintains the client's phobia. Next, we plan how the consultee will use an intervention with a strong research base, namely systematic desensitization. Because the consultee has had limited experience with the intervention, I retrain her and monitor her handling of the case. I show her how to apply the general technique to the specific needs of the client by helping her develop a personalized strategy. I give her some books and videotapes so that she can do some independent studying. I role-play systematic desensitization procedures with her, taking the role of her client. We design an evaluation that includes not only the successful completion of the desensitization strategy, but also whether or not the client actually flies in an airplane with acceptable levels of anxiety. We then arrange for a follow-up session in three

months. When she feels ready, the consultee prepares to follow through on what she has learned.

Behavioral Technology Training Approach. When I consult from a behavioral technology training approach, I focus on enhancing my consultees' general and/or specific skills in this area. The Center, particularly the child and adolescent program, was receiving more and more requests for assistance with implementing PBS and RTI programs in schools. Three of the staff members had served as school-based professionals in the past but were not familiar with recent initiatives related to PBS and RTI programs and their implementation.

Because of my expertise in behavioral technology and my many years of working with school systems in such training, I was retained to train the entire staff of the child and adolescent program in PBS and RTI program implementation with a focus on multitiered interventions.

My goal is to increase the consultees' skills in conducting functional behavioral assessment (FBA) so that they in turn can train selected school personnel in its effective use. The consultees are trained in evidence-based instructional and behavioral interventions for the universal, strategic, and intensive levels. Focus is placed on rewarding positive behaviors through various behavioral techniques.

I make sure that the consultees have enough accurate information on PBS and RTI, have developed related competencies, and have a positive attitude toward the use of these skills. The consultees should learn as best they can, integrate their knowledge about behavioral technology approaches into their consultation skills, and attempt to create a positive attitude toward the use of behavioral technology in the classroom.

Based on input from all the parties involved, including school personnel, I develop and implement a training plan using lectures, modeling, behavioral rehearsal, feedback, and reinforcement as my primary tools. Modeling followed by rehearsal and practice with feedback are stressed so that the consultee is able to perform the required skills well. I go to great lengths to demythologize

PBS and RTI and provide special focus on classroom management procedures, such as conducting observations and establishing token economies and "time-out" procedures. I have the Center's director announce specifically why this training is important to the consultees and the Center; he also comments on the types of rewards the consultees can expect from participation in the training.

I evaluate the training in several ways, first with a questionnaire that reveals attitudes toward the training itself and then with a test that has the consultees state specifically what they have learned and their attitudes toward their newly acquired knowledge and skills. A very important part of the evaluation comes six months later, when I observe the staff consult with teachers and other school staff on either PBS and/or RTI. At that time, I assess the degree to which they have transferred their knowledge and skills to actual school settings and how effectively they use those skills.

Behavioral System Approach. My goal in this approach is to enhance the efficiency and effectiveness of the Center in terms of its stated function. The director invites me to "take a look at the Center" and then make some recommendations. He notes that the Center is growing very rapidly and that its affairs are in a constant state of disarray.

As an expert in behavioral technology and systems theory, I accomplish my goals by collaboratively guiding the director and program heads through defining and assessing the system, making selected interventions, and evaluating the effects. I use behavioral technology to help the organization function more efficiently.

As joint collaborators, the consultees determine what is to be done in consultation and how the results of consultation will be used. To accomplish this, they provide me with as much accurate information as they can. As the change agents within the Center, they have both the power and perspective to accomplish the goals of consultation.

I proceed by helping the consultees define the Center in terms of its structure and activities. We observe what goes on in the everyday routine for a week, share our perceptions, and come to a consensus. Once we have characterized the Center adequately, we are ready to assess it. We design questionnaires and arrange to observe the various subsystems to evaluate the overall system. We try to answer the question: What are the effects of the Center's structure and activities on the behavior of its members? The major answer we obtain is that there is lack of direction among the members because there are no defined goals and objectives for the various programs the Center offers. The consultees and I determine that the highest priority must be given to having each program develop, spell out, and adhere to a set of behavioral goals and objectives. We next set behavioral outcome goals that include what is to be accomplished, when, by whom, and under what conditions.

Criteria are set up to assess the quality of these goals, which are then evaluated. I suggest that the various programs modify their activities and structure to coincide with their newly written behavioral goals and objectives. The consultees agree. We then develop an evaluation to determine how well each program behaves according to its specific goals and objectives. I arrange for a follow-up in six months to help the consultees discuss these evaluations and make appropriate adjustments.

Organizational Consultation

Education/Training Approach. As I consult with the Center within the education/training framework, I attempt to enhance the overall effectiveness of the organization by improving the professional effectiveness of the members of the substance-abuse program with respect to cocaine-related substance-abuse counseling. I assume that a blend of didactic and experiential learning is the best approach. The members of the substance-abuse team would probably need information related to cocaine abuse and some skills in working with drug abusers.

As a consultant using this approach, I function as an expert technological advisor, teacher, and trainer. Because I realize that the staff of the substance-abuse program is small and consists of skilled professionals, I tailor my consultation to their specific needs and am quite specific in the education and training I provide them.

The role of the consultees is that of learners. They have all volunteered for the consultation and meet my expectations that they will be interested and cooperative learners and will invest themselves in the consultation process. They realize that they need some assistance in working with cocaine abusers and are highly involved in the entire consultation process.

My first step is to conduct a needs assessment of the consultees to make sure that they perceive a need for education and training in cocaine abuse. Furthermore, I want to assess what they know and can already do in relation to working with cocaine abusers; I also want to determine what they must learn in order to work more effectively with cocaine abusers. I construct a questionnaire to acquire this information and hold a brief meeting with each consultee. I then hold one meeting with the entire group to determine whether the information I received from them accurately reflects their perceptions of their needs.

I plan the education/training based on the results of the needs assessment, which indicates that the staff requires information and training in diagnosing cocaine abuse, particularly in determining patterns of pathological use, impairments of social and occupational functioning related to its use, duration of the disturbance, and the probability of relapse into abuse. Utilizing the principles of adult learning, I assume that the participants are self-directing, can discuss many of their own experiences pertinent to the topic, and are ready to learn. For the primary tools of consultation, I plan a series of activities around the expressed needs of the consultees: lectures with audiovisual aids, several small group discussions, modeling and practice of diagnostic skills related to cocaine abuse, and feedback. I determine that four, two-hour sessions are needed to accomplish the goals of consultation.

As I implement the education/training consultation, I create a climate of mutual respect and am particularly careful not to "speak down" to the consultees or flaunt my knowledge of cocaine abuse. I am very open about what I know and don't know about the topic and about my experiences in working with cocaine abusers.

During the course of consultation, I include some of my own successes and failures with cocaine abusers. I remain flexible, keep a professional, yet light, atmosphere, and use humor when appropriate. I provide a great deal of time for practice of the skills required by the consultees, particularly during the last two sessions. In evaluating the education and training, I use pre- and postintervention questionnaires on the consultees' knowledge of cocaine abuse and behavioral checklists to determine their levels of functioning in applying their newly acquired skills. I have them evaluate the consultation in terms of its effect, adequacy, and value. Finally, I arrange for a follow-up meeting in 60 days to assess the impact of the training and to iron out any anticipated problems.

Program Approach. As a consultant with a program orientation, I am very much interested in working with the Acme Human Services Center in evaluating the relative success of its employee-assistance programs. The goal of a program evaluation consultation is to improve current decision making about how a program should function. I have been hired to answer the question "To what degree are the goals of the employee assistance program being met?" In addition, I have been retained to assist the Center director and the program heads to be more effective program evaluators in their own right.

My role is that of technological expert in program evaluation. I attempt to provide accurate, timely, and useful information to the director and program heads. I use as much of a collaborative approach as the skills of the consultees permit. I meet with the consultees to review the goals of the employee-assistance program, develop a possible program evaluation design, and present it to the consultees for their feedback. I then obtain their feedback and redesign the evaluation accordingly. Much of my time is spent in preparing and planning the evaluation design.

The consultees provide me with as much information as possible about the program, for such information will be needed when I design the evaluation. I spend a lot of time with the consultees to become very familiar with the program and ask the director to give the head of the employee-assistance program a great deal of time so that she will feel free to cooperate. I also discuss with the director what she intends to do with the results of the program evaluation. Her reply indicates that my evaluation will be used for modifying the programs (if necessary) and for running the program on a day-to-day basis.

After preparing the program evaluation design, I collect some of the data and have consultees collect the rest. To evaluate the goals of the employee-assistance program, data is collected on how many clients are served, the effects of the services for them, attitudes of clients and providers toward the program, and attitudes of members of the organizations in which employee-assistance programs are provided (including those who did not partake of the services). We collected this data by using questionnaires and surveys, observing the programs (but not the direct delivery of services to clients), conducting interviews of a few randomly selected volunteer service providers and clients, and examining the program's records on the number of clients for the various services offered and the duration of those services.

After collecting the data, I analyze them, bearing in mind the four standards of proper evaluation: accuracy, utility, feasibility, and propriety. I keep all the appropriate parties involved and apprised of my findings as they emerge. My findings indicate that only 3 percent of the employees use the employee-assistance program for an average of three contacts. Reasons for this scant participation are the stigma of being seen going to a counselor at work and fear that confidentiality will somehow be broken. Attitudes of clients and service providers are quite positive in terms of the perceived effectiveness of the services provided. Nonusers of the program indicate that they would be more likely to participate if services

were provided at the Center, not at the work site, and if the program did not have a reputation for serving only substance abusers. Intervention measures that counselors took with their clients resulted in positive gains by the clients.

My final task is to present this data to the director and program head. I suggest that all personnel involved in the program be present at a "feedback meeting," in which I outline the results of the evaluation and facilitate a planning session based on the evaluation. At that meeting, I use graphics to explain the evaluation and what the data represent and mean. I avoid jargon but take care not to appear condescending.

I then facilitate a planning session in which plans are made to publicize the program more thoroughly and promote it as a positive growth experience for the participants. Plans are also made to permit the employees the option of coming to the Center for services. I then summarize the evaluation, describe the next steps in which the consultees engage, and make arrangements for a follow-up visit.

Doctor–Patient Approach.   The director had no idea why there was friction between the child and adolescent program and the adult program. When an organization knows that something is wrong but doesn't know the reason, the doctor–patient model of consultation can be very helpful. As a consultant using this approach, my job is to find out what is wrong and prescribe a solution. The organization has purchased my expertise in diagnosis and prescription concerning the conflict between the two programs. I realize that my very presence is an intervention that affects how the problem will be diagnosed. Because of this, I spend time building effective relationships with the parties involved in and affected by the consultation to increase the probability that the information obtained from the parties involved will be straightforward and honest.

My primary goal is to define the problem that is causing friction between the two programs and recommend a viable solution. I assume that the friction is merely a symptom of some broader problem. At this time, I am not concerned about helping the organization enhance its diagnostic and prescriptive abilities. In the doctor–patient approach, I function as an expert.

I create relationships with the appropriate parties, collect and analyze information, make a diagnosis, and prescribe a solution. I must be able to "read" the organization and determine what data to obtain and how to obtain it. The consultees are the "patients"; I need them to describe the symptoms of the problem as they see them. I attempt to create conditions in which they can provide truthful, complete information, and so I ensure that they understand and are willing to implement my solution. I gather data about the organization's purpose, structure, internal relationships, leadership, and program for rewards. I gather this data by interviewing each member of each program about their program and their perceptions of the other program. Confidentiality is assured to all involved.

From these interviews, the child and adolescent program emerges as one that perceives itself to be out of favor with the director; the members see themselves as "second-class citizens" in her eyes and they question how they fit into her future plans. Some members even think that the entire program might be scrapped so that the organization could become involved to a greater degree in the more profitable adult service area. In addition, the head of the adult program is seen as a favorite of the director who has undue influence in the day-to-day operation of the entire agency. These factors have caused the strain between the two programs.

Based on this analysis, I formulate some solutions that are tailored to the organization and its capability for solving its own problems. First, I recommend a series of group meetings between the members of the two programs using third-party conflict resolution. Second, I recommend that the director make a written statement concerning the short- and long-term future of each program. Third, I recommend that she should appoint all program heads to an advisory committee that he will chair. Finally, I encourage her to implement these changes.

Process Approach.   The Center's director knows that the leadership style of the organization must change. She used to believe that an effective leader needed to control all the factors related to running an organization: employees' work-related behavior, record keeping, and decision making. This procedure worked relatively effectively until the Center started to grow in size and complexity. The director then continually found herself in a reactive posture she described in this way: "I feel like I am running from one brush fire to another. I am putting in 16-hour days. All the stress is affecting how I relate to clients and my employees. I think I need my own personal employee-assistance program!"

As a process consultant, I realize that leadership is a process variable in managing any organization. The director already knows that leadership style changes are imperative, so I am confident that some substantial progress can be made in changing how the organization is managed.

She has asked me to observe him in action for one week to get a feel for how she manages, and she also asked me to observe each of the program heads for two days. These observations give me some ideas about their decision-making styles and underlying assumptions about the nature of human beings that inevitably influence leadership style. My goals as a process consultant are to help the director and the program heads become aware of their everyday leadership and decision-making behaviors and to help them identify and modify them in ways that are consistent with their goals. I accomplish these outcomes by being a facilitator of self-discovery for each consultee.

I assist in gathering data to shed light on leadership and decision-making procedures as they relate to the current state of affairs within the organization. In addition, I help the consultees diagnose what is being done and what yet needs to be done. The director's goal is to delegate more authority, decision-making responsibility, and administrative tasks to the program heads. The program heads' goal is to develop leadership and decision-making skills that are necessary for their new responsibilities. Their roles are those of active collaborators; they must translate their vague perceptions into specific insights and then act on those insights.

I provide minimum structure in carrying out my assignment and use clarifying questions and probes to stimulate the consultees' thoughts on their own current behavior. As human service professionals with administrative experience, the consultees have decision-making and problem-solving skills on which I can capitalize. They also suggest interventions they think would be helpful. In this case, they ask for feedback on their leadership and decision-making skills. I proceed by helping the consultees set goals and by observing them as they attempt to accomplish them. I help the consultees gather data concerning employees' perceptions of the leadership styles and decision-making procedures within the organization.

Based on all this data, I help the consultees diagnose their problem—the need for practice in leadership and decision-making skills that involve input from all levels of the organization. I act as "director" and set up several role-playing situations in which the consultees practice the new skills. The director, for example, practices setting agendas for meetings, delegating authority, soliciting input from subordinates, and creating a strategic planning committee.

The heads practice confrontation meetings, assertive behavior, and conflict resolution skills.

After each role-playing segment, I coach the consultees in how they can increase their leadership and decision-making skills in an interpersonally effective manner. In addition, I make a few structural recommendations concerning how lines of authority can be set up within a small organization like the Center. I then help them develop ways to monitor their own progress in these areas.

Ecological Perspective

In using the ecological perspective, I consult employing a preventative approach. My "client" is the Center itself—a unique institution and not "just another human service center." Therefore, my first task is to become very familiar with the internal environment at the Center and with the community surrounding it. Therefore, I conduct an environmental assessment. I examine the history of the Center's development in the community and review its orientation procedures for new staff and how people are acknowledged on an everyday basis. I then interview selected mental health professionals from the community, who do not work directly with the Center.

My interventions are aimed at helping the organization develop long-term adaptive processes so it can continue to flourish as its external and internal environments change. I empower the staff to help one another and scan the entire organization for the resources (i.e., people, events, and places) that are over- and underused. I believe that the power for change resides in the consultees, so, as I build strong collaborative relationships with all the staff, I try to develop strong relationships with the consultees and make special note of their strengths.

Though the staff feel well paid and professionally appreciated, the interviews with selected staff members reveal a conflict between two teams and a general concern over having any voice in how the Center should be run. I help the members set up a network of effective communication in which they can support and act as resources for each other. I also suggest that the director establish work groups to enhance staff "ownership" of what goes on in the Center. I encourage the staff to develop special events at work that are not work related, such as "birthday breaks" and fun "bull sessions." Finally, I help develop a procedure for a community advisory group and an internal professional development group. My written report to the director (with a copy to each staff member) summarizes the elements and findings of the consultation and schedules two follow-up sessions three and six months later.

SCHOOL-BASED CONSULTATION EXAMPLE

This section first provides a typescript of a consultation session between a school-based professional and a teacher concerning a child who is disrupting the teacher's classroom learning environment. Next, I provide a collaboration session between the same two parties about the same child. After reading both typescripts, you may want to reflect on how they were similar and how they were different.

Background

Ms. Gentry, a fifth-grade teacher, has requested the assistance of Ms. Hall, a school-based professional, in dealing with a student who has difficulty with self-control. Ms. Gentry and Ms. Hall have met before to discuss other students. They have a good rapport with one another and share a strong respect for each other's professional abilities.

C1 (CONSULTANT):   Ms. Gentry, hi, it's good to see you. How's it going?

T1 (TEACHER):   Oh, better I guess. You know I really appreciate your meeting with me. I'm so frustrated. This kid is really disrupting the whole class, and I don't know what to do about it.

C2:   This is Tommy. He's the 10-year-old you mentioned the other day....

T2:   Yes. You know he's a bright kid, but I just can't get him to stay focused. He's always out of his seat with a thousand excuses ... the bathroom, the water fountain, the trash can. And, of course, this interferes with the work of the other students. As you know, we tested him but he doesn't qualify for any special services. He's of normal intelligence, and there are no LD or ADHD indications.

C3:   Hmm. Okay, let me see ... no special needs, normal IQ, but he consistently gets out of his seat, and when he's up he's not only not working himself, but he also gets others off task. Anything else?

T3:   No that's about it. You know, he's not a bad child. He doesn't mean to cause problems. He's just very social and very active.

C4:   Okay, so there don't seem to be emotional problems either. He's just out of control and doesn't seem able to follow the class rules.

T4:   Right. He just acts without thinking. He's not manipulative or mean. He needs to learn to control himself. I don't know what to do! I've got to do something. Tommy's not learning a thing, and he's keeping the rest of the class from learning too. My test scores this year are going to stink. Can you help?

C5:   Yes, we can work together on this. We could use the problem-solving formula we've used in the past. We'll get some more details on what's going on with Tommy. Goals will probably help once I get a more precise picture of what's going on. We'll establish some realistic goals and then design a plan. If it's okay with you, we'll use this little form I've developed to help us save time. (See Figure 13.1.)

T5:   Thanks. I appreciate your listening and your help. Maybe we could use a plan like the one we used for Jimmy. You know, it's nice to have a counselor like you. Your plans are sensible and easily implemented.

Global Goals

1. *Tommy learns to realize potential.*
2. *More effective learning environment for the whole class.*

Specific Goals

Tommy remains in seat during seatwork and discussion.

Plan:
Noted Obstacles:
Baseline Data:
Monitoring Data:
Conclusions:

Tommy develops insight as to how his behavior affects others.

Plan:
Noted Obstacles:
Baseline Data:
Monitoring Data:
Conclusions:

Tommy participates in discussion.

Plan:
Noted Obstacles:
Baseline Data:
Monitoring Data:
Conclusions:

Tommy follows directions.

Plan:
Noted Obstacles:
Baseline Data:
Monitoring Data:
Conclusions:

FIGURE 13.1   Consultation summary sheet

Consultant and Teacher Reflections

CONSULTANT: *At times it may be easier to utilize a ready-made form. This form can either be completed independently or during an interview with the teacher. With some teachers, this may lower the initial resistance to the consultative process. Some teachers become quite protective of their planning time. They may get as little as 45 minutes a day for planning and grading. These behaviors seem to call for a behavioral management situation. Does Ms. Gentry have the time and skills to apply the consistency required to implement a behavior management program?*

TEACHER: *I wonder what is going on with this child. There's something wrong because he is not doing the work. Could it be my teaching style or approach to him? How am I going to explain his behavior if the principal walks in to observe the class? Worse yet, what if the entire class gets off task while the principal is there in my room? Well, at least this consultant is listening to me and seems to understand. I really need that. I wonder if the consultant is going to get the impression that I can't motivate or control the class. I wonder if the consultant will think I complain too much.*

C6: Well, thanks. Let's hope we can make some changes for the better. Okay, you basically said, "Good kid, good intentions, average IQ, no emotional or learning problems, just out of control." Tell me more. How long has this been going on?

T6: Tommy's behavior has been a problem since the beginning of the year. I've tried different techniques in dealing with Tommy's behavior, but nothing seems to work. For example, after leaving his seat in the middle of a test, he knocked a little girl's paper off her desk. She became very upset and wasn't able to finish her test. This seemed to be the last straw so to speak. At this time, I called for a parent–teacher conference with Tommy's mother and father. When I informed them of the problem, they seemed surprised and concerned. During this time, I asked them about Tommy's behavior at home. His parents told me that they usually did not have problems with Tommy at home, except at bedtime. His parents don't sound very strict. I got the impression that their expectations of him are only that he eat

with the family and be in bed on time. Tommy basically decides what he does with his time. His mother felt that Tommy's behavior could easily be controlled by explaining the rules to him. She didn't seem to understand that I had already made several attempts to control his behavior, including explaining the rules, but always failed.

C7: That's got to be frustrating to have tried different types of behavior control and gotten nowhere and then find that there are not many expectations at home. Maybe we can design something new that gets better results. Is that your primary concern?

T7: That is definitely my primary concern because his behavior is not only disrupting his academic achievement but disrupting the concentration of the class as a whole.

C8: I think we have a pretty good idea about the nature of the problem. Now let's talk a little bit about goals. What would you like to see happen regarding Tommy's behavior?

Consultant and Teacher Reflections

CONSULTANT: *Tommy's parents sound loose. I wonder what kind of messages Tommy's parents send him about how to respond to Ms. Gentry's expectations? I also wonder if Tommy's acting-out behavior is a result of lack of control, attention getting, rebelliousness, or something else. A behavior management program may be effective with the first two causes, but, if he is motivated by rebelliousness, I wonder if such a program would work.*

TEACHER: *Well maybe I am too strict. Who knows? You know I tried those things I mentioned to the consultant, but did I try hard enough and long enough and do them correctly? Why are these parents so lenient with this child?*

T8: Basically, I would like for Tommy to be able to perform up to his potential in the classroom. He needs to get some control over his behavior in order to concentrate. He needs to change his behaviors so he's not distracting to the other kids in the classroom.

C9: Those things really seem to go hand in hand. If he is able to gain some control over his behavior, he should be less likely to disturb the other children in the class. You would also like him to work more toward his academic potential. Those really seem like good global goals for Tommy. In order to help him most effectively, we need to clarify two things: What do we mean by saying Tommy will be working to his academic potential? And regarding behavior—what would Tommy be doing if he did have more control over his actions? Do you agree that these are the two areas we should focus on?

T9: I believe that his behavior is affecting his academic performance and, if changed, will positively impact his performance in class. So, I believe his behavior should be the main focus of our intervention.

C10: Okay, do you mind if I jot this down as we go? Let's begin with Tommy's having more control over his behavior. Can you list five things that you would like to see Tommy doing that he's not doing now? Or five behaviors that you'd like to see him do less frequently? This will help us set some specific goals.

T10: First of all, I would like Tommy to be aware of other children and how

his behavior affects them. I would like for him to remain in his seat more often. I would like for him to be able to listen and interact appropriately in class discussions. And I would like for him to be able to follow instructions better.

C11: Those four suggestions seem like very good ones for a start. Let me summarize our goals: We talked about the global goals of helping Tommy to learn and achieve up to his potential as well as to obtain some control over his behavior in order for you to have a more effective learning climate for the whole class. The more specific goals that you stated include giving him some insight into how his behavior affects others. You would also like him to remain in his seat more. You want him to participate in class discussions. And lastly, you would like him to follow instructions more consistently. Are those some of the ideas that you had in mind?

T11: Yes. That about sums it up.

C12: Okay, now let's take each of these goals and see how we might measure progress in each area. For example, how would we know that Tommy better understands how his behavior affects other children in the classroom?

T12: I don't know, maybe through observations or his journaling. I would imagine if other goals are progressing that he would have a better understanding about how his behavior is affecting others.

C13: Sure, progress in other areas may give us some insight. That sounds really good. I did have one thought. What would happen if you had a

5- or 10-minute weekly meeting with Tommy to discuss some things that happened during that day or the week to create an awareness of other people's feelings? For example, you could say, "I wonder how Mary felt when you went by and knocked down her paper?"

T13: 5 or 10 minutes ... I could do that. I certainly spend more time on him than that now.

C14: We could use that then as one means of measuring progress toward our goal. Does that sound okay?

T14: Yes.

C15: Well, let's move on to the next goal of having Tommy stay in his seat more often. How do you think we might measure progress toward that goal?

T15: I suppose I could watch and observe over time. Perhaps take some data each day and note how the behavior decreases over time.

C16: Yes. One of the things we could do in this situation would be to take a baseline of Tommy's behavior as well as determining the standard amount of times other kids get out of their seats in a day. Then, as you said, we can observe and collect data to measure progress over time. What about measuring progress with listening and interacting during lessons? How would you measure progress regarding this goal?

T16: I'm not sure, can we talk about that?

C17: I see what you mean. That is a difficult goal to identify. How about eye contact? It's an indicator of attentiveness. Maybe you might note how well Tommy is maintaining eye contact. If you take note of how often he is able to maintain eye contact throughout the day, these behaviors may be a good measure of attentiveness. Perhaps we could come up with more specifics about that, but for now that seems like a good general technique for obtaining information. Then interaction of course implies....

T17: Right, that he's participating in class discussions and answering questions.

C18: Again, we could take a baseline of frequency of behavior then compare it over time. You know, you've got enough to do. Why don't I determine this baseline data for you unless you think my presence will make Tommy act differently? We haven't discussed a plan yet, but I would be willing to come into the class at some point in the day and get this data for you so you would still be able to concentrate on the rest of the class.

T18: Okay, thanks.

C19: Let's move on to our goal of following instructions. How would you measure progress toward that goal?

T19: I would observe his behaviors, establish a baseline, and note progress over time in the form of following instructions during the day or week.

C20: So, we would actually measure progress by Tommy becoming more compliant. I do think that though we are focusing primarily on changing Tommy's behavior, we may have to change some of your techniques and classroom management behaviors. For example, you may have to give Tommy more attention at the beginning of the implementation relative to other children in the class. Is this all right with you?

T20: I can do that.

Consultant and Teacher Reflections

CONSULTANT: *If Tommy realizes that other students resent his behavior, it may worsen the situation. We need to emphasize how his popularity will grow with more participation and compliant behavior. How can I get Ms. Gentry to realize the importance of emphasizing his growth in popularity rather than the negative side of his current behavior? Journaling is such a subjective measure to use for feedback. The negative impact Tommy's behavior has had on others may well be too sensitive for him to directly express in a journal or interview with Ms. Gentry. Is this an appropriate measure of any of our goals? Test scores are probably more important than Ms. Gentry is letting on. Perhaps they themselves should be the target of change here. The focus on improving test scores could keep Ms. Gentry fully focused and invested in the process while providing some concrete feedback for Tommy.*

TEACHER: *Setting up goals and measuring progress. Is this going to work? What if I put all of this time and energy into Tommy and he doesn't change? Why does everything mean more work for me? At least the consultant seems to think that the things I will try will work and is willing to help out in the process. But give Tommy more attention? How can I possibly do that?*

C21: I believe we've come up with enough goals. Now I think we're ready to take a look at what techniques you've tried so far. This will probably give us some clues as to what directions we will take with any further plan and will also give us ideas about the best ways to work

with Tommy. So, what have you tried so far, and what have you found to be helpful?

T21: When I first noticed Tommy's deviant behaviors, I would simply remind him to remain in his seat or to pay attention to the lesson, but he often would not comply. Then I moved his desk to the front of the class where I hoped he would better be able to concentrate, but this did not seem to help. I moved on to the removal of privileges such as time at recess as well as setting up a parent–teacher conference, which I mentioned previously. None of these things seemed to improve Tommy's behavior, though some worked better than others. The removal of privileges improved Tommy's behavior for a short period of time, but I don't enjoy using negative reinforcement with children. Especially since the effects seem to lessen after a few days. Tommy's mother suggested that I might reward him, but I have not implemented a plan using a reward system.

C22: You've really tried several good things. I'm a little concerned that none of them have been effective with Tommy. I understand your hesitance to use negative reinforcement, and since it has been only minimally effective, we won't include that in our plan. Do you feel that there is anything that you haven't tried that may be effective?

T22: No, I've tried all my usual tricks. I'm really frustrated with Tommy and his behavior. So, I don't really know where to go from here. I can usually get through to kids, but nothing seems to work with Tommy.

C23: Since his parents suggest that he enjoys rewards, perhaps we could design a system of positive reinforcement. Kids his age really respond to rewards. Do you have any ideas in this area?

T23: Mrs. Jones uses some sort of system of sticker reinforcement that I could use for the whole class.

C24: That's a good idea. Tommy wouldn't feel singled out, and maybe he could benefit from some peer modeling. You can even take this system a step further by creating really cool stickers with clip art to get the kids really enthusiastic. Does that sound like something you would have time for? I know how busy you are.

T24: Sure that sounds like a good idea. I believe you're right in the effectiveness of the entire class. As much as Tommy doesn't realize how his behavior affects others, he does seem to be influenced by his peers and their behaviors.

C25: Right, that really builds in the peer modeling idea. When he sees other kids performing in a certain way for a certain reward, Tommy may get the idea. Okay, it seems like we have a lot of good ideas. How about if we take the goals and create some rules and a reward system? To keep this manageable in terms of time, we'll only keep records on Tommy's behavior.

T25: Maybe this will work. Tommy will know what's expected and will respond to the positive reinforcement he's used to at home.

C26: Of course, the structure of your class will be slightly different as a result of record keeping. We also want the reinforcement to be consistent. Do you anticipate any problems or difficulties in this area?

T26: Listen, the way I feel today, I will try anything.

C27: I know students like Tommy can be a real challenge. The next step, then, is that we need to outline a plan of action. We have our basic goals. We know what we want to accomplish. I see the plan as using a peer-modeling program based on sticker reinforcement to facilitate appropriate behavior for Tommy. Let's try to put the logistical aspects of the plan into operation. What do you think would be the first step in putting this program into place?

T27: Well, I feel like I need to touch base with Tommy's parents again to let them know what we're doing. Then perhaps present the idea to Tommy himself.

C28: You're right. Tommy is a vital part of this plan, but perhaps presenting the program to the class as a whole rather than isolating Tommy would create less self-consciousness in Tommy about his behavior. To assure the effectiveness of this program for Tommy you could give him a little more attention—more eye contact and one-on-one time—in addition to making sure he's meeting his goals.

T28: Right.

C29: I told you I'd do the baselines, so I'll take care of that.

T29: Okay.

C30: So, we'll start by talking to his parents. Then the second step would be for me to come in and baseline some of his behaviors. Then thirdly, you should develop a procedure for presenting the reward system to the class.

T30: Okay.

C31: Now that we know what we're going to do and how we're going to do it, when do you think you would be ready to start?

T31: Anytime, as soon as possible. It should only take me a few days to set up a meeting with Tommy's parents. You can come to the classroom whenever you have time within the next couple of weeks. Then we could proceed with the implementation of the reward system.

C32: Okay, I can come in about 9 AM on Wednesday. How does that sound?

T32: That would be fine.

C33: Look, I know you have very little free time, but I would like to give you a pamphlet on token economies that may act as a reference during the implementation of the plan. Then we need to figure out how our plan might be making progress.

T33: Well, we will be able to look at Tommy's baselines and then follow his progress. We could even plot the data we collect in class on a graph so that we have concrete evidence of change. Yeah, that works.

Consultant and Teacher Reflections

CONSULTANT: *The negative reinforcement probably did not work because it is not used at home. I'm glad Ms. Gentry is not insisting on the use of negative reinforcement! I need to make sure that these techniques are clearly spelled out to Ms. Gentry and that they are implemented with integrity and for long enough to be effective. I'm not sure that what she has tried previously has been thoroughly implemented at a*

level consistent enough to be effective. I'm concerned about altering her class structure to assist record keeping. How can I minimize the level of intrusiveness this will make into her regular classroom routine?

TEACHER: *Okay, I am only investing 5–10 minutes a day on Tommy. That doesn't sound like much, but I seldom get time to breathe as it is. Is it fair that Tommy gets all of this extra attention when other better-behaved students get less? Am I taking too much time away from Tommy? Maybe some of the other teachers are correct. Maybe there is no point in all of this extra effort for one child who doesn't "deserve it." Yet the consultant seems to think there is hope. I wonder. Okay. Sticker program for the entire class … maybe Terry and Jackie's behavior can be addressed at the same time. What about the record keeping for all of this? That could be a lot. I wonder what system I could use that I'll feel comfortable with? All right. Nine, Wednesday morning. That's math time. What kind of process do I need to use for the consultant to get a baseline on Tommy? I can't forget to call Tommy's parents. I wish the consultant had offered to do that. She knows more about this than I do.*

C34: Good. Okay, what have we left out?

T34: I don't know. I feel good about this plan. It will definitely be a step in a positive direction for my class and Tommy.

C35: Can we schedule a time to get back together for about 20 minutes, perhaps during your planning period on Monday? Then we can make sure everything is ready and you can let me know some specific things I should look for regarding Tommy on Wednesday.

T35: Okay.

C36: I feel really good about our plan of action. We've put together a lot of good ideas, and I think it has a good chance of being successful. Now, let me be sure I've got this straight....

T36: Okay. We've gone through a problem-solving process in which we identified the problem as being certain aspects of Tommy's behavior. We then developed a plan involving peer modeling and a sticker reward system, which we used to develop a system of implementation.

C37: Great. So you feel good about this?

T37: Sure.

C38: Well, listen, I really appreciate working with you, and I hope we can do this again. Tommy is fortunate to have a teacher like you. The kids respond to you, and I can see why. With all you've got going on, you're still concerned about helping, not blaming, children like Tommy.

T38: Thanks. I try. And I guess if this doesn't work, we'll try something else.

Consultant and Teacher Reflections

CONSULTANT: *Ms. Gentry seems to have bought into this process. I'm encouraged that she is approaching this from a broad-based perspective. I need to remember to reinforce her and to mention, in an appropriate way, her efforts to the principal. Hmm ... I wonder if I should say anything to the principal. If I did, it could be misinterpreted by Ms. Gentry as well as others. Better not. This is the fourth case in which a token economy has been used this month. Maybe I should conduct some staff development training on the next workday. That would save a lot of us some time and perhaps plant some seeds for some future requests for consultation.*

TEACHER: *Baseline, sticker reward system, monitoring—these are going to take time. I'll try them, but I'm not sure about all of this. Well, okay, I'll try it for a few weeks.*

SCHOOL-BASED COLLABORATION EXAMPLE

Background

Ms. Gentry, a fifth-grade teacher, and Ms. Hall, a school-based professional, decide to collaborate to assist a student who has difficulty with self-control. Ms. Gentry and Ms. Hall collaborated before to discuss other students. They have a good rapport with one another and share a strong respect for each other's professional abilities. As you read this case, be sure to compare and contrast it with the preceding consultation case. In that way, you will notice both the similarities and differences between these two services. For example, in this case, you note that the school-based professional takes much more responsibility for some of the outcome of the case than in the preceding example of consultation.

C1 (COLLABORATOR): Ms. Gentry, hi, it's good to see you. How's it going?

T1 (TEACHER): Oh, better I guess. You know I really appreciate your meeting with me. I'm so frustrated. This kid is really disrupting the whole class, and I don't know what to do about it.

C2: This is Tommy. He's the 10-year-old you mentioned the other day. I have noticed him in the hallway a lot recently.

T2: Yes. You know he's a bright kid, but I just can't get him to stay focused. He's always out of his seat with a thousand excuses ... the bathroom, the water fountain, the trash can. And, of course, this interferes with the work of the other students. As you know, we tested him but he doesn't qualify for any special services. He's of normal intelligence, and there are no LD or ADHD indicators.

C3: Hmm. Okay, let me see ... no special needs, normal IQ, but he consistently gets out of his seat, and when he's up, he's not only not working himself, but he also gets others off task. I notice in the hall that he "gets in the faces" of other students a lot but in a playful manner. Anything else?

T3: No, that's about it. You know, he's not a bad child. He doesn't mean to cause problems. He's just very social and very active.

C4: Okay, so there don't seem to be emotional problems either. He's just out of control and doesn't seem able to follow the class rules. You know, that's exactly how he is in the hallway.

T4: Right. He just acts without thinking. He's not manipulative or mean. He needs to learn to control himself. I don't know what to do! I've got to do something. Tommy's not learning a thing, and he's keeping the rest of the class from learning too. My test scores this year are going to stink. I sure

would like for us to try to work together to help him.

C5: Me too. We could use the problem-solving formula we've used in the past. We'll get some more details on what's going on with Tommy. Goals will probably help once we get a more precise picture of what's going on. We'll establish some realistic goals and then design a plan. You can be in charge of the classroom part of it, and I will counsel with him and be responsible for that. I think he will be willing to work with me, and I'll work on changing the same behaviors you're trying to change in class. If it's okay with you, we'll use that little form we developed last year to help us save time. (See Figure 13.1; the teacher and the collaborator would use the same form that was used in the consultation example with the exception of adding a line for "Responsible Party" to indicate who is responsible for each goal.) You know, I really enjoy working with you. Together, we have a better chance of helping Tommy than either one of us would have alone.

T5: Maybe we could use a plan like the one we used for Jimmy. You know, it's nice to have a counselor like you. Your plans are sensible and easily implemented.

Collaborator and Teacher Reflections

COLLABORATOR: *At times it may be easier to utilize a ready-made form. This form can either be completed independently or during an interview with the teacher. Some teachers may prefer to use a different form or none at all. It is more important to create the conditions in which the teacher is willing to add his or her expertise to assist me in putting together and implementing my part of the plan. For example, I know she can help me determine the things that Tommy and I can work on in counseling. Some teachers become quite protective of their planning time. They may get as little as 45 minutes a day for planning and grading. By collaborating, I might help Ms. Gentry to be even more willing to spend the time it takes to help Tommy. These behaviors seem to call for a behavioral management situation. Does Ms. Gentry have the time and skills to apply the consistency required to implement a behavior management program?*

TEACHER: *I wonder what is going on with this child. There's something wrong because he is not doing the work. Could it be my teaching style or approach to him? How am I going to explain his behavior if the principal walks in to observe the class? Worse yet, what if the entire class gets off task while the principal is there in my room? Well, at least Ms. Hall and I are going to work together. She listens to me and seems to understand. I really need that. I wonder if Ms. Hall is going to get the impression that I can't motivate or control the class. I wonder if she will think I complain too much. I'm glad she is going to work with Tommy in counseling. That way I am not*

responsible for everything about getting him changed. Perhaps by working together, we can make good progress in a short amount of time.

C6: Well, thanks. Let's hope by working together and each having "a piece of the pie" in helping Tommy that we can make some changes for the better. Okay, you basically said, "Good kid, good intentions, average IQ, no emotional or learning problems, just out of control." That's my read on this too. Let's share some more about our perceptions of Tommy. For example, I am curious how long this has been going on.

T6: Tommy's behavior has been a problem since the beginning of the year. I've tried different techniques in dealing with Tommy's behavior, but nothing seems to work. For example, after leaving his seat in the middle of a test, he knocked a little girl's paper off her desk. She became very upset and wasn't able to finish her test. This seemed to be the last straw so to speak. At this time, I called for a parent–teacher conference with Tommy's mother and father. When I informed them of the problem, they seemed surprised and concerned. At this time, I asked them about Tommy's behavior at home. His parents told me that they usually did not have problems with Tommy at home, except at bedtime. His parents don't sound very strict. I got the impression that their expectations of him are only that he eat with the family and be in bed on time. Tommy basically decides what he does with his time. His mother felt that Tommy's behavior could easily be controlled by explaining the rules to him. She didn't seem to understand that I had already made several attempts to control his behavior, including explaining the rules, but always failed.

C7: That's got to be frustrating to have tried different types of behavior control and gotten nowhere and then find that there are not many expectations at home. Maybe we can design something new that gets better results. Is that your primary concern?

T7: That is definitely my primary concern because his behavior is not only disrupting *his* academic achievement but disrupting the concentration of the class as a whole.

C8: I think we have a pretty good idea about the nature of the problem. Now let's talk a little bit about goals. What would we like to see happen regarding Tommy's behavior?

Collaborator and Teacher Reflections

COLLABORATOR: *Tommy's parents sound loose. I wonder what kind of messages Tommy's parents send him about how to respond to Ms. Gentry's expectations? Maybe we need to involve them in our attempts to help Tommy. I also wonder if Tommy's acting-out behavior is a result of lack of control, attention getting, rebelliousness or something else. A behavior management program may be effective with the first two causes, but if he is motivated by rebelliousness, I wonder if such a program would work. All of this makes me think that I should work with him in counseling.*

TEACHER: *Well maybe I am too strict. Who knows? You know I tried those things I mentioned to Ms. Hall, but did I try hard enough and long enough and do them correctly? Why are these parents so lenient with this child? Maybe Ms. Hall and I should make a home visit part of the plan.*

T8: Well, for my part, I would like for Tommy to be able to perform up to his potential in the classroom. He needs to get some control over his behavior in order to concentrate. He needs to change his behaviors so he's not distracting to the other kids in the classroom.

C9: I agree. That's what I want to do. Those things really seem to go hand in hand. If he is able to gain some control over his behavior, he should be less likely to disturb the other children in the class. We would also want him to work more toward his academic potential. Those really seem like good global goals for Tommy. In order to help him most effectively, we need to clarify two things: What do we mean by saying Tommy will be working to his academic potential? And regarding behavior—what would Tommy be doing if he did have more control over his actions? I think that these are the two areas we should focus on. Do you agree?

T9: I believe that his behavior is affecting his academic performance and, if changed, will positively impact his performance in class. So, I believe his behavior should be the main focus of our intervention. Okay, I will jot this down as we go along.

C10:   Great. Let's begin with Tommy's having more control over his behavior. Let's list some things that we would like to see Tommy doing that he's not doing now. Or some behaviors that we'd like to see him do less frequently. This will help us set some specific goals. For example, I want him to walk down the hallway without disturbing others. I also want him to learn better social skills through the counseling I'll be providing him.

T10:   For me, well let's see. First of all, I would like Tommy to be aware of other children and how his behavior affects them. I would like for him to remain in his seat more often. I would like for him to be able to listen and interact appropriately in class discussions. And I would like for him to be able to follow instructions better.

C11:   Those four suggestions seem like very good ones for a start. Let's summarize our goals: We talked about the global goals of helping Tommy to learn and achieve up to his potential as well as to obtain some control over his behavior in order for you to have a more effective learning climate for the whole class. The more specific goals that we stated include giving him some insight into how his behavior affects others. We would also like him to remain in his seat more. We want him to participate in class discussions. And lastly, we would like him to follow instructions more consistently.

T11:   We also want him to learn better social skills and behave properly in the hallway. I know one thing, he's not going to be in the hallway much anymore. At any rate, we are going to have to figure out how we know what kind of progress is being made.

C12:   Good point. Let's take each of these goals and see how we might measure progress in each area. For example, how would we know that Tommy better understands how his behavior affects other children in the classroom?

T12:   I don't know, maybe through observations or his journaling. I would imagine if other goals are progressing that he would have a better understanding about how his behavior is affecting others.

C13:   Sure, progress in other areas may give us some insight. That sounds really good. I did have one thought. What would happen if you had a 5- or 10-minute weekly meeting with Tommy to discuss some things that happened during that day or the week to create an awareness of other people's feelings? For example you could say, "I wonder how Mary felt when you went by and knocked her paper off her desk?"

T13:   5 or 10 minutes … I could do that. I certainly spend more time on him than that now.

C14:   We could use that then as one means of measuring progress toward our goal. Does that sound okay?

T14:   Sounds okay to me. Well, let's move on to the next goal of having Tommy stay in his seat more often. How do you think we might measure progress toward that goal?

C15: What's your take on this?

T15: I suppose I could watch and observe over time. Perhaps take some data each day and note how the behavior decreases over time.

C16: Yes. One of the things we could do in this situation would be to take a baseline of Tommy's behavior as well as determining the standard amount of times other kids get out of their seats in a day. Then, as you said, we can observe and collect data to measure progress over time. What about measuring progress with listening and interacting during lessons? How would you measure progress regarding this goal?

T16: I'm not sure, can we talk about that?

C17: I see what you mean. That is a difficult goal to identify. How about eye contact? It's an indicator of attentiveness. Maybe you might note how well Tommy is maintaining eye contact. If you take note of how often he is able to maintain eye contact throughout the day, these behaviors may be a good measure of attentiveness. Perhaps we could come up with more specifics about that, but for now that seems like a good general technique for obtaining information. Then interaction of course implies....

T17: Right, that he's participating in class discussions and answering questions.

C18: Again, we could take a baseline of frequency of behavior and then compare it over time. You know, you've got enough to do. Why don't I determine this baseline

data for you unless you think my presence will make Tommy act differently? We haven't discussed a plan yet, but I would be willing to come into the class at some point in the day and get this data for you so you would still be able to concentrate on the rest of the class. I'd like to share this information with you. Maybe you can give me some ideas for working with him in counseling after you look at it.

T18: Okay, thanks. Now let's talk about him following directions.

C19: Good idea. Our goal is for him to follow instructions better. How can we measure progress toward that goal?

T19: I would observe his behaviors, establish a baseline, and note progress over time in the form of following instructions during the day or week.

C20: So, we would actually measure progress by Tommy becoming more compliant. I do think that though we are focusing primarily on changing Tommy's behavior that we may have to change some of your techniques and classroom management behaviors. For example, you may have to give Tommy more attention at the beginning of the implementation relative to other children in the class. Is this all right with you?

T20: I can do that. In your counseling with him, you can reinforce these behaviors. I wonder if he should be in a group rather than one-on-one with you. I guess I keep going back to the social skills and the fact that the group is a great place to practice them in vivo. We can talk about that later.

Collaborator and Teacher Reflections

COLLABORATOR: *If Tommy realizes that other students resent his behavior, it may worsen the situation. We need to emphasize how his popularity will grow with more participation and compliant behavior. How can I get Ms. Gentry to realize the importance of emphasizing his growth in popularity rather than the negative side of his current behavior? Journaling is such a subjective measure to use for feedback. The negative impact Tommy's behavior has had on others may well be too sensitive for him to directly express in a journal or interview with Ms. Gentry. Is this an appropriate measure of any of our goals? Test scores are probably more important than Ms. Gentry is letting on. Perhaps they themselves should be the target of change here. The focus on improving test scores could keep Ms. Gentry fully focused and invested in the process while providing some concrete feedback for Tommy. I'm glad Ms. Gentry is willing to make some suggestions, like the group suggestion, to me. It shows that we are truly collaborating here. It's nice to have some external validation of my ideas, or even some new ones from an informed source.*

TEACHER: *Setting up goals and measuring progress. Is this going to work? What if I put all of this time and energy into Tommy and he doesn't change? Why does everything mean more work for me? At least Ms. Hall seems to think that the things I will try will work and is willing to help out in the process. But give Tommy more attention? How can I possibly do that? I like how Ms. Hall was open to my idea about working with Tommy in a group. It is nice to see that I can help her some as*

she is helping me. Maybe we will get somewhere on all of this and I won't end up having to do all of the work.

C21:   I believe we've come up with enough goals. Now I think we're ready to take a look at what techniques we've tried so far. This will probably give us some clues as to what directions to take with Tommy. It will help us to develop a better plan and figure out some possible ways to work with Tommy. I don't have anything to report because I haven't had him in counseling before and haven't really done anything about his behavior in the classroom. What about you? What have you tried so far, and what have you found to be helpful with him in the classroom?

T21:   When I first noticed Tommy's deviant behaviors, I would simply remind him to remain in his seat or to pay attention to the lesson, but he often would not comply. Then I moved his desk to the front of the class where I hoped he would better be able to concentrate, but this did not seem to help. I moved on to the removal of privileges such as time at recess as well as setting up a parent–teacher conference, which I mentioned previously. None of these things seemed to improve Tommy's behavior, though some worked better than others. The removal of privileges improved Tommy's behavior for a short period of time, but I don't enjoy using negative reinforcement with children. Especially since the effects seem to lessen after a few days. Tommy's mother suggested that I might reward him, but I have not implemented a plan using a reward system. By the way, we need to involve the parents in this one. I think they are a piece of what's wrong.

C22: I agree with involving the parents. I think you've tried several good things. I'm a little concerned that none of them have been effective with Tommy. I understand your hesitance to use negative reinforcement, and since it has been only minimally effective, we won't include that in our plan. Do you feel that there is anything that you haven't tried that may be effective?

T22: No, I've tried all my usual tricks. I'm really frustrated with Tommy and his behavior. So, I don't know where to go from here. I can usually get through to kids, but nothing seems to work with Tommy. Since his parents suggest that he enjoys rewards, perhaps we could design a system of positive reinforcement. Kids his age really respond to rewards. Do you have any ideas in this area?

C23: Well, sometimes sticker reinforcement works well with students like Tommy.

T23: Mrs. Jones uses some sort of system of sticker reinforcement that I could use for the whole class.

C24: That's a good idea. Tommy wouldn't feel singled out, and maybe he could benefit from some peer modeling. Does that sound like something you would have time for? I know how busy you are.

T24: Sure, that sounds like a good idea; I was on the same track as you

when you started talking. I can even take this system a step further by creating cool stickers with clip art to get the kids really enthusiastic. I believe we're right in the effectiveness of the entire class. As much as Tommy doesn't realize how his behavior affects others, he does seem to be influenced by his peers and their behaviors.

C25: Right, that really builds in the peer modeling idea. When he sees other kids performing in a certain way for a certain reward, Tommy may get the idea. Okay, it seems like we have a lot of good ideas. How about if we take the goals and create some rules and a reward system? We have to keep this thing manageable.

T25: To keep this manageable in terms of time, we'll only keep records on Tommy's behavior. Maybe this will work. Tommy will know what's expected and will respond to the positive reinforcement he's used to at home.

C26: Of course, the structure of your class will be slightly different as a result of record keeping. We also want the reinforcement to be consistent. Do you anticipate any problems or difficulties in this area?

T26: Listen, the way I feel today, I will try anything. I can do this.

C27: I know students like Tommy can be a real challenge. Part of me is wondering how I am going to convince him that counseling is in his best interest. Well, back to the reward system. The next step, then, is that we need to outline a plan of action. We have our basic goals. We know what we want to accomplish. I see the plan as using a peer-modeling program based on sticker reinforcement to facilitate appropriate behavior for Tommy. Let's try to put the logistical aspects of the plan into operation.

T27: Well, I think the first step in putting this program into place is to touch base with Tommy's parents again to let them know what we're doing. Then we could present the idea to Tommy himself.

C28: You're right. Maybe we should use your idea of a home visit to enlist their support and maybe their participation. Tommy is a vital part of this plan, but perhaps presenting the program to the class as a whole rather than isolating Tommy would create less self-consciousness in Tommy about his behavior. To assure the effectiveness of this program for Tommy, you could give him a little more attention—more eye contact and one-on-one time—in addition to making sure he's meeting his goals.

T28: Right.

C29: I told you I'd do the baselines, so I'll take care of that.

T29: Okay. So, we'll start by talking to his parents. Then the second step would be for you to come in and baseline some of his behaviors. Third, I should develop a procedure for presenting the reward system to the class.

C30: That will work for me. I'll think about the visit to the home and how we should go about

approaching the parents. I'll think of some questions for you about how I might proceed with Tommy in counseling, like what he sees as rewarding and so forth.

T30: Okay.

C31: Now that we know what we're going to do and how we're going to do it, when do you think you would be ready to start?

T31: Anytime, as soon as possible. It should only take you a few days to set up a meeting with Tommy's parents. You can come into the classroom whenever you have time within the next couple of weeks. Then we could proceed with the implementation of the reward system. I will create a list of information on Tommy you can use in counseling. I am assuming you are still thinking about working with him in a group?

C32: Yes, I might have a couple of sessions one-on-one to gain a relationship and get him used to the process so he can be more ready for a group. About the baselining, I can come in about 9 AM on Wednesday. How does that sound?

T32: That would be fine.

C33: Look, I know you have very little free time, but I would like to give you a pamphlet on token economies that may act as a reference during the implementation of the plan. Then we need to figure out how our plan might be making progress.

T33: Well, we will be able to look at Tommy's baselines and then follow his progress. We could even plot the data we collect in class on a graph so that we have concrete evidence of change. Yeah, that works. By the way, I have put together some of his work so you can get a feel for what he does academically.

Collaborator and Teacher Reflections

COLLABORATOR: *The negative reinforcement probably did not work because it is not used at home. I'm glad Ms. Gentry is not insisting on the use of negative reinforcement! I need to make sure that these techniques are clearly spelled out to Ms. Gentry and that they are implemented with integrity and for long enough to be effective. I'm not sure that what she has tried previously has been thoroughly implemented at a level consistent enough to be effective. I'm concerned about altering her class structure to assist record keeping. How can I minimize the level of intrusiveness this will make into her regular classroom routine? I am concerned that the parents will play "No problem" with us and defend Tommy as being okay and imply that the problem is in the school. Ms. Gentry and I will need to make sure we are together on how we will approach the parents. I think Tommy can fit into a group. If his social skills are poor, the other kids may reject him pretty quickly. I guess individual counseling at the beginning will prevent some of that.*

TEACHER: *Okay, I am only investing 5–10 minutes a day on Tommy. That doesn't sound like much, but I seldom get time to breathe as it is. Is it fair that Tommy gets all of this extra attention when other better-behaved students get less? Am I taking too much time away from Tommy? Maybe some of the other*

teachers are correct. Maybe there is no point in all of this extra effort for one child who doesn't "deserve it." Yet Ms. Hall seems to think there is hope. I wonder. Okay. Sticker program for the entire class … maybe Terry and Jackie's behavior can be addressed at the same time. What about the record keeping for all of this? That could be a lot. I wonder what system I could use that I'll feel comfortable with? All right. Nine, Wednesday morning. That's math time. What kind of process do I need to use for Ms. Hall to get a baseline on Tommy? We can't forget to call Tommy's parents. We have to make sure we are on the same wavelength before we approach them. I don't like home visits, but this one may be worth it. Something has to change with Tommy. Ms. Hall knows more about this than I do, but I know Tommy better. I'm glad Ms. Hall is going to do group work with Tommy. I don't think that individual counseling as the only treatment would work that well with Tommy. I am glad that she was open to my advice.

C34: Good. Okay, what have we left out?

T34: I don't know. I feel good about this plan. It will definitely be a step in a positive direction for my class and Tommy.

C35: Can we schedule a time to get back together for about 20 minutes, perhaps during your planning period on Monday? Then we can make sure everything is ready and you can let me know some specific things I should look for with Tommy on Wednesday.

T35: Okay.

C36: I feel really good about our plan of action. We've put together a lot of good ideas, and I think it has a good chance of being successful. Now, let me be sure I've got this straight....

T36: Okay. We've gone through a problem-solving process in which we identified the problem as being certain aspects of Tommy's behavior. We then developed a plan involving peer modeling and a sticker reward system, which we used to develop a system of implementation. Then we developed a plan whereby we would try to engage the parents in helping him by making a home visit. You are going to work with Tommy in counseling and I am going to get you some ideas on things I think might work for you when you counsel him.

C37: Great. I feel good about this.

T37: Me too. I think that by working together on this we can hopefully help Tommy.

C38: Well, listen, I really appreciate working with you, and I hope we can do this again. Tommy is fortunate to have a teacher like you. The kids respond to you, and I can see why. With all you've got going on, you're still concerned about helping, not blaming, children like Tommy.

T38: Thanks. I try. And I guess if this doesn't work, we'll try something else. By the way, a lot of counselors would just come in and work out something for *me* to do. Then they would go off and work with someone else. It makes me feel real good to know that I have a partner in this. I have support and someone who is working

toward the same ends. It's a nice feeling to know that we are in this together.

Collaborator and Teacher Reflections

COLLABORATOR: *Ms. Gentry seems to have bought into this process. I'm encouraged that she is approaching this from a broad-based perspective. I need to remember to reinforce her and to mention, in an appropriate way, her efforts to the principal. Hmm … I wonder if I should say anything to the principal. If I did, Ms. Gentry as well as others could misinterpret it. Better not. Ms. Gentry's investment in this goes to show how sometimes collaboration is a better way to go than consultation. I think either service would work with her but I can think of many teachers who would want me to work with their students while they are working with the student also. This is the fourth case in which a token economy has been used this month. Maybe I should conduct some staff development training on the next workday. That would save a lot of us some time and perhaps plant some seeds for some future requests for collaboration. Better yet, I should ask for a few minutes at our next faculty meeting and discuss collaboration and consultation. It never hurts to keep these ideas in front of teachers and principals.*

TEACHER: *Baseline, sticker reward system, monitoring, and a home visit—these are going to take time. But so is Ms. Hall's counseling Tommy. I'll try my end of this for a few weeks. After all I won't be alone. It's not like we aren't going to help one another with each of our responsibilities in helping Tommy. All I can say is that I am relieved I'm not the only one responsible for helping Tommy change here.*

TABLE 13.1 **The Major Focus of Several Consultation and Collaboration Approaches**

APPROACH	MAJOR FOCUS
Mental Health	
Client-Centered Case	Helping a consultee with a client (with minimal contact with the consultee)
Consultee-Centered Case	Considers work-related problem to reside in the consultee; helping consultee by focusing on case
Program-Centered Administrative	Helping an administrator fix a program-related problem
Consultee-Centered Administrative	Helping an administrator and other consultees develop their skills to improve the mental health aspects of the organization and its programs
Behavioral	
Training	Training consultees to improve their general and/or specific skill areas of behavioral technology
System	Assisting an organization in being more effective by using behavioral technology
Case	Helping a consultee apply behavioral technology to a case
Organizational	
Educational/Training	Training or educating consultees to be more effective in some area
Program	Assisting an organization with some aspect of a program, frequently evaluation
Doctor–Patient	Entering an organization, diagnosing a problem, and prescribing a solution
Process	Assisting consultees in becoming better decision makers and problem solvers in the future
Ecological	
Generic	Changing the human–environment interface

SUMMARY

This chapter encourages you to begin assessing your own personal model of consultation and collaboration. It has applied the various approaches to mental health, behavioral, organizational, and ecological consultation to some work-related problem within a particular organization. Table 13.1 summarizes the major focus of each approach. In addition, we compared two transcripts of similar cases involving school-based consultation and collaboration to help you differentiate between these two services.

SUGGESTIONS FOR EFFECTIVE PRACTICE

- Remember to develop and follow your own personal model of consultation and collaboration.
- Read case studies and transcripts of consultation and collaboration cases often to maintain a

sense of how others deal with the nuts and bolts of effective practice.

- Get as much experience in consultation and collaboration as you can.

QUESTIONS FOR REFLECTION

1. Which of the approaches just described in the Acme case most emphasize the quality of the consultation relationship?

2. Of the Acme case problems just described, in which would consultation be the most difficult to evaluate adequately?

3. In the Acme case, do you see similarities among behavioral system consultation, doctor–patient consultation, and process consultation? Explain your answer.

4. Would you proceed in a manner different from mine if you were asked to perform process consultation with Acme? If so, how?

5. What similarities did you notice in the school-based consultation and collaboration transcripts?

6. What differences did you detect in the school-based consultation and collaboration transcripts?

7. Based on your reading of this chapter, which approach appeals to you the most? Why?

8. In which of the cases discussed would you most like to have been the consultant or a collaborating professional? Why?

9. With which approach would you have the most difficulty in the role of consultant or collaborator? Why?

10. For which approaches would you actively seek out additional training?

SUGGESTED SUPPLEMENTARY READINGS

Curtis, R., & Van Horne, J. W. (2014). School-wide collaboration to implement a positive behavioral interventions support program. In A. M. Dougherty (Ed.), *Casebook of psychological consultation and collaboration* (6th ed.). Belmont, CA: Brooks/Cole Cengage. This case presents systems-level collaboration involving multiple stakeholders while maintaining a personal, one-on-one approach to smooth the transition process.

Dougherty, A. M. (Ed.). (2014d). Cases for further practice. In *Casebook of psychological consultation and collaboration* (6th ed.). Belmont, CA: Brooks/Cole Cengage. This chapter provides a wealth of cases to provide the reader with common cases encountered by consultants and collaborators, each with extenuating circumstances that at once provide challenges, yet invite creativity in case management.

PART IV

✳

Professional Issues and Epilogue

Part IV of this text is designed to familiarize you with the professional issues, such as those that are ethical or legal in nature, and to assist you in determining how you can effectively manage them in your practice through sound decision making.

Chapter 14 explores the ethical and legal issues consultants and collaborators can face and makes recommendations for effectively resolving them in a professional manner. The epilogue contains my parting thoughts to you, the reader.

14

✳

Ethical and Legal Issues

Throughout their careers, all consultants and collaborators encounter ethical, professional, and legal dilemmas about which they must make decisions (Pack-Brown, Thomas, & Seymour, 2008). Decisions of this type require sound judgment. Frequently, the problems do not suggest clear and specific courses of action for the consultant to resolve them. This should not be surprising, for most consultation issues are complex and ethical dilemmas will be frequent. Consequently, ethics training should be a part of consultants' professional development throughout their careers (Neukrug & Milliken, 2011).

In this chapter, we will examine how ethical, professional, and legal issues may affect your consultation practice. We will also examine how consultants can make ethical decisions regarding these issues and thereby engage in effective practice. Even with the ethics codes of professional organizations as guides, there are few cut-and-dried answers when it comes to dealing with the ethics of consultation.

Consultants frequently have to depend on their sound professional judgment when they make ethical decisions. For example, you could face issues related to the ambiguity about how to proceed in providing consultation in extreme situations such as those involving disasters (Halpern & Tramontin, 2007) or you could have to determine adversity of the impact of consultee actions on client welfare (Gutkin, 2012). However, studying the issues that consultants encounter will provide you with a better understanding of the importance of ethics and the complexity of consultation.

Furthermore, exposure to these ideas can help you develop the competencies and professional perspective necessary for effectively delivering your consultation services.

Here are some questions to consider as you read this chapter:

- What professional and ethical obligations do consultants have beyond those to their consultees and their client systems?

- What are the basic legal issues that consultants encounter?

- Why are ethics codes, while limited in providing specific actions, important to guiding the practice of consultants and collaborators?

- What are some professional and ethical issues related to consultant effectiveness?

- How do multicultural issues affect the ethical practice of consultation?

CASE EXAMPLE

Consider the following scenario of an ethical dilemma:

You are a consultant working with a group of consultees in a human service organization. The consultees are all section heads within the organization, and you are training them in becoming more effective decision makers. It was clear from the outset that you were in no way to report to the organization's administration your opinions about any of the section heads' decision-making abilities. It was further understood by all the parties involved that you were to maintain total confidentiality about all aspects of the consultation.

After two months of training, the chief administrator asks you to evaluate the decision-making skills of a particular section head so that a personnel decision can be made about her.

The administrator assures you that the information will not go beyond your conversation with her and that no one will know that you ever said anything about the section head's decision-making skills. When you reiterate that confidentiality was guaranteed at the outset of the training, the administrator becomes angry, demands that you share the requested information, and threatens to terminate consultation immediately if you do not cooperate.

What would you do if you were the consultant in this case study? Would you be tempted to share the information secretly? What are your ethical obligations to the section head? What are your ethical obligations to the organization in which consultation is occurring? What is your ethical obligation to your profession? As you can see from this scenario, consultants must develop ethical standards as part of their professional practice.

Although ethics has been a neglected topic in consultation in the past, it has been receiving more attention in recent years (Thomas, 2010). For example, for a period of time, one journal dedicated to consultation, the *Journal of Educational and Psychological Consultation*, had a column entitled "Legal and Ethical Issues in Consultation" (Pruett, 1998). While very little has been written about specific ethical issues related to consultation and collaboration, these services are receiving increasing attention in the codes of ethics of many professional organizations. Several ethical, legal, and professional issues have arisen as consultation has become more widely practiced and as the number of people directly and indirectly affected by consultants' behavior has grown. Therefore, consultants need to become increasingly aware of the ethical and professional dilemmas they will encounter. For example, when consulting with organizations, human service consultants may encounter and have to make decisions about issues related to informed consent, coercion, risk to people, the limits of confidentiality, and the probability of the success of selected interventions (Wesley & Buysse, 2006). A school-based consultant may face the issue since the problem with the client system may be more due to the learning environment in a given classroom or the home situation than to some characteristic of the student who is the client system (Gutkin, 2012).

As members of the helping professions, consultants have an obligation to behave in such a way that they bring no harm to themselves, their consultees, the client system, the organizations involved, or society at large. Because consultation is by nature complex, the consultant is frequently caught in ethical dilemmas. In addition, consulting is a powerful activity that involves changing the parties involved. Finally, our society is demanding a higher level of accountability for human service professionals and the parties with whom they consult.

Just as ethical issues are receiving more attention in consultation, so too are legal issues. Ethical issues are distinct from legal issues (McNamara, 2008). Since consultants can be sued for malpractice or breach of contract and can encounter a variety of other legal difficulties, they need to learn about the laws affecting their practices and act in a manner that reflects that knowledge.

ETHICS AND PROFESSIONAL ISSUES

As it pertains to consultation, *ethics* refers to standards of moral and professional conduct.

Morality, on the other hand, deals with perceptions of right and wrong behavior and is based on judgments of behavior from a broad view such as religion or culture (Corey, Corey, & Callanan, 2011). You may want to note that there has been some discussion about morality and its relationship to consulting with organizations (Fuqua & Newman, 2006, 2009). For example, Fuqua and Newman (2006, 2009) raise the ethical issues surrounding the fact that members of an organization have responsibility for certain outcomes without the concomitant authority to execute those outcomes.

Ethical conduct comes from putting together an awareness of an ethical code and its underlying principles (Bersoff, 1996). Ethical issues in the mental health professions are regulated both by laws and professional codes (Remley & Herlihy, 2010). Ethics represent aspirational goals that reflect the ideal standards of the profession and are enforced by the appropriate organization (Remley, 2007). Corey et al. (2011) distinguish between *mandatory ethics* and *aspirational ethics*. Mandatory ethics refers to complying with minimal standards, a kind of "dos and don'ts" way of behaving. From this

perspective, professionals basically look outside of themselves, such as to rules of an organization, for guidance in dealing with ethical dilemmas (Newman, Gray, & Fuqua, 1996). Although the concept of mandatory ethics is useful, the complexity of the consulting relationship does not easily lend itself to using mandatory ethics (Newman et al., 1996). Consider, for example, the complexity of issues related to confidentiality due to the triadic nature of consultation.

Aspirational ethics refers to "the attempt to accomplish the maximum in moral and ethical outcomes" (Newman et al., 1996, p. 231). The concept of aspirational ethics can help the professional aim for the highest standards of professional behavior and go beyond the "letter of the law" (Corey et al., 2011). Compared to mandatory ethics, aspirational ethics are more general. Examples of aspirational goals include integrity and social responsibility (Newman et al., 1996).

When a counselor or psychologist functions in the capacity of a consultant and follows broad, written ethical guidelines, such guidelines are typically referred to as an *ethics code*.

An ethics code serves to discourage inappropriate practice and protects the recipients of the services being rendered. In a positive sense, ethics codes stress adherence to rigorous professional standards, clarify expectations, and promote exemplary behavior. Ethics codes help human service professionals to effectively serve society and the people with whom they work (Ponton & Duba, 2009).

Most human services professions have codes of ethics to guide practice (Jacob, 2008). Recent ethics codes, such as those of the American Counseling Association (ACA) and the American Psychological Association (APA), have both a mandatory and an aspirational component. The standards of practice of the ethics code tend to deal with mandatory ethics, while the codes of ethics typically deal with aspirational ethics.

Because codes of ethics tend to be general, they do not dictate specific courses of action. Further, the ethical codes of most human service professional groups contain very few, if any, guidelines specific to the practice of consultation. However, by having a strong understanding of pertinent ethics codes, consultants will be able to anticipate, and to some degree, prevent ethical issues from developing and use appropriate ethical decision making when they do (Williams & Armistead, 2011). In your practice, you will often face ethical dilemmas with no specific guidance for action. Each consultant can only apply the code of ethics of his or her profession and make the best possible professional decisions when applying the code to a particular situation. Many consultants belong to various professional organizations. Most of these organizations—for example, the ACA, the APA, the American School Counselors Association (ASCA), the National Board for Certified Counselors (NBCC), the National Association of Social Workers (NASW), the National Association of School Psychologists (NASP), the American Mental Health Counselors Association (AMHCA), and the National Organization for Human Services Education (NOHSE)—have developed a code of ethics. Thus, many consultants enjoy the privilege of having (and have the responsibility of following) some general guidelines that apply to the professional behavior of any human service professional.

By belonging to one of these organizations, members of the helping professions agree to adhere to that organization's code. Some organizations, such as the ACA, have specific statements about the ethical conduct of consulting behavior. The result is that there are some guidelines for acting as a professional in the general areas of competence (e.g., not providing services for which one is not competent) and responsibility (e.g., maintaining confidentiality) (Fuqua, Newman, Simpson, & Choi, 2012; Robinson & Gross, 1985). But there are few guidelines specific to consulting behavior, such as applying principles of confidentiality in an organizational setting.

In conclusion, consultants can use the ethics codes of their organizations only as general guidelines. These guidelines cannot identify appropriate actions for all situations, and the final decision for what constitutes a correct course of action in a given situation rests with the professional (Wesley & Buysse, 2006). Consultants are well advised to

strictly follow the ethics code of their profession for a variety of reasons, including avoiding potential legal liability (Wheeler & Bertram, 2008). Further, there is an issue that the ethics codes of many mental health organizations may be subject to cultural bias (Pedersen, 1997). As Pedersen (1997) notes, "not only do ethical guidelines need to be interpreted in each situation, but they must also be interpreted for and within each cultural context" (p. 230). Thus, developing personal methods for making ethical decisions is crucial for the consultant. On the other hand, recent editions of codes of ethics such as those of ASCA (2010) contain standards on items such as multicultural and social justice advocacy and leadership. The bottom line is that consultants, within the broad guidelines, need to make informed, sound, responsible, and culturally competent judgments (Corey et al., 2011; Pack-Brown et al., 2008).

In consultation and collaboration, ethical issues are often multidimensional and very complex. As a result, these issues can be a challenge to resolve effectively. There are many gray areas that require decision-making skills. The process entails not only learning information about ethical standards but also learning how to define and work through a variety of difficult situations (Dailor & Jacob, 2011; McNamara, 2008; Williams & Armistead, 2011).

To assist human service professionals in making such judgments, I recommend the following steps, which have been assembled from a variety of sources by Corey et al. (2011):

1. Identify the problem or dilemma.

2. Identify the potential issues involved.

3. Review the relevant ethics codes.

4. Know the applicable laws and regulations.

5. Obtain consultation from trusted colleagues.

6. Consider possible and probable courses of action.

7. Enumerate the consequences of various decisions.

8. Decide on what seems to be the best course of action. (pp. 24–26)

Just like any other decision-making process, ethical decision making is not typically linear and the consultant's emotions will be involved. For an alternative decision-making strategy based upon constructivism, consult Cottone (2001).

Here is a brief example of ethical decision making. You are a school counselor working with a teacher regarding a student with whom the teacher is having difficulty. A school administrator drops by your office and casually mentions your consultation relationship. The administrator asks for your opinion about this first-year teacher and her ability to handle students like the one who constitutes the client system. The problem is whether you should discuss the teacher's competency with the administrator. Potential issues include being asked for information by parties who fall outside of the consultation contract, issues related to informed consent from the teacher, confidentiality of information, the rights of the consultee and client system, to name a few. Pertinent to this example, you thoroughly review the ACA and ASCA ethical codes and related laws of your state. You contact and discuss the matter with one of your graduate school professors, your school district supervisor, and a fellow counselor in your district that is known for integrity. You examine the options that result from your discussions and look at your own thinking on the matter. You look for possible courses of action but only see one that is ethically viable for you. The consequences of the actions are basically possible relational issues with the administrator asking the question for not being compliant by answering it directly. You examine the consequences of not answering because you see answering the question as ethically unacceptable. You then professionally and politely empathize with the administrator's request. You then relate that you cannot share the requested information. You explain how you made your decision and then cite the ethical standards of ACA and ASCA that led to your decision. You then affirm that you are willing to do anything that is ethically responsible to support the school and its personnel.

In addition to mastering and using an ethical decision-making process, consultants themselves can engage in peer consultation activities (Gottlieb, 2006). Peer consultation is a process in which professional development activities and support are mutually provided by one or more professionals. For example, if I am experiencing difficulty with some of my consultation activities. I might seek some consultation for the consultant. Peer consultation can occur in support group types of venues and by telephone or the Internet. Peer consultation activities can be valuable in assisting consultants to cope with ethical dilemmas, prevent legal entanglements, and enhance their professional competence.

What kinds of professional and ethical issues do consultants face in their practices? The following issues are all involved, and I will address them throughout this chapter: values, multicultural issues, competence, training, the consultant–consultee–client relationship, the rights of the consultees, group work, and interventions. I have also included a discussion of ethical issues related to crisis/disaster consultation, organizational and school-based consultation, and Web-consulting in this chapter because human service professionals are increasingly being called upon to deal with these types of issues.

Values and the Consultant

As in any helping relationship, values play an integral role in the consultation process (Remley & Herlihy, 2010; Wesley & Buysse, 2006). The consultant, the consultee, the members of the client system, and the parties-at-interest to consultation all have values formed by their life experiences, and each party involved in or affected by consultation is in turn influenced by each other's values. It would be naive for consultants to think that their own values do not influence the consultation process while thinking that those of the other parties do. Clearly, it is important for consultants to possess a reflective understanding of their values and how they influence the practice of consultation. In fact, the ethics codes of the ACA (2005), the APA (2002), the ASCA (2010), and the NBCC (2005) note that self-awareness, including awareness of one's values, is important when consulting. Consequently, consultants will want to understand the role their own values take on in the creation and resolution of the ethical dilemmas they face in their practice.

A significant professional issue for consultants is the degree to which they let their values dictate their behavior in consultation. Consultants who impose their values on consultees or other parties-at-interest are on very shaky ethical ground because they are depriving others of their due freedom. There are, however, some sets of values that inform consultants' work. Community psychologists, for example, tend to value self-determination, and that value will affect the consultation process (Prilleltensky, Peirson, & Nelson, 1998). At the other extreme, when consultants are overly cautious about imposing their values on others involved in consultation, they risk rendering the consultation impotent. A middle ground appears to be one in which consultants are aware of their values, make a commitment not to impose them on others, and go about the consultation process as effectively as they can.

Value Conflicts. In our culturally diverse society, the potential for value conflicts is high.

When consultants' and consultees' values do conflict, effective progress in consultation can be blocked. The bottom-line for consultants is whether or not to refer the consultee to another consultant. Just as when value conflicts arise in other helping relationships such as counseling (Corey et al., 2011), there are no easy conflict resolution solutions in consultation. Consultants experiencing value conflicts should be honest with themselves in determining whether they can remain objective enough to work with those with whom they disagree.

When value conflicts do occur, they are typically best met head-on. The consultant can model effective conflict resolution skills for the consultee as they work through the conflict, and together they can determine whether and how consultation is still feasible. There are three areas in which value conflict issues are likely to arise in consultation: worldviews (including cultural perspectives), views of organizations, and views of the client or client

system. Consider the following examples of values conflicts:

Example 1: Differences in Worldviews. Gene and Phil, both mental health professionals, are consulting regarding several clients in Phil's caseload. Gene's cultural background is different from Phil's. As consultation ensues, Gene is increasingly disturbed by Phil's apparent lack of concern about being prompt for their sessions. When Gene questions him on this, Phil notes that from his perspective, time is a convenience for humans to use and not an indicator of politeness. Phil relates that in his culture, time just "happens" and is viewed more as a convenient way to track events rather than something that drives events. Gene's view is that time is very critical and important and that every act on the job must be completed in an efficient and timely fashion. To act otherwise is certainly unprofessional and possibly unethical. If you were Gene, how would you attempt to manage these different views so that effective consultation might take place? Should Gene refer Phil to another consultant? Do you think Gene is open to examining his view of life and accommodating differing views?

Example 2: Differences in Views of Organizations. Bobbie is a mental health consultant assigned to work with the law enforcement professionals in a large urban police department. Bobbie has to negotiate constantly between the often conflicting values associated with mental health and law enforcement. When a high-ranking police officer used a consultation session to deal with ways to prevent bypassing the chain of command, Bobbie inadvertently made light of the situation and was puzzled when the police officer did not return for a second consultation session. Why do you think that one minor slip-up caused the officer not to return? In what ways do you think Bobbie could have prevented such a slip-up? What Bobbie didn't recognize was the taboo in law enforcement circles against bypassing the chain of command, whereas in a mental health setting, such behavior might be viewed as inappropriate and worthy of reprimand but is certainly not such a big deal.

A perceived value difference concerning views of behavior probably caused the officer's absence. Because the officer did not perceive the consultant to be knowledgeable about or respectful of law enforcement values, he prematurely terminated consultation.

Example 3: Differences in Views of the Client System. A consultant working with the administrator of a substance-abuse program in a human service agency finds that the administrator thinks of the program's clients as "welfare bums" who are "sponging off" society and the agency. The consultant, in contrast, views the clients as sick and in need of rehabilitation. How would you proceed if you were the consultant? How would you specifically deal with the value conflict in which you find yourself? Clearly, this situation has no easy answer.

In summary, because values are connected to every important decision made during the consultation process, consultants must be aware of their own values (Corey et al., 2011) and make a commitment not to impose them on consultees. The consultant's values can, however, be used to make appropriate decisions. The issue concerns how much consultants should allow their values to influence their behavior in consultation and when they should reveal their values (Snow & Gersick, 1986). When value conflicts emerge, the consultant should deal with them in a nondefensive, professional manner.

Multicultural Issues

Multicultural issues are important elements in ethical and professional decision making (see, e.g., the APA (2003), the ASCA (2010), and the NASP (2010b). Ethical practice dictates that consultants take the cultural context of consultees and client systems into account. In fact, some authors (e.g., Ingraham, 2000, 2003, 2007; Tarver Behring & Ingraham, 1998) have called for making culture a central component in the field of consultation. Increasingly, our society is becoming culturally diverse (Kanel, 2007; Tomes, 2011). This diversity

is reflected in the workplace (Sue, 2008) and in organizations such as schools. As a result, as a consultant or collaborator, you will most likely have contact with people with varying cultural backgrounds. When working with consultees or fellow collaborators who are culturally different or with consultees or fellow collaborators whose clients are culturally different, you may well encounter many ethical dilemmas and issues (Corey et al., 2011). Ethics codes typically underscore the helper's responsibility to take cultural contexts into consideration when delivering services. For example, the ethics codes of the ACA (2005), the APA (2002), the ASCA (2010), the NASW (2008), and the NASP (2010b) all cite respect for cultural diversity as essential to best practices, and diversity perspectives have been incorporated into these codes. In their practice, consultants can place themselves in ethical jeopardy by ignoring diversity factors because such neglect can infringe upon rights of consultees with different worldviews and values or by not promoting fairness and nondiscrimination.

The experiences of growing up in a different culture can create language patterns, learning styles, and ways of acting that differ from those of the majority culture. For example, speech in high-context cultures, such as Native American cultures, relies heavily on nonverbal aspects of communication, whereas low-context cultures like that of the majority culture rely more heavily on the use of words (Miranda, 1993). It is easy to imagine a person from a low-context cultural background wanting a person from a high-context cultural background to think, act, and speak more concretely and quickly. The implications for the development of ethical dilemmas in consultation and collaboration are obvious.

People from differing cultural, ethnic, or racial backgrounds can vary in a variety of ways, including values, language patterns, and child-rearing patterns (Thomas, Correa, & Morsink, 1995). Obviously, there can be differences within cultural groups regarding these same constructs, which make generalization difficult (Kocet, 2009; Tobias, 1993). As a result, specific cultural characteristics may assist professionals with information in dealing with consultees, fellow collaborators, and their clients to the degree those people possess those characteristics. Nonetheless, working effectively with people from differing cultural backgrounds requires knowledge of and respect for their cultural heritage and worldviews (D'Andrea & Heckman, 2008; Ingraham, 2007, 2008; Ramirez & Smith, 2007).

To practice ethically, consultants need to demonstrate sensitivity to and respect for cultural differences when they provide their services to families, schools, or any other organization (Arredondo, Tovar-Blank, & Parham, 2008; Hogan, 2007; Remley & Herlihy, 2010). If consultants or collaborators do not take such differences into account, they can inadvertently cause difficulties in the helping relationship or exploit others. When consultants or collaborators do not act with multicultural sensitivity or competence, they often become frustrated in attempts to be of service, get locked into their "expert" role, and become more content oriented (as opposed to process oriented) (Dougherty, 1996–1997). There is some likelihood that the effectiveness of their communication will suffer.

Consultants and collaborators have a professional and ethical obligation to be aware of the influence of their culture and gender on their work with people of different cultural identities (Lum, 2011; Ramirez & Smith, 2007). Consultants and collaborators should recognize that their models of service delivery and perhaps even their ethics codes are deficient in the areas related to ethnic, racial, and cultural diversity (Jackson & Hayes, 1993; Soo-Hoo, 1998; Weinrach & Thomas, 1998).

Clearly, multicultural influences need to be taken into account when providing consultative and collaborative services (Holcomb-McCoy & Bryan, 2010; Romney, 2008; Tomes, 2011). Consultants and collaborators should possess an awareness and comprehension of their own cultural group and the cultural group of their consultees and fellow collaborators. Consultants need perceptual sensitivity toward their own personal values and beliefs as well as those of consultees and fellow collaborators, and they should

have a comprehension of the impact of the experiences of the mainstream culture on the parties involved in the helping process.

The Case of Sidney.   Sidney is a Caucasian consultant who has a private consulting practice in a large urban area. Sidney is contacted by a minority neighborhood group because of his reputation for advocacy work. The neighborhood group is interested in forming a network that provides neighborhood members access to resources related to their personal and social welfare as well as enhancing their own sense of empowerment.

Sidney agrees to provide consultation free of charge. As he begins work with the consultees from the neighborhood organization, he starts out by sharing the importance of advocacy. As he continues, many members of the group believe him to be condescending. He even occasionally uses terms like "you people" and "you need to get on with it!" When one of the members approaches Sidney about his behavior, Sidney explodes and says: "I am helping you people and not even charging you! You're lucky I just don't stop the whole deal right now. Remember, I am an expert on advocacy for disenfranchised groups." How could Sidney's worldview have gotten him in this unfortunate predicament? What values was Sidney using that seemed to make the consultation go awry? Assuming that Sidney had good intentions, what might you suggest to him about the way he went about trying to help?

The Case of Maria.   Maria, a Hispanic counselor, is consulting with Michael, an African American psychologist, about one of Michael's cases. As Michael describes the case of an abused child, Maria immediately focuses in on the family unit for discussion and directs Michael to talk more in a "family therapy" mode. Maria is aware of her own strong views about how families influence the individual family members and how treatment should focus on the entire family and perhaps the extended family. When Michael refocuses the discussion on the child, Maria confronts what she believes to be Michael's resistance. Maria ends up persuading

Michael to look at the problem from her perspective. Do you see any possible ethical conflicts for Maria in this case? Can you identify any ways in which Maria could have acted differently when consulting with Michael? Could cultural variables have played a part in the way both Maria and Michael conceptualized the case?

Consultant Competence

The issue of consultant competence has received much attention: the ethics codes of the major organizations in which many consultants have membership (e.g., the ACA [2005], the APA [2002], the ASCA [2010], the NASP [2010b]) all make statements to the effect that members should deliver only those services and accept only those positions for which they are qualified. The ethics code of the NBCC (2005) explicitly makes this statement for consulting. These qualifications are usually determined by the consultant's training and experience and are particularly challenging in situation involving organization consultation (Fuqua et al., 2012). In addition, most ethics codes strongly recommend obtaining peer consultation or supervision when clinical, ethical, or legal concerns arise in order to obtain a deeper and broader understanding of related issues (Raines & Dibble, 2011). Consultants need to bear in mind, from an ethical perspective, the actions that may result from their input during consultation.

The parameters of competence are maintaining high levels of professionalism, knowing one's professional limitations, knowing when to decline and refer, and avoiding consultation activities when personal concerns could affect professional performance (Corey et al., 2011; Williams & Armistead, 2011).

Maintaining High Levels of Professionalism.

Consultants can do several things to maintain high levels of professional competence:

- belong to and participate in professional organizations
- obtain the appropriate national and state credentials, certificates, and licenses for the profession in which they are trained

- participate in professional development activities in general
- participate in professional development activities (both didactic and experiential) that pertain to the consultation services they deliver or would like to deliver, including those related to multicultural contexts
- keep proper records
- co-consult with more experienced colleagues
- consult under the supervision of a trusted colleague or a designated supervisor
- remain knowledgeable about the ethics code for their profession

Underlying the maintenance of professionalism is consultants' desire to grow in their work.

Consultants with such a growth orientation attempt to stretch themselves so that the depth and breadth of their knowledge and skills increase. This willingness to grow professionally also provides consultees a positive role model that stimulates their growth and desire to participate more fully in consultation. Indeed, most ethics codes advocate that their organization's members engage in professional development maintain competence (Raines & Dibble, 2011).

Record keeping in clinical consultation, although not well defined from the perspective of ethical codes, is becoming increasingly important. Thomas (2010) suggests that it is often a good idea for consultants to engage in record keeping for the purposes of continuity, meeting an organization's policies, and documenting financial transactions.

The Case of Roger.   After Roger earned his doctorate in a human service profession, he proudly thought that he had "done it all." He became an active consultant and worked with many community groups on what he liked to call "family dynamics." Mary was one of Roger's consultees several years before. When she again became one of his consultees, Mary got the eerie feeling that she was hearing the very same thing she had heard from Roger almost 10 years earlier.

New terms like *empowerment* were thrown in for some of the same old ideas. When Mary challenged Roger and asked him his views on family systems and codependency as they related to the topic being discussed in the consultation, Roger became flustered, noted quickly that there was probably no connection, and promptly changed the subject. Has Roger kept updated in his field? Do you feel he has behaved ethically or has a high level of professionalism?

Knowing One's Professional Limitations.   Prior to entering a consultation relationship, consultants must assess whether their personal and professional competence is adequate for the task. Although it is easy to suggest ways of maintaining high levels of professionalism as a consultant, it is more difficult to suggest methods of knowing one's limitations. Most ethical codes such as those of the ACA (2005) and the APA (2002) state that knowledge of one's limitations and/or abilities is essential. The ACA *Code of Ethics* (2005) makes direct reference to consultant competency.

Probably the most important thing that consultants can do in recognizing their limitations is to make a commitment to maintain high levels of objectivity and integrity while placing the needs of the consultee and the organization above their own. By asking themselves the following four questions in order, consultants can stay focused on their limitations:

1.   What can I do, given this situation?

2.   What is the right thing to do in this situation?

3.   Do I have the ability to do the right thing?

4.   What is the right thing to do that is in the best interests of the consultee and the organization?

By carefully pondering these questions, consultants are less likely to make errors in judgment with respect to their limitations. There is no substitute for the combination of personal and professional self-awareness and the commitment to put forth one's best effort when consulting.

When assessing their professional limitations, mental health professionals also may well want to seek consultation regarding ethical dilemmas and issues (Raines & Dibble, 2011). The consultant may be able to assist the practitioner in developing a deeper and richer understanding of related ethical issues and, as a result, new options may emerge and legal entanglements avoided.

The Case of Shirley.   Shirley recently received her master's degree in one of the helping professions, which included taking a course in consultation. She received a phone call from a church group offering her a fee for providing a workshop on eating disorders. Although Shirley was not knowledgeable about eating disorders, she took the consultation. She studied the topic for a week and then presented a two-day workshop.

How well do you think Shirley knows her professional limitations? Did she have the right to conduct a workshop just because the group asked her to? If you were Shirley's work supervisor, how would you handle the situation if you became aware of it?

Knowing When to Decline and Refer.   When consultants realize they are "in over their heads" in terms of what is expected of them, they need to decline providing consultation services and make an appropriate referral. The story of the consultee walking up to a consultant and asking, "Are you an expert in X?," to which the consultant responds, "Sure, just give me an hour," should never occur. Several professional organizations' ethical codes state that services should be delivered only if it is anticipated that the provider can effectively manage the existing problem as well as any others that may arise.

A related issue involves the representation of oneself as a consultant. Consultants must state explicitly what they stand for, who they represent, and what they can and cannot do as consultants. This obligation to represent oneself honestly and accurately includes advertising. The ACA (2005) and the APA (2002) all make explicit statements with regard to honest disclosure about oneself both in person and through advertising.

Closely tied to the issue of representing oneself honestly is the issue of remuneration. Consultants typically charge the "going fee" for a given type of consultation service with a given type of organization in a given geographic area. The ACA (1995) specifically states that its members must refuse any type of remuneration when consultation recipients are due those services through the member's organization. Consultants must consider for each potential consultation whether they are in a position to charge fees in the first place and, if so, how much.

How do consultants respond when they are asked to provide services for which they are not qualified? The answer lies in referral procedures. Consultants have the responsibility to determine at the outset of consultation (in exploring organizational needs) whether or not they can be of assistance. When consultants determine that they cannot be of assistance, they should consider making a referral to a qualified consultant; even if a referral is not possible, the provision of services should be declined anyway.

Consultants sometimes decline to offer their services when the time required for consultation is longer than they have available. Thus, it would be unethical for consultants to take on a two-year project when at the outset they know they would be available for only six months.

The Case of Jackie. Jackie holds a doctorate in a helping profession and has been working with a mental health center for 10 years. She is actively seeking another professional position in another part of the country and is approached by a community group to consult with them in developing a two-year self-advocacy project for the homeless in the area. Although Jackie has a great deal of expertise and interest in this area, she refers the community group to another consultant because of the possibility that she might be relocating. This scenario reflects a common concern in our mobile society: The consultant may not be around to finish what he or she agreed to complete. In this case, Jackie clearly knew when to decline and refer.

When Personal Concerns Affect Professional Performance. Consultants, of course, have the same kinds of personal concerns and problems as anyone else, and these can negatively affect their

professional performance to the degree that consultation services are not adequate.

In this case, the consultant should consider stopping the services and making an appropriate referral. In fact, the APA code of ethics (2002) states that when members suffer from personal concerns that affect professional functioning, they should "take appropriate measures, such as obtaining professional consultation or assistance and determine whether they should limit, suspend, or terminate their work-related duties" (APA, 2002, p. 9). Therefore, consultants who are experiencing high levels of stress should be particularly aware of their ability to provide adequate professional services.

Consultants need to be aware of their personal needs throughout each phase of the consultation process and should take measures so that those needs do not replace the needs of the consultee (Corey et al., 2011); such an awareness decreases the probability that the consultant will behave unethically. If an exception must be made with regard to consulting despite a lack of competence, Wallace and Hall (1996) suggested that this should be done only when certain conditions are present:

- if it can be clearly established that there is no other consultant in the area who is better qualified
- if the consultant possesses parallel training and experience for the consulting task
- if the consultant has adequate time to prepare for the consulting task
- if the consultant makes all these limitations clear to the employing agency
- if it is a crisis situation that requires immediate intervention

Training as an Ethical Issue

Training is actually an aspect of consultant competence. Consultants must make sure they have the adequate training to perform the services for which they contract (ACA, 2005; ASCA, 2010; Fagan, 2008; Hylander, 2012; NASP, 2010b; Pryzwansky, 2011). Consultation is not "watered-down" counseling/psychotherapy and its skills do not come naturally from being trained in these methods (Caplan, Caplan, & Erchul, 1994).

Although there are some guidelines for training related to consultation and collaboration in many accrediting agencies, it is ultimately up to individual consultants to decide whether they have received sufficient training to deliver competent services in a given consultation situation. The development of ethical behavior in consultants has most likely been enhanced by the focus in recent literature on consultation training (see Gutkin, 2002; Meyers, 2002). There has been a paucity of empirical research conducted on training in consultation, but recent literature in the field has critically examined the training needs of prospective consultants (see, e.g., Alpert & Taufique, 2002b).

With regard to school-based consultants, it is safe to assume that most have adequate training in consultation and collaboration. The training of community-based consultants, however, is apparently not as well articulated. Regardless of how they receive training, consultants are still ethically bound to determine whether they are adequately trained to provide services in each consultation situation as it arises (Dailer & Jacob, 2011). Training programs still need to examine how multicultural variables are taken into consideration in the preparation of consultants and collaborators (Arra, 2010).

The Consultant–Consultee–Client Relationship

The consultant–consultee–client relationship is very complex. What obligation, for example, does the consultant have to the consultee's client? What parameters of this relationship relate to the consultant and consultee? Can the consultant–consultee–client relationship be examined only in the context of the organization in which consultation is occurring? It is critical that consultants have a sense of how the results of the consultation process will impact all of the parties involved (Remley & Herlihy, 2010). In general, the consultant–consultee–client relationship can be examined in isolation or within an organizational

context; both views shed light on ethical issues. When considered in isolation, ethical issues revolve around each party's obligations and how well these are fulfilled. For example, the use of coercive techniques on the part of the consultant may be ethically questionable as these techniques may well damage the consultant–consultee relationship (Wilson, Erchul, & Raven, 2008).

In an organizational context, ethical issues go beyond the isolated relationship. For example, when confidentiality is to be maintained, where within the organization do we set its limits? Ethical issues can emerge when an ecological perspective is taken. For example, if ecological assessment suggests that the organizational context may be precipitating the client system's behavior, then the ethical issue becomes one of determining what really constitutes the client system and whether the consultant should become an advocate for the client system. Next we'll consider the ethical issues surrounding the complex consultant–consultee–client relationship in terms of work-related focus, dual relationships, and freedom of choice.

Work-Related Focus. The code of ethics of the ACA (2005) states that the focus of the consultation relationship, from the outset and throughout, should be on work-related problems and not on the parties involved. It can be inferred from this code that personal relationships with consultees and their clients is questionable ethical behavior. Further, this same code of ethics also implies that the consultation relationship should be contractual and based on well-defined, mutually agreed-upon expectations (e.g., nature of the problem, goals of consultation, and desired results). This straightforward assumption must also be considered in light of the fact that the consultant and consultee represent their respective organizations (Snow & Gersick, 1986); either party may have obligations to others not directly involved in but directly affected by consultation. Attempting to sort out these obligations can be very difficult.

The Case of Sheila. Sheila is a talented school counselor with a knack for relating effectively to students and teachers alike. As part of her consultation role, Sheila's principal asked her to conduct a teacher support group to focus on work issues. Sheila agreed and, as the support group developed, some members increasingly asked for help on personal domestic issues such as relationships with spouses and children and eating disorders. Sheila expressed her concerns that the group was getting too far away from its original intent and tried to refocus the group.

Was Sheila right in refocusing the group? Might she have taken any other measures under referral to help the members meet their perceived needs? If you were Sheila, would you find it somewhat difficult not to let the group go where it wanted to go?

Dual Relationships. Increasing attention has been paid to dual relationships in consultation (Dougherty, 1992b, 2006a, 2006b; Herlihy & Corey, 2006; Moleski & Kiselica, 2005; Thomas, 2010). Among others, the APA code of ethics (2002) and the ASCA (2010) suggest a thorough assessment of the potential for harm before engaging in such relationships. *Dual relationships* are those in which a professional has more than one role with another person. As an extreme example, a consultant experiencing sexual intimacy with a consultee has dual relationships—one professional, the other personal. Dual relationships can occur due to a shift in roles. For example, a consultant may be appointed to an administrative position in which a current consultee now also becomes a subordinate. Dual relationships frequently cause conflicts of interest as well as role conflicts. Maintaining two professional roles in the consultation relationship can be particularly hazardous to consultants and their consultees.

The two potentially most common second roles in consultation relationships are counselor/psychotherapist and supervisor. There is often a fine line between where consultation ends and counseling begins. Therefore, it is relatively easy for a consultant who is a trained counselor or therapist to move the consultation relationship into one that also provides counseling or therapy. When this occurs, the act of counseling contaminates the consultation relationship by focusing on personal

problems and by deemphasizing the work-related problems on which consultation was contracted.

The use of counseling or psychotherapy in the consultation relationship, when it occurs, usually results once the consultant has determined that the basis for the work-related problem resides more in the personal issues of the consultee than in the client. Rather than providing direct counseling services to the consultee, consultants should refer the consultee for assistance. Dual relationships also occur when supervision is somehow incorporated into the consultation relationship.

It is relatively easy for the consultant who has had supervisory training and administrative experience to include supervisory activities in what should be an exclusively consultative relationship. Because supervision implies the use of evaluation, control, and power over someone, supervision violates the peer nature of the consultation relationship. Use of supervision in consultation allows the consultant to build an illegitimate power base, creates the potential for conflicts of interest, and violates the original consultation contract.

What are some of the potential problems that result from a dual role relationship? There are several reasons for caution when determining whether to engage in dual relationships (Dougherty, 2006b):

- The complexity of the consultation process has led to difficulties in determining the boundaries of the consultant's role and consequent difficulties in discriminating between appropriate and inappropriate practice.

- The difficulties in defining consultation lead to difficulties in defining the roles of consultants.

- Multiple roles in relationships can cause conflicts of interest that can reduce the efficacy of consultation.

- Multiple roles can cause the consultee to have contradictory expectations.

- Trained counselors can zero in on affective concerns and personal problems. Therefore, there is a possible danger for turning consultation into counseling.

- Consultees may have an obligation to their organizations not to use consultation for personal purposes (e.g., counseling).

- Publicity about a consultant engaging in dual role relationships could dissuade potential consultees from seeking consultation.

The bottom-line question consultants must ask themselves concerning dual relationships is, "Do the potential conflicts outweigh the potential benefits of serving in both capacities?" (Herlihy & Corey, 2006). As I have noted elsewhere (Dougherty, 2006b), consultants should be very cautious about engaging in dual professional relationships. Extreme caution should be used before engaging in supervision or counseling relationships with consultees (Knoff, 1988). I agree with the position of Kitchener and Harding (1990) that human service professionals "should never enter such relationships when the potential for harm is high unless there are strong offsetting, ethical benefits for the consumer and the risks are clearly discussed" (p. 153).

The Case of Freddie. Freddie, a social worker, is consulting with Norma, the director of a religious counseling center, about some problems she is having with some of the staff at the center.

As Norma is discussing the problems, she brings up some very significant aspects of her private life that are affecting her relationships with the staff. Out of the blue, Norma asks Freddie for personal counseling as well as consultation. If Freddie agrees, is he involved in an inappropriate dual relationship? If he agrees to the dual role, how can Freddie assess whether the benefits outweigh the possible dangers? If you were Freddie, what would you do?

Freedom of Choice. Providing consultees and their clients with freedom of choice is one of the major ethical obligations of consultants. Ethical issues related to freedom of choice concern assurances that the consultee is acting in the client's best interests. They also therefore concern the creation of dependence, the misuse of co͟u͟, and inappropriate manipulation of ͟ ͟consultants.

Consultees should always perceive that they have the freedom to do whatever they wish with consultants' recommendations (Kratochwill & Pittman, 2002). This freedom relieves the consultant from being responsible for the consultee's behavior, assuming that the consultee acts in a professionally responsible manner. This requires consultants to take certain steps when they consider consultees' actions to be negative (Snow & Gersick, 1986). The first step is to point out the inappropriate behavior to the consultee. Beyond this, there is little consensus as to how the consultant should proceed. The consultant may have the option of pointing out the consultee's behavior to the consultee's employer or may terminate the consultation relationship, thereby placing the consultee's behavior beyond the consultation relationship.

Consultees cannot have complete freedom of choice if they are dependent on their consultant. This issue is addressed by the ACA (2005), whose code of ethics specifically states that the consultation relationship should be such that the consultee does not become dependent on the consultant and learns increased self-direction.

It is the consultant's responsibility to make sure that dependence does not occur. Because the very purpose of consultation is to assist consultees and their organizations to function more effectively and autonomously, it is unethical for consultants to create and maintain dependence on the part of consultees (NBCC, 2005).

Closely related to the issue of dependence is that of power. The potential for an imbalanced power relationship is a common ethical issue for consultants (Corey et al., 2011). One of the most common abuses of power in the consultation relationship occurs when the consultant violates the peer nature of the relationship and pressures the consultee to get something accomplished. For example, a consultant might push a certain plan of action on the consultee. Social influence on the part of the consultant is to be used in such a manner that the consultee's behavior is in no way coerced (Wesley & Buysse, 2006). Consultants need to remember that, although the consultation relationship is equal in terms of status, it is unequal in terms of need. This inequality due to need raises issues related to how the consultant maintains the peer nature of the consultation relationship. The consultant is helping the consultee meet a need. If the consultant gets anything out of this process, it is simply as a by-product. When consultants take a collaborative stance toward consultation whenever possible, the misuse of power is minimized.

A second abuse of power involves misusing the relationship with the consulting organization's administrators to achieve something that should be accomplished through other channels. For example, a consultant might ask an administrator to send through channels a memo concerning preferred action plans when it was agreed at the outset of consultation that consultees would develop action plans independent of the administration.

A third misuse of power occurs when a consultee is forced to participate in consultation. Because such coercion violates the voluntary nature of consultation, it is unethical behavior. In addition, consultants must ensure that their consultees are not receiving undue pressure to participate from their administrators.

A fourth misuse of power relates to the advocacy role a consultant might take on for personal reasons (Brown, 1988). For example, a mental health consultant might exploit the director of a program for the homeless who prefers to go through proper channels by demanding immediate change in the program. In this case, the consultant's hidden agenda might be to gain a power position with the program's board of directors.

Consultees cannot have freedom of choice if they are being manipulated by consultants (Newman, 1993). Therefore, from the outset, consultants should discuss with their consultees the ways in which consultants will attempt to influence them. Consultants can maintain their consultees' freedom of choice by discussing their own values and by helping consultees to critically consider consultants' suggestions on their own merits (Hughes, 1986). This can also be accomplished by ensuring that there is agreement and understanding in terms of the goals of consultation (ACA, 2005). In summary, clear expectations concerning the relationship,

avoidance of dual relationships, and freedom of choice for all parties involved contribute to maintaining ethical behavior on the part of consultants.

The Case of Teresa. Teresa is an internal consultant in the human resource development department of a large psychiatric hospital. Part of her role is to consult with heads of other departments on topics such as "total quality management." Marcie, one of the hospital's department heads, was told by her supervisor that she had to get help in running her department from Teresa. Teresa is keenly aware that Marcie needs some assistance and at the same time has a negative attitude about consultation. If Teresa proceeds with consultation with Marcie, is Marcie's freedom of choice being violated? If you were Teresa, how would you handle this situation in an ethical manner?

Rights of Consultees

Closely related to the issues concerning the consultant–consultee–client relationship are those surrounding the rights of consultees, which include two major issues: confidentiality and informed consent. As it applies to consultation, confidentiality can be viewed as an ethical responsibility of the consultant to protect the consultee and the consultee's clients from inappropriate disclosure of information shared within the consultation relationship. The ethics codes of the ACA (2005) implicitly deals with confidentiality as it relates to consultation, while that of the APA (2002) mentions it explicitly. Informed consent refers to sharing with the consultee information pertinent to consultation so that the consultee will know what is involved and will participate fully and effectively in the process. Consultants will want to be aware that consultees may not be knowledgeable about the dynamics of consultation or they have different expectations for the process (Wesley & Buysse, 2006). Consequently, there is an obligation for the consultant to duly inform them about the consultant's position regarding consultation matters. The codes of ethics of the ACA (2005) and the APA (2002) mention informed consent, although not specifically regarding the practice of consultation.

Confidentiality. Confidentiality in consultation and collaboration is both important and complex (Jacob & Hartshorne, 2007). Confidentiality is meant to protect privacy and promote trust (Taylor & Adelman, 1998). Consultees should feel safe in stating their concerns (Gutkin & Curtis, 2009). Even unintended breaches of confidentiality can severely damage the consultation relationship. The consultant is obligated to develop guidelines that safeguard the confidentiality of parties involved in consultation and collaboration as well as educate consultees about the nature and limits of confidentiality (Corey et al., 2011). These guidelines should be developed during the entry stage and put into the consultation contract (Rosenfield, 2008). In fact, it is a good idea for the contract to state clearly how information gathered during consultation will be used, by whom, and when (Jacob, 2008). Guidelines should be structured to protect the consultee's oral and written communications and records (Robinson & Gross, 1985). It is a good idea to follow the practice noted in the APA (2002) ethics code of protecting the identity of parties involved in consultation and sharing only that information necessary to achieve the purposes of consultation. In other words, it is important to use the "need-to-know principle" (Jacob & Hartshorne, 2007; Thomas, 2010).

Consultation is by definition tripartite, which implies that three parties (and possibly more) can have knowledge of information that is disclosed during consultation. The simplest example is a consultee sharing information about a client to a consultant. In a more complex example, an external agency might require a report from a consultant about some aspect of consultation.

The potential for several parties to acquire information may create trust issues in consultation and makes confidentiality a primary ethical concern for consultants. The consultant must create procedures for determining what information is to be shared with whom, when, how, for what reasons, and what the likely impact of sharing will be.

Consultants can increase their awareness of the complexity of confidentiality by asking themselves the following questions:

- What can I tell my own organization about what is said both in consultation and in the consultee organization?

- With whom can I share information in the consultee organization?

- What steps do I need to take to ensure the safety of computer-accessible information?

Posing and answering such complex questions at the outset of consultation, getting consensus on the answers, and publicizing this consensus can prevent problems from occurring later on in the consultation process. There is no such thing as total confidentiality. Confidentiality has limits and it is up to the consultant to forge some agreement concerning those limits (Gutkin & Curtis, 2009). In collaboration, this is also true due to the advent of the use of collaboration in teams, interagency collaboration, and interdisciplinary teamwork (ACA, 2005; ASCA, 2010; Jacob, 2008). The limits of confidentiality refer to those instances that would dictate that confidentiality be set aside. It is usually assumed that consultants must get permission from their consultees or from members of the organization affected by the consultation before sharing information. But in cases where permission is not granted, what do consultants do when they have what they feel are good reasons for revealing the information? Specifically, what should consultants do when they determine that a consultee is mistreating a client or that a program is counterproductive for the client system? There are no clear-cut answers in determining when confidentiality should be set aside in consultation. I am of the opinion that confidentiality should be set aside when consultants determine to the best of their ability that the best interests of society are not being met, or the client system is being violated in some way. When setting aside confidentiality, the consultant determines and takes responsibility for who is to be told, what they are to be told, and in what manner.

The second way in which the limits of confidentiality are discussed involves the concept of anonymity (Snow & Gersick, 1986). Such a strategy is in line with the APA ethical principles, which state: "Psychologists do not disclose confidential information that reasonably could lead to the identification of a … person or organization with which they have a confidential relationship unless they have obtained prior consent of the person or organization or the disclosure cannot be avoided …" (APA, 2002, p. 8). When maintaining confidentiality, the consultant can share information only with the permission of the consultee or an appropriate member of the organization. When maintaining anonymity, the consultant can share the information but must protect its source. The use of anonymity has the advantage of facilitating a flow of information, which can be critical to the success of consultation that focuses on an organization as a whole. Using anonymity can be a very useful strategy for consultants: It prevents them from having "one helping hand tied behind their backs" when they have information that could be helpful if it were shared but are restrained from sharing by a lack of permission to do so.

The Case of Gus.   Gus, a mental health consultant with a large number of community service agencies, is asked to consult for six months with several of the staff in an area nursing home concerning the use of reminiscences as a tool for improving the quality of life of the elderly.

Midway through the consultation period, Gus is approached by the administrator of the nursing home. She relates that she is going to have to cut several of the staff in a downsizing move and would like Gus's opinion on whom to lay off. As a consultant, what ethical issue is Gus facing? Does the fact that the administrator hired Gus give her any rights with regard to her request?

Informed Consent.   Informed consent is very important in delineating the rights of consultees (Herlihy & Corey, 2006; Remley & Herlihy, 2010; Thomas, 2010). To determine whether they want to be involved in consultation in the first place, consultees need to be as fully informed as possible about the nature and goals of consultation, issues of confidentiality, their right to privacy, the voluntary nature of participation, and complete freedom in following or not following through on

the consultant's recommendations. Consultants will want to bear in mind that consultees may not be knowledgeable about the complexities of consultations and related ramifications such as those related to the amount of time a consultee may need to invest. Consultees have the right to know about how any information obtained from the consultation process will be used (Newman, 1993). The guidelines suggested by Corey et al. (2011) for counselors and therapists who work with clients seem quite appropriate for consultants and their consultees. ACA (2005) makes direct reference to informed consent in consultation.

Informed consent should be considered an ongoing process and not a one-time event (Remley & Herlihy, 2010). This view of informed consent prevents the consultant from making the mistake of overloading the consultee with too much information at the outset of consultation, and it permits candid discussion of the most critical information about which the consultee needs to be apprised.

Even though consultants should view informed consent as an ongoing process, they must still ask themselves what consultees need to know at the outset. Providing the consultee with a copy of the ethics code of the consultant's discipline can be a good starting point. A good practice for answering this question is for consultants to place themselves in their consultees' shoes and ascertain what they would like to know at the outset of consultation. By empathizing with their consultees, consultants are in a better position to answer questions patiently and provide information. Instead of merely being a routine exercise, the sharing of information to obtain informed consent can be a rapport-building event for consultant and consultee.

The Case of Sid.   As part of his job as a staff development specialist in a community mental health center, Sid provides a group of consultees an instrument designed to assess their ability to work effectively on a team. Based on their performance on the instrument and other measures, the consultees will be assigned to autonomous work teams. As the training is winding up, several of the consultees' supervisors contact Sid regarding what he found out about the consultees' suitability as team members. If Sid shares what he knows, is he violating the consultees' right to informed consent? What is Sid's obligation to the center in this situation? Does the employing organization have any rights in this situation? How could this problem have been avoided in the first place?

The Consultant and the Group

For a variety of reasons, such as professional and/or personal support, an increasing amount of a consultant's practice is with a group of consultees, including peer consultation, or part or all of an organization (see Conyne & Mazza, 2007; Paisley & Milsom, 2007; Thomas, 2010). Because consultation with groups raises unique ethical and professional issues, it is given separate consideration here. If you are interested in consulting with groups, I strongly recommend that you refer to the *Professional Standards for the Training of Group Workers* (2000) published by the Association for Specialists in Group Work (ASGW).

Consulting with Groups with Caseloads. When a consultant considers working with the same group of consultees for an extended length of time, a basic issue that is raised is one of competence. To what degree is the consultant experienced and trained in group consultation? How aware is the consultant of group process and group dynamics? Because consulting with a group is much different from and more complex than working with an individual consultee, it is critical that consultants have some form of training in group consultation before embarking on such a venture.

A second issue that reemerges when consulting with a group is informed consent. To what degree have the consultees been made aware of the differences between individual and group consultation? Has participation been made voluntary? Have the consultees been made aware of what is expected of them within the group? As in individual consultation, informed consent should be an ongoing process. Typically, group consultation is an elected activity for consultees (Thomas, 2010).

A third issue that resurfaces in group consultation is confidentiality. Clearly, the consultant cannot guarantee confidentiality for anyone in the group except him- or herself (Thomas, 2010). In fact, many consultees will subscribe to professional standards such as those of the ASGW (2000), which specifically mention that group cases be discussed only for professional consultation and educational purposes. Even in these cases, group members should be informed of any limits to confidentiality regarding their cases. Because most consultees are also professionals, it is not unreasonable to expect them to live up to their obligations with respect to confidentiality. Many authors (e.g., Corey et al., 2011) suggest that group leaders encourage confidentiality by providing a written policy statement at the outset and/or casually but seriously mentioning confidentiality throughout the life of the group.

A final issue that reemerges is that of cultural sensitivity. ASGW (2000) points out the importance of collaborative consultation with targeted populations to enhance the ecological validity of planned group interventions. This is an important factor whether one is consulting with groups about caseloads or with training groups.

The Case of Lucy. Lucy, a mental health practitioner who is consulting with a group of school counselors about their cases, is very concerned about confidentiality because the consultation is occurring at a variety of school sites. She prepares a statement about confidentiality, distributes it during the first meeting with the consultees, and mentions confidentiality intermittently throughout the course of the consultation relationship. In your opinion, has Lucy acted in an ethical manner? Is there anything else she could do to encourage confidentiality? What are the consultees' obligations regarding confidentiality in this situation?

Issues in Intervention

The ethical as well as the technical adequacy of interventions must be determined (Fuqua et al., 2012; Newman, Robinson-Kurpius, & Fuqua, 2002). Three important intervention areas that involve ethical issues are individual-versus systems-level interventions, use of assessment data, and the empirical validity of interventions (Newman, 1993).

When considering individual-level interventions, the consultant needs to determine that the intervention is not meant merely to accommodate the organization's needs and are in the best interest of the client system (Fuqua et al., 2012; Jacob, 2008). Consultants will need to avoid cultural bias in their assessment activities (Diller, 2007). For example, it would be unethical for a consultant to recommend a certain developmental guidance program for use by teachers merely as a way to cut the number of school counselors in a school. If the consultant determines through ecological assessment that the system is "sick," interventions at the individual level may also be ethically questionable because of their marginal effect on the problem (Gutkin, 2012).

The use of assessment data can present many ethical issues (Fuqua, Newman, & Dickman, 1999). Primary among these is the improper use of assessment devices so that freedom of choice and the principle of informed consent are violated (Newman et al., 2002). The potential for unethical behavior occurs often in personnel decisions. Consultants need to make sure that all parties-at-interest are properly informed about the use of any assessment instruments.

Consultants should also bear in mind the impact of culture on assessment procedures and consider using multiple assessment and "indigenous consultants" (an appropriate representative of the client system's cultural group) in both assessment and intervention in crosscultural consultation (Diller, 2007; Quintana, Castillo, & Zamarripa, 2000). For example, research-based interventions should be made available as culturally appropriate. On the other hand, culturally sensitive decisions

need to be made in selecting interventions, such as those using concrete reinforcers (Sheridan, 2000).

Consultants must make every effort to see that their interventions have some desired effect. There has been very little attention paid to this in the consultation literature. The scale and scope of available interventions makes their selection, implementation, and evaluation very difficult.

Consultants should be familiar with the empirical research as it relates to the efficacy of interventions and should attempt to make sound judgments when selecting interventions. There is limited research that suggests that consultants may have ethical issues in following up on interventions and questionable assessment procedures (Dailor & Jacob, 2011).

The Case of Ozzie.   Ozzie is hired as a consultant by a human service agency to help determine if the child and adolescent services sections could be combined as a cost-cutting measure. As Ozzie is gathering data, the director of the agency pushes the reorganization as the only recommendation she wants to hear. Ozzie determines that the reorganization is not an appropriate strategy because it would put an excessive burden on the personnel who serve the agency's clients. In his report, Ozzie suggests that reorganization is not a feasible alternative and makes other cost-cutting recommendations. Did Ozzie act in an ethical manner? What types of pressure do you believe he experienced when the director attempted to influence him? Did Ozzie attempt to recommend the best possible solution?

Issues Related to Crisis/Disaster Consultation

Consultants are increasingly being called upon to provide service in crisis and disaster situations (McCarroll & Ursano, 2006; Stock, 2007). Tragedies like those of September 11 and at Virginia Tech University have called attention for the need for organizations to implement or create crisis management plans and have shown the need for training organizational personnel in how to react to crises/disasters and related events such as workplace violence. Areas of ethics important in crisis situations include: self-awareness, dual relationships, confidentiality, elder/child abuse, informed consent, and supervision/training (Kanel, 2007; McCarroll & Ursano, 2006; Stock, 2007). Consultants will want to bear in mind the acute vulnerability of the client system in crisis and disaster situations as well as the fact that the resulting chaotic environment will heighten ethical considerations (Halpern & Tramontin, 2007). In addition, consultants will need to assure that cultural competence is exhibited when engaging in crisis consultation in that responses to a crisis vary to a given culture (Remley & Herlihy, 2010).

Issues in Organizational Consultation and School-based Consultation

Mental health/human service professionals, both internal and external, are increasingly being called upon to provide services at the organizational level. A school psychologist might, for example, assist a site-based management team in developing methods for incorporating evidence-based social emotional learning programs. In another example, a clinical mental health counselor might work with the board of directors of a church group in examining and revising the administrative structure of the church's operation in order to facilitate effective communication. Organizational consultation is one of the most complex types of consultation. Consequently, the ethical issues can also be highly complex (Block, 2000). Confidentiality may be an important issue due to the fact that the organization is the client system (Fuqua et al., 2012; Kratochwill & Pittman, 2002; Newman et al., 2002). The goal of organizational consultation is to help the organization function more effectively in some specified way. Ethical issues can easily arise when this overarching goal is being pursued. If you review the case example at the beginning of this chapter, you will note how easily ethical dilemmas can arise during organizational consultation.

The nature of organizations can lead to a variety of ethical issues for consultants (Newman et al., 2002):

- Consultants have significant ethical responsibility to ensure the proper effects of interventions, and those effects can be difficult to determine at the organizational level.
- Consultants frequently rely exclusively on the subjective reports of consultees, although consultees can have biased and distorted views of the organization and its functioning.
- Conflicts of interest within the organization itself can complicate the goals of consultation.
- Differing views of the organization can make setting goals difficult.
- Voluntary participation on the parts of consultees can be difficult to ascertain.

Fuqua et al. (2012) point out that several ethical issues consultants face when working with individual consultees become even more complex in organizational consultation:

- confidentiality (e.g., information shared with multiple parties)
- informed consent (e.g., dealing with people who may feel forced to cooperate)
- power (e.g., different organizational members have different levels of power in the organization)
- determining who constitutes the client system (e.g., determining the client system's nature prior to data gathering)

Because of the complexity of organizational consultation, consultants may want to consider adopting *aspirational ethics* (Fuqua & Newman, 2009; Newman et al., 2002). Aspirational ethics is also called *virtue ethics* (Wilczenski & Cook, 2011). Virtue ethics attempts to integrate the character of the professional with his or her practice. Virtue ethics looks at the reasoning that facilitates ethical decision making and subsequent behavior. Aspirational ethics is not based on the question "What shall I do?" but on the question

"Who shall I be?" (Newman et al., 2002; Wilczenski & Cook, 2011). Principle ethics, on the other hand, refer to duty (Wilczenski & Cook, 2011).

The use of virtue ethics by consultants lays the foundation for moral considerations as part of the organizational consultation process. By taking this orientation, consultants will continually be examining their own behavior in terms of whether it is the right course of action to take (Fuqua & Newman, 2006, 2009). This orientation considers consultation to have powerful moral influences. These influences can be used to promote moral discourse in the organization, impact the organization's leadership structure, and impact the moral elements of the organization's structure (Fuqua & Newman, 2006, 2009). Fuqua and Newman (2009) have expanded their views on the consultant as being a leader in facilitating moral discourse in the organization by looking at ethical issues that could arise during the various types of activities involved in the consultation process. In the relationship-building phase, these authors point out the moral imperative related to striking strong rapport with the consultee. In another example, these authors note that a major point in problem exploration is "who is at the table" in defining the problem to be addressed by consultation.

In school settings, many ethical issues take on particular significance, for example, confidentiality, informed consent (Dougherty, 1992a; Jacob, 2008), and multicultural issues. As every practicing human service professional knows, maintaining confidentiality in a school is difficult, because there is a tendency in many schools for personnel to share information about students in inappropriate ways (Jacob, 2008). It is easy to imagine how breaking teacher confidentiality unnecessarily could have disastrous effects. School-based counselors and psychologists must ensure that the limits to confidentiality are clearly defined and mutually agreed upon for each consultation and collaboration relationship (Jacob & Hartshorne, 2007).

Many school professionals are just becoming familiar with their own roles as consultants and collaborators, and the persons with whom they work such as teachers, administrators, and parents are often not familiar with exactly what constitutes consultation and collaboration, including how the two differ (Hughes, Barker, Kemenoff, & Hart, 1993). Therefore, counselors and psychologists need to educate the persons to whom they are providing these services as to their nature whenever necessary. As an example, time constraints in schools often create conditions for very brief informal consultation. Consultants will want to be alert for ethical issues related to the welfare of the client system and the integrity of the consultation process (Harrison, 2004).

Multicultural issues clearly affect school consultation and collaboration. The changing demographics of the student population in our society dictate that school-based professionals will encounter such issues in their daily practice. For example, the use of interpreters can raise issues of confidentiality in school settings (Lopez, 2000). In another example, school-based consultants will need to ensure that assessment and intervention practices are culturally appropriate and fair (Castillo, Quintana, & Zamarripa, 2000; Jacob, 2008).

School-based counselors and psychologists and external consultants may have to deal with the ethical issue of deciding whether to end a consultation or collaboration relationship and engage in more advocating roles to ensure that children in schools receive the services to which they are entitled (Clare, 2009; Huey, 2011). Counselors and psychologists can be placed in the predicament of trying to help a system that truly does not want assistance and, as a result, the students in the system suffer. In this case, the professional faces the dilemma of trying to change events through consultation or collaboration, or disengaging and taking a proactive, advocating role for the students in the system. Ethical issues can arise in terms of the quality with which interventions are selected and delivered, such as in their use with RTI (response to intervention) (Jacob, 2008).

Finally, school-based consultants need to be quite knowledgeable about and follow their professional organization's codes of ethics, such as those of ASCA (2010) and NASP (2010b).

The Case of Bryan. Bryan is a human resource development specialist in a community college. A trained counselor, Bryan has been asked to assist the academic affairs committee of the college to make recommendations for new programs to the college's president. As Bryan attempts to assist the group in making its decision, it becomes obvious that a lot of the committee members are allowing politics rather than the best interests of the college to guide their decision making. Bryan asks the group for some time to share his thoughts on the committee's processes to date. At a meeting, he directly, yet professionally, shares his views that the committee may be having their own special interests in mind when determining the academic future of the college. Was Bryan, in your opinion, using aspirational ethics in this situation? Was he taking a big risk with the group? What would you have done in this situation?

Issues Related to the Use of Technology

Computer technology and the Internet have provided millions of people with additional communication and information sources (Haberstroh, Parr, Bradley, Morgan-Fleming, & Gee, 2008). As telecommunications and technology continue to impact our society, so too do they have the potential to affect how consultation is delivered (Florell, 2011; Raines & Dibble, 2011). With the onset of e-mail, list servs, chat rooms, voice over Internet protocol (VOIP), instant messaging, smart phones, and file transfer protocols, consultants are able to develop a variety of methods for providing consultation, often to consultees in rural areas or to save time. For example, a group of counselors can engage in peer consultation via a VOIP, e-mail, or a chat group (Miller, 2006). In another example, a mental health consultant may deal with a consultee about a case exclusively through e-mail. There is some evidence that consultees perceive the use of e-mail as effective in helping

them accomplish the goals of consultation (Kruger et al., 2001) and that consultants can help facilitate an online support community for beginning teachers (Babinski, Jones, & DeWert, 2001). Although there is no data that demonstrates the amount of consultation that occurs over the Internet, there were at least 88 online counseling Web sites located (Shaw & Shaw, 2006).

Extrapolating from the ideas of various authors (ACA, 2005; AMHCA, 2002; ASCA, 2010; Corey et al., 2011; Haberstroh, 2009; ISMHO, 2000; Meyers, Meyers, & Grogg, 2004; Remley & Herlihy, 2010; Wheeler & Bertram, 2008) on Web counseling and applying them to consultation suggests the following consultation applications on the information highway: computer-based networking with consultees regarding cases, marketing of services via Web pages, delivery of consultation services over the Internet and through videoconferencing, data collection and assessment through the use of computer-assisted instruction, videoconferencing with more than one consultee at various remote sites, and the delivery of self-help materials and resources with the consultant being "on call" to assist as needed. As a side note, advances in technology have the potential to impact the way consultants use face-to-face meetings in unique ways. For example, face-to-face meetings may be used more for relationship building and less for the transmittal of information (Corey et al., 2011; Sampson, Kolodinsky, & Greeno, 1997).

However, the impact of technology on consultation raises a variety of ethical issues (Haberstroh et al., 2008; Malone, 2007; Miller, 2006; Remley & Herlihy, 2010; Shaw & Shaw, 2006). The APA (2002) has included a section in its code of ethics regarding the use of technology in service delivery; ACA (2005) and ASCA (2010) both have a separate set of standards. Other organizations such as the NBCC (2007) have adopted standards for Web-counseling. Consultants can adapt and use standards such as these and APA (2002) and ACA (2005) to assist them in dealing with related ethical issues that arise in their practice.

Issues raised by the use of what I refer to as "Web-consulting" can be categorized as technology-related aspects of the basic issues already discussed in this chapter. These include obtaining permission to consult with members of an organization without physically entering the system and confidentiality. Confidentiality and technology can provide some challenging issues related to confidentiality, for example, protection of election information (Florell, 2011). Examples of issues related to confidentiality include the privacy of material sent over the Web, the use of encryption methods, how long transmission will be preserved, difficulties in verifying the identity of the parties involved, crisis situations being dealt with from remote locations, and appropriate procedures for releasing information with other electronic sources (NBCC, 2005; Shaw & Shaw, 2006). In a related issue, consultants will want to remember that lack of attention to information security can violate consultee confidentiality (APA, 2002; Shaw & Shaw, 2006). Consultants need to ensure that the messages they receive and send electronically are protected as needed, and that the consultee has access to privacy when sending information to the consultant.

Another issue revolves around location-specific factors. Consultants need to make sure they assess the impact of local variables as they attempt to assist consultees. For example, a mental health counselor should be aware of the limitations imposed on the counseling activities of school personnel prior to making recommendations regarding interventions.

Consultants should also be aware of how relationship development can be affected by technology. Trusting relationships tend to develop rich and more valid discourse than do those based on superficial acquaintance. Consultants will want to keep this in mind as they determine the depth of relationship necessary to accomplish the goals of consultation. A minimal consideration is contact with consultees over the phone or through videoconferencing. Little has been written in the area of Web-consulting. The bottom line is that potential benefits need to outweigh the potential risks.

A Note on Collaboration and Ethical Issues

The emergence of collaboration as alternative service to consultation requires some clarification relative to professional issues. Some codes of ethics such as that of the ASCA (2010), among others, have specific standards related to collaboration. As you will recall, collaboration often involves the use of a team, in which the various individual collaborators, each with a unique contribution to make, work together to assist the client system. Teams can be made up of members who are all internal to the organization, such as a school-based team assisting in the implementation of RTI program. Or team members may come from a variety of organizations as in interagency collaboration, such as systems of support team for a family. In both cases, there are ramifications for ethical issues that would hold in consultation but not collaboration due to the nature of collaboration (Caplan et al., 1994). First, not all collaborators may have the freedom to participate or not in the team effort. Consider a school that has only one school counselor; that counselor may not have a choice but to participate as a team member in the implementation of a SEL program that requires his or her expertise. Consequently, whereas consultation assumes the voluntary participation of the consultee, collaboration does not automatically assume the voluntary participation of team members. Second, confidentiality is assumed in consultation, whereas in collaboration, pertinent material may have to be distributed among team members. Finally, in consultation, the consultee can accept or not accept the consultant's recommendations, whereas in collaboration, such freedom is not necessarily presumed due to each team member's unique knowledge and skills to which other team members typically defer. In conclusion, the areas of freedom of participation, confidentiality, and acceptance of recommendations are likely to have ethical issues surrounding them in consultation than they would in collaboration.

THE CONSULTANT
AND THE LAW

Relatively little has been written on the legal issues that concern consultants, but more is being written on legal issues for mental health professionals (Egan, 2010; Sales, Miller, & Hall, 2005; Williams & Armistead, 2011). Most professional organizations, for example, the ASCA (2010) and the APA (2002) note the importance of knowing and respecting the law (Jacob, 2008; Wheeler & Bertram, 2008).

Relatively few guidelines on professional behavior exist to guide the courts when consultants encounter legal entanglements. Still, as members of the helping professions, consultants deliver their services in a socio-legal environment and should be aware of legal matters that affect them (Stone & Zirkel, 2010; Swenson, 1997). For example, school-based consultants need to be aware of the legal considerations of sharing information about students.

Some authors such as Remley and Herlihy (2010) caution that lawsuits brought against human service professionals, although few, are on the rise. Consultants will want to remember that mandatory law, if it applies to a given consultation situation, takes precedence over ethical or other concerns, and consultants who violate the law are subject to legal consequences (Stone & Zirkel, 2010; Wheeler & Bertram, 2008). Because consultants have no control over what consultees do with the consultant's input, consultants are typically not held accountable for subsequent consultee actions resulting from the consultation. However, Remley and Herlihy (2010, p. 350) point out that: "It is, possible, however, that an individual who retains a consultant may have a legal cause of action based on contract principles against a consultant who gives wrong or poor advice that the consultee relies on." The bottom line is: When dealing with issues that may have legal ramifications, consultants may well want to consider seeking legal advice (Remley & Herlihy, 2010).

Malpractice

We'll now consider a legal issue of paramount importance to consultants: malpractice. Human service professionals are accountable for the quality of their services. In malpractice, the service recipient is in some way damaged by improper services offered without good faith or through neglect or ignorance. Malpractice cases allege that the professional induced in some way psychological, financial, or physical damage on someone in the course of providing services (Sales et al., 2005). Corey et al. (2011) note that malpractice is the failure to render professional services or to exercise the appropriate degree of skill that is ordinarily expected of professionals in a given situation. Consultants can be sued for performing the wrong services or for failing to provide the correct services. How can the right or wrong type of service be determined? Applying what generally happens to professional counselors (i.e., professionals with no well-defined professional identity in the eyes of the law) (Anderson, 1996) in a similar situation leads to this conclusion: The court would attempt to determine whether a typical professional consultant would act in a way similar to the way the consultant in question acted. An answer in the affirmative would likely lead to no liability, whereas a negative answer could lead to liability (Anderson, 1996). Tort lawsuits are the most common type involving malpractice (Wheeler & Bertram, 2008). To determine whether a consultant was guilty of malpractice, a court would seek answers to the following questions:

- Did the defendant (consultant) have a professional obligation to the plaintiff?
- Was that duty breached by the consultant?
- Is there a causal link between the breach and the damage to the plaintiff?

To answer these questions, the court would probably attempt to determine whether the consultant showed *requisite skill and care* (Anderson, 1996). However, because these terms are not yet adequately defined for consultants, courts tend to rely on already-established standards for related professions that perform consultation for defining standards for appropriate professional consulting behavior (Anderson, 1996). Courts often use the *ordinary reasonable person* concept, which refers to the evaluation of a legal issue from "... the standpoint of what would be the most reasonable course of action to most reasonable nonprofessional people," namely, people who are always reasonable, prudent, careful, informed, and up to standard (Harrison, 2004, pp. 139–140).

Malpractice suits can occur in just about any area of consultation practice. A recent literature review of the causes of malpractice (Corey et al., 2011; Wheeler & Bertram, 2008) suggests the following behaviors that could cause legal entanglements for consultants:

- misrepresenting one's training and skills
- failing to respect integrity and privacy
- using improper diagnosis and assessment techniques
- using improper methods to collect fees
- making inappropriate public statements (libel and slander)
- failing to honor agreements (breach of contract)
- failing to keep adequate records
- failing to provide for informed consent
- providing poor advice

Of these torts, those based on lack of skill are the most prevalent (Wheeler & Bertram, 2008). In summary, consultants can be sued for malpractice whenever there is the likelihood that they have provided services either without the proper skill or without the proper care.

Avoiding Legal Entanglements

It is safe to assume that the vast majority of consultants want to avoid legal entanglements.

How should they go about doing this? It is most important that consultants learn about any state laws that may have implications for their practices (Remley & Herlihy, 2010). Ignorance of the law is not an excuse if a consultant is called into court. In addition, when ethical codes and the law could collide, such as in advocacy situation, it is critical for consultants to keep a systems view of events and use their political and collaborative skills (Stone & Zirkel, 2010).

Consultants are not held legally accountable for negligence of the consultee (Remley & Herlihy, 2010). However, consultants should provide proper services—only those services in which they are skilled—with care. The old adage "An ounce of prevention is worth a pound of cure" could not be truer when it comes to avoiding legal entanglements.

Consultants should consider joining a professional organization that has an ethics code and should adhere to that code's principles and standards. Such adherence facilitates delivering consultation services with the proper skill and care and assists the consultant in determining standards of professional conduct.

Consultants need a personal and professional growth orientation based on a healthy and honest self-awareness. By setting high standards for themselves, consultants can avoid many missteps that could lead to legal entanglements (Williams & Armistead, 2011). Knowledge of one's limitations and abilities as a person and as a professional enhances a consultant's ability to make the correct decision concerning whether a given consultation service should be undertaken in the first place. Consultants can participate in professional development activities that review the law as it relates to their profession (Rowley & MacDonald, 2001) and seeking peer consultation when ethical/legal concerns arise (Raines & Dibble, 2011). Consultants should do well each of the little things their profession demands of them:

- Use a written contract.
- Keep accurate records.
- Discuss fees at the outset of consultation.
- Discuss confidentiality and its limits as a matter of course at the outset of every consultation relationship.

CASE 14.1   Ethics for School Consultants

Terry is a consultant based in a junior high school, and she is consulting with a newly hired and inexperienced in-school human service professional, Burt. Burt is conducting a group for students who received more than three Fs on their latest report card and has asked Terry to consult with him regarding "helping these kids out." As Burt describes the group's progress, Terry notices that he has not informed the group of its purpose or made any attempt to promote confidentiality. She also notes that Burt talks to teachers readily about the members' behavior and puts several of the members down by calling them "air heads." At the same time, he exhibits a commitment to the members and to the success of the group.

It is apparent to Terry that Burt does not want feedback on his behavior but rather desires techniques for more effectively helping the students in the group. Terry feels very frustrated during two of her consultation sessions with Burt and perceives him as having a low level of self-awareness and being impervious to how others might perceive him. She has come to resent what she sees as a basic contradiction in Burt—namely, his enthusiasm to help students and the disrespectful way in which he talks about them outside of the group.

During a third session, as Burt keeps asking for techniques to achieve this or that, Terry becomes angry not only at Burt but at herself for being angry with Burt. In the middle of the session, she excuses herself for a couple of minutes to check on an appointment. While out of the room, she uses some stress management techniques on herself. Her internal dialogue is saying things like, "It's awful that he talks about kids that way and still thinks he's committed to help them." As she continues to process her feelings, Terry begins to manage her anger effectively and realizes what she wants to do.

Upon returning to the room and before Burt can start talking again, Terry tells him that she has something to discuss. She briefly shares her perception that the reason Burt is having trouble with his group may not be due only to the kids but perhaps also his own actions in and out of the group. Terry assures Burt that she believes in his commitment to the students, mentions the behavior that she is concerned with, and asks

him if that is the image he wants to project to students, parents, and staff members.

In a gentle, yet straightforward, way, Terry refers to the ACA *code of ethics* and some of the questions she has about Burt's conduct. As Terry is talking, Burt shows surprise and becomes genuinely interested in what she is saying. He notes that his attitude may be because of his father's flippant attitude about life. He praises Terry for her sensitivity and perceptiveness and asks her to help him work on his attitudes and behavior, saying, "After all, if my personal life is messing up my professional life, I guess I'd better start there." Terry shares with Burt her appreciation for his willingness to look closely at himself and his interest in counseling. Because she is a school consultant, Terry points out that she feels very uncomfortable doing this and details how being both his counselor and his consultant might destroy their ability to work effectively together. She mentions to Burt the positive results of counseling she received from a local therapist and refers Burt to that counselor.

When Burt comes back for two more consultation sessions, the mood of the relationship is relaxed and yet very work oriented, with Burt speaking compassionately of one of the group member's difficulties.

Commentary

This case illustrates the importance of self-awareness on the part of consultants. If Terry had not possessed a strong sense of self-awareness and insight into herself, her anger might well have jeopardized her relationship with Burt. This case further demonstrates how easy it is for consultants to slip into possibly damaging dual relationships with their consultees. Given Terry's feelings of anger toward Burt combined with her strong willingness to help him, she might easily have trapped herself in a relationship that involved both consultation and counseling. By taking such steps, consultants can dramatically reduce the likelihood of legal entanglement. Consultants who know what they are doing and why they are doing it have relatively little to fear, even though the boundaries of their professional behavior remain relatively indistinct in the eyes of the law.

- Make sure that any advertising or promotional activities provide current and accurate information.
- Foster open communication at all times.

- Seek peer consultation from a trusted colleague or a supervisor when in doubt about proper procedure.

CASE 14.2   Ethics for Community Consultants

Cindy is the director of a prerelease center for incarcerates preparing for parole. Cindy and her five staff members all have master's degrees in one of the helping professions.

The center runs a coeducational seven-week program for incarcerates who are eligible for parole no more than six months after the program's conclusion. Part of the center's role is to assess the suitability of the program participants for early parole.

The center staff have been experiencing difficulties in communicating with incarcerates who are known to suffer from substance abuse. At a needs-assessment meeting, the staff concluded that they would like to hold a communication skills workshop that focused on working with substance abusers. As a result, Cindy contacts Sharon, a social worker in the community.

Sharon has several years' experience in corrections and an excellent reputation for conducting workshops and making presentations. Cindy contracts with Sharon for a four-day workshop on "Communicating Effectively with the Substance-Abusing Incarcerate." Sharon does an outstanding job in conducting the workshop. The staff are very open about their views and feelings about communication and how the center responds to known substance abusers. An evaluation of the workshop indicates that the staff felt very positive about the knowledge and skills they had gained from the workshop.

Two weeks later, Cindy calls Sharon to tell her that she is being promoted to a new position and that her immediate supervisor has asked her to choose an interim director from the staff of the center. Cindy also states that she values Sharon's opinion highly and that she realized how close Sharon got to each staff member during the workshop. Cindy asks Sharon to analyze

each staff member, rank them, and name her top three choices for the interim director position. Sharon feels uneasy as she talks with Cindy. She puts off agreeing or rejecting Cindy's proposal by telling her she will respond before the week is over. As Sharon considers the reasons for her uneasiness, she realizes that Cindy's request is inappropriate.

After all, Sharon was not hired to evaluate anyone but to conduct a workshop. Further, if she were to comply with Cindy's request, she would be depriving the staff members of their right to know about and consent to Sharon's imparting information (in this case, impressions) about them to their director. As Sharon reviews her professional organization's code of ethics, she realizes that her uneasiness was well founded. She calls Cindy and politely, yet assertively, denies her request.

Commentary

As you see from this case, Cindy put Sharon, perhaps inadvertently, in an ethical dilemma revolving around both informed consent of consultees and knowing one's limitations as a consultant. For Sharon to comply with Cindy's request for information about the workshop participants would clearly violate the consultees' right to informed consent. Further, when Cindy asked Sharon to analyze and rank the workshop members, Cindy was assuming that Sharon has expertise in staff evaluation procedures. Sharon did not, in fact, possess those skills and was put in the position of having to decline Cindy's request for an additional reason; namely, she did not possess the expertise to do what Cindy was asking regardless of whether the consultees had consented to being evaluated.

Seeking peer legal consultation can be an advisable activity for a mental health practitioner on some occasions (Raines & Dibble, 2011). For example, a mental health professional may want to engage in consultation regarding legal advice about federal, state, and local statutes, and case law.

SUMMARY

This chapter has presented an introduction to the closely related ethical, professional, and legal issues that pertain to consultation in the human services professions. The complexity of consultation increases the complexity of the ethical issues consultants face in their work.

Consultants can maintain professional standards by being aware of issues involving values, multicultural elements, competence, training, the consultation relationship, the rights of consultees and their clients, the use of technology, and consultation in groups. Collaboration and consultation differ some in terms of potential ethical issues in the areas of freedom of participation, confidentiality, and freedom to use or not use recommendations. Most legal issues that consultants encounter concern malpractice.

Consultants can maintain a sense of ethical and professional responsibility and avoid legal entanglements by being committed to their own personal and professional growth. Finally, for consultants to be more confident in their ethical behavior, more specific ethics codes and more deliberate training of consultants in ethical decision making are needed.

SUGGESTIONS FOR EFFECTIVE PRACTICE

- Strictly adhere to the ethical code of your profession.

- Seek out consultation from trusted colleagues when you are in doubt about how to proceed in consultation or collaboration.

- Avoid legal entanglements by documenting all procedures you employ and by rigorously adhering to your profession's ethical code.

- Only consult in areas in which you have expertise.

QUESTIONS FOR REFLECTION

1. If ethical guidelines are by definition general in nature, how can consultants apply them in specific situations?

2. To what degree do you agree that ethics codes of most human service organizations are culturally biased? Explain your position.

3. As a consultant-in-training, how would you want to be trained in ethical decision making?

4. To what degree do consultants require specific training to consult in a given area?

5. What are the consultant's professional and ethical obligations to the consultee?

6. What are the consultant's professional and ethical obligations to the consultee's client?

7. In what ways are consultants most likely to violate the rights of their consultees during consultation?

8. How does a consultant go about developing a personal and professional growth orientation?

9. If you were a judge in a court of law and a consultant was being sued for malpractice, what information would you want to know to determine whether malpractice had occurred?

10. How can there ever be a code of ethics for consultants when there are so many different professional groups whose members perform consultation as one of their primary functions?

SUGGESTED SUPPLEMENTARY READINGS

I hope you are interested in learning more about the ethical, professional, and legal issues that affect consultants. I strongly recommend the following readings for study and reflection:

American Counseling Association. (2005). *Code of ethics and standards of practice* (rev. ed.). Alexandria, VA: Author.

American Psychological Association. (2002). *Ethical principles of psychologists and code of conduct* (rev. ed.). Washington, DC: Author.

Corey, G., Corey, M. S., & Callanan, P. (2011). *Issues and ethics in the helping professions* (8th ed.). Belmont, CA: Brooks/Cole. This book provides a wealth of information for professionals and students in any of the human service professions. Ethics and issues specifically related to consultation are given adequate coverage, and the authors' ideas on several issues have relevance for consultants. Chapter 3, "Values and the Helping Relationship," provides excellent information that consultants can extrapolate and apply to their practices. Chapter 4, "Multicultural Perspectives and Diversity Issues"; Chapter 6, "Confidentiality: Ethical and Legal Issues"; and Chapter 7,

"Managing Boundaries and Multiple Relationships" all present important information that consultants can use in developing their own standards of conduct and making related decisions.

National Association of School Psychologists. (2010). *Principles for professional ethics*. Bethesda, MD: Author. Available from: http://www.nasponline .org/standards/2010standards/1_Ethical_Principles.pdf.

Epilogue

I hope you have enjoyed and benefited from this book. Providing consultation and collaboration can be among the most challenging and enjoyable professional activities in which you engage.

As you reflect on what you have read and practiced, let me leave you with some concluding thoughts.

There are a variety of strategies available to you to promote consultation and collaboration services in your work setting. McLean (2006) has identified several successful approaches to finding the "points of focus" (p. 45). You can make a point to learn the ins-and-outs of your organization, including its people. This task allows you to be able to identify the needs for consultation and collaboration at both the individual and organizational levels. You can proactively publicize and promote awareness of your services within the organization. These processes assist the members of the organization to determine how your work can assist them and the organization. When you share examples of their work and related successes, others in the organization are more likely to trust your expertise as well as make connections about how they can benefit from consultation and collaboration. When you are visible frequently and engaging others at all levels of the organization, you are more likely to be invited to engage in activities related to organizational level and individual level initiatives that lead to consultation and/or collaboration. Engage your immediate supervisor as champion of your consultation and collaboration services and invite those who have engaged in consultation or collaboration with you to share their experiences with others in the organization.

In the final analysis, there is no "one-minute manager" type of consultation or collaboration. To be accomplished effectively, these services take time and planning—a difficult prospect in the "quick fix" society in which we live. The "Catch–22" is that effective consultation and collaboration take time, yet time is often hard to come by. The consultant and collaborator need to balance time and quality. Finding creative ways to provide services such as over the phone and so forth is important. That said, remember quick fixes are short-lived and typically lead to diminishing returns.

Appreciate the challenge of the complexity of these services. Take care not to be overwhelmed by all the variables that affect their processes. There are several ways to go about expertly performing each approach to consultation and collaboration. Most of the approaches are highly flexible with regard to how consultation and collaboration might proceed. If you give your best effort when you consult and collaborate and trust the process, then anxiety and doubt will not overburden you.

To enhance your effectiveness as a consultant and as a collaborator, continue your professional and personal development. You will need to become familiar with the literature on consultation and collaboration, have some supervised field experience in performing them, gain a sense of the organizational context in which they occur, and possess some degree of knowledge of who you are as a person. Taken together, these will provide a cognitive map to guide your practice.

When in doubt, consider using collaboration. Collaboration minimizes the probability of a negative experience and at the same time maximizes the input into the problem-solving process. It is also empowering by nature.

Consultation and collaboration involve relationships among humans—they need to be performed with a personal touch. Each is more than a science, an art, or a craft: Each is all of these things along with commitment—to oneself as a helper, to the people with whom one is working, and to the ever-challenging task of trying to help others work more effectively.

Good luck and best wishes!

✳

Glossary of Key Terms Used in the Book

Because consultation and collaboration are neither well-defined nor have adequately developed their own identity, many of the terms used about them in the literature are vague and confusing.

Therefore, the glossary that follows contains some key terms used throughout this book.

It is very important that you familiarize yourself with these terms to avoid confusion as you continue reading.

advocacy a role consultants take on when they believe a certain course of action should be taken.

advocacy consultation an expansion of the role of advocacy to a method of consultation entirely devoted to furthering some course of action.

behavioral consultation one of the three major types of consultation; it attempts to assist consultees and their client systems through a systematic, problem-solving approach based on behavioral technology.

client in some approaches to mental health and behavioral consultation, the person with whom the consultee is having a work-related or caretaking-related problem; in this instance, the client constitutes the client system (see below). One of the goals of consultation is to improve the functioning of the client.

client system the person, group, organization, or community with whom the consultee is having a work-related or caretaking-related problem. One of the goals of consultation is to improve the functioning of the client system.

collaboration a service provided by a professional in which there is a shared responsibility for the outcome of the problem-solving process, including participation in interventions. Collaboration often occurs in teams of professionals and stakeholders working toward the same ends. Collaboration is characterized by mutual, reciprocal consultation among the parties involved.

collaborative consultation the method of relating most consultants use when working with their consultees; it allows both parties to pool their strengths and resources in their efforts (however, the consultee typically carries out the plan developed in consultation). Any model of consultation can be implemented collaboratively.

complementarity the idea that both the consultant and the consultee each bring unique competencies to the consultation process that supplement each other.

consultant a person, typically a human service professional, who delivers direct service to another person (consultee) who has a work-related or caretaking-related problem with a person, group, organization, or community (client system).

consultation a type of helping relationship in which a human service professional (consultant) delivers assistance to another person (consultee) so as to solve a work-related or caretaking-related problem the consultee has with a client system.

consultee the person, often a human service professional or a caretaker (e.g., a parent, teacher, or supervisor), to whom the consultant provides assistance with a work-related or caretaking-related problem. One of the goals of consultation is to improve the current and future functioning of the consultee.

cross-cultural consultation consultation in which the relationship consists of parties who are culturally different from one another.

cultural competence a set of knowledge, skills and attitudes in people and organizations that enable people and organizations to work effectively in cross-cultural contexts.

diagnosis the second of the four stages of the consultation process. In this stage, the problem to be solved in consultation is defined. Thus, in its simplest form, diagnosis is the equivalent of problem identification. In its more complex form, it is an ongoing process in which the target problem is continually redefined and worked on by gathering, analyzing, interpreting, and discussing data.

direct service the assistance a consultant provides a consultee or that a consultee provides a client system. When consultants work with consultees they are providing direct service to them. When consultees work with client systems, they provide direct service to them. This term is frequently contrasted with indirect service.

disengagement the last of the four stages in the consultation process; it involves the winding down of consultation, including evaluation of the consultation, postconsultation planning, reduced contact, follow-up, and termination.

diversity differences among groups based on characteristics such as race, gender, ethnicity.

entry the first of the four stages of the consultation process; it involves exploring the presenting problem, formulating a contract, and physically and psychologically entering the system in which consultation is to occur.

external consultant a consultant not permanently employed in the organization in which consultation is to occur.

generic model of consultation a model of consultation that contains those characteristics common to the various types of consultation and the approaches to these types. It is what distinguishes consultation as a unique helping relationship.

human service organization a broad term describing an organization that provides some form of contact with clients and aims to improve the well-being of those clients and, therefore, of society. Counseling centers, mental health centers, Head Start programs, homes for the mentally retarded, and social services departments are all examples of human service agencies.

implementation the third of the four stages of the consultation process; it is the stage in which action is taken on the problem. It begins with formulating and choosing a problem-solving plan and includes implementing and evaluating that plan.

indirect service that type of service provided to the client system by the consultant. The consultant affects the well-being of the client system by helping the consultee help the client system more effectively. It is one of the characteristics of consultation that differentiates it from other helping relationships.

internal consultant a consultant who is employed in the organization in which consultation is to occur.

mental health consultation one of the three major types of consultation; it attempts to focus on the psychological well-being of all the parties involved in consultation. Its ultimate goal is to create a more mentally healthy society.

multicultural consultation an approach to consultation that takes into account how cultural issues affect the consultation process.

organization a group of people put together for a common purpose. Almost all consultation, regardless of the type, occurs within some type of organization. It is one of the factors that influence the processes and outcomes of consultation.

organization contact person the person in the organization in which consultation is being considered who initially contacts (or is contacted by) the consultant. This person is often a mid-level administrator who may or may not become a consultee. This person usually paves the way for the consultant's entry into the organization.

organizational consultation one of the three major types of consultation; its primary goal is the enhancement of an organization's effectiveness. The organization itself is the client system, and the members of the organization involved in consultation are the consultees. Consultants frequently work together in teams when performing organizational consultation.

outreach extending or making known available services to a target population.

parties-at-interest (stakeholders) those people (who usually belong to the organization in which consultation occurs) who are not directly involved in consultation but are affected by the consultation process in some way. Parties-at-interest typically include contact persons and administrators. If the consultant belongs to an organization (for example, a mental health center), then those members of the consultant's organization indirectly affected by the consultation are also parties-at-interest.

tripartite composed of three parts. With respect to consultation, it refers to the three parties involved: consultant, consultee, and client system.

work-related problem the kind of problem considered to be suitable for the primary focus in consultation. In the case of consultation with people such as parents, the term *caretaking-related problem* is sometimes used instead. This term is often contrasted with *personal problems*, which are not directly dealt with in consultation.

References

Adelman, H. S., & Taylor, L. (2003). On sustainability of project innovations as systemic change. *Journal of Educational and Psychological Consultation, 14*, 1–25.

Adelman, H. S., & Taylor, L. (2007). Systemic change for school improvement. *Journal of Educational and Psychological Consultation, 17*, 55–77.

Adelman, H. S., & Taylor, L. (2008). Best practices in the use of resource teams to enhance learning supports. In A. Thomas & J. Grimes (Eds.), *Best practices in school psychology* (5th ed., pp. 1689–1705). Bethesda, MD: National Association of School Psychologists.

Akin-Little, K. A., Little, S. G., Braym, M. A., & Kehle, T. J. (Eds.). (2009). *Behavioral interventions in schools: Evidenced-based positive strategies*. Washington, DC: American Psychological Association.

Akin-Little, K. A., Little, S. G., & Delligatti, N. (2004). A preventative model of school consultation incorporating perspectives from positive psychology. *Psychology in the Schools, 41*, 155–162.

Allen, K. (2011). Introduction to the special issue: Cognitive behavioral therapy in the school setting—Expanding the school psychologist's toolkit. *Psychology in the Schools, 48*, 215–222. doi: 10.1002/pits.20546

Allen, S. J., & Graden, S. J. (2002). Best practices in collaborative problem solving for intervention design. In A. Thomas & J. Grimes (Eds.), *Best practices in school psychology* (4th ed., pp. 565–582).

Washington, DC: National Association of School Psychologists.

Alpert, J. L., & Duckworth Smith, H. (2003). Terrorism, terrorism threat, and the school consultant. *Journal of Educational and Psychological Consultation, 14*, 369–385.

Alpert, J. L., & Taufique, S. R. (2002a). Consultation training: A field in need of review, revision, and research. *Journal of Educational and Psychological Consultation, 13*(1&2), 7–11.

Alpert, J. L., & Taufique, S. R. (2002b). Consultation training: 26 years and three questions. *Journal of Educational and Psychological Consultation, 13*(1&2), 13–33.

Altschaefl, M. R. (2014). Problem-solving (behavioral) consultation: School-based applications. In A. M. Dougherty (Ed.), *A casebook of psychological consultation and collaboration* (6th ed., pp. 22–43). Belmont, CA: Brooks/Cole Cengage.

Amada, G. (1993). The role of the mental health consultant in dealing with disruptive college students. *Journal of College Student Psychotherapy, 8*, 121–127.

Amatea, E. S., Daniels, H., Bringman, N., & Vandiver, F. M. (2004). Strengthening counselor-teacher-family connections. *Professional School Counseling, 8*, 47–55.

American Counseling Association. (1995). *Ethical standards for internet on-line counseling*. Alexandria, VA: Author.

American Counseling Association. (2005). *Code of ethics and standards of practice* (rev. ed.). Alexandria, VA: Author.

American Mental Health Counselors Association. (2000). *Code of ethics* (rev. ed.). Alexandria, VA: Author.

American Psychological Association. (1993). Guidelines for providers of psychological services to ethnic, linguistic, and culturally diverse populations. *American Psychologist, 48*(1), 45–48.

American Psychological Association. (2002). *Ethical principles of psychologists and code of conduct* (rev. ed.). Washington, DC: Author.

American Psychological Association. (2003). Guidelines on multicultural education, training, research, practice, and organizational change for psychologists. *American Psychologist, 58*, 377–402.

American School Counselor Association. (2005). *ASCA national model: A framework for comprehensive school counseling programs* (2nd ed.). Alexandria, VA: Author.

American School Counselor Association. (2010). *Ethical standards for school counselors* (rev. ed.). Alexandria, VA: Author.

Andersen, M. N., Hofstadter, K. L., Kupzyk, S., Daly, E. J., III., Bleck, A. A., Collaro, A. L., et al. (2010). A guiding framework for integrating the consultation process and behavior analytic practice in schools: The treatment validation consultation model. *Journal of Behavior Assessment and Intervention in Children, 1*(1), 53–84.

Anderson, B. S. (1996). *The counselor and the law* (4th ed.). Alexandria, VA: American Counseling Association.

Anderson, W. R., Frieden, B. J., & Murphy, M. J. (Eds.). (1977). *Managing human services*. Washington, DC: International City Management Association.

Anderson-Butcher, D., Lawson, H. A., Iachini, A., Bean, G., Flaspohler, P. D., & Zullig, K. (2010). Capacity-related innovations resulting from the implementation of a community collaboration model for school improvement. *Journal of Educational and Psychological Consultation, 20*, 257–287. doi: 10.1080/10474412.2010.500512

Anton-Lahart, J., & Rosenfield, S. (2004). A survey of preservice consultation training in school psychology programs. *Journal of Educational and Psychological Consultation, 15*, 41–62.

Armenakis, A. A., & Burdg, H. B. (1988). Consultation research: Contributions to practice and directions for improvement. *Journal of Management, 14*, 339–365.

Armenakis, A. A., Burdg, H. B., & Metzger, R. O. (1989). Invited commentary: Current issues in consultant selection. *Consultation, 8*, 133–142.

Armstrong, M. I., & Evans, M. E. (2010). Fostering and unnatural act: Does policy make a difference in collaboration in systems of care? *Best Practices in Mental Health, 6*, 27–38.

Arra, C. T. (2010). An examination of cross-cultural curriculum development and student cross-cultural competencies in a school-based consultation course. *Journal of Educational and Psychological Consultation, 20*, 169–183. doi:10.1080/10474411003785537

Arredondo, P. (1996). *Successful diversity management initiatives*. Thousand Oaks, CA: SAGE.

Arredondo, P., Shealy, C., Neale, M., & Winfrey, L. L. (2004). Consultation and interprofessional collaboration: Modeling for the future. *Journal of Clinical Psychology, 60*, 787–800.

Arredondo, P., Toporek, R., Brown, S. P., Jones, J., Locke, D. C., Sanchez, J., et al. (1996). Operationalization of the multicultural counseling competencies. *Journal of Multicultural Counseling and Development, 24*(1), 42–78.

Arredondo, P., Tovar-Blank, Z. G., & Parham, T. A. (2008). Challenges and promises of becoming a culturally competent counselor in a sociopolitical era of change and empowerment. *Journal of Counseling & Development, 86*, 261–268.

Ashford, S. J., & Cummings, L. L. (1983). Feedback as an individual resource: Personal strategies of creating information. *Organizational Behavior and Human Performance, 32*, 370–398.

Association for Counselor Education and Supervision, and American School Counselor Association (ACES/ASCA), Joint Committee on the Elementary School Counselor. Working Paper, April 2, 1966.

Association for Specialists in Group Work. (2000). *Professional standards for the training of group workers* (rev. ed.). Alexandria, VA: Author.

Athanasiou, M. S. (2001). Using consultation with a grandmother as an adjunct to play therapy. *Family Journal, 9*, 445–450.

Athanasiou, M. S., Geil, M., Hazel, C. E., & Copeland, E. P. (2002). A look inside school-based consultation: A qualitative study of the beliefs and practices of school psychologists and teachers. *School Psychology Quarterly, 17,* 258–298.

Atkinson, D. R. (2004). *Counseling American minorities* (6th ed.). Boston: McGraw-Hill.

Auster, E. R., Feeney-Kettler, K. A., & Kratochwill, T. R. (2006). Conjoint behavioral consultation: Application to the school-based treatment of anxiety disorders. *Education and Treatment of Children, 29,* 243–256.

Babinski, L. M., Jones, B. D., & DeWert, M. H. (2001). The role of facilitators and peers in an online support community for first year teachers. *Journal of Educational and Psychological Consultation, 12,* 151–169.

Babinski, L. M., & Rogers, D. L. (1998). Supporting new teachers through consultee-centered group consultation. *Journal of Educational and Psychological Consultation, 9,* 285–308.

Bacon, E. H., & Dougherty, A. M. (1992). Consultation in preschool settings. *Elementary School Guidance and Counseling, 27,* 24–32.

Bahr, M. W., & Kovaleski, J. F. (2006). The need for problem-solving teams. *Remedial and Special Education, 27,* 2–5.

Baker, S. B., Robichaud, T. A., Westforth Dietrich, V. C., Wells, S. C., & Schreck, R. E. (2009). School counselor consultation: A pathway to advocacy, collaboration, and leadership. *Professional School Counseling, 12,* 200–206.

Baker, S. B., & Shaw, M. C. (1987). *Improving counseling through primary prevention.* Columbus, OH: Merrill.

Ball, C., Pierson, E., & McIntosh, D. E. (2011). The expanding role of school psychology. In M. A. Bray & T. J. Kehle (Eds.), *The oxford handbook of school psychology* (pp. 47–60). New York: Oxford Press.

Bandura, A. (1977). *Social learning theory.* Englewood Cliffs, NJ: Prentice-Hall.

Bandura, A. (1982). Self-efficacy mechanism in human agency. *American Psychologist, 37,* 122–147.

Bangert, A. W., & Baumberger, J. P. (2005). Research and statistical techniques used in the journal of counseling and development: 1990-2001. *Journal of Counseling and Development, 83,* 480–487.

Barak, A. (1994). A cognitive-behavioral educational workshop to combat sexual harassment in the workplace. *Journal of Counseling & Development, 8,* 595–602.

Bardon, J. (1986). Psychology and schooling: The interrelationships among persons, processes, and products. In S. N. Elliot & J. C. Witt (Eds.), *The delivery of psychological services in schools: Concepts, processes, and issues* (pp. 53–80). Hillsdale, NJ: Erlbaum.

Barlow, D. H., Hayes, S. C., & Nelson-Gray, R. O. (1999). *The scientist practitioner* (2nd ed.). New York: Pergamon Press.

Barlow, D. H., Nock, M. K., & Hersen, M. (2009). *Single case experimental designs: Strategies for studying behavioral change* (3rd ed.). Boston: Allyn & Bacon.

Barnett, D., Hawkins, R., & Lentz, F. E., Jr. (2011). Intervention adherence for research and practice: Necessity or triage outcome? *Journal of Educational and Psychological Consultation, 21,* 175–190. doi: 10.1080/10474412.2011.595162

Barnett, D., & Lentz, F. E., Jr. (1993). Functional outcome analysis: A good heuristic that went a bridge too far. *School Psychology Quarterly, 8,* 231–237.

Barnett, D., VanDerHeyden, A. M., & Witt, J. C. (2007). Achieving science-based practice through response to intervention: What it might look like in preschools. *Journal of Educational and Psychological Consultation, 17,* 31–54.

Batsche, G. M., Castillo, J. M., Dixon, D. N., & Forde, S. (2008). Best practices in linking assessment to intervention. In A. Thomas & J. Grimes (Eds.), *Best practices in school psychology* (5th ed., pp. 177–193). Bethesda, MD: National Association of School Psychologists.

Beaver, B. R., & Busse, R. T. (2000). Informant reports: Conceptual and research bases of interviews with parents and teachers. In E. S. Shapiro & T. R. Kratochwill (Eds.), *Behavioral assessment in schools* (2nd ed., pp. 257–287). New York: Guilford Press.

Beckhard, R. (1979). Organization changing through consulting and training. In D. P. Sinha (Ed.), *Consultants and consultant styles* (pp. 17–44). New Delhi, India: Vision Books.

Beer, M. (1980). *Organization change and development: A systems view.* Glenview, IL: Scott, Foresman.

Beer, M., & Walton, R. E. (1990). Developing the competitive organization: Interventions and strategies. *American Psychologist, 45*(2), 154–161.

Begeny, J. C. (2006). Assessing pre-service teachers' training in empirically-validated behavioral instruction practices. *School Psychology Quarterly, 21,* 262–285.

Bellman, G. M. (1990). *The consultant's calling.* San Francisco: Jossey-Bass.

Bemak, F., Murphy, S., & Kaffenberger, C. (2005). Community-focused consultation: New directions and practice. In C. Sink (Ed.), *Contemporary school counseling* (pp. 327–357). Boston: Houghton Mifflin.

Benn, A. E., Jones, G. W., & Rosenfield, S. (2008). An analysis of instructional consultants' questions and alternatives to questions during problem identification interview. *Journal of Educational and Psychological, 18*(1), 54–80.

Bergan, J. R. (1977). *Behavioral consultation.* Columbus, OH: Merrill.

Bergan, J. R., & Kratochwill, T. R. (1990). *Behavioral consultation and therapy.* New York: Plenum.

Bergan, J. R., & Tombari, M. L. (1976). Consultant skill and efficiency and the implementation and outcomes of consultation. *Journal of School Psychology, 14*(1), 3–14.

Bernard, M. E., & DiGiuseppe, R. (2000). Advances in theory and practice of rational-emotive behavioral consultation. *Journal of Educational and Psychological Consultation, 11*(3&4), 333–355.

Berninger, V. W., Fayol, M., & Alston-Abel, N. (2011). Academic interventions: What school psychologists need to know for their assessment and problem solving consultation roles. In M. A. Bray & T. J. Kehle (Eds.), *The oxford handbook of school psychology* (pp. 553–566). New York: Oxford Press.

Berrios, R., & Lucca, N. (2006). Qualitative methodology in counseling research: Recent contributions and challenges for a new century. *Journal of Counseling and Development, 84,* 174–186.

Bersoff, D. N. (1996). The virtue of principle ethics. *The Counseling Psychologist, 24*(1), 86–91.

Bianco-Mathis, V., & Veazey, N. (1996, July). Consultant dilemmas: Lessons from the trenches. *Training and Development Journal,* 39–42.

Bidell, M. P. (2011). School counselors and social justice advocacy for lesbian, gay, bisexual, transgender, and questioning students. *Journal of School Counseling,*

9(10). Retrieved from http://www.jsc.montana.edu/articles/v9n10.pdf

Blader, J. C., & Gallagher, R. (2001). Consultation to administrators. *Child and Adolescent Psychiatric Clinics of North America, 10,* 185–197.

Blake, R. R., & Mouton, J. S. (1983). *Consultation: A handbook for individual and organization development* (2nd ed.). Reading, MA: Addison-Wesley.

Blase, J., & Blase, J. J. (2006). *Teachers bring out the best in teachers: A guide to peer consultation for administrators and teachers.* Thousand Oaks, CA: Corwin Press.

Block, P. (2000). *Flawless consulting: A guide to getting your expertise used* (2nd ed.). San Francisco: Jossey-Bass.

Blom-Hoffman, J., & Rose, G. S. (2007). Applying motivational interviewing to school-based consultation: A commentary on "Has consultation achieved its primary prevention potential?," an article by Joseph E. Zins. *Journal of Educational and Psychological Consultation, 17,* 151–156.

Bloom, B. L. (1984). *Community mental health: A general introduction* (2nd ed.). Pacific Grove, CA: Brooks/Cole.

Boss, R. W. (1993). The psychological contract. In R. T. Golembiewski (Ed.), *Handbook of organizational consultation* (pp. 65–74). New York: Marcel Dekker, Inc.

Brack, G., Jones, E. S., Smith, R. M., White, J., & Brack, C. J. (1993). A primer on consultation theory: Building a flexible world view. *Journal of Counseling and Development, 71,* 619–628.

Braden, J. P., & Tayrose, M. P. (2008). Best practices for school psychologists in educational accountability: High stakes testing and educational reform. In A. Thomas & J. Grimes (Eds.), *Best practices in school psychology* (5th ed., pp. 575–588). Bethesda, MD: National Association of School Psychologists.

Bradley, D. F. (1994). A framework for the acquisition of collaborative consultation skills. *Journal of Educational and Psychological Consultation, 5,* 51–68.

Bramlett, R. K., & Murphy, J. J. (1998). School psychology perspectives on consultation: Key contributions to the field. *Journal of Educational and Psychology Consultation, 9,* 29–55.

Bramlett, R. K., Murphy, J. J., Johnson, J., & Wallingsford, L. (2002). Contemporary practices in school psychology: A national survey of roles and referral problems. *Psychology in the Schools, 39,* 327–335.

Brehm, J. W. (1966). *A theory of psychological reactance.* New York: Academic Press.

Briesch, A. M., & Chafouleas, S. M. (2009). Exploring student buy-in: Initial development of an instrument to measure likelihood of children's intervention usage. *Journal of Educational and Psychological Consultation, 19,* 321–336. doi:10.1080/10474410903408885

Brigman, G., & Webb, L. (2008). An individual psychology approach to school counselor consultation. *Journal of Individual Psychology, 64,* 506–515.

Brown, D. (1988). Empowerment through advocacy. In D. J. Kurpius & D. Brown (Eds.), *Handbook of consultation: An intervention for advocacy and outreach* (pp. 5–17). Alexandria, VA: American Association for Counseling and Development.

Brown, D. (1993). Defining human services consultation. In J. E. Zins, T. R. Kratochwill, & S. N. Elliott (Eds.), *Handbook of consultation for children* (pp. 46–69). San Francisco: Jossey-Bass.

Brown, D. (1997). Implications of cultural values for crosscultural consultation with families. *Journal of Counseling and Development, 76,* 29–35.

Brown, D., Kurpius, D. J., & Morris, J. R. (1988). *Handbook of consultation with individuals and small groups.* Alexandria, VA: American Association for Counseling and Development.

Brown-Chidsey, R., Steege, M. W., & Mace, F. C. (2008). Best practices in evaluating the effectiveness of interventions using case study data. In A. Thomas & J. Grimes (Eds.), *Best practices in school psychology* (5th ed., pp. 2177–2191). Bethesda, MD: National Association of School Psychologists.

Bryan, J. (2010). Engaging clients, families, and communities as partners in mental health. *Journal of Counseling & Development, 87,* 507–512.

Bryan, J. A., & Griffin, D. (2010). A multidimensional study of school-family-community partnership involvement: School, school counselor, and training factors. *Professional School Counseling, 14,* 75–86.

Buerkle, K., Whitehouse, E. M., & Christenson, S. L. (2009). Partnering with families for educational success. In T. B. Gutkin & C. R. Reynolds (Eds.), *The handbook of school psychology* (4th ed., pp. 655–680). Hoboken, NJ: Wiley.

Burnham, J. J. (2009). Contemporary fears of children and adolescents: Coping and resiliency in the 21st century. *Journal of Counseling & Development, 87,* 28–35.

Burns, M. K. (2004). Curriculum-based assessment in consultation: A review of three levels of research. *Journal of Educational and Psychological Consultation, 15,* 63–78.

Burns, M. K., Wiley, H. I., & Viglietta, E. (2008). Best practices in implementing problem-solving teams. In A. Thomas & J. Grimes (Eds.), *Best practices in school psychology* (5th ed., pp. 1633–1644). Bethesda, MD: National Association of School Psychologists.

Busse, R. T., & Beaver, B. R. (2000). Informant report: Parent and teacher interviews. In E. S. Shapiro & T. R. Kratochwill (Eds.), *Conducting school-based assessments of child and adolescent behavior* (pp. 235–251). New York: Guilford Press.

Busse, R. T., Kratochwill, T. R., & Elliott, S. N. (1999). Influences of verbal interactions during behavioral consultations on treatment outcomes. *Journal of School Psychology, 37,* 117–143.

Butler, W. M., Leitenberg, H., & Fuselier, G. D. (1993). The use of mental health professional consultants to police hostage negotiation teams. *Behavioral Sciences and the Law, 11,* 213–221.

Buysse, V., Schulte, A. C., Pierce, P. P., & Terry, D. (1994). Models and styles of consultation: Preferences of professionals in early intervention. *Journal of Early Intervention, 18,* 302–310.

Calderon, J., Subotnik, R., Knotek, S., Rayhack, K., & Gorgia, J. (2007). Focus on the psychosocial dimensions of talent development: An important potential role for consultee-centered consultants. *Journal of Educational and Psychological Consultation, 17,* 347–367.

Campbell, C. A. (1992). The school counselor as consultant: Assessing your aptitude. *Elementary School Guidance and Counseling, 26,* 237–250.

Campbell, C. A. (1993). Strategies for reducing parent resistance to consultation in the schools. *Elementary School Guidance and Counseling, 28,* 83–91.

Caplan, G. (1970). *The theory and practice of mental health consultation.* New York: Basic Books.

Caplan, G. (1974). *Support systems and community health: Lectures in concept development.* New York: Behavioral Publications.

Caplan, G. (1977). Mental health consultation: Retrospect and prospect. In S. C. Plog & P. I. Ahmed

(Eds.), *Principles and techniques of mental health consultation* (pp. 9–21). New York: Plenum.

Caplan, G. (1993a). Epilogue. In W. P. Erchul (Ed.), *Consultation in community, school, and organizational practice* (pp. 205–213). Washington, DC: Taylor & Francis.

Caplan, G. (1993b). Mental health consultation, community mental health, and population-oriented psychiatry. In W. P. Erchul (Ed.), *Consultation in community, school, and organizational practice* (pp. 41–55). Washington, DC: Taylor & Francis.

Caplan, G., & Caplan, R. B. (1993). *Mental health consultation and collaboration.* San Francisco: Jossey-Bass.

Caplan, G., & Caplan, R. B. (1999). *Mental health consultation and collaboration.* Prospect Heights, IL: Waveland. (Original work published in 1993).

Caplan, G., Caplan, R. B., & Erchul, W. P. (1994). Caplanian mental health consultation: Historical background and current status. *Consulting Psychology Journal: Practice & Research, 46,* 2–12.

Caplan, G., & Caplan-Moskovich, R. B. (2004). Recent advances in mental health consultation and mental health collaboration. In N. M. Lambert, I. Hylander, & J. H. Sandoval (Eds.), *Consultee-centered consultation: Improving the quality of professional services in schools and community organizations* (pp. 21–35). Mahwah, NJ: Erlbaum.

Caplan-Moskovich, R. B., & Caplan, G. (2004). In N. M. Lambert, I. Hylander, & J. H. Sandoval (Eds.), *Consultee-centered consultation in low feasibility settings* (pp. 187–201). Mahwah, NJ: Erlbaum.

Cappella, E., Hamre, B. K., Kim, H. Y., Henry, D. B., Frazier, S. L., Atkins, M. S., et al. (2012, March 19). Teacher consultation and coaching within mental health practice: Classroom and child effects in urban elementary schools. *Journal of Consulting and Clinical Psychology.* Advance online publication. doi: 10.1037/a0027725

Carlisle, H. (1982). *Management: Concepts, methods, and applications* (2nd ed.). Chicago: Science Research Associates.

Carlson, C. (2006). Single parenting and step-parenting. In G. G. Bear & K. M. Minke (Eds.), *Children's needs III: Development, prevention, and intervention* (pp. 783–797). Bethesda, MD: National Association of School Psychologists.

Carlson, D. L. (2007). From dodge city to emerald city: The importance of Joseph E. Zins' work in teacher education programs: A commentary on "The scientific base linking social and emotional learning to school success," a chapter by a chapter by Joseph E. Zins, Michelle R. Bloodworth, Roger P. Weissberg, and Herbert J. Walberg. *Journal of Educational and Psychological Consultation, 17,* 219–223.

Carlson, J., Dinkmeyer, D., Jr., & Johnson, E. J. (2008). Adlerian teacher consultation: Change teachers, change students! *The Journal of Individual Psychology, 64,* 480–493.

Carlson, J., Watts, R. E., & Maniacci, M. (2006). *Adlerian therapy: Theory and practice.* Washington, DC: American Psychological Association.

Carr, E. G. (2007). The expanding vision of positive behavior support: Research perspectives on happiness, helpfulness, hopefulness. *Journal of Positive Behavior Support, 9,* 3–14.

Carson, A. D., & Lowman, R. L. (2002). Individual-level variables in organizational consultation. In R. L. Lowman (Ed.), *Handbook of organizational consulting psychology: A comprehensive guide to theory, skills, and techniques* (pp. 5–26). San Francisco: Jossey-Bass.

Carter, R. T., & Morrow, S. L. (2007). Qualitative research: Current and best practices. *Counseling Psychologist, 35,* 205–208.

Castillo, E. M., Quintana, S. M., & Zamarripa, M. X. (2000). Cultural and linguistic issues. In E. S. Shapiro & T. R. Kratochwill (Eds.), *Conducting school based assessments of child and adolescent behavior* (pp. 274–306). New York: Guilford Press.

Cataldo, C. G., Raelin, J. D., & Lambert, M. (2009). Reinvigorating the struggling organization the unification of Schein's oeuvre into a diagnostic model. *Journal of Applied Behavioral Science, 45*(1), 122–140.

Champion, D. P., Kiel, D. H., & McLendon, J. A. (1990, February). Choosing a consulting role. *Training and Development Journal,* 66–69.

Cherniss, C. (1993). Preentry issues revisited. In R. T. Golembiewski (Ed.), *Handbook of organizational consultation* (pp. 113–118). New York: Marcel Dekker, Inc.

Cherniss, C. (1998). Teacher empowerment, consultation, and the creation of new programs in schools.

Journal of Educational and Psychological Consultation, 8, 135–152.

Chowanec, G. D. (1993). TQM: Evaluating service quality. *Consulting Psychology Journal, 45,* 31–32.

Christ, T. J. (2008). Best practices in problem analysis. In A. Thomas & J. Grimes (Eds.), *Best practices in school psychology* (5th ed., pp. 159–176). Bethesda, MD: National Association of School Psychologists.

Christenson, S. L. (1995). Families and schools: What is the role of the school psychologist? *School Psychology Quarterly, 10,* 118–132.

Christenson, S. L., & Buerkle, K. (1999). Families as educational partners for children's school success: Suggestions for school psychologists. In C. R. Reynolds & T. B. Gutkin (Eds.), *The handbook of school psychology* (3rd ed., pp. 709–744). New York: Wiley.

Clare, M. M. (2009). Decolonizing consultation: Advocacy as the strategy, diversity as the context. *Journal of Educational and Psychological Consultation, 19,* 8–25. doi:10.1080/10474410802494929

Clare, M. M., Jimenez, A., & McClendon, J. (2005). Toma el tiempo: The wisdom of migrant families in consultation. *Journal of Educational and Psychological Consultation, 16,* 95–111.

Clark, A. J. (2010). Empathy: An integral model in the counseling process. *Journal of Counseling & Development, 88,* 348–356.

Clark, M. A., & Breman, J. C. (2009). School counselor inclusion: A collaborative model to provide academic and socio-emotional support in the classroom setting. *Journal of Counseling & Development, 87,* 6–11.

Codding, R. S., & Smyth, C. A. (2008). Using performance feedback to decrease classroom transition time and examine collateral effects on academic achievement. *Journal of Educational and Psychological Consultation, 18,* 325–345. doi:10.1080/10474410802463312

Cohen, E., & Osterweil, Z. (1986). An "issue-focused" model of mental health consultation with groups of teachers. *Journal of School Psychology, 24*(3), 243–256.

Cohen, R., Linker, J. A., & Stutts, L. (2006). Working together: Lessons learned from school, family, and community collaborations. *Psychology in the Schools, 43,* 419–428. doi:10.1002/pits.20156

Colbert, R. D., Vernon-Jones, R., & Pransky, K. (2006). The social change feedback process: Creating a new role for counselors in education reform. *Journal of Counseling and Development, 84,* 72–82.

Comstock, D. L., Hammer, T. R., Strentzsch, J., Cannon, K., Parsons, J., & Salazar, G, II. (2008). Relational-cultural theory: A framework for bridging relational, multicultural, and social justice competencies. *Journal of Counseling & Development, 86,* 279–287.

Conoley, C. W., Conoley, J. C., & Gumm, W. B., II. (1992). Effects of consultee problem presentation and consultant training on consultant problem definition. *Journal of Counseling and Development, 71,* 60–62.

Conoley, C. W., Conoley, J. C., Ivey, D. C., & Scheel, M. J. (1991). Enhancing consultation by matching the consultees' perspectives. *Journal of Counseling and Development, 69,* 546–549.

Conoley, C. W., Conoley, J. C., & Reese, R. J. (2009). Changing a field of change. *Journal of Educational and Psychological Consultation, 19,* 236–247. doi: 10.1080/10474410903106836

Conoley, J. C., & Conoley, C. W. (1982). The effects of two conditions of client-centered consultation on student-teacher problem descriptions and remedial plans. *Journal of School Psychology, 20,* 323–328.

Conoley, J. C., & Conoley, C. W. (1985). The school consultant as advocate: A perspective for trainers. *School Psychology International, 6*(4), 219–224.

Conoley, J. C., & Conoley, C. W. (1990). Staff consultative work in schools. In N. Jones & N. Frederickson (Eds.), *Refocusing educational psychology* (pp. 84–103). London: Falmer.

Conoley, J. C., & Conoley, C. W. (1992). *School consultation: Practice and training* (2nd ed.). Boston: Allyn & Bacon.

Conoley, J. C., & Conoley, C. W. (2010). Why does collaboration work? Linking positive psychology and collaboration. *Journal of Educational and Psychological Consultation, 20,* 75–82.

Conoley, J. C., & Gutkin, T. B. (1986). School psychology: A re-conceptualization of service delivery realities. In S. N. Elliott & J. C. Witt (Eds.), *The delivery of psychological services in schools* (pp. 393–424). Hillsdale, NJ: Erlbaum.

Conoley, J. C., & Haynes, G. (1992). Ecological perspectives. In R. D'Amato & B. Rothlisberg (Eds.), *Psychological perspectives on interaction* (pp. 177–189). White Plains, NY: Longman Publishing.

Conoley, J. C., & Wright, C. (1993). Caplan's ideas and the future of psychology in the schools. In W. P. Erchul (Ed.), *Consultation in community, school, and organizational practice* (pp. 177–192). Washington, DC: Taylor & Francis.

Conyne, R. K., & Mazza, J. (2007). Ecological group work applied to schools. *Journal for Specialists in Group Work, 32,* 19–29.

Conyne, R. K., & O'Neil, J. M. (Eds.). (1992). *Organizational consultation: A casebook.* Newbury Park, CA: Sage.

Conyne, R. K., Rapin, L. S., & Rand, J. M. (1997). A model for leading task groups. In H. Forester-Miller & J. A. Kottler (Eds.), *Issues and challenges for group practitioners* (pp. 117–130). Denver, CO: Love Publishing Company.

Cook, D. W. (1989). Systematic need assessment: A primer. *Journal of Counseling and Development, 67,* 462–464.

Cook, L., & Friend, M. (2010). The state of the art of collaboration on behalf of students with disabilities. *Journal of Educational and Psychological Consultation, 20,* 1–8.

Cooper, S., & Hodges, W. F. (Eds.). (1983). *The mental health consultation field.* New York: Human Sciences Press.

Cooper, S., & Leong, F. T. L. (2008). Introduction to the special issue on culture, race, and ethnicity in organizational consulting psychology. *Consulting Psychology Journal: Practice and Research, 60,* 133–138. doi:10.1037/0736-9735.60.2.13

Cooper, S., Wilson-Stark, K., Peterson, D. B., O'Roark, A., & Pennington, G. (2008). Consulting competently in multicultural contexts. *Consulting Psychology Journal: Practice and Research, 60,* 186–202. doi: 10.1037/0736-9735.60.2.186

Cooper, S. E., Monarch, N., Serviss, S. T., Gordick, D., & Leonard, L. H. (2007). Professional preparation and continuing education for beginning, entry, midlevel, and senior consulting psychologists. *Consulting Psychology Journal: Practice and Research, 59,* 1–16.

Cooper, S. E., & O'Connor, R. M., Jr. (1993). Standards for organizational consultation assessment and evaluation instruments. *Journal of Counseling and Development, 71,* 651–660.

Corey, G. (2009). *Theory and practice of counseling and psychotherapy* (8th ed.). Belmont, CA: Brooks/Cole Cengage.

Corey, G., Corey, M. S., & Callanan, P. (2011). *Issues and ethics in the helping professions* (8th ed.). Belmont, CA: Brooks/Cole Cengage.

Costello, M., Phelps, L., & Wilczenski, F. (1994). Children and military conflict: Current issues and treatment implications. *School Counselor, 41,* 220–225.

Cottingham, H. E. (1956). *Guidance in the elementary schools: Principles and practice.* Bloomington, IL: McKnight & McKnight.

Cottone, R. R. (2001). A social constructivism model of ethical decision making in counseling. *Journal of Counseling and Development, 79*(1), 39–45.

Council for Accreditation of Counseling and Related Educational Programs. (2009). *2009 standards.* Retrieved from http://www.cacrep.org/doc/ 2009%20Standards%20with%20cover.pdf

Covey, S. R. (1991). *Principle-centered leadership.* New York: Simon and Schuster.

Cowan, R. J. (2007). The use and perceived utility of peer mediated systems for school psychologists: A commentary on "Introduction to developing peer-mediated support systems for helping professionals: Are we ready to practice what we preach?" an article by Joseph E. Zins, and on "Consultation with professional peers: A national survey of the practices of school psychologists," an article by Joseph E. Zins and John J. Murphy. *Journal of Educational and Psychological Consultation, 17,* 185–189.

Cowan, R. J., & Sheridan, S. M. (2003). Investigating the acceptability of behavioral interventions in applied conjoint behavioral consultation: Moving from analog conditions to naturalistic settings. *School Psychology Quarterly, 18,* 1–21.

Cowles, C. A., & Washburn, J. J. (2005). Psychological consultation on program design of intensive management units in juvenile correctional facilities. *Professional Psychology: Research and Practice, 36,* 44–50.

Cox, D. D. (2005). Evidence-based interventions using home-school collaboration. *School Psychology Quarterly, 20,* 473–497.

Cox, T. (2001). *Creating the multicultural organization.* San Francisco: Jossey-Bass.

Creswell, J. W. (2011). Controversies in mixed methods research. In N. K. Denzin & Y. S. Lincoln (Eds.), *The sage handbook of qualitative research* (4th ed., pp. 269–283). Thousand Oaks, CA: Sage.

Crone, D. A., Hawken, L. S., & Bergstrom, M. K. (2007). A demonstration of training, implementing, and using functional behavioral assessment in 10 elementary and middle school settings. *Journal of Positive Behavioral Interventions, 9,* 15–29.

Crose, R., & Kixmiller, J. S. (1994). Counseling psychologists as nursing home consultants: What do administrators want? *Counseling Psychologist, 22,* 104–114.

Culross, R. (2007). Cross-disciplinary perspectives on consultation in gifted education: An overview. *Journal of Educational and Psychological Consultation, 17,* 269–271.

Cummings, G. C., & Worley, C. G. (2009). *Organization development & change* (7th ed.). Mason, OH: South-Western Cengage Learning.

Cummings, J. A., Harrison, P. L., Dawson, M. M., Short, R. J., Gorin, S., & Palomares, R. S. (2004a). The 2002 conference on the future of school psychology: Implications for consultation, intervention, and prevention services. *Journal of Educational and Psychological Consultation, 15,* 239–256.

Cummings, J. A., Harrison, P. L., Dawson, M. M., Short, R. J., Gorin, S., & Palomares, R. S. (2004b). Follow-up to the 2002 futures conference: Collaborating to serve all children, families, and schools. *Journal of Educational and Psychological Consultation, 15,* 335–344.

Curtis, M. J., Castillo, J. M., & Cohen, R. M. (2008). Best practices in system-level change. In A. Thomas & J. Grimes (Eds.), *Best practices in school psychology* (5th ed., pp. 887–901). Bethesda, MD: National Association of School Psychologists.

Curtis, M. J., & Stollar, S. A. (1996). Applying principles and practices of organizational change to school reform. *School Psychology Review, 25,* 409–417.

Curtis, R., & Van Horne, J. W. (2014). School-wide collaboration to implement of a positive behavioral interventions support program. In A. M. Dougherty (Ed.), *A casebook of psychological consultation and collaboration* (6th ed., pp. 154–173). Belmont, CA: Brooks/Cole Cengage.

Dahir, C. A., & Stone, C. B. (2009). School counselor accountability: The path to social justice and systemic change. *Journal of Counseling & Development, 87,* 12–20.

Dahir, C. A., & Stone, C. B. (2012). *The transformed school counselor* (2nd ed.). Belmont, CA: Brooks/Cole Cengage.

Dailor, A. N., & Jacob, S. (2011). Ethically challenging situations reported by school psychologists: Implications for training. *Psychology in the Schools, 48,* 619–631.

Daly, E. J., III, Martens, B. K., Skinner, C. H., & Noell, G. H. (2009). Contributions of applied behavioral analysis. In T. B. Gutkin & C. R. Reynolds (Eds.), *The handbook of school psychology* (4th ed., pp. 84–106). Hoboken, NJ: Wiley.

Daly, E. J., III, & Murdoch, A. (2000). Direct observation in the assessment of academic skills problems. In E. S. Shapiro & T. R. Kratochwill (Eds.), *Behavioral assessment in schools: Theory, research, and clinical foundations* (2nd ed., pp. 46–73). New York: Guilford Press.

D'Amato, R. C., Zafiris, C., McConnell, E., & Dean, R. S. (2011). The history of school psychology: Understanding the past to not repeat it. In M. A. Bray & T. J. Kehle (Eds.), *The oxford handbook of school psychology* (pp. 9–46). New York: Oxford Press.

Damon, S., Riley-Tillman, T. C., & Fiorello, C. (2008). Comparing methods of identifying reinforcing stimuli in school consultation. *Journal of Educational and Psychological Consultation, 18,* 31–53. doi:10.1080/10474410701864123

D'Amour, D., Ferrada-Videla, M., San Martin Rodriquez, L., & Beaulieu, M. D. (2005). The conceptual basis for interprofessional collaboration: Core concepts and theoretical frameworks. *Journal of Interprofessional Care, Suppl 1,* 116–131.

D'Andrea, M., & Heckman, E. F. (2008). Contributions to the ongoing evolution of the multicultural counseling movement: An introduction to the special issues. *Journal of Counseling & Development, 86,* 259–260.

Daniels, T. D., & Dewine, S. (1990). Communication process as target and tool for consultancy intervention: Rethinking a hackneyed theme. *Journal of Educational and Psychological Consultation, 2,* 303–322.

Darnell, A. J., & Kupermine, G. P. (2006). Organizational culture competence in mental health service delivery: A multilevel analysis. *Journal of Multicultural Counseling and Development, 34,* 194–207.

Das, A. K. (1995). Rethinking multicultural counseling: Implications for counselor education. *Journal of Counseling and Development, 74*(1), 45–52.

David, R. J., & Strang, D. (2006). When fashion is fleeting: Transitory collective beliefs and the dynamics of TQM consulting. *Academy of Management Journal, 49,* 215–233.

Davidson, M. M., Waldo, M., & Adams, E. M. (2006). Promoting social justice through prevention interventions in schools. In R. L. Toporek, L. H. Gerstein, N. A. Fouad, G. Roysircar, & T. Israel (Eds.), *Handbook for social justice in counseling psychology* (pp. 117–129). Thousand Oaks, CA: Sage.

Davis, K. M. (2005). School-based consultation. In C. Sink (Ed.), *Contemporary school counseling* (pp. 297–326). Boston: Houghton Mifflin.

Davison, M., & Gasiorowski, F. (2006). The trend of coaching: Adler, the literature, and marketplace would agree. *The Journal of Individual Psychology, 62,* 188–201.

Deck, M. D. (1992). Training school counselors to be consultants. *Elementary School Guidance and Counseling, 26,* 221–228.

Dedrick, R. F., & Greenbaum, P. E. (2011). Multilevel confirmatory factor analysis of a scale measuring interagency collaboration of children's mental health agencies. *Journal of Emotional and Behavioral Disorders, 19,* 27–40.

Deitz, P. E., & Reese, J. T. (1986). The perils of police psychology: 10 strategies for minimizing role conflicts when providing mental health services and consultation to law enforcement agencies. *Behavioral Sciences and the Law, 4,* 385–400.

Delbecq, A. L., Van de Ven, A. H., & Gustafson, D. H. (1986). *Group techniques for program planning: A guide to nominal group and Delphi processes.* Middleton, WI: Green Briar Press.

Demers, C. (2007). *Organizational change theories.* Thousand Oaks, CA: Sage.

Denton, C. A., Hasbrouck, J. E., & Sekaquaptewa, S. (2003). The consulting teacher: A descriptive case study in responsive systems consultation. *Journal of Educational and Psychological Consultation, 14,* 41–73.

Denzin, N. K., & Lincoln, Y. S. (Eds.). (2011). *The SAGE handbook of qualitative research* (4th ed.). Thousand Oaks, CA: Sage.

Dewar, A. L. (1980). *The quality circle guide to participation management.* Englewood Cliffs, NJ: Prentice-Hall.

Dickinson, D. J., & Bradshaw, S. P. (1992). Multiplying effectiveness: Combining consultation with counseling. *School Counselor, 40,* 118–124.

Diller, J. V. (2007). *Cultural diversity: A primer for human services.* Belmont, CA: Thomson–Brooks/Cole.

Dinkmeyer, D., Jr. (2006). School consultation using individual psychology. *Journal of Individual Psychology, 62,* 180–187.

Dinkmeyer, D., & Caldwell, E. (1970). *Developmental counseling and guidance: A comprehensive school approach.* New York: McGraw-Hill.

Dinkmeyer, D., & Carlson, J. (1973). *Consultation: Facilitating human potential and change processes.* Columbus, OH: Merrill.

Dinkmeyer, D., Jr., & Carlson, J. (2001). *Consultation: Creating school-based interventions* (2nd ed.). Philadelphia: Taylor & Francis.

Dinkmeyer, D. C., Pew, W. L., & Dinkmeyer, D. C., Jr. (1979). *Adlerian counseling and psychotherapy.* Monterey, CA: Brooks/Cole.

Dixon, A. L., & Tucker, C. (2008). Every student matters: Enhancing strengths-based school counseling through the application of mattering. *Professional School Counseling, 12,* 123–126.

Dixon, A. L., Tucker, C., & Clark, M. A. (2010, Bottom of For). Integrating social justice advocacy with national standards of practice: Implications for school counselors. *Counselor Education and Supervision, 50,* 103–115.

Dixon, D. N., & Dixon, D. E. (1993). Research in consultation: Toward better analogues and outcome measures. *Journal of Counseling and Development, 71,* 700–702.

Doll, B., & Cummings, J. (2008). Best practices in population-based school mental health services. In A. Thomas & J. Grimes (Eds.), *Best practices in school psychology* (5th ed., pp. 1333–1347). Bethesda, MD: National Association of School Psychologists.

Doll, B., Haack, K., Kosse, S., Osterloh, M., & Siemers, E., & Pray, B. (2005). The dilemma of pragmatics: Why schools don't use quality team consultation practices. *Journal of Educational and Psychological Consultation, 16,* 127–155.

Doll, B., Spies, R., & Champion, A. (2012). Contributions of ecological school mental health services to students' academic success. *Journal of Educational and Psychological Consultation, 22,* 44–61.

Domitrovich, C. E., & Greenberg, M. T. (2000). The study of implementation: Current findings from effective programs that prevent mental disorders in school-aged children. *Journal of Educational and Psychological Consultation, 11,* 193–221.

Douce, L. A. (1993). AIDS and HIV: Hopes and challenges for the 1990's. *Journal for Counseling and Development, 71,* 259–260.

Dougherty, A. M. (1992a). School consultation in the 1990s. *Elementary School Guidance and Counseling, 26,* 163–164.

Dougherty, A. M. (1992b). Ethical issues in consultation. *Elementary School Guidance and Counseling, 26,* 214–220.

Dougherty, A. M. (1996–97, Fall/Winter). The importance of effective communication in consultation. *The Consulting Edge, 4,* 1–2, 4–7.

Dougherty, A. M. (2006a). Dual role conflicts in consultation. In B. Herlihy & G. Corey (Eds.), *Boundary issues in counseling* (2nd ed., pp. 91–93). Alexandria, VA: American Counseling Association.

Dougherty, A. M. (2006b). Managing role conflicts in school counseling. In B. Herlihy & G. Corey (Eds.), *Boundary issues in counseling* (2nd ed., pp. 179–182). Alexandria, VA: American Counseling Association.

Dougherty, A. M. (2014a). *Casebook of psychological consultation and collaboration* (6th ed.). Belmont, CA: Brooks/Cole Cengage.

Dougherty, A. M. (2014b). Foundations of consultation and collaboration. In A. M. Dougherty (Ed.), *A casebook of psychological consultation and collaboration* (6th ed., pp. 2–20). Belmont, CA: Brooks/Cole Cengage.

Dougherty, A. M. (2014c). Implications for effective practice. In A. M. Dougherty (Ed.), *A casebook of psychological consultation and collaboration* (6th ed., pp.176–205). Belmont, CA: Brooks/Cole Cengage.

Dougherty, A. M. (2014d). Cases for further practice. In A. M. Dougherty (Ed.), *A casebook of psychological consultation and collaboration* (6th ed., pp. 206–215). Belmont, CA: Brooks/Cole Cengage.

Dougherty, A. M., & Dougherty, L. P. (1991). Using your school counselor as an organizational consultant. *American Middle School Education, 12*(2), 37–44.

Dougherty, A. M., Dougherty, L. P., & Purcell, D. (1991). The sources and management of resistance to consultation. *School Counselor, 38,* 178–186.

Dougherty, A. M., Henderson, B. B., & Lindsey, B. (1997). The effectiveness of direct versus indirect confrontation as a function of stage of consultation: Results of an exploratory investigation. *Journal of Educational and Psychological Consultation, 8,* 361–372.

Dougherty, A. M., Henderson, B. B., Tack, F. E., Deck, M. D., Worley, V., & Page, J. R. (1997). The relation of facilitative conditions, consultant experience, and stage of consultation to consultees' perceptions of the use of direct confrontation. *Journal of Educational and Psychological Consultation, 8,* 21–40.

Dougherty, A. M., Tack, F. E., Fullam, C. B., & Hammer, L. A. (1996). Disengagement: A neglected aspect of the consultation process. *Journal of Educational and Psychological Consultation, 7,* 259–274.

Dougherty, A. M., & Taylor, B. L. B. (1983). Evaluation of peer helper programs. *Elementary School Guidance and Counseling, 18*(2), 130–136.

Drum, D. J., & Valdese, L. E. (1988). Advocacy and outreach: Applications to college/university settings. In D. J. Kurpius & D. Brown (Eds.), *Handbook of consultation: An intervention for advocacy and outreach* (pp. 38–60). Alexandria, VA: American Association for Counseling and Development.

Dufrene, B. A., Parker, K., Menousek, K., Zhou, Q., Harpole, L. L., & Olmi, D. J. (2012). Direct behavioral consultation in Head Start to increase teacher use of praise and effective instruction delivery. *Journal of Educational and Psychological Consultation, 22,* 159–186.

Duncan, C. F. (1995). Cross-cultural school consultation. In C. C. Lee (Ed.), *Counseling for diversity: A guide for school counselors and related professionals* (pp. 128–141). Boston: Allyn & Bacon.

Dunson, R. M., III, Hughes, J. N., & Jackson, T. W. (1994). Effect of behavioral consultation on student and teacher behavior. *Journal of School Psychology, 32,* 247–266.

DuPaul, G. J. (2011). Collaboration between medical and educational professionals: Toward a proactive, integrated, and cost-efficient system of care. *Journal of Educational and Psychological Consultation, 21,* 166–168. doi:10.1080/10474412.2011.571523

Durlak, J. A. (2009). Prevention programs. In T. B. Gutkin & C. R. Reynolds (Eds.), *The handbook of school psychology* (4th ed., pp. 905–920). Hoboken, NJ: Wiley.

Dustin, D., & Ehly, S. (1984). Skills for effective consultation. *School Counselor, 32,* 23–29.

D'Zurilla, T. J., & Goldfried, M. R. (1971). Problem solving and behavior modification. *Journal of Abnormal Psychology, 78,* 107–126.

Eagle, J. W., Dowd-Eagle, S. E., & Sheridan, S. M. (2008). Best practices in school community partnerships. In A. Thomas & J. Grimes (Eds.), *Best practices in school psychology* (5th ed., pp. 953–967). Bethesda, MD: National Association of School Psychologists.

Easton, J. E., & Erchul, W. P. (2011). An exploration of teacher acceptability of treatment plan implementation: Monitoring and feedback methods. *Journal of Educational and Psychological Consultation, 21,* 56–77. doi:10.1080/10474412.2011.544949

Egan, G. (1985). *Change agent skills in helping and human service settings.* Pacific Grove, CA: Brooks/Cole.

Egan, G. (2006). *Essentials of skilled helping.* Belmont, CA: Wadsworth Thomson.

Egan, G. (2010). *The skilled helper* (9th ed.). Belmont, CA: Brooks/Cole Cengage.

Elias, M. J., & Leverett, L. (2011). Consultation to urban schools for improvements in academics and behavior: No alibis. No excuses. No exceptions. *Journal of Educational and Psychological Consultation, 21,* 28–45. doi:10.1080/10474412.2010.522877

Elliott, S. N., & Busse, R. T. (1993). Effective treatments with behavioral consultation. In J. E. Zins, T. R. Kratochwill, & S. N. Elliott (Eds.), *Handbook of consultation services for children* (pp. 179–203). San Francisco: Jossey-Bass.

Elliott, S. N., Busse, R. T., & Shapiro, E. S. (1999). Intervention techniques for academic performance problems. In C. R. Reynolds & T. B. Gutkin (Eds.), *The handbook of school psychology* (3rd ed., pp. 664–685). New York: Wiley.

Epstein, J. L., & Van Voorhis, F. L. (2010). School counselors' roles in developing partnerships with families and communities for student success. *Professional School Counseling, 14,* 1–14.

Erchul, W. P. (1987). A relational communication analysis of control in school consultation. *Professional School Psychology, 2*(2), 113–124.

Erchul, W. P. (1993a). Reflections on mental health consultation: An interview with Gerald Caplan. In W. P. Erchul (Ed.), *Consultation in community, school, and organizational practice* (pp. 57–72). Washington, DC: Taylor & Francis.

Erchul, W. P. (1993b). Selected interpersonal perspectives in consultation research. *School Psychology Quarterly, 8,* 38–49.

Erchul, W. P. (1999). Two steps forward, one step back: Collaboration in school-based consultation. *Journal of School Psychology, 37,* 191–203.

Erchul, W. P. (2009). Gerald Caplan: A tribute to the originator of mental health consultation. *Journal of Educational and Psychological Consultation, 19,* 95–105. doi:10.1080/10474410902888418

Erchul, W. P. (2011). School consultation and response to intervention: A tale of two literatures. *Journal of Educational and Psychological Consultation, 21,* 191–208.

Erchul, W. P., & Chewning, T. G. (1990). Behavioral consultation from a request-centered relational communication perspective. *Professional School Psychology, 5,* 1–20.

Erchul, W. P., & Conoley, C. W. (1991). Helpful theories to guide counselors' practice of school-based consultation. *Elementary School Guidance and Counseling, 25,* 204–211.

Erchul, W. P., DuPaul, G. J., Bennett, M. S., Grissom, P. F., Jitendra, A. K., Tresco, K. E., et al. (2009). A follow-up study of relational process and consultation outcomes for students with attention deficit hyperactivity disorder. *School Psychology Review, 38,* 28–37.

Erchul, W. P., & Martens, B. K. (2002). *School consultation: Conceptual and empirical bases of practice.* New York: Kluwer/Plenum.

Erchul, W. P., & Raven, B. H. (1997). Social power in school consultation: A contemporary view of

French and Raven's bases of power model. *Journal of School Psychology, 35,* 137–171.

Erchul, W. P., Raven, B. H., & Ray, A. G. (2001). School psychologists' perceptions of social power bases in teacher consultation. *Journal of Educational and Psychological Consultation, 12,* 1–23.

Erchul, W. P., Raven, B. H., & Whichard, S. M. (2001). School psychologist and teacher perceptions of social power in consultation. *Journal of School Psychology, 39,* 483–497.

Erchul, W. P., & Schulte, A. C. (1993). Gerald Caplan's contributions to professional psychology: Conceptual underpinnings. In W. P. Erchul (Ed.), *Consultation in community, school, and organizational practice* (pp. 3–39). Washington, DC: Taylor & Francis.

Erchul, W. P., & Schulte, A. C. (1996). Behavioral consultation as a work in progress. *Journal of Educational and Psychological Consultation, 7,* 345–354.

Erchul, W. P., & Sheridan, S. M. (2008). Overview: The state of scientific research in school consultation. In W. P. Erchul & S. M. Sheridan (Eds.), *Handbook of research on school consultation* (pp. 3–12). New York: Erlbaum.

Erchul, W. P., Sheridan, S. M., Ryan, D. A., Grissom, P. F., Killough, C. E., & Mettler, D. W. (1999). Patterns of relational communication in conjoint behavioral consultation. *School Psychology Quarterly, 14,* 121–147.

Erhardt, K. E., Barnett, D. W., Lentz, F. E., Jr., Stollar, S. A., & Reifin, L. H. (1996). Innovative methodology in ecological consultation: Use of scripts to promote treatment acceptability and integrity. *School Psychology Quarterly, 11,* 149–168.

Ervin, R. A., & Erhardt, K. E. (2000). Behavior analysis and school psychology. In J. Austin & J. E. Carr (Eds.), *Handbook of applied behavioral analysis* (pp. 113–131). Reno, NV: Context Press.

Esler, A. N., Godber, Y., & Christenson, S. L. (2008). Best practices in supporting home-school collaboration. In A. Thomas & J. Grimes (Eds.), *Best practices in school psychology* (5th ed., pp. 917–936). Bethesda, MD: National Association of School Psychologists.

Fagan, T. K. (2008). Trends in the history of school psychology in the United States. In A. Thomas & J. Grimes (Eds.), *Best practices in school psychology* (5th ed., pp. 2069–2085). Bethesda, MD: National Association of School Psychologists.

Fall, M. (1995). Planning for consultation: An aid for the elementary school counselor. *The School Counselor, 43,* 151–156.

Farmer, T. W. (2000). The social dynamics of aggressive and disruptive behavior in school: Implications for behavior consultation. *Journal of Educational and Psychological Consultation, 11*(3&4), 299–321.

Faust, V. (1968). *The counselor-consultant in the elementary school.* Boston: Houghton Mifflin.

Feld, J. K., Bergan, J. R., & Stone, C. A. (1987). Behavioral consultation. In C. A. Maher & S. G. (Eds.). *A behavioral approach to education of children and youth* (pp. 183–219). Hiillsdale, NJ: Erlbaum

Ferguson, E. D. (2006). Work relations that enhance the well-being of organizations and individuals. *Journal of Individual Psychology, 62,* 80–84.

Fine, N., & Kontos, S. (1992). Indirect service delivery through consultation: Review and implications for early intervention. *Journal of Early Intervention, 16,* 221–233.

Finello, K. M. (2011). Collaboration in the assessment and diagnosis of preschoolers: Challenges and opportunities. *Psychology in the Schools, 48,* 442–453. doi:10.1002/pits:20556

Finn, C. A., & Sladeczek, I. E. (2001). Assessing the social validity of behavioral interventions: A review of treatment acceptability measures. *School Psychology Quarterly, 16,* 176–206.

Fisher, R., & Brown, S. (1988). *Getting together.* New York: Penguin.

Fisher, R., Ury, W., & Patton, B. (1991). *Getting to yes: Negotiating without giving in* (2nd ed.). New York: Penguin.

Flanagan, S. G., Cray, M. E., & Meter, D. V. (1983). A facility-wide consultation and training team as a catalyst in promoting institutional change. *Analysis and Intervention in Developmental Disabilities, 3,* 151–169.

Flaspohler, P. D. (2007). Making a difference in research and practice: A commentary on "Consulting to facilitate planned organizational change in schools," an article by Joseph E. Zins and Robert J. Illback. *Journal of Educational and Psychological Consultation, 17,* 125–132.

Florell, D. (2011). Using advancing technologies in the practice of school psychology. In T. M. Lionetti, E. P. Snyder, & R. W. Christner (Eds.), *A practical guide to building professional competencies in school psychology* (pp. 227–244). New York: Springer.

Flyvbjerg, B. (2011). Case study. In N. K. Denzin & Y. S. Lincoln (Eds.), *The sage handbook of qualitative research* (4th ed., pp. 301–316). Thousand Oaks, CA: Sage.

Froiland, J. M. (2011). Response to intervention as a vehicle for powerful mental health interventions in the schools. *Contemporary School Psychology, 15,* 35–42.

Ford, C. H. (1979). Developing a successful client-consultant relationship. In C. R. Bell & L. Nadler (Eds.), *The client-consultant handbook* (pp. 8–21). Houston, TX: Gulf Publishing.

Forman, S. G. (1995). Organizational factors and consultation outcome. *Journal of Educational and Psychological Consultation, 6,* 191–195.

Forman, S. G., & Selman, J. S. (2011). Systems-based service delivery in school psychology. In M. A. Bray & T. J. Kehle (Eds.), *The oxford handbook of school psychology* (pp. 628–646). New York: Oxford Press.

Forneris, T., Danish, S. J., & Fries, E. (2009). How perceptions of an intervention program affect outcomes. *Journal of Educational and Psychological Consultation, 19,* 130–149. doi: 10.1080/10474410902888673

Foster, S. L., & Lloyd, P. J. (2007). Positive psychology principles applied to consulting psychology at the individual and group level. *Consulting Psychology Journal, 59,* 30–40.

Frank, J. L., & Kratochwill, T. R. (2008). School-based problem-solving consultation. In W. P. Erchul & S. M. Sheridan (Eds.), *Handbook of research on school consultation* (pp. 13–30). New York: Erlbaum.

Freer, P., & Watson, T. S. (1999). A comparison of parent and teacher acceptability ratings of behavioral and conjoint behavioral consultation. *School Psychology Review, 28,* 672–684.

French, J. L. (1990). History of school psychology. In T. B. Gutkin & C. R. Reynolds (Eds.), *The handbook of school psychology* (2nd ed., pp. 3–20). New York: Wiley.

French, J. R. P., & Raven, B. H. (1959). The bases of social power. In D. Cartwright (Ed.), *Studies in social power* (pp. 150–167). Ann Arbor, MI: Institute for Social Research.

French, W. L., & Bell, C. H., Jr. (1999). *Organization development: Behavioral science interventions for organization improvement* (6th ed.). Englewood Cliffs, NJ: Prentice-Hall.

French, W. L., Bell, C. H., Jr., & Zawacki, R. A. (Eds.). (1978). *Organization development: Theory, practice, and research.* Dallas, TX: Business Publications.

Friend, M., & Cook, L. (1996). *Interactions: Collaboration skills for school professionals* (2nd ed.). New York: Longman.

Froehle, T. C., Mullen, C., Pappas, V., Tracy, M., & Chait, J. (1999). Using group decision support systems to brainstorm and evaluate consultation interventions. *Consulting Psychology Journal: Research and Practice, 31,* 181–190.

Froehle, T. C., & Rominger, R. L., III. (1993). Directions in consultation research: Bridging the gap between science and practice. *Journal of Counseling and Development, 71,* 693–699.

Fullmer, D. W., & Bernard, H. W. (1972). *The school counselor consultant.* Boston: Houghton Mifflin.

Fuqua, D. R., & Kurpius, D. J. (1993). Conceptual models in organizational consultation. *Journal of Counseling and Development, 71,* 607–618.

Fuqua, D. R., & Newman, J. L. (2006). Moral and ethical issues in human systems. *Consulting Psychology Journal: Practice and Research, 58,* 206–215.

Fuqua, D. R., & Newman, J. L. (2009). Consultation as a moral process. *Consulting Psychology Journal: Practice and Research, 61,* 136–146. doi:10.1037/a0015496

Fuqua, D. R., Newman, J. L., & Dickman, M. M. (1999). Barriers to effective assessment in organizational consultation. *Consulting Psychology Journal, Practice and Research, 51,* 14–23.

Fuqua, D. R., Newman, J. L., Simpson, D. B., & Choi, N. (2012, April 2). Who is the client in organizational consultation? *Consulting Psychology Journal: Practice and Research.* Advance online publication. doi:10.1037/a0027722.

Gallessich, J. (1982). *The profession and practice of consultation.* San Francisco: Jossey-Bass.

Gallessich, J. (1985). Toward a meta-theory of consultation. *Counseling Psychologist, 13*(3), 336–354.

Garland, F. N. (1993). Combat stress control in the postwar theater: Mental health consultation during redeployment phase of operation desert storm. *Military Medicine, 158,* 334–337.

Garrett, J. N. (1998). Local interagency coordinating council personality: A factor in consultation. *Journal of Educational and Psychological Consultation, 9,* 261–266.

Gerstein, L. H. (2006). Counseling psychology's commitment to strengths: Rhetoric or reality? *The Counseling Psychologist, 34,* 276–292.

Gerstein, L. H. (2007). Counseling psychology's commitment to strengths: Rhetoric or reality? *The Counseling Psychologist, 34,* 276–292.

Getty, K. C., & Erchul, W. P. (2009). The influence of gender on the likelihood of using soft social power strategies in school consultation. *Psychology in the Schools, 46,* 447–458. doi:10.1002/pits.20389

Gibbons, K. A., & Silberglitt, B. (2008). Best practices in evaluating psychoeducational services based on student outcome data. In A. Thomas & J. Grimes (Eds.), *Best practices in school psychology* (5th ed., pp. 2103–2116). Bethesda, MD: National Association of School Psychologists.

Gibbs, J. T. (1980). The interpersonal orientation in mental health consultation: Toward a model of ethnic variations in consultation. *Journal of Community Psychology, 8,* 195–207.

Gibbs, L. E. (2003). *Evidence-based practice for the helping professions: A practical guide with integrated multimedia.* Pacific Grove, CA: Thomson Learning.

Gibson, G., & Chard, K. M. (1994). Quantifying the effects of community mental health consultation interventions. *Consulting Psychology Journal, 46,* 13–25.

Gilmore, T. N. (1993). Issues in ending consultancies. In R. T. Golembiewski (Ed.), *Handbook of organizational consultation* (pp. 253–261). New York: Marcel.

Glaser, E. M. (1981). Ethical issues in consultation practice with organizations. *Consultation, 1*(1), 12–16.

Glidewell, J. C. (1959). The entry problem in consultation. *Journal of Social Issues, 15*(2), 51–59.

Gmeinder, K. L., & Kratochwill, T. R. (1998). Short-term, home-based intervention for child noncompliance using behavioral consultation and a self-help manual. *Journal of Educational and Psychological Consultation, 9,* 91–117.

Godber, Y. (2008). Best practices in program evaluation. In A. Thomas & J. Grimes (Eds.), *Best practices in school psychology* (5th ed., pp. 2193–2205). Bethesda, MD: National Association of School Psychologists.

Golden, L., & Cook, K. (2010). The parent consultation center. *The Family Journal: Counseling and Therapy for Couples and Families, 18,* 423–426.

Goldstein, B. S. C., & Harris, K. C. (2000). Consultant practices in two heterogeneous Latino schools. *School Psychology Review, 29,* 368–377.

Golembiewski, R. T. (1993a). Role analysis technique. In R. T. Golembiewski (Ed.), *Handbook of organizational consultation* (pp. 357–358). New York: Marcel Dekker, Inc.

Golembiewski, R. T. (1993b). Toward a process orientation. In R. T. Golembiewski (Ed.), *Handbook of organizational consultation* (pp. 383–386). New York: Marcel Dekker, Inc.

Golembiewski, R. T., & Rauschenberg, F. (1993). Third-party consultation: Basic features and one misapplication. In R. T. Golembiewski (Ed.), *Handbook of organizational consultation* (pp. 393–398). New York: Marcel Dekker, Inc.

Gongora, J. N. (2004). Using consultee-centered consultation in a network intervention with health providers. In N. M. Lambert, I. Hylander, & J. H. Sandoval (Eds.), *Consultee-centered consultation: Improving the quality of professional services in schools and community organizations* (pp. 171–185). Mahwah, NJ: Erlbaum.

Gonzalez, J. E., Nelson, J. R., Gutkin, T. B., & Snwery, C. S. (2004). Teacher resistance to school-based consultation with school psychologists: A survey of teacher perceptions. *Journal of Emotional and Behavioral Disorders, 12,* 30–37.

Gottlieb, M. C. (2006). A template for peer ethics consultation. *Ethics & Behavior, 16,* 151–162.

Graden, J. L. (2004). Arguments for change to consultation, prevention, and intervention: Will school psychology ever achieve this promise? *Journal of Educational and Psychological Consultation, 15,* 345–359.

Granda, K. (1992, May). Consultant personal and working framework and its impact on member-authority relations in small groups. Doctoral dissertation, northwestern university, Evanston, IL.

Gravois, T. A. (2012). Consultation services in schools: A can of worms worth opening. *Consulting Psychology Journal: Practice and Research, 64,* 83–87.

Gravois, T. A., & Gickling, E. E. (2008). Best practices in instructional assessment. In A. Thomas & J. Grimes (Eds.), *Best practices in school psychology* (5th ed., pp. 503–518). Bethesda, MD: National Association of School Psychologists.

Gravois, T. A., Groff, S., & Rosenfield, S. (2009). Teams as value-added consultation services. In T. B. Gutkin & C. R. Reynolds (Eds.), *The handbook of school psychology* (4th ed., pp. 808–820). Hoboken, NJ: Wiley.

Gravois, T. A., Knotek, S., & Babinski, L. M. (2002). Educating practitioners as consultants: Development and implementation of the instructional consultation team consortium. *Journal of Educational and Psychological Consultation, 13*(1&2), 113–132.

Gravois, T. A., & Rosenfield, S. A. (2006). Impact of instructional consultation teams on the disproportionate referral and placement of minority students in special education. *Remedial and Special Education, 27*, 42–52.

Gray, C. L., Gutkin, T. B., & Riley, T. R. (2001). Acceptability of rewards among high school teachers, parents, students, and administrators: Ecological implications for consultation at the high school level. *Journal of Educational and Psychological Consultation, 12*, 25–43.

Greenberg, M. T., Weissberg, R. P., O'Brien, M. U., Zins, J. E., Fredericks, L., Resnik, H., et al. (2003). Enhancing school-based prevention and youth development through coordinated social, emotional, and academic learning. *American Psychologist, 58*, 466–474.

Greenwood, C. R., & Kim, J. M. (2012). Response to intervention (RTI) services: An ecobehavioral approach. *Journal of Educational and Psychological Consultation, 22*, 79–105. doi: 10.1080/10474412.2011.649648

Gregory, B. T., Armenakis, A. A., Moates, K. N., Albritton, M. D., & Harris, S. G. (2007). Achieving scientific rigor in organizational diagnosis: An application of the diagnostic funnel. *Consulting Psychology Journal: Practice and Research, 59*, 79–90.

Greiner, L. E., & Metzger, R. O. (1983). *Consulting to management: Insights to building and managing a successful practice.* Englewood Cliffs, NJ: Prentice-Hall.

Gresham, F. M. (2006). Response to intervention. In G. G. Bear & K. M. Minke (Eds.), *Children's needs III: Development, prevention, and intervention* (pp. 525–540). Bethesda, MD: National Association of School Psychologists.

Gresham, F. M. (2011). Response to intervention: Conceptual foundations and evidenced-based practices. In M. A. Bray & T. J. Kehle (Eds.), *The oxford handbook of school psychology* (pp. 607–618). New York: Oxford Press.

Gresham, F. M., & Kendall, G. K. (1987). School consultation research: Methodological critique and future research directions. *School Psychology Review, 16*, 303–316.

Gresham, F. M., & Lemanek, K. L. (1987). Parent education. In C. A. Maher & S. G. Forman (Eds.), *A behavioral approach to education of children and youth* (pp. 153–181). Hillsdale, NJ: Erlbaum.

Gresham, F. M., & Lopez, M. F. (1996). Social validation: A unifying concept for school-based consultation research and practice. *School Psychology Quarterly, 11*, 204–227.

Gresham, F. M., & Noell, G. H. (1993). Documenting the effectiveness of consultation outcomes. In J. E. Zins, T. R. Kratochwill, & S. N. Elliot (Eds.), *Handbook of consultation services for children* (pp. 249–273). San Francisco: Jossey-Bass.

Gresham, F. M., & Vanderwood, M. (2008). Quantitative research methods and designs in consultation. In W. P. Erchul & S. M. Sheridan (Eds.), *Handbook of research in school consultation* (pp. 63–87). New York: Erlbaum.

Gresham, F. M., Watson, T. S., & Skinner, C. H. (2001). Functional behavioral assessment: Principles, procedures, and future directions. *School Psychology Review, 30*, 156–172.

Grier, B. C., & Bradley-King, K. L. (2011). Collaborative consultation to support children with pediatric health issues: A review of the biopsychoeducational model. *Journal of Educational and Psychological Consultation, 21*, 88–105. doi:10.1080/10474412

Griffin, D. (2011). Parent involvement with African American families in expanded school mental health practice. *Advances in School Mental Health Promotion, 4*, 16–26.

Griffin, D., & Farris, A. (2010). School counselors and collaboration: Finding resources through community asset mapping. *Professional School Counselor*, 248–265.

Griffin, D., & Galassi, J. P. (2010). Parent perceptions of barriers to academic success in a rural middle school. *Professional School Counseling, 14*, 87–100.

Grigsby, R. K. (1992). Mental health consultation at a youth shelter: An ethnographic approach. *Child and Youth Care Forum, 21*, 247–261.

Grissom, P. F., Erchul, W. P., & Sheridan, S. M. (2003). Relationships among relational communication processes and perceptions of outcomes in conjoint behavioral consultation. *Journal of Educational and Psychological Consultation*, *14*, 157–180.

Gruman, D. H., & Hoelzen, B. (2011). Determining responsiveness to school counseling interventions using behavioral observations. *Professional School Counseling*, *14*(3), 183–190.

Gueldner, B., & Merrell, K. (2011). Evaluation of a social-emotional learning program in conjunction with the exploratory application of performance feedback incorporating motivational interviewing techniques. *Journal of Educational and Psychological Consultation*, *21*, 1–27. doi: 10.1080/10474412.2010.522876

Guishard, M., Fine, M., Doyle, C., Jackson, J., Staten, T., & Webb, A. (2005). The Bronx on the move: Participatory consultation with mothers and youth. *Journal of Psychological and Educational Consultation*, *16*, 35–54.

Guli, L. A. (2005). Evidence-based parent consultation with school-related outcomes. *School Psychology Quarterly*, *20*, 455–472.

Gutkin, T. (1993). Conducting consultation research. In J. E. Zins, T. R. Kratochwill, & S. N. Elliot (Eds.), *Handbook of consultation services for children* (pp. 227–248). San Francisco: Jossey-Bass.

Gutkin, T. B. (1996). Patterns of consultant and consultee verbalizations: Examining communication leadership during initial consultation interviews. *Journal of School Psychology*, *34*(3), 199–219.

Gutkin, T. B. (1997). An introduction to the mini-series: The social psychology of interpersonal influence with adults. *Journal of School Psychology*, *35*, 105–106.

Gutkin, T. B. (1999a). Collaborative versus directive/ prescriptive/expert school-based consultation: Reviewing and resolving a false dichotomy. *Journal of School Psychology*, *37*, 161–190.

Gutkin, T. B. (1999b). The collaboration debate: Finding our way through the maze: Moving forward into the future: A response to Erchul (1999). *Journal of School Psychology*, *37*, 229–241.

Gutkin, T. B. (2002). Training school-based consultants: Some thoughts on grains of sands and building anthills. *Journal of Educational and Psychological Consultation*, *13*(1&2), 133–146.

Gutkin, T. B. (2009). Ecological school psychology: A personal opinion and a plea for change. In T. B. Gutkin & C. R. Reynolds (Eds.), *The handbook of school psychology* (4th ed., pp. 463–496). Hoboken, NJ: Wiley.

Gutkin, T. B. (2012). Ecological psychology: Replacing the medical model paradigm for school-based psychological and psychoeducational services. *Journal of Educational and Psychological Consultation*, *22*, 1–20. doi:10.1080/10474412.2011.649652

Gutkin, T. B., & Curtis, M. J. (1999). School-based consultation theory and practice: The art and science of indirect service delivery. In C. R. Reynolds & T. B. Gutkin (Eds.), *The handbook of school psychology* (3rd ed., pp. 598–637). New York: Wiley.

Gutkin, T. B., & Curtis, M. J. (2009). School-based consultation: The science and practice of indirect service delivery. In T. B. Gutkin & C. R. Reynolds (Eds.), *The handbook of school psychology* (4th ed., pp. 591–635). Hoboken, NJ: Wiley.

Haberstroh, S. (2009). Strategies and resources for conducting online counseling. *Journal of Professional Counseling: Practice, Theory & Research*, *37*, 1–20.

Haberstroh, S., Parr, G., Bradley, L., Morgan-Fleming, B., & Gee, R. (2008). Facilitating online counseling: Perspectives from counselors in training. *Journal of Counseling and Development*, *86*, 460–470.

Hagermoser Sanetti, L. M., & Simonsen, B. (2011). Positive behavioral supports. In M. A. Bray & T. J. Kehle (Eds.), *The oxford handbook of school psychology* (pp. 647–665). New York: Oxford Press.

Hagermoser Sanetti, L. M., & Fallon, L. M. (2011). Treatment integrity assessment: How estimates of adherence, quality and exposure influence interpretation of implementation. *Journal of Educational and Psychological Consultation*, *21*, 209–232. doi: 10.1080/10474412.2011.595163

Hagermoser Sanetti, L. M., & Kratochwill, T. R. (2009). Toward developing a science of treatment integrity: Introduction to the special series. *School Psychology Review*, *38*, 445–459.

Hagermoser Sanetti, L. M., & Kratochwill, T. R. (2011). An evaluation of the treatment integrity planning protocol and two schedules of treatment integrity self-report: Impact on implementation and report accuracy. *Journal of Educational and Psychological Consultation*, *21*, 284–308. doi:10.1080/ 10474412.2011.620927

Hall, L. E. (2005). *Dictionary of multicultural psychology: Issues, terms, and concepts.* Thousand Oaks, CA: Sage.

Halpern, J., & Tramontin, M. (2007). *Disaster mental health: Theory and practice.* Pacific Grove, CA: Brooks/Cole Thomson.

Harris, A. M. (2007). Systematic consultation in a multilingual setting. In G. Esquivel, E. C. Lopez, & S. Nahari (Eds.), *Handbook of multicultural school psychology* (pp. 137–155). Mahwah, NJ: Erlbaum.

Harris, K. C., & Klein, M. D. (2004). An emergent discussion of itinerant consultation in early childhood special education. *Journal of Educational and Psychological Consultation, 15,* 123–126.

Harrison, M. I., & Shirom, A. (1999). *Frames and models in organizational diagnosis.* Thousand Oaks, CA: Sage.

Harrison, T. C. (2004). *Consultation for the helping professions.* Boston: Pearson.

Haverkamp, B. E., Morrow, S. L., & Ponterotto, J. G. (2005). A time and place for qualitative and mixed methods in counseling psychology research. *Journal of Counseling Psychology, 52,* 123–125.

Haynes, R., Corey, G., & Moulton, P. (2003). *Clinical supervision in the helping professions.* Pacific Grove, CA: Brooks/Cole.

Hays, D. G., & Wood, C. (2011). Infusing qualitative traditions in counseling research design. *Journal of Counseling & Development, 89,* 288–295.

Hays, P. A. (2001). *Addressing cultural complexities in practice.* Washington, DC: American Psychological Association.

Hazel, C. E. (2007). Timeless and timely advice: A commentary on "Consultation to facilitate planned organizational change in schools," an article by Joseph E. Zins and Robert J. Illback. *Journal of Educational and Psychological Consultation, 17,* 125–132.

Heller, K., & Monahan, J. (1983). Individual-process consultation. In S. Cooper & W. F. Hodges (Eds.), *The mental health consultation field* (pp. 19–25). New York: Human Sciences Press.

Hellkamp, D. T. (1996). A multidisciplinary collaborative management and consulting model: The inner workings and future challenges. *Journal of Educational and Psychological Consultation, 7,* 79–85.

Henderson, J. L., MacKay, S., & Peterson-Badali, M. (2010). Interdisciplinary knowledge translation: Lessons learned from a mental health: Fire service collaboration. *American Journal of Community Psychology, 46,* 277–288.

Henning-Stout, M. (1993). Theoretical and empirical bases of consultation. In J. E. Zins, T. R. Kratochwill, & S. N. Elliot (Eds.), *Handbook of consultation services for children* (pp. 15–45). San Francisco: Jossey-Bass.

Henning-Stout, M. (1994). Consultation and connected knowing: What we know is determined by the questions we ask. *Journal of Educational and Psychological Consultation, 5,* 5–21.

Heppner, P. P., Kivlighan, D. M., Jr., & Wampold, B. E. (2008). *Research design in counseling* (3rd ed.). Belmont, CA: Thomson Brooks/Cole.

Herlihy, B., & Corey, G. (2006). *Boundary issues in counseling* (2nd ed.). Alexandria, VA: American Counseling Association.

Hershfeldt, P. A., Pell, K., Sechrest, R., Pas, E. T., & Bradshaw, C. P., (2012). Lessons learned coaching teachers in behavior management: The PBIS*plus* coaching model. *Journal of Educational and Psychological Consultation, 22,* 280–299.

Hintze, J. M., Volpe, R. J., & Shapiro, E. S. (2008). Best practices in the systematic direct observation of student behavior. In A. Thomas & J. Grimes (Eds.), *Best practices in school psychology* (5th ed., pp. 319–335). Bethesda, MD: National Association of School Psychologists.

Hoard, D., & Shepard, K. N. (2005). Parent education as parent-centered prevention: A review of school-related outcomes. *School Psychology Quarterly, 20,* 434–454.

Hodges, W. F., & Cooper, S. (1983). General introduction. In S. Cooper & W. E. Hodges (Eds.), *The mental health consultation field* (pp. 19–25). New York: Human Sciences Press.

Hoffman, M. A., Phillips, E. L., Noumair, D. A., Shullman, S., Gray, J., Homer, J., et al. (2006). Toward a feminist and multicultural model of consultation and advocacy. *Journal of Multicultural Counseling and Development, 34,* 116–128.

Hogan, M. (2007). *Four skills of cultural diversity competence: A process for understanding practice* (3rd ed.). Belmont, CA: Wadsworth Thomson.

Hogan, M. (2012). *Four skills of cultural diversity competence* (4th ed.). Belmont, CA: Wadsworth.

Hohenshil, T. H. (1996). Editorial: Role of assessment and diagnosis in counseling. *Journal of Counseling and Development, 75,* 64–67.

Hojnoski, R. L. (2007). Promising directions in school-based systems level consultation: A commentary on "Has consultation achieved its potential?" an article by Joseph E. Zins. *Journal of Educational and Psychological Consultation, 17,* 157–163.

Hojnoski, R. L., & Missal, K. N. (2006). Addressing school readiness: Expanding school psychology in early education. *School Psychology Review, 35,* 602–614.

Holcomb-McCoy, C. (2004). Assessing the multicultural competence of school counselors: A checklist. *Professional School Counseling, 7,* 178–186.

Holcomb-McCoy, C. (2009). Cultural considerations in parent consultation. *Professional Counseling Digest.* ACAPCD-25. Retrieved January 29, 2012, from http://counselingoutfitters.com/vistas/ACAPCD/ACAPCD-25.pdf

Holcomb-McCoy, C., & Bryan, J. (2010). Advocacy and empowerment in parent consultation: Implications for theory and practice. *Journal of Counseling and Development, 88,* 259–268.

Holcomb-McCoy, C., & Coker, A. D. (2009). Multicultural consultation. In C. C. Lee, D. A. Burnhill, A. L. Butler, C. P. Hipolito-Delgado, M. Humphrey, O. Munoz, & H. Shin (Eds.), *Elements of culture in counseling* (pp. 177–192). Upper Saddle River, NJ: Pearson.

Holtz, H., & Zahn, D. (2004). *How to succeed as an independent consultant* (4th ed.). Hoboken, NJ: Wiley.

Hopko, D. R., & Hopko, S. D. (2003). Employee assistance programs: Opportunities for behavior therapists. *Behavior Therapist, 26,* 310–304.

Houk, J. L., & Lewandowski, L. J. (1996). Consultant verbal control and consultee perceptions. *Journal of Educational and Psychological Consultation, 7,* 107–118.

House, R. M., & Walker, C. M. (1993). Preventing AIDS through education. *Journal of Counseling and Development, 71,* 282–289.

Huckabay, M. A. (2002). The issue of dependency in organizational consultation: A response to Arvum Weiss's article. *Gestalt Review, 1,* 18–25.

Huey, W. C. (2011). The revised 2010 ethical standards for school counselors. *Georgia School Counselors Association Journal, 18,* 6–12.

Hughes, J. (1983). The application of cognitive dissonance theory to consultation. *Journal of School Psychology, 21,* 349–357.

Hughes, J. N. (1986). Ethical issues in school consultation. *School Psychology Review, 15,* 489–499.

Hughes, J. N. (2000). The essential role of theory in the science of treating children: Beyond empirically supported treatments. *Journal of School Psychology, 38,* 301–330.

Hughes, J. N., Barker, D., Kemenoff, S., & Hart, M. (1993). Problem ownership, casual attributions, and self-efficacy as predictors of teachers' referral decisions. *Journal of Educational and Psychological Consultation, 4*(4), 369–384.

Hughes, J. N., & DeForest, P. A. (1993). Consultant directiveness and support as predictors of consultation outcomes. *Journal of School Psychology, 31,* 355–373.

Hughes, J. N., & Falk, R. S. (1981). Resistance, reactance, and consultation. *Journal of School Psychology, 19,* 134–141.

Hughes, J. N., Hasbrouck, J. E., Serdahl, E., Heidgerken, A., & McHaney, L. (2001). Responsive systems consultation: A preliminary evaluation of implementation and outcomes. *Journal of Educational and Psychological Consultation, 12*(3), 179–201.

Hughes, J. N., Lloyd, L., & Buss, M. (2008). Empirical and theoretical support for an updated model of mental health consultation for schools. In W. P. Erchul & S. M. Sheridan (Eds.), *Handbook of research in school consultation* (pp. 343–360). New York: Erlbaum.

Hylander, I. (2003). Toward a grounded theory of the conceptual change process in consultee-centered consultation. *Journal of Educational and Psychological Consultation, 14,* 263–280.

Hylander, I. (2012). Conceptual change through consultee-centered consultation: A theoretical model. *Consulting Psychology Journal: Practice and Research, 64,* 29–45.

Hyman, A. (1993). A model for psychological consultation with retarded adults living in community residences. *Journal of Developmental and Physical Disabilities, 5,* 369–376.

Ikeda, M. J., Tilly, W. D., Stumme, J., Volmer, L., & Allison, R. (1996). Agency-wide implementation of problem solving consultation: Foundations, current implementation, and future directions. *School Psychology Quarterly, 11,* 228–243.

Illback, R. J., & Zins, J. E. (1993). Organizational perspectives in child consultation. In J. E. Zins, T. R. Kratochwill, & S. N. Elliott (Eds.), *Handbook for consultation services for children* (pp. 87–109). San Francisco: Jossey-Bass.

Individuals with Disabilities Education Act. Washington, DC: U.S. Government Printing Office.

Individuals with Disabilities Education Improvement Act of 2004. Public law 108-446. (2004). Washington, DC: U.S. Government Printing Office.

Ingraham, C. L. (2000). Consultation through a multicultural lens: Multicultural and cross-cultural consultation in schools. *School Psychology Review, 29,* 320–343.

Ingraham, C. L. (2003). Multicultural consultee-centered consultation: When novice consultants explore cultural hypotheses with experienced teacher consultants. *Journal of Educational and Psychological Consultation, 14,* 329–362.

Ingraham, C. L. (2004). Multicultural consultee-centered consultation: Supporting consultees in the development of cultural competence. In N. M. Lambert, I. Hylander, & J. H. Sandoval (Eds.), *Consultee-centered consultation: Improving the quality of professional services in schools and community organizations* (pp. 133–170). Mahwah, NJ: Erlbaum.

Ingraham, C. L. (2007). Focusing on consultees in multicultural consultation. In G. Esquivel, E. C. Lopez, & S. Nahari (Eds.), *Handbook of multicultural school psychology* (pp. 99–118). Mahwah, NJ: Erlbaum.

Ingraham, C. L. (2008). Studying multicultural aspects of consultation. In W. P. Erchul & S. M. Sheridan (Eds.), *Handbook of research in school consultation* (pp. 269–291). New York: Erlbaum.

Ingraham, C. L., & Meyers, J. (2000a). Annotated bibliography for the mini-series on multicultural and crosscultural consultation in schools. *School Psychology Review, 29,* 426–428.

Ingraham, C. L., & Meyers, J. (2000b). Introduction to multicultural and cross-cultural consultation in schools: Cultural diversity issues in school consultation. *School Psychology Review, 29,* 315–319.

International Society for Mental Health Online. (2000). *Suggested principles for the online provision of mental health principles.* Retrieved February 3, 2007, from http://www.ismho.org/suggestions.html

Ivey, A. E., Ivey, M. B., & Zalaquett, C. P. (2012). *Essentials of intentional interviewing* (2nd ed.). Belmont, CA: Brooks Cole Cengage.

Jackson, D. N., & Hayes, D. H. (1993). Multicultural issues in consultation. *Journal of Counseling and Development, 72*(2), 144–147.

Jacob, S. (2008). Best practices in developing ethical school psychological practice. In A. Thomas & J. Grimes (Eds.), *Best practices in school psychology* (5th ed., pp. 1921–1932). Bethesda, MD: National Association of School Psychologists.

Jacob, S., & Hartshorne, T. S. (2007). *Ethics and law for school psychologists* (5th ed.). Hoboken, NJ: John Wiley & Sons.

James, R. K., & Crews, W. (2014). Systems consultation: Working with a metropolitan police department. In A. M. Dougherty (Ed.), *A casebook of psychological consultation and collaboration* (6th ed., pp. 101–130). Belmont, CA: Brooks/Cole Cengage.

James, R. K., & Dougherty, A. M. (1985). Doing your own dog and pony show: A guide for the perplexed school counselor. *School Counselor, 20,* 11–18.

Janis, I. L., & Mann, L. (1977). *Decision making: A psychological analysis of conflict, choice, and commitment.* New York: Free Press.

Jason, L. A., Pokorny, S. B., Ji, P., & Kunz, C. (2005). Developing community-school-university partnerships to control youth access to tobacco. *Journal of Educational and Psychological Consultation, 16,* 201–222.

Jeltova, I., & Fish, M. C. (2005). Creating school environments responsive to gay. Lesbian, bisexual, and transgender families: Traditional and systemic approaches for consultation. *Journal of Educational and Psychological Consultation, 16,* 17–33.

Jennings, K. R. (1988). Testing a model of quality circle processes: Implications for practice and consultation. *Consultation, 7*(1), 19–28.

Jerrell, J. M., & Jerrell, S. L. (1981). Organizational consultation in school systems. In J. C. Conoley (Ed.), *Consultation in schools* (pp. 133–156). New York: Academic Press.

Johnson, J. J., & Pugach, M. C. (1996). The emerging third wave of collaboration: Beyond problem solving. In W. Stainbach & S. Stainback (Eds.), *Controversial issues confronting special education* (2nd ed., pp. 196–204). Boston: Allyn & Bacon.

Kahn, B. B. (2000). A model of solution-focused consultation for school counselors. *Professional School Counseling, 3*, 248–254.

Kahnweiler, W. M. (1979). The school counselor as consultant: A historical review. *Personnel and Guidance Journal, 57*, 374–379.

Kamberelis, G., & Dimitriadis, G. (2011). Focus groups: Strategic articulations of pedagogy, politics, and inquiry. In N. K. Denzin & Y. S. Lincoln (Eds.), *The sage handbook of qualitative research* (4th ed., pp. 545–561). Thousand Oaks, CA: Sage.

Kamphaus, R. W., Reynolds, C. R., & Imperato-McCammon, C. (1999). Roles of diagnosis and classification in school psychology. In C. R. Reynolds & T. B. Gutkin (Eds.), *The handbook of school psychology* (3rd ed., pp. 292–306). New York: Wiley.

Kampwirth, T. J. (2006). *Collaborative consultation in the schools* (3rd ed.). Upper Saddle River, NJ: Merrill-Prentice Hall.

Kanel, K. (2007). *A guide to crisis intervention* (3rd ed.). Pacific Grove, CA: Brooks/Cole Thomson.

Kanfer, F. H., & Goldstein, A. P. (Eds.). (1991). *Helping people change* (4th ed.). New York: Pergamon Press.

Karg, R. S., & Wiens, A. N. (2005). Improving diagnostic and clinical interviewing. In G. P. Koocher, J. C. Norcross, & S. S. Hill, III (Eds.), *Psychologists' desk reference* (2nd ed., pp. 13–16). New York: Oxford University Press.

Katz, D., & Kahn, R. L. (1990). *The social psychology of organizations* (4th ed.). New York: Wiley.

Kazdin, A. E. (2001). *Behavior modification in applied settings* (6th ed.). Pacific Grove, CA: Brooks/Cole.

Kazdin, A. E. (2011). *Single-case research designs* (2nd ed.). New York: Oxford University Press.

Kelleher, C., Riley-Tillman, T. C., & Power, T. J. (2008). An initial comparison of collaborative and expert-driven consultation on treatment integrity. *Journal of Educational and Psychological Consultation, 18*, 294–324. doi:.10.1080/10474410802491040

Keller, H. R. (1981). Behavioral consultation. In J. C. Conoley (Ed.), *Consultation in schools: Theory,*

research, and procedures (pp. 59–99). New York: Academic Press.

Kelley, R. E. (1981). *Consulting: The complete guide to a profitable career.* New York: Scribner's.

Kelly, J. G. (1983). Consultation as a process of creating power: An ecological view. In S. Cooper & W. F. Hodges (Eds.), *The mental health consultation field* (pp. 153–171). New York: Human Sciences Press.

Kelly, J. G. (1987). An ecological paradigm: Defining mental health consultation as a preventative service. *Prevention in Human Services, 4*(3–4), 1–36.

Kelly, J. G. (1993). Gerald Caplan's paradigm: Bridging psychotherapy and public health practice. In W. P. Erchul (Ed.), *Consultation in community, school, and organizational practice* (pp. 75–85). Washington, DC: Taylor & Francis.

Kennedy, E. K., Frederickson, N., & Monsen, J. (2008). Do educational psychologists "walk the talk" when consulting? *Educational Psychology in Practice, 24*, 169–187.

Keys, S. G., Bemak, F., Carpenter, S. L., & King-Sear, M. E. (1998). Collaborative consultant: A new role for counselors serving at-risk youths. *Journal of Counseling & Development, 7*, 123–133.

Kirst-Ashman, K. K., & Hull, G. H., Jr. (2012). *Generalist practice with organizations and communities* (5th ed.). Belmont, CA: Brooks/Cole.

Kitchener, K. S., & Harding, S. S. (1990). Dual role relationships. In B. Herlihy & L. B. Golden (Eds.), *American association for counseling and development ethical standards casebook* (4th ed., pp. 146–154). Alexandria, VA: American Association for Counseling and Development.

Kloos, B., McCoy, J., Stewart, E., Thomas, R. E., Wiley, A., Good, T. L., et al. (1998). Bridging the gap: A community-based, open systems approach to school and neighborhood consultation. *Journal of Educational and Psychological Consultation, 8*, 175–196.

Knoff, H. M. (1988). Clinical supervision, consultation, and counseling: A comparative analysis for supervisors and other educational leaders. *Journal of Curriculum and Supervision, 3*, 240–252.

Knoff, H. M. (1996). The interface of school, community, and health care reform: Organizational directions toward effective services for children and youth. *School Psychology Review, 25*, 446–464.

Knoff, H. M. (2008). Best practices in strategic planning, organizational development, and school effectiveness. In A. Thomas & J. Grimes (Eds.), *Best practices in school psychology* (5th ed., pp. 903–916). Bethesda, MD: National Association of School Psychologists.

Knoff, H. M., McKenna, A. E., & Riser, K. (1991). Toward a consultant effectiveness scale: Investigating the characteristics of effective consultants. *School Psychology Review, 20,* 81–96.

Knoff, H. M., Sullivan, P., & Liu, D. (1995). Teachers' ratings of effective school psychology consultants: An exploratory factor analysis study. *Journal of School Psychology, 33,* 39–57.

Knotek, S. E. (2003). Making sense of jargon during consultation: Understanding consultees' social language to effect change in student study teams. *Journal of Educational and Psychological Consultation, 14,* 181–207.

Knotek, S. E. (2004). Evaluation issues and strategies in consultee-centered consultation. In N. M. Lambert, I. Hylander, & J. H. Sandoval (Eds.), *Consultee-centered consultation: Improving the quality of professional services in schools and community organizations* (pp. 391–400). Mahwah, NJ: Erlbaum.

Knotek, S. E. (2006). Administrative crisis consultation after 9/11: A university's system response. *Consulting Psychology Journal: Practice and Research, 58,* 162–173.

Knotek, S. E. (2012). Utilizing culturally responsive consultation to support innovation implementation in a rural school. *Consulting Psychology Journal: Practice and Research, 64,* 46–62.

Knotek, S. E., Babinski, L. M., & Rogers, D. L. (2002). Consultation in new teacher groups: School psychologists facilitating collaboration among new teachers. *California School Psychologist, 7,* 39–50.

Knotek, S. E., Kaniuka, M., & Ellingsen, K. (2008). Mental health consultation and consultee-centered approaches. In W. P. Erchul & S. M. Sheridan (Eds.), *Handbook of research in school consultation* (pp. 127–145). New York: Erlbaum.

Knotek, S. E., Kovac, M., & Bostwick, E. (2011). The use of consultation to improve academic and psychosocial outcomes for gifted students. *Journal of Applied School Psychology, 27,* 359–379. doi: 10.1080/15377903.2011.616577

Knotek, S. E., Rosenfield, S., Gravois, T. A., & Babinski, L. (2003). The process of orderly reflection and conceptual change during instructional consultation. *Journal of Educational and Psychological Consultation, 14,* 303–328.

Knotek, S. E., & Sandoval, J. (2003). Current research in consultee-centered consultation. *Journal of Educational and Psychological Consultation, 14,* 243–250.

Kocet, M. M. (2009). Multicultural ethical perspectives. In C. C. Lee, D. A. Burnhill, A. L. Butler, C. P. Hipolito-Delgado, M. Humphrey, O. Munoz, & H. Shin (Eds.), *Elements of culture in counseling* (pp. 193–210). Upper Saddle River, NJ: Pearson.

Koonce, D. A., & Harper, W., Jr. (2005). Engaging African American parents in the schools: A community-based consultation model. *Journal of Educational and Psychological Consultation, 16,* 55–74.

Kormanski, C., & Eschbach, L. (1997). From group leader to process consultant. In H. Forester-Miller & J. A. Kottler (Eds.), *Issues and challenges for group practitioners* (pp. 133–164). Denver, CO: Love Publishing Company.

Kottman, T. (1995). *Partners in play.* Alexandria, VA: American Counseling Association.

Kottman, T., & Dougherty, A. M. (2014). Adlerian case consultation with a teacher. In A. M. Dougherty (Ed.), *A casebook of psychological consultation and collaboration* (6th ed., pp. 61–78). Belmont, CA: Brooks/Cole Cengage.

Kovach, B. E. (1998). Pyramids, circles, and teams: Confronting leadership issues. *Consulting Psychology Journal, 50,* 164–172.

Kratochwill, T. R. (2008). Best practices in school-based problem-solving consultation: Applications in prevention and intervention systems. In A. Thomas & J. Grimes (Eds.), *Best practices in school psychology* (5th ed., pp. 1673–1688). Bethesda, MD: National Association of School Psychologists.

Kratochwill, T. R., & Bergan, J. R. (1990). *Behavioral consultation in applied settings: An individual guide.* New York: Plenum.

Kratochwill, T. R., Elliott, S. N., & Busse, R. T. (1995). Behavioral consultation: A five-year evaluation of consultant and client outcomes. *School Psychology Quarterly, 10,* 87–110.

Kratochwill, T. R., Elliott, S. N., & Carrington Rotto, P. (1995). Best practices in school-based behavioral consultation. In A. Thomas & J. Grimes (Eds.), *Best practices in school psychology* (3rd ed., pp. 519–537). Washington, DC: National Association of School of Psychologists.

Kratochwill, T. R., Mace, F. C., & Bissel, M. S. (1987). Program evaluation and research. In C. A. Maher & S. G. Foreman (Eds.), *A behavioral approach to education of children and youth* (pp. 253–288). Hillsdale, NJ: Erlbaum.

Kratochwill, T. R., & Pittman, P. H. (2002). Expanding problem-solving consultation training: Prospects and frameworks. *Journal of Educational and Psychological Consultation, 13*(1&2), 69–95.

Kratochwill, T. R., Sheridan, S. M., Carlson, J., & Lasecki, K. L. (1999). In C. R. Reynolds & T. B. Gutkin (Eds.), *The handbook of school psychology* (3rd ed., pp. 350–382). New York: Wiley.

Kratochwill, T. R., & Shernoff, E. S. (2004). Evidence-based practice: Promoting evidenced-based practice interventions in school psychology. *School Psychology Review, 33*, 34–48.

Kratochwill, T. R., & Stoiber, K. C. (2000a). Empirically supported interventions and school psychology: Conceptual and practice issues-part II. *School Psychology Quarterly, 15*, 233–253.

Kratochwill, T. R., & Stoiber, K. C. (2000b). Uncovering critical research agendas for school psychology: Conceptual dimensions and future directions. *School Psychology Review, 29*, 591–603.

Kratochwill, T. R., & Van Someren, K. R. (1985). Barriers to treatment success in behavioral consultation: Current limitations and future directions. *Journal of School Psychology, 23*, 225–239.

Kratochwill, T. R., & Van Someren, K. R. (1995). Barriers to treatment success in behavioral consultation: Current limitations and future directions. *Journal of Educational and Psychological Consultation, 6*, 125–143.

Kress, J. S., Cimring, B. R., & Elias, M. J. (1998). Community psychology consultation and the transition to institutional ownership and operation of intervention. *Journal of Educational and Psychological Consultation, 8*, 231–253.

Kruger, L. J., & Struzziero, J. (1998). Computer-mediated peer support of consultation: Case description and evaluation. *Journal of Educational and Psychological Consultation, 8*, 75–90.

Kruger, L. J., Struzziero, J., Kaplan, S. K., Macklem, G., Watts, R., & Weksel, T. (2001). The use of e-mail in consultation: An exploratory study of consultee outcomes. *Journal of Educational and Psychological Consultation, 12*, 133–149.

Kurpius, D. J. (1978). Consultation theory and process: An integrated model. *Personnel and Guidance Journal, 56*(6), 335–338.

Kurpius, D. J., Brack, G., Brack, C. J., & Dunn, L. B. (1993). Maturation of systems consultation: Subtle issues inherent in the model. *Journal of Mental Health Consultation, 15*, 414–429.

Kurpius, D. J., & Fuqua, D. R. (1993a). Introduction to the special issues. *Journal of Counseling and Development, 71*, 596–597.

Kurpius, D. J., & Fuqua, D. R. (1993b). Fundamental issues in defining consultation. *Journal of Counseling and Development, 71*, 598–600.

Kurpius, D. J., Fuqua, D. R., & Rozecki, T. (1993). The consulting process: A multidimensional approach. *Journal of Counseling and Development, 71*, 601–606.

Kurpius, D. J., & Lewis, J. E. (1988). Introduction to consultation: An intervention for advocacy and outreach. In D. J. Kurpius & D. Brown (Eds.), *Handbook of consultation: An intervention for advocacy and outreach* (pp. 1–4). Alexandria, VA: American Association for Counseling and Development.

Kurpius, D. J., & Rozecki, T. (1992). Outreach, advocacy, and consultation: A framework for prevention and intervention. *Elementary School Guidance and Counseling, 26*, 176–189.

Lambert, N. M. (2000). School psychology—more than the sum of its parts: Legends on journeys through time. *School Psychology Review, 29*, 120–137.

Lambrechts, F., Bouwen, R., Grieten, S., Huybrechts, J., & Schein, E. H. (2011). Learning to help through humble inquiry and implications for management research, practice, and education: An interview with Edgar H. Schein. *Academy of Management Learning & Education, 10*(1), 131–147.

Lambrechts, F., Grieten, S., Bouwen, R., & Corthouts, F. (2009). Process consultation revisited: Taking a relational practice perspective. *Journal of Applied Behavioral Science, 45*(1), 39–58.

Larney, R. (2003). School-based consultation in the United Kingdom: Principles, practice and effectiveness. *School Psychology International, 24*, 5–19.

LaRoche, M., & Maxie, A. (2003). The considerations in addressing cultural differences in psychotherapy.

Professional Psychology: Research and Practice, 35, 194–200.

LaRoche, M., & Shriberg, D. (2004). High stakes exams and Latino students: Toward a culturally sensitive education for Latino children in the United States. *Journal of Educational and Psychological Consultation, 15,* 205–223.

Larson, J. (2008). Best practices in school violence prevention. In A. Thomas & J. Grimes (Eds.), *Best practices in school psychology* (5th ed., pp. 1291–1307). Bethesda, MD: National Association of School Psychologists.

Larson, T., & Samdal, O. (2007). Implementing second step: Balancing fidelity and program adaptation. *Journal of Educational and Psychological Consultation, 17,* 1–29.

Latham, G. P., & Lee, T. W. (1986). Goal setting. In E. A. Locke (Ed.), *Generalizing from laboratory to field settings* (pp. 101–117). Lexington, MA: Lexington Books.

Lawson, H. A. (1998). Academically based community scholarship, consultation as collaborative problemsolving, and a collective-responsibility model for the helping fields. *Journal of Psychological and Educational Consultation, 9,* 195–232.

Ledford, G. E. (1990). Smart clients, foolish questions: On dumb questions and the clients who love them. *Consultation, 9,* 323–328.

Lee, C. C. (1995). School counseling and cultural diversity: A framework for effective practice. In C. C. Lee (Ed.), *Counseling for diversity: A guide for school counselors and related professionals* (pp. 3–17). Boston: Allyn & Bacon.

Lee, C. C., & Richardson, B. L. (1991). *Multicultural issues in counseling: New approaches to diversity.* Alexandria, VA: American Counseling Association.

Lee, C. C., & Rodgers, R. A. (2009). Counselor advocacy: Affecting systems change in the public area. *Journal of Counseling & Development, 87,* 284–287.

Lehman, C., Salaway, J. L., Bagnato, S. J., Grom, R. M., & Willard, B. (2011). Prevention as early intervention for young children at risk: Recognition and response in early childhood. In M. A. Bray & T. J. Kehle (Eds.), *The oxford handbook of school psychology* (pp. 369–378). New York: Oxford Press.

Lentz, F. E., Allen, S. J., & Erhardt, K. E. (1996). The conceptual elements of strong interventions in school settings. *School Psychology Quarterly, 11*(2), 118–136.

Leong, F. T. L., & Huang, J. L. (2008). Applying the cultural accommodation model to diversity consulting in organizations. *Consulting Psychology Journal: Practice and Research, 60,* 17–185. doi: 10.1037/0736-9735.60.2.170

Lerner, R. M. (1995). *America's youth in crisis: Challenges and opportunities for programs and policies.* Thousand Oaks, CA: Sage.

Lewin, K. (1945). Research center for group dynamics. *Sociometry, 8*(2), 9.

Lewin, K. (1951). *Field theory in social sciences.* New York: Harper & Row.

Lewis, J. A., & Lewis, M. D. (1986). *Counseling programs for employees in the workplace.* Pacific Grove, CA: Thomson Brook/Cole.

Lewis, J. A., Lewis, M. D., Daniels, J. A., & D'Andrea, M. J. (2003). *Community counseling: Empowerment strategies for a diverse society* (3rd ed.). Pacific Grove, CA: Brooks/Cole Thomson.

Lewis, J. A., Lewis, M. D., Daniels, J. A., & D'Andrea, M. J. (2011). *Community counseling: Empowerment strategies for a diverse society* (4th ed.). Pacific Grove, CA: Brooks/Cole Cengage.

Lewis, J. A., Lewis, M. D., & Souflee, S., Jr. (1991). *Management of human service programs* (2nd ed.). Pacific Grove, CA: Brooks/Cole.

Lewis, T. J., & Newcomer, L. L. (2002). Examining the efficacy of school-based consultation: Recommendations for improving outcomes. *Child & Family Behavior Therapy, 24,* 165–181.

Li, C., & Vazquez-Nuttall, E. (2009). School consultants as agents of social justice for multicultural children and families. *Journal of Educational and Psychological Consultation, 19,* 26–44. doi: 10.1080/10474410802462769

Lincoln, Y. S., & Guba, E. G. (1985). *Naturalistic inquiry.* Newbury Park, CA: Sage.

Lindberg, S. P. (1996). The mental health counselor and hospice. In W. J. Weikel & A. J. Palmo (Eds.), *Foundations of mental health counseling* (2nd ed., pp. 229–231). Springfield, IL: Thomas Books.

Lippitt, G. (1969). *Organizational renewal: Achieving viability in a changing world.* New York: Dutton.

Lippitt, G., & Lippitt, R. (1986). *The consulting process in action* (2nd ed.). La Jolla, CA: University Associates.

Lochman, J. E., Dunn, S. E., & Klimes-Dougan, B. K. (1993). An intervention and consultation model from a social cognitive perspective: A description of the anger coping program. *School Psychology Review, 22,* 458–471.

Lochman, J. E., Lampron, L. B., Gemmer, T. C., Harris, S. R., & Wyckoff, G. M. (1989). Teacher consultation and cognitive-behavioral interventions with aggressive boys. *Psychology in the Schools, 26,* 179–188.

Locke, E. A., & Latham, G. P. (2002). Building a practically useful theory of goal setting and task motivation: A 35-year odyssey. *American Psychologist, 57,* 705–717.

Lopez, E. C. (2000). Conducting instructional consultation through interpreters. *School Psychology Review, 29,* 378–388.

Lopez, E. C. (2006). Targeting English language learners, tasks, targets, and treatments in instructional consultation. *Journal of Applied School Psychology, 22,* 59–79.

Lopez, E. C. (2007). Termination is a time to look back and move forward: Farewell from the editor. *Journal of Educational and Psychological Consultation, 17,* 263–265.

Lopez, E. C., & Truesdell, L. (2007). Multicultural issues in instructional consultation for English language learning students. In G. Esquivel, E. C. Lopez, & S. Nahari (Eds.), *Handbook of multicultural school psychology* (pp. 71–98). Mahwah, NJ: Erlbaum.

Lopez-Baez, S. I., & Paylo, M. J. (2009). Social justice advocacy: Community collaboration and systems advocacy. *Journal of Counseling and Development, 87,* 276–283.

Lott, B. (2003). Recognizing and welcoming the standpoint of low-income parents in the public schools. *Journal of Educational and Psychological Consultation, 14,* 91–104.

Lott, B., & Rogers, M. R. (2005). School consultants working for equity with families, teachers, and administrators. *Journal of Educational and Psychological Consultation, 16,* 1–16.

Love, K. B. (2007). Close but no cigar (yet): A commentary on "Has consultation achieved its primary prevention potential?" An article by Joseph E. Zins. *Journal of Educational and Psychological Consultation, 17,* 165–169.

Luiselli, J. K. (2002). Focus, scope, and practice of behavioral consultation to public schools. *Child & Family Behavior Therapy, 24,* 5–21.

Lum, D. (2011). *Culturally competent practice: A framework for understanding diversity & justice issues* (4th ed.). Belmont, CA: Brooks/Cole Thomson.

Lundberg, C. C. (1993). Knowing and surfacing organizational culture. In R. T. Golembiewski (Ed.), *Handbook of organizational consultation* (pp. 535–547). New York: Marcel Dekker.

Lusky, M. B., & Hayes, R. L. (2001). Collaborative consultation and program evaluation. *Journal of Counseling and Development, 79*(1), 26–38.

Lutzker, J. R., & Martin, J. A. (1981). *Behavior change.* Pacific Grove, CA: Brooks/Cole.

MacLennan, B. W., Quinn, R. D., & Schroeder, D. (1975). The scope of community mental health consultation. In E. V. Mannino, B. W. MacLennan, & M. E. Shore (Eds.), *The practice of mental health consultation* (pp. 3–24). Rockville, MD: National Institute of Mental Health.

MacMann, G. M., Barnett, D. W., Allen, S. J., Bramlett, R. K., Hall, J. D., & Ehrhardt, K. E. (1996). Problem solving and intervention design: Guidelines for the evaluation of technical adequacy. *School Psychology Quarterly, 11,* 137–148.

MacNealy, M. S. (1999). *Strategies for empirical research in writing.* Boston: Allyn & Bacon.

Maher, C. A. (1993). Providing consultation services in business settings. In J. E. Zins, T. R. Kratochwill, & S. N. Elliott (Eds.), *Handbook of consultation services for children* (pp. 317–328). San Francisco: Jossey-Bass.

Malone, J. F. (2007). Ethical guidelines, legal and regulatory issues in distance counseling. In J. F. Malone, R. M. Miller, & G. Walz (Eds.), *Distance counseling: Expanding the counselor's reach and impact* (pp. 133–148). Ann Arbor, MI: Counseling Outfitters.

Maloney, H. N. (1991). Congregational consultation. *Prevention in Human Services, 1*(3), 289–315.

Mang, M. (2004). Use of metaphors, parables, and anecdotes in consultee-centered consultation: School-based applications. In N. M. Lambert, I. Hylander, & J. H. Sandoval (Eds.), *Consultee-centered consultation: Improving the quality of professional services in schools and community organizations* (pp. 301–312). Mahwah, NJ: Erlbaum.

Mann, P. A. (1983). Transition points in consultation entry, transfer, and termination. In S. Cooper & W. E. Hodges (Eds.), *The mental health consultation field* (pp. 99–105). New York: Human Sciences Press.

Mannino, F. V., MacLennan, B. W., & Shore, M. E. (Eds.). (1975). *The practice of mental health consultation.* New York: Gardner.

Manz, P. H. (2007). Cultivating fertile grounds: Enhancing and extending the scientific base of social and emotional learning: A commentary on "The scientific base linking social and emotional learning on school success," a chapter by Joseph E. Zins, Michelle R. Bloodworth, Roger P. Weissberg, and Herbert J. Walberg. *Journal of Educational and Psychological Consultation, 17,* 211–218.

Manz, P. H., Mautone, J. A., & Martin, S. D. (2009). School psychologists' collaborations with families: An exploratory study of the interrelationships of their perceptions of professional efficacy and school climate, and demographic and training variables. *Journal of Applied School Psychology, 25,* 47–70. doi: 10.1080/1537900802484158

Margolis, H., McCabe, P. P., & Alber, S. R. (2004). Resolving struggling readers' homework difficulties: How elementary school counselors can help. *Journal of Educational and Psychological Consultation, 15,* 79–110.

Margulies, N., & Raia, A. P. (1972). Emerging issues in organization development. In N. Margulies & A. P. Raia (Eds.), *Organizational development: Values, process, and technology* (pp. 475–478). New York: McGraw-Hill.

Marks, E. S. (1995). *Entry strategies for school consultation.* New York: Guilford.

Marshall, C., & Rossman, G. B. (1995). *Designing qualitative research* (2nd ed.). Thousand Oaks, CA: Sage Publications.

Martens, B. K., & Ardoin, S. P. (2002). Training school psychologists in behavior support consultation. *Child and Family Behavior Therapy, 24,* 147–163.

Martens, B. K., & DiGennaro, F. D. (2008). Behavioral consultation. In W. P. Erchul & S. M. Sheridan (Eds.), *Handbook of research in school consultation* (pp. 147–170). New York: Erlbaum.

Martens, B. K., Kelly, S. Q., & Diskin, M. T. (1996). The effects of two sequential-request strategies on teachers' acceptability and use of a classroom intervention. *Journal of Educational and Psychological Consultation, 7,* 211–221.

Martens, B. K., Lewandowski, L. J., & Houk, J. L. (1989). The effects of entry information on the consultation process. *School Psychology Review, 18,* 225–234.

Matuszek, P. A. (1981). Program evaluation as consultation. In J. C. Conoley (Ed.), *Consultation in schools* (pp. 179–200). New York: Academic Press.

Mazade, N. A. (1983). In conclusion the past, present, and future in consultation. In S. Cooper & W. E. Hodges (Eds.), *The mental health consultation field* (pp. 233–242). New York: Human Sciences Press.

McAdams, C., Shillingford, M. A., & Trice-Black, S. (2011). Putting research into practice in school violence prevention & intervention: How is school counseling doing? *Journal of School Counseling, 9*(12). Retrieved from http://www.jsc.montana.edu/articles/v9n12.pdf

McCarroll, J. E., & Ursano, R. J. (2006). Consultation to groups, organizations, and communities. In E. C. Ritchie, P. J. Watson, & M. J. Friedman (Eds.), *Interventions following mass violence and disasters: Strategies for mental health practice* (pp. 193–205). New York: Guilford.

McDougal, J. L., Clonan, S. M., & Martens, B. K. (2000). Using organizational change procedures to promote the acceptability of prereferral intervention services: The school-based intervention team project. *School Psychology Quarterly, 15,* 149–171.

McGivern, J. E., Ray-Subramanian, E. H., & Auster, E. R. (2008). Best practices in establishing effective helping relationships. . In A. Thomas & J. Grimes (Eds.), *Best practices in school psychology* (5th ed., pp. 1613–1631). Bethesda, MD: National Association of School Psychologists.

McGowan, S. (1993). Employees, managers work it out after layoffs. *Guidepost, 35*(10), 1–10.

McKenna, S. A., Rosenfield, S., & Gravois, T. A. (2009). Measuring the behavioral indicators of instructional consultation: A preliminary validity study. *School Psychology Review, 38,* 496–509.

McKevitt, B. C., & Braaksma, A. D. (2008). Best practices in developing a positive behavior support system at the school level. In A. Thomas & J. Grimes (Eds.), *Best practices in school psychology* (5th ed., pp. 735–747). Bethesda, MD: National Association of School Psychologists.

McLean, G. N. (2006). *Organization development*. San Francisco: Berrett-Koehler Publishers.

McLeod, B. D., Southam-Gerow, M. A., & Weisz, J. R. (2009). Conceptual and methodological issues in treatment integrity measurement. *School Psychology Review*, 38, 541–645.

McNamara, K. (2008). Best practices in the application of professional ethics. In A. Thomas & J. Grimes (Eds.), *Best practices in school psychology* (5th ed., pp. 1933–1941). Bethesda, MD: National Association of School Psychologists.

McNamara, K., Rasheed, H., & Delamatre, J. (2008). A statewide study of school-based intervention teams: Characteristics, member perceptions, and outcomes. *Journal of Educational and Psychological Consultation*, 18, 5–30. doi:10.1080/10474410701864107

Meade, C. J., Hamilton, M. K., & Yuen, R. K.-W. (1982). Consultation research: The time has come the walrus said. *Counseling Psychologist*, 4, 39–51.

Meeks, S. (1996). Psychological consultation to nursing homes: Description of a six-year practice. *Psychotherapy*, 33, 19–29.

Meichenbaum, D. (1977). *Cognitive-behavior modification: An integrative approach*. New York: Plenum.

Meichenbaum, D. (1985). *Stress inoculation training*. New York: Pergamon Press.

Mellin, E. A. (2009). Unpacking interdisciplinary collaboration in expanded school mental health: A conceptual model for developing the evidence base. *Advances in School Mental Health Promotion*, 2, 4–14.

Mellin, E. A. (2011). Mental health counseling in community settings: History, models, and trends. In S. C. Nassar-McMillan & S. G. Niles (Eds.), *Developing your identity as a professional counselor: Standards, settings and specialties* (pp. 206–231). Belmont, CA: Cengage Learning.

Mellin, E. A., Anderson-Butcher, D., & Bronstein, L. (2011). Strengthening interprofessional team collaboration: Potential roles for school mental health professionals. *Advances in School Mental Health Promotion*, 4, 51–61.

Mellin, E. A., Bronstein, I. R., Anderson-Butcher, D., Amorose, A., Ball, A., & Green, J. H. (2010). Measuring interprofessional collaboration in expanded school mental health: Model refinement and scale development. *Journal of Interprofessional Care*, 24, 524–523.

Mellin, E. A., Hunt, B., & Nichols, L. M. (2011). Counselor professional identity: Findings and implications for counseling and interprofessional collaboration. *Journal of Counseling and Development*, 89, 140–147.

Melnick, J. (2003). Making the learning last. *Gestalt Review*, 7, 1–4.

Mendoza, D. W. (1993). A review of Caplan's Gerald Caplan's Theory and practice of mental health consultation. *Journal of Counseling and Development*, 71, 629–635.

Merrell, K. W., Ervin, R. A., & Gimpel, G. A. (2006). *School psychology for the 21st century*. New York: Guilford Press.

Merron, K. (1993). Let's bury the term "resistance." *Organization Development Journal*, 11(4), 77–86.

Metropolitan Area Child Study Research Group. (2007). Changing the way children "think" about aggression: Social cognitive effects of a preventative intervention. *Journal of Consulting and Clinical Psychology*, 75, 160–167.

Meyers, A. B., Meyers, J., & Gelzheiser, L. (2001). Observing leadership roles in shared decision making: A preliminary analysis of three teams. *Journal of Educational and Psychological Consultation*, 12(4), 277–312.

Meyers, A. B., Meyers, J., Graybill, E. C., Proctor, S. L., & Huddleston, L. (2012). Ecological approaches to organizational consultation and systems change in educational settings. *Journal of Educational and Psychological Consultation*, 22, 106–124. doi: 10.1080/104744412.2011.64964

Meyers, J. (1981). Mental health consultation. In J. C. Conoley (Ed.), *Consultation in schools: Theory, research, and procedures* (pp. 35–58). New York: Academic Press.

Meyers, J. (1985). Consultation as a basis for delivery of school psychological services. *Programs in School Psychology*, 40(1), 3–4.

Meyers, J. (2002). A 30 year perspective on best practices for consultation training. *Journal of Educational and Psychological Consultation*, 13(1&2), 35–54.

Meyers, J., Brent, D., Faherty, E., & Modafferi, C. (1993). Caplan's contributions to the practice of psychology in schools. In W. P. Erchul (Ed.), *Consultation in community, school, and organizational practice* (pp. 99–122). Washington, DC: Taylor & Francis.

Meyers, J., Gaughan, E., & Pitt, N. (1990). Contributions of community psychology to school psychology. In T. B. Gutkin & C. R. Reynolds (Eds.), *The handbook of school psychology* (2nd ed., pp. 198–217). New York: Wiley.

Meyers, J., Meyers, A. B., & Grogg, K. (2004). Prevention through consultation: A model to guide future developments in the filed of school psychology. *Journal of Educational and Psychological Consultation, 15,* 257–276.

Meyers, J., & Nastasi, B. K. (1999). Primary prevention in school settings. In C. R. Reynolds & T. B. Gutkin (Eds.), *The handbook of school psychology* (3rd ed., pp. 764–799). New York: Wiley.

Meyers, J., Proctor, S. L., Graybill, E. C., & Meyers, A. B. (2009). Organizational consultation and systems intervention. In T. B. Gutkin & C. R. Reynolds (Eds.), *The handbook of school psychology* (4th ed., pp. 921–940). Hoboken, NJ: Wiley.

Meyers, J., Roach, A. T., & Meyers, B. (2009). Engaging in the debate: A critique for Blueprint III. *Journal of Educational and Psychological Consultation, 19,* 197–223. doi:10.1080/10474410903117239

Meyers, J., Truscott, S. D., Meyers, A. B., Varjas, K., & Collins, A. S. (2008). Qualitative and mixed methods designs in consultation research. In W. P. Erchul & S. M. Sheridan (Eds.), *Handbook of research in school consultation* (pp. 89–114). New York: Erlbaum.

Meyers, J., & Yelich, G. (1989). Cognitive-behavioral approaches in psychoeducational consultation. In J. N. Hughes & R. J. Hall (Eds.), *Cognitive-behavioral psychology in the schools* (pp. 501–535). New York: Guilford.

Michaels, C. A., & Lopez, E. C. (2005). Collaboration and consultation in transition planning: Introduction to the mini-theme. *Journal of Educational and Psychological Consultation, 16,* 255–261.

Miller, D. D., & Kraft, N. P. (2008). Best practices in communicating with and involving parents. In A. Thomas & J. Grimes (Eds.), *Best practices in school psychology* (5th ed., pp. 937–951). Bethesda, MD: National Association of School Psychologists.

Miller, T. W. (2006). Telehealth issues in consulting psychology practice. *Consulting Psychology Journal: Practice and Research, 58,* 82–90.

Minke, K. M. (2006). Parent-teacher relationships. In G. G. Bear & K. M. Minke (Eds.), *Children's needs III: Development, prevention, and intervention* (pp. 73–85).

Bethesda, MD: National Association of School Psychologists.

Minke, K. M., & Anderson, K. J. (2005). Family-school collaboration and positive behavior support. *Journal of Positive Behavior Interventions, 7,* 181–185.

Miranda, A. H. (1993). Consultation with culturally diverse families. *Journal of Educational and Psychological Consultation, 4,* 89–93.

Miranda, A. H. (2008). Best practices in increasing cross-cultural competence. In A. Thomas & J. Grimes (Eds.), *Best practices in school psychology* (5th ed., pp. 1739–1749). Bethesda, MD: National Association of School Psychologists.

Moe, J. L., & Perera-Diltz, D. (2009). An overview of systemic-organizational consultation for professional counselors. *Journal of Professional Counseling: Practice, Theory & Research, 37,* 27–37.

Moe, J. L., Perera-Diltz, D., & Sepulveda, V. (2010). Are consultation and social justice advocacy similar? Exploring the perceptions of professional counselors and counseling students. *Journal for Social Action in Counseling and Psychology, 3,* 106–123.

Moleski, S. M., & Kiselica, M. S. (2005). Dual relationships: A continuum ranging from the destructive to the therapeutic. *Journal of Counseling and Development, 83,* 3–11.

Moore-Thomas, C., & Day-Vines, N. L. (2010). Culturally competent collaboration: School counselor collaboration with African American families and communities. *Professional School Counseling, 14,* 53–63.

Morasky, R. L. (1982). *Behavioral systems.* New York: Praeger.

Mortola, P., & Carlson, J. (2003). "Collecting an anecdote": The role of narrative in school consultation. *The Family Journal: Counseling and Therapy for Couples and Families, 11,* 7–12.

Moseley-Howard, G. S. (1995). Best practices in considering the role of culture. In A. Thomas & J. Grimes (Eds.), *Best practices in school psychology* (3rd ed., pp. 337–345). Washington, DC: National Association of School Psychologists.

Myers, B., & Arena, M. P. (2001). Trail consultation: A new direction in applied psychology. *Professional Psychology: Research and Practice, 32,* 386–391.

Myrick, R. D. (2003). *Development guidance and counseling: A practical approach* (4th ed.). Minneapolis, MN: Educational Media.

Nabors, L. A., Ramos, V., & Weist, M. D. (2001). Use of focus groups as a tool for evaluating programs for children and families. *Journal of Educational and Psychological Consultation, 12*(3), 243–256.

Nadler, D. A. (1977). *Feedback and organization development: Using data-based methods.* Reading, MA: Addison-Wesley.

Nadler, L. (1980). *Corporate human resources development: A managerial tool.* New York: Van Nostrand Reinhold.

Nagle, R. J., & Gagnon, S. G. (2008). Best practices in planning and conducting needs assessment. In A. Thomas & J. Grimes (Eds.), *Best practices in school psychology* (5th ed., pp. 2207–2223). Bethesda, MD: National Association of School Psychologists.

Nahari, S. G., Martines, D., & Marquez, G. (2007). In G. Esquivel, E. C. Lopez, & S. Nahari (Eds.), *Handbook of multicultural school psychology* (pp. 119–136). Mahwah, NJ: Erlbaum.

Nastasi, B. (2004). Meeting the challenges of the future: Integrating public health and public education for mental health promotion. *Journal of Educational and Psychological Consultation, 15*, 295–312.

Nastasi, B. (2005). School consultants as change agents in achieving equity for families in public schools. *Journal of Educational and Psychological Consultation, 16*, 113–125.

Nastasi, B. K. (2006). Multicultural issues in school psychology practice: Introduction. *Journal of Applied School Psychology, 22*, 1–11.

Nastasi, B. K., & Varjas, K. (2008). Best practices in developing exemplary mental health programs in schools. In A. Thomas & J. Grimes (Eds.), *Best practices in school psychology* (5th ed., pp. 1349–1360). Bethesda, MD: National Association of School Psychologists.

Nastasi, B. K., Varjas, K., Bernstein, R., & Jaysena, A. (2000). Conducting participatory culture-specific consultation: A global perspective on multicultural consultation. *School Psychology Review, 29*(3), 401–413.

National Association of School Psychologists. (2000). *Professional conduct manual.* Bethesda, MD: Author.

National Association of School Psychologists. (2010a). *Model for comprehensive and integrated school psychological services.* Bethesda, MD: Author. Retrieved from http://www.nasponline.org/standards/2010standards/2_PracticeModel.pdf

National Association of School Psychologists. (2010b). *National association of school psychologists principles for professional ethics.* Bethesda, MD: Author. Retrieved from http://www.nasponline.org/standards/2010standards/1_Ethical_Principles.pdf

National Association of School Psychologists. (2010c). *Standards for graduate preparation of school psychologists.* Bethesda, MD: Author. Retrieved from http://www.nasponline.org/standards/2010standards/1_Graduate_Preparation.pdf

National Association of Social Workers. (2008). *Code of ethics* (rev. ed.). Silver Springs, MD: Author.

National Board for Certified Counselors. (2005). *National board for certified counselors code of ethics.* Retrieved December 2, 2011, from http://www.nbcc.org/Assets/Ethics/nbcc-codeofethics.pdf

National Board for Certified Counselors. (2007). *The practice of internet counseling.* Retrieved December 2, 2011, from http://www.nbcc.org/Assets/Ethics/internetCounseling.pdf

Neilsen, E. H. (1984). *Becoming an OD practitioner.* Englewood Cliffs, NJ: Prentice-Hall.

Nelson, G., Amio, J. L., Prilleltensky, I., & Nickels, P. (2000). Partnerships for implementing school and community prevention programs. *Journal of Educational and Psychological Consultation, 11*, 121–145.

Nelson, J. A., Robles-Pina, R., & Nichter, M. (2008). An analysis of Texas high school counselors' roles: Actual and preferred counseling activities. *Journal of Professional Counseling: Practice, Theory and Research, 36*, 30–46.

Neukrug, E. S. (2012). *The world of the counselor* (2nd ed.). Belmont, CA: Brooks/Cole Cengage.

Neukrug, E. S., & Milliken, T. (2011). Counselors' perceptions of ethical behaviors. *Journal of Counseling & Development, 89*, 206–216.

Newell, M. (2010a). Exploring the use of computer simulation to evaluate the implementation of problem-solving consultation. *Journal of Educational and Psychological Consultation, 20*, 228–255. doi: 10.1080/10474412.2010.500511

Newell, M. (2010b). The implementation of problem solving consultation: An analysis of problem conceptualization in a multiracial context. *Journal of Educational and Psychological Consultation, 20*, 83–105. doi:10.1080/10474411003785529

Newell, M. L. (2012). Transforming knowledge to skill: Evaluating the consultation competence of novice school-based consultants. *Consulting Psychology Journal: Practice and Research, 64*, 8–28.

Newell, M. L., & Newell, T. S. (2011). Problem analysis: Examining the selection and evaluation of data during problem-solving consultation. *Psychology in the Schools, 48*, 943–957. doi:10.1002/pits.20606

Newman, D. S. (2012). A grounded theory of supervision in preservice consultation training. *Journal of Educational and Psychological Consultation, 22*, 247–270.

Newman, J. L. (1993). Ethical issues in consultation. *Journal of Counseling and Development, 72*(2), 148–156.

Newman, J. L., & Fuqua, D. R. (1984). Data-based consultation in student affairs. *Journal of College Student Personnel, 25*, 206–212.

Newman, J. L., Gray, E. A., & Fuqua, D. R. (1996). Beyond ethical decision making. *Consulting Psychology Journal, 48*, 230–236.

Newman, J. L., Robinson-Kurpius, S. E., & Fuqua, D. R. (2002). Issues in the ethical practice of consulting psychology. In R. L. Lowman (Ed.), *Handbook of organizational consulting psychology: A comprehensive guide to theory, skills, and techniques* (pp. 733–758). San Francisco: Jossey-Bass.

Nicoll, W. G. (1992). A family counseling and consultation model for school counselors. *School Counselor, 39*, 351–361.

Noell, G. H. (1996). New directions in behavioral consultation. *School Psychology Quarterly, 11*, 187–188.

Noell, G. H. (2002). Direct assessment of clients' instructional needs: Improving academic, social, and emotional outcomes. In M. L. Kelley, D. Reitman, & G. H. Noell (Eds.), *Practitioners guide to empirically based measures of school behavior* (pp. 63–68). New York: Kluwer Academic/Plenum Publishers.

Noell, G. H. (2008). Research examining the relationships among consultation process, treatment integrity, and outcomes. In W. P. Erchul & S. M. Sheridan (Eds.), *Handbook of research in school consultation: Empirical foundations for the field* (pp. 315–334). Mahwah, NJ: Erlbaum.

Noell, G. H., & Gresham, F. M. (1993). Functional outcome analysis: Do the benefits of consultation and prereferral intervention justify the costs? *School Psychology Quarterly, 8*, 200–226.

Noell, G. H., Roane, H. S., VanDerHeyden, A. M., Whitmarsh, E. L., & Gatti, S. L. (2000). Programming for the generalization of communication to the classroom following assessment and training outside of the classroom. *School Psychology Review, 29*, 429–442.

Noell, G. H., & Witt, J. C. (1996). A critical re-evaluation of five fundamental assumptions underlying behavioral consultation. *School Psychology Quarterly, 11*, 189–203.

Noell, G. H., & Witt, J. C. (1998). Toward a behavior analytic approach to consultation. In T. S. Watson & F. M. Gresham (Eds.), *Handbook of child behavior therapy* (pp. 41–57). New York: Plenum Press.

Noell, J. C., Witt, J. C., Slider, N. J., Connell, J. E., Gatti, S. L., Williams, K. L., et al. (2005). Treatment implementation following behavioral consultation in schools: A comparison of three follow-up strategies. *School Psychology Review, 34*, 87–106.

Ochoa, S. H., & Rhodes, R. L. (2005). Assisting parents of bilingual students to achieve equity in public schools. *Journal of Educational and Psychological Consultation, 16*, 75–94.

O'Connell, J. J. (1990). Process consulting in a content field: Socrates in strategy. *Consultation, 9*, 199–208.

O'Connell, L. M. (2008). Systemic and organizational obstacles in the tale of the reading coach: A commentary. *Journal of Educational and Psychological Consultation, 18*, 156–168. doi:10.1080/10474410802022431

O'Driscoll, M. P., & Eubanks, J. L. (1992). Consultant and client perceptions of consultant competencies: Implications for OD consulting. *Organization Development Journal, 10*(4), 53–59.

Oher, J. M. (1993). Survey research to measure EAP customer satisfaction: A quality improvement tool. *Employee Assistance Quarterly, 8*(4), 41–75.

O'Keefe, D. J., & Medway, F. J. (1997). The application of persuasion research to consultation in school psychology. *Journal of School Psychology, 35*, 173–193.

Olivos, E. M., Gallagher, R. J., & Aguilar, J. (2010). Fostering collaboration with culturally and linguistically diverse families of children with moderate to severe disabilities. *Journal of Educational and Psychological Consultation, 20*, 251–267.

O'Neill, P., & Trickett, E. J. (1982). *Community consultation.* San Francisco: Jossey-Bass.

Ortiz, S. O. (2006). Multicultural practices in school psychology practice: A critical analysis. *Journal of Applied School Psychology, 22*, 151–167.

Ortiz, S. O., Flanagan, D. P., & Dynda, A. M. (2008). Best practices in working with culturally diverse children and families. In A. Thomas & J. Grimes (Eds.), *Best practices in school psychology* (5th ed., pp. 1721–1738). Bethesda, MD: National Association of School Psychologists.

Osterweil, Z. O. (1987). A structured process of problem definition in school consultation. *School Counselor, 34*(5), 345–352.

Osterweil, Z. O. (1988). A structured integrative model of mental health consultation in schools. *International Journal for the Advancement of Counseling, 11*, 37–49.

Otani, A. (1989). Client resistance in counseling: Its theoretical rationale and taxonomic classification. *Journal of Counseling and Development, 67*, 458–461.

Ouyang, M., & Conoley, J. C. (2007). Consultation for gifted Hispanic students: 21st-century public school practice. *Journal of Educational and Psychological Consultation, 17*, 297–314.

Padgett, D. K. (Eds.). (2004). *The qualitative research experience.* Pacific Grove, CA: Thomson Learning.

Paisley, P. O., & Milsom, A. (2007). Group work as an essential contribution to transforming school counseling. *Journal for Specialists in Group Work, 32*, 9–17.

Pack-Brown, S. P., Thomas, T. L., & Seymour, J. M. (2008). Infusing professional ethics into counselor education programs: A multicultural/social justice perspective. *Journal of Counseling and Development, 86*, 296–302.

Parr, G. (1993). Educational reforms in Texas and their implications for school counselors. *School Counselor, 41*, 44–47.

Parsons, R. D. (1996). *The skilled consultant.* Boston: Allyn & Bacon.

Parsons, R. D., & Meyers, J. (1984). *Developing consultation skills.* San Francisco: Jossey-Bass.

Patton, M. Q. (1986). *Utilization-focused evaluation.* Beverly Hills, CA: Sage.

Pearrow, M. M., & Pollack, S. (2009). Youth empowerment in oppressive systems: Opportunities for school consultants. *Journal of Educational and Psychological Consultation, 19*, 45–60. doi: 10.1080/10474410802494911

Pedersen, P. B. (1997). The cultural context of the American counseling association code of ethics. *Journal of Counseling and Development, 76*, 23–28.

Pellitteri, J. (2000). Music therapy in the special education setting. *Journal of Educational and Psychological Consultation, 11*(3&4), 379–391.

Pena, R. A. (1996). Multiculturalism and educational leadership: Keys to effective consultation. *Journal of Educational and Psychological Consultation, 7*, 315–325.

Perera-Diltz, D. M., Moe, J. L., & Mason, K. L. (2011). An exploratory study in school counselor consultation engagement. *Journal of School Counseling, 9*(13). Retrieved from http://www.jsc.montana.edu/articles/v9n13.pdf

Peterson, J. S. (2007). Consultation related to giftedness: A school counseling perspective. *Journal of Educational and Psychological Consultation, 17*, 273–296.

Petri, L. (2010). Concept analysis in interdisciplinary collaboration. *Nursing Forum, 45*, 73–81.

Petti, T. A., Cornely, P. J., & McIntyre, A. (1993). A consultative study as a catalyst for improving mental health services for rural children and adolescents. *Hospital and Community Psychiatry, 44*, 262–265.

Petty, R. E., Heesacker, M., & Hughes, J. N. (1997). The elaboration likelihood model: Implications for the practice of school psychology. *Journal of School Psychology, 35*, 107–136.

Phelps, L. (2011). Pediatric health-related disorders: Prevention and early intervention. In M. A. Bray & T. J. Kehle (Eds.), *The Oxford handbook of school psychology* (pp. 685–695). New York: Oxford University Press.

Piersel, W. C., & Gutkin, T. B. (1983). Resistance to school-based consultation: A behavioral analysis of the problem. *Psychology in the Schools, 20*, 311–320.

Plummer, K. (2011). Critical humanism and queer theory. In N. K. Denzin & Y. S. Lincoln (Eds.), *The Sage handbook of qualitative research* (4th ed., pp. 195–207). Thousand Oaks, CA: Sage.

Polkinghorne, D. E., & Gribbons, B. C. (1999). Applications of qualitative research strategies to school psychology research problems. In C. R. Reynolds & T. B. Gutkin (Eds.), *The handbook of school psychology* (3rd ed., pp. 108–136). New York: Wiley.

Ponterotto, J. G. (2005). Qualitative research in counseling psychology: A primer on research paradigms and philosophy of science. *Journal of Counseling Psychology, 52*, 126–136.

Ponton, R. F., & Duba, J. D. (2009). The ACA code of ethics: Articulating counseling's professional covenant. *Journal of Counseling & Development, 87,* 117–121.

Portman, T. A. A. (2009). Faces of the future: School counselors as cultural mediators. *Journal of Counseling & Development, 87,* 21–27.

Prein, H. (1987). Strategies for third-party interventions. *Human Relations, 40,* 699–720.

Prilleltensky, I., Peirson, L., & Nelson, G. (1998). The application of community psychology values and guiding concepts to school consultation. *Journal of Educational and Psychological Consultation, 8,* 153–173.

Prochaska, J. O., & DiClemente, C. C. (1984). *The transtheoretical approach: Towards a systematic eclectic framework.* Homewood, IL: Dow Jones Irwin.

Pruett, M. K. (1998). Statement of purpose for legal and ethical issues in consultation. *Journal of Educational and Psychological Consultation, 9,* 73–74.

Pryzwansky, W. B. (2003). Finally, a contemporary treatment of consultee-centered consultation. *Journal of Educational and Psychological Consultation, 14,* 363–368.

Pryzwansky, W. B. (2011). APA 2010 ABPP convocation address. Consultation and collaboration: Time for the story. *The Specialist, 30*(1), 10–14.

Pryzwansky, W. B., & Noblit, G. W. (1990). Understanding and improving consultation practice: The qualitative case study approach. *Journal of Educational and Psychological Consultation, 1,* 293–307.

Puuitio, R., Kykyri, V. L., & Wahlstrom, J. (2008). Constructing asymmetry and symmetry in relationships within a consulting system. *Systemic Practice & Action Research, 21*(1), 35–54.

Quintana, S. M., Castillo, E. M., & Zamarripa, M. X. (2000). Assessment of ethnic and linguistic minority children. In E. S. Shapiro & T. R. Kratochwill (Eds.), *Behavioral assessment in schools: Theory, research and clinical foundations* (2nd ed., pp. 435–463). New York: Guilford Press.

Quirk, M. P., Strosahl, K., Kreilkamp, T., & Erdberg, P. (1995). Personality feedback consultation to families in a managed mental health care practice. *Professional Psychology Research and Practice, 26,* 27–32.

Racine Gilles, C. N., Kratochwill, T. R., Felt, J. N., Schienebeck, C. J., & Vaccarello, C. A. (2011). Problem-solving consultation: Applications in evidenced-based prevention and intervention. In M. A. Bray & T. J. Kehle (Eds.), *The oxford handbook of school psychology* (pp. 666–682). New York: Oxford Press.

Raforth, M. A., & Foriska, T. (2006). Administrator participation in promoting effective problem-solving teams. *Remedial and Special Education, 27,* 130–135.

Raines, J. C., & Dibble, N. T. (2011). *Ethical decision making in school mental health.* New York: Oxford University Press.

Ramirez, S. Z., Lepage, K. M., Kratochwill, T. R., & Duffy, J. L. (1998). Multicultural issues in school-based consultation: Conceptual and research considerations. *Journal of School Psychology, 36,* 479–509.

Ramirez, S. Z., & Smith, K. A. (2007). Case vignettes of school psychologists' consultations involving Hispanic youth. *Journal of Educational and Psychological Consultation, 17,* 79–93.

Randolph, D. L., & D'Ilio, V. R. (1990). Factors influencing perceptions of consultant effectiveness. *Psychology: A Journal of Human Behavior, 27*(13), 12–19.

Randolph, D. L., & Graun, K. (1988). Resistance to consultation: A synthesis for counselor-consultants. *Journal of Counseling and Development, 67,* 182–184.

Ratts, M. J., & Hutchins, A. M. (2009). ACA advocacy competencies: Social justice advocacy at the client/student level. *Journal of Counseling & Development, 87,* 269–275.

Rawlings, D. (2000). Collaborative leadership teams: Oxymoron or new paradigm? *Consulting Psychology Journal, 52,* 36–48.

Reese, R. J., Conoley, C. W., & Brossart, D. F. (2006). The attractiveness of telephone counseling: An empirical investigation of client perceptions. *Journal of Counseling & Development, 84,* 54–60.

Register, D. (2002). Collaboration and consultation: A survey of board certified music therapists. *Journal of Music Therapy, 39,* 305–321.

Remley, T. P. (1988). Consultative advocacy differentiated from legal advocacy. In D. J. Kurpius & D. Brown (Eds.), *Handbook of consultation: An intervention for advocacy and outreach* (pp. 18–26). Alexandria, VA: American Association for Counseling and Development.

Remley, T. P. (1993). Consultation contracts. *Journal of Counseling & Development, 72*, 157–158.

Remley, T. P. (2007). The relationship between law and ethics. In B. Herlihy & G. Corey (Eds.), *American Counseling Association ethical standards casebook* (6th ed., pp. 285–292). Alexandria, VA: American Counseling Association.

Remley, T. P., & Herlihy, B. (2010). *Ethical, legal, and professional issues in counseling* (3rd ed.). Upper Saddle River, NJ: Merrill/Prentice-Hall.

Reschly, A. L., & Christenson, S. L. (2012). Moving from "context matters" to engaged partnerships with families. *Journal of Educational and Psychological Consultation, 22*, 62–78. doi:10.1080/10474412.2011.649650

Reschly, D. J., & Bergstrom, M. K. (2009). Response to intervention. In T. B. Gutkin & C. R. Reynolds (Eds.), *The handbook of school psychology* (4th ed., pp. 434–460). Hoboken, NJ: Wiley.

Rhoades, M. M., & Kratochwill, T. R. (1992). Teacher reactions to behavioral consultation: An analysis of language and involvement. *School Psychology Quarterly, 7*, 47–59.

Riley, R. W. (1996). Improving America's schools. *School Psychology Review, 25*, 477–484.

Riley-Tillman, T. C., & Chafouleas, S. M. (2003). Using interventions that exist in the natural environment to increase treatment integrity and social influence in consultation. *Journal of Educational and Psychological Consultation, 14*, 139–156.

Rimehaug, T., & Helmersberg, I. (2010). Situational consultation. *Journal of Educational and Psychological Consultation, 20*, 185–208. doi:10.1080/10474412.2010.500509

Roach, A. T., Kratochwill, T. R., & Frank, J. L. (2009). School-based consultants as change facilitators: Adaptation of the concerns-based adoption model (CBAM) to support the implementation of research-based practices. *Journal of Educational and Psychological Consultation, 19*, 300–320. doi:10.1080/10474410802463304

Robertson, P., Deck, M. D., & Isenhour, G. E. (2014). Education/Training consultation with school personnel. In A. M. Dougherty (Ed.), *A casebook of psychological consultation and collaboration* (6th ed., pp. 80–100). Belmont, CA: Brooks/Cole Cengage.

Robinson, B. A., & Elias, M. J. (1993). Stabilizing classroom-based group interventions: Guidelines for special services providers and consultants. *Special Services in the Schools, 8*, 159–177.

Robinson, S. E., & Gross, D. R. (1985). Ethics of consultation: The Canterville ghost. *Counseling Psychologist, 13*(3), 444–465.

Rockwood, G. R. (1993). Edgar Schein's process versus content consultation models. *Journal of Counseling and Development, 71*, 636–638.

Rogers, C. R. (1961). *On becoming a person*. Boston: Houghton Mifflin.

Rogers, M. R. (2000). Examining the cultural context of consultation. *School Psychology Review, 29*, 414–418.

Romney, P. (2008). Consulting for diversity and social justice: Challenges and rewards. *Consulting Psychology Journal: Practice and Research, 60*, 139–156. doi:10.1037/0736-9735.60.2.139

Rosen, C. S., Young, H. E., & Norris, F. H. (2006). On a paved road with good intentions, you still need a compass. In E. C. Ritchie, P. J. Watson, & M. J. Friedman (Eds.), *Interventions following mass violence and disasters: Strategies for mental health practice* (pp. 206–223). New York: Guilford.

Rosenfield, S. A. (1985). Teacher acceptance of behavioral principles. *Teacher Education and Special Education, 8*(3), 153–158.

Rosenfield, S. A. (1987). *Instructional consultation*. Hillsdale, NJ: Erlbaum.

Rosenfield, S. A. (1991). The relationship variable in behavioral consultation. *Journal of Behavioral Consultation, 1*, 329–336.

Rosenfield, S. A. (1992). Developing school-based consultation teams: A design for organizational change. *School Psychology Quarterly, 7*, 27–46.

Rosenfield, S. A. (2002). Developing instructional consultants: From novice to competent to expert. *Journal of Educational and Psychological Consultation, 13*(1&2), 97–111.

Rosenfield, S. A. (2004). Consultation as dialogue: The right words at the right time. In N. M. Lambert, I. Hylander, & J. H. Sandoval (Eds.), *Consultee-centered consultation: Improving the quality of professional services in schools and community organizations* (pp. 337–347). Mahwah, NJ: Erlbaum.

Rosenfield, S. A. (2008). Best practices in instructional consultation and instructional consultation teams. In A. Thomas & J. Grimes (Eds.), *Best practices in school psychology* (5th ed., pp. 1645–1659). Bethesda, MD: National Association of School Psychologists.

Rosenfield, S. A., & Gravois, T. A. (1996). *Instructional consultation teams: Collaborating for change.* New York: Guilford.

Rosenfield, S., & Gravois, T. A. (1999). Working with teams in the school. In C. R. Reynolds & T. B. Gutkin (Eds.), *The handbook of school psychology* (3rd ed., pp. 1025–1040). New York: Wiley.

Rosenthal, S. L. (1993). Educational consultation in the context of a medical setting. *Journal of Educational and Psychological Consultation, 4*(4), 391–394.

Rotheram-Borus, M. J., Bickford, B., & Milburn, N. G. (2001). Implementing a classroom-based social skills training program in middle childhood. *Journal of Educational and Psychological Consultation, 12*(2), 91–111.

Rowley, W. J., & MacDonald, D. (2001). Counseling and the law: A cross-cultural perspective. *Journal of Counseling and Development, 79,* 422–429.

Royse, D. (2011). *Research methods in social work* (6th ed.). Belmont, CA: Brooks/Cole.

Rubin, H. (2002). *Collaborative leadership.* Thousand Oaks, CA: Sage.

Ruby, S. F., Crosby-Cooper, T., & Vanderwood, M. J. (2011). Fidelity of problem solving in everyday practice: Typical training may miss the mark. *Journal of Educational and Psychological Consultation, 21,* 233–258. doi:.10.1080/10474412.2011.598017

Russell-Chapin, L. A., & Stoner, C. R. (1995). Mental health counselors as consultants for diversity training. *Journal of Mental Health Counseling, 17,* 146–156.

Ryan, T., Kaffenberger, C. J., & Carroll, A. G. (2011). Response to intervention: An opportunity for school counselor leadership. *Professional School Counseling, 14,* 211–221.

Safran, J. S., & Safran, S. P. (2001). School-based consultation for asperger syndrome. *Journal of Educational and Psychological Consultation, 12*(4), 385–395.

Sales, B. D., Miller, M. O., & Hall, S. R. (2005). *Laws affecting clinical practice.* Washington, DC: American Psychological Association.

Saltzman, C. (2011). Being helpful and sometimes not. *Psychodynamic Practice, 17*(1), 57–71.

Salzman, M. B. (2005). Contextualizing the symptom in multicultural consultation: Anger in a cultural-historical context. *Journal of Educational and Psychological Consultation,16,* 223–237.

Sampson, J. P., Jr., Kolodinsky, R. W., & Greeno, B. P. (1997). Counseling on the information highway: Future possibilities and potential problems. *Journal of Counseling and Development, 75,* 203–212.

Sander, J. B., Sharkey, J. D., Olivarri, R., Tanigawa, D. A., & Mauseth, T. (2010). A qualitative study of juvenile offenders, student engagement, and interpersonal relationships: Implications for research directions and preventionist approaches. *Journal of Educational and Psychological Consultation, 20,* 288–315. doi:10.1080/10474412.2010.522878

Sandland, K., & Dougherty, A. M. (1985). Using the nominal group technique with incarcerates. *Journal of Offender Counseling, 6,* 25–30.

Sandoval, J. (1996). Constructivism, consultee-centered consultation, and conceptual change. *Journal of Educational and Psychological Consultation, 7,* 89–97.

Sandoval, J. (2003). Constructing conceptual change in consultee-centered consultation. *Journal of Educational and Psychological Consultation, 14,* 251–261.

Sandoval, J. (2004). Conceptual change in consultee-centered consultation. In N. M. Lambert, I. Hylander, & J. H. Sandoval (Eds.), *Consultee-centered consultation: Improving the quality of professional services in schools and community organizations* (pp. 37–44). Mahwah, NJ: Erlbaum.

Scarborough, J. L., & Culbreth, J. R. (2008). Examining discrepancies between actual and preferred practice of school counselors. *Journal of Counseling and Development, 86,* 446–459.

Schein, E. H. (1969). *Process consultation: Its role in organization development* (1st ed.). Reading, MA: Addison-Wesley.

Schein, E. H. (1978). The role of the consultant: Content expert or process facilitator? *Personnel and Guidance Journal, 56*(6), 339–343.

Schein, E. H. (1987). *Process consultation: Lessons for managers and consultants* (Vol. 2). Reading, MA: Addison-Wesley.

Schein, E. H. (1988). *Process consultation: Its role in organization development* (2nd ed., Vol. 1). Reading, MA: Addison-Wesley.

Schein, E. H. (1990a). Back to the future: Recapturing the OD vision. In E. Massarick (Ed.), *Advances in organization development* (Vol. 1, pp. 13–26). Norwood, NJ: Ablex.

Schein, E. H. (1990b). Models of consultation: What do organizations of the 1990s need? *Consultation, 9,* 261–275.

Schein, E. H. (1990c). Organizational culture. *American Psychologist, 45*(2), 109–119.

Schein, E. H. (1993). Legitimating clinical research in the study of organizational culture. *Journal of Counseling and Development, 71,* 703–708.

Schein, E. H. (1999). *Process consultation revisited: Building the helping relationship.* Reading, MA: Addison-Wesley.

Schein, E. H. (2004). *Organizational culture and leadership.* San Francisco: Jossey-Bass.

Schein, E. H. (2006). Consultation and coaching revisited. In M. Goldsmith & L. S. Lyons (Eds.), *Coaching for leadership* (2nd ed., pp. 17–25). San Francisco: Wiley.

Schein, E. H. (2010). The role of organization development in the human resource function. *OD Practitioner, 42*(4), 6–11.

Schein, E. H., & Greiner, L. E. (1977). Can organization development be fine tuned to bureaucracies? *Organization Dynamics, 5*(3), 48–61.

Schellenberg, R., & Grothaus, T. (2011). Using culturally competent responsive services to improve student achievement and behavior. *Professional School Counseling, 14,* 222–230.

Schmidt, S. W., Glass, J. S., & Wooten, P. (2011). School counselor preparedness: Examining cultural competence regarding gay, lesbian, and bisexual issues. *Journal of School Counseling, 9*(11). Retrieved from http://www.jsc.montana.edu/articles/v9n11.pdf

Schulte, A. C., Easton, J. E., & Parker, J. (2009). Advances in treatment integrity research: Multidisciplinary perspectives on the conceptualization, measurement, and enhancement of treatment integrity. *School Psychology Review, 38,* 460–475.

Schulte, A. C., & Osborne, S. S. (2003). When assumptive worlds collide: A review of definitions of collaboration in consultation. *Journal of Educational and Psychological Consultation, 14,* 109–138.

Sears, R., Rudisill, J., & Mason-Sears, C. (2006). *Consultation skills for mental health professionals.* Hoboken, NJ: Wiley.

Seligman, M. P., & Csikszentmihalyi, M. (2000). Positive psychology: An introduction. *American Psychologist, 60,* 410–421.

Shadish, W. R., Cook, T. D., & Campbell, D. T. (2002). *Experimental and quasi-experimental designs for generalized causal influence.* Boston: Houghton Mifflin.

Shapiro, E. S. (2008). Best practices in setting and monitoring goals for academic skill improvement. In A. Thomas & J. Grimes (Eds.), *Best practices in school psychology* (5th ed., pp. 141–157). Bethesda, MD: National Association of School Psychologists.

Shaw, H. E., & Shaw, S. F. (2006). Critical ethical issues in online counseling: Assessing current practices with an ethical intent checklist. *Journal of Counseling and Development, 84,* 41–53.

Shaw, S. R., & Brown, M. B. (2011). Keeping pace with changes in health care: Expanding educational and medical collaboration. *Journal of Educational and Psychological Consultation, 21,* 79–87. doi: 10.1080/10474412.2011.571549

Shaw, S. R., Glaser, S. E., & Ouimet, T. (2011). Developing the medical liaison role in school settings. *Journal of Educational and Psychological Consultation, 21,* 106–117. doi:10.1080/10474412.2011.571479

Shaw, S. R., & Woo, A. H. (2008). Best practices in collaborating with medical personnel. In A. Thomas & J. Grimes (Eds.), *Best practices in school psychology* (5th ed., pp. 1701–1717). Bethesda, MD: National Association of School Psychologists.

Sheeley, V. L., & Herlihy, B. (1986). The ethics of confidentiality and privileged communication. *Journal of Counseling and Human Service Professions, 1*(1), 141–148.

Sherblom, S. A., & Bahr, M. W. (2008). Homosexuality and normality: Basic knowledge and practical considerations in school consultation. *Journal of Educational and Psychological Consultation, 18,* 81–100. doi: 10.1080/10474410701634419

Sheridan, S. M. (1992). Consultant and client outcomes of competency-based behavioral consultation training. *School Psychology Quarterly, 7,* 245–270.

Sherlock, J. J., & Smith, K. (2014). Process consultation in a workplace setting. In A. M. Dougherty (Ed.), *A casebook of psychological consultation and collaboration* (6th ed., pp. 131–151). Belmont, CA: Brooks/Cole Cengage.

Sheridan, S. M. (1993a). Functional outcome analysis: Do the costs outweigh the benefits? *School Psychology Quarterly, 8,* 227–230.

Sheridan, S. M. (1993b). Models for working with parents. In J. E. Zins, T. R. Kratochwill, & S. N. Elliott (Eds.), *Handbook of consultation services for children* (pp. 110–133). San Francisco: Jossey-Bass.

Sheridan, S. M. (1997). Conceptual and empirical bases of conjoint behavioral consultation. *School Psychology Quarterly, 12,* 119–133.

Sheridan, S. M. (2000). Considerations of multiculturalism and diversity in behavioral consultation with parents and teachers. *School Psychology Review, 29,* 344–353.

Sheridan, S. M., Bovaird, J. A., Glover, T. A. S., Garbacz, S. A., Witte, S., & Kwon, K. (2012). A randomized trial examining the effects of conjoint behavioral consultation and the mediating role of the parent-teacher relationship. *School Psychology Review, 41,* 23–46.

Sheridan, S. M., Clarke, B. L., Knoche, L. L., & Edwards, C. P. (2006). The effects of conjoint behavioral consultation in early childhood settings. *Early Education and Development, 17,* 593–617.

Sheridan, S. M., Eagle, J. W., Cowan, R. J., & Mickelson, W. (2001). The effects of conjoint behavioral consultation: Results of a 4-year study. *Journal of School Psychology, 39,* 361–385.

Sheridan, S. M., Eagle, J. W., & Doll, B. (2006). An examination of the efficacy of conjoint behavioral consultation with diverse clients. *School Psychology Quarterly, 21,* 396–417.

Sheridan, S. M., & Kratochwill, T. R. (2008). *Conjoint behavioral consultation* (2nd ed.). New York: Springer.

Sheridan, S. M., Kratochwill, T. R., & Bergan, J. R. (1996). *Conjoint behavioral consultation.* New York: Plenum.

Sheridan, S. M., Swanger-Gagne, M., Welch, G. W., Kwon, K., & Garbacz, S. A. (2009). Fidelity measurement in consultation: Psychometric issues and preliminary examination. *School Psychology Review, 38,* 476–495.

Sheridan, S. M., Warnes, E. D., Woods, K. E., Blevins, C. A., Magee, K. L., & Ellis, C. (2009). An exploratory evaluation of conjoint behavioral consultation to promote collaboration among family, school, and pediatric systems: A role for pediatric school psychologists. *Journal of Educational and*

Psychological Consultation, 19, 106–129. doi: 10.1080/104774410902888566

Sheridan, S. M., Welch, M., & Orme, S. F. (1996). Is consultation effective? A review of outcome research. *Remedial and Special Education, 17,* 341–354.

Short, R. J., Moore, S., & Williams, C. (1991). Social influence in consultation: Effect of degree and experience on consultees' perceptions. *Psychological Reports, 68,* 131–137.

Short, R. J., & Talley, R. C. (1999). Services integration: An introduction. *Journal of Educational and Psychological Consultation, 10*(3), 193–200.

Shosh, M. (1996). Counseling in business and industry. In W. J. Weikel & A. J. Palmo (Eds.), *Foundations of mental health counseling* (2nd ed., pp. 232–241). Springfield, IL: Thomas Books.

Shriberg, D., & Fenning, P. (2009). School consultants as agents of social justice: Implications for practice: Introduction to the special issue. *Journal of Educational and Psychological Consultation, 19,* 1–7. doi: 10.1080/10474410802462751

Shultz, J. (1984). Historical overview of OD counseling. In R. J. Lee & A. M. Freedman (Eds.), *Consultation skills reading* (pp. 1–3). Arlington, VA: National Training Labor Institute.

Silverman, M. M. (1993). Commentary: Consultation in a campus context: Collaboration, cooperation, and coordination. *Journal of College Student Psychotherapy, 7*(3), 49–55.

Simcox, A. G., Nuijens, K., & Lee, C. C. (2006). School counselors and school psychologists: Collaborative partners in promoting cultural competent schools. *Professional School Counselor, 9,* 272–277.

Simola, S. K. (2005). Organizational crisis management: Overview and opportunities. *Consulting Psychology Journal: Practice and Research, 57,* 180–192.

Sink, C. (Ed.). (2011a). *Mental health interventions for school counselors.* Belmont, CA: Brooks/Cole.

Sink, C. (2011b). School-wide responsive services and the value of collaboration. *Professional School Counseling, 14,* 1.

Skinner, B. F. (1953). *Science and human behavior.* New York: Macmillan.

Skinner, C. H., Dittmer, K. I., & Howell, L. A. (2000). Direct observation in school settings: Theoretical issues. In E. S. Shapiro & T. R. Kratochwill (Eds.),

Behavioral assessment in schools (2nd ed., pp. 19–77). New York: Guilford Press.

Sladeczek, I. E., Elliott, S. N., Kratochwill, T. R., Robertson-Mjaanes, S., & Stoiber, K. C. (2001). Application of goal attainment scaling to a conjoint behavioral consultation case. *Journal of Educational and Psychological Consultation, 12,* 45–58.

Slonski-Fowler, K. E., & Truscott, S. D. (2003). General education teachers' perceptions of the prereferral intervention team process. *Journal of Educational and Psychological Consultation, 15,* 1–39.

Smith, R. M., & Nevin, A. (2005). Conceptualizing liberatory roles for educational and psychological consultants: Implications for transition planning. *Journal of Educational and Psychological Consultation, 16,* 263–286.

Smith, S. D., Reynolds, C. A., & Rovnak, A. (2009). A critical analysis of the social advocacy movement in counseling. *Journal of Counseling & Development, 87,* 483–491.

Snow, D. L., & Gersick, K. E. (1986). Ethical and professional issues in mental health consultation. In R. V. Mannino, E. J. Trickett, M. Shore, M. G. Kidder, & G. Levin (Eds.), *Handbook of mental health consultation* (pp. 393–431). Rockville, MD: National Institute of Mental Health.

Snyder, E. P., Quirk, K., & Dematteo, F. (2011). Consulting with families, schools, and communities. In T. M. Lionetti, E. P. Snyder, & R. W. Christner (Eds.), *A practical guide to building professional competencies in school psychology* (pp. 69–81). New York: Springer.

Sommers-Flanagan, J. (2007). Single session consultations for parents: A preliminary investigation. *The Family Journal, 15,* 24–29.

Soo-Hoo, T. (1998). Applying frame of reference and reframing techniques to improve school consultation in multicultural settings. *Journal of Educational and Psychological Consultation, 9,* 325–345.

Speight, S. L., & Vera, E. M. (2009). The challenge of social justice for school psychologists. *Journal of Educational and Psychological Consultation, 19,* 82–92.

Sperry, L. (2005). Establishing a consultation agreement. In G. P. Koocher, J. C. Norcross, & S. S. Hill, III (Eds.), *Psychologists' desk reference* (2nd ed., pp. 666–669). New York: Oxford University Press.

Staton, A. R., Benson, A. J., Briggs, M. K., Cowan, E., Echterling, L. G., Evans, W. F., et al. (2007). *Becoming a community counselor.* Boston: Houghton Mifflin.

Stayer, E. M., & Dillard, J. W. (1986). A factor analysis approach to selecting a consultation style. *Psychology: A Quarterly Journal of Human Behavior, 23*(4), 1–8.

Steen, S., & Noguera, P. A. (2010). A broader and bolder approach to school reform: Expanded partnership roles for school counselors. *Professional School Counseling, 14,* 42–52.

Steele, E. (1975). *Consulting for organizational change.* Amherst: University of Massachusetts Press.

Stenger, M. K., Tollefson, N., & Fine, M. J. (1992). Variables that distinguish elementary teachers who participate in school-based consultation from those who do not. *School Psychology Quarterly, 7,* 271–284.

Sterling-Turner, H. E., Watson, T. S., & Moore, J. W. (2002). The effects of direct training and treatment integrity on treatment outcomes in school consultation. *School Psychology Quarterly, 17,* 47–77.

Stock, H. V. (2007). Workplace violence: Advances in consultation and assessment. In A. M. Goldstein (Ed.), *Forensic psychology: Emerging topics and expanding roles* (pp. 511–549). Hoboken, NJ: Wiley.

Stoiber, K. C., & Kratochwill, T. R. (2000). Empirically supported interventions and school psychology: Rationale and methodological issues-Part I. *School Psychology Quarterly, 15,* 75–105.

Stoiber, K. C., & Vanderwood, M. L. (2008). Traditional assessment, consultation, and intervention practices: Urban school psychologists' use, importance, and competence ratings. *Journal of Educational and Psychological Consultation, 18,* 264–292. doi: 10.1080/10474410802269164

Stone, C. B., & Zirkel, P. A. (2010). School counselor advocacy: When law and ethics may collide. *Professional School Counseling, 13,* 244–247.

Strein, W., & Koehler, J. (2008). Best practices in developing prevention strategies for school psychology practice. In A. Thomas & J. Grimes (Eds.), *Best practices in school psychology* (5th ed., pp. 1309–1322). Bethesda, MD: National Association of School Psychologists.

Stroh, L. K., & Johnson, H. H. (2006). *The basic principles of effective consulting.* Mahwah, NJ: Erlbaum.

Strong, S. R. (1968). Counseling: An interpersonal influence process. *Journal of Counseling Psychology, 15*, 215–224.

Studer, J. R. (2005). *The professional school counselor.* Belmont, CA: Brooks/Cole Thomson.

Suarez-Orozco, C., Onaga, M., & Lardemelle, C. D. (2010). Promoting academic engagement among immigrant adolescents through school-family-community collaboration. *Professional School Counseling, 14*, 15–26.

Sue, D. W. (2008). Multicultural organizational consultation: A social justice perspective. *Consulting Psychology Journal: Practice and Research, 60*, 157–169. doi:10.1037/0736-9735.60.2.157

Sue, S. (1998). In search of cultural competence in psychotherapy and counseling. *American Psychologist, 53*, 440–448.

Sugai, G., & Horner, R. (1999). Discipline and behavioral support: Practices, pitfalls, and promises. *Effective School Practices, 17*, 10–17.

Sugai, G., Horner, R., & McIntosh, K. (2008). Best practices in developing a broad-scale system of school-wide positive behavior support. In A. Thomas & J. Grimes (Eds.), *Best practices in school psychology* (5th ed., pp. 765–779). Bethesda, MD: National Association of School Psychologists.

Sugai, G., Horner, R. H., Dunlap, G., Hieneman, M., Lewis, T. J., Nelson, C. M., et al. (2000). Applying positive behavior support and functional behavioral assessment in schools. *Journal of Positive Behavior Interventions, 2*(3), 131–143.

Sugai, G., Sprague, J. R., Horner, R. H., & Walker, H. M. (2000). Preventing school violence: The use of office discipline referrals to assess and monitor school-wide discipline interventions. *Journal of Emotional and Behavioral Disorders, 8*, 94–101.

Sulkowski, M. L., Wingfield, R. J., Jones, D., & Coulter, W. A. (2011). Response to intervention and interdisciplinary collaboration: Joining hands to support children's healthy development. *Journal of Applied School Psychology, 27*, 118–133.

Swenson, C. C., Randall, J., Henggeier, S. W., & Ward, D. (2000). The outcomes and costs of an interagency partnership to serve maltreated children in state custody. *Children's Services: Social Policy, Research, and Practice, 3*, 191–209.

Swenson, L. C. (1997). *Psychology and law* (2nd ed.). Pacific Grove, CA: Brooks/Cole.

Tack, F. E., & Morrow, D. F. (2014). Mental health case consultation. In A. M. Dougherty, *A casebook of psychological consultation and collaboration* (6th ed., pp. 44–60). Belmont, CA: Brooks/Cole Cengage.

Tanyu, M. (2007). Implementation of prevention programs: Lessons for future research and practice: A commentary on "Social and emotional learning: Promoting the development of all students," a chapter by Joseph E. Zins and Maurice J. Elias. *Journal of Educational and Psychological Consultation, 17*, 257–262.

Tarver Behring, R. K., & Ingraham, C. L. (1998). Culture as a central component of consultation: A call to the field. *Journal of Educational and Psychological Consultation, 9*, 57–72.

Tarver Behring, S., Cabello, B., Kushida, D., & Murguia, A. (2000). Cultural modifications to current school-based consultation approaches reported by culturally diverse beginning consultants. *School Psychology Review, 29*, 354–376.

Tashakkori, A., & Teddlie, C. (Eds.). (2003). *Handbook of the mixed methods in the behavioral and social sciences.* Thousand Oaks, CA: Sage.

Taylor, L., & Adelman, H. S. (1998). Confidentiality: Competing principles, inevitable dilemmas. *Journal of Educational and Psychological Consultation, 9*, 267–275.

Taylor, R. D., & Dymnicki, A. B. (2007). Empirical evidence of social and emotional learning's influence on school success: A commentary on "Building academic success on social and emotional learning: What does the research say?," a book edited by Joseph E. Zins, Roger P. Weissberg, Margaret C. Wang, and Herbert J. Walberg. *Journal of Educational and Psychological Consultation, 17*, 225–231.

Teddlie, C., & Tashakkori, A. (2011). Mixed methods research: Contemporary issues in an emerging field. In N. K. Denzin & Y. S. Lincoln (Eds.), *The sage handbook of qualitative research* (4th ed., pp. 285–299). Thousand Oaks, CA: Sage.

Theodore, L. A., Dioguardi, R. J., Hughes, L., Aloiso, D., Carlo, M., & Eccles, D. (2009). A class-wide intervention for improving homework performance. *Journal of Educational and Psychological Consultation, 19*, 275–299. doi: 10.1080/10474410902888657

Thomas, C. C., Correa, V. L., & Morsink, C. V. (1995). *Interactive teaming.* Englewood Cliffs, NJ: Prentice-Hall.

Thomas, J. T. (2010). *The ethics of supervision and consultation: Practical guidance for mental health professionals*. Washington, DC: American Psychological Association.

Thomas, R. T., Jr. (2006). Coaching in the midst of diversity. In M. Goldsmith & L. S. Lyons (Eds.), *Coaching for leadership* (2nd ed., pp. 229–236). San Francisco: Wiley.

Thousand, J. S., Villa, R. A., Paolucci-Whitcomb, P., & Nevin, A. (1996). A rationale and vision for collaborative consultation. In W. Stainback & S. Stainback (Eds.), *Controversial issues confronting special education* (2nd ed., pp. 205–218). Boston: Allyn & Bacon.

Tichy, N. M. (1983). *Managing strategic change: Technical, political, and cultural dynamics*. New York: Wiley.

Tilly, W. D., III. (2008). The evolution of school psychology to science-based practice. In A. Thomas & J. Grimes (Eds.), *Best practices in school psychology* (5th ed., pp. 17–36). Bethesda, MD: National Association of School Psychologists.

Tingstrom, D. H., Little, S. G., & Stewart, K. J. (1990). School consultation from a social psychological perspective: A review. *School Consultation and Social Psychology, 27*, 41–50.

Tobias, L. L. (1990). *Psychological consulting to management*. New York: Brunner/Mazel.

Tobias, R. (1993). Underlying cultural issues that effect sound consultant/school collaboratives in developing multicultural programs. *Journal of Educational and Psychological Consultation, 4*, 237–251.

Tomes, Y. I. (2011). Building competency in cross-cultural school psychology. In T. M. Lionetti, E. P. Snyder, & R. W. Christner (Eds.), *A practical guide to building professional competencies in school psychology* (pp. 35–49). New York: Springer.

Toporek, R. L., Gerstein, L. H., Fouad, A., Roysircar, G., & Israel, T. (Eds.). (2006). *Handbook for social justice in counseling psychology*. Thousand Oaks, CA: Sage.

Toporek, R. L., Lewis, J. A., & Crethar, H. C. (2009). Promoting systemic change through the ACA advocacy competencies. *Journal of Counseling and Development, 87*, 260–269.

Topping, K. J., & Ehly, S. W. (2001). Peer assisted learning: A framework for consultation. *Journal of Educational and Psychological Consultation, 12*, 113–132.

Trickett, E. J. (1986). Consultation as a preventative intervention: Comments on ecologically based case studies. *Prevention in Human Services, 4*, 187–204.

Trickett, E. J., Kelly, J. G., & Vincent, T. A. (1984). The spirit of ecological inquiry in community research. In E. Susskind & D. C. Klein (Eds., pp. 331–406), *Community research*. New York: Praeger.

Trickett, E. J., & Rowe, H. L. (2012). Emerging ecological approaches to prevention, health promotion, and public health in the school context: Next steps from a community psychology perspective. *Journal of Educational and Psychological Consultation, 22*, 125–140. doi:10.1080/10474412.2011.649651

Trolley, B. C., Haas, H. S., & Patti, D. C. (2009). *The school counselor's guide to special education*. Thousand Oaks, CA: Corwin.

Truscott, S. D. (2008). New opportunities and familiar foundations: The journal of educational and psychological consultation in its eighteenth year. *Journal of Educational and Psychological Consultation, 18*, 1–4. doi:10.1080/10474410801938306

Truscott, S. D., & Albritton, K. (2011). Addressing pediatric health concerns through school-based consultation. *Journal of Educational and Psychological Consultation, 21*, 169–174. doi: 10.1080/10474412.2011.574583

Truscott, S. D., Cosgrove, G., Meyers, J., & Eidle-Barkman, K. A. (2000). The acceptability of organizational consultation with prereferral intervention teams. *School Psychology Quarterly, 15*, 172–206.

Truscott, S. D., Kreskey, D., Bolling, M., Psimas, L., Graybill, E., Albritton, K., et al. (2012). Creating consultee change: A theory-based approach to learning and behavioral change processes in school-based consultation. *Consulting Psychology Journal: Practice and Research, 64*, 63–82.

Tseng, S. H., Liu, K., & Wang, W.-L. (2011). Moving toward being analytical: A framework to evaluate the impact of influential factors on interagency collaboration. *Children and Youth Services Review, 33*, 798–803. doi:10.1016/j.childyouth.2010.11.028

Turco, T. L., & Skinner, C. H. (1991). An analysis of consultee verbal responses to structured consultant questions. *TACD Journal, 19*(1), 23–32.

Tysinger, P. D., Tysinger, J. A., & Diamanduros, T. (2009). Teacher expectations on the directiveness continuum in consultation. *Psychology in the Schools, 46*, 319–332. doi:10.1002/pits.20378

Uhlemann, M. R., Lee, D. Y., & Martin, J. (1994). Client cognitive responses as a function of quality of counselor verbal responses. *Journal of Counseling and Development, 73,* 198–203.

Upah, K. R. F. (2008). Best practices in designing, implementing, and evaluating quality interventions. In A. Thomas & J. Grimes (Eds.), *Best practices in school psychology* (5th ed., pp. 209–223). Bethesda, MD: National Association of School Psychologists.

United States Bureau of the Census. (2000). *2000 U. S. Census.* Washington, DC: U. S. Government Printing Office.

Vanderheyden, A. M., & Witt, J. C. (2008). Section commentary on effective consultation. In W. P. Erchul & S. M. Sheridan (Eds.), *Handbook of research in school consultation* (pp. 115–124). New York: Erlbaum.

Van Velsor, P. (2009). School counselors as social-emotional learning consultants: Where do we begin? *Professional School Counseling, 13,* 50–58.

Vernberg, E. M., & Reppucci, N. D. (1986). Behavioral consultation. In E. V. Mannino, E. J. Trickett, M. F. Shore, M. G. Kidder, & G. Levin (Eds.), *Handbook of mental health consultation* (pp. 49–80). Rockville, MD: National Institute of Mental Health.

Walker, J. M. T., Shenker, S. S., & Hoover-Oempsey, K. V. (2010). Why do parents become involved in their children's education? Implications for school counselors. *Professional School Counseling, 14,* 27–41.

Wallace, W. A., & Hall, D. L. (1996). *Psychological consultation.* Pacific Grove, CA: Brooks/Cole.

Walton, R. E. (1987). *Managing conflict: Interpersonal dialogue and third party roles* (2nd ed.). Reading, MA: Addison-Wesley.

Walz, G. R. (2007). More than an introduction. In J. F. Malone, R. M. Miller, & G. Walz (Eds.), *Distance counseling: Expanding the counselor's reach and impact* (pp. 1–7). Ann Arbor, MI: Counseling Outfitters.

Washburn, J. J., Manley, T., Jr., & Holiwski, F. (2003). Teaching on racism: Tools for consultant training. *Journal of Educational and Psychological Consultation, 14,* 387–399.

Watson, T. S., & Robinson, S. L. (1996). Direct behavioral consultation: An alternative to traditional behavioral consultation. *School Psychology Quarterly, 11,* 267–278.

Watson, T. S., & Steege, M. W. (2003). *Conducting school-based functional behavioral assessments.* New York: Guildford.

Watson, T. S., Steege, M. W., & Turner, H. (2011). Functional assessment of behavior. In M. A. Bray and T. J. Kehle (Eds.). *The oxford handbook of school psychology* (pp. 187–204). NY: Oxford Press.

Watson, T. S., Sterling, E., & McDade, A. (1997). Demythifying behavioral consultation. *School Psychology Review, 26,* 467–474.

Watson, T. S., & Sterling-Turner, H. (2008). Best practices in direct behavioral consultation. In A. Thomas & J. Grimes (Eds.), *Best practices in school psychology* (5th ed., pp. 1661–1672). Bethesda, MD: National Association of School Psychologists.

Webster, L., Knotek, S. E., Babinski, L. M., Rogers, D. L., & Barnett, M. M. (2003). Mediation of consultee's conceptual development in new teacher groups: Using questions to improve coherency. *Journal of Educational and Psychological Consultation, 14,* 281–301.

Weinrach, S. G., & Thomas, K. R. (1998). Diversity-sensitive counseling today: A postmodern clash of values. *Journal of Counseling and Development, 76,* 115–122.

Weiss, H. (1996). Family-school collaboration: Consultation to achieve organizational and community change. *Human Systems, 7,* 211–235.

Welch, M. (2000). Collaboration as a tool for inclusion. In S. E. Wade (Ed.), *Inclusive education: A casebook and readings for prospective and practicing teachers* (pp. 71–96). Mahwah, NJ: Lawrence Erlbaum.

Welch, M., & Tulbert, B. (2000). Practitioners' perspectives of collaboration: A social validation and factor analysis. *Journal of Educational and Psychological Consultation, 11*(3&4), 357–378.

Welfel, E. R. (2002). *Ethics in counseling and psychotherapy: Standards, research, and emerging issues* (2nd ed.). Pacific Grove, CA: Brooks/Cole.

Werner, J. L., & Tyler, J. M. (1993). Community-based interventions: A return to community mental health center's origins. *Journal of Counseling and Development, 71,* 689–692.

Wesley, P. W., Bryant, D., Fenson, C., Hughes-Belding, K., Tout, K., & Susman-Stillman, A. (2010). Treatment fidelity challenges in a five-state consultation study. *Journal of Educational and Psychological Consultation, 20,* 209–227.

Wesley, P. W., & Buysse, V. (2006). Ethics and evidence in consultation. *Topics in Early Childhood Special Education, 26,* 131–146.

Westaby, J. D. (2006). How different survey techniques can impact consultant recommendations: A scientist practitioner study comparing two popular methods. *Consulting Psychology Journal: Practice and Research, 58,* 195–205.

Wheeler, A. M., & Bertram, B. (2008). *The counselor and the law* (5th ed.). Alexandria, VA: American Counseling Association.

White, S. W., & Kelly, F. D. (2010). The school counselor's role in school dropout prevention. *Journal of Counseling & Development, 88,* 227–236.

White Kress, V. E., Eriksen, K. P., Rayle, A. D., & Ford, S. J. W. (2005). The DSM-IV-TR and culture: Considerations for counselors. *Journal of Counseling and Development, 83,* 97–104.

Wickstrom, K. F., & Witt, J. C. (1993). Resistance within school-based consultation. In J. E. Zins, T. R. Kratochwill, & S. N. Elliott (Eds.), *Handbook of consultation services for children* (pp. 159–178). San Francisco: Jossey-Bass.

Wilczenski, F. L., & Cook, A. L. (2011). Virtue ethics in school counseling: A framework for decision making. *Journal of School Counseling, 9*(7). Retrieved from http://www.jsc.montana.edu/articles/v9n7.pdf

Wilczynski, S. M., Mandal, R. L., & Fusilier, I. (2000). Bridges and barriers in behavioral consultation. *Psychology in the Schools, 37,* 495–504.

Wilkinson, L. A. (2005). Bridging the research-to-practice gap in school-based consultation: An example using case studies. *Journal of Educational and Psychological Consultation, 16,* 175–200.

Wilkinson, L. A. (2006). Monitoring treatment integrity. *School Psychology International, 27,* 426–438.

Willems, E. P. (1974). Behavioral technology and behavioral ecology. *Journal of Applied Behavioral Analysis, 7,* 151–156.

Williams, B. B., & Armistead, L. (2011). Applying law and ethics in professional practice. In T. M. Lionetti, E. P. Snyder, & R. W. Christner (Eds.), *A practical guide to building professional competencies in school psychology* (pp. 13–33). New York: Springer.

Williams, J. M., & Greenleaf, A. T. (2012). Ecological psychology: Potential contributions to social justice and advocacy in school settings. *Journal of Educational and Psychological Consultation, 22,* 141–157. doi: 10.1080/10474412.2011.649653

Williams, W. L. (2000). Behavioral consultation. In J. Austin & J. E. Carr (Eds.), *Handbook of applied behavioral analysis* (pp. 375–397). Reno, NV: Context Press.

Willis, J. O., & Dumont, R. (2006). And never the twain shall meet: Can response to intervention and cognitive assessment be reconciled? *Psychology in the Schools, 43,* 901–908.

Wilson, K. E., Erchul, W. P., & Raven, B. H. (2008). The likelihood of use of social power strategies by school psychologists when consulting with teachers. *Journal of Educational and Psychological Consultation, 18,* 101–123. doi:10.1080/10474410701864321

Witt, J. C. (1990a). Complaining, precopernian thought and the univariate linear mind: Questions for school based behavioral consultation research. *School Psychology Review, 19,* 367–377.

Witt, J. C. (1990b). Face-to-face verbal interaction in school-based consultation: A review of the literature. *School Psychology Quarterly, 5,* 199–210.

Witt, J. C., & Elliott, S. N. (1983). Assessment in behavioral consultation: The initial interview. *School Psychology Review, 12,* 42–49.

Witt, J. C., Gresham, F. M., & Noel, G. H. (1996a). What's behavioral about behavioral consultation? *Journal of Educational and Psychological Consultation, 7,* 327–344.

Witt, J. C., Gresham, F. M., & Noel, G. H. (1996b). The effectiveness and efficiency of behavioral consultation: Differing perspectives about epistemology and what we know. *Journal of Educational and Psychological Consultation, 7,* 355–360.

Wizda, L. (2004). An instructional consultant looks to the future. *Journal of Educational and Psychological Consultation, 15,* 277–294.

Wolf, R. S., & Pillemer, K. (1994). What's new in elder abuse programming? *The Gerontologist, 34,* 126–129.

Woodward, A., & Davis, T. (2009). Student support and community collaboration. *ASCA School Counselor, 46,* 19–23.

Yetter, G. (2010). Assessing the acceptability of problem-solving procedures by school teams: Preliminary development of the pre-referral intervention team inventory. *Journal of Educational and Psychological Consultation, 20,* 139–168. doi: 10.1080/10474411003785370

Young, H. L., & Gaughan, E. (2010). A multiple method longitudinal investigation of pre-referral intervention team functioning: Four years in rural schools. *Journal of Educational and Psychological Consultation, 20,* 106–138. doi:10.1080/10474411003785438

Ysseldyke, J. E., Burns, M., Dawson, M., Kelley, B., Morrison, D., Ortiz, S., et al. (2006). *School psychology: A blueprint for training and practice III.* Bethesda, MD: National Association of School Psychologists.

Ysseldyke, J. E., Burns, M., & Rosenfield, S. (2009). Blueprints on the future of training and practice in school psychology: What do they say about educational and psychological consultation? *Journal of Educational and Psychological Consultation, 19,* 177–196. doi:10.1080/10474410903106448

Ysseldyke, J. E., Lekwa, A. J., Klingbeil, D. A., & Cormier, D. C. (2012). Assessment of ecological factors as an integral part of academic and mental health consultation. *Journal of Educational and Psychological Consultation, 22,* 21–43. doi:10.1080/10474412.2011.649641

Zins, J. E. (1993). Enhancing consultee problem-solving skills in consultation. *Journal of Counseling and Development, 72*(2), 185–190.

Zins, J. E. (1995). Has primary prevention achieved its potential? *The Journal of Primary Prevention, 15,* 285–301.

Zins, J. E. (1998). Expanding the conceptual foundations of consultation: Contributions of community psychology. *Journal of Educational and Psychological Consultation, 8,* 107–110.

Zins, J. E. (2002). Building a strong future for educational and psychological consultation. *Journal of Educational and Psychological Consultation, 13*(1&2), 5–6.

Zins, J. E., Bloodworth, M. R., Weissberg, R. P., & Walberg, H. J. (2004). The scientific base for linking social and emotional learning to school success.

In J. E. Zins, R. P. Weissberg, M. C. Wang, & H. J. Walberg (Eds.), *Building academic success on social and emotional learning: What does the research say?* (pp. 2–22). New York: Teachers College Press.

Zins, J. E., Bloodworth, M. R., Weissberg, R. P., & Walberg, H. J. (2007). The scientific base linking social and emotional learning to school success. *Journal of Educational and Psychological Consultation, 17,* 191–210.

Zins, J. E., & Curtis, M. J. (1984). Building consultation into the educational service delivery system. In C. A. Maher, R. J. Illback, & J. E. Zins (Eds.), *Organizational psychology in the schools: A handbook for professionals* (pp. 213–242). Springfield, IL: Thomas.

Zins, J. E., Elias, M. J., Greenberg, M. T., & Pruett, M. K. (2000). Promoting quality implementation in prevention programs. *Journal of Educational and Psychological Consultation, 11,* 173–174.

Zins, J. E., & Erchul, W. P. (2002). Best practices in school consultation. In A. Thomas & J. Grimes (Eds.), *Best practices in school psychology* (4th ed., pp. 625–643). Bethesda, MD: National Association of School Psychologists.

Zins, J. E., & Illback, R. J. (1995). Consulting to facilitate planned organizational change in schools. *Journal of Educational and Psychological Consultation, 6,* 237–245.

Zins, J. E., Kratochwill, T. R., & Elliott, S. N. (1993). Current status of the field. In J. E. Zins, T. R. Kratochwill, & S. N. Elliott (Eds.), *Handbook of consultation services for children* (pp. 1–12). San Francisco: Jossey-Bass.

Zins, J. E., Weissberg, R. P., Wang, M. C., & Walberg, H. J. (Eds.). (2004). *Building school success through social and emotional learning.* New York: Teachers College Press.

Name Index

Adams, E. M., 170
Adelman, H. S., 13, 157, 273, 274, 295, 296, 356
Adler, A., 271, 277, 278, 283
Aguilar, J., 285
Akin-Little, K. A., 113, 274, 300
Alber, S. R., 282
Albritton, M. D., 7, 87, 275, 301
Allen, K., 234, 268, 294
Allen, S. J., 54, 97, 98, 101, 111, 112, 276
Allison, R., 291
Alpert, J. L., 24, 46, 298, 352
Alston-Abel, N., 113
Altschaefl, M. R., 223, 237
Amada, G., 178
Amatea, E. S., 282
American Counseling Association (ACA), 33, 37, 38, 343, 344, 345, 347, 349, 350, 351, 352, 354, 355, 356, 357, 362, 368
American Mental Health Counselors Association (AMHCA), 344, 362
American Psychological Association (APA), 32, 33, 343, 344, 345, 347, 349, 350, 351, 353, 355, 357, 362, 363, 364, 368
American School Counselor Association (ASCA), 6, 7, 11, 24, 267, 271, 284, 296, 344, 345, 347, 349, 351, 353, 356, 362, 363, 364
Amio, J. L., 284
Andersen, M. N., 209, 217, 233, 236
Anderson, B. S., 364, 365
Anderson, K. J., 227, 231, 234, 285, 286, 293

Anderson, W. R., 7, 126, 135
Anderson-Butcher, D., 7, 38, 39, 116, 160, 161, 170, 251, 270, 272, 273
Anton-LaHart, J., 6, 209
Ardoin, S. P., 110, 113, 123, 234, 272
Arena, M. P., 6
Armenakis, A. A., 45, 72, 87, 105
Armistead, L., 344, 349, 364, 365
Armstrong, M. I., 289, 290, 291
Arra, C. T., 32, 286, 292, 352
Arredondo, P., 6, 12, 28, 29, 30, 32, 33, 34, 168, 246, 247, 248
Ashford, S. J., 105
Association for Counselor Education and Supervision (ACES), 271
Association for Specialists in Group Work (ASGW), 358
Association of Counselor Education and Supervision (ACES), 271
Athanasiou, M. S., 141, 147, 283
Atkinson, D. A., 33
Auster, E. R., 9, 29, 59, 101, 229, 230

Babinski, L. M., 35, 280, 301, 362
Bacon, E. H., 300
Bagnato, S. J., 300
Bahr, M. W., 32, 37, 273, 274, 291
Baker, S. B., 18, 169, 269
Ball, C., 6, 250, 251, 294, 297, 298
Bandura, A., 210, 211, 216
Bangert, A. W., 144
Barak, S., 247
Bardon, J., 30
Barker, D., 361
Barlow, D. H., 142, 143, 144

Barnett, D. W., 13, 35, 110, 121, 122, 124, 126, 226, 294, 300
Batsche, G. M., 89, 97
Baumberger, J. P., 144
Bean, G., 273
Beaulieu, M. D., 14
Beaver, B. R., 93
Beer, M., 158, 255
Begeny, J. C., 281
Bell, C. H., Jr., 67, 68, 71, 84, 85, 87, 96, 97, 113, 114, 115, 116, 118, 121, 131, 148, 157, 158, 165, 241, 242, 264
Bellman, G. M., 30, 62, 72, 239
Bemak, F., 20, 268, 288
Benn, A. E., 31, 47, 80, 165, 279
Bergan, J. R., 44, 46, 53, 89, 96, 121, 142, 209, 212, 213, 214, 215, 216, 217, 219, 220, 221, 222, 223, 224, 237, 238
Bergstrom, M. K., 6, 8, 87, 227, 234, 294
Bernard, M. E., 175, 271
Berninger, V. W., 113
Bernstein, R., 286
Berrios, R., 47, 141, 143
Bersoff, D. N., 343
Bertram, B., 344, 362, 364, 365
Bianco-Mathis, V., 28
Bickford, B., 273
Bidell, M. P., 295
Blader, J. C., 273
Blake, R. R., 242, 244
Blase, J. C., 300
Blase, J., 300
Blevins, C. A., 229, 267

Subject Index